North Carolina WOMEN

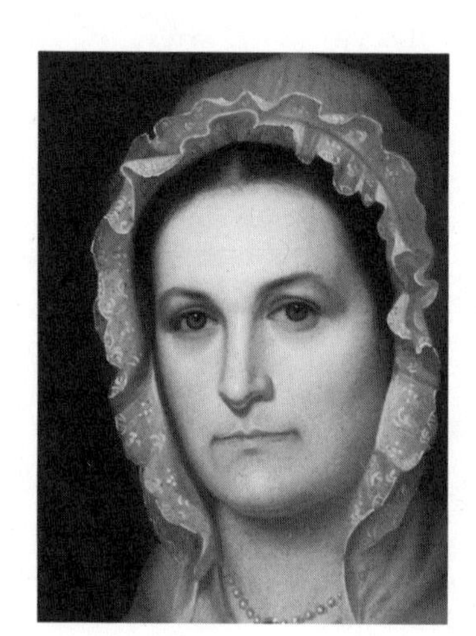

North Carolina WOMEN Making History

Margaret Supplee Smith & Emily Herring Wilson

FOREWORD BY DORIS BETTS

The University of North Carolina Press Chapel Hill and London

Designed by Richard Hendel
Set in Minion and Castellar
by Keystone Typesetting, Inc.
Manufactured in the United States of America
The paper in this book meets the guidelines for
permanence and durability of the Committee on
Production Guidelines for Book Longevity of the
Council on Library Resources.
Library of Congress Cataloging-in-Publication Data
Smith, Margaret Supplee.
North Carolina women: making history /
Margaret Supplee Smith and Emily Herring Wilson.
p. cm.
Includes bibliographical references and index.
ISBN-13: 978-0-8078-2463-4 (alk. paper)
ISBN-10: 0-8078-2463-1 (alk. paper)
ISBN-13: 978-0-8078-5820-2 (pbk. : alk. paper)
ISBN-10: 0-8078-5820-x (pbk. : alk. paper)
1. Women—North Carolina—History. I. Wilson,
Emily Herring. II. Title.
HQ1438.N5S55 1999
305.4'09756—dc21 98-25243
CIP

03 02 01 00 99 5 4 3 2 1
10 09 08 07 06 5 4 3 2 1

Grateful acknowledgment is made to the North
Carolina Department of Cultural Resources for
its role in bringing this book to fruition.

FOR OUR CHILDREN

Susan Brett

and

Eddie, Sally, and Julie

Contents

Foreword

Circumstances and Winners Change

History, they say, is always written by the winners—those successful beneficiaries of war or major social change. Although the "battle between the sexes" may be metaphoric, men have historically been declared its winners, at least in public; and ever since Eve, men have kept nearly all the record books, which have concentrated on explorers, kings, and generals.

But circumstances and winners change, as the Greeks and Romans learned.

It is a lesson Americans have also learned. After the Union won the Civil War, for instance, both the conflict and its aftermath were chiefly recorded by northern historians. After African Americans won the civil rights movement, the Uncle Remus version of southern culture entered a long period of reexamination.

Another change in circumstances and winners occurred after American women won the vote. Historian Kemp Battle, a professor at the University of North Carolina at Chapel Hill, had opposed woman suffrage and in 1918 said that "women are inferior in physical strength and must inevitably pass through periods of sickness and weakening of nervous power." When a U.S. congressman expressed a similar opinion several years ago, men *and* women laughed him to scorn.

But some circumstances change only gradually and unevenly. The patronizing attitudes of both these men seem almost enlightened when compared with a law, still on the North Carolina statute books in 1864, that allowed a husband to use toward his wife "such degree of force as is necessary to control an unruly temper and make her behave herself." By 1874 a court decision repudiated his right to whip his wife with a "switch no thicker than his thumb," but fifty years had to pass before a wife would be permitted to sue a husband for physical injury and keep the money awarded her.

Even after wives were no longer classified as the property of their husbands, many women themselves curtsied their way out of recorded history, saying that ladies should only be mentioned in newspapers when they married or died. Some collaborated with the role advocated by Cornelia Phillips Spencer: "Her true sphere in the world . . . is a subordinate one. I did not say *inferior*, young ladies, I said *subordinate*. There can be but one head and the man is the head."

The South, especially, seemed to like dividing women into types, like Picasso's "goddesses or doormats." Anne Firor Scott in *The Southern Lady* depicts the southern (white) belle ("beautiful, graceful, accomplished in social charm, bewitching in coquetry, yet strangely steadfast in soul, she is perhaps the most winsome figure in the whole field of our fancy") who matures into the southern lady. If a member of the lower classes, she is a tomboy who grows up to be a "good ol' girl," exhibiting spunk and independence, something like that coal miner's daughter, singer Loretta Lynn. Until recently, many depictions of black southern women have been of stereotypical mammy-cooks possessing primitive folk-wisdom and earthy sexuality.

For many years this social culture, driven largely by ideals of male patriarchy (sometimes benevolent, sometimes not), lifted white southern ladies onto pedestals where the thinner air rendered them too delicate for politics or the professions, or else worked poorer and darker southern women almost to death on hardscrabble farms, in cotton mills, and in richer women's kitchens.

For most of North Carolina history, a woman's place was in the home, either working there herself or supervising the work of other women, herself in the service of her family. Even today, 85 percent of American women and 90 percent of women worldwide give birth and manage increasingly busy lives in context of the demands of home and motherhood.

In the years before contraception was widely available, motherhood was so frequent and unremitting, and death in childbirth so commonplace, that it is understandable women seldom made it onto the printed page except for weddings and obituaries, much less the pages of history. Of our one hundred counties, only three—Dare, Wake, and Mecklenburg—are named for women: a lost baby girl, a governor's wife, and a king's wife. In William Powell's *North Carolina: A Proud State in Our Nation* (1988), designed for the middle school grades, the twenty index entries for women refer mostly to demographic generalities, with passing mention of Clara Barton, Harriet Tubman, and astronaut Sally Ride. In the much longer but earlier standard state history (Lefler and Newsome's *North Carolina: The History of a Southern State*, now out of print), the third edition in 1979 mentions few female names. Since 1963, when Governor Terry Sanford appointed a commission to study the status of women in North Carolina, there has been a trickling of articles and specialized histories, such as Elna Green's *Southern Strategies* (1997), about the suffrage movement in the South, but no overview of the role of women in the general history of the Tar Heel state.

If there had been earlier histories of North Carolina women, too many would have been unable to read their own stories. Even wealthy girls from prominent families used to be "finished" in school without being really educated; poor girls were needed at home. Literate women did write diaries and family letters, but not ballots or legislation. Even as circumstances moved forward with slow changes, politicians emphasized the homebody role for women, and pushed for their higher education and their right to vote so they might engage in "social housekeeping," to nurture society on a larger scale. Charles Duncan McIver, founder in 1893 of the all-female State Normal and Industrial College (now the University of North Carolina at Greensboro), urged women students to "see the real needs of the world and then do something about it."

Winners and circumstances do not change without setbacks, detours, and delays. By 1897, our all-male legislature referred a woman suffrage bill to the Committee on Insane Asylums. Later, North Carolina rejected state and federal suffrage amendments and for years would not even ratify the Nineteenth Amendment after it had become law. Senator Sam Ervin called the Equal Rights Amendment (ERA) the "most destructive piece of legislation to ever pass Congress," and the state legislature agreed, steadily defeating it from 1973 to 1982, when the deadline passed.

By 1998, although women had become 6 out of 50 in the North Carolina Senate and 23 in a 120-member state house, it is uncertain that the voting outcome would have changed.

Yet, despite how slowly some circumstances change, women have in the twentieth century accumulated victories peculiar to their needs: in education, both as students and teachers; with the first reliable control of childbearing; at work outside the home; in government and public life; and by new laws that offered them protection and opened opportunity.

Now at last Tar Heel women have won enough victories to produce and enjoy this well-earned history of their efforts and achievements.

Smith and Wilson's history—a first for North Carolina and by its scope, approach, and comprehensiveness perhaps the first for any state— traces how Tar Heel women have lived in, worked for, and contributed to home, state, and nation up to the middle of this still-changing century.

No other record exists that so thoroughly brings into general history their heretofore unwritten histories at home, on farms, and eventually in public life. Some of the women presented here were leaders who laid the groundwork for improved opportunity for all women and for the rise of feminism. Forty-seven of them took early the stance of American patriots at the Edenton Tea Party in 1774. But in this largely rural state, generations of other hardworking women, taken for granted at home and abroad, achieved little fame or recognition.

The late twentieth century has seen a rediscovery of the complex lives of great-great-great-grandmothers with resulting change in the nation's history. By the early 1990s, women's studies programs existed on 650 campuses nationwide, with general courses in women's history and literature offered at another 600 or so. In classrooms and the media, an accelerating reexamination of past heroines, female artists, and civic leaders has produced an explosion of women's topics to study, with researchers finding role models and foremothers in all walks of life. Smith and Wilson's volume brings that new emphasis home to North Carolinians.

Because circumstances and winners keep changing, women scholars—like men writing earlier histories—apply selectivity to the past. Today women admire Gertrude Weil and Nell Battle Lewis who fought for suffrage here, noting that when finally allowed to vote in 1920 for the first time, Tar Heel women turned out in such numbers that ballot counting was delayed. But when women were more accepting of a subordinate societal role, many admired Mary Hilliard Hinton during those same years, and she is remembered in these pages as well but in perspective. A governor's niece and state leader of the Daughters of the American Revolution who worked hard *against* suffrage, she voted in 1920 only as a "duty" to prevent black domination. Like some women who were, in her day, reluctant to embrace change, Hinton agreed with state senator Willie M. Person of Franklin County. He was still shielding Mrs. Person from the risks of venturing to the polls, and he wanted to protect both her and the state from woman suffrage when he said, "Why, my cook would vote when my wife would not!"

Changing circumstances also affect which women in history seem major influences in one decade, but minor when seen through a longer lens. Anna Morrison Jackson, Stonewall's widow, was greatly admired during the years southerners devoted time and energy to memorializing the Civil War. Hailed as the first lady of the South and visited with deference by both Theodore Roosevelt and Woodrow Wilson, she died in 1915 in her native Charlotte after fifty-two years of widowhood. In her honor, all stores and government offices closed and public schools held memorial services. She, too, finds a place in Smith and Wilson's history, but circumstances and winners have changed a great deal since then, and today's readers will be more interested in, for example, Ella May Wiggins, killed in a drive-by shooting in Gastonia during the Loray Mill strikes in 1929. She was supporting five children on $9 a week, but the minimum salary for state teachers then (nearly all of them women) was $400 a year.

This sifting of history and biography causes some names to rise to time's surface while others drift out of sight, some lives to shine while some only reflect the light of others. Well known is the Tar Heel story of Siamese twins Eng and Chang Bunker, perhaps from prurient imaginings about how they fathered so many children by the sisters they married. But who remembers Mollie and Christie McCoy, of Columbus County, Siamese twins born slaves and exhibited by Barnum's circus, given matching brooches by the queen of England before they died in 1912? Their story still awaits the storyteller. And readers, proud to learn in these pages that white as well as black women organized against lynching, must also face the history of white women taking part in the Wilmington race riot of 1898, campaigning for the disenfranchisement of blacks in 1900, baking fragrant yeast loaves for legislators while conducting an oh-so-suthun-belle lobby against the ERA not long ago. Women have joined men in quoting scripture to justify bias; Virginia suffragette Mary Johnston finally included "answers to St. Paul" in her speeches, and gay rights advocates need to look up and borrow them today. We sing the sad ballad of how Tom Dula murdered Naomi Wise, but Frankie Silver—in 1833 the first North Carolina woman executed by hanging— chopped her husband to bits with an ax and burned them in the fireplace. Her song—or his—awaits a balladeer.

Smith and Wilson do not pretend that all North Carolina women should climb off the paternalistic pedestal and onto the more modern feminist version. The book's theme is that heroes and villains come in both genders and that all belong in the history books.

Precisely because circumstances and winners do change, and because Smith and Wilson acknowledge in their introduction that the years between 1945 and 2000 moved at such dizzying speed through so many major changes that a separate history will be needed, this long overdue book already demands its sequel.

Bringing North Carolina's heretofore untold "her-story" into the mainstream of "his-story" makes clear to men as well as women the mutual benefit of knowing the *whole* story that generations of Tar Heels have shared. To have in schools, libraries, and homes this readable and carefully researched history is a joyful circumstance for all readers, who will realize anew how much better our shared future becomes when we learn from the shared past.

Everybody wins.

Doris Betts

Preface

The publication of *North Carolina Women: Making History* marks the culmination of a massive and complex effort to document the contributions of women to the building of our state. Beginning in the mid-1980s with the North Carolina Women's History Project at the state's Museum of History, the endeavor could not have succeeded without the dedicated effort and tangible support of a large number of individuals and organizations committed to the study of North Carolina women. Funding from the American Association for State and Local History, the North Carolina Literary and Historical Association, the North Carolina Museum of History Associates, the Woman's Club of Raleigh, and the North Carolina Humanities Council underwrote research-related expenses, especially travel, during the 1980s. Additionally, the Sara Lee Corporation, the Cannon Foundation, and the Z. Smith Reynolds Foundation were major contributors to the exhibition. Special acknowledgments are due John D. Ellington, North Carolina Museum of History administrator until 1994; Janice C. Williams, formerly head of the Education Branch and now associate director of the North Carolina Museum of History; Marion E. Gwyn, administrative assistant to John Ellington; Eve R. Williamson, executive director of the North Carolina Museum of History Associates; and Mabel Claire Hoggard Maddrey and Gladys Strawn Bullard of the Woman's Club of Raleigh, who solicited and supported funding for research and the collection of artifacts. Suellen M. Hoy, assistant director of the North Carolina Division of Archives and History from 1981 to 1987, supported all aspects of the Women's History Project. Coauthor Margaret Supplee Smith was curator of a major exhibition on women's history that opened the new museum building in 1994. Coauthor Emily Herring Wilson wrote the introductory video for the exhibition.

With support and encouragement from William S. Price Jr., then director of the North Carolina Division of Archives and History, Elizabeth F. Buford hosted a luncheon on January 10, 1989, at the suggestion of Jan Proctor, Barbara K. Allen, and Martha McKay of the Women's Forum of North Carolina, who felt the need for a published history of women in our state. Margaret Supplee Smith attended this meeting as coordinator of the Women's History Project of the North Carolina Museum of History. Buford agreed to chair a committee on the Women of North Carolina Publication Project on behalf of the Forum, an honorary leadership organization for women, and the North Carolina Department of Cultural Resources. When Jeffrey J. Crow became director of the North Carolina Division of Archives and History, he continued support for the publication. Terrell Armistead Crow served as chief researcher for the Women's History Project in its crucial initial stages. Joanie B. Cotten, Myrle L. Fields, Phyllis R. Whitehurst Russell, Rita A. Cashion, and Jennifer A. McCrory sent solicitation letters and tracked donations. Research funding and the authors' expenses were assisted by Jerry C. Cashion, head of the Research Branch of the Division of Archives and History; James C. McNutt, director of the Museum of History; Renné C. Vance, business officer for the Department of Cultural Resources; and Betty Ray McCain, who became the state's Secretary of Cultural Resources in 1993.

Members of the Women's Forum who served on the Women's History Project Committee are, as follows: Barbara K. Allen, Mimi Cunningham, Jeannette Hyde, Rae McNamara Jarema, Mary Turner Lane, Betty Ray McCain, Martha McKay, Neill McLeod, Helen Martikainen, Ruth Mary Meyer, and Kathy Baker Smith. Additional individual donations were received from the following Forum members: Lauren J. Brisky, Carol Ann Douglas, Tennala A. Gross, Mary Turner Lane, Donald O. and Meyressa H. Schoonmaker, and Winifred J. Wood. More recently, the North Carolina Federation of Women's Clubs provided assistance in the distribution of copies of the publication throughout the state.

Corporate donations to support research and writing for both the exhibition and the book were received from IBM, thanks to Dorothea L. Bitler; Southern Bell, thanks to R. David Lane; Kaiser Permanente Foundation, thanks to Alvin W. Washington; Josephus Daniels Charitable Foundation, thanks to Frank A. Daniels Jr.; Captive-Aire Systems, thanks to Robert L. Luddy; and A. J. Fletcher Foundation, thanks to Thomas H. McGuire. Diane S. Rodger of Tarheel Concepts donated mugs and tiles with the North Carolina Women's History Exhibit logo, which were sold in the Museum of History's gift shop; Frances H. Whitley, gift shop manager, targeted proceeds from the sale of these items for the project.

Staff members at the University of North Carolina Press have supported the many-faceted funding of this publication with good humor and generosity of spirit. They have remained constant and encouraging partners in this effort.

Funding for the publication of *North Carolina Women: Making History* has been a major public and private under-

Acknowledgments

Our writing of this book began a decade ago as part of the North Carolina Women's History Project. In the mid-1980s the North Carolina Museum of History (NCMOH), a section of the North Carolina Division of Archives and History (NCDAH) of the Department of Cultural Resources, began a monumental effort to see that women were fully incorporated into the state's history. John D. Ellington, then director of the museum, observed that the museum's major attention paid to women had been in exhibiting gowns of governors' wives every four years. The move to a new building provided just the occasion to showcase the state's first major women's history exhibit and to initiate an ambitious public history program of conferences, lectures, curriculum materials, brochures, and publications. Under the impetus of Suellen Hoy and Elizabeth F. Buford of the NCDAH director's office, Terrell Crow and other staff members of the division began compiling materials from the vast archives of books, manuscripts, letters, documents, and artifacts that became the nucleus for the exhibition and this book. Margaret Supplee Smith served as coordinator of the North Carolina Women's History Project and guest curator for the women's history exhibition.

In April 1994 *North Carolina Women Making History* was one of four exhibitions opening the new North Carolina Museum of History in Raleigh. Although viewers will discover many similarities between the exhibition and the book, the book develops the history of North Carolina women in more detail and in greater breadth than the exhibit format permits. During the many years of research, site visits, interviews, and writing, the scope of the book enlarged far beyond the authors' original intent—to become more ambitious and inclusive, but, we hope, to the reader's edification and delight. The women's history exhibit drew hundreds of thousands of visitors. When it closed after two years, some materials were reconstituted into a traveling exhibition, others were stored, and the permanent legacy of the North Carolina Women's History Project was still to come. Writing this book now became the task that was ours.

It is our pleasure to acknowledge the many people and institutions that have helped us bring this book to completion.

The early stages of research were made possible by two grants, one from the American Association for State and Local History and the other from the North Carolina Humanities Council, in what was an unprecedented demonstration of council support for a book. The Council's executive director, Alice Barkley, was a perceptive and enthusiastic supporter. Throughout the 1980s and early 1990s the Associates of the North Carolina Museum of History regularly funded intern and staff research on women's history that was used both for the exhibit and the book. The Graduate Research and Publication Fund of Wake Forest University supported us significantly with several grants for photographic and manuscript preparation; Dean of the Graduate School Gordon Melson was there every time we needed him, and we are grateful that he was always generous. Elizabeth F. Buford obtained funds from members of the Women's Forum of North Carolina and the North Carolina Department of Cultural Resources toward publication costs. Emily Wilson was awarded residencies at the McDowell Colony and at the Virginia Center for the Creative Arts.

In conducting our research we have benefited from the knowledge and kindness of staffs at the North Carolina Division of Archives and History; Duke Manuscript Collection; Friends Historical Collection; Greensboro Historical Museum; University Archives, Jackson Library of the University of North Carolina at Greensboro; John C. Campbell Folk School; Library of Congress; Moravian Archives; Museum of Early Southern Decorative Arts; North Carolina Collection and the Southern Historical Collection, both of the University of North Carolina at Chapel Hill; Oberlin College Archives; Old Salem, Inc.; Pack Memorial Library; Salem College Library; Tryon Palace Historic Sites and Gardens; and the Z. Smith Reynolds Library of Wake Forest University. Special thanks go to Stephen Catlett, Jerry Cotten, Virginia Daley, Sally Gant, Hilarie M. Hicks, Frank Horton, Elen Knott, Rachel Kuhn, Paula W. Locklair, William McRae, Steve Massengill, Richard Schrader, Rose Simon, George Stevenson, Susan Taylor, Carole Treadway, and Isabel Zuber.

Because this volume is so closely tied to the research, exhibition, and programs on women's history of the North Carolina Museum of History and the North Carolina Division of Archives and History, the staffs of those institutions, past and present, played uncommonly critical roles in its development. William S. Price Jr., John D. Ellington, and Elizabeth F. Buford believed that a book rather than a catalog was necessary to ensure the permanent place of women in North Carolina's history. Jacquelyn Dowd Hall, Beverly Jones, Susan Levine, Theda Perdue, Anne Firor Scott, and Carole Troxler composed an advisory board that initially established a framework for the exhibit that was important for our thinking about the book. Janice C. Williams, in her new capacity as associate director of the North Carolina Museum of History (now its own division), has consistently sustained institutional support for the book, as have NCMOH director James McNutt, NCDAH director Jeffrey Crow, and Secretary of Cultural Resources Betty Ray McCain.

For their research skills, knowledge of the state's material culture, and imagination and insight, we are especially grateful to Tom Belton, Vicki Berger, Catherine Bishir, Louise Benner, John Lee Bumgarner, Carole Chamberlain, Jim Cowles, Carey Crane, Wesley Creel, Jeffrey Crow, Terrell Armistead Crow, John Durham, Obelia Exum, Edward Flowers, Marion Gwyn, Gerry Herring, Eloise Jackson, Darryl Ketchum, Ruth Little, Faye Lovern, Jackson Marshall, Lea Walker Marshall, Tammy Martin-Hawkins, Joe A. Mobley, Debra Nichols, William "Billy" Oliver, Nancy Pennington, Sally Peterson, Patricia Phillips, Keith Strawn, James Sumner, Martha Tracy, Rhonda Tyson, Marianne Wason, and Janice C. Williams. Even after ten years, Tom Belton always promptly returned telephone calls and seemed genuinely pleased to answer a research query. Eric N. Blevins and D. Kent Thompson provided much of the photography, especially of objects from the NCMOH and NCDAH, and Nancy Pennington supplied her superb organizational skills to keep track of those photographs, as well as ones from other archives. North Carolina Women's History Project interns who generated initial research include Karen Lynne Cox, Kirsten Fischer, Jennifer Herndon, Lynn Hudson, Lu Ann Jones, Marjolein Kars, Angela Narron, and Lisa O'Neil. Intern Claudia Colhoun worked hard on a project whose completion lay so far in the future that we hope she is as pleased as we are that the book is finally done.

Equally important were the many scholars and friends who generously read and commented on our manuscript at various stages, among them Mary Jane Berman, Gene Capps, Jill Carraway, Stephen Claggett, Jeffrey Crow, Terrell Crow, Barbara R. Duncan, Paul D. Escott, John Mack Faragher, Gloria Fitzgibbon, Edward Flowers, Linda Flowers, Nancy Hewitt, LeAnne Howe, Lu Ann Jones, Marty Lentz, Dolly McPherson, Sydney Nathans, Linda Nielsen, Billy Oliver, Theda Perdue, Laura A. W. Phillips, Charles Wadelington, Alan Watson, Sarah Watts, Judith White, Raymond Winslow, Ned Woodall, Jean Yellin, Richard Zuber, and especially Elizabeth Phillips. Many people went out of their way to help us track down information or obtain photographs, including Dan Becker, Louise Benner, Carter B. Cue, Irene Disosway, Sarah Downing, Linda Edmisten, Ed Hendricks, Rick Jackson, David Liden, Laurey-Faye Long, Suzanne H. McDowell, Steve Massengill, Brenda O'Neal, Howell Smith, Irene Smith, Mitzi Schaden Tessier, Sarah Tillett Thomas, Rhonda Tyson, Mary Beth Sutton Wallace, and David "Giz" Womack. Susan Faust and Harry B. Titus offered continuing support over a long project.

We are grateful for the close reading of the manuscript by Wilson Angley, Catherine Bishir, and Anne Firor Scott and the editorial skills of Catherine Hutchins and Stevie Champion. We are indebted to the professionalism of the University of North Carolina Press staff: Iris Tillman Hill, Kate Torrey, and David Perry in the manuscript's initial stages; editors Elaine Maisner and Pam Upton and designer Richard Hendel as we transformed the manuscript into a book. Academic computing specialist Randy A. Riddle and the staff of the Wake Forest University Microcomputer Center helped smooth out the many complexities of a computer-generated manuscript.

Behind every author is support at home. In our case, we had more than moral support. Ed Wilson read the manuscript with an acute sensitivity to language, and Jackson Smith stepped up when photographic needs arose. We are grateful to them both. Finally, we need to thank each other for more than a decade of an intellectually stimulating, always challenging, and mutually supportive collaboration. We made each other laugh, cry, and lose sleep—but we got the job done.

Introduction

North Carolina history books for most generations of students contained the names of very few women—Queen Elizabeth and Virginia Dare come to mind. Of course, students had grandmothers who told them stories and mothers who taught them, but when they got up from the supper table to read their schoolbooks, they entered a house of history unlike any house they had ever lived in: where were the women? Seventeen women were among the settlers of the Lost Colony; between 1830 and 1840 women became a majority of North Carolinians; in 1920 more women were employed in textiles and tobacco in North Carolina than in any other southern state; and by the end of the twentieth century women made up about half of the state's workforce. Like most things taken for granted, women's roles in the making of North Carolina—and other states of our country—went unexamined for a very long time.

By contrast, this book draws together research on North Carolina women over centuries into a comprehensive narrative. As such, it goes against the trend in current historiography to take one segment of the past and illuminate a larger picture by thoroughly analyzing a microcosm. We have tried to see as much of the whole as possible because so much has been missing. Since we started this book almost a decade ago, new research and scholarly interpretations on women have been published and more are in the works, so that in the future the picture begun here will be redrawn in ever more detail and complexity, reinterpreted, revised, and expanded.

This first-ever history of North Carolina women, like its subject, evolved slowly. We began by trying to educate ourselves, reading as much as we could about American women and North Carolina women. Like most historians, some days we felt that we were in a race against time. The project—to gather what had already been researched, to stay current with recent scholarship, and to weave it all together into a readable history—was daunting. By the time we had written our way from prehistory to the end of World War II, we had to impose limitations: the second half of the twentieth century was so monumental that it would require a book of its own. There was more than enough to do between the first chapter on Native American women and the last chapter on women during World War II.

From the beginning we relied on the work of many scholars. Our method was twofold. A great deal of research had already been done; it not only put in our hands the materials we needed, but also in citing our sources we would be able to recognize how early and how long researchers had worked. Then, as time and resources permitted, we could conduct our own research to fill in some of the missing pieces.

Although we learned from many historians, we relied especially on the work of two scholars who published in the first half of the twentieth century and two who published in the second half. Guion Griffis Johnson's *Ante-Bellum North Carolina: A Social History* (1937) and Julia Cherry Spruill's *Women's Life and Work in the Southern Colonies* (1938) have been for us, as for many other writers, essential and incomparable. Two later books helped shape our understanding of the broader themes of women's history. In *At Odds: Women and the Family in America from the Revolution to the Present* (1984), Carl Degler considered how women's growing individuality in terms of activities outside their families—whether volunteer or paid—conflicted with their conventional role in the family. Sara M. Evans's *Born for Liberty: A History of Women in America* (1989) posited an active role for women in shaping their own history. She explored a major theme in women's history: women's roles in the private and public spheres, not as irreconcilable opposites but as opportunities for women to transform public life through an awareness of the traditional concerns of the home—education, health, and welfare. In developing this theme in our own research, we learned how the movement from the home into public places changed North Carolina as well as women's lives.

Despite the work of many historians, however, there were missing chapters, especially in the sixteenth, seventeenth, and eighteenth centuries. Even in later periods, information was not uniformly available on all groups of North Carolina women. To try to complete the picture, we turned to many different kinds of information. In using visual images from the *North Carolina Women Making History* exhibit, we created an illustrative history: needlework, clothing, jewelry, and household furnishings help us see the way women lived. In analyzing the architecture of houses and the composition of paintings, we discovered places where women worked and lived and ways in which they were represented. Archaeological shards, baskets and bowls, public records and oral histories, statistical data and demographic studies all supplied vital evidence.

At the same time that we tried to create a sense of the sweep and flow of a long, complex historical narrative, we attempted to mention as many individual women as possible. Present throughout our narrative are vignettes of many lives. Because written records favor white literate women and women in public life, they occupy a disproportionate share of the history. Nineteenth-century gentry women left copious journals and letters, whereas slave voices were heard in less obvious ways but not widely until oral interviews with former slaves were undertaken and published in the 1930s by the Works Progress Administration. During the same period sociologist Margaret Jarman Hagood documented the lives of tenant farm women. More recently, historians Lu Ann Jones and Anne Radford Phillips researched the lives of yeoman farm women, and Glenda Elizabeth Gilmore and Anastatia Sims studied middle-class clubwomen, black and white.

Women were not always on the same side: Native American women saw their land and lives destroyed by the arrival of settlers, whose women helped establish permanent homesteads; white women slaveowners controlled the lives of black slave women; women suffragists were opposed by women antisuffragists; the wives of millowners had little in common with women who worked in the mills. Only by considering the particular contours of individual lives as well as the broad constraints of gender, race, class, religion, and geography can we begin to understand the complexities and diversity of women's history.

With women at the center, the conventional pace of history changes. Anne Firor Scott has observed that many of the activities with which women are involved—maintaining households, rearing families, educating children, caring for the sick and the elderly—are long-term, private, and incremental rather than public and dramatic. To become aware of a history that is as familiar to us as our own lives, we asked basic questions. What did women do in North Carolina? How were their lives different from men's? How did women's lives differ from one another? What perspectives and experiences did race, class, geography, marital status, religion, and age impose? What impact did women have on the values and life of the state?

As we began to move through the centuries, two important themes emerged: first, women's importance in the economies underlying North Carolina's agrarian history and urban development, and second, women's significance in shaping values, at first in the privacy of their homes, then increasingly in the public sphere. Religion was central in most lives, and women became the mainstay of congregations. Because North Carolina remained a rural state well into the twentieth century, many women continued to practice the time-honored traditions of an agrarian society. When the farm could not support the family and wage work was necessary, women became the largest—and the lowest paid—labor force in the tobacco and textile industries. Even as women gave up their independence on the farm for dependence on paid jobs in small towns and cities, they gained access to more opportunities and activities. But the public life available in towns and cities was controlled mostly by men in government and business. Women found themselves in low-paying jobs at the same time that urbanization offered more housing, more consumer goods, and more entertainment—all of which cost more money. Having less and wanting more was common for many women, and the conservative and religious values of rural families were sometimes at odds with the values of a growing urban economy.

This history is presented through chronological narratives followed by biographical essays, fleshing out as fully as possible a small number of lives, not completely representative of many others but the most representative that we could find. We did not choose anyone now (1998) living as a subject for biography, and in selecting only twenty-two women from the past, we knew that our choices would sometimes be questioned, especially by readers who have their own favorite North Carolina women. But we were forced to impose limits on ourselves and hope that each woman whom we did include would, in various ways, be representative of many others. And we also made a great effort to include by name hundreds of women throughout the narrative chapters, often speaking in their own voices, from every part of the state, and from as many different homes and backgrounds and occupations as we could document. From these examples, we hope that other historians will find a rich field for further biographical research.

The book begins with an examination of the essential role that women—Native American, European, and African—played in settling North Carolina. Chapter 1, "The First Settlers of This Land," looks at Native American women, who lived in a culture in which they were the farmers, kinship and property were traced through the female line, and men and women played different but equally important roles. Following the narrative is a biographical essay on Cherokee War Woman Nanye'hi, later called Nancy Ward, whose native culture underwent dramatic changes after the arrival of Anglo-American settlers. Chapter 2, "The Most Industrious Sex in That Place," considers women and settlement and hypothesizes that white women settlers probably did not envision the New World as men did, that is, as "a Golden Age" or "Paradise," but in terms of what the new land offered them: smaller dreams of establishing families, building homes, planting gardens. On the North Carolina frontier in the Albemarle, men and women shared the same hardships and responsibilities, and the scarcity of people and the struggle to survive meant that gender and race did not always determine who did what. In that early society the boundaries between public and private, family and institution, owner and slave were still somewhat fluid.

By the eighteenth century North Carolina society had become more complex, and Chapter 3, "A Pattern of Industry," establishes something of a dialectic between women on the settled coast and those living in the backcountry; between those who purchased household items and those who engaged in home production; and among those who were slaves, those who owned slaves, and those who did not own slaves. Eighteenth-century rhetoric lauded the "notable housewife," and despite women's contributions to Revolutionary struggles, by 1800 women were less visible in the public sphere than previously. The biographies that follow this narrative are those of Rebecca Bryan Boone, who, as the wife of Daniel Boone and the mother of ten children, was a hardworking frontierswoman, and Ann Matthews Jessop, a Quaker minister in the New Garden community of present-day Guilford County. Enslaved women at Somerset plantation in the eastern part of the state and Moravian women in the Piedmont community of Salem represent women who lived collective lives.

The historic narrative continues with an examination of the lives of women in the traditional slaveholding agrarian society that was antebellum North Carolina and the ways they responded to the changes brought by the Civil War, Emancipation, and Reconstruction. Chapter 4, "A Hardier Mold," explores the centrality of family, kin, and church in black and white women's lives, whether slave or free, and considers the development of education and religion as they opened new horizons for some women, particularly those living in towns. Chapter 5, "The Labor of Her Own Hands," analyzes women's work on the farm, in the house, and in schools; it argues that women's domestic, agricultural, and industrial labor—slave and free black, planter and yeoman—undergirded Carolina's antebellum economy.

Chapter 6, "Women Entered the Struggle," focuses on women's role in the Civil War and after, from their support for the war within the gentry to yeoman resistance to the black sense that the end of slavery would bring opportunity with freedom. Women's "proper place" was challenged by their visible actions on the homefront, on the battlefield, and in new occupations. The hope of former slaves that education, industriousness, and justice would guarantee their civil rights was jeopardized by the unwillingness of whites to consider blacks as anything but inferior. The biography of Harriet Jacobs, who left Edenton and escaped to the North, where she joined the abolition movement, tells the story of how she came to write *Incidents in the Life of a Slave Girl*, under the name "Linda Brent." Although Jacobs's narrative contains fictionalized elements, it contributes to our historic understanding of enslaved women's lives in North Carolina. Other women in this period are Catherine Devereux Edmondston, who kept a journal about her life as a plantation mistress in Halifax County during the Civil War; Cornelia Phillips Spencer, who wrote and advocated for the University of North Carolina in Chapel Hill, where she lived, and for public education statewide; and Rhoda Strong Lowry, who as the wife of a guerrilla Indian fighter in Robeson County persevered through the tumultuous days of Reconstruction.

As the narrative moves into the modern period, we see that by 1920 North Carolina, though still predominantly rural, had become the most industrialized state in the South, based on a significant workforce of women. Race and class, as well as gender, strongly affected the opportunities available in this changing world. Chapter 7, "The Task That Is Ours," looks at how family life and women's work were reshaped by the realities of a different economy, New South industrialization, and the increasing urbanization that occurred between the end of Reconstruction and the first decade of the twentieth century. A biographical essay tells the story of Anna Julia Haywood Cooper, who graduated from St. Augustine's College in Raleigh, a recently created institution supported by the Freedmen's Bureau for the education of newly freed African Americans. Sallie Southall Cotten was inspired by her role as "lady manager" of North Carolina's exhibit at the 1893 Chicago World's Fair to return home and organize white middle-class women in a federation of women's clubs. A woman's entry into business is represented in the life of Julia Westall Wolfe, whose Asheville boardinghouse figures prominently in her son Tom's novel, *Look Homeward, Angel*.

Chapter 8, "More Was Expected of Us," explores how some women continued to stake out a feminine domain within public life by using the strategy of "organized womanhood" in suffrage, World War I activities, and labor reform and other social movements. Race and class dramatically affected the opportunities each had. Charlotte Hawkins Brown returned from Massachusetts, where she was educated, to her native North Carolina as a teacher for the American Missionary Association and stayed to build Palmer Memorial Institute for black children. Jane Simpson McKimmon pioneered in the state's home demonstration movement for women. Olive Dame Campbell, instrumental both in preserving folk traditions and in introducing new concepts into mountain life, and Mary Martin Sloop, concerned for children isolated in mountain communities, founded schools in western North Carolina. Active in support of many progressive causes—woman suffrage, voter education, child labor reform, and collective bargaining—Gertrude Weil was a well-known public woman who enjoyed family wealth and status. At the other end of the spectrum, Ella May Wiggins worked in textile mills and was a labor organizer. A popular balladeer, Wiggins was murdered on her way to sing for the union.

Chapter 9, "Turning Point or Temporary Gain," examines North Carolina women's role in World War II, a time that some historians consider a period of revolutionary change for women but others see as a period of only temporary change. Despite extraordinary events, some women continued to live as they had always lived: Minnie Evans, self-taught artist, and Elizabeth Lawrence, gardener and garden writer, fulfilled their ambitions in private lives. The postwar landscape for African Americans began to change under the leadership of early civil rights protesters like Pauli Murray, who later challenged laws and customs affecting blacks and women. Gladys Avery Tillett became a quintessential public woman, her life's work spanning the years between woman suffrage and unsuccessful efforts to pass the Equal Rights Amendment in 1982.

With the conclusion of the narrative and biographical essays, we move into an Epilogue, where, stepping back from history, we write in our own voices about the last half century. As children born just before America's entry into World War II, we have been part of the changes since that conflict and recognize the obstacles still faced by many women. In 1998, while others were perhaps looking ahead to the twenty-first century, we found ourselves looking back and seeing history as connected to the present in ways we had not even begun to consider.

After almost a decade of work, we are exhilarated by the realization that we have completed our journey; we have walked in many women's footsteps and have hoped to leave a few of our own. Although neither of us is a native of North Carolina, we have lived and worked in Winston-Salem for many years. In the course of our studies, travels, and conversations, we have come to feel at home in the state, on familiar ground. As women, we have had the intense satisfaction of knowing our own history. When Dorothy Spruill Redford "began as a woman alone, drifting in both time and place" to discover her African American roots in the eastern North Carolina slave community of Somerset, she said, "By traveling backward I had found an entire community of relatives I never knew existed."[1] We hope our readers will find just such a community of kinfolk in this history.

I

Prehistory through the Eighteenth Century

CHAPTER 1

The First Settlers of This Land

Native American Women

Indian legends and religious rituals celebrate women as givers of life and creators of the necessities for a settled domesticity—pottery, weaving, basketry, and farming. Native American women lived in a society where kinship was traced through the female line, where women controlled the communally owned land, and where men and women played different but equally important roles.

The arrival of the Europeans destroyed native culture, by disease and by design, and dramatically undercut the status and rights of women. By 1838, when the Cherokee were removed to present-day Oklahoma, women had already been displaced from their traditional place of power.

The history of women in North Carolina began thousands of years ago, when Asians walked across the wide Bering land bridge created by the advance and retreat of continental glaciers and the rise and fall of sea levels during the latter stages of the Ice Age. These small bands of nomadic people, women and men, followed tracks laid down by large animals, or they struck out on their own as circumstances required. They may have migrated eastward across arctic Canada, eventually finding a long narrow corridor of ice-free land on the eastern side of the Rockies that they followed south. Or perhaps they wended their way down the Pacific coast. After many generations, people moved southward and eastward across the North and South American continents. Eventually, some groups settled in the highlands and forests and on the coasts of what is now North Carolina.[1]

Tuscarora, who inhabited the Coastal Plain from the Roanoke to the Neuse Rivers, remembered how their ancestors endured a long, cold trip from the west in search of food. Over and over these stories were told until they became legend. In one, the speaker is an old woman telling her great-grandson how their people followed the rising sun to eventually find a forest with abundant food. When the travelers returned west for the people they had left behind, they discovered that the climate had warmed and the ice bridge on which they had crossed the great sea had disappeared. The Cherokee believe that they have always lived in the Great Smoky Mountains. Kana'ti, the first man, and Selu, the first woman, lived at Shining Rock, near present-day Waynesville in Haywood County, and the first Cherokee village was Kituwah, near present-day Bryson City in Swain County.[2]

Native people also had creation legends in which women played essential roles. According to the Tuscarora, the earth was created when the Great Chief of Skyland banished a pregnant woman and the animals from the upper spiritual world to the lower watery world. Water monsters held a meeting to decide what to do with the woman, and eventually the Great Turtle volunteered to hold her. The turtle's back was covered with dirt to form the earth, which was called the Great Island. In time, the woman gave birth to twins, one of whom was the Good Spirit or Master of Life and the other, the Evil Spirit or Master of Death. Thus Tuscarora explained the origin of good and evil in the world. For Algonquians, who lived along the coastal estuaries and rivers, the earliest human was a woman who coupled with a god, conceived, and gave birth to the first children. Siouans, who lived in the Piedmont and the lower Coastal Plain, believed that all humans descended from four women—Pash, Sepoy, Askarin, and Maraskin—who established four tribes.[3]

In Algonquian, Catawba, and Cherokee beliefs, the sun was female and the moon, male. The Cherokee legend of Grandmother Spider told how an old female spider created the light in the sky and the creatures on the earth. Spinning an intricate web to connect both spiritual and natural worlds, she taught her people skills to improve their lives—pottery, weaving, and basketry. Another Cherokee story—of Selu (Corn) and Kana'ti (the Lucky Hunter)—explained how women were linked to farming. Kana'ti furnished the game, always in plentiful supply from a secret cave, and Selu provided corn and beans. When their son and a "wild boy," who grew from the blood of the game killed by Kana'ti, set the animals free, there was no meat available, and corn and beans became their main diet. Selu rubbed her stomach, and her basket was half filled with corn. She then rubbed under her armpits, and the basket was filled to the top with beans. When she realized that the wild boys were going to kill her, Selu taught them how to grow corn, thus ensuring that her people would always have food.[4]

These ancient legends identify women in four significant roles: as life givers, as indispensable to the earth and its processes, as intermediaries between the natural and spiritual worlds, and as different from men but equally important. We can infer from the traditional stories that women were regarded with respect in native cultures long before Europeans and Africans set foot on the land known today as North Carolina.

How the Sun Came

When Grandmother Spider came to the place of the sun people, she was so little and so quiet no one noticed her. She reached out gently, gently, and took a tiny bit of the sun, and placed it in her clay bowl. Then she went back along the thread that she had spun, with the sun's light growing and spreading before her, as she moved from east to west. And if you will notice, even today a spider's web is shaped like the sun's disk and its rays, and the spider will always spin her web in the morning, very early, before the sun is fully up.
—Marriott and Rachlin, *American Indian Mythology*, 32.

Women in Prehistory

Twelve thousand years ago North Carolina was glacial and dry. Although scant evidence remains of the earliest cultures, common sense suggests that finding food and surviving were the most critical activities. Weapons, stone tools, and bone needles and awls have been found by archaeologists in prehistoric sites such as the Hardaway Site in Stanly County. From these fragments we know that Paleo-Indians moved around in small bands in pursuit of the large animals such as mammoths and bisons, which were still extant in the final stages of the Ice Age. They also hunted small game, fished, collected shells, and gathered plants.[5]

The Archaic tradition emerged about ten thousand years ago and lasted approximately seven thousand years. The climate had moderated, and people's diet reflected the changes in animal and plant life produced by the warmer temperatures. There was less dependence on large animals and more on smaller ones like deer, elks, bears, and turkeys. Oak, hickory, and other deciduous trees provided acorns, nuts, and fruits that could be gathered at certain times of the year. People, though still few in numbers, were dispersed rather widely across the landscape. They tended to return to familiar locales—summer camps on river banks or seashores and winter camps in the uplands—season after season, year after year. From these semipermanent camps Archaic Indians gathered plants, fished in streams, collected shellfish, and hunted game.[6]

What roles did women play in this hunter-gatherer-forager culture? Archaeology can reveal what foods were important in prehistoric cultures, but it cannot disclose who was responsible for gathering and preparing them. Ethnohistoric observations and cross-cultural studies, however, are clear on two points: gender tended to determine subsistence tasks, and women traditionally gathered plants while men hunted game. Thus we can surmise that women supplied the group with wild plants, roots, bark, berries, nuts, and seeds, an important contribution as plant foods constituted the majority of Archaic people's diet. Presumably women also prepared the food—grinding acorns, hickory nuts, or chestnuts with a simple mortar and pestle, or cooking, by placing hot stones in vessels like a soapstone bowl (Fig. 1-1).[7]

During the third prehistoric period, known as the Woodland, starting about five thousand years ago and lasting through the arrival of the Europeans in the 1600s, two major inventions associated with women in legends appeared—the creation of pottery and the development of horticulture. Making pots and cultivating crops did not surface overnight, but by the end of the Woodland period, those activities had transformed native culture. Indians continued to depend on hunting, gathering, and fishing, but they increasingly relied on crops like corn, squash, sunflowers, gourds, and beans they cooked and stored in ceramic vessels. They did not have to forage constantly for food, and as a result of a more stable diet, they sustained larger populations. Life was still precarious, but as they had closer around them more of the things needed for survival, they probably developed attachments to place. And "place" meant more permanent villages located on the fertile floodplains near streams and rivers and surrounded by fields of corn and beans.[8]

Cultivating plants—horticulture—expanded the gathering activity in which the women had long been engaged. The entire process was gradual, and the domestication of plants is thought to have occurred in three different episodes separated by many years. The first was the cultivation of bottle gourds, about 9,000 years ago. Then, around 5,500 years ago, a variety of highly nutritious plants with oily and starchy

FIGURE 1-1. *Late Archaic bowl*, soapstone, 2000–500 B.C. (Courtesy of the Douglas Rights Collection, Museum of Anthropology, Wake Forest University)

FIGURE 1-2. *Late Woodland vessel* from Donnaha site, Yadkin County, clay, A.D. 1000–1500. (Courtesy of the Museum of Anthropology, Wake Forest University)

seeds and weedy greens such as sumpweeds, goosefoots, and sunflowers began to be cultivated. Some 1,000 years ago, the third phase began, with the growing of maize (corn). Years of collecting wild plants meant that women were familiar with the best specimens. They harvested tasty ones, ignored or discarded inedible ones, and observed species that tended to germinate and thrive. Eventually they encouraged some plants while removing others, and in this way they actively managed their gardens. Ultimately they planted seeds deliberately, tended the plants, and harvested the crop.[9]

Just as earlier women learned how to cultivate plants like sumpweeds and sunflowers, their descendants probably approached maize production in a purposeful fashion. They applied the knowledge they had gained in growing local domesticated plants to adapt maize—which had originated in Mesoamerica—to the climatic and soil conditions of the Southeast. Trial and error certainly guided their efforts. By A.D. 1100, both maize and squash were cultivated up and down the flood plain of the upper Yadkin Valley, along the Coastal Plain, and in the Mountains. After A.D. 1200, beans also were grown across prehistoric North Carolina. New tools were devised to cultivate the new crops, such as shell hoes on the Coastal Plain and chipped stone hoes in the Piedmont. Cultivating crops must have been precarious in its early stages, but ultimately women provided a food supply that did not depend on the vagaries of hunting or gathering.[10]

The development of agriculture and the technology of pottery went hand in hand (Fig. 1-2). Corn and beans took longer to cook than wild and semicultivated plants, so new utensils and methods of cooking were required (Fig. 1-3). Certainly pottery helped make women's work easier. Ceramics were more durable and adaptable containers than the earlier soapstone vessels or woven baskets. Clay vessels made it possible to save surplus and leftover food and to haul and store water. We can speculate that as work habits became more efficient and expressive, women turned to one another to share their successes, and in this way the definition of women's collective working took shape.[11]

The manufacture of ceramics is often considered one measure by which a society becomes less nomadic and more sedentary. And yet pottery is also a means by which contact

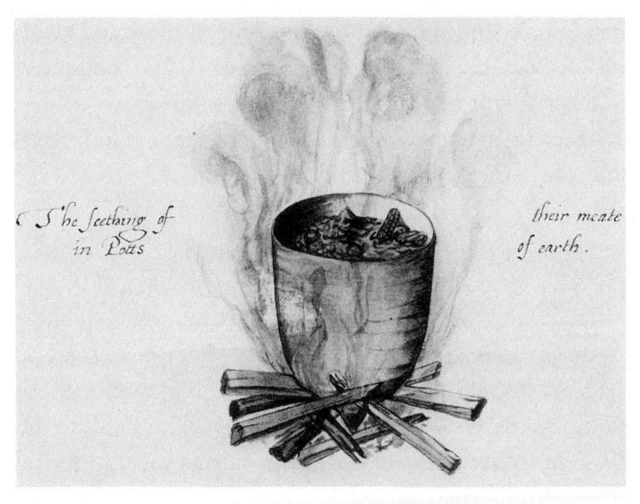

FIGURE 1-3. John White (fl. 1577–93), *The seething of their meate in Potts of earth*, watercolor, America or England, ca. 1585–86. Of the Algonquians, Roanoke chronicler Thomas Harriot observed: "Their woemen know how to make earthen vessells with special Cunninge and that so large and fine." De Bry XV, in Hulton, *America 1585*, 121. Ceramic cooking pots were designed to stand firmly in the fire and permitted women to heat foodstuffs at higher temperatures for longer periods of time, thus increasing the potential range of foods in the everyday diet as beans and corn became available. (British Museum; Hulton, *America 1585*, Plate 44)

and interaction between communities can be traced. Although the mass, weight, bulk, and breakability of earthenware would seem to preclude its being carried long distances by a people who traveled on foot, the archaeological record is full of examples of pottery traded between far-flung communities. Women traded the goods they produced in the historic period: it is possible that their female ancestors also traveled from their villages to exchange ceramics for other goods.

A fourth prehistoric tradition, called Mississippian, was briefly established in the south-central Piedmont (present-day Montgomery County) and the Mountains when Peedee Indians invaded from the south in the 1400s. Gaining only a temporary foothold, Mississippian society was more structured than the Woodland and emphasized political and religious organization, militarism, and social hierarchies based on heredity and military exploits. The Cherokee participated extensively in the Mississippian traditions, and during this period their agriculture provided surpluses that fueled their extensive trade with other southeastern tribes.[12]

Most North Carolina Indians participated in the Late Woodland pottery-making and horticultural traditions. There were about thirty different tribes and three major linguistic groups: the Siouans, the ancestors of the Catawba; the Iroquois, to which the Tuscarora and Cherokee belonged; and the Algonquians, which included the Roanokes, Secotans, and Croatans. The Late Woodland natives lived in villages scattered along the banks of rivers and coastal estuaries, and they depended on a mix of hunting, fishing, and planting of crops like maize, beans, pumpkins, and sunflowers cultivated with hand tools. Men and women existed in a balanced interchange, each playing a different but indispensable role in the group's survival.

FIGURE 1-4. John White (fl. 1577–93), *Theire Sitting at meate*, watercolor, America or England, ca. 1585–86. John White's drawings, made in 1585 when Europeans first came into contact with coastal Algonquians, delineate a world in which parity seems to have existed between the sexes. Here a man and a woman sit in similar positions, their heads at comparable heights, and eat from a common platter. Both wear deerskin mantles, and both are ornamented—the man with his ear bobs, the woman a necklace. (British Museum; Hulton, *America 1585*, Plate 41)

Native Americans and European Contact

This Late Woodland horticultural tradition was what the European immigrants encountered as they traveled across the North Carolina landscape from the late 1500s through the 1700s. They were confronted with a matrilineal culture far different from their own (Fig. 1-4). Indians sought survival before surplus, they valued communal sharing, and women held considerable power and autonomy. Europeans, on the other hand, came from a patriarchal culture that emphasized individual initiative and a market economy, one in which a man held absolute authority over his wife, children, servants, and slaves. Native cultures had developed through centuries of living close to the land in the three distinct geographic regions recognized then—as now: Coastal Plain, Piedmont, and Mountains.[13]

About one hundred years after the first English attempts at settlement in 1585, approximately 10,000 Native Americans such as the Tuscarora, Algonquians, and Siouans lived in North Carolina east of the Mountains and 32,000 Cherokee lived in the mountain areas that now form parts of Tennessee, Georgia, and North Carolina. All of these tribes followed similar patterns of accommodation to the Europeans: resistance where possible, but ultimately defeat and, in many cases, the agony of death from the diseases brought by the settlers. Some of the smaller Algonquian tribes, such as the Hatteras, Yeopins, and Machapungas living in present-day Dare, Currituck, and Pasquotank Counties, were not placed on reservations, but by the 1670s the Chowans were relocated to a reservation in present-day Gates County. Many of the Tuscarora who remained in North Carolina after their defeat at Nooherooka in 1713 eventually moved north to join Iroquois tribes in New York and Pennsylvania, though some remained on a reservation in what is now Bertie County. Siouan-speaking tribes scattered throughout the Piedmont tried to survive by forming a confederation known as the Catawba Nation and eventually resettled in South Carolina. The only Native American North Carolinians to survive the 1700s were the Cherokee, whose mountain land was less desirable to Europeans who wanted to farm.[14]

In the small villages occupied by Native Americans during the warm months, women's culture was predominant: nurturing children, tending gardens, cultivating the larger fields, preparing meals, hauling water and firewood, making baskets and pottery, and caring for the sick. Their daily activities were visible to all, and open, arborlike wooden dwellings made it easy for the women to get together for news and conversation. European Americans thought that Indian men were lazy because they witnessed summer village life when the men were resting, exercising, playing games, or fishing. In winter, when men were away hunting, those who remained behind—the elderly, children, and women—retreated to enclosed dwellings, but still the women's work was evident. "The whole care of the house falls upon the women," Philadelphia naturalist William Bartram observed of the Cherokee in the 1760s. The women "then obliged to undergo a good deal of labor, such as cutting and bringing home the winter's wood, which they toat [*sic*] on their back or head a great distance, especially those of the ancient large towns, where the commons or old fields extend some miles to the woodland."[15]

Women did work hard, and because they lived in a culture characterized by matrilineality, matrilocality, and maternal control of household goods and resources, they owned the crops they grew and the household objects they made. In matrilineal culture, a woman's ability to bear children was a source of tremendous power, and within her family, clan, and community she wielded considerable authority.

FIGURE 1-5. John White (fl. 1577–93), *A chiefe Herowans wyfe of Pomeoc and her daughter of the age of 8 or 10 yeares*, watercolor, America or England, ca. 1585–86. The little girl holds a doll dressed in Elizabethan clothing. (British Museum; Hulton, *America 1585*, Plate 33)

Matrilineality: "She Keeps the Children and Property"

Matrilineality means that the entire social structure revolves around women. They not only give birth to children; they also give them a lifelong social identity (Fig. 1-5). North Carolina Indian children traced their bloodline through their mothers rather than through their fathers as in the European patrilineal system. Children belonged to their mothers' clans and were identified by their clan symbols in a society in which clans provided the basic social organization (Fig. 1-6). For example, the seven matrilineal Cherokee clans, divided into white or peace clans and red or war clans, determined political alignments.[16]

The origin of Siouan culture of the upland parts of Virginia and North Carolina was described by seventeenth-century German explorer John Lederer: "From four woman, viz., *Pash, Sepoy, Askarin* and *Maraskarin*, they divide the race of Mankinde; which they therefore divide into four Tribes, distinguished under several names. They very religiously observe the degrees of Marriage, which they limit not to distance of Kindred, but difference of Tribes, which are continued in the issue of the Females."[17]

For Siouans and other North Carolina Native Americans, reckoning kinship meant that "blood" relatives—male or

FIGURE 1-6. *Siouan gorget* with rattlesnake motif from burial SKl, shell, late Woodland period, ca. 1500. (Courtesy of the Collection of the Research Laboratories of Archaeology, University of North Carolina at Chapel Hill)

female—came only from the mother's side of the family. This practice surprised the Europeans, who, though patrilineal, included the mother's family in the bloodline. "The children always fall to the Woman's lot," English explorer John Lawson observed in 1709. "It often happens, that two *Indians* that have liv'd together, as Man and Wife, in which Time they have had several Children; if they part, and another Man possesses her, all the Children go along with the Mother, and none with the Father."[18] Indian fathers officially had little to do with their children, who were not considered part of their clan or lineage. For example, a Cherokee mother could kill her infant at birth or immediately after and not be punished. If a father killed his child, even accidentally, he was subject to clan vengeance. Furthermore, the major male influence in the child's life came directly through the mother. Her brothers (the child's uncles) rather than her husband were responsible for passing along male culture.[19]

Typical of many horticultural societies, a man joined his wife's household, which often included her mother and sisters. Matrilocality differed from English tradition, in which a woman came as outsider to her husband's home and focused her energies on that individual patriarchal household. If a Native American couple divorced, a procedure that was relatively easy and could occur at the instigation of either partner, the woman and children stayed with her family and the man returned home to his mother. "Marriage gives no right to the husband over the property of his wife," William Bartram noted in the mid-eighteenth century, "and when they part she keeps the children and property belonging to them." Indeed, the women owned the bark-covered Algonquian houses and fields abundant with maize, pumpkins, and sunflowers depicted by John White (Fig. 1-7).[20]

Native American women also were free to have as many sexual partners before marriage as they wanted and to select their husbands. Once married, their unions "are no farther binding, than the Man and Woman agree together," observed John Lawson. "Either of them has Liberty to leave the other." The women's sexual freedom challenged European American standards of appropriate sexual conduct, according to which men could be sexually active but "good" women were to be chaste before marriage and faithful afterward. In contrast, Indian girls as well as boys enjoyed sexual freedom. "The Girls at 12 or 13 Years of Age, as soon as Nature prompts

FIGURE 1-7. Theodore De Bry (ca. 1528–98), *The Towne of Secota (Indian village of Secotan)*, engraving. John White's 1585 rendering of the Algonquian town of Secotan shows the corn crop in three stages—"newly sprong," "green," and "ripe"—and small garden plots of pumpkins and sunflowers that the women cultivated in cooperative, all-female work groups. (Hulton, *America 1585*, Figure 24)

them, freely bestow their Maidenheads," wrote Lawson. That females could select and change mates, without fear of retribution from men or of damage to their reputations, shocked him. Lawson noted that an Indian woman could give "her Favours on whom she most affects, changing her Mate very often" and that the "Multiplicity of Gallants [was] never . . . a Stain to a Female's Reputation, or the least Hinderance of her Advancement." He concluded, "the more *Whorish*, the more *Honourable*, and they of all most coveted, by those of the first Rank, to make a Wife of."[21]

Native American women's sexual autonomy challenged the proprietary manner with which European Americans regarded women. "The *Flos Virginis*, so much coveted by the *Europeans*," Lawson noted in 1709, "is never valued by these Savages." Some thirty years later, Edenton doctor John Brickell observed that the Indian men "do not seem so very careful of their Females as the *Europeans*, having no Bars or Partitions to keep the Men at a distance from the Women." The notion of women as valuable property to be guarded—from other predatory men—permeates much of European American descriptions of sexual freedom among Native American women.[22]

Irish trader James Adair understood the relationship between women's sexual autonomy and political authority. He found the Cherokee

> an exception to all civilized or savage nations, in having no laws against adultery; they have been a considerable while under petticoat-government, and allow their women full liberty to plant their brows with horns as oft they please, without fear of punishment. On this account their marriages are ill observed, and of short continuance; like the Amazons, they divorce their fighting bed-fellows at their pleasure, and fail not to execute their authority, when their fancy directs them to a more agreeable choice.[23]

Although sexual equity drew the attention of western observers, Indian women and men had another, more pressing concern: their day-to-day quest for survival. In this, women and men had separate and distinctive roles to play, governed by cycles both daily and seasonal. Men's work came in intensive bouts, such as pursuing game for days or weeks at a time, followed by similarly long periods of inactivity because they generally did not take care of the children or perform domestic chores. Women's work tended to be more even, more constant, more integrated into the daily pattern of life. They had little "leisure" time, for their responsibility for children, domestic life, and farming was continual.

In horticultural societies men typically helped clear the land and prepared the plots for planting; women planted, tended, and harvested the crops. In the 1580s the chronicler of the Roanoke voyages, Thomas Harriot, described Algonquian men and women sharing the initial tasks of preparing the ground to plant corn: "the men with woodden instruments, made almost in forme of mattocks or hoes with long handles; the women with short peckers or parers, because they use them sitting, of a foot long and about five inches in bredth." Once the soil was prepared, men's work was done, and women, "beginning in one corner of the plot, with a pecker they make a hole, wherein they put foure graines, with that care they touch not one another."[24]

Garden plots cultivated by women were a distinctive feature noted by travelers. In the 1770s James Adair wrote that every dwelling had "a small field" close by, and some years later William Bartram mentioned the "little plantations" of corn and beans scattered among the Cherokee village dwellings. Women tended both garden plots and the larger fields located farther away. As Cherokee towns lost population in the 1700s and contracted in size, cultivating distant fields became more difficult, and the fields were moved closer to the women's household domain.[25]

Women also collected wild vegetables, berries, nuts, and seeds, which continued to be an important part of the Native American diet. There was a seasonal urgency to their quest. They found blackberries, strawberries, and raspberries in the summer and nuts—chestnuts, chinquapins, pecans, hickory nuts, black walnuts—and roots like the "wild sweet potato" (or wild morning glory) in the fall. After the first frost, they collected persimmons. The women knew the location of muscadines or scuppernongs, the times when seeds like the cockspurgrass or chenopodium were likely to flourish, and medicinal uses for ginseng and snakeroot.[26]

Women living near the coastal waters gathered clams and oysters, an activity that presented a change of pace and elements of play along with work for the all-female groups, which included children and older women. Shellfish were valued for more than food. Shells, or wampum made from shells, were an important commodity that coastal people could exchange for goods found in the Piedmont or the Mountains, like clay, salt, or mica.[27]

Maintaining households and caring for families were also women's work. "*Indian* Womens Work is to cook the Vituals for the whole Family," reported John Lawson, "and to make Mats, Baskets, Girdles of Possum-Hair, and such-like." Pottery could be made at home along with other household tasks (Fig. 1-8). Because of their knowledge of the uses of plants as contraceptives, and because they may have avoided pregnancy by prolonged nursing of infants, women generally had only two to three children, in contrast to the much larger families of European American settlers. "I never saw a Scold amongst them," observed Lawson, "and to their Children

FIGURE 1-8. *Cherokee check stamped cooking pot*, clay, 1800s. The stamped design was made with a wooden paddle. (Courtesy of the Collection of the Research Laboratories of Archaeology, University of North Carolina at Chapel Hill)

they are extraordinarily tender and indulgent; neither did I ever see a Parent correct a Child, excepting one Woman."[28]

On the autumn and winter hunting trips, women and children frequently accompanied men and boys, establishing hunting camps great distances from home. An observer of the Virginian Algonquians reported, "as the men goes further a huntinge the weomen goes before to make houses, always carrienge ther mattes with them." Deer hunting involved hours of labor by hunters and women. In the eighteenth century, when "burdening" was practiced, the women carried heavier loads than the hunters. Women also processed deerskins into clothing or other items, preserved meat, and manufactured a variety of bone implements. Just as men had specific roles to play in women's plant-growing activities, women had clearly defined tasks to support a successful deer hunt.[29]

Such a clear division of labor reflects the conviction that women and men had contrasting roles in their economy. The Cherokee story of Selu and Kana'ti explains the origins of hunting and farming and expresses a belief in the opposition of men and women, animals and plants. In the exchange of gifts that marked the Cherokee marriage ceremony, the man would bring game he had killed and the woman, corn she had grown. The seasons associated with women's and men's economic activities also differed, with women cultivating crops in the summer and men hunting game in the winter. Even so, the sharp woman/plant/warm and man/hunt/cold duality was probably moderated by reality: in a subsistence culture everyone had to work every day for food. In the warm months men occasionally fished and hunted and helped women with the farming, and during the cold season women occasionally participated in hunting parties and collected food. Among coastal Algonquians, for example, groups of men and women worked cooperatively in setting traps on deer drives and in building houses, the men getting the poles and the women making the mats for the walls. The organization of labor by sex also was blurred by age. Overall, however, most day-to-day activities were carried out in same-sex groups and, as such, encouraged identification with one's own gender.[30]

Women's work extended beyond their immediate households and encompassed trade with different tribes and with Europeans. Sharing a common residence with female kin undoubtedly facilitated women's control over their communal resources, which they were free to trade. Cherokee women's right to trade is considered proof that they owned the land and the crops they grew. Thomas Harriot mentioned trading with Algonquian women for corn in the 1580s, and James Adair, with Cherokee women for processed deerskins in the 1770s. John Lawson reported that shells, pottery, wooden bowls, baskets, and mats were "often transported to other *Indians*, that perhaps have greater Plenty of Deer and other Game." Roots gathered in the mountain forests and ground to make red powder for paint were traded to coastal Indians who held "this Scarlet Root in great Esteem, and sell it for a very great Price, one to another." Women adapted their traditional crafts to the European trade and absorbed the new wares into already existing patterns. They substituted glass beads for shells, iron pots for clay vessels, and cloth for fur, and transformed copper kettles into ornaments.[31]

That Algonquian women were traders has been well documented. In 1584 English explorer Arthur Barlowe described the high-status women accompanying Granganimeo, Chief Wingano's brother, in an initial trading visit with the English, at which Granganimeo exchanged twenty deerskins for a bright tin dish to be used as a necklace called a gorget. Later, the women returned to the English ship on their own and, in the first of many trading occasions, brought leather and coral. These women held a strong position because early English explorers needed the corn and other foodstuffs that they grew.[32]

Siouan women had produced and traded baskets, mats, and deerskins long before the English arrived. Indeed, the cane baskets that William Byrd's men took back to Virginia from the Siouan Piedmont in the 1700s were the products of a craft tradition that was flourishing in the 1540s when Hernando de Soto passed through. Women did not wait for the traders to come to them: there are instances of Siouan women traveling to colonial towns to sell pottery.[33]

Cherokee women were also known as traders. Both colonial traders and British troops depended heavily on the Cherokee for basic supplies like corn and beans, chickens and pigs, all raised by the women, and women used manufactured trade goods like iron hoes in their farming. Their trading activities were a matter of consternation to the colonial government, which equated commercial traffic with sexual traffic and considered the women's selling corn a subversive activity. A group of Cherokee women from a village known for its mulberry bark creations expressed an awareness of their economic and political importance when they sent a present to England's Queen Anne. They entrusted English emissaries to carry to "that good Woman" a special example of their handwork, "a large carpet made of mulberry bark for herself to sit on and twelve small ones for her Counsellours." Cherokee women turned their plant gathering to entrepreneurial advantage and capitalized on the colonial demand for medicinal herbs. By 1760 they were the Southeast's largest suppliers of Indian pink, ginseng, and Virginia snakeroot. They also participated in the male-dominated deerskin trade, which by the mid-1700s had evolved from a subsistence activity to a major economic endeavor.[34]

Among the Cherokee, men and women approached their respective trading ventures differently—the men embracing a market economy and trading deerskins for whatever price they could get, the women exercising caution and discretion based on traditional values. Women gave corn freely within their community, in keeping with cultural notions of hospitality, but charged a high price on the outside market. The women also seem to have rationed their sales of plants such as ginseng, which was particularly valued as part of Cherokee ritual, to ensure that an adequate supply remained for use in their community.[35]

Native American Women and Spirituality

Indian women's work was an integral part of everyday life and of ceremonial ritual that drew the whole community together. Rituals provided sacred counterparts to the yearly cycles of obtaining food. The most important of the celebrations held by nearly every tribe in the Southeast was the Green Corn Ceremony, a thanksgiving for a successful corn crop in late summer or early autumn. The renewal ceremony provided an opportunity for the tribe to restore balance and harmony within the community and in the cosmos. It was also a time to ensure the well-being of the tribe—fertility, abundance, long life, and freedom from disease—for the next year. Grievances were forgiven and marriages either dissolved or renewed. Cherokee women, as daughters of Selu, played an important part in the Green Corn Ceremony, in which an old woman presented the new corn crop. During this time Cherokee men and women separated from one another. Men could not use the word *agehya* (woman): instead, they had to refer to "one who owns a house." For their part, women fasted, purified themselves, cleaned their houses and cooking vessels, renewed their hearths, and joined with other women in the sacred songs and dances.[36]

Indians believed that the natural world is animated by the spiritual, and both men and women sought to transcend their earthly experience to attain spiritual knowledge. Both men and women retreated from communal tribal life, often at the peak of their most sex-linked activities—before hunting and war parties for men and during menstruation, pregnancy, and birthing for women. Women were considered extremely powerful during these special times: they were isolated because they might be dangerous, killing crops or draining men of their strength before war or hunting. In Cherokee culture, a menstruating woman was forbidden to touch a man and withdrew to a small dwelling built for her isolation. At the end of her period, she emerged, bathed, dressed in clean clothing, and reentered the community. To some observers, such seclusion has been considered evidence that women were seen as unclean polluters. Others have viewed this practice as an opportunity for women to withdraw from their daily labor on a regular basis, often in concert with other women in their households who more than likely would have been on similar menstrual cycles. Through these periodic retreats women could rest, fast, meditate, and attain spiritual wisdom.[37]

Native American Women and Power: "Female Issue Carrying the Heritage"

Women's political power was based on the matrilineal kinship system and their position in a ranked society. They exerted the most power at the village level, where they controlled the domestic front, clan relations, and much of the economy. This authority was significant because Indian life centered on the local village and daily, intimate contact with kin and tribe.

Just as inheritance passed through the female line, positions of power, insofar as they were hereditary, were reckoned the same way. Algonquian leadership descended through the oldest sister of the chief. The English, who were familiar with the hierarchal structure of royalty, regarded high-status women as "queens." John Lawson explained that the chief of the Keyauwee, whom he visited in 1701, "got this Government by Marriage with the Queen; the Female Issue carrying the Heritage." Although the English made no mention of women chieftains in North Carolina, Spanish explorers recorded the

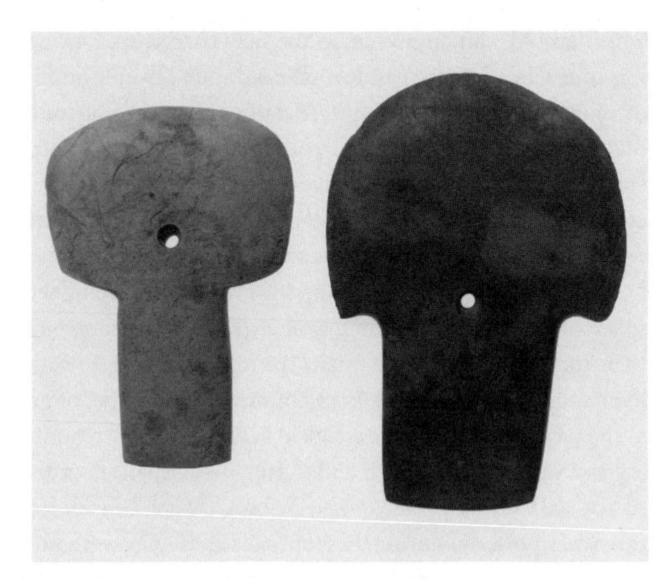

FIGURE 1-9. *Spatulate axes* found in association with a young adult female at Porter site in Wilkes County, Mississippian, ca. 1450. (Courtesy of the Archeology Laboratory, Wake Forest University)

names of the most powerful chieftains of the most powerful towns—and some of those names belonged to women. In 1540 de Soto, visiting a town near present-day Camden, South Carolina, found it ruled by a woman, the "Lady of Cofitachequi." Twenty-five years later Juan Pardo, one of de Soto's captains, met two female chiefs on his explorations along the Yadkin River, at Guatari, near Salisbury.[38]

The woman whose grave remains were discovered at an upper Yadkin River site may have been a chieftain, for the polished green stone axes buried with her are symbols of authority. They date from the mid-fifteenth century and can be traced to Coosa (in present northern Georgia), a Mississippian center that de Soto considered the most powerful sixteenth-century chiefdom (Fig. 1-9). How they ended up in a Late Woodland village in present-day Wilkes County is unknown, but their presence implies a social, economic, and political relationship in which the symbols of a powerful Mississippian culture were held by a woman many miles away.[39]

A young Saura woman who lived along the Dan River in the Piedmont about three hundred years ago must have held a prominent position in her Siouan-speaking culture. Although only about eighteen years old when she died, she was treated with considerable respect in death. The valuable objects buried with her included an English silver-plated brass spoon dated 1624 and two pairs of iron scissors. Her burial garment was deerskin ornamented with more than 36,000 small glass and shell beads and copper bells, the sort of dress that would have been worn during dancing or ceremonial activities (Fig. 1-10).[40]

Cherokee women had an active role in tribal government. Because Cherokee traditions were matrilineal and matrilocal and governance was by the clans, women had equal power with men in making decisions for their tribes. A few exceptional women were called "Beloved" or "War" women because they had distinguished themselves in battle. They were expected to speak at the town council, at which all the major political decisions were made, and had the power to decide the fate of captives. The best known of these leaders was Nanye'hi, also known as Nancy Ward, whose biography follows this section. In 1789 a Cherokee woman wrote Benjamin

FIGURE 1-10. *Reconstruction of a Saura woman* dressed in a recreated deerskin garment, ca. 1700. The original garment was found in association with a young female, Burial 1, SKvIA, Stokes County. (Based on the Collection of the Research Laboratories of Archaeology, University of North Carolina at Chapel Hill; courtesy of the North Carolina Museum of History)

Franklin that she had entreated her people to make peace with the new American nation, stating: "I am in hopes that if you Rightly consider that women is the mother of All—and the Woman does not pull Children out of Trees or Stumps nor out of old Logs, but out of their Bodies, so that they ought to mind what a woman says." As Native Americans adapted to the changes brought by white settlers, women sometimes acted as intermediaries and gained another source of power.[41]

The Impact of European Contact on the Status of Native American Women

In 1584 Arthur Barlowe wrote of having been entertained by the wife of Granganimeo, the brother of the Algonquian chief Wingano. Barlowe had met her earlier, when she and her daughter had accompanied her husband on a trading visit to his ship. He described her as "very well favored, of meane stature, and very bashfull: she had on her backe a long cloke of leather, with the furre side nexte to her bodie, and before her a peece of the same; about her forehead, she had a broad bande of white Corrall, . . . in her eares she had bracelets of pearles, hanging downe to her middle."[42] No sketch of her survives, but John White painted another high-status woman, the wife of the herowan (chief) of Secotan (Fig. 1-11).

Some days later Barlowe went to visit Granganimeo, who lived in a small village of about nine houses on the northern end of Roanoke Island in present-day Dare County. Granganimeo was away, and his wife received the travelers kindly and took great care to provide for their comfort. She served them fish, venison, melons, and fruits from clay pots on wooden plates. While the Englishmen were enjoying their meal, two or three male Indians arrived from hunting with bows and arrows, alarming them. The hostess chased the hunters away and had her attendants break their bows and arrows. When the Englishmen prudently decided to sleep on their boats, she lamented their seeming distrust and sent them bowls of provisions and mats for protection against the rain. She also posted men and women to sit all night as guards, further evidence to the Englishmen of her kindness and consideration.

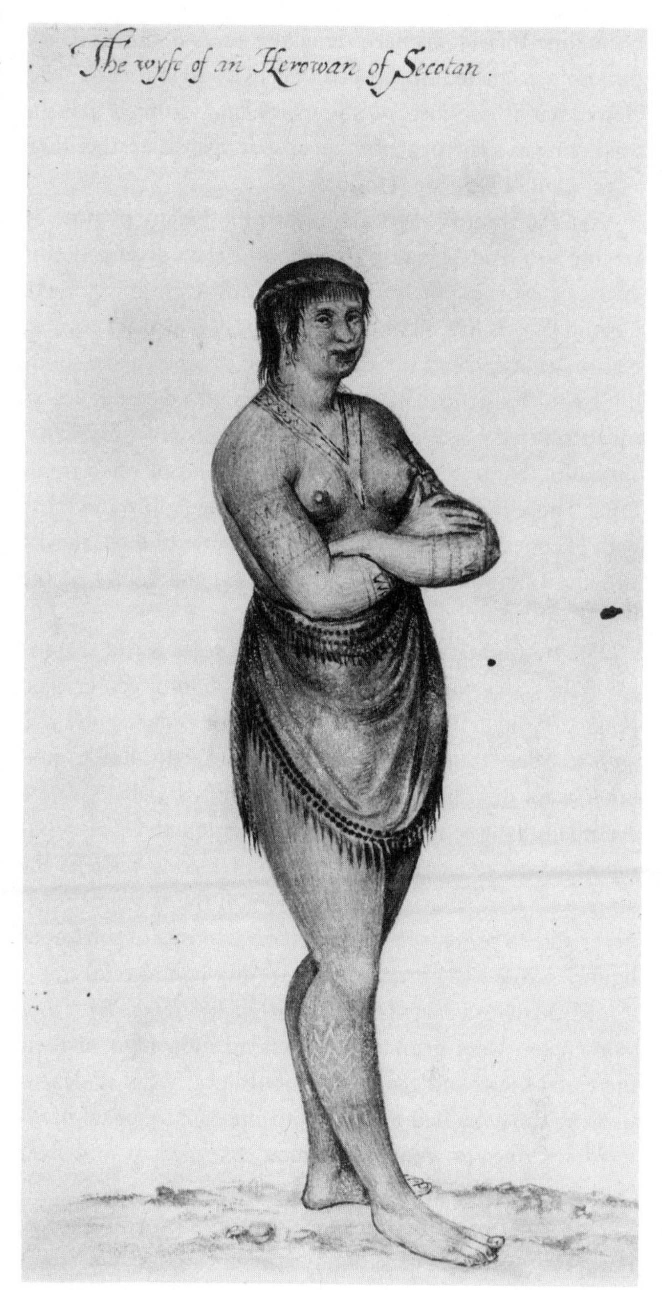

FIGURE 1-11. John White (fl. 1577–93), *The wyfe of an Herowan of Secotan*, watercolor, America or England, ca. 1585–86. Dressed in fringed deerskin mantle and adorned with jewelry appropriate to her high status, the wife of an Algonquian chief stands confidently, her tattooed arms crossed and her gaze direct. (British Museum; Hulton, *America 1585*, Plate 37)

Barlowe described a complicated mix of similarities and differences in cultural attitudes between the Algonquians and the English. A distinctive similarity was that Algonquian society was ranked. Those individuals in charge made the laws, governed the people, and enjoyed privileges that included wearing elaborate clothing and adornments and enjoying special trading options with other Indian tribes and with the English. Granganimeo's wife's high rank permitted her to command her neighbors to carry the Englishmen to shore, wash their feet, break the hunters' weapons, and spend the night guarding them. But because she lived in a society that traced matrilineal kinship and practiced matrilocality and maternal control of property, she was in charge of her own household and its provisions. Indeed, it was her hospitality to offer. In this scenario two cultural systems collided: she came from a culture in which sharing was essential to survival and hospitality was highly valued. The English had no inkling that it was her prerogative to extend hospitality. Barlowe designated his hostess only as Granganimeo's wife, viewed her as her husband's property, and assumed that she was acting as a surrogate for her absent husband rather than as an agent of her own resources.

The European Americans destroyed Indian culture by waging war and bringing disease, and they displaced survivors by usurping their lands. By the mid-1700s most North Carolina tribes had all but ceased to exist as distinct entities. Native American culture was subverted in other, more subtle but equally destructive ways. Trade created a dependence on manufactured goods in a formerly self-sufficient culture. Assimilation led to a rejection or concealment of one's traditions. Those Indians who survived interacted more and more with European Americans and, as in the case of the Catawba and the Cherokee, increasingly reflected the values of the dominant culture.

The traditional balance between the sexes was disrupted when the Catawba adapted to a market economy centered on pottery. Women became the sole family providers, and men, with few deer to hunt and no wars left to fight, had to find other ways of contributing to their family's welfare. Some eventually evolved from hunters and warriors to farmers, but many turned to alcohol, exacerbating tensions between the sexes. "All the persuasion and power of the women . . . is never able to prevent . . . the deleterious effects of spirituous liquor," wrote one observer in 1772. Although alcohol traditionally had been part of the men's ritual life, by the late 1700s women too were drinking, perhaps an indication of their increased social and economic importance. What is clear is that the Catawba had to cope with the consequences of altered sex roles as women and men struggled to find their place in a changed world.[43]

The Cherokee, in a different scenario, seemed to accept European American ideas about women's appropriate status as being subordinate rather than complementary. This led to a shift from a matrilineal to a patrilineal system.[44]

The place of a Cherokee woman in her society, like that of all Native American women, had long been rooted in her connection to the land. But throughout the 1700s and early 1800s, European American settlers ignored the horticultural basis of Woodland Indian culture in the Southeast and thereby women's importance. By considering Indians as hunters and gatherers rather than as farmers, white settlers who wanted their land could rationalize that Indians only occupied the land but did not own it. Government agents and zealous missionaries, on the other hand, envisioned a Cherokee society patterned after the English model, in which the man farmed and headed a household composed only of his wife and children. As Cherokee men emulated white culture, and either took up farming themselves or with African slaves, they took away women's traditional autonomy on the land.[45]

In 1817 War Woman Nancy Ward and twelve other women sent a warning to the Cherokee National Council, which was considering ceding a large amount of land to the U.S. government. Two years later women again raised their voices to oppose the giving of Cherokee land to individuals: "The land was given to us by the Great Spirit above as our common right, to raise our children upon, & to make support for our rising generations . . . hold out to the last in support of our common rights, as the Cherokee nation has been the first settlers of this land." When the federal government appropriated Cherokee land, it appropriated the women's matrilineal heritage.[46]

The position of Cherokee women, like that of Algonquians, was also jeopardized by the European reluctance to recognize their authority. By dealing with the warrior hierarchy in the Cherokee Nation rather than with traditional leaders, Europeans elevated young men at the expense of older men and women.[47]

Cherokee women's culture was further undermined by the European American's narrowly defined expectation of a woman's proper role. Early European visitors were shocked that Indian women did not spin and weave—defining activities for women in their culture. (Native American women

Entreaty to Cherokee Council, 1817

The Cherokee ladys now being present at the meeting of the Chiefs and warriors in council have thought it their duties as mothers to address their beloved Chiefs and warriors now assembled.

Our beloved children and head men of the Cherokee nation we address you warriors in council[. W]e have raised all of you on the land which we now have, which God gave us to inhabit and raise provisions[. W]e know that our country has once been extensive but by repeated sales has become circumscribed to a small tract and never have thought it our duty to interfere in the disposition of it till now, if a father or mother was to sell all their lands which they had to depend on[,] which their children had to raise their living on[,] which would be bad indeed and to be removed to another country[. W]e do not wish to go to an unknown country which we have understood some of our children wish to go over the Mississippi but this act of our children would be like destroying your mothers. Your mother and sisters ask and beg of you not to part with any more of our lands. . . .

—Perdue, "Nancy Ward," 97.

did, of course, process deerskins into clothing and other household furnishings.) George Washington ordered Indian agents to procure looms and spinning wheels and directed the Cherokee, "Your wives and daughters can soon learn to spin and weave." In 1825 Cherokee leader Elias Boudinot proudly documented his people's progress in Americanization: the 467 looms and 1,600 spinning wheels owned by the Cherokee in 1810 had increased to 762 looms and 2,488 spinning wheels by 1825.[48]

By the 1820s the autonomy of Cherokee women deteriorated even more when prominent Cherokee men embraced the white middle-class ideology of feminine domesticity espoused by the ever-increasing Protestant missionaries. As one Cherokee man described women's proper role, "They sew, they weave, they spin, they cook our meals and act well the duties assigned them by Nature as mothers"—no more heading households, no more trading corn and ginseng, and no more speaking up in town councils or negotiating treaties.[49]

Cherokee women lost their traditional legal and political rights through this process of cultural assimilation. Nanye'hi's participation at the Hopewell Conference in 1785 was the last official act of a woman at a treaty negotiation. When the Cherokee council established a national police force in 1808 to keep order and "to give protection to children as heirs to their father's property and to the widow's share," it nullified matrilineal inheritance patterns and officially acknowledged the patriarchal family as the norm. And yet traditional ways and respect for women's authority undoubtedly continued: fully one-third of the households on the removal lists of 1835 were still headed by women. In 1810 a council of all seven matrilineal clans (though with no women represented) abolished the practice of blood vengeance, one of the clan's major functions. From that time on, the national police and tribal courts, rather than one's kin, apprehended and punished all wrongdoers.[50]

FIGURE 1-12. *Cherokee basket*, ca. 1830s. This basket is believed to have been carried from North Carolina to Oklahoma on the Trail of Tears in 1838. (Courtesy of the Oklahoma Museum of Natural History, University of Oklahoma)

FIGURE 1-13. Robert Lindneux, *The Trail of Tears*, oil on canvas. (Courtesy of the Woolaroc Museum, Bartlesville, Oklahoma)

In 1827 Cherokee men drafted a constitution patterned after that of the United States and, in so doing, excluded Cherokee women: "No person but a free male citizen who is full grown shall be entitled to vote." By eradicating women's participation in politics, tribal leaders eliminated the effectiveness of the one group that had steadfastly opposed land cession. By the time the Cherokee were removed to present-day Oklahoma in 1838 (Figs. 1-12, 1-13), the women had, for some time, been removed from their traditional roles in their tribal community.[51]

What, then, is the story of Native American women in North Carolina? For thousands of years they held esteemed positions in their culture based on their economic authority and their place in matrilineal kinship. Their activities, essential to the well-being of society, were celebrated in a ceremonial cycle that gave shape and meaning to life. Many of their traditions were changed by European settlement, but much of the spirit of those traditions remains, not least the belief that men and women, though different, are complementary and are necessary for balance in a good society.

Nanye'hi / Nancy Ward

1738?–1822

Burton Jones, *Monument erected to Nanye'hi/Nancy Ward*, Watauga County, Tennessee. (From Foreman, *Indian Women Chiefs*)

As Nanye'hi, War Woman of the Cherokee Nation, and Nancy Ward, friend of the American settlers, she embodied two different worlds. Nanye'hi was brought up in a culture in which there was balance between the roles of women and men; later, when she became War Woman, she acquired exceptional authority in tribal matters. After the death of her Cherokee husband, Kingfisher, she married a white trader, Bryant Ward, and acquired another name and a familial understanding of a different culture. By the end of her long life she had adapted to many changes that undermined Cherokee traditions, but she argued in Anglo-American and Cherokee councils against ceding more land to the white man. In 1838, sixteen years after her death, most of her tribe was removed to the Southwest. The smaller Eastern Band of Cherokee remained on what would become the Qualla Boundary, land that it purchased and that is held in trust by the federal government. The story of Nancy Ward, much of it missing from documented history, speaks to the complexity of acculturation.[1]

The "famous Indian woman Nancy Ward" appears in eighteenth-century government records of traders and agents, in the correspondence of Thomas Jefferson, and later in a popular nineteenth-century history by Theodore Roosevelt. She became the subject of romanticized accounts as "Pocahontas of the West" and has been included in biographical dictionaries. Recently, a longer study of her life was published in a collection of women's biographies.[2]

Because there was no written Cherokee language during most of her life, there are no records of what her own people said about her. That they awarded her the special title of "War Woman" (sometimes used interchangeably with "Beloved Woman," or "Ghighau") while she was still very young is compelling evidence of her importance to the Cherokee.[3] When in 1781 Thomas Jefferson instructed American agents to give Nancy Ward (as she came to be called after her marriage to Bryant) and her family special consideration, he probably did so because she sided with the Americans during the Revolutionary War. Although she received protection, she was unable to prevent the Virginia militia from burning her town of Chota and other Cherokee villages. About one hundred years after Jefferson's recognition of her special status, Theodore Roosevelt wrote that when the Overhill Cherokee were "laid waste," members of the family of Nancy Ward "were treated as friends, not prisoners."[4]

This is the story of how she came to occupy an important position in Indian and American history.

Historians believe that Nanye'hi was born around 1738 in Chota on the Little Tennessee River. (This land was then in North Carolina but later became part of Tennessee.) Although the lives of the Cherokee had already been changed by explorers and settlers, Chota was a large and important village—the capital and a "city of refuge"; it probably accommodated members of each of seven or more clans, numbering in the hundreds. Nanye'hi belonged to the Wolf clan of her mother, Tame Doe. Her father is thought to have been a Delaware. Her mother's brother, Attakullakulla, called "The Little Carpenter" by white men because of his ability to cobble together agreements, was a prominent leader in the Wolf clan and one of several Cherokee chiefs who had been to England in 1730 and had met King George II. Afterward, he worked vigorously as a spokesman for Anglo-American alliances. Because of the primacy of the female line, Attakullakulla was the dominant male figure in Nanye'hi's life.

Cherokee women had freedom to

choose their partners as long as they did not marry within their own clan, and when she was in her early teens, Nanye'hi wed Kingfisher, a member of the Deer clan. She gave birth to two children, Fivekiller and Catherine, who, of course, belonged to their mother's clan, and the family—Nanye'hi, Kingfisher, Fivekiller, Catherine, and Tame Doe—probably shared a household, which according to custom belonged to the women. Nanye'hi and other women raised and prepared food and maintained the family. During the winter months Kingfisher joined other men in hunting. Because demand for furs and skins increased among the settlers, Kingfisher no doubt began to hunt more aggressively, went greater distances from home, and stayed away for longer periods as deer became less plentiful. When he returned with meat, he might also have traded furs and hides for the iron and steel implements that Nanye'hi used with her earthen bowls. Kingfisher's trades presumably also brought bracelets, glass beads, ribbons, scissors, and steel needles.

In 1755, about the time that she might still have been nursing her younger child, Nanye'hi's life took a dramatic turn. The Cherokee had long been at war with their ancient enemies, the Creeks, and Nanye'hi was called upon to help. It was not unusual for women to travel with war parties in order to carry wood and water and prepare food for the warriors, and Nanye'hi left her children in the care of other women and accompanied Kingfisher to Georgia. What happened next lifted her out of the ranks of the now-anonymous Cherokee women of the eighteenth century and into a role in history. At the Battle of Taliwa in northern Georgia, Kingfisher was killed, and Nanye'hi apparently was at his side and took his place. She must have known how to chew bullets to make them more deadly, to load a gun, and to shoot to kill. As part of the Cherokee warring expedition, Nanye'hi helped to defeat the Creeks, and in that decisive victory she became a special leader. After returning to Chota, she received the title of "War Woman," a position held by only a few women (usually under similar circumstances). At the time, she was only sixteen or seventeen years old.

Because Nanye'hi had succeeded in a culture known for its tests in battle, she was regarded as an exceptional person and given a special role. She was entitled to speak and to vote in the Council of Chiefs, to lead the Woman's Council, to take part in ceremonies of the clan, and to spare the lives of captives. She also acquired status with male settlers, who were used to dealing with women only as translators, wives, mistresses, or traders. When she spoke in treaty conferences, the men initially must have been startled to hear a woman speak in public about important political issues.

With Nanye'hi's marriage to Bryant Ward and the birth of their daughter, Elizabeth, she moved closer to the Anglo-American culture. A marriage between a Cherokee and a white, whether brief or long-term, was not uncommon, and, in addition to providing the pleasures of an affectionate relationship, the alliance could be of great usefulness to both. Each could learn the other's culture and language. These advantages undoubtedly accrued to the Wards. Although Bryant may have lived some of the time in Nancy's household, he may have had no more than a casual relationship with her own two children, but he could have taught them some English words and brought them dolls and trinkets. The children, the house, and, in a larger sense, the village were hers. After a few years, Bryant Ward left the Cherokee Nation to return to a white wife and family in South Carolina. According to later reports from his son, Bryant continued to regard Nancy Ward with great respect and affection—she was later an honored guest in his home.

By 1763, after the British defeated the French in the protracted Seven Years' War (French and Indian War in America), the issue of which European power would dominate the new country had been settled. But conflict was far from over, and soon the colonies would be at war with England in a fight for their own independence. Both the British colonial government and the colonies needed allies among the Indians. A majority of the Cherokee, perhaps hoping that the king would protect their land, sided with the British, but Nancy Ward allied herself with the American settlers. Her choice could have been motivated by friendship and the belief that the Cherokee had goods and services to trade. She was weary of war. She may have assumed the role of "cultural broker."[5] Whatever the motivation, soon after the Revolution began, Nancy Ward threw her support to the Americans.

Her alliance with white settlers did not take her away from her own life among the Cherokee. In 1766, when Cherokee warriors were planning to advance on the Watauga settlement, she probably played a duplicitous role. As Beloved Woman she had authority to serve the black drink to warriors in a religious ceremony of purification before battle, but she is thought to have warned the white settlers of the Cherokee attack. One of the settlers illegally living along the Holston River was a Mrs. William Bean, the wife of a Virginian who had started the first permanent settlement. Away from home when Nancy Ward's message was delivered, Bean was captured on the road by some Cherokee warriors. Various stories later reported how Nanye'hi, acting on her authority as a Cherokee War

Woman, had arrived just as Bean was about to be burned at the stake. Because she was permitted to make decisions about captives, the Cherokee had to obey when she ordered Bean's release. Her warning to the settlers and her rescue of Bean became the stuff of American legends. But historians also note that she did not intervene to save the life of the young boy who was burned to death at the stake.[6]

Duplicity could have been responsible for many broken treaties and the general state of conflict that existed between the Cherokee Nation and the Americans. After a peace agreement had been made, it was common for both sides to violate its terms. The mutual confusion, suspicion, and aggression throughout most of Ward's life created in her a longing for peace. Acting on her own freedom within the Cherokee Nation, she could, if she chose, warn white settlers of advancing Cherokee war parties. During treaty negotiations between the two groups, she acted as a Cherokee representative. By the time Americans had established their independence from the colonial government, Native Americans no longer posed a threat to the country's autonomy.

As Cherokee losses mounted, the women sometimes acted as defenders of their own rights. Speaking at a treaty conference between the Cherokee and the Americans on the Long Island of the Holston in 1781, Nancy Ward said, "Our cry is all for peace; let it continue. The peace must last forever. Let your women's sons be ours; our sons be yours. Let your women hear our words." For the time being, no more land was ceded.[7]

As a Cherokee representative designated to meet U.S. commissioners at Hopewell, South Carolina, in 1785, she sat with thirty-six chiefs and more than nine hundred other Cherokee, some of them women. Introduced by the venerated Chief Old Tassel, she spoke for "the young warriors I have raised in my town, as well as myself" and urged the forging of a "chain of friendship" between Cherokee and American. "I look on you," she told the Americans, "and the red people as my children." But this time, notes Theda Perdue, Americans had little sympathy and took more Cherokee land as punishment for their having sided with the British during the Revolution.[8]

Cherokee women were often present at peace negotiations. Ward's uncle, Attakullakulla, once chided Americans for failing to include women in their negotiations. Reflective of the loss of status is her response when she addressed the peace conference at Hopewell. "You know," she said to the Americans, "that women are always looked upon as nothing."[9]

After the war she returned to Chota, where she taught butter making and cheese making (skills she is said to have learned from Mrs. Bean), raised cattle, and cultivated lands. Her own daughter Elizabeth, married to Joseph Martin, the North Carolina agent to the Cherokee, was reported in 1799 to be living in a home "on a fine plantation" near the Hiwassee River. There, with the help of black slaves, the Martins raised livestock, corn, wheat, and cotton. Their household goods included implements for carding, spinning, and weaving.[10]

Meanwhile, as they tried to adapt to the powerful presence of the settlers, the Cherokee continued to cede lands to the American government and Chota was virtually surrounded. But Nancy Ward continued to play a role in clan governance, and in 1817, apparently too old or too ill to attend the Cherokee council, she and twelve other women sent a message (and her walking cane, so the story goes) urging the council to hold on to remaining lands: "Nancy Ward to her children Warriors to take pity and listen to the talks of your sisters, although I am very old yet cannot but pity the situation in which you will hear of their minds. I have a great many grand children which I wish them to do well on our land."[11] By now, however, the influence and force of the Americans were too great to be resisted, Cherokee councils acted like patriarchal councils of white governance, and the War Woman of Chota no longer had any power.

Land where she was living was ceded by the Cherokee in the Hiwassee Purchase of 1819, and Nancy Ward left Chota (perhaps before 1819) to live in a place belonging to the Cherokee Nation in the Ocoee River Valley (now in eastern Tennessee). There she opened an inn that served travelers passing on the federal road from Georgia to Nashville, Tennessee. Her son Fivekiller and her brother Longfellow lived nearby. She became known as "Granny Ward," a wise old woman, and died at about age eighty-five. (Five years later, when the constitution of the Cherokee Nation was drafted, the delegates to the convention decided that only Cherokee men would have seats in the General Council and be able to vote.)

When Nanye'hi died, according to a story told by her great-grandson, a light rose from her body and flew toward Chota. A Tennessee chapter of the Daughters of the American Revolution (DAR) later erected a marker over her grave. The great-grandson's vision and the DAR's recognition reflected the two worlds of Nanye'hi and Nancy Ward.[12]

CHAPTER 2

The Most Industrious Sex in That Place

Women on the Carolina Frontier, 1587–1729

"Women were necessary for the founding of permanent homes," wrote pioneer historian of colonial southern women Julia Cherry Spruill. Alone, men "could establish only temporary camps in the wilderness." Although their stories must be reconstructed from fragmentary evidence, women played a more critical role in the earliest settlements of North Carolina—Roanoke Island in the 1580s and the Albemarle region and beyond in the 1660s and afterward—than their cultural and legal status indicates. On the North Carolina frontier, women and men had to work together. Women shared the same hardships, responsibilities, and dangers. Given the scarcity of people and the struggle to survive, gender and race did not always determine who did what.[1]

Women's lives were shaped by childbearing and the needs of their families. Yet domestic duties did not necessarily cut a woman off from public issues. Boundaries between the private world of the family and the public arenas of government and religion were fluid on the frontier. Because no public buildings were erected until the 1700s, people's homes served as taverns, courts, and meeting houses. As government and the legal system became more institutionalized, opportunities for white women as well as black men and women became more restricted.

Women played both symbolic and actual roles in the European settling of the land that became North Carolina. Virgin land awaiting conquest was the image, sexual and economic, invoked by early chronicler Richard Hakluyt in 1587, when he urged Sir Walter Raleigh: "If you persevre only a little longer in your constancy, your bride will shortly bring forth new and most abundant offspring, such as will delight you and yours." Some eighty years later single women were recruited with the promise that they would think North Carolina was a "Golden Age, when Men paid a Dowry for their Wives; for if they be but Civil, and under fifty years of Age, some honest Man or other, will purchase them for their Wives." The new land may have been a bride to be taken, but it needed a wife to help settle it. Men envisioned the New World as a paradise of opportunity and adventure. Women tempered their enthusiasm with more ancient obligations. They probably held different images as to what the new land offered them, smaller dreams, of establishing families, building homes, planting gardens. They would have been less interested in penetrating an unfamiliar wilderness and more concerned with cultivating a familiar garden. They understood that the New World was a place to continue what they valued in the Old as well as a space to start anew.[2]

The wilderness demanded courage and perseverance, and it fostered skills and self-reliance unusual for European women in the 1600s. George Fox, the Englishman who founded Quakerism, visited the Albemarle in 1672; when his boat was stuck in shallow water, he was rescued by the wife of a government official who arrived in her own canoe to deliver him to shore. In his 1709 book, North Carolina chronicler John Lawson observed, "Many of the Women are very handy in Canoes, and will manage then with great Dexterity and Skill, which they become accustomed to in this watry Country." Lawson also noted that the women were "ready to help their Husbands in any servile Work, as Planting. . . . Pride seldom banishing good Houswifry."[3]

Queen Elizabeth I, neither bride nor housewife, sent English explorers to the New World with her sponsorship of Sir Walter Raleigh's two attempts to establish colonies on Roanoke Island in the 1580s (Fig. 2-1). Elizabeth I understood that an English presence could check growing Spanish dominance in America and simultaneously fill England's coffers with New World bounty. A woman ruler in a man's world, she was shrewd enough to use her gender to strengthen her authority. Instead of compromising her power (as marriage and a family inevitably would have done), the Virgin Queen ruled with the advice of her trusted male councillors as a *feme sole* (a woman alone). When she permitted Raleigh to name the new English territories "Virginia" after her, she was surely aware of the dual imagery of the Virgin Queen and the virgin land.

Roanoke Voyages, 1584–1587

Ordinary people—one hundred males (ninety-one adults and nine boys) and seventeen women—sailed from Portsmouth harbor on April 26, 1587, to establish an English colony on Roanoke Island. The first two Roanoke ventures, a reconnaissance expedition in 1584 and an aborted settlement in 1585–86, had been composed of soldiers and adventurers intent on privateering and raiding Spanish shipping. The 1587 attempt was to be a colony of families—women and

FIGURE 2-1. Marcus Gheerearts, *Portrait of Queen Elizabeth I*, 1592, oil. (Courtesy of the National Portrait Gallery, London)

children along with men—that invested their own resources in the venture and had a stake in its success. The prospective settlers planned to grow crops on plots of land, to which they all had deeds, rather than depending on native people for food. Instead of a military man, John White, the artist who had depicted the Algonquian Indians on the 1585–86 trip, would be the governor.[4]

Little is known about the colonists, but it is believed that most were artisans and farmers recruited from London and from Devon and Cornwall Counties in western England. The sole record of their existence remains the list of 117 names from John White's official log. Almost 80 percent were men, four out of five of them apparently single. Women made up a little less than 15 percent. Slightly more than half of the women can be identified as members of a family group, but the others may have emigrated alone, perhaps as indentured servants. We can speculate about family relationships by matching names on White's list of the people who "safely arrived" on Roanoke Island and "remained to inhabite there" and by including the two children born on the island before White's return to England. About seventy-four men, one to three boys, and seven women cannot be linked to a family group, but thirty-six people may have belonged to nine to eleven families. Elizabeth Viccars and Joyce Archard both had husbands and sons, whereas seven to nine women appear to have been married but with no children. Four to six families consisted of fathers and sons, or brothers, or other male relatives. The ages of the eleven children are unspecified, but White's reference to a child "sucking" a woman's breast on the voyage indicates that at least one was an infant.[5]

Shortly after the colonists' arrival on Roanoke in July 1587, Elyoner Dare and Margery Harvie gave birth; so they were probably four to five months pregnant when they left England. Elyoner Dare was John White's daughter, and her husband, Ananias, had been a bricklayer and tiler in London before becoming one of his father-in-law's twelve assistants. White wrote that on August 18 Elyoner "was delivered of a daughter in Roanoke," and "because this childe was first Christian borne in Virginia, she was named Virginia" (Fig. 2-2). Margery Harvie's child was the second born on Roanoke, and although White noted this baby's birth, he neglected to record its sex and first name.[6]

The Roanoke colonists had arrived too late to plant crops, and their relations with the Algonquians were unfriendly enough that they could not depend on them for assistance.

FIGURE 2-2. "Baptism of Virginia Dare, the first white child born in America," Dare County. Virginia Dare's grandfather, John White, painted pictures of the Algonquian Indians he saw on his 1585 Roanoke voyage, but he only recorded her birth in his official log and evidently returned to England from Roanoke in 1587 without depicting her birth or baptism. At least no contemporary images have been found. Later artists, focusing on her white race and Anglican faith, have imagined her baptism in a far more elaborate setting than would have existed on the Roanoke frontier. (From John Clark Ridpath, *People's History of the United States* [Philadelphia: Historical Publishing Co., 1895]; photograph courtesy of the Outer Banks History Center, Manteo)

John White reluctantly agreed to go back to England for more supplies and set sail just nine days after his granddaughter's birth. His return was delayed for three years by England's continuing battles with Spanish and French fleets and other misfortunes. When he finally reached Roanoke on August 16, 1590, he found the colony abandoned, houses dismantled, possessions scattered, and only a carved CROATOAN near the entrance to a palisade of trees. Stormy weather, ship mishaps, and scarce supplies prevented a search for the lost colonists, and White left again, reaching Plymouth, England, in late October. After Queen Elizabeth's death in 1603 and Sir Walter Raleigh's fall from royal favor shortly afterward, Raleigh's rights to the New World reverted to King James, who could make his own grants.[7]

Although the Roanoke colonists failed to establish a permanent colony, they provided the first instance in North Carolina in which white women were among the settlers. Only settlements composed of men and women had a chance for survival, as in the more successful English joint-stock ventures twenty years later at Jamestown, Virginia, and thirty-three years afterward at Plymouth, Massachusetts. A colony exclusively of soldiers—young, male, feisty, dependent on natives for food—had small chance for success.[8]

Proprietary North Carolina, 1663–1729

For about seventy years after Roanoke, little settlement occurred in North Carolina. In the 1650s, however, women and men, black and white, bound and free, enslaved and indentured, began a steady, though generally undocumented, migration. Overflowing from the Virginia tidewater, they headed for Roanoke, Carolano, South Virginia, or "Southward," as the northern shore of the Albemarle Sound was variously named. The majority were small landowning farmers, such as Dorothy and John Harvey who were living at the "Southward" by 1659; others were freed indentured servants. They came to plant tobacco on land both cheap and fertile that they got from the Yeopin Indians, a branch of the Algonquians. Landless laborers were willing to inhabit unclaimed land or locate in backwoods when they were unable to purchase the better tracts along the waterways.[9]

Some settlers were runaways, hoping for a fresh start, who gave North Carolina the reputation of harboring "rude and desperate" men, the "sinke of America, the Refuge of our Renagadoes." A missionary for the Society for the Propagation of the Gospel in Foreign Parts, the Reverend John Urmstone, characterized North Carolina as "a nest of the most notorious profligates upon earth. Women forsake their husbands come in here and live with other men." Anna Sothel, a New England widow who had moved to the Albemarle, in 1694 advised her sister, "You write me that your son is intended into this Country to se me I should be glad to se any of my relations but the Country is sickly and the Inlet bad and a dangerous place to corrupt youth that I cannot give him the least Incouragement."[10]

After 1663, settlers obtained land by headright grants (the right to receive a parcel of land) from the Lords Proprietors. These eight loyal supporters of Charles II were permitted to establish the provincial colony of Carolina by charters of 1663 and 1665. Political turmoil, civil war, revolution, and the execution of Charles I in 1649 had diverted England's attention from its colonies. When Charles II was restored to the throne in 1660, the Crown turned its attention to the province of Carolina. At that time barely five hundred white people lived on the Albemarle frontier. As whites increasingly took up land along the rivers and creeks of the Albemarle, the Yeopins abandoned their villages in Perquimans Precinct and left for a reservation in Camden County. New Englanders and English immigrants joined those from Virginia, and Quakers became a dominant force. The colony's population continued to grow, though the exact numbers are unknown. By 1675 isolated farmsteads dotted the northern shore of the sound and both sides of the Chowan River. By 1700, as whites relentlessly encroached on land occupied by the Tuscarora, settlement extended as far south as the Pamlico and Neuse River basins.[11]

According to *A Brief Description of the Province of Carolina on the Coasts of Floreda*, a 1666 pamphlet to promote the Cape Fear region, the Lords Proprietors extended 100 acres to every head of household—man or woman—plus an additional 100 acres for a spouse, each child, and each manservant and 50 acres for each female servant and slave (Fig. 2-3). On expiration of their service, males were to receive 100 acres and females, 50 acres. Although most land patents went to white males, some early ones also were granted to women, blacks, and Indians. Other inducements to emigrate were self-governance, freedom of worship, low taxes, and no customs duties. Single women, even those pushing fifty years, were encouraged with promises of marriage.[12]

How many women accepted the Proprietors' offer as either heads of household or indentured servants? Little is known about indentured women in North Carolina, certainly much less than about their counterparts in Maryland or Virginia, for those in North Carolina tended to be part of the overland migration from Virginia rather than arriving in a port and being documented on a ship's list. Indenture bonds exist, however, for three women—Elizabeth Jersey, Katherine Gardner, and Alice Gardner—who exchanged four years of service for passage from England to North Carolina in 1684 (Fig. 2-4). There may have been more white servants

A Brief DESCRIPTION
OF
The Province
OF
CAROLINA
On the COASTS *of* FLOREDA.
AND
More perticularly of a *New-Plantation* begun by the *ENGLISH* at *Cape-Feare*, on that River now by them called *Charles-River*, the 29th. of *May*. 1664.

Wherein is ſet forth
The *Healthfulneſs* of the *Air*; the *Fertility* of the *Earth*, and *Waters*; and the great *Pleaſure* and *Profit* will accrue to thoſe that ſhall go thither to enjoy the ſame.

Alſo,
Directions and advice to ſuch as ſhall go thither whether on their own accompts, or to ſerve under another.

Together with
A moſt accurate MAP of the whole *PROVINCE*.

London, Printed for *Robert Horne* in the firſt Court of *Greſham-Colledge* neer *Biſhopſgate ſtreet*. 1666.

FIGURE 2-3. Robert Horne, *A Brief Description of the Province of Carolina on the Coasts of Floreda and More Particularly of a New-Plantation Begun by the English at Cape-Feare . . .* 1666. Horne's promotional pamphlet declared: "If any Maid or single Woman have a desire to go over, they will think themselves in the Golden Age, when Men paid a Dowry for their Wives; for if they be but Civil, and under 50 years of Age, some honest Man or other, will purchase them for their Wives." (Courtesy of the North Carolina Collection, University of North Carolina at Chapel Hill)

than black slaves in the first fifty years of the colony's existence. Virginia residents Mary Fortsen and Katherine Woodward were among the earliest recipients of Carolina land patents granted heads of households. Fortsen was married and Woodward probably widowed; there is no evidence that they ever settled on their extensive land grants on the "Paspetanke" river in the Albemarle region.[13]

Though willing to grant women heads of household equal incentives to emigrate to Carolina, the Lords Proprietors did not consider women equal to men. Like other Europeans, the Proprietors believed in the patriarchal Judaeo-Christian tradition in which women are subordinate to men, and they accepted the cultural assumptions about women's inferiority and dependence. Just as God reigns over all human beings, this philosophy claimed, the husband is to rule with absolute authority over his family and household.[14] As a sixteenth-century English minstrel song put it:

> I would be right as any roe
> To praise Women, where that I go,
> A Woman is a worthy wight,
> She serveth man both day and night,
> Thereto she putteth all her might.
> A Woman is a worthy thing,
> She doth the wash and doth the wring,
> "Lully, lully," she dothe thee sing,
> And yet she hath but care and woe.[15]

Inevitably New World conditions undermined the European patriarchal ideal, and, at least initially, a principle was established—white women were eligible to obtain land allotments.

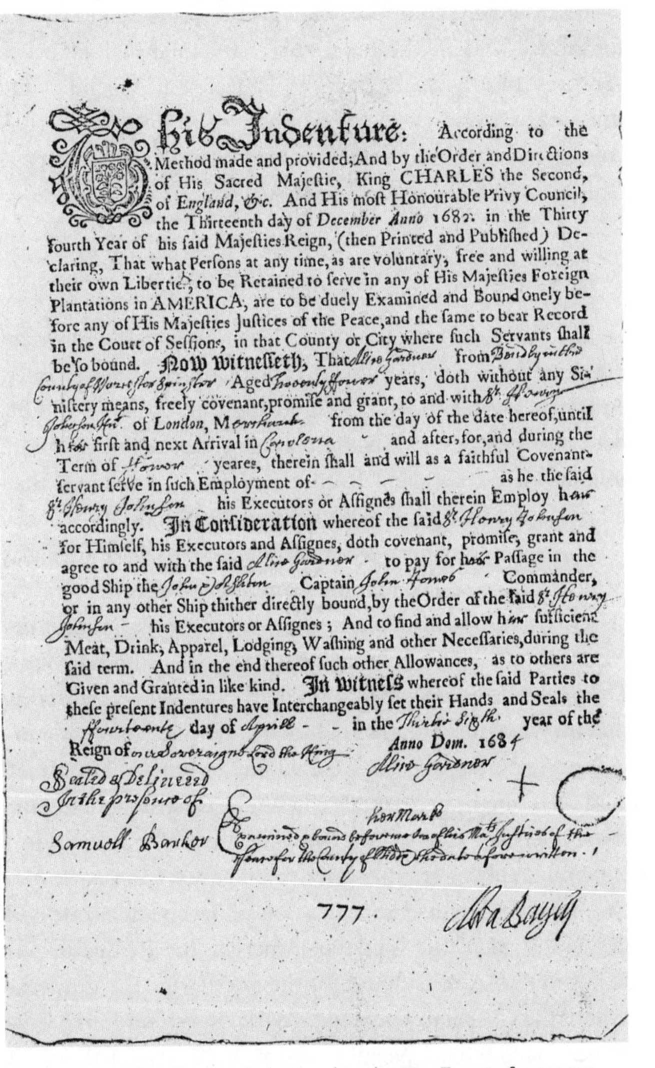

This Indenture: According to the Method made and provided; And by the Order and Directions of His Sacred Majeſtie, King CHARLES the Second, of *England*, &c. And His moſt Honourable Privy Council, the Thirteenth day of *December Anno* 1682. in the Thirty fourth Year of his ſaid Majeſties Reign, (then Printed and Publiſhed) Declaring, That what Perſons at any time, as are voluntary, free and willing at their own Liberties, to be Retained to ſerve in any of His Majeſties Foreign Plantations in AMERICA, are to be duely Examined and Bound onely before any of His Majeſties Juſtices of the Peace, and the ſame to bear Record in the Court of Seſſions, in that County or City where ſuch Servants ſhall be ſo bound. Now witneſſeth, That Alice Gardner from [illegible] Spinster Aged twenty four years, doth without any Siniſtery means, freely covenant, promiſe and grant, to and with Sr. Henry Johnson Knt. of London, Merchant from the day of the date hereof, until her first and next Arrival in Carolina and after, for, and during the Term of four yeares, therein ſhall and will as a faithful Covenant-ſervant ſerve in ſuch Employment of- as he the ſaid Sr. Henry Johnson his Executors or Aſſignes ſhall therein Employ her accordingly. In Conſideration whereof the ſaid Sr. Henry Johnson for Himſelf, his Executors and Aſſignes, doth covenant, promiſe, grant and agree to and with the ſaid Alice Gardner to pay for her Paſſage in the good Ship the [illegible] Captain John [illegible] Commander, or in any other Ship thither directly bound, by the Order of the ſaid Sr. Henry Johnson his Executors or Aſſignes; And to find and allow her ſufficient Meat, Drink, Apparel, Lodging, Waſhing and other Neceſſaries, during the ſaid term. And in the end thereof ſuch other Allowances, as to others are Given and Granted in like kind. In Witneſs whereof the ſaid Parties to theſe preſent Indentures have Interchangeably ſet their Hands and Seals the fourteenth day of Aprill - - in the Thirty Sixth year of the Reign of our Sovereigne Lord the King Anno Dom. 1684

Sealed & Delivered In the presence of Samuell Barker

Alice Gardner + her Mark

777

FIGURE 2-4. *Alice Gardner indenture bond*, 1684. Twenty-four years old, Gardner agreed to serve four years in exchange for passage to North Carolina. (Courtesy of the North Carolina Division of Archives and History)

African women, on the other hand, received no land. There is evidence that some Africans may have accompanied Spanish explorers in the 1540s, but their first presence in North Carolina is difficult to determine. Dutch traders had introduced slavery in Jamestown in 1619, and as Virginia planters moved into the Albemarle area after 1650, the more prosperous brought with them indentured servants and slaves. The Lords Proprietors' 1666 offer to slaveowners of fifty acres for every slave, male or female, over fourteen years of age further encouraged slavery. Throughout the late 1600s slavery slowly but steadily spread throughout the colony. Most blacks came overland from Virginia or, from the 1720s on, from South Carolina rather than directly from Africa. By 1712 about eight hundred black slaves lived in the colony.[16]

One way in which the experience of enslaved blacks mirrored that of white immigrants was that men came first and in disproportionately large numbers. Women followed later. It was not long, however, before black women's reproductive labor was considered every bit as valuable as black men's productive labor.

White Women and Family: "Send Me Safely Delivered of the Child"

The women whose lives can be extrapolated from the colonial records provide powerful testimony of the likelihood of frequent pregnancy, young widowhood, and multiple marriages on the frontier. Ann Marwood Durant was newly married when she and her husband George moved from Northumberland County, Virginia, around 1661 to settle in present-day Perquimans County on an extensive tract of land known today as Durant's Neck. The first of her nine children was probably born in Virginia; the rest were born in North Carolina. She had three sons and six daughters, almost an average of one child every two years for twenty-two years. Although the oldest child died shortly before his twelfth birthday, all the others lived to adulthood. Durant is an atypical first-generation pioneer woman in that she lived her entire married life with one husband.[17]

Widowhood and remarriage were common in the seventeenth century because of high mortality rates. Hannah Baskel Phelps moved to the Albemarle from Salem, Massachusetts, in 1664 with her second husband Henry, the brother of her first husband Nicholas. Hannah and Henry's family consisted of her children Jonathan and Hannah and his son John. Widowed in the 1670s, she married a third time, and possibly again in the 1690s, giving her four husbands over a forty-five-year period. Anna Willix Riscoe also had a succession of husbands. Originally from New England, she was widowed by June 1683, when she married a prominent Chowan County planter, Captain James Blount Sr. After Blount's death in 1686, she wed Seth Sothel (notorious as one of the most "arbitrary" and "corrupt" governors during the Proprietary period). Sothel died in 1693, leaving his "Deare & entirely well beloved wife" widowed again, and sometime between September 1694 and April 1695 she took a fourth husband, Colonel John Lear of Virginia.[18]

Diana Harris Foster White Mercer followed a similar pattern. With her first husband, Thomas Harris, she had her only child, John. Thomas Harris had a son Thomas from an earlier marriage, though it is not clear if the young Thomas came to the Albemarle with his parents in 1665. Widowed at thirty-three, Diana brought her son (and possibly her stepson) to her second marriage, to William Foster, who had two children of his own. At the time of her third marriage, to Thomas White, fourteen years her junior and heavily in debt, Diana Foster was fifty years old and the proprietor of a successful inn. Disparities in age and status were not unusual on the frontier. Diana married her fourth husband, Thomas Mercer, about whom little is known, when she was sixty. She was married twelve years to Harris, seven years to Foster, two years to White, and two to Mercer. The length between her first and second marriages was three years; second and third, seven years; and third and fourth, eight years. North Carolina's balanced sex ratio may have resulted in older widows remarrying less quickly than in the Chesapeake, where women were scarcer.[19]

The marital journeys of Phelps, Sothel, and Harris exemplify another pattern similar to that of women living in the Chesapeake region: widows remarried far more frequently than widowers. Historians have suggested that women on the frontier enjoyed more favorable status and more freedom than those in more settled regions. Frequent remarriage could have enhanced a woman's position through the accumulation of estates, children, and stepchildren. Diana Harris was able to offer the inn she and her first husband Thomas Harris had established to her second and third husbands. Anna Riscoe Blount Sothel Lear made three auspicious marriage alliances that increased her social and economic prominence.[20]

In 1709 John Lawson asserted that North Carolina women "marry very young; some at Thirteen or Fourteen; and She that stays til Twenty, is reckon'd a stale Maid; which is a very indifferent Character in that warm Country." Yet a study of marriage ages of men and women born before 1740 in Perquimans County (where approximately 50 families lived in 1670 and about 150 families in 1710) indicates that early colonial women did not marry as young as Lawson claimed. More than 50 percent first married after age twenty, only 2 percent at ages fourteen and fifteen, and none at thirteen

FIGURE 2-5. *Mrs. Elizabeth Freake and Baby Mary*, Boston, ca. 1674. No pictures of women living on the North Carolina frontier exist, but New Englander Elizabeth Freake was depicted holding her baby daughter in a domestic setting. (Courtesy of the Worcester Art Museum, Worcester, Massachusetts; gift of Mr. and Mrs. Albert W. Rice)

years. (Although Ann Durant's birthdate is unknown, both Diana Harris Foster and Hannah Phelps had reached their twentieth birthdays when they married for the first time.)[21]

The daughters of the first settlers may have married at slightly younger ages than their mothers (as in the Chesapeake), although the Albemarle evidence is too slight to support generalizations. Hannah Phelps's daughter, also named Hannah, married at age eighteen. Both Hannah and Ann Durant's oldest daughter, Elizabeth (whose age at marriage is unspecified), were widowed in their mid-twenties with young children, remarried, and died when they were around thirty, leaving behind minor children. In both cases, the grandmothers stepped in to protect their grandchildren. Ann Durant reared Elizabeth's young daughters, Ann and Elizabeth, and Hannah Phelps went to court twice, in 1685 and 1689, to safeguard the property of her young grandson from his stepfather.[22]

"The Women are very fruitful; most Houses being full of Little Ones," wrote John Lawson. "It has been observ'd, that Women long marry'd, and without Children, in other Places, have removd to *Carolina*, and become joyful Mothers." Ann Durant did bear eight more children after her arrival in Perquimans, but Harris had only one. Perhaps Lawson was trying to encourage settlement with his enthusiastic hyperbole (Fig. 2-5).[23]

Black Women and Family: "Together with Her Increase"

For slave women living in the early Albemarle, creating and maintaining kinship ties were fraught with obstacles. Slaves' legal status was that of chattel or movable property, which meant that they could be sold and moved from one plantation to another. The slave status of a baby was determined by its mother, regardless of who the father was. Slave children could be separated from their mothers, though usually not before the age of two. Forming a family was difficult because there were many more black men than black women, and most slaves lived on small, isolated farmsteads that had only one or two other slaves. Moreover, once a family was formed, parents might have to cope with the loss of a child or spouse by sale or inheritance.[24]

Slave families consisting of parents and children may have been moved south from Virginia by white planters in the 1650s; however, headright lists, the earliest evidence of slavery in the colony, give little information about kinship groups. The earliest slave family identified in colonial records is that of "Manuell & Frank his wife," listed in the 1695 inventory of Governor Seth Sothel's estate as it passed to planter Thomas Pollock, of Chowan County, early North Carolina's largest landowner. Fourteen years later, five other slave families appeared on a listing of Pollock's property—"Rowman and his wife Judith," "London and his wife Betty," "Thom and his wife Nancy," "Jackfiddle and his wife Grace," and "Scipio and one Negro Woman named Moll Scipio's wife, two Negro boys named Tom and Scipio ye Sons of ye Sd Scipio and Moll."[25]

Because of the fluidity of frontier Albemarle and the still-emerging definition of slavery (which included Native Americans as well as blacks), early slavery was not as structured and therefore not as rigid as it later became. Thus Manuell and Frank had limited autonomy over their daily lives. They regularly hired themselves out to work for other planters. They owned a bed, bedclothes, and a gun. They lived as a married couple with five children—three daughters, two of whom were named Hannah and Molina, and two sons, Charles and Manuell. Even so, family survival was subject to the will and whim of slaveowners. In 1709 Thomas Pollock divided his estate among his three sons, and Frank and her five children were separated from one another to make an equitable division among his heirs (Manuell had died by that time).[26]

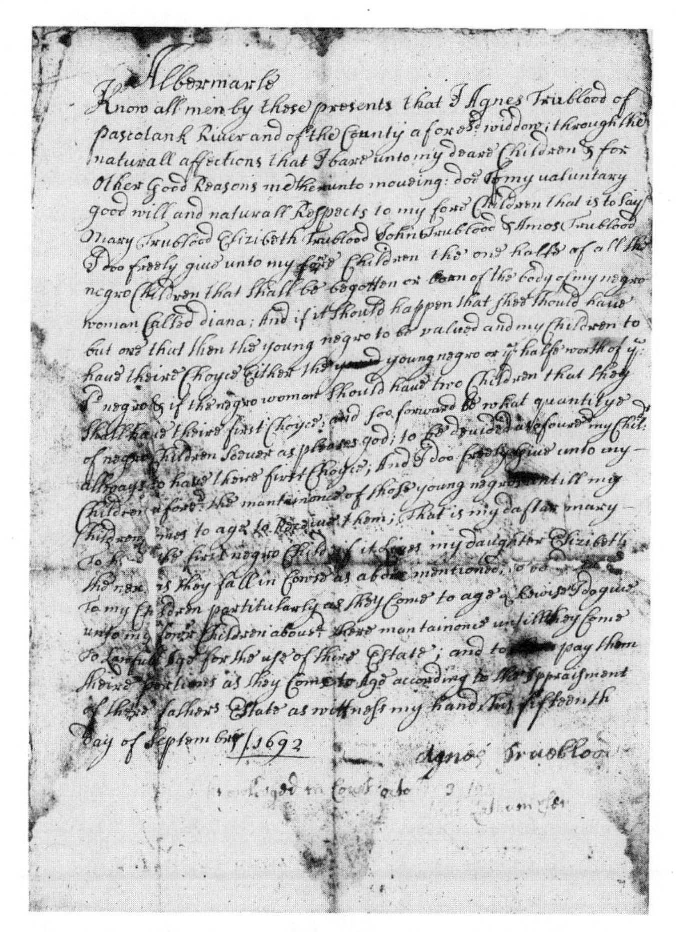

Albermarle
Know all men by these presents that I Agnes Trueblood of
Pascotank River and of the County aforesd widdow; through the
naturall affections that I bare unto my deare Children & for
Other Good Reasons me thereunto mouving: doe of my valuntary
good will and naturall Respects to my foure Children that is to say
Mary Trueblood Elizibeth Trueblood John Trueblood & Amos Trueblood
I doe freely give unto my said Children the one halfe of all the
negro Children that shall be begotten or born of the body of my negro
woman Called diana; And if it should happen that shee should have
but one that then the young negro to be valued and my Children to
have theire Choyce either the [illegible] young negro or ye halfe worth of ye
negro & if the negro woman should have two Children that they
shall have theire first Choyce; and soe forward to what quantity ye
of negro Children soever as pleases god; to be devided as foure my Chil-
allways to have theire first Choyce; And I doe freely give unto my
Children afores the manteinance of those young negros untill my
Children comes to age to Receive them; That is my daughter Mary
to [illegible] the first negro Child [illegible] my daughter Elizibeth
the next as they fall in Course as above mentioned; [illegible]
to my Children particularly as they Come to age & [illegible] I doe give
unto my foure Children above there manteinance untill they Come
to Lawfull Age for the use of theire Estate; and to [illegible] pay them
theire portions as they Come to Age according to the Appraisment
of theire fathers Estate as witness my hand the fifteenth
day of September 1692
Agnes Trueblood
[illegible] in Court [illegible]

FIGURE 2-6. *Will of Agnes Trueblood*, Pasquotank County, 1692. (Cited in Brinn, "Blacks in Colonial North Carolina," 99–100; courtesy of the Secretary of State Collection, Council Minutes, North Carolina Wills and Inventories, Wills, 1663–1789, 32:16)

A slave mother could also lose her children when owners equalized their own children's inheritance by bequeathing to them a slave woman "together with her increase"—children yet unborn. The first known instance of this practice was in 1692, when Quaker Agnes Fisher Trueblood, who lived at the Narrows of the Pasquotank (later Elizabeth City), left to her four children "one halfe of all the negro Children that shall be begotten or born of the body of my negro woman Diana" (Fig. 2-6).[27]

Although slaves lived with the threat of separation by sale or inheritance, there are examples of longtime relationships. Of the five couples listed by Pollock in 1709, four—Rowman and Judith, Scipio and Moll, London and Betty, and Tom and Nancy—were still together when the planter died in 1722. Unrecognized in law, slave marriages clearly existed in fact. Many planters did not acknowledge black family ties and referred to the children only by the mother's name. Others recognized family groups in the listing of their slaves, as the Pollock descendants continued to do well into the nineteenth century.[28]

A degree of personal autonomy may have been possible for slave women, as well as for men. "Negro Betty" inherited "one sow about three years old" in 1696 as a measure of her owner's gratitude for her caregiving. There are also instances in which women exercised independence and enterprise beyond domestic tasks. A slave named Jenny sold six pairs of buttons, a "turkey cocke," and two sticks of whalebone to a free white woman, Mary Guthrie, in exchange for "two fouls of Dunghill Cockes." "Sarah" appears several times in the colonial records (though Sarah was a common name and may refer either to a single slave or to several of the same name): in one instance, Sarah hid corn for a white man in exchange for a remnant of lace; in another, she sold corn for her own profit. In 1706, "An Act Concerning Servants and Slaves" forbade slaves to "buy, sell, trade, or trucke, borrow, or lend to or with any Servant or Servants, Slave or Slaves without the Lycence and Consent of his or their Master or Owner." Initially blacks received the same judicial treatment as whites, but the creation of a comprehensive slave code and the establishment of slave courts in 1715 signaled the tightening of restrictions and regulation of slavery.[29]

White Women and Public Life

The intermingling of public and domestic life found in the early Albemarle allowed some white women to assume responsibilities for legal, political, and religious activities that later generations of women could hardly imagine. As public buildings were not constructed until the 1720s, the various seventeenth-century courts, the council, and the General Assembly met in private homes. Just when local or precinct courts were established is uncertain, but they were in place by 1679. The justices of the precinct courts were authorized to investigate "felonies, witchcraft, inchantments, sorceries, magic arts, trespasses, forestallings, regratings [the buying up of grain or provisions to resell at a profit in the same market], and extortions," as well as other crimes, and to prove wills and landrights. Although the majority of Albemarle women made do with crude, impermanent housing in remote areas, others had dwellings conveniently located on waterways that served both as local gathering places and seats of government. For those women, innkeeping was probably a short step from frontier hospitality. Inundated with visitors, they could charge for meals and lodging, and they were able to participate in public life.[30]

For about twenty years beginning in the early 1670s, Diana Harris and her successive husbands operated a popular inn in their residence near Muddy Creek in centrally located Perquimans Precinct. Referred to variously in the records as "the house of Thomas Harris," "the house of William Foster,"

The deposition of Diana Harris aged 32 yeares or thereabouts saith that Thomas Miller being in hir house in discourse sd yt of all Religions in the world Cavalrs are the veriest rogues & Tho. Willis answered why soe & Thomas Miller replyed againe how can there be righteous dealing when ye King hath his hand in a whores plackett & further saith not.

Diana hir Harris
x
mark

—Saunders, *Colonial Records of North Carolina*, 1:316, November 1697.

by the name of her third husband, Thomas White, and in 1694 as the "House of Mrs. Diana Forster," the inn was a frequent meeting place for the General Court. Thomas Harris was one of the earliest clerks of the Perquimans Precinct Court, and William Foster was a justice of the county court of Albemarle in 1684. Diana Harris had ample opportunity to become familiar with court proceedings, and after marrying the heavily indebted Thomas White, she regularly appeared before the court to collect debts owed her prior to the marriage—there were nearly fifty suits involving her either individually or with her husband. Harris also participated in colonial politics as a supporter of "Culpeper's Rebels," a group of local planters who resisted the ironfisted use of power over their trade by Thomas Miller, the newly appointed deputy governor and customs collector. When Miller arrested George Durant as a "Traytour" in December 1677 for selling his tobacco without paying the required tax and was, in turn, seized by Durant and his followers and placed on trial, Diana Harris testified against him. Known as Culpeper's Rebellion, the colonists' resistance is considered one of the first popular uprisings against unjust and arbitrary government action.[31]

Ann Marwood Durant is an early example of a political wife. Her husband George, the colony's largest exporter of tobacco, was frequently away opposing the Proprietors' policies or pursuing his occupation as a mariner. Ann acted in his stead and conducted other businesses in her own name. The mother of nine children, she operated an inn in their Perquimans Precinct home north of Albemarle Sound where she was right in the hub of public events in the colony. During Culpeper's Rebellion the "rebels" established new assemblies and councils at the Durant home. Miller was tried in court there, where stocks and a pillory were erected. Durant is the first woman attorney-in-fact on record in North Carolina (1673) and represented herself, her husband, and others in court proceedings held at the inn. In 1673 she successfully brought suit to retrieve lost wages for a seaman, Andrew Ball, and later defended her husband's and her own interests as well. In 1675 her husband appointed her his attorney, and in 1688 he named her executrix of his estate.[32]

Seventeenth-century North Carolina's informal legal system permitted laypeople to handle their own court cases, and other women's names also appear in the early public records as they prosecuted and defended their interests. Margaret Bird, Jane Bayley, and Mary Clarke served as executrices for their husbands' estates and for those of others. Esther Pollock, Thomas Pollock's second wife who died in 1712, designated someone other than Pollock to be the executor of her estate and that of her first husband, William Wilkinson, who had died eight years earlier.[33]

A small but significant number of women also represented themselves and other parties as attorneys-in-fact. Margaret Culpepper presented the inventory of Valentine Bird's estate at two separate court sessions in 1680 and successfully prosecuted her own case to collect a debt from William Therrill (she was awarded 1,500 pounds of tobacco). In a 1694 court session Susanna Heartley joined with Major Alexander Lillington to collect a debt from Colonel William Wilkinson for a Captain George Clark, and Anne Stuart Senior proved six headrights for "four negroes, one English servant, and Argill Simons." Elinor Moline represented her husband Robert in 1695, evidently with such vehemence that she was sentenced to fifteen stripes on her back for "abusive words" against the deputy governor and council. (The punishment might have been due to her Quaker husband's politics at a time of growing political tensions between Quakers and non-Quakers in the Albemarle.) Anne Ros traded in whale oil and went to court to defend her rights. Certainly the longest female participation in the colonial courts is that of Juliana Hudson Taylor Laker. Laker pursued her legal interests, protecting her property rights and defending herself against charges of "unreasonable correctings," with determination, competence, and occasional vindictiveness for almost fifty years.[34]

When courts became more formal and structured at the close of the Proprietary period, women lost out. By the late 1720s the higher courts and by the 1730s the lower courts began meeting in public buildings constructed especially for judicial proceedings, and male professional attorneys were in charge. In the last three years before her death in 1738, even the resourceful Juliana Laker engaged attorneys to handle her legal affairs.

Although organized religion barely existed in the early days of the Albemarle, religious tolerance was one of the inducements the Lords Proprietors used to attract colonists, and Quakers from both England and New England settled among those of the officially established Anglican faith. The first recorded Quaker meeting in the Albemarle was held by William Edmundson of Ireland at the home of Hannah and Henry Phelps in May 1672. (The first recorded Quaker meeting in Massachusetts, in 1658, had also been held at Hannah's house.) In November 1672, when Quaker leader George Fox traveled to the Albemarle, he stopped first at the home of Mary and Joseph Scott where he held a meeting; then he and his entourage "passed by water four miles to Henry Phillips' [Phelps] house" and held a meeting there. Quaker meetings continued at Hannah's house even after Henry's death and her marriage to James Hill. Not until the eighteenth century were public places of worship established: the first Quaker meetinghouse was built in Perquimans in 1704, followed by a second in 1706; and in 1707 Anglicans erected their first church building.[35]

> The ordinary Women take care of Cows, Hogs, and other small Cattle, make Butter and Cheese, spin Cotton and Flax, help to sow and reap Corn, wind Silk from the Worms, gather Fruit, and look after the house.
>
> —English pamphleteer John Oldmixon on South Carolina women. (Oldmixon, "British Empire" [1708], 372)

White Women in the Household: "Pride Seldom Banishing Good Housewifery"

Seventeenth-century women gained status from their role as housewives in a society in which the basic economic foundation was the household, and their at-home work had important financial implications. Domestic tasks took on new meaning with the development of the status of yeoman in sixteenth-century England. In these early independent agricultural families—the yeomanry—women and men were assigned their position from the house and its land. Women were given the name and status of "huswives," as important counterparts to their "husbands." Books on husbandry in the Tudor period such as Master Fitzherbert's *The Book of Husbandry* (1534) and Thomas Tusser's *The Five Hundred Points of Good Husbandrie* (1577) also included "points of Huswiferie." In a yeoman partnership, the more "huswifelie" the "huswife," the more she helped "bring in the golde."[36]

The Albemarle settlers transferred the yeoman tradition to the New World, wherein each gender performed tasks essential to the family's survival: women prepared food and clothing, soap, candles, and medicines and cared for the children and infirm; men provided manual labor for field and home.

In North Carolina, as in the Chesapeake, men and women who did not establish households and farm their own land could work for decades and never gain an economic foothold. More than two-thirds of the early settlers raised some hogs or cattle, subsistence crops, and a money crop such as tobacco, corn, or wheat without slave or servant labor. The husband's domain was typically a backwoods farm in the midst of the coastal forest. Tree stumps were left to decay, animals foraged freely, and cultivating crops took precedence over maintaining buildings. Virginian William Byrd, who visited the colony in the early 1700s when he was surveying the boundary line between Virginia and North Carolina, thought that North Carolina farms showed few "Tokens of Husbandry or Improvement." John Lawson observed that although some of the men in North Carolina were "very laborious, and make great Improvements in their Way . . . the easy Way of living in that plentiful Country, makes a great many Planters very negligent." Women, on the other hand, were "the most industrious Sex in that Place."[37]

Looking after the house was only part of a housewife's job, for, depending on family resources, she also had charge of a separate kitchen, smokehouse, dairy, henhouses, vegetable and herb gardens, and servant and slave quarters. The division of household chores into housewifery and husbandry meant that girls learned from their mothers how to care for the house, the dairy, the gardens, and the younger children, while boys helped their fathers in the fields. Mothers taught their daughters the domestic skills critical to the functioning of every colonial household. As children and as adults, females contributed significantly to the domestic economy, and the value of their household labor was understood and appreciated (Fig. 2-7). Lawson commented, "The Girls are not bred up to the Wheel, and Sewing only; but the Dairy and Affairs of the House they are very well acquainted withal; so that you shall see them, whilst very young, manage their Business with a great deal of Conduct and Alacrity."[38]

As most of the settlers' time, labor, and resources were invested in land, labor, and crops, what they put into buildings and furnishings was generally minimal, and women commonly kept house in small cabins built more for shelter than for permanence. Byrd wrote that "most of the Houses in this part of the Country are Log-houses, covered with Pine or Cypress shingles," and the shoddy construction permitted "a very free passage of the air through every part of it." There is little trace of the first two generations of North Carolina settlers, and none of the earliest wooden houses has survived. If the family prospered, impermanent houses were replaced with more permanent buildings, but even these tended to be modest log or frame structures. The 40-by-20-foot dwelling of "all sawed worke"—probably a frame covered with clapboard or riven wood instead of logs—that Perquimans Pre-

FIGURE 2-7. "Countrywoman of the Time." In *A New Voyage to Carolina* (1709, pp. 90–91), John Lawson wrote of the pioneer women: "As for those Women, that do not expose themselves to the Weather, they are often very fair, and generally as well featur'd, as you shall see anywhere, and have very brisk charming Eyes, which sets them off to Advantage." Edward Eggleston, *A History of the United States and Its People* (New York: Appleton and Co., 1888). (Courtesy of the Outer Banks History Center, Manteo)

cinct merchant Francis Godfrey and his wife Joanne were building when he died in 1675 had framing costing nearly eight pounds, a far greater amount than most other houses of the period.[39]

Although most householders had few possessions, even as early as the 1680s some had a considerable number of domestic goods that provide clues to women's work patterns and efforts to create comfortable environments. A few household inventories survive from the 1600s, mostly for more prosperous Albemarle families. Margaret Bird and her husband Captain Valentine Bird, one of the wealthiest planters in the Albemarle, had extensive furnishings, including two bedsteads, a couch, a cradle, two feather beds, two small chests (one with drawers), two tables with frames, ten chairs, a looking glass, a dressing box, and a large amount of tableware and household linens. Joane Godfrey, whose merchant husband Francis's inventory is the most detailed of those surviving from that period, also oversaw a wide assortment of household furnishings—numerous chairs, tables, carpets, mirrors, and cupboards. Anna Sothel, when widowed by her third husband (Proprietary governor Seth Sothel), by contrast, had few household furnishings: only one "old Bedd" and two tables and old chairs in the hall; a bed, six chairs, and two pairs of old andirons in the chamber; a few pans and "A small parasell" of pewter and brass in the kitchen; and miscellaneous items in the dairy. Probably Bird did not use all her fifteen bedsheets or seventeen pillows nor Godfrey her thirteen pewter dishes and twenty-three pewter plates. Such a quantity of tangible domestic possessions, especially imported items, may have represented, along with land and slaves, a capital investment.[40]

No matter how many or how few her household possessions, the average housewife's central activity was cooking at the open hearth either in the hall or in a separate kitchen—a time-consuming and hazardous chore. Cooking often required a variety of pots and a formidable array of andirons, pothooks, racks, and cradles that a woman had to handle summer and winter. A woman who could lift a fifty-pound cast-iron pot onto a spit over a hot fire had strength as well as skill.[41]

Cookware was extremely sturdy and served a family for years as it passed through several generations (Fig. 2-8). Margaret Bird's cooking equipment included a brass kettle, a brass skillet, a frying pan, three other skillets, four large iron pots ranging in size from 33 to 50 pounds, six metal mortar and pestles, a wooden mortar, and a hand mill. To manipulate the massive pots, pans, and skillets, she had three spits, three pairs of pothooks, a rack, a flesh fork, a cradle, and andirons. Joane Godfrey had at her disposal a brass chafing dish, a brass mortar and pestle, two brass skillets, a brass skimmer, two iron kettles, three iron pots, an eight-gallon brass kettle, two frying pans, a meal sifter, a grater, three pairs of pothooks, a white earthen basin, two butter tubs, and scales with brass weights. Such an array of equipment provides material evidence that contradicts the widespread description of early American cooking as a single pot stew of meat and vegetables. Anna Sothel, by contrast, was left with the sparest of kitchen furnishings—three "old iron pots, frying pans," a pair of andirons and pot hooks, a spit, a hand mill, and a grindstone.[42]

Women supplemented a diet heavy in meat—fresh, salted,

FIGURE 2-8. *Earthenware mug*, ca. 1690, found in the Roanoke River near the Hogtown site, Martin County. Although extensive cooking and eating implements of the time document that women spent much of their time preparing food, few utensils exist today, and unbroken archaeological remains are rare. (Office of State Archaeology, North Carolina Archaeology and Historic Preservation; photograph courtesy of the North Carolina Museum of History)

or cured pork, mutton, bacon, and wild game—fish, and shellfish from their dairies and gardens. Milking and gardening, the province of women in England, remained so in America. Women's close association with dairy production is confirmed by the colonial documents, in which females ending indentured service or apprenticeships were given a calf or heifer to start out in life. Dorothy Harvey's father bequeathed to her "four cows and a Heifer" as part of her inheritance. Women's gardens provided fresh vegetables and herbs important to the household diet and health (almost every household possessed a mortar and pestle for grinding herbs) and gave women a place of their own to cultivate. Orchards were also women's responsibility, and the apples, pears, quince, peaches, apricots, plums, figs, and cherries provided variety, at least within seasonal limitations, and most could be preserved by drying.[43]

Women were also responsible for textile production within the household. Household linens were highly prized, sometimes worth more than the actual house itself, and linens were passed, along with valued clothing, buttons, and silk stockings, through estates. "By their good Houswifry," women, wrote Lawson, "make a good deal of Cloath of their own Cotton, Wool, and Flax; some of them keeping their Families (though large) very decently apparel'd, both with Linnens and Woollens." According to Lawson, housewives "have no occasion to run into the Merchant's Debt, or lay their Money out on Stores for Cloathing." It is clear from the large amounts of imported cloth found in merchants' inventories that Albemarle women used manufactured textiles and that Lawson exaggerated their commitment to making cloth. In fact, there is not as much textile equipment in extant inventories as one might expect: the Sothels, the Birds, and the Godfreys owned neither spinning wheels nor looms.[44]

Caretaking was also women's work—tending infants and young children, nursing the sick and elderly, training children, and overseeing orphans, apprentices, slaves, or servants who might be part of the household. Indeed, the isolated households served the multiple functions later provided by schools, hospitals, and welfare institutions. Whether women also nurtured emotional bonds within the family is currently being debated as historians try to understand when and how the earlier function of the family as an economic entity changed to one in which emotional and affectionate ties became dominant. It is an important question but difficult to answer, for the early Albemarle evidence consists of land grants and court records—wills, inventories, and litigation; few women's letters and no diaries or journals survive.[45]

Two consumer goods, beds and pewter plates, considered markers of a shift to increased domestic comfort and sociability, do appear in Albemarle inventories. The bedstead was the most important article of furniture in seventeenth-century houses. It was costly, its massive size connoted permanence and comfort, and it usually occupied a place of honor in the parlor. The term "bed" usually referred to what we call a mattress and took many different forms, though feather beds were a mark of wealth and among the most valuable of all household possessions; poorer people slept on straw pallets. According to her father's will, in 1659 pioneer settler Dorothy Harvey had "a Feather Bed and Bolster a Rugg and Blankett, and a pair of Sheets," and he bequeathed

> I give and bequeath all the rest of my wearing Apparrell both Lynnen and woollen to my said Couson Dorothy Tooke & Joane Tooke to be equally divided betwixt them.
> —Will of Dorothy Harvey, dated November 14, 1682, proved January 1682 (1683). (North Carolina Division of Archives and History)

her "a small Feather Bed with a Canvas Ticking." Margaret Bird had two feather beds and two bedsteads, Joane Godfrey had five feather beds, and both women had a wide variety of sheets and pillows. The Sothel household did not have much in the way of bedding—one "old Bedd" with two sheets and blanket and another bed and bolster. The Bird and Godfrey households also used pewter tableware—plates, porringers, basins, tankards. The accumulation of pewter, silver, and other luxury items that transformed eating from a survival activity to an elegant ritual raises the possibility that their families gathered for extended, sociable meals. And yet utensils such as forks, which indicate an even more leisurely and genteel approach to eating typical of English noble households of the time, do not appear in any of the Albemarle inventories.[46]

Living on the colonial frontier required women to do more than housewifery. Besides operating an inn or providing some sort of board and lodging, Ann Marwood Durant made shirts and leather breeches, furnished coffins, arranged funerals, and supplied commodities like cloth, thread, planks, and nails. Sometimes early colonial women took on men's roles and acted, in effect, as their husbands' surrogates. On the other hand, it would have been unusual for a man to cross over to the domestic sphere. Women could be counted on to parlay their domestic talents into earning money or to help out in the fields, if the need arose, or to master the flat-bottomed skiffs across Albemarle waterways. There are no accounts of men preparing meals or spinning thread in their wives' absence.[47]

Married Women and Common Law

Women's rights and status were limited under the "common law" that the colonists transferred from England to the Virginia and North Carolina colonies. Married women, and by extension, single and widowed women, were particularly disadvantaged because of several underlying principles. Common law recognized property rights over personal liberties. Marriage was regarded as a lifelong contract, with specific terms defined by the state, to which both husband and wife were legitimately bound. Divorce was virtually impossible, and marriage ended only with death. Most significantly, marriage changed a woman's legal identity but not a man's. Husband and wife became one person, and, legally, the husband was the one. When a woman married, her legal and economic identity was subsumed under that of her husband. He was considered head of the family and guardian of his wife's rights. She became a *feme covert* (a covered, protected, married woman) and a legal nonentity, except in an equity court, which moderated common law and provided another forum for settling cases. No doubt the frontier's somewhat more lenient laws and even more relaxed enforcement meant that the Albemarle colonists did not follow every letter of the legal system—whether common, statutory, or equity—but probably made use of whatever served their needs at the time.[48]

Single women, on the other hand, had many of the same legal options as men in that they could take responsibility for their own affairs. Spinsters and widows were considered to be *feme sole*. They could buy and sell property, make wills and contracts, sue in court, execute deeds, administer estates, and serve as guardians. They could not sit on juries, serve as government officials, or hold office in local councils or courts. Married women whose husbands were absent so often that the women needed to serve as a legal surrogate might be designated *feme sole traders* (married women who could engage in business transactions as if they were unmarried), but such action was unusual.[49]

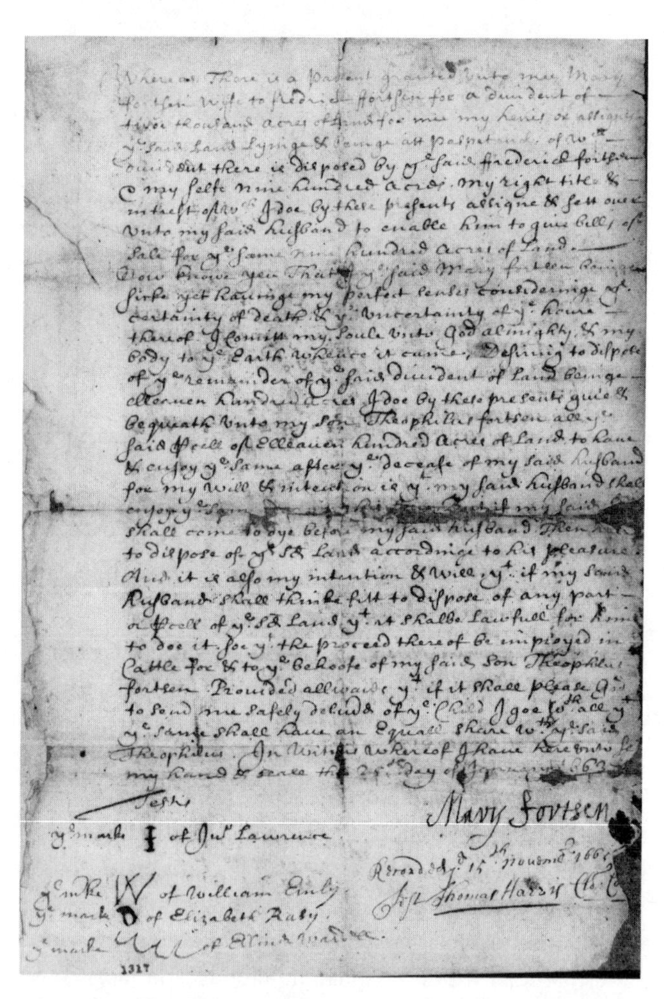

Whereas There is a Patent granted unto me Mary [illegible] wife to ffederick ffortsen for a divident of two thousand acres of land for me my heires or assignes ye said land lyinge & beinge att [illegible] of [illegible] [illegible] But there is disposed by ye said ffrederick fortsen & my selfe nine hundred acres. my right title & interest of w[illegible] I doe by these presents assigne & sett over unto my said husband to enable him to give bills of sale for ye same nine hundred acres of land.

Now know yee That I ye said Mary fortsen beinge sicke yet havinge my perfect senses considering ye certainty of death & ye uncertainty of ye houre thereof I committ my soule unto God almighty & my body to ye earth whence it came, Desiring to dispose of ye remainder of ye said divident of land beinge eleaven hundred acres I doe by these presents give & bequeath unto my son Theophilus fortsen all ye said ffrell of Elleaven hundred acres of land to have & enjoy ye same after ye decease of my said husband for my will & intention is yt my said husband shall enjoy ye [illegible] but if my said [illegible] shall come to dye before my said husband Then [illegible] to dispose of ye sd land accordinge to his pleasure. And it is also my intention & will, yt if my said husband shall thinke fitt to dispose of any part or ffell of ye sd land yt it shallbe lawfull for him to doe it so yt the proceed thereof be imployed in Cattle for & to ye behoofe of my said Son Theophilus fortsen Provided allwaies yt if it shall please God to send me safely delivred of ye Child I goe wth all yt ye same shall have an equall share wth ye said Theophilus. In witness whereof I have hereunto set my hand & seale this 28th day of [illegible] 1663

Testis

ye marke I of Jno Lawrence

ye marke W of William Emly

ye marke [illegible] of Elizabeth Raby

ye marke [illegible] of [illegible]

Mary Fortsen

Recorded ye 15th November 1665

Test Thomas Harris Cl[illegible]

1317

FIGURE 2-9. *Mary Fortsen's will* dated January 28, 1663, and probated on November 15, 1665. Although women are generally absent from colonial public records, Mary Fortsen's will is the oldest document of its kind surviving in North Carolina from the 1660s. Fortsen is the first woman known to have owned land in North Carolina. (Courtesy of the North Carolina Division of Archives and History)

Thus married women could only hope that their husbands were both kind and clever. Whatever real and personal property a woman brought to a marriage became his. The only way a woman could keep her property was by a prenuptial contract, generally a device used by widows to ensure inheritance for their children. In 1696 Hannah Wood complained to the court that her husband had taken away "the wearing Clothes of your petitioner and her Children without any process at Law." She argued that the loss of clothing was "hazardous," especially "Now winter is Comming on." Diana Harris Foster White inherited a substantial estate from her first husband Thomas Harris, increased it with her second husband William Foster, only to see it destroyed by her third husband Thomas White. Her marriage to White, fourteen years her junior and heavily in debt, was a disaster. Within a year, he had ruined his wife's business, an inn she had operated with her previous husbands for twenty-five years, and sold much of her property to cover his debts. Diana White sued, unsuccessfully, for separate maintenance, arguing that White had sold most of her household goods and furniture and ejected her from her home, leaving her "destitute of a Convenient Lodging and all other necessaries."[50]

Although common law specified that married women had no separate property rights, the case of Mary Fortsen, one of the earliest patent holders of North Carolina land with 2,000 acres on the Pasquotank River, is an intriguing exception (Fig. 2-9). Ordinarily her husband would have held the patent; even if it were made out to her, he would have had legal ownership. Because married women had limited rights to own or dispose of property, few of them made wills. Mary Fortsen's will, however, indicates that she believed she had the right to dispose of her property and that she was literate. She identified herself as the "wife to Frederick Fortsen" and the mother of Theophilus, both of whom were alive and well at the time she wrote her will, and she was pregnant with a second child: "if it shall please God to Send me Safely delivered of the Child . . . that the Same shall have an Equall Share with the said Theophilus." Fortsen's will is evidence that in North Carolina a *feme covert* could own land and have the legal right to provide for her children, living and unborn. How could this be? Perhaps Mary and Frederick had a prenuptial agreement, especially likely if Theophilus were her son from a previous marriage. Perhaps common law was overlooked when it was deemed unsuitable for frontier conditions, or perhaps equity sometimes outweighed married women's unequal legal rights.[51]

On the frontier women and men did what had to be done to survive, and a woman's industrious housewifery could make the difference between success and failure. Private lives and public roles were closely intertwined, and women's place was often in the thick of the action, both political and legal. At the same time, the unusual accomplishments of a privileged few did not alter women's culturally and legally sanctioned subordinate status. By 1715 slave laws began to tighten, and in 1741 even harsher legal and judicial restraints reinforced slaves' inferior status. In 1729, when the English king replaced the Lords Proprietors, North Carolina had become a royal colony. Both the government and the legal system were more institutionalized, and possibilities for white women as well as black men and women were more restricted.

And yet many formidable women ventured to the New World, planted gardens on the frontier, bore children, established households, and flourished. What this legacy of achievement meant for their daughters would have to be measured in the eighteenth century.

CHAPTER 3

A Pattern of Industry

Women from the Colonial to Republican Eras

A woman on the North Carolina frontier in the early 1700s was admired by Virginian William Byrd for being "civil" and modest "in her carriage" yet able to "carry a gunn in the woods and kill deer, turkeys, &c., shoot down wild cattle, catch and tye hoggs, knock down beeves with an ax." Throughout the eighteenth century, as a steady influx of Germans, Scots-Irish, Highland Scots, and English settlers flowed into the North Carolina backcountry, new generations of women continued to adapt to frontier conditions with similar robust ingenuity.[1]

By contrast, many white women in the towns and plantations along the coast had more rigidly defined gender roles. They were expected to be "most excellent" wives, "fond" mothers, and "notable" housewives within the private space of increasingly complex households. Slavery was slow to take hold—in the 1760s fewer than 1 percent of North Carolina households owned the twenty or more slaves that characterized a "plantation," but by 1800 slavery was well established. Whereas women of the slaveholding classes benefited from the labor of slaves, enslaved black women were expected to work like men, reproduce as women, and exist at a subsistence level. Native American women experienced a loss of their matrilineal status and their stewardship of land, paralleled by a century-long decline in the Indian population.[2]

By 1800 women were less visible in the public sphere than previously. Despite their contributions to the Revolutionary struggles, the cultural, economic, and legal position of women was restricted in ways that their early colonial mothers could not have anticipated. Furthermore, their economic role within the household, as recognized in the traditional concept of dower rights, was eroded by the 1784 state constitution, which relegated women to a dependent status similar to that of children.

North Carolina's population, fueled by immigration and a high birthrate, increased ninefold during the 1700s. The new colonists brought with them a variety of languages, cultures, and religions. In 1710 Swiss and Germans founded New Bern in Craven County. Newcomers to the Piedmont in the mid-1700s spoke Gaelic or German as well as English and followed the Moravian, Lutheran, German Reformed, and Presbyterian faiths. Starting in 1730, Highland Scots migrated in successive waves, heaviest in the 1770s, to establish farms and towns in the Cape Fear region. Scots-Irish, Germans, Scots, Irish, and Welsh, many of them the younger children of first- and second-generation Pennsylvania farmers, left their homes to travel down the Shenandoah Valley on the Great Wagon Road, arriving in North Carolina in the 1730s and, in rapidly growing numbers, the 1750s and 1760s. Mostly "plain folks," they bought large tracts of land in Anson, Granville, Mecklenburg, Orange, and Rowan Counties, built log houses, reared large families, grew their own food and some cash crops, and raised pigs, sheep, and cows—generally without slave labor. Many of their children and grandchildren were by the late 1700s moving even farther west to the mountain wilderness of North Carolina, Tennessee, and Kentucky and across the Mississippi River to Missouri. Rebecca Boone, whose biography follows this chapter, is the best-known pioneer woman, and many women like her faced hardships, persevered in the drudgery of frontier housekeeping, and created satisfying lives (Figs. 3-1, 3-2). Even as they came from different cultures, their lives had much in common once they settled in North Carolina. While the men mostly farmed, the women dwelled within the domestic sphere, a circumscribed world obligated by the duty of caring for children, the aged, and the infirm; constrained by the daily routine of preparing food, cloth, and other necessities; bounded by gardens, kitchens, and dairies; and tied to the house, whether log or brick, small or large, on the Coastal Plain or in the backcountry.[3]

Women and Domestic Life

Cheap and available land brought people to the colony, and the lineal family, through which land was conveyed from one generation to the next, formed the center of the social, political, legal, and economic structure. In the 1700s men and women, girls and boys, free and slave, young and old, typically lived within the protection of the family and the confines of the household. Women spent the majority of their time caring for their families, but as economic situations, geographic locations, and sizes of the households varied, so did the duties of the women in those households.[4]

Regardless of economic circumstances, girls learned early that they were destined for domestic life (Fig. 3-3). In privileged families, boys were prepared to enter public life and the professions, and they might be sent away for their schooling. Girls were normally taught at home by their mothers or

FIGURE 3-1. *Charlotte Reeves Robertson*, oil on canvas, Northampton County. Charlotte emerges from the historical record as the ever-intrepid pioneer woman. Born and reared in gentle circumstances, she married James Robertson and immediately moved west, to Orange County, to the Watauga River Valley, and finally to Nashborough (Nashville) along the Cumberland River on what was then considered North Carolina land. James spent much of his married life away from home, leaving Charlotte to rear their thirteen children, establish a school on the frontier, and gain renown as a heroine at the Battle of the Bluffs. (Courtesy of the Tennessee State Museum, Tennessee Historical Society Collection, Nashville)

tutors. In his will of 1731, planter John Baptista Ashe of Bath directed that his two sons receive "as liberal an Education as the profits" afford, including instruction in Latin, Greek, and French. One son was to pursue "ye Law" and the other, "Merchandize." Daughter Mary, on the other hand, was to be instructed in the domestic arts.[5] Children who were apprenticed also received training based on their gender. Boys learned a trade; girls were instructed in "the art and mystery of Carding and Spinning" or the "business of housewifery." The 1741 apprentice bond for orphan Elizabeth Deputy of Chowan County specified that her master should teach her "to read write knit Sow spin and cook," and when her time was up, he would pay her "freedom dues"—generally, a cow, calf, and spinning wheel.[6]

Women's place as domestic was reinforced by the division of property. In 1722 Frederick Jones left his library of books and extensive landholdings in Craven, Hyde, and Beaufort Precincts to his three sons; to his three daughters he willed household furnishings, jewelry, clothing, and slaves. Jones gave oldest daughter Jane her mother's diamond wedding ring and large pair of diamond earrings, damask tablecloths and napkins, holland sheets and pillowcases, and "All her Mothers Child bede Linnen." In 1753 James Robertson of Pasquotank County bequeathed land to his sons but "to my Daughter, Euphan, one Feather bed and furniture" and "to my Daughter, Salley, . . . one Fether Bed and Furniture." In 1774 Samuel Swann left his son all of his "mathematical books, classick, latin, and greek." His wife Jane received his books on "divinity and religion." In 1778 William Barwick left his wife Druscilla a large Bible, his son the family dictionary.[7]

Foreign visitors commented on North Carolina women's domesticity. A paragon of "domestic" accomplishments, "a most excellent wife and a fond mother," whose garden and dairy showed "her industry" is how Scotswoman Janet Schaw described her American sister-in-law, who lived near Wilmington in 1775. Spanish traveler Francisco de Miranda

FIGURE 3-2. Washington Bogart Cooper, *Charlotte Reeves Robertson at an advanced age*, oil on canvas, ca. 1835. (Courtesy of the Tennessee State Museum, Tennessee Historical Society Collection, Nashville)

FIGURE 3-3. "Ehre Vater Artist" (attributed), *Birth and Baptismal Certificate of Sarah Zimmerman* (born in Friedland, March 10, 1777), watercolor and ink on paper, Rowan County (later Forsyth), ca. 1800. The circular legend at the bottom of Sarah Zimmerman's illustrated Taufscheine reads: "It is a commendable thing for a boy to apply his mind to the study of good letters; they will always be useful to him; they will procure him the love and favour of good men, which those that are wise, value more than riches and pleasure." (Courtesy of the Collection of Old Salem, Winston-Salem)

> I will that my daughter be taught to write and read & some feminine accomplishments which may render her agreeable; And that she be not kept ignorant as to what appertains to a good house wife in the management of household affairs.
> —John Baptista Ashe, 1731. (Grimes, *North Carolina Wills and Inventories*, 16–17)

wrote that the "entire lives" of the married women he met in New Bern in 1783 were "domestic." Indeed, they "maintain a monastic seclusion" and "separate themselves from all intimate friendships and devote themselves completely to the care of home and family."[8]

Housewifery on the Frontier: "All with Their Own Hands"

Today the log house where Rachel and John Allen lived with their many children stands silent, but two hundred years ago it was filled with the sounds of Rachel and her four daughters preparing meals, spinning at a wheel, and making soap and candles. Rachel had been reared in Pennsylvania and moved to the North Carolina Piedmont when she married. John had been thirteen when he accompanied his widowed mother and four siblings from Pennsylvania to join Quaker relatives in Cane Creek Friends Meeting in Orange County. Seventeen years later, in 1779, he returned to Pennsylvania to find a bride, possibly because of the scarcity of women of his faith on the frontier. John and Rachel had twelve children and created a hard-working but comfortable life. Rachel's economic contribution to the family was as essential as John's; besides her household labors, she became midwife and healer for their Snow Camp neighbors.[9]

Built three years after their marriage, the Allens' cabin had one all-purpose room, dominated by a massive stone fireplace that was the source of the household cooking, heating, and lighting (Fig. 3-4). Front and back doors provided light and ventilation (window glass was costly and hard to get). In the yard adjacent to the house was an ash hopper for making soap, which was Rachel's responsibility, and nearby were vegetable and herb gardens and poultry pens to supplement the main diet of corn and pork. Cooking, eating, sleeping, making cloth, mending clothes, repairing tools, and reading books occurred in the main room, a sleeping loft, and the front and rear porches. Stools provided seating, and the few

FIGURE 3-4. *Main room of Rachel and John Allen Log House*, Alamance County, built ca. 1782, now the Alamance Battleground State Historic Site. (Courtesy of the North Carolina Division of Archives and History)

possessions not in use were stored in chests. Amid the sounds of the women's housework and the children's voices was the measured ticking of the grandfather clock brought by Rachel from Pennsylvania to her new backcountry home. Ten of the Allen children grew to adulthood in that tiny cabin; the oldest, however, was married and gone by the time the youngest was born.

Women living on the eighteenth-century frontier were not expected to be tidy housekeepers but to provide the household necessities that sustained a self-sufficient way of life. With little cash or access to the consumer items arriving in North Carolina ports, backcountry families depended on homegrown food and homespun cloth. Looms, spinning wheels, and cards were basic equipment in many households (Fig. 3-5). Rachel Allen owned two spinning wheels, hackles, and cards. In Halifax and Orange Counties in the 1770s about half the households had spinning wheels, and some 75 percent had flax wheels and looms that were used in linen and wool production. Clothmaking could be tedious and time-consuming, but it also gave women an opportunity for craftsmanship, self-expression, and pride (Plate 1). When Mary Meyers of Rowan County left her daughter and granddaughters her spinning wheel and weaver's reeds in 1784, she also specified various bed linens, such as a "counterpain" and a "Read Spotted Coverlid," that she wanted to pass along to them.[10]

Textile production provides one of the keys to how self-sufficient frontier households actually were and what economic role women played in home production. In 1767 royal governor William Tryon stated that there were in the "southern and western settlements [backcountry] spinning wheels and looms for the manufacture of cotton, wool, and flax, but no greater quantities of stuffs or coarse cloths are made than will supply the respective families in which they are worked." Tryon noted that when families had no looms, they could "send their woolen and linnen yarn to their neighbors to weave." A study of female spinners in Rowan County from 1753 to 1790 suggests that not all women spun, and some spinners may have produced thread for the market as well as for their families. Backcountry women sometimes created barter arrangements in which they spun and wove for each other and supplemented their family economy by exchanging surplus cloth.[11]

> Tho', in truth, the Distemper of Laziness seizes the Men oftener much than the Women. These last Spin, weave, and knit, all with their own Hands, while their Husbands, depending on the Bounty of the Climate, are Sloathfull in every thing but getting of Children, and in that only Instance make themselves useful Members of an Infant-Colony.
> —William Byrd, 1728. (Boyd, *William Byrd's Histories*, 66)

The Wife turns Soldier, & the Husband spining

FIGURE 3-5. *Man spinning and woman soldiering*, English Role Reversal Prints. No household task was more symbolic of women's domestic role than spinning. It was unthinkable that a man would learn how to spin. When Moravian bishop Joseph Spangenberg asked the Salem brothers in 1756, "How would it be, if you, like many of our Brethren in Nazareth and Bethlehem, too, were to help spin in the evenings or when at other times the weather is bad so that you cannot do anything outdoors," they refused. (From *Catchpenny Prints: 163 Popular Engravings from the Eighteenth Century* [New York: Dover Publications, 1970])

Black and White Women in Town

As early Carolina coastal society took shape and urban centers like Edenton, New Bern, and Wilmington tied to an emerging plantation culture developed, many white women took on new roles and different expectations. Town life was more sociable, and women could visit friends and family who lived nearby, attend church and social gatherings, shop for fresh provisions at the town markets, and purchase cloth and household goods at stores. Whereas backcountry households tended to be poor or "middling," those on the coast spanned a wider range—some poor or humble and others large, complex, multiracial households. Slave women helped white women in their housekeeping, and even women who were not slaveholders endorsed the trappings of gentry life.[12]

The image of the house and the housewife changed during the eighteenth century. For elite families, the home was becoming a space for recreation, leisure, and sociability as well as a place for work, sleep, and prayer. Little by little there was more house for women to look after, more rooms and more possessions, as well as more activities. Jean Innes Corbin, the widow of two wealthy men, owned eight looking glasses, five mahogany tables, twelve leather-bottomed chairs, and a backgammon table, among many other items that suggest that her New Hanover County household was an arena for amusements and entertainment. As early as the 1730s, the emerging ranks of merchants, professionals, and planters lived in what royal governor George Burrington described as "good Brick and wooden Mansions with Suitable outhouses" and orchards and gardens "handsomely laid out." Being a notable housewife came to mean keeping a clean house, well furnished and well managed, executed with proper modesty and household help (Fig. 3-6). When Julia Cherry Spruill published her pioneer study of southern colonial women, she concluded that the home was the "only field" in which "superior women" could "distinguish themselves" and that being a successful housewife took "individual initiative and executive ability."[13]

Many coastal households had at least a few slaves, and some had white indentured servants. Although white women who had slaves sometimes complained of the difficulties in managing them, these slaveowning women were spared the physical labor of keeping house. Whether they were white or black, women had the responsibility to cook, clean, wash, produce textiles, and care for the children. If slave women were in the household, they did those jobs. In 1775 Wilmington visitor Janet Schaw described a slave woman washing clothes, one of the most arduous household tasks: "cloaths coarse and fine, bed and table linen, lawns, cambricks and muslins, chints, checks" were thrown together in a "copper with a quantity of water and a large piece of soap" and set to boiling while the "Negro wench turns them over with a stick." Textiles were frequently the province of slave women, and in the evenings, they would spin, weave, and sew cloth for both the white families and their own. Young white girls learned early to command slaves, like the four-year-old who was "strutting about in the yard after Susanna (whom she has ordered to do something) with her work in her hand & an Air of as much importance as if she had been Mistress of the family."[14]

Slave women who cleaned and cooked for white families also had their own households to run, children to care for, and families to clothe and feed within the restricted sphere of the slave quarters. Edenton doctor John Brickell observed in 1737 that slaves supplemented the limited provisions supplied by their owners with gardens, hunting, and fishing. Janet Schaw wrote that blacks were the "only people that seem to pay any attention to the various uses" to which "wild vegetables" could be put. Schaw wrote that they cultivated their "little piece of land" to supplement their meager daily allowance of one quart of Indian corn, and their gardens were "much better than their Master. There they rear hogs and poultry, sow calabashes, etc. and are better provided for in every thing than the poorer white people with us."[15]

Such resourcefulness was less practiced in more affluent households. Brickell complained that "women do not over burthen themselves with care and Industry; otherwise there would not be such continual calls for those necessarys from *Europe*." Schaw implied that Cape Fear women were too lazy for home production of candles or soap. Even though "they

> They tell me however that the Mrs of this place is a pattern of industry, and that the house and every thing in it was the produce of her labours. She has (it seems) a garden, from which she supplies the town with what vegetables they use, also with mellons and other fruits. She even descends to make minced pies, cheese-cakes, tarts and little biskets, which she sends down to town once or twice a day, besides her eggs, poultry, and butter, and she is the only one who continues to have Milk. They tell me she is an agreeable woman, and I am sure she has good sense, from one circumstance,—all her little commodities are contrived so, as not to exceed one penny a piece, and her customers know she will not run tick [give credit].
>
> —Janet Schaw, Journal. (E. W. Andrews, *Journal of a Lady of Quality*, 178–79)

FIGURE 3-6. *Maynard*, home of Mary and Cornelius Harnett (later called Hilton), New Hanover County. Notable housewife Mary Harnett's domain extended beyond her twelve-room house to include kitchen, dairy, gardens, and orchards. (From *Ballou's Pictorial Drawing Room Companion*, February 24, 1855; courtesy of the Cape Fear Museum, Wilmington)

Will be sold for cash, or exchanged for a fellow and a boy,
A likely WENCH and GIRL.

The wench is about 25 years of age, she is a good cook, washer and ironer—She can spin on the little and big wheel very well, and is a tolerable good seemstress. The girl is about nine or ten years of age, is very handy about a house and is very likely. I would be glad to exchange the Girl for a Yellow Boy about the same age.

W. H. Beatty

—Advertisement, *Fayetteville Gazette*, March 5, 1793.

have the finest ashes in the world . . . and tho' some housewives are so notable as to make it [soap] for themselves, which they do at no expence, . . . most of them buy it at the store at a monstrous price."[16]

In privileged households, food and textiles remained a woman's responsibility (Fig. 3-7). More than likely the mistress purchased family clothing and linens or supervised their manufacture by slaves, and her textile work was ornamental needlework, one of several "accomplishments" taught to elite girls (Fig. 3-8). Cooking could be an elaborate activity. The expanded variety of foods—meats such as beef, mutton, pork, venison, game, and fowl; fish and shellfish; vegetables like carrots, parsnips, turnips, mushrooms, asparagus, celery, cucumbers, corn, rice, beets, artichokes, potatoes, radishes, leeks, onions, spinach, and squash; as well as fruit, salads, breads, butter, and cheese—were prepared in complicated ways, often from recipes handed down from mother to daughter, by slave cooks. Meals developed into intricate affairs with a variety of courses, necessitating china and silver serving dishes to hold different foods, forks and knives as well as spoons, glassware, dishes, tea and coffee cups and pots.

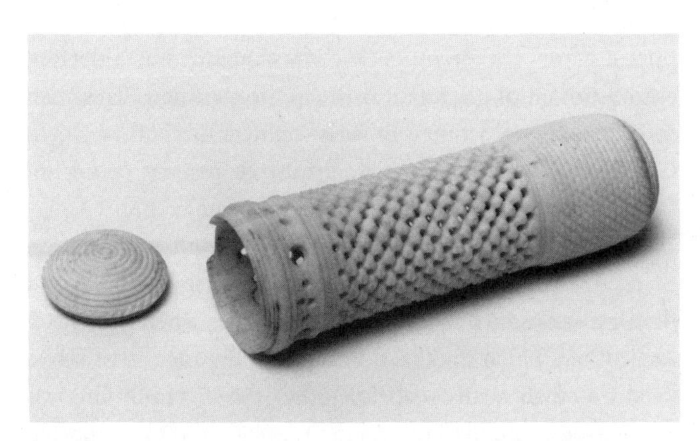

FIGURE 3-7. *Pin case*, ivory, ca. 1785. Few examples of eighteenth-century North Carolina needlework survive, but such elegant sewing accessories as this pin case are evidence of women's extensive textile activity. (Courtesy of the North Carolina Museum of History)

FIGURE 3-8. *Broderie Perse chintz appliqué*, by Harriet Williams, Pitt County, pre-1800. Williams combined imported English chintz of a floral tree with appliquéd flowers in a block quilt backed by homespun butternut dyed linen. (Courtesy of the North Carolina Museum of History)

The wealthy Wilmington widow Jean Innes Corbin had household furnishings so numerous that they were grouped under the headings of "Plate," "China," and "Glass"; they included "1 Milk pott & Sugar Tongs," "2 Butter boats" "10 Tea Spoons" "14 Silver knives" "20 do. forks" "3 Tea Potts" "17 Tea Cups" "25 Saucers." Carving was considered a female "accomplishment," and a 1764 poem satirizing female education described a properly trained young woman as one who "Can cut a fowl the modish way / And knows the art of drinking tea."[17]

Tea, as Carole Shammas has noted, became linked "with leisure-time sociability in the home, and with women" (Fig. 3-9). Tea drinking was a sign that a woman did not have to spend every moment of daylight working. In Edenton, Hannah Iredell received frequent callers at teatime and enjoyed the sociability that relieved what she sometimes found to be a boring domestic routine. Philadelphia visitor William Attmore described a small afternoon dinner party at the elegant home of Ann and John Wright Stanly in New Bern in 1787. After dinner the guests moved into the "tea room," where

FIGURE 3-9. *Family taking tea in library*, oil on canvas, 1730. Tea is the centerpiece of family sociability and camaraderie in this English painting of an upper-class family. The mother, fully in command of her elegant tea table as well as her husband and son, occupies the functional and emotional center of the household and the family. (Courtesy of the Tryon Palace Restoration, New Bern)

they were served tea from a black-penciled china tea set, arranged on a mahogany tea table and poured from a japanned teapot on a japanned tea board. The large number of tea pots and tea accessories owned by the Stanlys evokes the emerging pattern of consumption and sociability among the genteel classes in the late eighteenth century.[18]

Slave Women in North Carolina: "A Fruitful Woman amongst Them Being Much Valued by the Planters"

Slaves helped to create the good life for eighteenth-century gentry, whether working in house or field, but not until the nineteenth century do we hear stories from their point of view (Fig. 3-10). Early eighteenth-century author and doctor John Brickell described the origins of slavery in North Carolina: "The NEGROES are sold on the Coast of *Guinea*, to Merchants trading to those Parts, are brought from thence to *Carolina*, *Virginia*, and other Provinces in the hands of the *English*, are daily increasing in this Country, and generally afford a good Price." As chattel property, enslaved Africans found their legal rights curtailed first in 1715, then in 1741, their treatment harsh, and their punishments often cruel (Fig. 3-11). By the late 1700s one in three women in North Carolina was a slave.[19]

Women's experiences under slavery were different from those of men. From the beginning, they were subjected to sexual abuse. On the "middle passage," crossings from Africa to America, women were shackled and manacled in tight quarters, typically on the upper decks, where they were conveniently located for the seamen's sexual pleasure (Fig. 3-12). As slavery became institutionalized, women "breeders," a term that captures the harsh expectations of the slave system, were especially prized. "When these Women have no Children by the first Husband, after being a Year or two cohabiting together, the Planters oblige them to take a second, third, fourth, fifth, or more Husbands or Bedfellows," wrote Brickell, "a fruitful Woman amongst them being very much valued by the Planters, and a numerous Issue esteemed the greatest Riches in this Country." As mothers, women were less likely than men to run away, but they created other forms of resistance.[20]

Women's "reproductive labor" was important in boosting their owners' property values. More than half of the thirty-one slaves on Orange County plantation owner Richard Bennehan's 1778 tax listing were children. In July 1777 Bennehan had paid 250 pounds for Phebe, "a Small Wench" twenty-five years of age, and her three-year-old daughter Lucy. A year later Phebe alone was valued at 350 pounds. Esther, "a Wench about 50 years Old done Breeding," was listed at 250 pounds, and Nanny, "about 30 Sickly & Infirm[:] never had a child," was only 200 pounds. Aggy, about thirty years old, "Supposed to be done Breeding"—her youngest child was about ten or eleven—was worth 350 pounds. Brickell noted that it was not simply the "great Numbers" of slaves "born here" that the planters esteemed, but that they proved to be "more industrious, honest, and better Slaves than any brought from *Guinea*."[21]

Initially, almost twice as many men as women were transported across the Atlantic. One consequence was a delayed establishment of black family life in the colonies. Black men so outnumbered women in early-eighteenth-century North Carolina that, it is estimated, almost 40 percent could not form families (and in western counties, more than 60 percent). As a result, competition for black women was fierce. Brickell wrote that black men were "Jealously inclined, and fight most desperately amongst themselves when they Rival each other, which they commonly do." Because most slaves lived on small farms with few other slaves, family life was made even more difficult. As the number of male imported slaves increased, so did the number of women, who constituted almost half of the total black population by the 1770s,

FIGURE 3-10. Benjamin Henry Latrobe (1784–1820), *Overseer Doing His Duty*, watercolor, ink washes on paper, 1798. No images of eighteenth-century North Carolina slave women exist, but English architect Latrobe sketched two black women hoeing in a recently cleared field outside Fredericksburg, Virginia, under the looming presence of the overseer. According to Janet Schaw, who observed field slaves in the Cape Fear area, "the only instrument used is a hoe, with which they at once till and plant corn." (Benjamin Henry Latrobe Papers; courtesy of the Collection of Maryland Historical Society, Baltimore)

and there were more opportunities to create family and community life. In 1786 a small number of women were among eighty Africans delivered to planter Josiah Collins, who wanted to establish a rice plantation at his Somerset estate between Lake Scuppernong and the Chowan River. Life at Somerset, for these and other bondswomen, is the subject of a biography following this chapter.[22]

Little is known about the private lives of eighteenth-century slaves. Brickell wrote that their marriages were "generally performed among themselves," solemnized by the man giving the woman a "Present, such as a Brass Ring or some other Toy," and the woman's acceptance meant that she was his wife (Fig. 3-13). Although slaves were not legally allowed to marry, long-term unions were acknowledged and encouraged by slaveowners. Marriages between slaves on different plantations benefited the women's owners, for slave children were identified legally with their mother rather than their father and were considered the property of the planter to whom the mother belonged. The formation of families undoubtedly made it easier for white owners to control their slaves. Mothers were less likely to try to escape, and fathers might think hard about running away and leaving their families behind.[23]

Naming patterns show strong family ties: many of the eighty-five slaves listed by Jean Innes in her marriage contract with Francis Corbin in 1761 were sons named for their fathers, like George Junior or Sinclear Junior, and even girls had names like Delia Junior and Dinah Junior. Of the seventy-eight slaves listed in the 1789 inventory of New Bern merchant, shipowner, and distiller John Wright Stanly, fifty-one appear as members of a family group, and the other twenty-seven are listed as "Names of those who have not Husbands or Wives." By the late eighteenth century, ever increasing numbers of slaves were imported directly from Africa, and about one-third of North Carolina slaves were African. For them, family provided a structure in which Afri-

FIGURE 3-11. *Shackles*, Wake County, ca. 1800. (Courtesy of the North Carolina Museum of History)

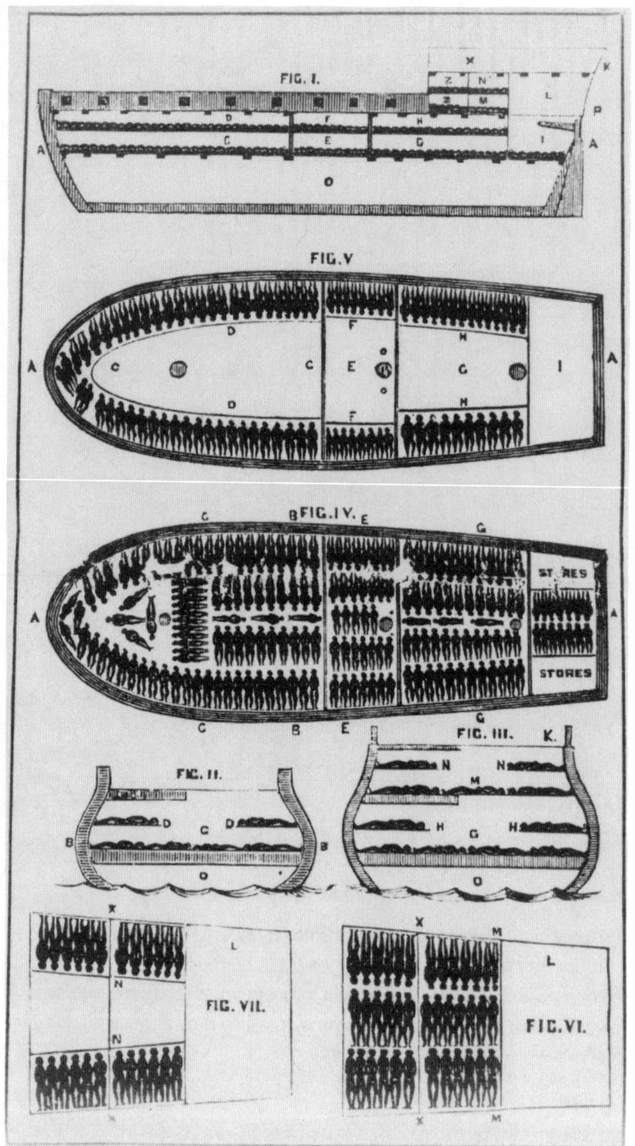

FIGURE 3-12. *A slave ship*, engraving. (Courtesy of the North Carolina Division of Archives and History)

can language, religion, work patterns, and naming of children were maintained.[24]

A slave family was most threatened by changing events in the lives of white owners, like marriage, death, economic setbacks, or migration. Marriages between planter families secured the planters' estates, but such alliances frequently threatened the stability of slave families, often dissolved to provide a young bride's dowry. "When a man marries his Daughters," observed royal governor William Tryon in 1765, "he never talks of his fortune in Money but 20, 30, or 40 slaves." In 1788 New Englander Elkanah Watson witnessed the dissolution of a slave family at a Wilmington auction. The mother "clung" to her young daughter and "implored with the most Agonizing supplication that they might not be separated."[25]

White Women and Family Life: "A Most Excellent Wife and a Fond Mother"

White girls learned early that marriage was their duty and motherhood their destiny. Females were expected to be modest before marriage and obedient afterward—patriarchal notions implicit and explicit in the literature, sermons, letters, law, and social customs of the time. Popular books like *The Art of Contentment* instructed a young woman to accept her status in life. *The Ladies Calling* taught the importance of modesty, meekness, compassion, affability, and piety in fulfilling the female roles of virgins, wives, and widows. How modest and how obedient women were in reality we can only imagine, but the ideal was stated in the *Spectator* by a matron who wrote: "I am married, and I have no other concern but to please the man I love; he is the end of every care I have; if I dress, it is for him; if I read a poem, or a play, it is to qualify myself for a conversation agreeable to his taste; he is almost the end of my devotions; half my prayers are for his happiness."[26]

> The mothers took care of the girls, they were train'd up under them, and not only instructed in the family duties necessary to the sex, but in those accomplishments and genteel manners that are still so visible amongst them, and this descended from Mother to daughter.
> —Janet Schaw, Journal. (E. W. Andrews, *Journal of a Lady of Quality*, 154–55)

In 1775 the *North Carolina Gazette* advised good wives to be neat in dress and sweet in temper; it concluded with this warning:

FIGURE 3-13. Anonymous, *Old Plantation*, watercolor on paper, late 1700s. This painting, found in Columbia, South Carolina, may depict a slave wedding on a central South Carolina plantation. The couple at center right is about to "jump" the stick (the familiar "jumping the broom" wedding ceremony documented in slave narratives), as their companions celebrate with music and dancing that represent a blend of African and southern North American cultures. (Courtesy of the Abby Aldrich Rockefeller Folk Art Center, Williamsburg, Virginia)

> . . . her Wit must never be display'd,
> Where it the husband's province might invade:
> Be she content sole *Mistress* to remain,
> Nor poorly strive for the *Mastership* t'obtain
> This would occasion Jars, intestine Strife,
> Imbitter all the sweets of nuptial Life:
> Then let her not for Government contend,
> But use this policy to gain her end—
> Make him *believe* he holds the Sov'reign Sway
> And she may *rule*, by seeming to *obey*.

Other newspaper articles, such as "The CHOICE of a HUSBAND" (1764), urged girls to select a mate wisely, for marriage, with its legal, social, and economic ramifications, was the critical event in determining the shape of women's lives, in a way that was not true for men. "HINTS for Young MARRIED WOMEN" (1788) cautioned wives to hide their "wit" and to "cease to command and learn to obey."[27]

It was in the domestic sphere that eighteenth-century women received respect. To venture into the public world of politics or war was to invite dismissal and ridicule. Even highly educated or notable women did not challenge the notion of women as inferior to men.

Single women whom Francisco de Miranda encountered in New Bern in the early 1780s enjoyed "complete freedom." He noted that they "take walks alone whenever they want to, without their steps being observed." Yet few young women chose to remain single, and the prevailing public attitude toward single women was unkind (Fig. 3-14). An unmarried female was an anomaly and seen as evading her obligation to marry and bear children. This view was reinforced after the Revolution by the expectation that it was women's patriotic duty to bear citizens for the new republic.[28]

Many marriages were based on mutual affection and respect, but they were frequently pragmatic arrangements as well. If a woman remained unmarried, she might well live out her life as a subordinate in someone else's household. It was better to take one's chances with a husband than remain dependent on a brother or father. Dowries were expected. Cumberland County planter Alexander McAllister noted succinctly, "Gerles without a porsion Stickes long on hand." Young women, too, had expectations. In 1793 Mary Jones of

FIGURE 3-14. Anonymous, *The Old Maid*, engraving, London, 1777. The *State Gazette of North Carolina* (January 16, 1790) described an "old maid" as a "cranky, ill-natured, maggotty, peevish, conceited, disagreeable, hypocritical, fretful, noisy, gibing, canting, censorious, out-of-the-way, never-to-be-pleased, good-for-nothing creature" who "enters the world to take up room, not to make room for others." (Courtesy of the Library of Congress, Washington, D.C.)

Wilmington described the man a friend had recently married as possessed "of a very good property . . . you see, I begin with the fortune it being esteemed by us Ladies the first ingredient in a husband."[29]

Particularly among the eighteenth-century planter and merchant elite, marriage reinforced social and economic ties linking old and new families of the Albemarle and Cape Fear. For instance, in the late 1600s and early 1700s the marriages of two sisters, Elizabeth and Anne Lillington, solidified their family's political and economic positions through several generations. Anne first married wealthy Albemarle planter Henderson Walker, then Edward Moseley, whom some consider the "single most important political figure" in early North Carolina. Elizabeth's second husband was Samuel Swann, collector of customs in the Albemarle region, with whom she had four children, and her third was Colonel Maurice Moore, the brother of Roger Moore, known in the Cape Fear area as "King Roger." Elizabeth's Swann children included Elizabeth, who married Cape Fear planter John Baptista Ashe; Sarah, who married Virginia lawyer Thomas Jones; John, who married Ann, a daughter of King Roger; and Samuel, who married Jane Jones. In the next generation Jane Swann married her first cousin Frederick Jones in 1758, further linking families with political and economic power in Virginia, the Albemarle, and Cape Fear (Fig. 3-15). The marriage of Anna Caswell, sixth child and third daughter of Richard Caswell (North Carolina's first governor under statehood), and her second husband William White in 1787 joined two Kinston merchant-planter-political families. Two prominent Edgecombe County families were joined when Joel Battle asked for the hand of Polly Johnston from her father—Battle sought "an Alliance with your Family" (Fig. 3-16).[30]

The courtship and marriage of Hannah Johnston and James Iredell, as chronicled in his diary and numerous letters

FIGURE 3-15. *Jane Swann miniature brooch*, New Hanover County, ca. 1750. Swann belonged to a wealthy planter family with interests in both the Albemarle and Cape Fear. Her elegant pink dress, fashionable black ribbon around the neck, and the tiny blue bird were appropriate attributes for a young woman of her social status. At eighteen she married her Virginia cousin Frederick Jones, and they had a family of two sons and six daughters. (Courtesy of the North Carolina Museum of History)

FIGURE 3-16. *Trousseau box*, wood, Edgecombe County, 1801. According to family tradition, when Polly Johnston left her father's house to marry Joel Battle, she carried her trousseau in this small wooden box. (Courtesy of the North Carolina Museum of History)

to her, reveal the range of emotions—mutual respect, affection, love, passion, disappointment, regret, sadness, anger—associated with romantic love. James was a well-connected and literate young Englishman who moved to Edenton in 1768, and Hannah was one of five sisters, all educated and lively, of the politically influential lawyer-planter Samuel Johnston, who owned one of the most impressive houses and libraries in the colony—at Hayes plantation, just across Queen Anne's Creek from Edenton (Fig. 3-17). Hannah's large family also included her brother's wife, Frances Cathcart, and her sister Anne, with whom she lived at Hayes; another sister, Jean Johnston Blair, in nearby Edenton; a cousin, Penelope Johnston Dawson, close-by on her plantation, Eden House, across the Chowan; and all their various children. The entire family seems to have captivated young James, who chose Samuel as his mentor and Hannah as his wife. Iredell wrote that the Johnstons were "all united by the tenderest ties of affection" and displayed "a general share of good sense, cultivated understandings, and engaging Manners of that I have never seen excelled, if equalled. They are truly Families of love." James admired Hannah for her "good sense, Goodness of Heart, Excellence of Conduct." He cherished her as a "sensible Woman who has read elegantly and judiciously." As he wrote, "Reason as well as Passion have carried my Heart captive—or rather, that Passion dictated, and Reason honoured and approved my Choice."[31]

Passion, greatly restrained by decorum, was an underlying theme throughout their courtship. Young women of marriage age typically were protected from matrimonial mistakes by strict rules of behavior and parental participation in their marital decisions. That Hannah was in her mid-twenties and her brother was her legal guardian might account for the nature of her less supervised courtship, in which James wrote freely of his affection for her, and they met frequently in shops, at friends' houses, and along the streets of Edenton.[32]

At the same time, their behavior conformed to eighteenth-century notions of propriety and to their social position. James asked formal permission of Hannah and her brother to court her. Once engaged, he wrote: "a most delightful task it indeed will be for me to employ my whole life in an affectionate attention to make *you* happy." As their marriage date drew near, James confessed: "I could not bear this Situation much longer. I rely greatly on your Goodness to shorten the time as much as possible." On July 18, 1773, James, age twenty-two, and Hannah, four years his senior, married. They had three children and a marriage that lasted twenty-five years, until James's death in 1798.[33]

The urbanity of the Iredells' courtship contrasts with the rustic pursuit of Hannah Plummer by Nathaniel Macon of Warren County, as renowned for its gambling as for its tobacco plantations. While courting the dazzling and wealthy Hannah Plummer, Nathaniel methodically drove off all her many suitors but one. In true Warren County fashion, according to legend, he challenged the lone remaining competitor to a game of cards in the lady's presence, the loser to

FIGURE 3-17. John Crowley, *Hannah Johnston Iredell*, 1806, oil on canvas, Chowan County. The only image of Iredell dates from when she was over seventy and had been widowed for a quarter of a century. (Courtesy of the North Carolina Division of Archives and History)

depart and come calling no more. Nathaniel lost, but instead of retreating with honor, he implored Hannah: "I have lost you fairly, but love is superior to fortune—I cannot give you up." She agreed, they married, and only her death less than ten years later, in January 1790, separated them.[34]

For Hannah Johnston and Hannah Plummer, love and property, passion and decorum were intertwined. The courtship of Sally Pomfret was somewhat different. Our evidence consists only of three letters from different suitors to the young North Carolina farm woman, and their direct language challenges the notion of polite eighteenth-century courtship discourse. In June 1782 an admirer wrote Sally, "Let not your chiefest glory be immurd in the nice Casket of Maidenhead withhold not what thou shoulest [*sic*] communicate." The following spring John Wallace pleaded, "[I]f it be a crime in mee to love O Most Adoriable it is your fair self, that hast raised such tumults in my breast, that I never since had my thoughts sease one Minuet of you since I has the Pleasure of your sweet Company." Less than a year later, Sally was still driving her suitors wild. Thomas Grafton wrote: "[Y]our Coldness to me I am afrade will Cause me to run Crasey."[35]

Courtship was one thing, married life another. For most women living in the eighteenth century, as for those in the seventeenth, marriage meant frequent pregnancy; infant mortality; childbirth complicated by illness, even death; widowhood, often at a young age; hasty remarriage; and very large families. For example, Penelope Skinner of Perquimans County married at age fifteen and within six years was widowed, remarried, and lost three children. In particular did childbirth and motherhood produce a precarious reality for most eighteenth-century women (Plate 2). Women had two dominant fears: their children's deaths and their own. Mary Blount married Charles Pettigrew in 1778, when she was twenty-eight and he was thirty-four, and in eight years of marriage, she had five children, only one of whom lived to maturity. In March 1786 Mary gave premature birth to twins who died within twelve hours, and ten days later she died of complications from their birth (Fig. 3-18).[36]

Judith Mordecai had six children in ten years of marriage to Jacob Mordecai, a merchant who later opened a popular female seminary in Warrenton. With the birth of her fourth child in 1790, Judith developed "an Inflammation of the Womb . . . attended With Very Painful and Debilitating Symptoms" due to the "Want of Skill in the Physician." Even so, as she informed her stepmother, she had a household to manage and the "attention My family required would not admit of My Useing endulgence tho I found my strength, Daily decrease." Pregnant a fifth time in 1792, she wrote, "My disorder returned With redoubled Voilence," and in 1793 it "Nearly brought me to the Brink of the Grave." She observed,

FIGURE 3-18. William Williams, *Mary Blount Pettigrew*, pastel, 1785, Washington County. Pettigrew sat for her portrait in 1785 and died a year later from complications following the birth of twins in March 1786. (Courtesy of the Collection of the Museum of Early Southern Decorative Arts, Old Salem, Inc., Winston-Salem)

"If I am so plesd as to have No farther addition in a small Way, I flatter myself I shall yet be a Hearty woman." That was not to be the case, for in early 1796 she died after still another baby. Her husband then married her half sister Rebecca, who had seven children and reared them and her stepchildren.[37]

Marriage had other shoals for a woman. Once married, she legally had to accept whatever her husband did. The double standard of the eighteenth century meant that husbands could dally while wives remained docile. Men complained of their wives' extravagance, disobedience, or neglect of domestic duties, but the major cause of women's unhappiness was their husbands' infidelity, which included liaisons with black women as well as white. When Boston patriot Josiah Quincy visited North Carolina in 1773, he commented that "enjoyment of a negro or mulatto woman is spoken of as quite a common thing; no reluctance, delicacy, or shame is made about the matter."[38]

What recourse did women have if their husbands were

unfaithful or their marriages unhappy? Divorce was virtually impossible, but a few enterprising women found ways to escape. Some simply left their husbands. Notices of wives who "bolted" can be found among the newspaper notices about fugitive slaves and stray horses. One unhappy couple, Mary and John Snow of Brunswick County, separated legally in 1768 only two years after their marriage. Mary was granted *feme sole* status and ownership of six slaves, numerous household items, eighteen chickens, one cow, a calf, a pair of rabbits, and any seeds or roots she wanted from the household garden. She also received a desk, "which you already have," noted John, and twenty-six pounds of butter, "more than your fair share." In 1775 Joseph and Mary M'Gehe of New Bern announced that they "solemnly agreed before God and the World, to be no longer Man and Wife, but for ever hereafter, be as if we had never been married." Such an agreement might not have held up in court, but according to Julia Cherry Spruill's reading of Anglican records, new marriages often followed such "divorces."[39]

Widowhood: "Recourse to Her Thirds"

Because marriage played such a shaping role in most women's lives, becoming a widow was as significant a passage as becoming a wife. Apart from the emotional loss, widowhood brought momentous changes in a woman's economic, social, and legal position. A man's death meant the dissolution of a family, and minor children who lost their fathers were considered orphans (whereas those whose mothers had died were not). Although a woman had worked as a helpmate with her husband in the family household, what they had accumulated did not belong to her. She was entitled only to a third of the family estate or whatever her husband chose to leave her. Her economic status depended on how much property she inherited, and that depended on both the size of her husband's estate and his generosity. After the husband's death, his land was surveyed and the widow's third was set off for her as a "dower tract," which, by custom and after 1784 by law, included the dwelling house. Women's lack of economic and legal status is underscored by the fact that men bequeathed their wives household items like spinning wheels and looms. Rachel Stout Allen's husband gave his land, over eight hundred acres, to his six sons, "excepting the terms on which I have left [their] mother her living," and she received "her riding mare named Gray and one cow named Nole and all my household furniture, excepting the clock, books, and desk."[40]

Although mortality rates declined during the eighteenth century, widowhood was still a common experience. A widow had three choices: to remarry and constitute a new household; to be a dependent in someone's household, often that of her oldest son; or to remain single and head her own household. Widows' legal status was that of *feme sole*, so they could own property and conduct business, yet only 2 to 5 percent of all households and probably never more than 10 percent were headed by women in eighteenth-century North Carolina. Few women chose independence, which was viable only for those who were financially well-off, had inherited businesses, or lived in town. Jean Johnston Blair was widowed in 1772 when her husband George, a prominent Edenton merchant, died, leaving her to care for and educate five small children, and in considerable debt. She auctioned off slaves, livestock, and household effects to settle debts but continued to own land in Onslow and Jones Counties and town lots in Edenton. Blair chose not to remarry. More than 70 percent of the marriage contracts in New Hanover County, for example, concerned widows who sought to secure their estates before remarrying.[41]

Dower rights gave widows only a life interest in their husbands' estate. For instance, Elizabeth Swann's husband left her "My plantation whereon I now live, with all the Land and Houses and appurtenances thereto belonging, for and dureing the term of her naturall Life," after which it would go to their son Samuel. Husbands often placed conditions on the women's remarriage or behavior. Patrick Campbell's 1775 will stipulated that his widow could use his plantation only "During her Widohood or as Long as she Behaves Well to My Children to be Judg By My Executors." In 1785 John Oliphant left his wife the use of the front room of his house, a slave, a good horse with saddle and bridle, her bed and furniture, her apparel, and her spinning wheel. If she remarried, she relinquished the room of her own and the slave. Ann Cogdell Stanly's husband, whose mercantile and distillery interests made him the wealthiest man in New Bern after the Revolution, provided handsomely for her in his 1788 will. She was designated executrix of his estate and guardian of his children, "in both cases to cease" if she remarried. She received an equal share with their children in his considerable estate, and she was to have first choice of her share. But if she remarried a widower, her share was nullified, and the items she was to receive were specifically enumerated—the residence, urban lots in New Bern, and "all my household and kitchen, furniture, plate, china, carriage, and carriage house, and the following Negroes." Although the specific provisions of these wills vary, they all indicate the husband's control of his widow and her total dependence on his allocation of household assets.[42]

After the Revolutionary War the state of North Carolina passed legislation that asserted the legal dower for widows "a very inadequate provision" and purported to secure "property values" and "dower rights." The law acknowledged that women's "prudence, economy, and industry" had helped to

> Furthermore, if such husband shall die leaving no child, or not more than two, then and in that case she shall be intitled to one-third part of the personal estate; but if such husband shall die leaving more than two children, then and in that case such widow shall share equally with all the children, she being intitled to a child's part.
>
> —The Laws of North Carolina, 1784, chap. xxii: *An Act to regulate the descent of Real Estates, to do away Entails, to make provision for Widows, and prevent frauds in the Execution of last Wills and Testaments*. (Clark, *State Records* 24: 572–77)

create their husbands' estate and therefore they were entitled to "share" in it. Although the legislation legally ensured a widow's access to her deceased husband's estate, it had the potential of adversely affecting her economic situation. Instead of receiving the customary widow's "third" of the estate, after the passage of this law, she shared an equal portion with her children. If there were more than two children, she received less than her dower's third.[43]

According to a study of dower petitions in New Hanover County between 1750 and 1800, it was generally upper-class women who contested their husbands' bequests. In 1791 Elizabeth MacLaine refused to accept her late husband Archibald's provisions whereby she received one house and its furnishings, plus $250 a year from her daughter and son-in-law. Using the new law, she received one-third of all Archibald's lands and personal inventory, plus houses in four counties. Mary Magdalene Toomer objected to the provisions of her attorney husband's will in 1799 and sued for her dower. Mary Toomer's "Thirds" included a plantation, eleven slaves, three lots in Wilmington, and a tannery, far more than her husband had left her. North Carolina patriot Willie Jones anticipated his wife's reaction to his bequest: "Now, as it is possible and indeed probable that my wife will not be satisfied with the provisions which I have hereinbefore made for her, and consequently could refuse to be bound by this very will. . . . I leave to my wife to do better for her self if she can."[44] Widowhood often necessitated that women had to do better for themselves than their husbands had provided.

Women and Public Work: "For Her Own Livelihood"

Few women engaged in work outside their immediate households in eighteenth-century North Carolina. It would have been unseemly for a married woman with a healthy husband to work outside the home unless she was assisting her husband in his trade or acting as his surrogate. Yet widowhood or other adversity compelled some women to earn their own way, and they had a better chance of finding work if they lived in town. Typically, women worked for pay doing the same domestic chores they did at home—cooking, cleaning, spinning, sewing, gardening, healing, and caring for children. For example, Margaret Clay, Catherine McNamara, and a Mrs. Eagen found work cleaning the New Hanover County Courthouse in Wilmington. The Moravian Single Sisters, whose biography follows this chapter, supported themselves and contributed to the community by doing laundry, sewing, and teaching in Salem.[45]

Maintaining inns, ordinaries, taverns, "victualling" houses, public houses—the early hospitality trade—was particularly a woman's occupation. Most taverns operated out of dwellings, exactly the sort of low-stakes financial endeavor that many widows could undertake. In Chowan, New Hanover, and Pasquotank Counties almost 20 percent of the tavern licenses were granted to women, and in Perquimans and Craven Counties, about 10 percent. Almost half of the licensed female ordinary keepers continued their deceased husband's business. Taverns were the only businesses that women inherited from their husbands in New Hanover County between 1750 and 1800.[46]

Serving men who were drinking and away from home was a rough business, and few women did it for more than a few years. Strong drinks were plentiful—cider, liquor, especially rum, for which the standard measure was by the quart, and beer, madeira, claret, and port—and patrons often rowdy. Two Wilmington innkeepers, Mrs. Lettice Blackmore and Mrs. Elizabeth Saunders, were found guilty of keeping "disorderly houses," "harboring Common Sailors," selling them liquor without the consent of their shipmaster, and thereby "injuring" maritime trade in the Cape Fear.[47]

Ferrykeeping was another women's occupation, closely associated with innkeeping (taverns were often located at ferry crossings). New Bern innkeepers Bridget Arthur and her husband also ran a ferry across the Neuse River. Operating a successful ferry business was partly a matter of being in the right place at the right time, for one had to live near a well-traveled water crossing, but it must also have been a matter of grasping opportunity. Many women apparently did. In 1715 Annie Willson was appointed to keep a "good and sufficient ferry" across the Perquimans River from her plantation to that of James Thickpenn. No other persons were "to presume to ferry over any horse or man within at least five miles either above or below that place." Elizabeth Hall was appointed in 1756 to maintain a ferry from her plantation in Beaufort County. Four widows petitioned to continue their deceased husbands' ferry business in Tyrrell County. Mary Taylor transported the post via the Bath Town Ferry for a

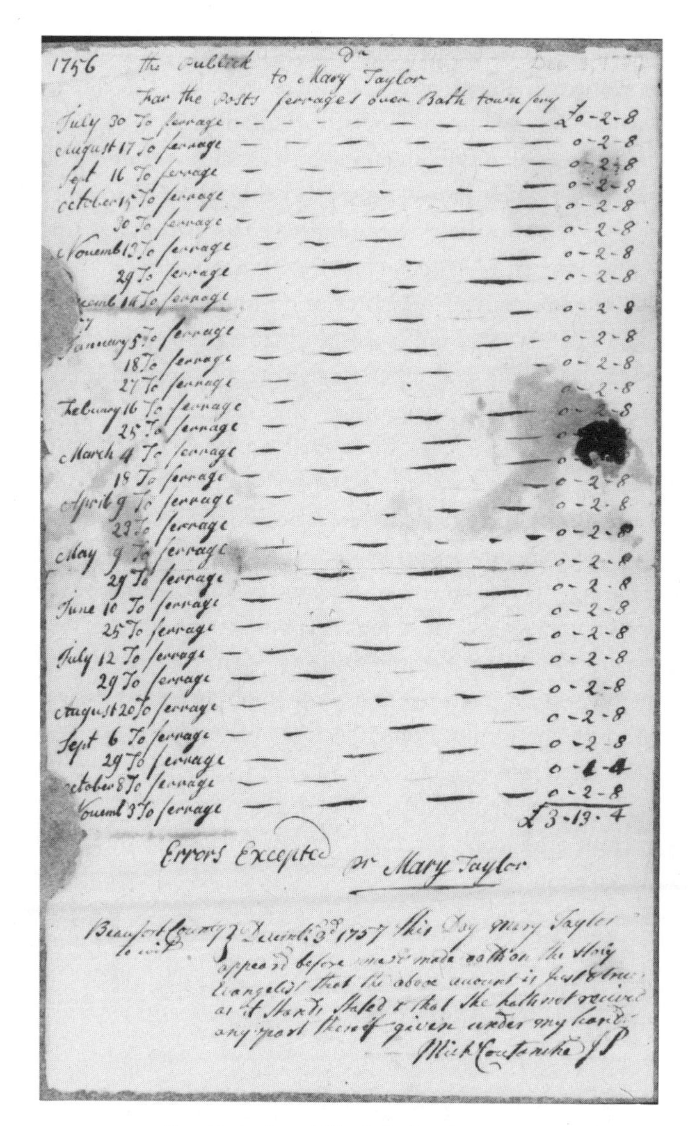

1756 The Publick Dr
to Mary Taylor
For the Posts ferrages over Bath town ferry

July 30	To ferrage	0-2-8
August 17	To ferrage	0-2-8
Sept 16	To ferrage	0-2-8
October 15	To ferrage	0-2-8
30	To ferrage	0-2-8
November 13	To ferrage	0-2-8
29	To ferrage	0-2-8
December 14	To ferrage	0-2-8
1757 January 5	To ferrage	0-2-8
18	To ferrage	0-2-8
27	To ferrage	0-2-8
February 16	To ferrage	0-2-8
25	To ferrage	0-2-8
March 4	To ferrage	[illegible]
18	To ferrage	0-2-8
April 9	To ferrage	0-2-8
23	To ferrage	0-2-8
May 9	To ferrage	0-2-8
29	To ferrage	0-2-8
June 10	To ferrage	0-2-8
25	To ferrage	0-2-8
July 12	To ferrage	0-2-8
29	To ferrage	0-2-8
August 20	To ferrage	0-2-8
Sept 6	To ferrage	0-2-8
29	To ferrage	0-1-4
October 8	To ferrage	0-2-8
November 3	To ferrage	0-2-8
		£3-19-4

Errors Excepted pr Mary Taylor

Beaufort County to wit } December 3rd 1757 This Day Mary Taylor appeared before me & made oath on the Holy Evangelist that the above account is just & true as it stands stated & that she hath not received any part thereof given under my hand
Mich Coutanche JP

FIGURE 3-19. *Mary Taylor ferry bill* to Beaufort County, 1757. Taylor's bill for ferrying the mail is a rare document verifying actual payment to a colonial woman. (Courtesy of the North Carolina Division of Archives and History)

year and a half from July 1756 to November 1757, every two weeks, summer and winter (Fig. 3-19). There were five female ferrykeepers in Cumberland County between 1762 and 1764 (though Margaret Livington had to surrender her license for "not being abel to give it Proper Attendence").[48]

Most eighteenth-century women could do plain sewing, but women with exceptional sewing skills, entrepreneurial spirit, and economic need might become dressmakers or milliners, open their own shops, and even sell fabric, buttons, and trim. Mary King used her sewing skills to create hats; she charged more for a single hat she made Salisbury tavern owner Elizabeth Steel than Ann Crosby charged Steel for an entire dress. Moravian widow Sarah Buttner opened a tailor shop in Salem that prospered so well that the church board felt compelled to reprimand her and refuse her request to hire more help—she was only to make enough money "for her own livelihood." Four Moravian women—Mary Elrod, Mary Flood, Elizabeth Hauser, and Mary Elizabeth Krause—and Hannah Bond of Onslow County were weavers. Surry County widow Anna Baker ran a spinning and weaving operation in her backcountry home and was one of the few women on the county tax list. Mary Carter Boone and Annas Newberry were among the seventy professional spinners identified as working in Rowan County between 1753 and 1790, evidence that spinning was part of a market economy and that the term "spinster" could refer to a woman's occupation as well as to her marital status. "Esther," apprenticed in 1781 in Salisbury to learn weaving and designated in 1785 in the Rowan County apprentice bonds as "artisan," is the only slave artisan to appear in Rowan County records and the only mulatto apprenticed to learn a trade.[49]

Most housewives had extensive experience attending to the sick, ill, injured, and aged in their own families, and some women became healers and midwives for their community (Fig. 3-20). Rachel Stout Allen's "receipt" book lists the varieties of illness she treated. "To make an ointment to cure a burn or scald," she writes, "take the tops of high RattleSnake in the Spring of the year and fresh may Butter and pound them well together." Allen was skilled in the use of roots and herbs; she also drew on published texts like *Culpepper's Herbal* (1740) or William Buchan's *Domestic Medicine* (1797). In a manner similar to that of an apothecary, she made various purges, emetics, syrups, cordials, and poultices and kept them on hand to use when needed. Midwifery and healing presented options for women who had to work, but certainly they represented a calling as well as an occupation.[50]

Childbirth in the eighteenth century took place in the woman's home with her female relatives in attendance and midwives, black or white, in charge. Among the midwives on call when a woman was ready to deliver a baby were Anna Maria Brendel Bonn in Salem and slave "Tamers" of Beaufort County. Agnes MacKinley advertised her credentials as a "college educated" and "physician trained" midwife shortly after arriving in Wilmington from Glasgow in 1798. Two years later, possibly in response to the challenge of MacKinley's

> As there is now no mid-wife in Salem and Sister S— will soon be confined, it was determined that Sister Bonn shall be appointed mid-wife and in addition her husband shall teach her to do other minor surgical work among the Sisters—to bind slight wounds, and the like.
>
> —Minutes of the Salem Board, February 1, 1774. (Fries et al., *Records of the Moravians*, 2:825)

FIGURE 3-20. *Mortar and pestle*, Buncombe County. This mortar and pestle is associated with Nancy Ashworth, who gathered herbs and prepared remedies to heal her neighbors in the mountains of Buncombe and Rutherford Counties. (Courtesy of the North Carolina Museum of History)

professional midwifery, a former tavern operator named Ann Austin, advertising her services in the Wilmington newspaper, claimed twenty years' experience as a midwife. What was once an informally acquired occupation, in which female midwives typically learned their art and skill from other women on the job, would eventually give way to professional training and male physicians (Fig. 3-21). But that change was not readily apparent in the late eighteenth century. Midwifery remained a woman's province longer in rural areas, with white and especially black women relying on midwives through the nineteenth century and into the twentieth.[51]

Women, War, and Politics: "American Ladies Follow the Laudable Example of Their Husbands"

For North Carolina women whose lives centered on the routine of household and family, the Revolutionary War and the political conflict leading to it brought both a major disruption of domestic life and the opportunity to participate in patriotic activities (Fig. 3-22). These were years of intense partisan feelings in the embattled colonies. In 1768 Anne Clarke Hooper of Wilmington wrote that she mentioned politics in her letters only because "its being talked of so much here." By 1781 her letters were admired by her patriot husband William for their "masculine patriotism and virtue."[52]

Colonials resisted British taxes on imported goods with economic boycotts, and as women managed the households where tea, cloth, and other foreign items were consumed, men expected their wives, sisters, and daughters to support the boycotts. Purchases from England were to cease and home production was to be stepped up. As early as 1767, women were encouraged to "wear none but your own country linen" and show "pride" in "cloaths of your make and spinning." The tedious task of textile production that many had happily set aside now took on political significance. Producing homespun became patriotic. Slave women found their workload increased to include spinning and weaving—although in North Carolina, planters undertook large-scale cloth manufacture reluctantly and not until 1774 or 1775. As one congressional delegate observed in resisting the shift to cloth production by slaves, slave women were "best employed about Tobacco."[53]

FIGURE 3-21. *A man-midwife, a newly discovered animal*, by Isaac Cruikshank. Male doctors venturing into midwifery were often viewed with skepticism, even ridicule, in the eighteenth century. (Frontispiece to *Man-midwifery*, dissected by S. W. Fores, London, 1793)

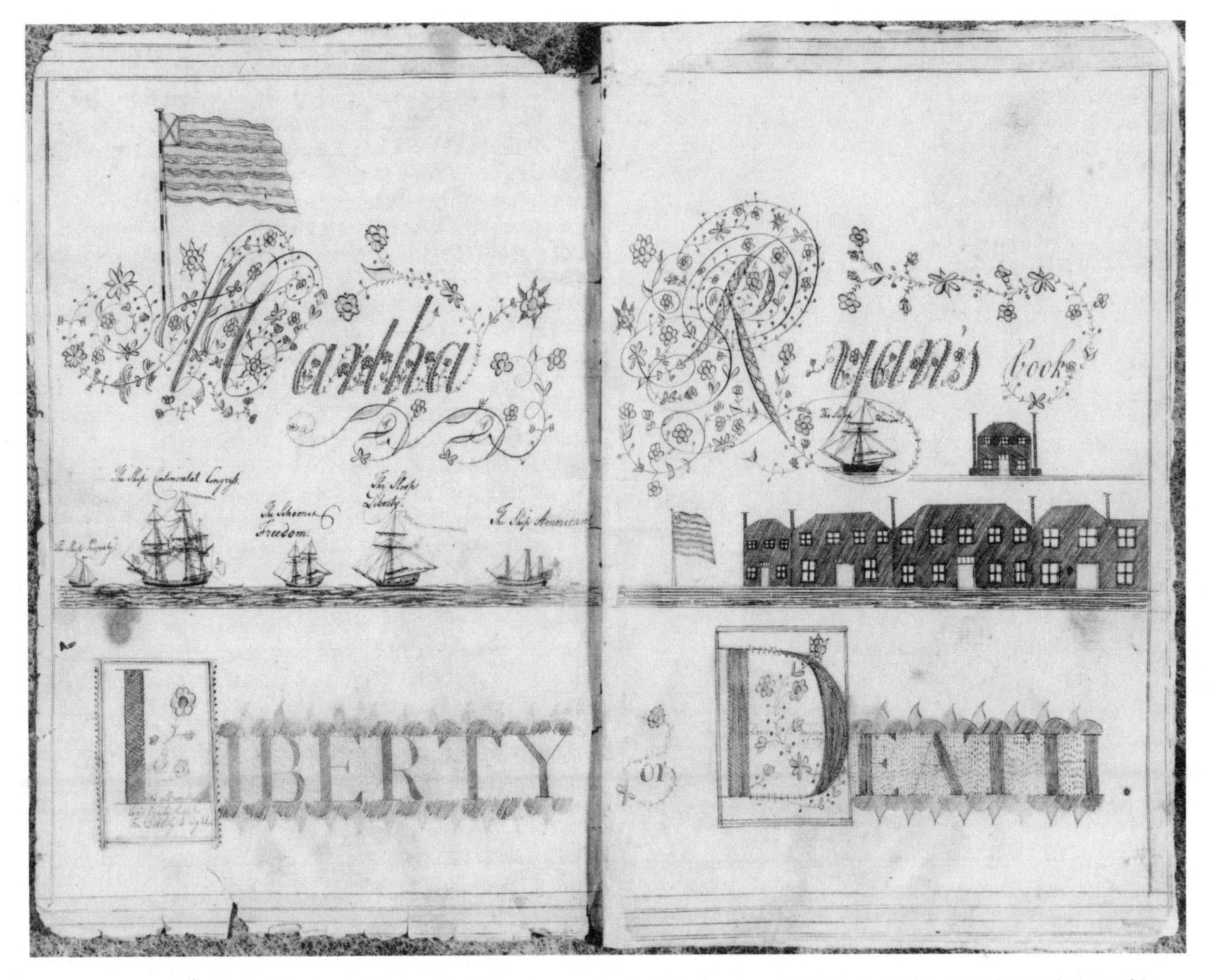

FIGURE 3-22. *Martha Ryan's cipher book*, Windsor, Bertie County, ca. 1781. Delicate flowers, patriotic flags, and full-masted ships decorate this schoolgirl's book. Inside the boxed "L" are the lines: "Let's all united / and freely fight / For Liberty & Right." (Courtesy of the Southern Historical Collection, University of North Carolina at Chapel Hill)

North Carolina families engaged in a variety of patriotic activities, following the actions of protesters in other parts of colonial America. The leaders had been those who had dumped cargoes of tea in the Boston harbor in 1773. Month by month after that signal event, protests spread to other colonies, among both women and men. "Ladies associations" and "patriotic guilds"—both terms have been used in connection with the Edenton women—sprang up and petitions against buying British goods were circulated. Janet Schaw reported that Wilmington ladies "burnt their tea in a solemn procession" to protest British policy. Young women of the "best families in Mecklenburg County" refused to "receive the Addresses of any young Gentlemen of that Place, except the brave Volunteers who cheerfully served" against the British.[54]

In October 1774 more than fifty women from prominent families in Edenton and neighboring counties, including Penelope Barker, Penelope Johnston Dawson, and Jean Johnston Blair, signed a proclamation agreeing to follow the example of the provincial deputies of North Carolina and "*not* to drink any more *tea*, nor wear any more British cloth"—an act of defiance now known as the "Edenton Tea Party" (Fig. 3-23). A writer to a London newspaper enclosed a copy of the Edenton women's resolve, which was printed on January 16, 1775 (Fig. 3-24). Fifteen days after its appearance, James Iredell's brother Arthur wrote to inquire: "Pray are You become Patriotic? I see, by the News Papers, the Edenton Ladies have signalized themselves, by their protest agst Tea Drinking. The name of Johnston I see among others; are any of my Sisters [that is, sisters-in-law] Relations Patriotic Heroines? Is there a Female Congress at Edenton too? I hope not, for we Englishmen are afraid of the Male Congress, but if the Ladies, who have ever, since the Amazonian Era, been esteemed the most formidable Enemies, if they, I say, should

FIGURE 3-23. John Wollaston, *Penelope Barker* (1728–96), oil on canvas. A member of Edenton's elite, Barker is credited as the leader of the Edenton Tea Party of 1774. While Thomas Barker (her third husband—she was widowed twice) spent seventeen years in London, first to negotiate trade relations for North Carolina and then unable to get home because of the war, she managed their substantial estates in Edenton and Bertie County, including about fifty slaves. (Courtesy of Cupola House, Edenton, Chowan County)

attack us, the most fatal consequences is to be dreaded." The women's action, though ridiculed at the time by British men, has been heralded as the first example of American women claiming a voice in public discourse (Fig. 3-25).[55]

For Hooper, Iredell, and the ladies in Edenton, Wilmington, and Charlotte, political activity reflected their class in-

negative, then they would make us slaves; to attempt which is contrary to every good principle of humanity and of the Britiſh conſtitution."

Extract of a letter from North Carolina, Oct. 27.

" The Provincial Deputies of North Carolina having reſolved *not* to drink any more *tea*, nor wear any more Britiſh cloth, &c. many ladies of this Province have determined to give a memorable proof of their patriotiſm, and have accordingly entered into the following honourable and ſpirited aſſociation. I ſend it to you, to ſhew your fair-countrywomen, how zealouſly and faithfully American ladies follow the laudable example of their huſbands, and what oppoſition your Miniſters may expect to receive from a people thus firmly united againſt them:

" *Edenton, North Carolina, Oct. 25, 1774.*

" As we cannot be indifferent on any occaſion that appears nearly to affect the peace and happineſs of our country, and as it has been thought neceſſary, for the public good, to enter into ſeveral particular reſolves by a meeting of Members deputed from the whole Province, it is a duty which we owe, not only to our near and dear connections who have concurred in them, but to ourſelves who are eſſentially intereſted in their welfare, to do every thing as far as lies in our power to teſtify our ſincere adherence to the ſame; and we do therefore accordingly ſubſcribe this paper, as a witneſs of our fixed intention and ſolemn determination to do ſo.

Abagail Charlton	Mary Blount
F. Johnſtone	Elizabeth Creacy
Margaret Cathcart	Elizabeth Patterſon
Anne Johnſtone	Jane Wellwood
Margaret Pearſon	Mary Woolard
Penelope Dawſon	Sarah Beaſley
Jean Blair	Suſannah Vail
Grace Clayton	Elizabeth Vail
Frances Hall	Elizabeth Vail
Mary Jones	Mary Creacy
Anne Hall	Mary Creacy
Rebecca Bondfield	Ruth Benbury
Sarah Littlejohn	Sarah Howcott
Penelope Barker	Sarah Hoſkins
Elizabeth P. Ormond	Mary Littledle
M. Payne	Sarah Valentine
Elizabeth Johnſton	Elizabeth Cricket
Mary Bonner	Elizabeth Green
Lydia Bonner	Mary Ramſay
Sarah Howe	Anne Horniblow
Lydia Bennet	Mary Hunter
Marion Wells	Treſia Cunningham
Anne Anderſon	Elizabeth Roberts
Sarah Mathews	Elizabeth Roberts
Anne Haughton	Elizabeth Roberts."
Elizabeth Beaſly.	

Extract of a letter from Amſterdam, Jan. 10.

" Capt. John de Groot, who ſailed from Gi-

FIGURE 3-24. *(opposite) Association Signed by Ladies of Edenton*, October 25, 1774. A group of Edenton women entered into public discourse. An American correspondent noted that the resolve was sent "to shew your fair countrywomen, how zealously and faithfully, American ladies follow the laudable example of their husbands, and what opposition your matchless Ministers may expect to receive from a people thus firmly united against them." (From "Extract of a letter from North Carolina, Oct. 27," *Morning Chronicle and London Advertiser*, January 16, 1775; courtesy of the North Carolina Division of Archives and History)

FIGURE 3-25. Philip Dawe, *Edenton Tea Party*, London, 1775. This caricature is the first evidence that the Edenton women's political resolution published in the London newspaper was connected to a "tea party"—an allusion to the colonists' boycott and women's special affinity for tea drinking and sociability. (Courtesy of the North Carolina Collection, University of North Carolina at Chapel Hill)

terests as well as their men's political involvement. Widow Elizabeth Maxwell Steel's tavern in the Piedmont backcountry town of Salisbury represented another path by which women could enter the public world of political discourse. Along with financial independence, tavernkeeping offered Steel the opportunity to participate in political discussion in a way impossible for women sequestered within their households. The "Widow Steel" also kept abreast of political activity outside her region; writing her brother-in-law in Pennsylvania, she asked for northern news and added, "I am a great politician you know." Steel is remembered today for providing crucial support for the patriot cause at a critical moment in the Revolutionary War. She gave two sacks of gold and silver coin—real money when that commodity was scarce—to General Nathanael Greene, who had stopped at her tavern one evening in gloomy spirits over the patriots' prospects (Fig. 3-26). According to popular lore, Steel's generosity so cheered Greene that he overcame his depression and made a courageous effort at the Battle of Guilford Courthouse (Fig. 3-27). Though the patriots lost that battle, historians believe that their valiant stand set the stage for Cornwallis's defeat at Yorktown.[56]

Women made successful spies and smugglers. Although Hannah Millikan Blair had a baby every year during the Revolution, she managed to smuggle food and medicine to patriots hiding in the woods near Greensboro. Martha McGee Bell foiled Cornwallis and reported his troop strength and ammunition supplies to Greene's army. Fourteen-year-old Margaret McBride spied for the patriots in Guilford County, and Yadkin County tavernkeeper Elizabeth Pledge Poindexter (granddaughter of a Cherokee chief and his British wife, and mother of twelve children) supplied the American soldiers with information about British troop movements near the Yadkin River.[57]

For Loyalist women, war was harder. Often they were cut off from their network of friends and relatives, their properties were confiscated, and their husbands were long gone. Elizabeth Catherine DeRosset, a Tory living in Wilmington where patriot sympathies were intense, refused to vacate her home and leave her household possessions. She wrote, "Things must go a great length before I fly my own house, as the moment I do so, I presume, it might be pillaged." Her "age and infirmity" persuaded the committee in charge of the tea boycott to make a "gracious" exception in her case, and she was permitted to "drink some tea." Another North Carolina Tory had her property confiscated and complained how "humiliating" it was to rely on friends' charity. She knew she had "no prospect of returning it but my Gratitude" and was as "distressed" with that as with her "Misfortune."[58]

Probably the best-known Loyalist was Flora MacDonald,

FIGURE 3-26. *Female Patriotism—Mrs. Steel and General Green*, engraving, based on a painting by Alonzo Chappel, Rowan County. (From J. A. Spencer, *History of the United States* [1874–76]; courtesy of the North Carolina Museum of History)

FIGURE 3-27. *Guilford Courthouse battle flag*, silk, Guilford County, pre-1781. According to tradition, patriotic women made this flag, which was flown at the Battle of Guilford Courthouse. (Courtesy of the North Carolina Museum of History)

a bonafide Scottish heroine revered for her role in helping the Stuart pretender to the English Crown, "Bonnie Prince Charlie," escape from Scotland to France after his defeat by the English at the Battle of Culloden in 1746 (Fig. 3-28). Flora and her husband Allan had immigrated with their large family to the Cape Fear region in 1774 and settled on a plantation called "Killiegray" in Anson County. Their stay in North Carolina was brief—barely five years—for they had arrived at an inopportune time: they, along with other Scots Highlanders, had pledged loyalty to England, and the American Revolution was imminent. Allan joined the British forces, was among those roundly defeated at the Battle of Moore's Creek Bridge, and taken captive. Flora was left homeless and penniless when the Revolutionary state government took Killiegray. She returned to Scotland and was reunited with her husband after a separation of nearly six years.[59]

Patriot women shouldered the added responsibilities brought on by war and their husbands' absence within the familiar context of their own households. The war campaign in the South was extended from 1778 to 1781. Jean Johnston Blair wrote that "the prices of provisions and every thing else rise daily." Women coped with unprecedented problems—inflation, food and supply shortages, and epidemics. There are numerous examples of a woman's stepping into her husband's shoes and carrying on his business or farming, or of exhibiting unusual bravery or cunning in repelling troops intent on looting her home. Other women, homeless or impoverished by the war or wishing to care for their menfolk, became camp followers. The reality for most North Carolina women was that their home had become a battlefield. Even Quakers and Moravians, who had resisted being drawn into the war, helped nurse the injured on both sides. No one was safe. Houses could be plundered; food, firewood, and livestock stolen; slaves taken off. Marauding soldiers might abuse women "shamefully" or take the "Rings off Their fingers and the Buckles out of their shoes." Jean Blair remained steadfast as British troops advanced toward her Windsor home in 1781. She wrote: "The English are certainly at Halifax but I suppose they will be everywhere and I will fix myself here. It is as safe as any where else and I can be no longer tossed about." When Blair was faced with twenty unexpected guests for dinner one May day in 1781, she commented: "I hardly ever knew the trouble of house keeping before, a large family and continued confusion and not any thing to eat but salt meat and hoe cake and no conveniences to dress them." Women in New Bern used thorns for pins, and the entire town shared one needle because of wartime shortages.[60]

Although the continuing presence of British troops meant scarcity, trouble, and distress for white women, it created opportunities for black women and men to escape. Rumors about the British granting liberty kept slaves in a state of readiness. Jean Blair noted that "The Negroes bring Strange storys" and that her brother had lost "five or six" slaves among "many other things."[61]

Women traditionally support war efforts, and those in North Carolina were no different. An important question is,

FIGURE 3-28. Snuff box belonging to Flora and Allan MacDonald, Anson County. Pewter. (Courtesy of St. Andrews Presbyterian College, Laurinburg)

what did they get in return? What effect did the Revolutionary War and the subsequent creation of the republic and statehood have on the status of women? Historians disagree about the war's significance for women. Julia Cherry Spruill believes that the "Revolutionary War had no permanent effect on the status of women." Mary Beth Norton argues that the war politicized the domestic sphere, making public consequences of women's private actions more obvious. Linda Kerber sees change in the concept of republican motherhood, which created a new civic responsibility for women. Joan Hoff Wilson, on the other hand, does not believe that women received any noteworthy benefits from the Revolution. She views it as only one event in a century-long transformation of women into two groups, those who worked to varying degrees exclusively in the home and those who worked both inside and outside.[62]

Women's Status and Public Life: "It Is Not the Province of Our Sex"

Indeed, the events of the Revolution bring us to a more comprehensive question. How can we characterize the change in North Carolina women's role and status during the eighteenth century?

One clear gain was in education. The post–Revolutionary era's redefinition of women's family roles—in which a mother's impact on her children's character gained new significance—influenced the argument for female education. If children were perfectible and malleable, then gentle and correct mothering was crucial to their upbringing: educated women were likely to be better mothers. English writers Hannah More and Mary Wollstonecraft, both of whose works were read in North Carolina and elsewhere in the South, emphasized the importance of educated women in rearing children; a female academy in Duplin County was even named for Hannah More.[63]

Early Republican-era thought also contributed to changed opinions about educated women. Women were recognized as important because they influenced their children's patriotism—specifically male children, who were the virtuous citizens and statesmen of the future. Linda Kerber has called this new family role for women "Republican Motherhood." Dr. Benjamin Rush, a signer of the Declaration of Independence and social reformer, urged the education of women for the good of the country: educated women would teach their children the important principles of liberty, government, and Christianity. The assumption behind Republican arguments was that female education sustained the family and improved the nation. However, though educated women might be better wives and mothers, common sense and popular opinion held that education should in no way encourage women to seek a role beyond their proper place in family or society. Notwithstanding, Mary Beth Norton sees female education as one of the positive outcomes of the post–Revolutionary era.[64]

The evangelical movement that energized religion in the South also supported female education. In 1791 Methodist bishop Francis Asbury urged parents to provide a Christian education for daughters as well as sons. The daughters should attend separate schools, "under a gracious woman of abilities, to learn to read, write, sew, knit, mark and make their own clothing," but they should "have their religious exercises and instructions the same as your sons." In the early years of Methodism, both parents were accountable for the religious and secular training of their children, but eventually mothers became responsible for the religious instruction of the whole household. Again, the argument was based on a woman's role in the family, which was redefined to embody the Evangelical Woman—pious, moral, and the model of Christian discipleship.[65]

The post-Revolutionary acceptance of the notion of educated women would be realized eventually in the female academy movement of the early nineteenth century. More to the point of women's status, Julia Cherry Spruill wrote that there had been a "decline in the vigor and self-reliance of women in wealthier families and a lessening of their influence in public matters," a trend that even their participation in the war effort did not mitigate. What public rights did women gain? Was the woman of achievement of the early 1700s still the ideal in 1800?[66]

Even by the early 1700s, the unruly public world that had created some space for Albemarle women to maneuver in had become more stable but more closed. Early North Carolina's fractious public life has been described as economically self-interested and politically irresponsible. And yet, with the change from a Proprietary government to a Crown colony in 1729 and other developments through the 1700s, the established institutions of courts, church, law, and government became more orderly as well as male dominions, a pattern that continued after independence and statehood.

Whereas formerly women had defended their and others' rights in the provincial courts, as the judicial system became more fixed and professional attorneys replaced laypeople by the mid-eighteenth century, women no longer appear in the court records. The death in 1738 of Juliana Laker, whose litigation career spanned almost fifty years, coincided with the end of women's participation in the colonial courts. Women, like Martha Jones, who were not educated for the legal profession were now advised by the Tyrrell County Court that their petitions were rejected "for want of Legal Process." Women no longer served as attorneys, they litigated far less, and if they did litigate, it was with a husband as colitigant. The number of women accused of crimes such as theft or public disorder declined, even though women's proportion to men in the total population increased—further evidence that as more women retreated to private domains, fewer violated their moral or spatial boundaries.[67]

Even the spirited participation of North Carolina women before and during the Revolutionary War demonstrated a lessened sense of politics as women's proper sphere. This diminished role would have surprised their more outspoken grandmothers. A petition from Wilmington matrons asking the governor to rescind an order for the removal of wives of Tories from the state begins apologetically—"It is not the province of our sex to reason deeply upon the policy of the order": their "earnest supplications" were prompted only by the "distress of the innocent and helpless." In contrast to Diane Harris's feisty challenge to Proprietary officials in the late 1600s was Margaret McLean's timid request to royal governor Josiah Martin: "It is not for me, unacquainted as I am with the politics and laws, to say with what propriety this was done." New Englander Elkanah Watson's astonishment that a woman "appeared to be an active leader at the polls" in Warrenton in 1786 is testimony to how unusual it must have been by the late 1700s for women to take part in public life.[68]

One place where colonial women had a voice was at church. Quaker women had their say on an equal basis with men in meeting, and the monthly gatherings provided a training ground for many women who became traveling ministers for the Society of Friends. One of them was Ann Jessop, whose biography follows this chapter. Although men's monthly meetings could overrule women's, women generally controlled their own affairs. For instance, women

FIGURE 3-29. Charles Willson Peale, *John and Ann Stanly*, Craven County, ca. 1782. Young Ann and John Stanly were born to privilege, but different roles were expected of each: John to enter the public arena, and Ann to stand docilely in the shadows. John occupies half the canvas in an unobstructed pose, whereas Ann shares her space with the deer and, in a nurturing gesture, feeds it. The deer in this painting is not an affectation: the Stanlys actually had a deer park on their estate. (Courtesy of the Tryon Palace Restoration, New Bern)

in the Cane Creek Monthly Meeting handled sixteen disownments between 1751 and 1761 without ever consulting men.[69]

Women were among the most pious and devoted churchgoers, the mainstay of the established churches, and they were eagerly courted by the emerging evangelical Baptists and Methodists. They not only attended church in large numbers, but they also provided food, shelter, and medical care to the itinerant preachers. Some women, such as Margaret Hallowell, played prominent roles. Hallowell was a valuable member in the early days of the North Creek Baptist Church, which met in both Hyde and Beaufort Counties. She operated a mill and had a millpond where meetings (and baptisms) were frequently held. Another eminent Baptist woman, Martha Stearns Marshall, the sister of Shubal Stearns, who brought the New Light Baptist movement to North Carolina, was known as a "lady of good sense, singular piety, and surprising elocution." Sister Marshall preached in public and brought her audience to "tears" in the 1750s.[70]

In religion women functioned as independent entities rather than simply as offshoots of their husbands; in fact, a woman's conversion presumably could take place against her husband's wishes. Scholars differ on how much the religions associated with the Great Awakenings of the 1740s and 1750s affected women's equality within religion but agree that the emphasis on personal salvation convinced many women that their souls were as good as men's in the eyes of God. Yet by the 1780s and 1790s Baptist congregations increasingly voted to deny women a voice in church. Women ceased to speak as "sisters," although their physical presence continued to swell church memberships. As the churches became more established, women's participation became more circumscribed. Early Baptist histories refer to Martha Stearns Marshall's public-speaking ability, but after the first decade of the nineteenth century, all mention of her role as a public speaker disappears.[71]

Such changes in women's public activities were subtle, but the major revision in North Carolina law in 1784 made clear their increased economic and legal dependence. The traditional concept of dower had acknowledged women's economic role within the household, both in terms of property they might have brought to the marriage and labor they contributed to its prosperity. This new law relegated women to the dependent status of children. A decade later, dower rights were legally abolished in North Carolina.[72]

As North Carolina society became more stable and its economy matured, and as new legal and political structures were established in the aftermath of the Revolutionary War and the formation of a new republican state, women were less visible in public affairs (Fig. 3-29). Throughout the colonial period, women had served effectively as "surrogate husbands," but one of the most striking aspects of the petitions by the widows of Tories attempting to reclaim their confiscated property was how little they knew about their husbands' affairs. Helen "Nelly" Blair Tredwell, outspoken as a young woman, corresponded with her uncle James Iredell about politics and literature and complained to her brother about men who assumed that women were "trifling sorts of creatures" who could not discuss "serious" topics. When she married and had children, Helen left political discussions behind and turned to her Aunt Hannah for housekeeping advice. Ann Steele, granddaughter of the "great politician" Elizabeth Maxwell Steel and daughter of the North Carolina Federalist legislator John Steele, wrote: "I make it an invariable rule to be silent on political subjects. In my opinion they are altogether out of a ladys sphere."[73]

At the beginning of the eighteenth century, North Carolina women could not have anticipated that their place would contract to a totally domestic sphere and their legal rights would be eroded. Native American and African American women living within the European American culture that had been transplanted to North Carolina had few legal rights and economic privileges to begin with and, therefore, little to lose.

Women continued to be essential to the European American settlement of North Carolina's coast and backcountry throughout the 1700s. By the end of the century, although they were secure in the private sphere and educational prospects seemed promising, their place in the public world was less assured.

Rebecca Bryan Boone

1739–1813

George Caleb Bingham, *Rebecca Boone* as depicted in *Daniel Boone Escorting Settlers through the Cumberland Gap*, oil on canvas, 1851–52. (Courtesy of the Washington University Gallery of Art, St. Louis)

From the Forks on the Yadkin River in Rowan County, Rebecca and Daniel Boone, their eight children, and a large number of relatives and friends set forth on a September morning in 1773. Prepared to follow traces only wide enough for a single file of horses, they aimed to cross the mountains into Kentucky. It would be a long journey and a dangerous one for white families determined to establish the first settlement in territory claimed by the Cherokee and the Shawnee. Those who stayed behind knew that they might never see them all again. A neighbor was later to remember, with the kind of drama Daniel Boone evoked in his admirers, "Even Daniel, in spite of his brave and manly heart, was seen to lift the lapel of his pouch to dry the tears from his eyes whilst his dear old Mother held him around his neck weeping bitterly."[1]

Rebecca's own good-byes gave her reason to weep: she was leaving her family and homeplace, she had a four-month-old baby (her other children were ages sixteen, fourteen, twelve, ten, seven, five, and three), and perhaps she did not feel the need to conquer Kentucky. Daniel's far-flung travels were old stuff to her. She knew what she had to do: as soon as the good-byes were said, she probably turned her attention to the children, the youngest riding in a basket across a pack saddle. Cattle and hogs were driven, and horses snorted and stamped under the weight of supplies, clothes, rifles, tools—everything they could carry to begin life in the new country. Ahead lay mountains and forests, and long nights of fitful sleep. Along parts of the trace, Indians watched the invasion. The presence of women and children was a sure sign of intent to settle, and both the Cherokee and the Shawnee had warned this Daniel Boone to stay out. But to blaze a trail for others to follow and to be the first white families to inhabit Kanta-ke—an Iroquois name for land where Indian women cultivated crops—that, and perhaps the danger also, drew their leader.[2]

In agreeing to accompany Daniel, Rebecca gave up the familiarity and security of her home country in North Carolina (present-day Davie County). She was selective in her choices—she had refused other requests to pick up and go—so there must have been something promising about Daniel's obsession to lay claim to land west of the mountains. By now they had been married seventeen years, and she must have realized that he was not going to be cured of wanderlust. She knew the risks of the adventure. Indeed, before the Boone party reached Kentucky—not until September 1775 would they be established in Boonesborough—the family experienced a heartbreaking loss: the oldest child, sixteen-year-old James, was tortured to death by Indians. A companion who escaped reported that at the end the boy had cried out for his mother. Rebecca was some three miles ahead in the main party. When she received the news of his death, she took from her saddlebag two linen sheets and instructed that his body and that of another boy be wrapped in them. The small, corroborative detail of the sheets tells us something more about eighteenth-century women's history than trail maps: linens were a woman's scarce and valuable possession, and Rebecca brought them with her to start housekeeping in a distant place; when her son died, she was both practical and perhaps sentimental in using them as shrouds. A few weeks later, when Daniel discovered that wolves had begun to dig up the grave, he reburied the bodies wrapped in his sturdy saddle blanket.[3]

To imagine these scenes more than two hundred years later is to return to the history of the American frontier and the story of an archetypal folk family, Rebecca and Daniel Boone. Legends of Daniel Boone entered American literature during his own lifetime—woven out of a rich mixture of oral, fictive, and historic materials—and in them we are given certain images of frontier women. Boone himself is often quoted as having said that all he needed for happiness was a good gun, a good horse, and a good wife. Rebecca Bryan Boone's fifty-seven years of marriage to Daniel apparently stood the test of her needs and his.

Rebecca Bryan came from a well-known family in Rowan County. The patriarch, Morgan Bryan, was a Welsh Quaker who had met his future wife, Martha Strode, when they both emigrated to America at the end of the seventeenth century, marrying and settling first in Pennsylvania and then moving on to Virginia in 1734. Morgan Bryan was one of a large number of emigrants leaving a more populated region for sparsely settled and cheap land in the South. (Daniel Boone's family emigrated from Pennsylvania to settle in North Carolina in 1751.)

Rebecca was born in western Virginia on January 9, 1739, to Joseph (Morgan's son) and Aylee Bryan. After Martha Bryan's death in 1747, when Morgan was nearly eighty years old, he moved his married sons and daughters with him to North Carolina, where he soon became the biggest landowner in the Yadkin Valley, with more than five thousand acres. The Bryan Settlement on Dutchman's Creek and the Bryan family name would come to occupy a central place in the developing backcountry of North Carolina.[4]

When Rebecca was fifteen, she met Daniel, who was nineteen, at one of the Bryan-Boone family weddings. They were well matched. Legend has it that when he tested her mettle during a party after the wedding by playfully cutting her apron with his knife, he was pleased that she had refused to show any temper. After about two years, in a courtship that may have waited for Daniel to return from hunting, Rebecca married him on August 14, 1756. They spent their first night in a cabin in the yard of Daniel's father, Squire Boone. According to custom, family members and friends accompanied the couple to the loft and tucked them in, then went downstairs to drink and be merry. Rebecca and Daniel set up housekeeping in Squire Boone's cabin, and she immediately became mother to two young boys, orphaned when Daniel's widowed brother died.

Nine months later, Rebecca gave birth to their first child, James. She had another child on an average of every two and a half years thereafter until she was forty-one—four daughters and six sons. In addition to her own biological children and the two nephews, Rebecca reared various others, including six motherless children of a widowed brother and a white child Daniel had found during an exchange of captives with Indians. Rebecca's mother had given birth to ten children and Daniel's mother, to eleven. Birthing a large number of babies was a familiar experience: either mother could have assisted in the delivery of her grandchildren, and Rebecca herself was an experienced midwife.[5]

Rebecca Bryan had very dark hair and very dark eyes—according to a relative, "one of the handsomest persons" she had ever seen. Like most eighteenth-century backcountry women, she was illiterate. Later testimonies from a granddaughter record that Rebecca was an excellent housekeeper, no small reputation considering the dirt of frontier life, especially in the rude forts where families often lived under constant threat of Indian attack. As a daughter in a large family, she was accustomed to the tremendous amount of work necessary to maintain a household—hauling water from the creek for cooking and washing, feeding the livestock and milking the cows, splitting wood and making fires, planting, weeding, and harvesting the garden, and spinning, weaving, and sewing to keep the family clothed. In addition to her domestic talents, Rebecca had a skill especially important to the frontier: she hunted small game near the family settlement and, according to legend, killed seven deer in a single outing. As John Mack Faragher observes, the work of women freed men to go hunting, and in this respect Rebecca Boone was a typical woman of the frontier. White frontierswomen lived, like Native American women, in a pattern of gender division of labor, doing the work in the home and the fields while men hunted.[6]

Because Bryan Settlement, near present-day Farmington, was close to Salisbury, a seat of government and trade, Rebecca could have heard discussions about the issues of the day—lawsuits, land deals, and the increasing resentment of families in the backcountry toward the eastern "establishment." As a member of the biggest landowning family, she was near the center of whatever activity was going on in the county.

For most of their marriage, a crowd of people lived in Rebecca and Daniel's house—often as many as twenty or so: their younger and adult children (and their spouses and children) and kin from both sides. Many hands may have helped, but given Rebecca's central place in the stories of her descendants, hers were the busiest. Although most men hunted, none of them seemed to have stayed away as long as Daniel Boone. A Moravian missionary traveling in Rowan County recorded having met Rebecca when Daniel had been gone for two years. "She is by nature a quiet soul, and of few words," the missionary noted. "She told me of her trouble, and the frequent distress and fear in her heart."[7] In other stories, however, there is a decided mischievousness about her: once she reportedly shot off her gun to get the attention of men who were languishing in their defense of a settlement. Family members agreed that Daniel was able to tease her, as well as to leave her—and return—apparently without any serious consequences to the marriage. When he tried to persuade her to take the children and move with him to other places, she refused more than once, and he abided by her decisions. After they had moved to Kentucky and Daniel was held captive by some Shawnee for several months, Rebecca—thinking him dead—packed up the children and returned home to North Carolina. She had the mark of the backcountry: she was resourceful and independent.

Rebecca Boone's most rooted years were in North Carolina. During their first year of marriage she and her husband moved from Squire Boone's cabin to the Bryan Settlement. Daniel, with the help of Rebecca's uncles, brothers, and brothers-in-law, built a large log house that was their home for the next ten years, longer than they would stay in any other place. Its fireplace had a hearth deep enough for hanging pots; and nearby, but separate from the house, there was a summer kitchen. Although Boones and Bryans owned slaves, apparently Rebecca and Daniel did not. (Faragher surmises that they probably would have if they could have afforded them.) Rebecca, like her mother, had help from her daughters in cooking and performing other household chores for the family.[8]

From the first months of their married life, Daniel Boone was gone from home, hunting, exploring farther and farther away, happy to be alone in the woods. Often he was accompanied by members of the Bryan or Boone families, and he began to take his son James with him when the boy was about six years old. The money that Daniel made selling furs and skins provided for his family's well-being.

But backcountry life was not exactly safe. Ruffians and plunderers were always capable of setting upon travelers and breaking down doors. Indian wars were raging, and the Cherokee frequently attacked homesteads in retaliation for the continued incursions by whites into their hunting grounds. By 1759 Cherokee had reached the Yadkin settlements, and the Boones picked up and moved to Culpeper County, Virginia. In Virginia Rebecca gave birth to their third child, Susannah.

Between 1760 and 1762 Daniel crossed the mountains, and when he returned, Rebecca had a new baby, Jemima, who has been called "Boone's Surprise." According to some accounts, Rebecca had given Daniel up for dead and had conceived the child with his brother Ned. Family members reported that she said Ned looked so much like Daniel that she could not help it. Daniel is supposed to have said, with a sigh, "Oh well, the race will be continued." In the several versions Faragher and others give of this story, Daniel Boone is a forgiving man for whom "all in the family" had no limits. Moreover, he is supposed to have confessed that he had been "obliged to be married in Indian fashion a couple of times."[9] As it turned out, Jemima Boone was his most attentive child. She alone remained in Boonesborough, Kentucky, to welcome her father when he returned in June 1778 from captivity among the Shawnee.

The Boones returned to Rowan County in 1762, but Daniel was restless. He proposed moving to Florida, and Rebecca refused. A fifth child, Levina, was born in 1766, and the same year the family packed again and moved a little farther west, near present-day Wilkesboro. In 1767 Daniel began exploring Kentucky. In 1768, when a daughter Rebecca was born, the Regulator rebellion stirred up the Boones and Bryans, who sympathized with the opposition to taxes and lack of representation. The rebellion gave Daniel a pressing reason to leave North Carolina, and, anyway, Kentucky drew him. In Kentucky, Daniel led survey parties and helped open up the Wilderness Road. By 1773 he had persuaded Rebecca and many other family members to return with him to Kentucky to settle a place to be called Boonesborough. The journey to Kentucky is described at the opening of this story.

In Boonesborough, where the Boones and Bryans had quickly "forted up" against Indian attacks, Rebecca gave birth to a ninth child, William, who died soon afterward. The next year Jemima and two other girls were kidnapped by Shawnee and rescued by

Daniel. A relative later reported that when Rebecca heard the news of Jemima's rescue, "She both laughed and cried, as she always did when she was over joyed."[10] (Jemima's rescue probably had much more importance in the Boone house than the news that reached Boonesborough in August 1776—the signing of the Declaration of Independence.) Rebecca Boone's life never was any easier or much different. In 1780 she had her tenth child, Nathan, who would be her last. Two years later her son Israel was killed in a Shawnee attack.

By the late 1790s Daniel and Rebecca were operating a tavern on the banks of the Ohio River, and Rebecca served as cook on boat trips when Daniel traded on the river, often transporting ginseng root to market. Once Rebecca, Daniel, and Nathan rode on horseback from Kentucky to visit some of Daniel's friends in Pennsylvania. According to those who saw her on this trip, Rebecca "was very pleasant and sociable, and spoke very freely of their affairs," whereas her husband was "stern looking, very taciturn and gloomy."[11] Perhaps Daniel was already considering his last move and realized that his wilderness adventures were almost over. He served out a term in the Virginia assembly (Kentucky was not yet a separate state), and Rebecca and Nathan went with him for the meetings in Richmond. He could still fail to turn up on schedule after a winter hunt, and Rebecca worried. They spent more time together, sometimes with married children, often in a small cabin where fat from bear bacon dripped from rafters. It is said that when Daniel began to suffer from rheumatism, Rebecca went hunting with him and carried his gun.

By the end of the 1790s game was mostly gone and also Daniel's sense of the rugged frontier. He and Rebecca moved from one small cabin to another, sometimes living with their children, perhaps with a kind of bafflement about where they belonged, owning no property and often in debt. But there was still one more journey to make, a last frontier for the Boones and Bryans to cross. Rebecca and their grown-up children were now leaders more than followers. In 1799 Rebecca and Daniel Boone and other family members moved from the United States to the Spanish territory of Upper Louisiana on the Missouri River. There, in a valley along a creek named Femme Osage, Rebecca and Daniel made their final home.

Rebecca had moved many times over many years, and she must have been a tired woman. The Bryan Settlement, where it all began, was far away. Her husband had survived attacks of every kind, including those on his character, and was already a subject of national fascination. When curiosity seekers and journalists found their way to the old man, Rebecca was there by his side, having her coffee and her clay pipe.

Rebecca Bryan Boone, seventy-four years old and still making apple butter in the last week of her life, died on March 18, 1813. Daniel Boone was more alone than he had ever been in his life, even in the wilderness. As one family member put it, "After Grandmother Boone died, he never was Contented." He lived for another seven years in Jemima's home, where he died in 1820.[12]

Ann Matthews Floyd Jessop

1738–1822

Marriage certificate of Ann Floyd and Thomas Jessop, Guilford County, 1765. (Courtesy of the Friends Historical Collection, Guilford College)

Women were the first lay ministers in the Society of Friends to carry the Light to the North American colonies. Friends, or Quakers, arrived in North Carolina as early as 1672, when William Edmondson of Ireland paid a visit. That same year George Fox, who had begun the Friends movement in England, visited and preached in the home of Hannah Phelps in the Albemarle region. By 1700 there were permanent settlements in Perquimans and Pasquotank Counties. By the 1740s, however, immigration had shifted westward. Abigail Pike rode about two hundred miles on horseback to the eastern Quarterly Meeting to ask that a new meeting be set up near the center of the colony at Cane Creek, in the southern part of present-day Alamance County. In 1754 a meeting was established at New Garden, about thirty-five miles from Cane Creek, where the first item of business was a request for marriage. Piedmont North Carolina replaced the Albemarle as the center for the Society of Friends. Wave upon wave of new settlers arrived from Pennsylvania, Maryland, Virginia, and northeastern North Carolina, and in 1781 forty-one families came from Nantucket Island.[1]

More educated and more prosperous than many of the state's yeoman families, the Quakers of New Garden bear comparison with the Moravians (the Unity of Brethren) of Salem: both were strictly sectarian, required members to marry within the faith and expelled offenders, kept meticulous records, opposed war and slavery, and were modest and hardworking. But whereas Moravians were governed by an intricate hierarchical network, Quakers taught no catechism and organized no clergy. Moravian women, who were essential members of a tightly governed economic and religious community, preserved tradition; Quaker women, conducting their own business meetings at home and traveling in their work, created change.[2] It is not surprising that many of the great social reformers in American history were Quaker women.

One of the Quaker ministers, called Publishers of Truth, was Ann Matthews Floyd, whose ministry was recorded at New Garden Meeting on September 28, 1765.[3] She was twenty-seven years old, widowed, and the mother of Elizabeth, age six. She probably had been a member at New Garden for five or six years and had already distinguished herself in speaking at meeting, for to become a preacher or Public Friend, she was subject to the New Garden members' appraisal of her qualifications. After she had been accepted and recorded, she was approved to preach. Before she could travel, however, she had to request a document, called a "minute," granting her permission. In this way Friends held the right to determine who would speak for them and where. The record keeping also helped meetings to keep up with the comings and goings of members.

No doubt Ann had already begun spending a good deal of time visiting New Garden Friends in their homes—scattered in the wilderness—as well as speaking in meeting. In the midst of this life, for a woman to take on a traveling ministry could only speak to her clear sense of who she was and what she had to do. It is also possible that Quaker women saw preaching as an adventure, and they could leave home "with permission." But travel was not only a spiritual quest. It surely was social as well. Ann would have had another woman to travel with her (and usually a man to accompany them on long journeys), and wherever she went, Friends would open their homes and their meeting to her. No salary was paid, but congregations were likely to raise money to cover expenses and to provide food and lodging. Mile by mile, home by home, meeting by meeting, Ann saw new places, met people, learned to comfort individuals and families and to speak in public. Meanwhile, at home, other Friends could help look after her family.

About a year after beginning her ministry, Ann Matthews Floyd made another choice. She wed Thomas Jessop at New Garden Meeting on January 1, 1766.[4] The ceremony was simple, then as now: the couple married themselves with an exchange of vows, facing one another, right hands joined. They promised to be "loving" and "faithful"; there was no mention of "obedient."

Perhaps Ann and Thomas had chosen the marriage date to symbolize a new beginning, which otherwise was clouded because Ann was a widow with one child and Thomas was twice a widower with eight children. Four of his children were adults and probably resided on neighboring farms that belonged to him. The four younger children—Caleb, sixteen; William, fourteen; Jacob, twelve; and Sarah, four—surely lived with Ann and Thomas. Thomas was experienced in caring for children: his first wife Sarah had died when Jacob was three and his second wife Hannah, when their daughter Sarah (apparently named for the first wife) was only two months old. Into this house Ann and her daughter Elizabeth went to live.

Thomas had been born in Yorkshire, England, in 1715, and as a small boy, following the death of his mother, had immigrated to New Bern with his father. After the death of his first wife, he moved with his children to the Piedmont. There he married Hannah, fathered three more children (two of whom died as infants), and became a widower for the second time. Thomas, like his father, had purchased land. Although he had significant family and farm responsibilities, he had material security. He was fifty-one years old at the time of his marriage to Ann, who was twenty-eight.

Ann had been born on October 10, 1738, in York, Pennsylvania. Records of the years between her birth and her marriage to Thomas in 1766 are incomplete. Her parents, Mary and Walter Matthews, were probably among the large number of Pennsylvania Quakers who migrated south to New Garden. In North Carolina they had another daughter, who, two months before Ann was recorded as a minister, was "disowned" by meeting for having married out of the faith.

Soon after their marriage, Ann and Thomas may have moved into a substantial log house situated on Brush Creek near present-day Guilford College. The size of the family recommended a large house, which Thomas could afford to build, but it would have been plain: chinked logs, a central fireplace, and loft space above. During their thirteen years together, the couple had more material wealth than many backwoods families—though comparable to that of the most prosperous Quaker landowners. Thomas brought from his father's estate in Perquimans County title to land there and English furnishings for the house. Ann had the use of pewter, brass, and iron cooking dishes and pots, linens, and household furniture—chests, chairs, tables, and beds. The sons working on Thomas's farms had tools, saddles, harnesses, and other implements, all of which were willed to them on his death. Because no inventory of Ann's personal possessions exists, what she brought to the marriage, either from her own parents or her first marriage, is unknown.

Over the course of little more than a decade, Ann gave birth to four children. John was born late in 1766 but died when he was two. Hannah, perhaps named for Thomas's second wife, was born in mid-1768; Jonathan was born in 1770 and Ann in 1777. Additionally, Ann was stepmother to her husband's adult children and, in the first years of their marriage, to his four adolescent children.

When Thomas died in 1783 at the age of sixty-eight, Ann was forty-five years old with three children in her care. Thomas's property was left to his sons; one-half the profits of the land was assigned to his widow, and his worldly goods went to his children—feather beds to Hannah and Ann, carpenter's and cooper's tools to Timothy and William, the blazed-face mare to Jonathan, and wearing apparel to the six sons. Jonathan inherited most of the land. Ann could continue to live in the home, and all the children received generous gifts—except Sarah, who got only five shillings. Sarah had displeased her father because she had fallen in love with a British officer during the Battle at Guilford Courthouse and married him (he died on their voyage to England). Ann did not let Thomas's anger stand in the way of her continued affection for Sarah; years later she would cross the Atlantic to visit her stepdaughter in Glasgow, Scotland.

After Thomas's death, Ann loaded up some of her household goods and with her three youngest children (Hannah, fifteen; Jonathan, thirteen; and Ann, six) set off for York, Pennsylvania, where she had a brother—also a Quaker minister—and other relatives. They traveled in a covered wagon, and at night Ann built fires as a precaution against wild animals.[5]

Ann had often visited York during her marriage, and she was regarded as an outstanding preacher at York Meeting. She would have had reason to believe that she could provide a home in York for herself and her children. She placed Jonathan as an apprentice to a cousin to learn the watchmaking and jewelry business. Daughter Ann died a year or so after the family arrived in York, and Hannah would look after her mother in Ann's later years.

Between 1783 and 1790 Ann traveled often between York and New Garden, speaking in meeting and visiting family. In 1785 she went to Nantucket Island, a Friends community from which many Quakers had emigrated to North Carolina. In 1790, at age fifty-two, she went to the British Isles, where she spent two years visiting Sarah and speaking in meetings.

Ann's particular gifts as a minister can be deduced from the records of her frequent travels. On September 4, 1793, in a proposal to return "again" to York, the clerk records that "Her life and conversation [are] orderly and her Ministry lively and edifying." In another record, she is described as a "Minister well approved amongst us." And in a letter written in 1881, about sixty years after her death, a great-granddaughter recalls that the family often said that Ann had been "a great preacher."[6]

She is also remembered for her service during the American Revolution, when she helped care for soldiers wounded at the Battle of Guilford Courthouse in 1781. Most Quakers refused to fight in the Revolutionary War, and they expelled from meeting those who did fight. They also refused to pay taxes to support the war. Consequently, Quakers were often accused of being British sympathizers. But when the Battle of Guilford Courthouse was fought in their own backyard, they declared themselves on neither side and tended the wounded and dying of both.

By the time British general Lord Charles Cornwallis had marched his troops twelve miles from Deep River Friends Meeting House to the Guilford Courthouse community, the presence of approximately 4,000 American and 2,000 British soldiers and the sounds of war had shattered the rural quiet. When the first skirmishes began in the early morning of March 15, 1781, the Jessops heard the shots. Jonathan Jessop, then about eleven years old, later recalled that all his family had taken refuge in the cellar, but he slipped out to watch the approaching British. By midday the battle shifted to the west, near Guilford Courthouse, and in the next hour and a half the woods were torn up by cannon shot. Casualties were great on both sides. By midafternoon the British had won, and General Nathanael Greene's army was in retreat. But British confidence and strength had been shaken by the fierce resistance. Historians observe that at Guilford Courthouse the British had won the battle but lost the war. Seven months later Cornwallis surrendered at Yorktown, Virginia.

The Guilford Courthouse battle lines stretched a half mile through the Quaker neighborhood. Both commanders left wounded soldiers in the hands of the Quakers, but there were so many casualties that moans continued in the sodden woods long into the night; many died where they had fallen. The Jessops and other Friends moved what wounded men they could into their own homes and into New Garden Meeting House, which served as a hospital. Near the meetinghouse the Friends began to dig graves for the dead.

According to a map drawn years later by Jonathan Jessop, remembering this scene of his boyhood, the house of Thomas and Ann Jessop was near the Great Salisbury Road, down which the British soldiers had marched on the afternoon of March 15, 1781, close to both the American and the British lines. Between daylight and dark, a farming community was turned into a battlefield, a religious meeting place into a hospital, a "little cove" into a cemetery. The quiet, plain, and peaceful Quaker life had been forever altered.

The vanquished General Greene, a former Quaker, issued an appeal to the Friends. "I address myself," he began, "to your humanity for the relief of the suffering. . . . As a people I am persuaded you disclaim any connection with measures calculated to promote military operations; but I know of no order of men more remarkable for the exercise of humanity and benevolence; and perhaps no instance ever had a higher claim upon you than the unfortunate wounded now in your neighborhood." He also warned the Friends against harboring British sympathies, reminding them that "free exercise" of their religion depended on an American victory. Finally, he asked that they tend the American wounded.[7]

The Quakers responded four days later. Describing the burdens of war left by both the Americans and the British, they reported that "upward of one hundred" were living in New Garden Meeting House, with "no means of provision, except what hospitality the neighborhood affords them." Promising what assistance they could provide to both the Americans at New Garden and the British in the hospital set up at the courthouse, they reaffirmed their neutrality, having "as yet made no distinction as to party and their cause."[8]

The wounded probably remained with the Friends for many weeks, maybe even months, and Friends' supplies and energies were often depleted. Farm work had been delayed or made impossible by the destruction, and health conditions were further undermined by an outbreak of smallpox.

The last phase of Ann Jessop's life records another distinction: her work as a horticulturist. She returned from Scotland with alfalfa seeds and other grasses and grafts of different varieties of fruit—apples, pears, and grape cuttings. In the spring of 1793, at Guilford, Ann employed a farmer by the name of Abijah Pinson, who was an expert grafter, to help her propagate fruit trees and establish orchards. Later Pinson started a large nursery in Surry County. According to the Quaker historian Addison Coffin, writing in 1890, fruit from Ann's orchards was sold "over a wide extent of country, and nurseries were started, in which none but the importation of 1792 was cultivated." The grafts were transported to Ohio, Indiana, Illinois, Missouri, and "every state west of the Mississippi."[9] Ann's son Jonathan has been credited with propagating the York Imperial apple in his nursery in York, Pennsylvania.[10] Two of her great-granddaughters married farmers and became "ranch women" near San Jose, California, where they raised prunes, peaches, apricots, and apples.

In 1802 Ann was living in New Garden with her daughter Hannah Willis and Hannah's family. (Jonathan, who did not return to live in North Carolina, had deeded to Hannah and her husband the land in New Garden that he had inherited from his father.) In 1817 she moved with the Willises to Highland County, Ohio, where she spent the last years of her life. She died on September 26, 1822, at the age of eighty-four and was buried at Fall Creek in a Friends burying ground.

Moravian Women

1753–1836

Old Salem guides, representing members of the Single Sisters' Choir, on the steps of the 1786 Single Sisters' House, Winston-Salem. (Courtesy of Old Salem, Winston-Salem)

When the European Moravian Church purchased land for settlement in Piedmont North Carolina in 1753, it began the process of putting down roots that were to nourish the New World with traditions affecting women. Driven out of Bohemia by religious persecution, the fifteenth-century fellowship of believers known as Unitas Fratrum (Unity of Brethren) had, by the eighteenth century, found a new home—and a new name, Moravians—in the province of Moravia (today, the Czech Republic). One of the leaders was Countess Erdmuth Dorothy Zinzendorf, the wife of the church father, Count Nicholas von Zinzendorf. "Mama" held important offices and often represented the church on diplomatic missions in Europe. After her death, the count's second wife, Anna Nitschmann, was the Moravian Chief Elderess. In his absence, Anna presided over all the work of the missionary-minded church and helped plan new church communities in Bethlehem, Pennsylvania, and Salem, North Carolina.

The old Unity of Brethren offered women in the New World a paradoxical benefit: by accepting the strict authority of the church, they acquired a status that most colonial women did not have. In Moravian communities, where property was owned by the church and wages, fees, and services were controlled by the central economy, there was more equity for women than in colonial American towns under civil and common law. Moravian women knew what was required of all believers: work, frugality, faith, and adherence to church rules.

After the Brethren built the first North Carolina Moravian settlement (in present-day Forsyth County), naming it Bethabara, meaning "House of Passage," women were admitted, either as proposed wives for the Single Brethren or as married women traveling with their husbands from Pennsylvania. In 1766 a party of four "Single Sisters" and twelve "Older Girls" walked most of the way from Bethlehem to Bethabara to establish the first Single Sisters' Choir—"Choir" being the name for groups organized by gender and marital status. Another small farming community was established at nearby Bethania, but the most important settlement was planned as a commercial town near the center of the tract, named Salem from the Hebrew word for "peace." Work there got under way in 1766, and despite bad weather, limited supplies, and spells of discouragement, the Moravians pressed on. By 1772 the major buildings in Salem were ready for occupancy, and families from Bethabara began to arrive. As the town grew, Moravians carved out a community that was incongruous with the surrounding wilderness of Indian trails and rude homesteads: a system of orderly (though muddy) streets, comfortable dwellings in the half-timbered style of Germanic architecture, medical care, shops and services, safety and security, and daily contact with other people living under the same rules. Salem residents, women and men, helped to pay for services out of the money they received as wages for their work. And because Moravians kept meticulous records, we know a good deal about how they lived.[1]

Every task was considered important to the well-being of the new town. Although Salem was specifically intended for trades and commerce, gardening was an essential part of life. While buildings were still under construction, the Single Sisters from Bethabara had gone to Salem to begin their garden.[2] Women were busy in many other ways: as housekeepers, midwives (trained by the town doctor), and governesses; teachers of school, music, sewing, and knitting; laundry workers; cooks, kitchen supervisors, and tavern workers; weavers, glove makers, tailor shop assistants, and milliners; potash makers, white tanners, cooper dyers, and coppersmiths; and bell ringers.[3] They smoked sausage and ham and made kraut and apple butter; scoured, carded, and spun wool; braided straw for hats; carried wood for fires and water for cooking—the list goes on and on. Work—women's and men's—was varied, skilled, and intended to serve the community.

Moravians were taught how to comport themselves as well as how to work and pray. Their behavior was carefully watched by others in the settlement, but especially close care was given to the conduct of women. Single Sisters could not walk with or near Single Brothers or enter any business where Single Brothers were likely to be seen. The tavern was off-limits to women, except the proprietor's wife and female servants who worked there. The good reputation of the Single Sisters was essential to the public and private needs of the town: they were eligible marriage partners. Although Moravian women and men married relatively late (women around age twenty-seven, men around thirty-six), they generally did marry. Men outnumbered women in most early colonial North Carolina settlements, but a balance was achieved more quickly among Moravians than was usual; in 1771, for example, there were 152 single unmarried men and 100 single women.[4] Marriages were arranged through a very efficient system. Church Elders regularly consulted with the head of the Single Sisters' Choir, asking that she pass along to a particular Single Sister a proposal of marriage in behalf of one of the Single Brethren or a widower. By a system called "the lot," Elders asked the Lord to approve or disapprove of proposals they put before Him. The lot was frequently used with regard to marriage. Elders took three pieces of paper—one signifying approval, one disapproval, and one a blank (meaning no action at that time). A piece of paper was drawn from a small bowl. In this way the church exercised some control over one of the most intimate aspects of a member's life and at the same time affirmed what it regarded as God's will.

As women's lives were governed, so they helped govern: women could vote as members of the important Elders Conference of the church and as heads of their separate organizations. Like Moravian men, they were, at every stage of their lives, from infancy to old age, part of the Choir system, which fostered personal growth and security. Beginning with the Choir for Little Girls, at the appropriate times females progressed to Choirs for Older Girls, Single Sisters, Married Couples, and Widows. There were also Choirs for Little Boys, Older Boys, Single Brethren, and Widowers. Single Sisters and Single Brothers lived in separate Choir Houses, where they worked, studied, and worshipped. In many respects, one's membership in a Choir was more important than one's membership in a family. Each woman wore a sign of her Choir in the color of the ribbons that tied her close-fitting cap: red for Older Girls, pink for Single Sisters, light blue for Married Sisters, and white for Widows. Children were looked after in church day nurseries almost from the time they were weaned. By age thirteen or fourteen, Older Girls had left their families and gone to live with the Single Sisters.

The Moravian Single Sisters had more varied opportunities for developing skills and self-confidence than many unmarried women in other places, and their contributions were essential to the community. In 1772 they made a profit from their school and laundry fees, and in 1784, when the tavern burned, they donated the building materials they had been buying to build their own house. They were able to construct it two years later, and in 1786, accompanied by a trombone salute, thirty-three Single Sisters and Older Girls moved into the Single Sisters' House. In 1820, having paid off the mortgage, the Sisters used their profits from an increase in the number of students they taught to cancel other debts of the town. After the Single Brothers' House closed in 1823 because young unmarried men were no longer willing to live there, the Single Sisters' Choir assumed its liabilities.[5]

The Single Sisters' Choir also provided teachers for a School for Little Girls, which opened in 1772 to educate children of Salem families. (The school was the forerunner of present-day Salem Academy and College.) The first director was Elisabeth Oesterlein, a member of the group of women and girls who had walked from Bethlehem to Bethabara in the fall of 1766. When she became head of the school, she was twenty-two years old. At first she had only four pupils, but from time to time Moravian parents in outlying communities sent their children to board with families in Salem so they could learn reading, writing, sewing, and knitting. In a few years the Elders had another plan for their successful Sister Oesterlein: the potter had spoken with them about his need for a wife. They chose Elisabeth (perhaps with the potter's approval or even petition); she accepted the proposal. Sister Catharine Sehner was then assigned to teach at the school; eleven years later, in 1791, she married Abraham Steiner, a Moravian minister, later head (or Inspector) of the girls' school.

In 1804 the School for Little Girls reached an important turning point. That year, in response to requests from non-Moravian families throughout North Carolina and bordering states who desired an education for their daughters and could afford the cost, the trustees voted to open a boarding school. By 1826 considerable interest was given the arrival of a new student, Sarah (Sally) Ridge, the daughter of a Cherokee chief, John, and his wife, Susanna, who had become a Moravian when she was converted by missionaries. Jane Ross, the daughter of John Ross, chief of the Cherokee Nation, also was enrolled but had to leave Salem in 1828. Both she and Sally Ridge accompanied their families when the Cherokee were forced to move westward on the Trail of Tears.[6]

The system that incorporated every individual into a uniform pattern of life and work also recognized exceptional achievers. One of those was Anna Catharina, whose story is somewhat fictionalized by a twentieth-century Single Sister and church archivist, Adelaide L. Fries. Anna Catharina was a leader in the Single Sisters' Choir in Bethlehem when she met Brother Martin Kalberlahn, one of the first ten men sent to start the settlement in Bethabara and the settlement's doctor, who on a trip back to Pennsylvania found himself a wife. Anna Catharina married Martin (in a ceremony with seven other couples) and accompanied him to North Carolina. On Kalberlahn's death from smallpox within months after their arrival, she changed the color of the ribbons on her cap from blue to white, a sign of her widowhood. Three years later, while she was looking after children in Bethabara, the Salem Elders sent a proposal of marriage from Brother Christian Reuter, the Moravian surveyor. Widow Anna Catharina accepted, and they were married. In 1772 they moved to Salem, where Christian built for them one of the first houses in the village. Anna became a leader in church activities for women and children. In 1777 Reuter died of a stroke, and Anna Catharine scarcely had time to tie her widow's ribbons before another proposal came, this one in behalf of John Casper Heinzmann, the minister of the nearby Friedland congregation. "It was difficult for me to decide to [marry]," Anna Catharina wrote in her church memoir, "as I was quite happy in my aloneness. But I had no permission in my heart to turn down the proposal and the call, since I had dedicated myself to the Savior for everything." She married Heinzmann and moved to Friedland, where she cared for children and women of the congregation until Heinzmann's death three years later.[7]

Sister Anna Catharina was sixty years old when she received yet another proposal, this time to wed Jacob Ernst, a minister living in Bethabara and a widower six years younger than Anna. After "another hard struggle," she accepted. They were married on January 24, 1786. The marriage was to be her longest, lasting until Jacob died in 1802. Although Anna Catharina never had children of her own, she was known as "Mother Ernst," well loved by the Moravian communities where she had lived and taught. She died in 1816 in her eighty-ninth year. Her gravestone in the Salem cemetery reads, "A life spent in the service of others."

The life of a black Single Sister, Anna Maria Samuel, is another example of exceptional service. Anna Maria was born in Bethabara in 1781 to Johann and Maria Samuel, who were slaves owned by the church and whose marriage had been arranged by church officials. Anna Maria attended congregational school with white Moravian children and at age eleven became a member of the Salem Older Girls' Choir and moved into the Single Sisters' House in Salem. For the next five years she participated in all the activities, attending Choir meetings, love feasts, festivals, foot washings, and morning devotions and was assigned work such as nursing the sick. In 1797 she and her brothers and sisters were freed by the courts after the church had emancipated their mother. Anna Maria moved out of the Single Sisters' House and returned to live in Bethabara, where she worked in the communal kitchen. She died soon afterward, in 1798, when she was only sixteen, and was buried in God's Acre in Bethabara. In 1800 after Johann Samuel was freed, the remaining members of the family rented a farm outside Bethabara, which now ended its communal economy.[8]

Sister Anna Maria had an exceptional life as the only black Moravian known to have lived in the Single Sisters' House. Other enslaved blacks were not permitted to be full participants in the life of the congregation. Individual Moravians could not own slaves, but slaves were owned by the church collectively and used in Salem businesses and homes; sometimes they were hired out to non-Moravian owners on nearby farms. The first record of the hiring of a slave woman dates from 1763, when an elderly woman named "Franke" was employed to work in the Salem tavern. As the need for labor outgrew the number of workers Moravians themselves could supply, church leaders sought to acquire more blacks. Throughout the 1770s the church bought or hired more black women and put them to work in the tavern kitchen and garden, in private homes, and on small farms in the area. As long as blacks were willing to be baptized in the faith, they were able to partake of some of the benefits enjoyed by white Moravians. Children were taught to read and write, and married couples lived and worked together. But as more workers were needed, church officials permitted more slave purchases. By 1822 blacks were no longer allowed to worship among whites, and a separate church was built for them on the edge of the town. Moreover, the Elders no longer officially recognized black marriages. By the eve of the Civil War, circumstances for blacks had changed dramatically because of the erosion of the few advantages provided them in Moravian communities.[9]

Advantages for white Single Sisters attracted new members. Whereas single men found it increasingly pleasurable and profitable to leave the church community, single women outside Salem experienced difficulty in making both a living and a life for themselves. Room, board, and opportunities to learn skills were available at the Moravian Single Sisters' House. By the first decade of the nineteenth century, more and more women asked to be taken in, not only women from other Moravian communities but non-Moravians as well. In 1836 over one hundred Single Sisters were living in Salem, but Single Brothers accounted for no more than eighteen.[10] As the years passed, the candlelit windows on the square in Salem looked in upon a place of security and comfort.[11]

The Bondswomen of Somerset Place

1786–1860

Somerset Place, Washington and Tyrrell Counties. (Courtesy of the North Carolina Division of Archives and History)

The Quarters fill with shadows. Within the hour the horn will blow, the sun will set, and out of the fields and gardens, sheds and houses, and into the lanes will come the bondswomen of Somerset Place. Their familiarity with one another will be reflected in the easy silence of their passage, hips and arms or hands touching or apart, but residing almost out of sight down the long corridor of history.

The public records speak of them as "wench" and "female slave," as "breeder" or "sickly & infirm." Letters and diaries of planter families call them "servants." They have first names—Fanny, Rose, Betty, Jenny, Lucy, Esther, Nanny, Aggy, and Suckey—and the surnames of their owners. Each is a piece of property: bought and paid for, taxed, and, if unsatisfactory, sold. Among themselves, they create families, which the laws of the state will neither recognize nor protect.[1]

The slaves of Somerset belonged to three generations of eastern North Carolina planters. In each generation the head of the house was named Josiah Collins. To recover what slave history exists requires us to consider the history of their owners, who kept the records.

On June 10, 1786, eighty recently enslaved Africans arrived at Edenton on the brig *Camden* and were delivered to the merchant-planter Josiah Collins, who had arranged in Boston to underwrite the cost of sending the ship to West Africa to procure start-up labor for his Somerset plantation. Because of the nature of the work to be done, most of those eighty Africans were men, but among them were women: Dunkey, Bird, Phoebe, Lid, Hagar, and perhaps others.[2]

Collins was partner in a commercial venture called the Lake Company, which had recently purchased thousands of secluded acres in Tyrrell and Washington Counties that included a large body of fresh water called Lake Phelps or Lake Scuppernong.[3] He wanted slaves—in the hottest months of summer—to dig a six-mile canal to connect the lake with the Scuppernong River, which empties into Albemarle Sound. Thereby he planned to have a navigable waterway over which to transport timber, rice, corn, and other commercial goods to and from his property. With a system of gates, as water was drained off the lake, irrigation ditches would be established and fields made suitable for the growing of crops.

Such a canal required dislodging ancient cypress trees—the most brutal kind of labor. Many slaves were destined to die for the ambitions of "Captain Collins" and his amazing, swamp-transforming canal. There is a legend that the Africans were imprisoned in cages as they dug, passing the mud through bars. Another legend tells us that after spending their evenings singing, the slaves became so homesick and haunted by their fate that they marched arm in arm into the lake, where some of them drowned.

When the canal was completed two years later, Collins began to move some of his female slaves from Edenton to Somerset. Perhaps some of them had been boarded with a free black woman living in Edenton, Sarah White, who could have helped them become acclimated to the new environment. Collins had bought them for a purpose: to provide wives for the West Africans and thus ensure the birth of children to increase his wealth in addition to enlarging the workforce. Women also worked at heavy plantation jobs, hauling wood from the cleared fields and carrying water many times a day. As Collins added to his slave labor, women became 60 percent of the field hands.[4]

In the late 1700s, as Collins was getting the place established, he moved slaves from his other plantations and bought others from local small farmers. He tried to keep families together, and sometimes in later years he united couples by purchasing the husband of one of the Collins female slaves from a nearby plantation—usually the Pettigrew estate of Bonarva, adjacent to Somerset. Slaves who did not know one another and sometimes spoke different dialects had to learn quickly to adapt to the master's needs. It was imperative for their well-being, as well as for the financial success of the plantation, that slaves established families and "blended" together in a network of kinship.

Edenton bondswomen must have found the wilderness of Somerset frightening, particularly in its early years. When the first female slaves arrived at Somerset, there were no white women: Josiah Collins was a widower and never remarried; Josiah II on his visits from Edenton to Somerset rarely brought his wife. Indeed, no member of the Collins family lived at Somerset until Josiah Collins III and his wife Mary moved into the recently completed big house in 1830. Throughout the plantation's history, blacks vastly outnumbered whites, and as early as 1800 black women outnumbered black men.

Despite the shocking changes of forced emigration by a wide range of ethnic groups to a foreign culture, within a decade of the arrival of the first slaves on the *Camden*, a village of sorts had formed in the Quarters. Marriages were made and kept, even under the most arduous conditions; children were born, and extended communal kinships were developed and maintained.[5]

In 1790, with the canal completed and work continuing on the ditches, Josiah Collins invited guests to Somerset to celebrate the Fourth of July, the anniversary of freedom for his new country. There was jousting and other pageantry, costumes, and plenty of food prepared by the bondswomen. At Christmas the slaves performed a pageant called the "John Koonering," staged for the entertainment of the Collinses' guests as well as for their own enjoyment.[6]

By 1800 Somerset began to look like a plantation, as permanent structures replaced the early temporary cabins. Recent studies indicate that the Quarters were built in a straight line along the shore of Lake Phelps, in sight of the big house and the master's bedroom window; they consisted of five two-story, four-room houses, like barracks, housing 115 slaves. Each house had chimneys at either end, fireplaces upstairs and down, and four apartments measuring about 20′ by 20′.[7] There must have been considerable crowding, the discomfort relieved somewhat in summer by a breeze that came—with insects—through the open windows. Men, women, and children usually were assigned to places according to family, so that there might have been a grandparent, one or more parents, children, and even aunts and uncles living together.

To the growing plantation were added an impressive barn, a gristmill, a machine to clean rice, about twenty additional cabins, a hospital to treat the slaves, and a chapel. The housing, medical care, and food were apparently better than most. Meals were cooked in large pots by the bondswomen and transported by wagons into the fields, where most of the enslaved men and women (including pregnant women) worked in the growing and harvesting seasons. It is likely that children under age ten were supervised in the Quarters by elderly bondswomen and perhaps elderly bondsmen.

The Collins slaves and the Pettigrew slaves on the adjacent plantation knew one another, were allowed to travel back and forth, and often were sent to help out on the other's plantation. The proximity of these estates was an advantage in terms of providing partners and extended families for the slaves. In addition, after Josiah Collins III moved to Somerset, he may have allowed some of the slaves he had brought from Edenton to return, at least for family visits. Almost from the beginning there were runaways from both plantations; some were captured, returned, and punished—enough to strike fear in the minds of slave masters. Sporadic resistance continued for many years, and Josiah Collins III was often alarmed over barn burnings and poisonings rumored to be the work of slaves. There is some evidence that seventeen Somerset slaves, accused of having tried to poison the overseer, were sold to a Louisiana plantation owner. Each rumor spurred tighter controls.

Yet in some ways it was better to be a slave at Somerset, where there was a kinship network, than to suffer the isolation of small farms. There were other benefits, too. The Collinses allowed slaves to have their own garden plots and raise crops—corn was a favorite—as well as meat for their own tables, and, sometimes, to sell what they raised—such as poultry—and the crafts they made, such as baskets and dolls. The slaves could also buy on credit from the company store. Although the quality of their food would have been inferior to what was served to the Collins family, there was the possibility of some variety and quantity because the plantation had an abundance of rice, corn, and wheat in good seasons, and there was a smokehouse.

Collins men owned 240 slaves in 1810. After the death of Josiah II in 1839, management of the land went to Josiah III and ownership of the land and slaves passed to the grandchildren. Fifty-nine slaves inherited in 1843 by a Collins granddaughter, Louisa, became the property of her husband and were marched to Marengo County, Alabama, to work on the recently purchased plantation of Faunsdale.[8] By 1860 Somerset worked nearly five hundred slaves. But that year, with the prospect of a Civil War, Mary Collins and her children fled to Hillsborough, leaving Josiah III and the slaves at Somerset. After the Emancipation Proclamation, many former slaves fled plantations to live in the upcountry as "refugees," with little means of enjoying their freedom.[9] By January 1, 1863, Collins tried to maintain the practice of keeping slave families together while moving some of them to two other plantations: sixty-six older men and women remained at Somerset; others were taken to work under new masters at Hurry Scurry in Orange County and Northwood in Vance County. Some were hired out for their own wages. At Northwood they planted corn and built cabins for themselves. But many slaves became sick; there was a drought and food was scarce. Few survived the long walk that would eventually bring them to the Roanoke River and the possibility of securing passage to freedom on a federal gunboat. In 1870 Mary Collins, widowed for several years, and her sons were unable to get Somerset started again, and she sold the estate to settle a debt.

Although available information is inadequate to draw a full portrait of the African women of Somerset, a few lives can be at least partially glimpsed. Among the first was a woman we know only as Fanny, whose subsequent marriage to Guinea Jack lasted about forty-nine years. It is thought that Guinea Jack was born in Africa in 1768, was among the eighty slaves transported on the *Camden*, and arrived at Somerset when he was eighteen or nineteen years old. He and Fanny had a son Will, born in 1790, the first of six recorded children. Fanny was nineteen when Will was born, and he was probably her first child.

Suckey, also called "Suck" and "Old Suck," a variation of Susan, was born in 1772, probably in Chowan or Bertie County, and through her line came many of the men and women who would comprise the artisans of Somerset Place. When she was fifteen, Suckey was sold by Penelope Dawson to Josiah Collins. In 1787 Suckey was taken to Somerset Place. Her first child—John Trotter—was recorded when she was twenty-five. (The boy had the same name as the overseer.) Two years later she had Polly, whom she perhaps named for a kinswoman, Poll, who had been sold at the same time by Penelope Dawson. Suckey's other children were a second Polly (1798), Cerena (1801), Rose (1803), Sarah (1807), Ben (1808), Suck or Susan (1812), and Chishire (1813), born when Suckey was forty-one.

According to a slave list, Suckey lived in Number One, the first of the two-story houses in the Somerset slave quarters. She shared space with children, grandchildren, a great-granddaughter, and sons-in-law. Additional family members lived close by.

Suckey was a busy servant and mother. Her tasks could have included making candles and lye soap, boiling clothes, building fires, cooking over the large open hearth in the kitchen for the big house and over her own fireplace in the Quarters, preserving meat for the salthouse, working in the garden, cutting flowers—heliotrope, geraniums, and myrtle—for Mrs. Collins, emptying chamber pots, putting linens on the beds, and picking cranberries in the bogs. At the beginning she may have worked in the field, but apparently she was intended to be in charge of the kitchen in the big house. Perhaps she helped serve the Christmas dinner to the Collins family and their many guests at 4:00 P.M. When she was sick—Collins slaves suffered (and many died) from smallpox, dysentery, whooping cough, lockjaw, typhoid fever, and accidents cutting timber and doing other dangerous work—she could have been cared for in the "hospital," which resembled one of the slave houses. A doctor, hired especially by the Collinses, was sometimes available to administer quinine and other medical care to the servants, as well as the family. When Suckey was pregnant, her tasks may have been lightened—perhaps more time at the spinning wheel or in the kitchen, less time in the field—but she would still have been expected to work hard, probably would also have attended other women in labor and nursed the sick and dying. Living until her seventies, she was one of the oldest people at Somerset and acquired the affectionate name "Old Suck," used by blacks and whites alike.

Another Somerset woman who stands out in the records is Charlotte Cabarrus, a free black woman born in

1800 and hired by Josiah Collins III in 1830. The only free black at Somerset, Charlotte, according to local history, lived in the Collins house and had authority over the head housekeeper. She looked after the Collins children but apparently she never had children of her own. She was paid one hundred dollars a year, and the family took her with them when they traveled to their home on Long Island, New York. When Collins, fearing Union soldiers, marched some 170 working slaves to western North Carolina, apparently Charlotte stayed behind to look after Somerset. She died November 26, 1860, on a Monday afternoon, "a large quantity of morphine" having been administered to ease her suffering. One of the Pettigrews writing of her death described her as "a most excellent character and an exemplary Christian and who will be greatly missed by Mr. Collins's family and all who visit the house." All the Collinses and other Pettigrews had by that time left their plantations, and the writer thought himself "the sole inhabitant of the Caucasian race." "Mr. Collins' place," he concluded, "seems a perfect graveyard."[10]

II

The Nineteenth Century through Reconstruction

CHAPTER 4

A Hardier Mold

Women, Family, and Society, 1800–1860

The nineteenth century was a time of increased opportunities for women nationally, but such changes occurred slowly in North Carolina, sometimes called the "Rip van Winkle state" for its provincial and conservative ways.[1] The lives of the majority of women, white or black, slave or free, were governed by traditional rural values centered on family, kin, and church—as were those of their mothers and grandmothers. Family formed the core of their existence, with frequent pregnancy and large families the norm. Kinship ties and religion provided meaningful support, helping white women endure isolation and black women survive slavery. Sickness and death were constant threats, and women's letters, diaries, and narratives are filled with a resigned faith in God's will. One significant change was that some North Carolinians believed that educated women made better wives and mothers, and young girls attended school in ever increasing numbers.

North Carolina women lived in an agrarian society where slavery and male authority were taken for granted. The removal of 17,000 Cherokee (4,000 from North Carolina) from their mountain homeland to present-day Oklahoma in 1838 ended the last vestiges of Native American women's matrilineal power. Although less than 30 percent of white North Carolinians owned slaves and only 3 percent could be designated as having the status of "planter," North Carolina was still a slave state. Law, church, and custom, founded on traditional English practice and hardened to sustain slavery, reinforced patriarchal attitudes in the home as well. Under North Carolina law, sole authority rested with master, husband, and father. In 1829 Chief Justice Thomas Ruffin wrote, "The power of the master must be absolute to render the submission of the slave perfect." Over thirty years later, in 1862, Chief Justice Richmond Pearson granted a husband the "power to use such a degree of force as is necessary to make the wife behave herself and know her place." The *North Carolina Standard* had noted in 1845 that there was "no essential difference between the legal condition of married woman and that of the slave." Poor white women who headed their own households and free black women were especially vulnerable in a society that expected white women to live under the protection of men and blacks to be slaves.[2]

By 1860 fifteen towns counted populations of one thousand or more: Wilmington, New Bern, Beaufort, Edenton, Elizabeth City, Kinston, Tarboro, Fayetteville, and Washington on or near the Coast; Raleigh, Warrenton, Henderson, Charlotte, and Salisbury in the Piedmont; and Hendersonville in the Mountains. Without changing the predominantly rural landscape of most people's lives, towns offered both white and free black women employment options and many white women their first opportunity to step outside their homes, claim a place in public life through church and benevolent work, and develop organizational skills that served them when war came.

Resonating in the voices of many North Carolina women in the 1800s is a recognition of their own strength in the midst of hard lives and harsh laws that restricted women's place. In 1824 Priscilla Bailey, who lived on a remote coastal plantation, wrote, "I find by daily experience I am of a hardier mold than I had the most distant idea."[3]

Black Women and Slavery: "Far More Terrible"

The brutal nature of slavery meant that most North Carolina black women endured the burdens of womanhood but enjoyed few of its benefits. Deborah Gray White has characterized female slaves as three times cursed—as blacks in a white world, as slaves in a free society, and as women in a patriarchal culture. They could expect racial hostility, unremitting labor, harsh punishment, and sexual and reproductive exploitation.[4] As Anne Firor Scott explains in *The Southern Lady: From Pedestal to Politics 1830–1930*, an elaborate mythology defined white women's proper place as a pedestal, where they were expected to be chaste, pious, and obedient. By contrast, black women were not regarded as "virtuous" and faced continual sexual harassment from their masters and other white men. Under North Carolina law, a white man could not be convicted of fornication, rape, or adultery with a slave woman.[5]

White women rarely acknowledged white men's sexual relations with black women, although Mary Boykin Chesnut of South Carolina noted, "Like patriarchs of old our men live all in one house with their wives and concubines and the mulattoes one sees in every family exactly resemble the white children." Hannah Crasson, who grew up on a plantation near Garner, thought her master good in that he did not whip his slaves, but she blamed him directly for the many "half white niggers."[6] Jacob Manson, a former slave from Warren County, thought that his owner, a Colonel Eden, did not have any white overseers on his plantation because Eden liked to have full access to his slave women without having any other "white man playin aroun' 'em."[7] When a female slave told his wife that the master was "forcing her" to let him have his way, Mrs. Eden replied, "Well go on you belong to him."[8]

In an era when respectable white women modestly (and ostentatiously) covered their bodies with voluminous dresses and mountains of petticoats, slave women frequently had only the scantiest of clothing. Mattie Curtis, who lived on a Granville County plantation near the Franklin County line, "went as naked as yo' han' til I was fourteen."[9] Although slave auctions were held every January 1, slaves wore no shoes and scarcely enough clothes "to keep a cat warm." The women wore only "a thin dress and a petticoat and one underwear."[10]

Black and white women often worked side by side, but this familiarity did not erase the barriers between them or protect black women from harm. Rena Raines described the Wake County plantation between Apex and Holly Springs where she lived as "a Hell on earth" after her master married a woman who "jist liked" to see slaves beat "almost ter death."[11] Mattie Curtis regarded her mistress as a devil who became more ornery and mean as war approached.[12] Sarah Debro's mother wept when Sarah was moved into the big house on the Orange County plantation to wait on "Miz Polly, to tote her basket of keys an' such." After freedom, Sarah's mother took her back, despite the daughter's tears and the white mistress's entreaties. The mother said, "You took her away from me an' didn' pay no mind to my cryin', so now I'se takin' her back home."[13]

FIGURE 4-1. *Cowrie shell*, Bennehan Plantation, Durham County, ca. 1800. Few material goods survived the passage from Africa. This cowrie shell of African origin discovered in the slave quarters at the Bennehan plantation may have been a treasured reminder of faraway kin irrevocably lost. (Courtesy of The Stagville Center, Durham)

Motherhood and Slavery

Motherhood enhanced a slave woman's status in her slave community and her value to her owner. In matrilineal African society, motherhood ensured a family line, protected property and inheritance, and passed rank and status on to the next generation (Fig. 4-1). Under North Carolina law, the status of the mother—free or slave—determined that of the child, and a slave woman's owner benefited materially by her motherhood.[14]

Temple Herndon Durham, a Chatham County slave who had eleven children, knew that "De more chillun a slave had de more dey was worth." Durham recalled that her only competition on her plantation was Lucy Carter—with twelve children—but Lucy's "chillun was sickly an' mine was muley strong an' healthy."[15] Fannie Moore, who had been born on a South Carolina plantation and later lived in Asheville, observed, "De 'breed womn' always bring mo' money den de res', ebben de men. When dey put her on de block dey put all her chillun aroun her to show folks how fas she can hab chillun."[16]

Although pregnancy sometimes resulted in lighter work schedules, pregnant slaves generally were not well cared for, nor were they safe from punishment or heavy work. Lucy Brown, a former slave from Person County, remembered her mother telling her that women sometimes gave birth "like a cow" in the field. There is an account of a pregnant woman forced to lie face down with her abdomen secured in a shallow hole dug by the overseer for her whipping.[17]

Slave mothers had to juggle caring for children with the demands of slavery. Celia Robinson, who lived in Franklin County and was about eight or ten years old at the end of the Civil War, remembered her mother telling her that the overseer gave her only fifteen minutes to leave the field, "go home and suckle dat thing," and be back at work. Filled with despair, Celia's mother "would go somewhere an' sit down an' pray de child would die."[18] Slave mothers did have the support of an extended family—"fictive kin" of neighbors and friends as well as grandmothers, mothers, aunts, and sisters—an African heritage that continued after slavery (Fig. 4-2). Jacob Manson remembered that the children on the Warren County plantation where he lived were looked after by "ole slave women" who were past their prime, while their mothers plowed or did other field work.[19]

Although some owners honored the bond between mother and child, the black family could not count on white people to respect its sanctity. Death, marriage, or debt in the owner's family often overrode good intentions, and slaves became property to be dispersed. A slaveowner might be reluctant to sell his slaves, yet give them as gifts to his children. In a study of ninety-two wills of North Carolina planters from 1800 to 1860, only eight directed executors to honor slave family relationships. Isaac Wright of Bladen County

FIGURE 4-2. *Doll* (attributed to slave[s]), homespun cotton and cotton thread, Bennehan Plantation, Orange County, ca. 1850. A doll found in the attic wall of the plantation may have been made by a slave for his or her children. Few such toys have survived, but dolls may have provided a girl both a plaything and practice in mothering skills. (Courtesy of The Stagville Center, Durham)

> A motherless chile sees a hard time.
> Oh Lord, help her on the road.
> Er sister will do de bes' she kin,
> Dis is a hard world, Lord, fer a motherless chile.
> —Slave song (D. G. White, *Ar'n't I a Woman*, 133)

stipulated that "families should be broken as little as practicable and also the relation of man and wife shall be respected as far as can be done without undue sacrifice of interest." Windsor slaveholder Thomas Turner explained to a prospective buyer how he "should be very sorry to separate them [Hannah and her five children], or to sell them to a person likely soon to separate them." But Turner had debts to settle, and he was forced to sell mother and children separately. The mother of eleven healthy children, Hannah already had seen her older six children sold away.[20]

> Know ye that I James Baker of the County of Ashe and State of North Carolina being moved by good and parental feeling toward my daughter Nancy Ray and her children do hereby give and bequeath to the said Nancy Ray one negro girl by the name of Violet age 14 years to labor for her and her children during the life time of my daughter . . . and after her death the said Negro girl, Violet I give with all her increase if any to the said children of the said Nancy Ray.
> —James Baker, November 24, 1840. (Reeves, *History of Early Ashe County*, 140)

In McDowell County, all sixteen children of Mary Barbour's mother Edith were sold as soon as they "got three years old."[21] Patsy Mitchner of Raleigh never saw her father, and her mother, sister, and brother were sold to a speculator and shipped to the "Mississippi bottoms in a box-car"; she never heard from her mother again.[22] Viney Baker, who never knew her father, lived with her mother on a plantation in present-day Durham County employing about one hundred slaves. One night she "lay down on de straw mattress wid my mammy, an' de nex' mo'nin' I waked up an' she wuz gone." A speculator had come in the night and "got my mammy widout wakin' me up." Baker was always "glad somehow" that she had been asleep so she did not have to see her mother taken away.[23]

Black Women and Marriage: "No Bossin'"

Because women and men both contributed economically to the slave family, the black man lacked the economic clout to force his wife into a subordinate position and they may have shared power more equally than did white couples. Most slaves married, lived in a nuclear family, with two parents and their children, and divided household tasks according to gender: women cooked, cleaned, and washed; men hunted, fished, and worked a garden plot (Fig. 4-3). A husband could use his skills to make life more endurable, but he could not use property to wield control over his wife, nor could he protect her from physical harm or sexual abuse.[24] And yet the slave family provided—away from the master's world—a home in which love, companionship, sexual gratification, respect, and understanding could exist. The selection of a good, dependable mate was probably the most significant decision a slave woman could make, and one she did not make lightly, as evidenced by the common practice of a woman's trying out several men before actually marrying one. For most slave couples, marriage was a serious, lifelong commitment broken only by separation or death. In 1833 George Pleasants, a slave living in Tennessee, wrote his wife, a slave in North Carolina, "I hope with godes helpe that I may be abble to rejoys with you on earth and . . . my dear wife I hope to meet you In paradise to prase god forever."[25]

FIGURE 4-3. David Hunter Strother (Porte Crayon), *Negroes at Home*. Depicted as "happy slaves" relaxing at home, most slaves did, in fact, live as nuclear families in their own quarters. The wife stands in the doorway to the cabin, the older woman sits to the side of the husband, and the children complete the extended family circle. (*Harper's New Monthly Magazine*, November 1859; courtesy of the North Carolina Division of Archives and History)

As in the eighteenth century, throughout North Carolina and the South generally, "jumping the broom" was the most common wedding ritual in the slave quarters. According to Willie Cozart, a former slave from Person County, owners agreed to slave marriages by simply telling the couple to "step over de broom." That was the "way" slaves married in those days, and poor "white folks" did the same.[26]

When Temple Herndon of Chatham County married Exter Durham, her owners gave the couple a big wedding. Temple was dressed all in white, the "weddin ma'ch played on de piano," the "tables filled wid flowers an' white candles," and such good food—"you ain't never seed de like of eats." Married by the African American preacher from the plantation church, the couple also observed the tradition of jumping over the broom to see which one of them would be the "boss" of their household. By jumping the broom, Temple and Exter enacted a ritual that many historians believe points to the more egalitarian nature of slave marriages. Each jumped backward over the broom, trying not to touch the handle. If they both could jump without "touchin' it," there would be "no bossin', dey jus' gwine be 'genial." After their wedding night in a cabin that "Mis' Betsy done all dressed up," Durham left the next day for his plantation in Orange County. He returned every Saturday night and stayed until Sunday evening.[27]

Temple and Exter had a "broad" marriage, meaning that they lived on different farms (as was true for almost a third of the marriages described in the slave narratives). Field slaves tended to marry one another, as did house servants. "Cross-marriages" between house and field slaves were more likely to involve couples who had different owners and lived on different plantations.[28] Broad marriages were clearly more advantageous for the woman's owner, who retained all the children the couple had, than for the man's. But broad marriages must have been an effective means for controlling a male slave, as the black man had to get his master's consent not only to marry, but also to leave his plantation to visit his wife. Some slave men were allowed to visit only on Christmas and other holidays; others were permitted to see their wives every Saturday evening or midweek.[29] Thus the mother was constantly present, whereas the father appeared on special occasions.

Free Blacks and Marriage

Slaves who married free blacks also endured the stresses of a broad marriage. Wake County slave Sarah Boon was tied to her plantation while her husband, a free black carpenter named James Boon, moved around looking for work. In 1850 Sarah was "lonesome" and asked her husband to "be sertin to answer [this] letter as soon as you get it." She begged him to return to the plantation, where the couple had a cabin, garden, and livestock. "Your hogs are running wild," she wrote, "and I fear they will all be destroyed." Despite her feelings of jealousy when she learned that he was seeing another woman, she wrote, "My Dear Husband, I freely forgive . . . I wish it to be banished from our memoreys and neve to be thought of again and let us take a new start." James Boon's lover, Mahala Buffalo, was a free black woman who could travel and marry him legally. According to the law, he and his slave wife, Sarah, were never married, and he owed her nothing.[30]

Slavery further limited the marital choices of free black women and men. An 1827 law forbade free blacks to migrate into the state; so in 1830 Thomas Day, a respected furniture maker and free black of considerable property in Caswell County, had to obtain a special dispensation from the General Assembly for his wife, Acquilla Wilson of Halifax, Virginia, a free woman of color whom he had married in 1829, to join him in North Carolina. Free black women had few potential marital partners, and, as a consequence, some of them married slaves or broke with custom and married cousins, uncles, and other relatives. Of the eighty free black families in Granville County, at least fifty shared one of the county's five oldest free black surnames for an extensive interlocking kinship network.[31]

There is an ongoing debate about the relative importance of black men and women in sustaining family, community, and culture. Some contemporary scholars have accentuated black men's historical significance in the family and minimized women's. Yet research by Deborah Gray White and Jacqueline Jones illustrates how crucial slave women were to the survival of the family and community. For example, in North Carolina between 1850 and 1860, more than 80 percent of the slaves who escaped were men. The majority of runaway slaves were young, between the ages of fifteen and thirty-five, which were prime childbearing years for women, who stayed put on the plantation tending to their families. It was not that fathers loved their children less, but rather that mothers were more necessary for their children's well-being, health, and safety. Most slave women chose family over freedom.[32]

FIGURE 4-4. *Backwoods family from the Turpentine forests, near Fayetteville*, engraving. The white woman, situated within the open doorway of the makeshift log cabin, holds a child in her arms while other children play nearby. (From Frederick Law Olmsted, *Our Slave States* [1856])

White Women and Family Life: "Most Intense Affection"

For white women in antebellum North Carolina, as for black women, family provided the primary source of strength and security and placed some of the greatest demands on emotions, energy, and health. With few legal rights, no financial assets (a woman's property became her husband's when they married), and very limited job opportunities, most women had to hope for a satisfactory marriage that afforded both financial security and emotional contentment. Once married, a woman's lot was cast with her husband (Fig. 4-4). If black women's sexual and reproductive activities were confined by slavery, then, as Victoria Bynum observed, white women's were limited by marriage. One young woman wrote, "Oh do you not regret" having to "renounce your childish pleasures, and amusements," to either become a "sedate old maid" or to have a "lord to rule over you and whose will you are obliged to obey." She wished, "Oh that I could be a girl forever."[33]

Two antebellum families suggest a range of possibilities in domestic life. When Phebe Caroline Jones Patterson of Caldwell County died of a stroke in 1869, her grieving husband Samuel wrote that she had been his "heart." Both members of prominent western Carolina families, the Pattersons had been married for forty-six years and enjoyed a fulfilling life on her family plantation, Palmyra (Fig. 4-5). Samuel Patterson recalled that he, their children, their grandchildren, kin, and friends had "clustered" around her with the "most intense affection"—indeed, "no man ever had a *better* wife."[34]

Rebecca Jane Haywood of Raleigh, on the other hand, found married life fatally stressful. While visiting her mother's family in Wilmington in 1834, she met and married Albert G. Hall, despite warnings about his poor character. The couple moved to isolated Washington County, and Rebecca's letters to her sister Eliza in Raleigh document her unhappy domestic circumstances. By 1836 Albert—an abusive womanizer—was in debt and taking his frustrations out on his wife. Rebecca, overwhelmed by responsibility for her three daughters, attributed her "hysteria" to the "constant din of children." In 1841 her second daughter, Alice, burned to death in an accident that Albert blamed on Rebecca, even though she had seared her hands trying to save her child. Her husband refused to let her have surgery, insisting that "he had been at more expense already than my hand was worth." Demoralized and dependent on drugs, Rebecca Hall died on August 16, 1842, barely thirty years old.[35]

Women who did not marry and have children were considered "deviant" and "peculiar." Single women were often objects of pity, even to themselves. Writing to her married sister in Orange County, Anna Bingham, of Redimon, Tennessee, revealed the loneliness she felt was her lot as a spinster: "Between [caring for] old *people*, puny *children*, and clothing all, besides attending to other things, we are busy

FIGURE 4-5. Anonymous, *Phebe Caroline Jones Patterson, husband Samuel F. Patterson, and son Rufus L. Patterson*, silhouette, Caldwell County, ca. 1842. The 1824 marriage of Phebe and Samuel joined two prominent western North Carolina families. (Courtesy of the North Carolina Museum of History)

old maids." With a mixture of resignation and despair, she added, "I think it is well for the world that some *can't help* being old maids." Unmarried white women had only a few options. If a relative had property, women of the gentry class might live as a dependent in that household, in return for which they were expected to be celibate and to assist with the housekeeping and child care. Poor women might head their own household, surviving on whatever wages they could make in a predominantly agrarian economy. Single women who did not value their reputations might pursue sexual relationships outside of marriage, but this risked losing all respectability.[36]

Courtship and White Women: "When Right Its the Woman Should Reighn"

Eligible marriage partners could be found at church, camp meetings, or school; rural social gatherings like corn huskings or quilting bees; during the "season" in town, at a spa, or at a beach resort; or at wedding parties or even funerals—all supervised situations bringing young people of similar backgrounds together, generally with the consent and participation of their parents (Fig. 4-6). Proximity played a major role in the choice of a mate, and in antebellum North Carolina it was common for a person to marry someone from a neighboring farm, the same county, the same church, or even the same family.[37]

Young women of the gentry were encouraged by their parents, their religion, and their schooling to express emotions in their letters. For these privileged women, courtship was a time to assert their sexual power; it even could be a game of sorts, in which the woman "kept score" of how many proposals she could elicit. As heiress Penelope Skinner of Edenton wrote her brother Tristim, "I refused three or four a week before last. So you see your little sister is not forgotten in the crowd." In the last weeks before graduating from her Hillsborough school in 1838, Penelope received additional proposals. "A lady told me the other day she expected I had more offers than any other Lady in the state. I said nothing but thought it very probable." In 1815 Ann Blount Shepard of New Bern exerted the leverage that courtship gave her. She agreed to marry Ebenezer Pettigrew only after he promised that if she lived at his Bonarva plantation on Lake Phelps in remote Tyrrell County for their first year of marriage—"the partner of his solitude for one year"—he would relocate to her more sociable hometown. Less than a month before their wedding, Ann casually informed Ebenezer that they might marry on May 10, unless she took "a whim" to attend her cousin's wedding instead.[38]

FIGURE 4-6. Porte Crayon, *Picnic and Party, Holtsburg Depot on the Yadkin River*, Davidson County. (*Harper's New Monthly Magazine*, August 1857; courtesy of the North Carolina Collection, University of North Carolina at Chapel Hill)

A woman's brief period of power ended once she married. Sarah Hawkins Polk wryly observed that her daughter, Susan, who was soon to be married, told her that her "Gentleman says he will never ask her to do anything against her will, all this is very clever before Marriage, when Right its the Woman should Reighn [*sic*]." But, after marriage, according to Mrs. Polk, "It's certainly Right the Husband should, as the Good Book says[,] be the 'Head of the Wife.' "[39]

As the century progressed, emotions were given greater weight in marital choices for gentry women, although wealth and property continued to be important. Edenton merchant James Norcum wanted his daughter Elizabeth to understand that no matter how "meritorious a man may be," he would not sanction a "connexion" with his daughter "to any man not in a condition to give [her] a comfortable & respectable support." Parents tried to influence their daughter's marital preferences, but at times they had to bow to her wishes, and increasingly they had less power.[40]

Three Courtship Stories

PENELOPE SKINNER

Penelope Skinner's father played a pivotal role in her courtship.[41] Nineteen-year-old Penelope, of a wealthy Chowan County family, could not find "anyone to suit my fancy" despite her numerous admirers while she was a student. After graduation in 1838, she became the mistress of her widowed father's plantation near Edenton. She enjoyed the freedom from school but missed her friends and the attentions of her many suitors. Within nine months, she had become melancholy, morose, and so lonely that, as she wrote her brother, "the next eligible offer I have I am gone; for anything would be better than this dull gloomy place." Her father expected her to "sit still" and listen quietly to the young gentlemen who came to court her, but Penelope envisioned a more active role.

She found three prospects: a Mr. French, about whom her father had strong reservations and whose character he charged her brother Tristim to investigate; an Edenton doctor named Thomas Warren, who had been enlisted as a character reference for French but had become a "constant visitor" at the Skinner home; and Mr. S, a man Penelope met at a resort. Although Mr. S was well liked by her friends, her father remained skeptical, and Penelope herself was irritated by being kept waiting for his letters. Eventually she conceded, "Well, I have discarded Mr. French." The "rascally" Mr. S was out, and Dr. Warren, who had "behaved so handsomely even when I had injured him so deeply," was her man. Scaling down her romantic expectations, Penelope began to value in Thomas qualities that would make for a "companionate"

> [Dr. Warren] is not rich, nor of great birth, but he is my equal and my *superior* in some respects. Everybody loves him. I have been anxious to marry a great man, one who would be distinguished in the world, more to please my Father than my myself. So I gave up on one whom I loved devotedly [Mr. French] for one whom I admired and who I knew would please my friends [Mr. S.] and now see what it has all come to. The most distinguished men do not make the happiest husbands by a great deal, neither does wealth for I have that and I am not happy.
> —Penelope Skinner to her brother Tristim.
> (Stowe, *Intimacy and Power*, 113)

marriage. Romantic love ceded to the prospect of a good match. In March 1840 Skinner married Warren, a good, honorable man, "devotedly attached to me and I to him so we can get along."

FRANCES WEBB

The courtship of Frances Webb was less worldly; she and her prospective husband were both deeply religious, and their evangelical fervor intensified and enriched their romantic aspirations.[42] Born in Halifax, Virginia, and educated there and in North Carolina, Frances had been taught by her parents that domestic duties were not to occupy all of her time and that it was her obligation to "train the minds and instruct the souls of others" when her school days were over. After schooling at home, she finished off her education with the Reverend D. C. Doak, a Presbyterian minister in Orange County. The Reverend Sidney Bumpass, a scholarly Methodist minister invited to attend her final examinations, was so charmed by her mastery of Greek culture that he immediately fell in love with her. As an itinerant minister, Sidney was in no position to press his suit, and Frances began teaching in Granville County.

Two years later, on December 20, 1841, Bumpass was appointed pastor of the Edenton Street Methodist Church in Raleigh, one of the few pastoral positions in North Carolina that provided a salary adequate for a married man. A few days later, he sent Frances a small New Testament with a hand-tooled white leather cover, in which he had marked several passages from the Second Epistle of John: "The elder to the elect Lady whom I love in Truth, now I beseech you, Lady, not as though I wrote a new commandment to you but one we had from the beginning, that we love one another. Having many things to say to you, I would not write with pen and ink but trust to come unto you and speak face to face, that our joy may be full." By Christmas, he had spoken to her parents and Frances had accepted his proposal. The following December Webb and Bumpass—she, twenty-two years old, and he, ten years her senior—were married by Mr. Doak. Frances Webb had found a mate suitably religious, moral, committed, intelligent, and passionate.

BESSIE LACY

Bessie Lacy and Thomas Dewey had a restrained yet emotionally charged courtship conducted mainly through correspondence.[43] Bessie, the daughter of a Presbyterian minister, grew up in a loving, demonstrative Evangelical Christian family in Raleigh; Thomas, a Guilford County planter's son, had ambitions for local public office. By 1851, when Thomas, the brother of a classmate of Bessie's, asked if they could correspond, Bessie had attended Edgeworth Female Academy in Greensboro and was teaching there. At first, she wrote politely, but eventually she became more intimate and revealing about her personal feelings and daily routines, even flirtatious, familiar, and teasing.

After they decided to marry and the day of their wedding approached, Bessie expressed an uneasiness about Dewey as a lifelong companion. Both she and Thomas were given to experiencing emotional shifts, but she more than he. She regressed into deferential behavior and asked him to forgive her "for all she does wrong," for being "a wicked child." Alternatively she became cool, assertive, direct. She expected him at the time "appointed"; he should "never, never again submit" to one of his "curious fits." Bessie wrote that if he was not in a good humor, she would "make" him "go straight home again, so he had better practice a smile all day." Perhaps she realized that courtship was one game, but marriage was another, with more daunting rules and roles. With foreboding, Bessie left the romantic harbor of courtship for the unknown shore of marriage.

Marriage and White Women: "I Am a Very Happy Wife"

What Bessie Lacy, Frances Webb, Penelope Skinner, and many young women of their generation and education envisioned was a marriage marked by mutual affection that assured intimate companionship instead of patriarchal authority. And some couples did seem to achieve this. Ann and Ebenezer Pettigrew, for example, reveal an easy reciprocity and affection in the letters written early in their marriage when they had to live apart for awhile. Ebenezer asked Ann to excuse his bad letter writing and to "view it with the eye of a wife," presumably with tolerance and understanding. Ann

FIGURE 4-7. *Wedding dress belonging to Anne Ruffin Cameron*, Orange County, 1832. Eighteen-year-old Anne Ruffin, a daughter of Chief Justice Thomas Ruffin of the state supreme court, wore this dress at her wedding to Paul Cameron, scion of one of North Carolina's largest plantation complexes, Fairntosh. (Courtesy of the North Carolina Museum of History)

noted that, if they lived together a "hundred years," at the end of that time they would be more "sincerely attached than in the commencement of our love and friendship."[44]

Likewise, companionship seemed to exist between John Herritage Bryan, a lawyer and congressman, and Mary Shepherd Bryan, a sister of Ann Shepherd Pettigrew. Before their marriage, John wrote Mary a letter in which he discussed political matters, explaining, "You see I am disposed to make you somewhat of a politician but every wife ought to know something about and take an interest in her husband's business & concerns." Mary was educated enough to meet his expectations, and she had an expectation of her own, that he take religion seriously. One of her friends assessed John's qualities as a husband: "Your *hearts chosen* unites all that is estimable & excellent, one thing only [is] wanting to render him all I could desire for you, and I trust ere long, with the man of talents & worth will be added the Christian."[45]

Most girls living in North Carolina were taught that marriage and motherhood were their natural destiny. But the shape their family lives would take was changing, even in rural areas. Two factors may have contributed to a companionate marital relationship: genteel girls' education was similar to that of boys of their class, and evangelical religion's emphasis on love, emotion, and connectedness led many women to seek a mutual intimacy in marriage (Fig. 4-7). The traditional view of the family as patriarchal and functional, with the wife giving unquestioning deference to her husband, slowly was being replaced by newer ideas of a family being more companionable, affectionate, and emotionally open (Fig. 4-8). Yet in most families, the husband had authority and seldom shared his power, a behavior reinforced by the younger age at which southern white women tended to marry—between eighteen and twenty (most women in the Northeast did not marry before age twenty-four).[46]

We do not know how happy Penelope Skinner was in her marriage (she died shortly afterward, and Dr. Warren inherited her fortune and made another auspicious match). Frances Webb's mission-oriented approach to life and sense of herself as a helpmate were realized in her marriage. After a year in Raleigh, she and her clergyman husband traveled together around the state to "build up" congregations of poorer churches, and she worked as a teacher to supplement

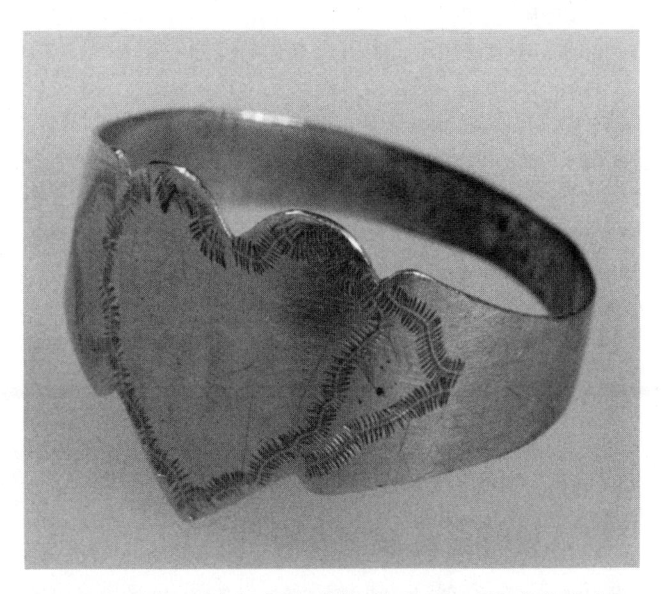

FIGURE 4-8. *Ring made by Nathaniel Vogler for Anna Maria Fischel*, for their wedding in December 1827, Forsyth County. Gold. (Courtesy of the Collection of Old Salem, Winston-Salem)

his salary. Eventually he left active ministry to pursue a dream they both shared—to publish a newspaper for the Methodists in North Carolina. Bessie Lacy also found deep satisfaction in her new role as wife and mother and enjoyed intimacy with her husband, for whom she served as "blanket saver" in bed. They moved to Charlotte, and she wrote to him with conviction, "I am a very happy wife, Tom, I assure you."[47]

Laws and Marriage: "She Knew When She Married Him"

But marriage did not ensure happiness. A North Carolina woman noted that "one does not always have a great deal of good humor to spare after marriage." Few North Carolinians tried to terminate their marriages legally, but more women than men sought divorces.[48] Divorce was almost impossible to obtain and carried both social stigma and economic hardship. Rebecca Haywood Hall and many women like her stayed in unhappy, violent, or dangerous marriages. A husband was legally obligated to provide his wife with food, housing, and clothing in a manner consistent with his economic situation—and he was well within his legal rights to "chastise his wife," so long as his weapon was "not thicker than his little finger."[49]

Until 1814 only the General Assembly could grant a divorce, a lengthy process in which each petition was considered and then debated by legislators. Impotence, adultery, and cruel abuse were the legal grounds for divorce (a divorced woman who had been cruelly abused was entitled to a third of her husband's annual income). Hundreds of divorce petitions poured in, but few were granted: one out of twenty petitions in 1810, four out of twenty-two in 1813. In 1814 the superior courts were given jurisdiction for divorce, although a decree was still not final until ratified by the General Assembly. This time-consuming and expensive practice continued until 1827, when the courts assumed sole authority. As chief justice from 1833 to 1852, Thomas Ruffin never granted a divorce for adultery or spousal abuse.[50]

A woman needed to protect herself and her property before she married, as after marriage the law was of little help. "If my advice would avail anything; it would be offered in the five words 'take care of your self,' " Paul Cameron advised his sister, Margaret, before her marriage at forty-two to George Mordecai. Cameron conceded, "It may be that a manly and generous spirit will secure to you your own—this is but justice to *you* considering the age and circumstances of the contracting parties." Margaret protected her estate with a marriage contract (thereby securing it for the Cameron family).[51]

For women without a prenuptial agreement, North Carolina law was clear—they had no rights. As Chief Justice John Louis Taylor stated in 1827: "It may be a hardship for a married woman who brings a fortune to her husband, to find herself and her children reduced to poverty; but she knew when she married him, that the law gave him an absolute property in all her personal estate." Taylor also noted that such adversity might have been avoided. By not making a prenuptial settlement, the wife "agreed to share his fortune, be it prosperous or adverse." In 1848 the law changed slightly: any income from property set aside for a married woman now was reserved for her sole use and benefit.[52]

At issue were the individual rights of a woman for her person and property against the interests of the state to preserve the patriarchal family and slaveholding. Women were considered the property of their husbands under common law, hence men's custodial role that could include physical punishment. Divorce was viewed not as a private affair between two people, but as an offense against public order. The state supreme court was divided as to how women's rights intersected with society's interests. Justice Richmond Pearson believed that the traditional family was weakened when women were granted greater control over their own property. Justice Thomas Ruffin saw women's right to control their own property as part of an individual family's power to secure its wealth, whomever their daughter chose as a husband.[53]

Not until 1868, when a coalition of black and white Republican legislators drafted a new constitution under Radical Reconstruction so North Carolina could reenter the Union, was there a dramatic change in women's rights. At that time, married women were recognized as individuals separate from their husbands and entitled to control their own property. Even so, they needed their husbands' written permission to sell their own property, a provision that remained in effect until 1964.[54]

Unmarried Women and the Law

Unmarried women were also disadvantaged under North Carolina law, but in different ways. Misbehavior was the most common legal charge leveled against women, and mostly against unmarried women, especially poor white and free black women who lacked a husband's protection. Laws against prostitution and fornication reflected society's interest in controlling women's sexuality and restricting racial mixing; they were applied more often to poor white women intimate with free black men, or free black women involved with slaves, than to black women and white men.[55]

Unmarried mothers, mostly poor white and free black women at the bottom of the social and economic ladder, were penalized by laws that allowed the state to take their children away from them. The statutes revealed a concern that an unmarried woman could not support her children and that the community should not be stuck with that responsibility. In 1810, for instance, an irate resident of the Cross Creek community in Wake County advertised for the whereabouts of one Betsy Fowler, who had arrived in town, given birth, and "absconded" three weeks later: "she could be compelled to take and maintain her child." Unmarried mothers who had money did not pose the same financial burden to the community and therefore did not generally lose their children. As in the eighteenth century, a father was required to support his children, and the mother (and midwife, if she knew) was legally bound to identify him. Justice Frederick Nash expressed society's viewpoint in 1854, when he wrote: "The community says to the marauder, you have no right to amuse yourself at the public expense; if we can catch you we will not punish you, but will compel you to do that which every principle of honor, justice, and humanity binds you to do."[56]

FIGURE 4-9. *Mary Eliza Battle (later, Dancy Pittman)*, miniature, Edgecombe County, ca. 1836. Seven years old when her portrait was painted, Mary Eliza had three brothers and two sisters and lived on Cool Springs plantation between Rocky Mount and Tarboro. (Private collection)

Motherhood and White Women: "Our Children Are Heavens Best Gift"

In North Carolina, where family was the center of economic and social life, being a mother was an important occupation. "I know well with whom we confide *our greatest treasures*—and our children are Heavens best gifts," wrote Temperance Williams, the new mother of a sixth child (and eventually, of nine).[57] Her fervent sentiments reflect an important shift occurring during the antebellum period, especially among the gentry, toward what we call today a child-centered family (Plate 3). Increasingly mothers and fathers lavished attention, love, and gifts on their children; worried about their health, education, and well-being; and reared them to take their place in the next generation (Figs. 4-9, 4-10, 4-11).[58]

Southern society "encouraged and celebrated maternal focus," writes Sally McMillen in *Motherhood in the Old South*, even though bearing children was dangerous and life-threatening. "I often think of the approaching critical period—its sufferings and its dangers," wrote Frances Webb Bumpass in her journal. She hoped to "be prepared for the event" but pondered, "What if death should come!" In Salisbury, as Mary Henderson's time to deliver came closer, she had her best clothes washed and starched, just in case, for her funeral.[59]

Birth control was generally not an alternative. Laura Lenoir Norwood of Hillsborough may typify many women with her remark, "I often feel startled at the thought of the size which my own family is attaining so rapidly."[60] The regularity with which most women had babies suggests that they either knew little about birth control or that they and their husbands found it unacceptable. North Carolina brigadier general William Dorsey Pender wrote his wife Fanny after one of her visits in 1862, "My mind was very much relieved to hear that you were not as I had imagined. . . . If you do not want children you will have to remain away from me, and hereafter when you come to me I shall know you want another baby."[61]

That widowers frequently married younger women reinforced the pattern of extended childbearing and contributed to the large size of southern families. Eliza Eagles Williams of Wilmington was seventeen when she married forty-two-year-old widower and state treasurer John Haywood of Raleigh. During their twenty-year marriage, she gave birth to twelve children. Her oldest daughter Betsy attributed her mother's ill health and "great and protracted sufferings . . . in a great measure to her becoming a mother early in life." Eliza had four children within the first five years of marriage. Shortly after the fourth child was born—"the Sunday after

FIGURE 4-10. Polly Johnston Battle, *Doll belonging to her daughter, Laura Battle Phillips*, Edgecombe County, ca. 1828. Polly made this doll for the last born of her twelve children, four-year-old Laura. Dressed in a green and white striped dress and white pantalets, Laura's doll is more elegant than the doll found in the slave quarters at Stagville (Fig. 4-2 above), but both served as models in mothering for their young owners. (Courtesy of the North Carolina Museum of History)

my breast was lanced"—she was expected by her husband to entertain thirty men at dinner over several nights until they had invited every member of the General Assembly. A year later, in 1804, she had a fifth child who almost died, after which she "unexpectedly fainted quite away, neither breathe nor pulse" and only roused herself to call out in a "Feeble voice . . . for God's Sake help me—so many little children." After a sixth child the following year, her mother Jane Williams wrote from Wilmington. Although Mrs. Williams referred to her daughter's frequent pregnancies in a discreet manner, her meaning is clear: "let me advise that Mr. Haywood talk less to you than he generally does directly after [your confinement begins]. I am well aware that his tenderness and joy impels him to it but to answer him as loud as you are obliged to do, is to much in yr exhausted state."[62]

Although doctors promoted their skills over those of midwives, their entry into obstetrics did not result in a corresponding decrease in mortality rates between 1800 and 1860. Infection was the primary cause of death, and in 1850 one in twenty-five white southern women died from childbirth—about twice as many as in the Northeast. Gentry women had higher death rates after childbirth than slave women and white farm women. In 1830 Ann Blount Pettigrew bled to death during the birth of her ninth child, and her husband Ebenezer, who was present, wrote an excruciating account of the ordeal for their children. The midwife, Mrs. Brickhouse, was unable to dislodge the placenta. Ann cried out, "O, Mrs. Brickhouse, you will kill me." In those "two efforts," wrote Ebenezer, "my dear Nancy" (as he called her) suffered "exceedingly and frequently exclaimed, 'O I shall die, send for the doctor.'" She died in her husband's arms.[63]

Pregnant women were given large doses of medicine by doctors who did not consider (or know) the potential dangers to either mother or infant. On isolated Fairntosh plantation in Orange County, Anne Ruffin Cameron, daughter of Justice Thomas Ruffin and wife of planter Paul Cameron, had three children in three years. She took morphine and laudanum to relieve headaches caused by malaria, an illness to which pregnant women were particularly susceptible. Enduring twelve pregnancies, difficult deliveries, sick children, and her son's death, Anne became so dependent on morphine and opium that she sometimes could not get out of bed or fulfill her domestic duties. Laura Norwood of Hillsborough took laudanum during her pregnancy, which alleviated her "entirely of pain but [made her] feel sick and miserably stupid today, as it always does."[64]

Women tended to put their baby's birth in the hands of God and give thanks for surviving childbirth. Of the more than 16,500 babies, black and white, born in North Carolina in 1850, one in six died before the first birthday, and more than one in four died before the age of five.[65] Mary Bethel, a Methodist minister's daughter, felt that "The Lord was with me at the birth of the child [her third] and gave me a safe and speedy delivery, thanks and praise to his holy name, he is my best friend, he has been with me in many trials." But when one of her children died, the deeply religious Bethel wrote: "Sometimes her remarks were so sweet and sensible, I was lead [*sic*] to exclaim, 'We must not love her too much, the Lord might take her.'" Salisbury's Mary Henderson buried five children but was resigned: "God doeth all things well. He gave and he surely had the right to take." With two surviving

FIGURE 4-11. *"Little Fanny" paper doll*, 1813. Along with homemade toys, manufactured playthings such as "The History of Little Fanny," a precursor of paper dolls, appeared in the early 1800s. Little Fanny came with a varied wardrobe, from beggar's rags to Empire gown. (Courtesy of the North Carolina Museum of History)

children, however, Henderson worried, "thinking it may be God's good pleasure to recall them and shuddering at the bare idea." Frances Webb Bumpass, sustained by her Methodist faith, wrote in 1844 on the birth of her first child: "Through the mercy and kindness of the Lord, my life has been prolonged, my suffering comparatively light, and my health soon restored and I am blessed with a little daughter."[66]

Widowhood

Seven years later, in December 1851, the death of the Reverend Sidney Bumpass, nine years after their marriage, thrust Frances Webb Bumpass into the role of widow, single mother of two daughters, and newspaper editor and publisher in a social climate that discouraged respectable women from engaging in any activity outside the home. Her husband had died shortly after beginning publication of a Methodist newspaper, the *Weekly Message*, in Greensboro. In deference to public disapproval of a woman's running a business, Mrs. Bumpass initially retained her husband's male manager. But he did so poorly that she took charge in 1852 and moved the presses to her house on South Mendenhall Street so she could perform her family duties more easily and avoid the taboo against ladies going downtown to work. With the assistance of servants, her daughters, and Greensborough Female College students, she ran the press for twenty years in her home (also a boardinghouse), producing one paper every week, straight through the Civil War and for six years afterward.[67]

The legal status of nineteenth-century women made widowhood particularly difficult unless the husband's will provided for the widow and children (Fig. 4-12). Mary McDonough Johnson, of Raleigh, left destitute with two sons (one of whom was the future president Andrew Johnson) on her husband's death, acquired a loom and started a spinning and weaving business; she became known as "Polly the Weaver." The wife of artist and teacher Jacob Marling, Louisa Marling had given private art lessons in her Raleigh home, but widowhood forced her to support herself by her sewing; in 1840 she supplied the candle shades for the chandeliers in the new capitol building in Raleigh. When the silversmith husband of the New Bern milliner Madame Huau died, her millinery was considered part of his estate and put up for sale in 1818 along

FIGURE 4-12. *Mary Eliza Battle Dancy and husband William F. Dancy*, Edgecombe County, 1858. Within two years of her wedding, Mary Eliza Battle of Cool Springs plantation—here standing beside William, her arms resting gently on his shoulder in a gesture of intimacy and affection—was widowed. She married her second husband, physician Dr. Newsom Jones Pittman, in 1868, after first securing her property, either at her own initiative or through her husband's generosity. Both of Mary Eliza's husbands had proposed marriage to her, been turned down, married other women who bore children and then died, and eventually had their proposals accepted by her. Dancy's two children from his first marriage accompanied Mary Eliza and him on their honeymoon, and Pittman delivered both of her Dancy children, including a son born a few months after his father's death. (Courtesy of the North Carolina Museum of History)

with his silversmith tools. The common-law principle that the wife's property was subsumed within that of the husband's applied, even though she had been engaged in a commercial activity distinct from that of her husband (Fig. 4-13).[68]

Young Women and Education: "A Dangerous Step"

In 1845 thirteen-year-old Bessie Lacy left her Raleigh home to attend Edgeworth Female Seminary in Greensboro. Although her father, the Reverend Drury Lacy, would miss her, he was confident that she would progress well in her studies. He worried, however, about her "disposition" and "morals": "It is a dangerous step to send any girl from *home*; its sacred influence keeps them from much harm." Williana Lacy also missed her daughter but understood the importance of formal schooling in developing academic and social skills. She knew that if Bessie had stayed at home, learning only what suited their "convenience" or when their "various avocations might leave an inch or two of the time to devote to [it] . . . this would not do for one who was growing up to young womanhood."[69]

> As women exercise a powerful influence in the domestic circle, and consequently in society, a proper education alone can enable her to exert this influence in the promotion of virtue and happiness.
>
> —Susan Nye Hutchison. (Hutchison, *Prospectus of the Raleigh Academy and Mrs. Hutchison's View of Female Education* [Raleigh: Mr. White, Printer, 1835], 5, as cited in Pope, "Preparation for Pedestals," 20)

Bessie Lacy and the privileged young women who attended Edgeworth, the Raleigh Female Academy, and other female schools across the state were among the first to benefit from changing attitudes toward educating women in the

FIGURE 4-13. Daniel Welfare, *Elizabeth Reuz and son, Samuel Zacharias Reuz*, Forsyth County, ca. 1825. Elizabeth Reuz was widowed shortly after this portrait (and a companion portrait of her husband Matthew, tavernkeeper and proprietor of Salem's Toy Shop) was painted. She secured her husband's business for her son. (Courtesy of the Collection of the Wachovia Historical Society, Winston-Salem)

FIGURE 4-14. Jacob Marling, *The Crowning of Flora: Raleigh Female Academy*, oil on canvas, Wake County, 1816. This painting provides a glimpse into the world of female education in Federal period North Carolina. The culmination of the academic year was commencement, when visitors were invited to attend the girls' examinations and to view their accomplishments in music and art. The young ladies, dressed in their best white gowns (in the gauzy high-waisted Empire fashion), have gathered under a shady grove of trees to crown the May queen. The female school experience encouraged intense friendships and fervent competition, both of which reached their peak in the ritual of the May Day festivities. Several children, black and white, stand—by race or age—on the margins of the ritual. (Courtesy of The Chrysler Museum, Norfolk, Virginia; gift of Edgar William and Bernice Chrysler Garbisch, 80.181.20)

nineteenth-century South (Fig. 4-14).[70] Although the rhetoric varied, the arguments supporting female education centered on a woman's special nature and her distinct role in the family as wife and mother. In 1811 less than a third of the women in Edgecombe County could write their names. By 1860 four out of five white women and one of every two free black women in the state were literate.[71]

This remarkable change was made possible by two developments—a private education system geared to the gentry and a free education system of common schools—both of which educated girls and boys. As Virginian Maria Campbell wrote in 1819 to her cousin, Mary Hume, a student at Salem Academy in Forsyth County: "In the days of our forefathers it was considered only necessary to learn a female to read the Bible—the ballance of her time was spent in domestic employments. They, to be sure, were very necessary. But why should a whole life be thus spent[?] . . . Things are happily taking a change. Daughters as well as sons are now thought of by the fond parent. Education is considered equally their due."[72]

Campbell's optimism was fueled by her own educational experience, which sustained her during the years she spent in isolation on her husband's plantations (she was childless, and he was frequently away on business). Her confidence reflected her gentry class perspective. Education traditionally served the interests of the upper class, maintaining that group's status and ensuring its place in public affairs. During the antebellum period, planters and merchants increasingly regarded their daughters' formal education as important as

The father of the family is abroad—a great part of *his* life is spent *from home*. *The Mother* of the family must give character to its interior government.
—William Hooper, President of Wake Forest College. (Hooper, *Address on Female Education, Delivered before the Sedgewick Female Seminary, February 27, 1847* [Raleigh: Weston R. Gales, 1848], 17, as cited in Pope, "Preparation for Pedestals," 19)

that of their sons. It may have been even more important, because formal schooling gave a young woman the status and accomplishments to "marry well."

As one of the few female schools in the state before 1820, Salem Academy in Forsyth County attained a premiere position (Fig. 4-15). In 1804, in response to local farmers' interest in educating their daughters, the Moravians expanded their educational programs to include a boarding school. By 1808 the school had about 40 students a term, by 1835 about 120, and by the 1850s more than 200, some from as far away as Texas and California. Salem Academy became so popular (and overcrowded) that in 1818 parents were urged not to try to enroll their daughters. Milton Academy, which opened in Caswell County in 1819, capitalized on this development: it proudly claimed that its curriculum had been planned in consultation with the superintendent of Salem Academy and was suitably "religious" and "ornamental" to prepare young girls "to be wives and mothers of the community" (Fig.4-16).[73]

Between 1820 and 1860 almost three hundred academies, many exclusively female, were established across the state. Practically every county had one, and Wake County had twelve. In Greensboro the New Garden Boarding School (later Guilford College) was established by Quakers in 1837; Greensborough Female College, by Methodists in 1838; and Edgeworth Female Seminary, by Governor John Motley Morehead to educate his daughters. St. Mary's School was founded by Episcopalians in 1842 on the campus of the former Episcopal School for Boys in Raleigh, with the support of Bishop Levi Silliman Ives and planter-banker Duncan Cameron. The Charlotte Female Institute (later Queens College), the Burwell Female School in Hillsborough, and the Mordecai Female Academy in Warrenton were other substantial institutions. But most female academies had a shaky existence, and many closed after a term or two. Still the number of female schools doubled in the 1840s and increased even more with the growth in the 1850s of denominational schools, more than two-thirds Baptist or Methodist. A student at the Burwell Female School remarked that, at least in Hillsborough, "if the coming generation are not all able to spell, read, and write, it will not be because there are no schools in the place."[74]

Once at school, young women were immersed in a social and intellectual world far different from what they had experienced at home (Fig. 4-17). Discipline, routine, manners, morals, and piety were watchwords. Some historians suggest that the girls' course of study centered around the ornamentals of needlework, art, and music, but the evidence from advertisements, school catalogs, and letters indicates that useful subjects were at the heart of the curriculum.[75] In 1823 William Polk advised his daughter Mary, a Salem Academy student, that she should not neglect her piano or harp, or her French, but they were "secondary accomplishments, tho' highly to be appreciated." In 1841 M. C. Stephens advised his granddaughter, Mary Ann Primrose, a Burwell School pupil, to emphasize academic subjects. He observed: "Nothing is so insipid as some young ladies I have seen, they have been asked to sing and play on some instrument or to exhibit their drawings to the visitors after doing which they retired to their seats and sit mumchanced until some dandy of a beau sidles up to them and talks of the weather or last ball or some such frivolities." Stephens felt that the minds of men and women were "equally vigorous," but that men have engaged "into a kind of conspiracy to keep women in the background—a prejudice has been excited against their improvement beyond a certain limit." He encouraged Mary Ann to develop her intellectual capabilities and not to be intimidated if "fools" called her a "blue stocking."[76]

Parental expectations were frequently high and exerted pressure on the young woman (Plate 4). Mary Blount Bryan of New Bern wrote her daughter Charlotte, who was attending school in Philadelphia, many letters reminding her that she should avail herself of all the advantages of her situation—converse in French, practice her music, read good books to "improve both heart and mind"—otherwise "it was not worth the expense of sending you there." She was concerned that Charlotte made little mention of practicing her music: "musical education was acquired by a great deal of application & money," and Charlotte must not neglect it. Her daughter should also "write oftener."[77]

School discipline was strict, intended to alleviate parental concern about daughters' welfare and to protect their morals. The different attitudes toward discipline in male and female schools underscore the different expectations for each sex. Boys' schools were plagued by rowdy and insubordinate pupils. Their undisciplined behavior reflected the gentry code of honor according to which males were expected to be

TERMS AND CONDITIONS
OF THE
BOARDING SCHOOL
FOR
FEMALE EDUCATION
IN
SALEM, N. C.

THE age of admittance of pupils is between 8 and 12 years. The age of 15 terminates their ſtay in the School: unleſs parents chooſe, to order their return home ſooner, or their deportment ſhould be ſuch, as not to admit their continuance in the School.

Every attention is paid to the health and morals of the pupils.

The branches taught are: Reading, Grammar, Writing, Arithmetic, Hiſtory, Geography, (German if deſired), plain Needlework, &c. Muſic and fine Needlework, including Drawing are two extra branches, in which inſtruction is given, if expreſsly deſired.

Entrance money is 5 Dollars

The quarterly expence for board and tuition, bedding included, is at preſent 20 Dollars, to be advanced every quarter. Waſhing is a ſeparate charge, viz. 2 Dollars per quarter for pupils under 12 years, and 4 Dollars for thoſe above that age. For inſtruction in Muſic and fine Needlework, each 2 Dollars per quarter. Cloathing, medecine, books, paper and other contingent expences are charged quarterly.

Punctual payment of the bills is expected, and a ſettlement in full at the removal of children.

The amount of the yearly expences collectively may be calculated at the rate of between 170 and 180 Dollars, more or leſs.

Parents may either, if they have it convenient, furniſh the articles of cloathing, or the pupils may be found here.

Every article of cloathing, they bring along, ſhould be marked, ſo as to ſtand waſhing.

The dreſs to be decent, avoiding extravagance.

Applications are to be made in writing, addreſſed to the Revd. Saml. Kramsch the preſent Inſpector of the Seminary at Salem, N. C.; informing him of the age, name and character of the child, the name and place of reſidence of the parents, guardians, &c. and it is requeſted, that no child may be brought or ſent without leave obtained from him in writing, appointing the time of admittance. It is deſirable, that ſuch as are applied for, ſhould have had the ſmall or kine pox and meaſles.

Parents and guardians &c. may reſt aſſured, that the underſigned will endeavour to merit their confidence by paying the moſt faithful attention to the education of pupils intruſted to his care.

Salem, N. C.
Apr. 5? 1806

Samuel Kramsch

FIGURE 4-15. *Terms and Conditions of the Boarding School for Female Education in Salem*, 1806. (Courtesy of Salem College, Winston-Salem)

FIGURE 4-16. Matilda Amalia Winkler (attributed), *Mourning Embroidery*, silk, crepe, chenille, ribbon, watercolor, ink, and paper on silk, Forsyth County, 1831. Five years after her brother Carl's death in 1826, sixteen-year-old Matilda Amalia Winkler made an embroidery portraying the family's grief. Using a variety of stitches to create dimensional shading, she depicted herself, her brother Ludwig, and sister Henrietta mourning at their older brother's tomb, to which is attached a poem: "Slow waves the Willow / O'er the Stone That points / where sleeps a Brother dear / Oft have I sought / the spot alone / to shed at ease / the solitary tear." She combined familiar mourning symbols of tomb, urn, and weeping willow trees with the more specifically Moravian crepe wreath and flower garland. (Courtesy of the Collection of Old Salem, Winston-Salem)

manly and to dominate their social inferiors—even, in this case, their teachers.[78]

Girls, on the other hand, were expected to be well behaved. Rules and regulations, exercise, and religious instruction served to control them at school and to prepare them for their future roles as wives and mothers. The last of the thirty-nine rules in Salem Academy's Code of Conduct is clear: The students were to exercise "prudence and economy" with pocket money, to waste nothing, and to put their clothes and everything else properly in its place, as "this will teach you also to husband your time and will be the means of your coming into the very important habit of economy and frugality, which is such an essential requisite for your sex for housekeeping." Extravagant dress was discouraged at most female academies. Margaret Burwell, owner and principal of the Hillsborough school, took that rule seriously and wrote to her daughter Fanny: "We have heard of three new scholars—two from Person and one from Granville. They are from the counties that *love dress* and the first thing I anticipate is the sight of a gold pencil hanging around the neck and a locket alongside. . . . I'll soon straighten the rest." St. Mary's eighteen rules emphasized piety, punctuality, consideration, obedience, frugality, and silence—"no romping, running, dancing." Girls were expected to exercise regularly, apparently by means of daily walks. "Works of fiction" were to be read only on Saturdays, and then only after all other duties were done, including a full two hours spent "at her needle" (Plate 5).[79]

These young women were the first generation of females for whom higher education was considered "equally their due." Being educated produced a major change in women's expectations and perspectives and affected both their domestic relations and their relationship to public life. An educated woman could reasonably expect a more companionate marriage, because she knew about more than simply how to keep house or direct servants and could relate more as an equal to her similarly educated husband on a variety of topics—from politics to literature. Furthermore, many girls who were taught piety and compassion at school became women who worked tirelessly for their church and community (Fig. 4-18).[80]

Southern academies survived longer than similar northern institutions. By 1870 female academies had been superseded by other institutions of higher learning that trained a broader range of women—some to enter the workforce as teachers and secretaries, others to influence the public sphere through good works and welfare. Salem, St. Mary's, Peace, Guilford, and Queens endured, but most others ceased to be "useful" and vanished (Fig. 4-19).

Public Education for Females

The number of North Carolinians who attended academies was about 25 percent of all those who received any education. The others attended common schools. The establishment of public schools in 1839 led to an explosion in students, from fewer than 3,000 enrolled in schools of any type in that year to 40,000 in the public system in 1853. Despite strong opposition to coeducation beyond the primary grades, girls were schooled along with boys.[81]

Education historically had been the province of the church and the powerful, but Republican-era ideology supported public education as a function of government—educated citizens make better voters and maintain a stable social order. Such thinking had been hard to sell in rural North Carolina, where fear of government "interference"

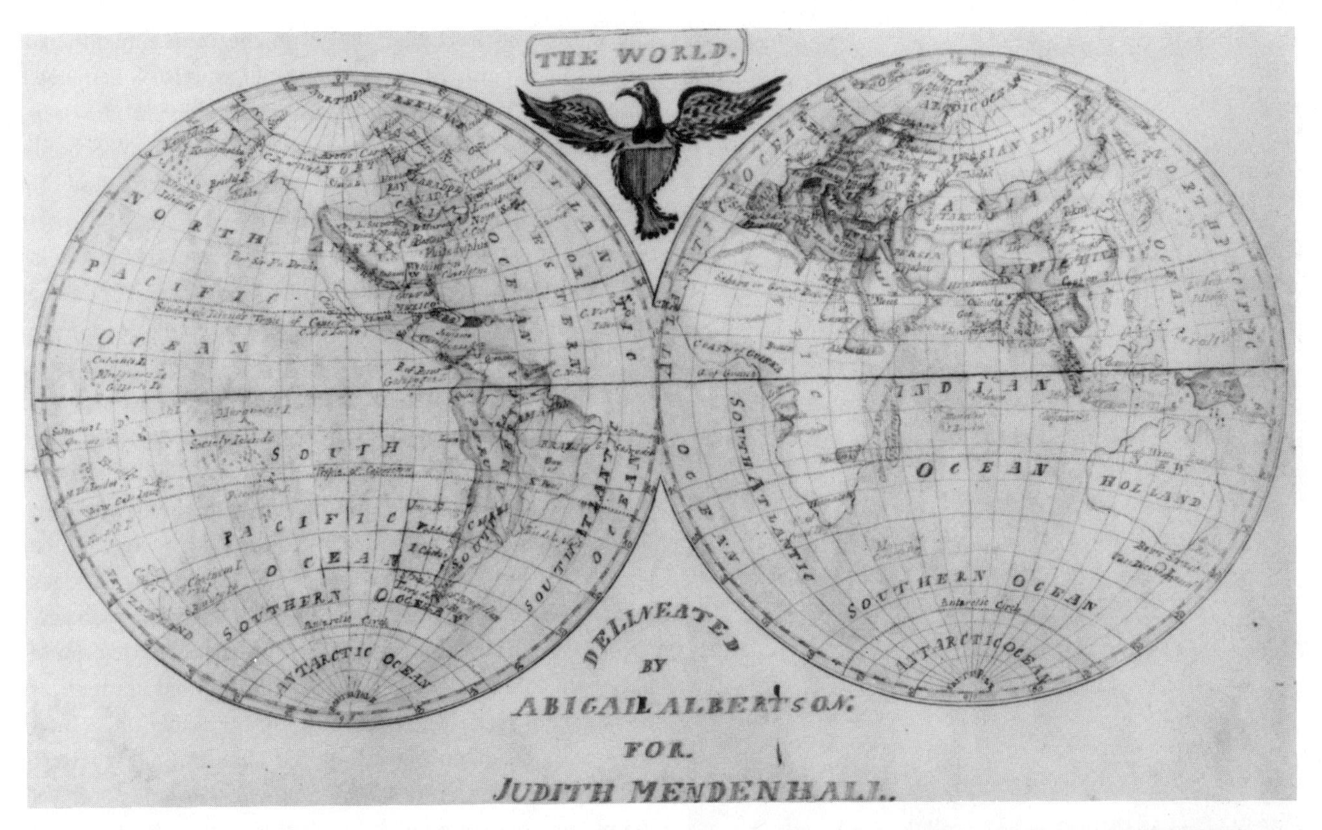

FIGURE 4-17. *The World Delineated by Abigail Albertson for Judith Mendenhall*, watercolor, Guilford County, 1817. Young women thrived in the stimulating world of academies. They developed close friendships and crushes on their classmates and teachers and participated in the rituals of friendship, such as telling secrets or exchanging special presents. (Courtesy of the Greensboro Historical Museum)

and higher taxes was strong, and anything free bore the stigma of being only for the poor. Despite the belief of the first state superintendent of common schools, Calvin Wiley, that establishing a system of public schools was a "vast and sublime moral obligation," resistance to public or "free" education was so intense that it took years of persuasion before a limited public school system was established. Starting in 1839 counties could apply for state funds, but the building of schoolhouses depended on private money. Teachers were scarce, terms lasted only three to four months, and equipment and textbooks varied greatly among schools. Just getting to school was difficult for rural children, and attendance was sporadic and irregular. Against these odds, by 1860 North Carolina had the best public school system in the South.[82]

Many daughters of farmers, whose families were the majority in North Carolina, may have yearned for schooling; however, they had little leisure time, and their labor was considered indispensable in the household. Many critics also believed that formal schooling did not prepare farm girls for their station in life. Farm periodicals of the time express a bias against higher education for rural young women. They should know how to wash, iron, cook, and sew—but be "ignorant of all that boarding schools can teach."[83]

In 1843 young farm women contemplating education beyond their station were cautioned, "It does not look well for farmers' daughters to be always talking about piano playing and the trilling of Signor Cantanini; while they do not know of what butter is made, and suppose a cow a rhinoceros." Behind the discussions about farmers' daughters' education lurked the concern that if the young girls used their minds, they might not be content to cook and clean. Although some young women did benefit from the limited public education that became available to all white North Carolinians in the 1840s, more boys than girls attended school. Higher education remained a luxury for daughters of the gentry.[84]

A young lady, with ever so fashionable education *if she possessed no knowledge of the kitchen, and the different departments of house-keeping*, however well she might show off in the parlour or drawing room, would make a farmer a very unsuitable companion."

—"Farmers' Daughters," *Farmer and Planter* 11 (June 1860): 189, as cited in Hagler, "Ideal Woman," 407

FIGURE 4-18. William Hart, *Bishop Levi Silliman Ives Confirming Female Students at St. Mary's*, oil on canvas, Wake County, 1846. This painting provides strong visual evidence for the merging of Christian piety and feminine compliance as part of the North Carolina female school experience. The bishop, his full face strongly lit, stands head and shoulders above the kneeling women, whose heads are bowed and faces modestly hidden. The students, all of whom have been identified, represent the virtues of "true womanhood" in their reverent, respectful demeanors. Their fashionable form-fitting dresses may emphasize an hourglass, womanly figure (rather than the girlish Empire dress of the 1816 Marling painting), but the girls still wear pure white. (Courtesy of St. Mary's, Raleigh)

As attitudes toward educating white women slowly changed, those toward educating blacks—men or women, slave or free—hardened. Those most interested in keeping blacks in a subordinate position argued that educated blacks were more likely to rebel, were harder to supervise, or might become uppity. After 1832, teaching a slave to read or write was illegal. Although there were instances of masters teaching slaves to read the Bible in hopes of encouraging obedience and acceptance of their lot, and of a few white children sharing books with a black playmate, a large number of the slaves who were interviewed in the 1930s remembered that being caught with a book meant trouble. Nonetheless, some slave women learned to read and write, and the overwhelming attendance of former slaves at Freedmen's Schools after the Emancipation is strong testimony to their desire to attain literacy and its benefits.

According to the 1850 census, 42 percent of free blacks in North Carolina were literate. In 1816 Quakers had opened a school for black children two days a week for three months, boys and girls both being taught to read and write, and boys learning to count as high as three. Before 1835 Presbyterians, Methodists, and especially Quakers had helped to educate free blacks (as well as some slaves) by establishing schools, Sunday schools, and Bible classes. Although public schooling was not provided for free black children, 217 were counted among the public schoolchildren in 1850. Most free black children were apprenticed, and the large numbers of girls apprenticed in spinning, weaving, and dressmaking could have benefited from the 1760 law requiring that apprentices be taught to read and write (although typically those lines were crossed out on blacks' apprenticeship bonds or were not there at all). An 1838 statute removed that obligation, yet many owners continued to teach their apprentices to read

FIGURE 4-19. *Salem Academy students*, Forsyth County, 1858. (Courtesy of the Collection of Old Salem, Winston Salem).

FIGURE 4-20. *Mary Jane Patterson*. A free black woman from Raleigh, Patterson was the first black woman in the United States to receive a B.A. degree—from Oberlin College in 1862. (Courtesy of the Oberlin College Archives)

and write. In Craven County, for instance, most free black apprentices in the 1850s were under indentures requiring that they be taught reading and writing.[85]

Free black young women of means were able to obtain good educations, although they generally left North Carolina to do so. For example, the children of Caswell County's celebrated free black cabinetmaker, Thomas Day, were educated at the Wilbraham Academy in Massachusetts. In 1847 Day asked the Salem Collegium to permit him to "send his 16-year-old daughter, educated in the North, to Brother Christian Frederick Sussdorf in order that he may give her music lessons." Several North Carolina free black women attended Oberlin College in Ohio, established in 1833 as an evangelical school for men and women "irrespective of color" (Fig. 4-20). Ann Hazle was a member of Oberlin's class of 1855. Little is known about Hazle, who has the distinction of being one of two women among Oberlin's black students who appear to have been pure African, instead of mulatto. Mary Jane Patterson, the first black woman in the United States to receive a B.A. degree, in 1862, was born in Raleigh in 1840 to free black parents. Her father was a skilled mason, and in the 1850s her parents moved the entire family to the North, where they prospered, acquired property, and saw four of their children graduate from Oberlin College.[86]

The opportunity for education transformed the lives and expectations of many young women, white and black, in early nineteenth-century North Carolina. Religion, also a powerful force, had the potential to be equally transformative and affected even larger numbers of women.

Women, Religion, and Benevolence: "The Liberality of the Ladies"

Promising the hope and salvation of a better life in heaven, Christianity taught obedience and resignation to one's lot on earth: "tho I have my bitters with my sweets in the midst of outward affliction I feel Christ within." Regardless of race or class, women often found solace and strength in organized religion. In addition to providing them the larger, transcendent goals of faith and personal conviction, it offered women the opportunity to express themselves as individuals, to bond with a larger community of people with similar interests, and to exert some power in their lives. In North Carolina, as nationwide, women swelled the ranks of the established and evangelical churches and were the mainstay of church-related organizations, whatever the denomination. Of all southern institutions, church was the most integrated racially and the only public body in which women members predominated.[87]

Religion gave black women hope in the midst of oppression. Willie Bost, a former slave from Newton, remembered that his mother would "sing an' pray to the Lord to deliver us out o' slavery." Even under threat of beatings, she and other slaves would sneak off to hold prayer meetings in the woods. Somehow, "somethin' inside" told them about God and "that there was a better place hereafter."[88] Women especially responded to the emotional release that spirituality provided, and most slaves practiced a religion that combined aspects of their African heritage with evangelical Christianity—singing, shouting, and dancing to praise the Lord and hoping in turn that the Lord would deliver some justice and retribution.[89]

Free women of color, as well as slave women, were attracted to the evangelical religions. Large numbers of free black women were among the early members of the Methodist and Baptist churches and were active participants at camp meetings.

Religion answered white women's needs both private and public. It sustained them through life's travails, promoted their moral centrality in the new ideal of a "family religion," and provided an entry into public life as they supported the work of the church. Esther Lowry of western North Carolina lost two daughters within a few weeks, but "it is the Lord's will and I want to be resigned to his gracias [*sic*] will." Catherine DeRosset of Wilmington each evening asked herself a series of questions such as, "Did I in the morning consider what particular Virtue I was to exercise, what Sin or Temptation to avoid, & what business I had to do through the day?"[90] In Fayetteville, an Episcopal minister noted that his church had a "new and handsome set of plate" that had been acquired through "the liberality of the ladies of the congregation." In Hillsborough in 1828, Episcopal "ladies of the congregation made enough with their needles to erect a tower to the church."[91]

Churchmen recognized and appreciated women's special affinity with religion, morality, piety, and charity. Revival preachers stressed the supposedly feminine qualities of emotion and intuition instead of "manly" reason and intellect as the basis for an authentic religious conversion. By spiritual nature and natural piety, women were seen as superior to men.[92]

Around the time of the Revolutionary War, evangelical sects of the Baptists, Methodists, and New Light Presbyterians challenged the established Anglican Church and sought women and blacks as members. In the 1830s and 1840s these groups split into northern and southern churches over the issue of slavery, but in the early days of the Second Awakening, evangelical ministries cut across race and class lines to produce a religious revival in the state. Evangelical religion, which places primary importance on an individual's personal relationship with God and on an intensely emotional conversion experience, appealed to people outside the traditional power hierarchy, many of whom were women, both white and black, rural, and illiterate. They were drawn to the promise of redemption and salvation if they accepted God's presence in their lives. Thousands of mostly poor and middling North Carolinians responded enthusiastically to the deeply felt and intensely emotional message of spiritual rebirth, personal experience, and individual worth. Blacks, free as well as slave, constituted a third of the state's Methodists in 1830 and more than a third of the Chowan Baptist Association in 1860.[93]

FIGURE 4-21. *Camp meeting in progress*, engraving. (From B. Weed Gorham, *Camp Meeting Manual*; courtesy of the North Carolina Division of Archives and History)

When Methodists and Presbyterians began erecting churches in Wilmington, Raleigh, Fayetteville, and other towns, white women of the middle and upper classes became fervent members. Overall, the shift was dramatic. In 1800 evangelical Protestant churches had few members and were radical outsiders. By 1860 they claimed 90 percent of the state's 157,000 white church members and were models of social and moral propriety. Baptists and Methodists were the two largest denominations, claiming 80 percent of all church members; Presbyterians had another 10 percent; and Episcopalians, Quakers, Lutherans, and Moravians made up the remaining 10 percent.[94]

Thousands of women, black and white, embraced God and were "awakened" or "reborn" at rural camp meetings—the centerpiece of the evangelical movement (Fig. 4-21). Conversion was often the turning point in many women's lives. To testify to their own religious experience and to be responsible for their own salvation were independent actions that challenged the notion of women's proper behavior as deferential to their husbands' will. After conversion, many women were active in their new religious community.[95]

Though most husbands accepted their wives' religious convictions, others felt their male authority undermined. Opposition could be passive, such as a man's interrupting a preacher's sermon to insist that his wife fetch him a drink of water, or direct, such as shooting a preacher in the leg because he had baptized his wife. Some men considered the interracial camp meetings sexually dangerous because so much passion and emotion was part of the conversion experience: church leaders more experienced in the dynamics of conversion consistently warned young unmarried itinerant ministers, "Converse sparingly and conduct yourself prudently."[96]

In successive waves of evangelical activity, from around 1800 to 1804, 1829 to 1835, and again in 1857, revivals crackled across North Carolina's rural landscape. Camp meetings were dramatic theater, religious revival, and social events where families set up their tents, met old friends, and listened to fervent preaching. Mary Jeffreys Bethel "wanted religion" and attended numerous camp meetings in North Carolina and Virginia during the summer of 1837 to "get blessed." Other women may have been as concerned about their personal appearance as about the state of their soul. In 1819, for example, when a young North Carolinian realized that she had no new clothes for the camp meetings, she defiantly stated, "them that dont like to see me in my old clothes will have to let me be." After witnessing a meeting of "about 400 souls" near Louisburg in Franklin County, Methodist bishop Francis Asbury observed: "There are evils here; the meeting not solemn; the women appeared to be full of dress, the men full of news."[97]

Camp meetings were important to the evangelical movement, and so were itinerant preachers and Christian women. Ministers regularly riding their circuits through the sparsely settled state were in large part responsible for the rapid spread of Methodism. Referring to those "pioneers in religion," Episcopalian Ann Blount Pettigrew voiced reservations from her plantation in Tyrrell County: "In these parts we should live without the Gospel sound were it not for the Methodists but notwithstanding I should dislike to belong to the Sect. Such scrutinizing into feelings & moralities & forms must be disagreeable."[98]

Yet large numbers of women felt differently. They testified and converted, examined their actions, held prayer meetings, worked tirelessly to win over friends and family members to God, and provided moral and physical support for the itinerant preachers. Black preachers were visible until 1831, when their public preaching was prohibited, and free black women opened their houses to them on their travels.[99]

Women were expected to leave the preaching of God's word to men, but Luzene Stanley Chipman of Guilford County began public preaching after her conversion from Quakerism to Methodism (Fig. 4-22). Throughout the Piedmont, she drew large crowds, which were attracted by her religious fervor and, as a Moravian diarist noted in 1832, curiosity to hear a woman preacher. Although Chipman felt called to reveal her religious convictions, she delayed writing her religious tract, *Earnest Entreaties and Appeals to the Unconverted with Persuasions to Religious Duties*, until 1852, when she was fifty-four years old, explaining: "I strove to excuse myself, because my services were called for by the public in another way, and the care of my family occupied all my time; but this I found to be of little avail, this concern still followed me and caused me many sleepless nights; I must encourage believers in their Christian duties, and tell sinners their career must lead to death."[100]

The importance of religion in women's lives can be explained in part by the state's agrarian setting. Church and camp meetings were important occasions for hardworking farm families to visit with kin and friends, and they were among the few public places where women could socialize with other women. Yet evangelical churches also flourished in towns.

Methodists and Presbyterians particularly appealed to genteel ladies.[101] Many urban women were attracted by the emphasis on religious feelings, salvation and spiritual rebirth, preaching, and rejecting worldly indulgences; men generally believed that the evangelicals were too emotional and their enthusiasms "unmanly." Women felt energized by their new faith, the sense of community they felt with other female converts, and opportunities for organized benevolent activity. By contrast, men found submitting to the presence of a greater power difficult and "heart-wrenching." Richard Rankin observed that although, "once, gentlemen had ridiculed the lowly evangelicals, suddenly they found themselves married to them." In New Bern, Edenton, and Wilmington competition from the Methodists caused the moribund Episcopal Church to try to accommodate evangelically inclined ladies by emphasizing spirituality more and ritual less. By the 1820s, however, Episcopal evangelism began to decline in North Carolina. Episcopal churches became High Church, which means that they emphasized external ritual, sacraments, and orthodoxy and rejected the "low" or more internally experienced faith of evangelicalism.[102]

The social appeal of the newly restored Episcopal Church was such that the Episcopal wife of William Hooper only reluctantly followed him when he became the president of Wake Forest College and joined the Baptist Church. Mrs. Hooper was "too worldly minded" to wish her daughters "to be baptists." She felt that "girls certainly make their way in the world and maintain a place in genteel society better as Presbyterians or Episcopalians than as baptists or methodists."[103]

Despite Mrs. Hooper's disdain for the evangelical sects, an important legacy of North Carolina's evangelical movement was the opportunity for women of all denominations to en-

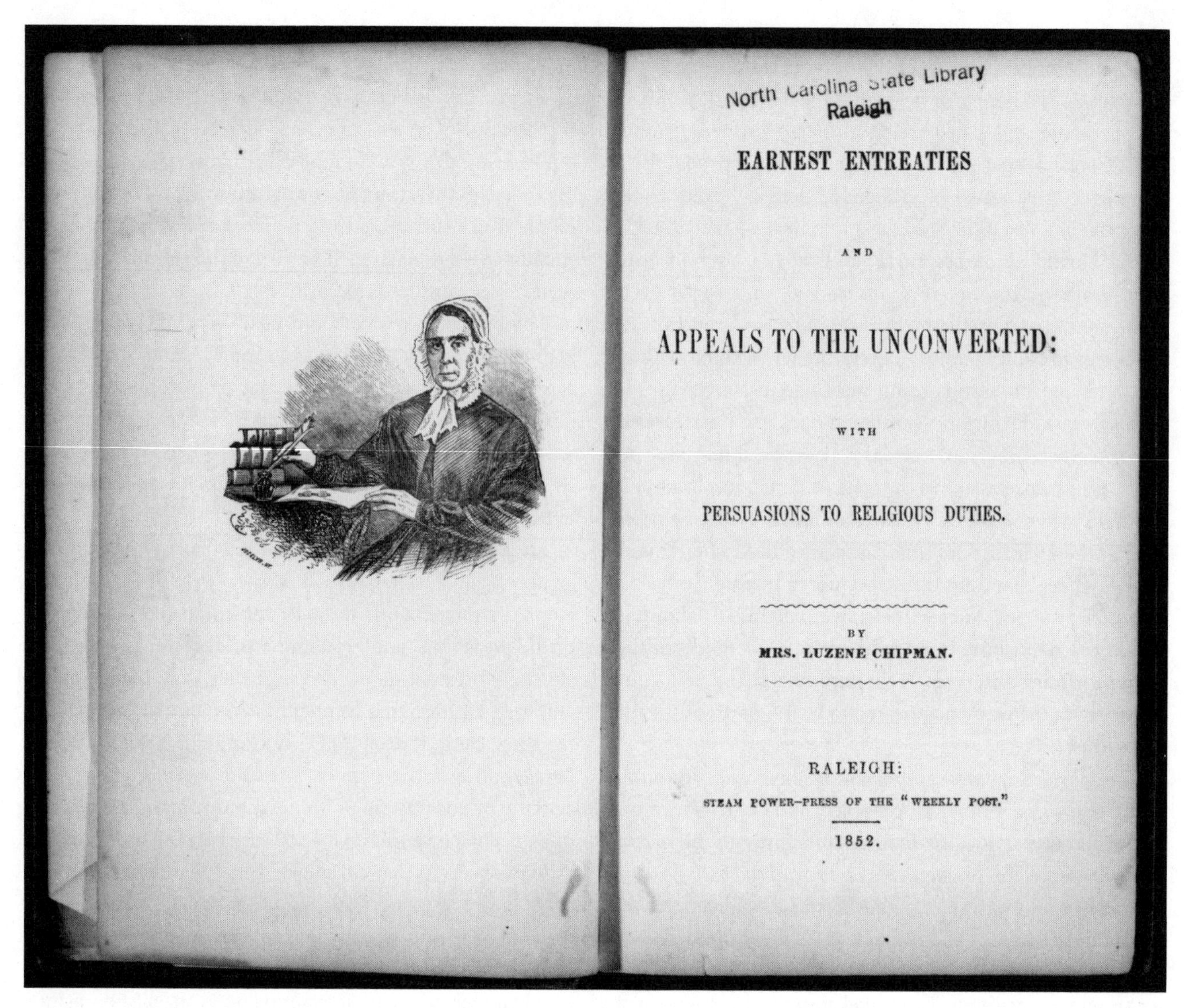

FIGURE 4-22. Luzene Chipman, *Earnest Entreaties and Appeals to the Unconverted, with Persuasions to Religious Duties*, Raleigh, 1852. (Courtesy of the North Carolina Division of Archives and History)

gage in organized benevolent activity and, in this way, to participate in shaping their communities. Such activities were considered entirely appropriate to women's nurturing and spiritual natures and, in North Carolina's growing towns, reinforced a developing class consciousness in which more privileged people—the "better classes"—felt a responsibility to help those less fortunate. In the rural South, female organizations were rare: kinship ties, demanding work routines, and distances undermined the establishment of women's voluntary associations. But in the region's few towns and cities, women traditionally had cared for the physical needs of the poor in their churches. Increasingly they organized prayer meetings, supported foreign and home missions, distributed Bibles and tracts, and taught Sunday school. Guion Griffis Johnson's pioneer study, *Ante-Bellum North Carolina*, points out that voluntary, organized charity in the state before 1860 was primarily "women's work."[104]

Women moved from helping "poor" individuals in their churches to assisting the "worthy poor" in their communities. In Raleigh, Fayetteville, Wilmington, Warrenton, and Elizabeth City, women organized charity schools for poor children. Female benevolent societies were incorporated in many North Carolina towns, including the Newbern Female Charitable Society (1812), Female Orphan Asylum of Fayetteville (1813), Female Benevolent Society of Wilmington (1817), Raleigh Female Benevolent Society (1821), Dorcas Society in Elizabeth City and Greensborough Female Benevolent Society (1830), Ladies Working Society of St. James Church in Wilmington (1833), and Female Benevolent Society of New Bern (1854). Local women started the Fayetteville Female

Orphan Asylum in 1813, but it had closed by 1830 when they organized the Female Society of Industry, which sponsored a school for the "relief and education of distressed and indigent children." Edward J. Hale of the *Fayetteville Observer* was "pleased to see that a portion of the Ladies of our town" were concerned with local matters, "instead of engaging in the common crusade of Foreign Missions."[105]

From 1810 almost every church had a benevolent society focusing on foreign missions or care for the poor. Baptist and Presbyterian women raised money for foreign missions, and missionary societies appeared across the state—near Fayetteville in 1815 and in Edenton and Sandy Creek in 1817, Raleigh in 1818, and Spring Hill in 1822.[106]

Many church workers found tract distribution an appealing benevolent activity. By 1818 two female tract societies had been formed in Cabarrus County and one in Raleigh. Furnishing Bibles, religious tracts, and pamphlets to the poor was considered part of home missionary work to promote religion (regardless of denomination), despite the fact that many of those receiving the literature could not read it. After her conversion to Presbyterianism, Eliza Haywood became active in the Raleigh Female Tract Society, serving as president from 1816 to 1822, except in 1817, when she delivered her tenth child. By 1828 a North Carolina Tract Society was formed (the state organization, linked to the national organization, was threatened when northern colleagues were critical of North Carolina and slavery). The year 1858 saw the establishment of the Charlotte Presbyterian Ladies' Tract Society, whose members were determined to touch "every destitute family" in Charlotte; they even reached out to strangers, distributing religious tracts to travelers on railroad cars. Two active members were educator Margaret Burwell, who with her husband directed the Charlotte Female Institute, and Bessie Lacy Dewey, whose husband Thomas was a banker in Charlotte's emerging market economy.[107]

Sunday schools also grew out of the revival activity of the Second Awakening, and most teachers were, like participants in the movement as a whole, young and female. In its first phase, Sunday school was considered a form of Christian benevolence because it involved teaching poor children to read and write. In 1816 a "tutoress from Salem Academy" taught a Sunday school, and within a year twenty of the children had learned enough to read the Testament. Soon afterward, a group of young women from Salem taught a school on Sunday afternoons "for poor neighbor's children." In 1818 Abigail Albertson of the Springfield Friends Meeting began giving lessons on Scripture to children in her own home. Within two years, her house could not accommodate all the children who wanted to attend, so she moved her Sunday school to the meetinghouse. Sunday schools, established in many counties throughout the state, were so successful that churches began organizing schools for "genteel" children as well.[108]

Some North Carolina women who took part in their church's benevolent work felt that they deserved more of a voice in church affairs. It is easy to hear the dissatisfaction with women's secondary role in the remarks of an unidentified member of the North Carolina Tract Society in 1859: "We may perfect ourselves in music and take a seat in the choir, or busy our fingers in fabricating ornaments for the church edifice, but is that all we are to be permitted to do? Are we capable of no holier, higher work?" Yet this woman knew her place: "As Southern women, we shrink from clamoring for our rights, we send no delegates to jostle with public speakers on the platform; but we would modestly ask of our brethren, wiser and more experienced than ourselves, to recognize and acknowledge our *right* to become fellow laborers in God's work." Frances Webb Bumpass, who taught Sunday school and organized the Women's Foreign Mission Society, believed that "too long" women had "hesitated, fearful, lest it be said they were stepping beyond their sphere."[109]

Most women's benevolence was biscuits and needles rather than bricks and mortar: they did not control their own money and rarely provided major financial support to their causes. Frances Pollock Devereux, a woman wealthy enough to be called the "Spanish Galleon," was also known for "doing good." She "founded and fostered" benevolent societies in New Bern and Raleigh, started a Lancasterian school in New Bern, and "engaged in the distribution of Religious tracts and similar acts of benevolence and mercy." She and her mother, Eunice Edwards Pollock, whose father was the New England evangelist Jonathan Edwards, helped found the Presbyterian Church in New Bern in 1817. Devereux left her fortune to groups and people she deemed worthy, rather than to her own family.[110]

Mary Sumner Blount, who died in 1822, showed a similar independence in her will (Fig. 4-23). Rather than leaving her entire estate to her heirs, she provided money to build the first Christ Episcopal Church in Raleigh and authorized her executors to withhold legacy benefits from any kin who contested her will.[111]

Abolition, Temperance, and Moral Reform: "Enlarge the Circle"

As long as benevolence stayed within the bounds of Christian charity, it was an appropriate activity for North Carolina

FIGURE 4-23. *Mary Sumner Blount*, oil on canvas, Wake County, 1820. (Mordecai Historic Park, Raleigh; photograph courtesy of the North Carolina Division of Archives and History)

women. But many women, imbued with evangelical passion for righting wrong, looked beyond their church work to improve and "perfect" society. They applied skills of organization, leadership, and persuasion they had developed in their church work to moral and social reform. When "doing good" developed into "being good" and appeared to challenge traditional ways, including slavery and male authority, these would-be reformers encountered hostility, especially as sectional feelings intensified in the 1850s.

For example, women's mission support and tract distribution were acceptable at the local and state levels, but when the benevolent groups were tied to national organizations critical of slavery, they were unwelcome. In 1858 the *North Carolina Presbyterian* advised an agent of the "American Missionary Society," whose headquarters were located in New York, to cease all abolition activities and to leave the state. A year later, the same periodical urged Christian people to run off an agent of the Boston Tract Society for distributing abolition literature.[112]

Most white women in North Carolina, like others in the South, did not generally participate in abolitionism, the major reform movement of the time. They accepted slavery and defended its existence. Moreover, they considered abolitionists to be dangerous radicals who were out to destroy the southern way of life. At the same time, they were aware of the abolition argument that slavery deprived blacks of a family life—a strong indictment in a region that identified preserving moral order with family stability. White women were also sensitive to another claim of abolitionists: that miscegenation, and its root cause, slavery, disrupted white families.[113]

Because of the strong Quaker presence in the state, North Carolina had more antislavery societies than any other southern state, and women were often active members. The Quakers' well-known opposition to slavery was based on their support of human rights over property rights, as was that of Wesleyan Methodists, who split from the Methodist Episcopal Church over the issue of slavery and even brought abolitionist ministers to the state.[114]

Quakers defied North Carolina law and custom when they purchased slaves and then transferred the titles to the Trustees of the North Carolina Yearly Meeting, effectively freeing the slaves—a practice that became illegal in 1827. From 1816 to 1834 the General Association of the Manumission Society of North Carolina, a branch of the Quaker Manumission Society, worked to free slaves (though what exactly should be done with the freed slaves was a point of contention) and to help the state's free blacks. The society's strongest support was in the counties known as the "Quaker Belt" of Guilford, Randolph, and Chatham, but some of its members were not Quakers. Within ten years after its formation, the manumission society had twenty-three chapters including those in Orange, Davidson, and Forsyth Counties as well.

Women were not admitted as members of the manumission societies; so in 1825, eight years before the establishment of the Female Anti-Slavery Society in Philadelphia, a group of Guilford County's Quaker women formed a female auxiliary to the men's group in Jamestown. In their petition to the General Association of the Manumission Society of North Carolina, signed by Elizabeth S. Mendenhall, the women noted their "inability to do much or add any strength to the arduous task," but they offered their stores of cloth and stockings and their sewing services to needy slaves. Other groups, such as the Springfield Female Branch Auxiliary and the Centre Female Auxiliary Society in Guilford County, were formed at about the same time. In 1827 there were five female manumission societies, and by 1830 forty-five groups in Guilford and surrounding counties had contributed money, sewing, and encouragement.[115]

FIGURE 4-24. *Mount Vernon Ladies' Association*. Although reformist activity was generally unacceptable for southern women, patriotic efforts to preserve George Washington's Mount Vernon were admissible. North Carolina women managed to raise large amounts of money yet preserve their anonymity. Delegate Letitia Morehead is depicted in the group surrounding the bust of George Washington. (Courtesy of the Mount Vernon Ladies' Association, Mount Vernon, Virginia)

Quaker protest against slavery in North Carolina had dissipated somewhat by the 1850s because so many Friends had left for Indiana, Ohio, and other free states. The migration placed greater responsibility on those who remained, and they became the main support for the Underground Railroad to help runaway slaves to reach freedom and the safety of Quaker families in Indiana and Ohio. Cousins Vestal and Levi Coffin of New Garden are credited with establishing the Underground Railroad around 1819, but their wives Alethea and Catherine were also instrumental.

Alethea Flukes Coffin had been married just two years when she and Vestal began their secret "railroad" work, with their farm the primary "depot" in the Guilford College area. After Vestal's death in 1826, Alethea carried on by herself, and for more than twenty-five years she hid slaves on her farm and directed them to the next "station." She delayed her move to the Midwest partly because of her commitment to the Underground Railroad, but in 1852 she joined her family and friends in Indiana and began her work on the northern end of the line. Catherine Coffin, Levi's wife, also provided food, shelter, and assistance to the next "station" for runaway slaves, first in North Carolina and, after she and her family emigrated, in Ohio. Over a twenty-year period, Catherine and Levi Coffin helped probably 3,300 slaves.[116]

Another worker on the Underground Railroad was Vina Curry, a freed slave who was a washerwoman at the New Garden Boarding School in Guilford County (where Alethea Coffin was the matron). Curry lent her dead husband's freedom papers to slaves who matched his description; the papers helped them escape with parties of westbound pioneers. Returning Quakers brought the papers back to be reused, enabling more than fifteen slaves to escape with Curry's help. Delphina Mendenhall of Randolph County was married to the second or third largest slaveowner in Guilford County, but she held firm to her Quaker values and was apparently also involved in the Underground Railroad; she assisted in a plan to resettle fugitive slaves to the West Indies, and she and her husband personally escorted many of his slaves to freedom in Ohio.[117]

Some historians have traced the seeds of feminism to abolitionism. However, because the Quaker women who engaged in antislavery activities were so far outside mainstream North Carolina and were generally regarded with hostility, it is unlikely that they attracted many non-Quaker women to their cause.

Temperance, by contrast, appealed to many nineteenth-century North Carolina white women who believed that the amount of liquor husbands consumed had a direct connection to family welfare. Temperance activities first appeared in the state in the 1820s as part of the growing national recognition that drunkenness harmed individuals, families, and society. In the Quaker community of Jamestown a temperance society was formed in 1834, nine years after the founding of the local female antislavery society, and included some of the same members. Women's names—Lydia Beard, Nancy Kiley, Polly Holland, Elizabeth and Mary Carpenter, Betsy Potter, Elizabeth S. Mendenhall, Eugenia Beeson, and Angeline Burton—appeared alongside those of men. In 1848 the Daughters of Temperance was organized as a female auxiliary to the Sons of Temperance. Within four years, there were twenty-nine chapters in the state, not surprising in light of the more than 230 stills in 1851 in Guilford County alone.[118]

Bessie Lacy Dewey, who had moved to Charlotte from Raleigh in the 1850s when she married her husband Thomas, wrote home that Charlotte was not a "pleasant place" because too many (even church members) "get on the rarest sort of drinking sprees & half a dozen who are drinkers by habit—not frolickers but soakers." Many women felt that it was their duty to protect homes, family, and community against the evils of alcohol, and some were even willing to speak up in public for temperance. But the antebellum temperance war in North Carolina was shortlived; by 1852 it was in decline, though temperance remained a controversial and divisive local issue. Anastatia Sims has observed that "feminine purity" was the motivation for reform activities of the 1830s and 1840s. Like religious benevolence, moral reform was rooted in women's "special nature," their interest in protecting home and family, and an evangelical belief in righteousness and morality.[119]

In 1826 Moses Swaim, chairman of the General Manumission Society, thanked the Female Society of Jamestown for its help. He added: "an enlarged participation . . . in the works of Justice, Benevolence, and Humanity . . . will enlarge the circle which Custom has *improperly prescribed* to [women's] action and usefulness and elevate them to *the sphere to which nature intended them to move*."[120]

Starting in the 1840s female reformism became increasingly unpopular in North Carolina, and by the 1850s it was no longer sanctioned socially. A northern outsider like Dorothea Dix was able by the use of two strategies to convince the General Assembly to pass legislation in 1848 to establish an insane asylum in North Carolina. First, she followed the standard procedure that she had developed in other state campaigns—inspecting existing facilities, presenting her findings, and arguing for reform. Although she found sympathy in the Democratic legislature, she failed to get financial support. Her second approach was more traditionally female. She become the devoted companion of Louisa Dobbin, the dying wife of the Democratic leader, James C. Dobbin, during the last days of her life. When Louisa asked how she could ever repay her kindness, Dix replied that she could urge her husband to pass the asylum bill. And then Louisa died. When the grief-stricken Dobbin recounted to his fellow legislators the story of his wife's death and Dix's extraordinary sympathy for those in acute circumstances, the bill was reconsidered, passed, and funded. Then Dorothea Dix, as she always did, traveled on to other states. Dix was masterful in making desperate private lives the concern of public men. But North Carolina women who persevered in reformist behavior risked losing respectability, male approval, and prospects for marriage.[121]

As the nation moved inexorably toward war, southern men felt that women had ventured too far into the public sphere and should restrict their "superior moral judgement" to their immediate household (Fig. 4-24). In conferences at Seneca Falls, New York, in 1848 and Worcester, Massachusetts, in 1850, some northern women had claimed their right to full citizenship in marriage, the workplace, and society. This horrified the North Carolina press—"Women made speeches—women acted on committees—and women claimed the right to vote, and in fact, to be men."[122]

North Carolina men admonished women to stay in their proper place. "Women's sphere is about the domestic altar," intoned the *Raleigh Register* in 1850. "When she transgresses that sphere and mingles in the miserable brawlings and insane agitations of the day, she descends from her lofty elevation, and becomes an object of disgust and contempt." Young women graduating from the Edgeworth Female Seminary in 1858 were warned by the commencement speaker, James A. Long, that to enter public life was "to soil your garments with matters that do not pertain to your position in society."[123]

CHAPTER 5

The Labor of Her Own Hands

Women and Work, 1800–1860

Most North Carolina women did not work for wages during the early nineteenth century. But that does not mean that they did not work, and work hard. Because the labor of most women, black and white, was domestic and agricultural, it is easy to overlook their essential role in the state's economy.

Women who had to earn money in antebellum North Carolina found their choices limited and their pay poor. There were few alternatives for the "helpless female born dependent on the labor of her own hands," noted Calvin Wiley, the state's major proponent of common schools.[1] Towns like Wilmington, Hillsborough, and Greensboro provided growing occupations in law, banking, and retail merchandising for white men, but such activities were considered inappropriate for women. Running boardinghouses, selling hats, making cloth, and teaching school were white women's options, whereas domestic work was black women's.

The growing acceptance of the separate spheres doctrine that was beginning to define middle-class male and female life in the urbanizing Northeast, where men went off to factory or office and women stayed at home, had little impact in small-town North Carolina. The concept of separate spheres was even less relevant in rural areas, where the household—whether farm or plantation—was the center of economic activity and productive labor for most men and women. As Elizabeth Fox-Genovese has noted, domestic ideals for southern white women, like northern white women, were centered on the home, but it was a different definition of home—not a "refuge from the workplace" but the "center of the workplace."[2]

Yeoman Women and Farm Households: "The Industry of His Wife"

The majority of white women in antebellum North Carolina were wives and daughters of nonslaveholding yeoman farmers, farm laborers, and tenants. From the Coastal Plain to the Mountains, and especially throughout the Piedmont, small family farms dominated the landscape. Farmers cultivated corn and wheat, tobacco and cotton; raised swine and poultry; and grew vegetables and herbs in their gardens. As in all traditional agricultural societies, women did their own work within the household and, when necessary, helped their husbands, and perhaps a hired hand, in the field. They were part of a domestic economy in which they shared the products of their labor.

Farm women were expected to be helpmates to their husbands, through good times and bad; a capable, thrifty wife could make the difference between survival and failure. For many nineteenth-century farm women, their self-sufficient lives were not so different from those of eighteenth-century women in the backcountry. They rose before daybreak, grew and prepared their family's food, spun and wove cloth, carried firewood and water, laundered and ironed clothes, made quilts and coverlets, manufactured soap and candles, slaughtered hogs and cured meat; and they sometimes worked in the field.

More than 70 percent of the white women who lived in North Carolina in 1860 belonged to families who owned no slaves.[3] According to agricultural periodicals of the time, the ideal southern farmwife cooked the food herself—not simply supervised someone's domestic labor—and knew how to preserve fruits and vegetables, butcher and cure meat, and make butter and cheese. The few recipe books belonging to women of the yeomanry that have survived, such as that of *M. Lewis*, demonstrate a no-frills approach to housekeeping—recipes for blackberry wine, tomato catsup, and "Leady Cake" and a series of dye recipes for cochineal, blue, yellow, scarlet, black, and green.[4]

The good farmwife tended a garden for family needs and perhaps some surplus cash, and she was practical in her cloth production. "If the farmer's family wants new clothes, the industry of his wife supplies them," declared a writer for the *Miner's and Farmer's Journal* of Charlotte in 1830. "When I see a farmer appear in company genteely dressed in homespun, I think of Solomon's description of a good wife."[5] A farm daughter "can wash and iron, make bread and butter, and cheese, cook a good farmer's dinner, and set the daintiest of little stitches in all kinds of plain sewing; and she has learned it all from that excellent, kind mother."[6]

Slave Women's Labor: "Slave Time Wuz Slave Time wid Us"

Between 1790 and 1862 a third of North Carolina's women worked as slaves. In 1840, 97 percent of female slaves lived on farms and plantations scattered across the rural landscape.[7] Their days started before sunrise and ended after sunset.

Louisa Adams, a former slave from Rockingham in Richmond County, recalled being awakened at the "time de chicken crowed, and we went to work just as soon as we could see how to make a lick wid a hoe."[8] "Jes wok, an' wok, an' wok. I nebbah know nothin' but wok," said Sarah Gudger, who lived in Buncombe County. She went into the field to chop wood and hoe corn "in any kine ob weathah, rain o' snow; it nebbah mattah."[9] After working a twelve- to fourteen-hour day for their owner, slave women returned home to take care of their own family. Betty Powers's mother cooked for fourteen people in addition to her field work. She was "up way befo' daylight fixin' breakfast and supper after dark." According to Louise Adams, "slave time wuz slave time wid us."[10]

The nature of a female slave's work depended on her age—lighter tasks for children and older women, although work was still expected—and the type and size of farm or plantation she lived on. A typical slave woman, as was true of most North Carolinians, lived on a small farm. Because more than half of the slaveowners owned five or fewer slaves, and almost 20 percent owned only one slave, a female slave usually worked in close proximity to her owner—in the house with the mistress or other slaves cooking, cleaning, washing, spinning or weaving, sewing, preserving foods; outside, tending animals and gardens and performing other domestic tasks; and, at harvest time, working in the field.[11]

If she lived on a large plantation where slaves had specialized occupations, she might be a house servant—but most slave women were field hands. At Somerset plantation in Washington County, which had more than three hundred slaves, 60 percent of the field hands were women. Female field hands performed much of the same backbreaking work as men but were considered a ¾ hand, with pregnant women counted as a ½ to ¼ hand. From daybreak to nightfall on weekdays and half a day on Saturdays, from spring through summer to autumn, women worked in all-female groups or alongside the men—cleaning ditches, planting seeds, chopping weeds, and harvesting crops. Halifax County planter Henry K. Burgwyn, whose Roanoke plantations raised corn, wheat, clover, cotton, and other crops, assigned his slave women such tasks as "raking up manure in stable yard," spreading and carting it, grubbing, stacking corn, fencing, and cleaning out irrigation ditches.[12]

Slave work often was organized along gender lines, but a former Warren County slave, Jacob Manson, recalled that the "women plowed an done udder work as de men did" (Plate 6).[13] According to Harry James Trentham, who had lived on a large plantation near Camden, South Carolina, "Some of de women plowed barefoot most all de time, an' had to carry dat row an' keep up with de men, an' den do dere cookin' at night."[14] Frederick Law Olmsted, who traveled in the South in the 1850s, observed that "the ploughs at work, both with single and double mule teams, were generally held by women, and very well held, too." He watched "with some interest for any indication that their sex unfitted them for the occupation" but found that "twenty of them were ploughing together, with double teams and heavy ploughs."[15]

WOMEN'S LABOR IN THE FIELD

The staple crop cultivation that dominated North Carolina's commercial agriculture, the relatively backward methods and technology, and increasingly exhausted soils that required extensive preparation ensured that field slaves worked long, hard hours year-round. Field hands customarily worked around twenty acres each; so a farmer with eight hands might have 160 acres in cultivation, 100 in cotton and 60 in corn. Corn had long been an important crop in the state (for people and animals), and in the northeastern counties, where there were large plantations, corn and wheat were staples. Cotton, which by the 1830s had become a staple commodity, was grown across the state but mainly in the eastern counties of Edgecombe, Bertie, Pitt, Martin, and Lenoir and in south-central counties, including Mecklenburg, Iredell, Union, Anson, and Richmond. Cotton had to be constantly attended. After planting in early spring, slaves spent long hours throughout the summer chopping cotton to get rid of weeds. From August through November, in what were often as many as six pickings, they harvested the cotton (Fig. 5-1).[16]

Tobacco, which in the nineteenth century was grown mainly in the Piedmont counties along the Virginia border, required even more intensive labor. In Warren County,

FIGURE 5-1. *Cotton basket*, Rowan County, ca. 1855. (Courtesy of the North Carolina Museum of History)

FIGURE 5-2. James E. Taylor (1839–1901), *Rice Culture on the Cape Fear River*, engraving. Rice plantations presented a cultural landscape that was predominantly black. Women played an important role in rice production in Africa and continued to do so in the American South, using their traditional methods and tools—hoes for breaking the ground, gourds for sowing, sickles for harvest, wooden flails for threshing, and mortars and pestles for pounding the rice. (From *Frank Leslie's Illustrated Newspaper*, October 20, 1866; courtesy of the North Carolina Division of Archives and History)

which was a major tobacco-growing area, slaves outnumbered whites 3 to 2 in 1820 and 2 to 1 in 1860. After planting and transplanting the young plants, field hands had to pinch off secondary stems, or suckers, to promote healthy growth. Like cotton, tobacco did not ripen all at once; so successive pickings were necessary, and following each, leaves had to be graded, looped, and cured.[17]

Rice cultivation required large numbers of workers spending long hours hunched over flooded, swampy, mosquito-infested fields. New Hanover and Brunswick Counties, which dominated North Carolina rice production, also had the largest number of slaves, the largest ratio of blacks to whites, and the largest plantations. The success of rice cultivation in the South generally was due in large part to the expertise of slaves, who were familiar with rice growing in Africa.[18]

Starting in early December and throughout the winter months, slave women prepared fields for planting (Fig. 5-2). In early spring they planted rice seedlings, after which floodgates were opened, and a sequence of flooding and draining followed until the rice was ready for harvest in late summer. They cut the rice with sickles and bound it in sheaves, then threshed it (Fig. 5-3). In early November, almost a year after they started the crop, the rice was in. Rice workers sometimes had greater autonomy and more free time than other field hands because they often worked on a "task system": Once the task was completed to the overseer's satisfaction, the rest of the day was theirs.[19]

WOMEN'S WORK AT THE BIG HOUSE

For slave women assigned to the plantation household, less autonomy and more supervision were likely, though there were trade-offs. Housework was easier than field labor, and house servants had more status, ate better food, and wore nicer clothing. "I was kept at de big house to wait on

FIGURE 5-3. *Rice winnowing basket*, county unknown, 1700s. After harvesting and threshing the rice plants, the women then separated the grain from the chaff by tossing the rice into the air from a winnowing basket and allowing the chaff to blow away while the heavier grain fell back into the basket. (Courtesy of the North Carolina Museum of History)

Mis' Polly," recalled Sarah Debro, a former Orange County slave who was a "house maid" as a child. "My dresses an' aprons was starched stiff. I had a clean apron every day. We had white sheets on the beds, an' we niggers had plenty to eat too, even ham."[20]

But domestic service had its disadvantages. House servants had little privacy or time off. They were subjected to continual supervision by their white owners and isolated from other slaves. They had to endure harsh punishments and sometimes sexual abuse. Because of their physical proximity to the white family, personal relationships between slaves and whites were extremely important. Louisa Adams of Richmond County remembered, "My missus was kind to me, but Mars. Tom was the buger."[21] Harriet Jacobs, whose biography follows the next chapter, allegedly endured sexual advances from her owner, Edenton doctor James Norcom, and the wrath of his wife.

Almost all household work was done by female slaves. In 1818 when Ann Blount Shepard Pettigrew of the Bonarva plantation complained that it "was the most disagreeable labour in the world that of making others work," she was not suggesting that she would prefer to do the housework herself. And when Anne Ruffin Cameron of the Bennehan-Cameron plantations "commenced gardening," it did not necessarily mean that she had her own hands in the soil, but that slaves "Jem and Demps [were] very busy in the front yard making a cedar hedge from either side of the piazza down to the enclosure around the grove." Although slaveholding women might write about gardening, sewing, cooking, nursing, child care, and other domestic tasks as if they themselves were performing those chores, they were, in fact, appropriating as well as directing the labor of slaves who actually cleaned the house, cooked the meals, spun and wove the cloth, cared for the children, made candles and soap, slaughtered the animals, and tended the gardens and dairy.[22]

Slave women's labor allowed white women to live more comfortably and to avoid much of the strenuous work that constituted nineteenth-century housekeeping in rural North Carolina. Former slave Betty Cofer, who lived on the Forsyth County plantation of Dr. Beverly Jones, recalled that "there was always two washerwomen, a cook, some hands to help her, two sewin' women, a house girl, an' some who did all the weavin' an' spinnin'."[23] Although some female slaves preferred plowing under a hot sun over hearing a white mistress's sharp tongue, hundreds of others favored the chores of a house servant over field work.[24]

Household positions often descended from mother to daughter. Training began early, when a girl of six or seven learned to clear the table, watch over other children (sometimes her own age or older), and develop the skills that would make her a valuable domestic worker as an adult. Sally, the "faithful and loved servant" of Ellen Mordecai of Raleigh, was the daughter of "Caroline—a personal maid and seamstress," the granddaughter of "one of the milkers and the weaver," and the great-granddaughter of a "personal family servant."[25] Ida Adkins, whose mother worked as a weaver at the big house on an Orange County plantation, stayed there, too, when she was a young girl, "pickin' up chips, sweepin' de yard an' such 'as dat."[26] Betty Cofer's mother was the cook on the Jones plantation in Forsyth County, and when Betty became old enough, she helped to set the table in the big dining room. Then she would put on "a clean white apron an' carry in the vituals and stand behind Miss Ella's chair." Betty Cofer was "claimed" by Ella, her master's daughter, and "waited on her an' most times slept on the floor in her room."[27] Mattie Curtis, who was born on a Granville County plantation, told of standing around the table to fan flies off the heads of white people with peacock feathers.[28]

The highest-status jobs tended to be those that stretched the boundaries of slavery, if not of gender—such as cooks, who had more privacy, some control over their time, and always enough to eat (Fig. 5-4), or seamstresses, who could use their sewing skills for creativity and self-expression. Midwives and healers sometimes practiced their craft away from the plantation, making them more mobile than most female slaves (Fig. 5-5). Ebenezer Pettigrew, for instance, sent a woman from his Bonarva plantation in Tyrrell County to nurse some neighbors down with a fever in nearby Washington County. Sarah McDonald, a Cumberland County slave who was "great on curing rheumatism" with herbs from her garden, went to Raleigh to nurse a white family.[29]

FIGURE 5-4. Porte Crayon, *The Cook*. (*Harper's New Monthly Magazine*, September 28, 1861; courtesy of the North Carolina Division of Archives and History)

In 1840 about 3 percent of the almost 74,000 female slaves of working age lived in the towns of Fayetteville, New Bern, Raleigh, and Wilmington. Undoubtedly, town life offered some of them opportunities for employment and enterprise unavailable in isolated rural settings. In Fayetteville, "Aunt Sally" made enough money selling cakes and beer to buy a measure of personal time, though her success caused resentment among white merchants, and they pressured her master to sell her. In Beaufort, slave women were "hired out" to work in the local fisheries (Fig. 5-6).[30]

REPRODUCTIVE LABOR: "PRETTY LIKELY . . ."

In 1819 Ebenezer Pettigrew wrote his wife Ann that the Negro woman he had bought for a cook already had a "child" and was "23 years of age and pretty likely." Pettigrew then mentioned that one of the men on his plantation already had taken a liking to her.[31] Just how callous a slaveowner was in his attitude toward women as "breeders" depended on the size and scale of his plantation operation, his personal interaction with slaves, and his own notions of morality. "Mr. Mordicia had his yeller gals in one quarter to dereselves, an' dese gals belong ter de Mordicia men, dere friends, an' de overseers," recounted Mattie Curtis, a former Wake County slave. She noted that when "a baby wuz born in dat quarter, dey'd sen' it over ter de black quarter at birth."[32]

> The colored people washed and shrouded the dead bodies. My grandmother wus one who did this. Her name was Sarah McDonald. She belonged to Capt. George McDonald. She had fifteen children and lived to be one hundred and ten years old. . . . She wus called black mammy because she wet nursed so many white children. In slavery time she nursed all babies hatched on her marstar's plantation and kept it up after the war as long as she had children.
> —Sarah Louise Augustus, former slave.
> (Rawick, *American Slave*, 14:53–54)

Jacob Manson, of Warren County, which had larger plantations and greater slave populations than were typical for North Carolina, commented: "A lot of de slave owners had certain strong, healthy slave men to serve de slave women. Ginerally dey give one man four women, an' dat man better not have nuthin' to do wid de udder women, an' de women better not have nuthin' to do wid udder men."[33] Some women resisted becoming mothers; others bore children in exchange for less work, more food, and better clothing.

Although active resistance, overt rebellion, and actual escapes by female slaves were rare, women did succeed in mitigating the harshness of slavery by various tactics. Some women confronted their situation directly with anger and verbal conflict, whereas others used more subtle means, such as breaking tools or feigning illness, to strike back. They

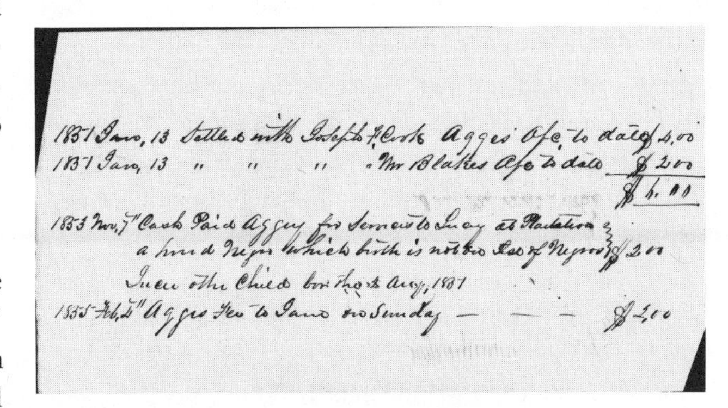

1851 Jan, 13 Settled with Joseph J. Cook Aggey's a/c to date $4.00
1851 Jan, 13 " " " Mr Blakes a/c to date $2.00
$6.00
1853 Nov, 7th Cash Paid Aggey for Services to Lucy at Plantation a hired Negro which birth is not [illegible] of Negroes $2.00
Lucy other Child born the [illegible] Aug, 1851
1855 Feb, 2 Aggey Fee to Jane on Sunday — — — $2.00

FIGURE 5-5. *Receipt for services* of slave midwife Aggey, Wake County, 1851–55. Slave healers were important to their community; they could also earn money. Aggey received two dollars for her services, but the fee was paid to her master. (From the Alonzo Mial Papers; courtesy of the North Carolina Division of Archives and History)

FIGURE 5-6. Porte Crayon, *Farming the Sea—Heading Herring*, Belvidere Fishery, Chowan County. (*Harper's New Monthly Magazine*, September 28, 1861; courtesy of the North Carolina Division of Archives and History)

could be too ill to work, and their pregnancy or womanly complaints would be hard for the overseer or owner to discount. Women who had passed the change of life and therefore could be put to heavy labor with no adverse effect on their "breeding" capabilities might feel "poorly" to avoid work. "I wish I could see a hearty negro woman—one who admitted herself to over forty who was not 'poorly,'" noted Catherine Edmondston, the mistress of the Looking Glass plantation in Halifax County, whose biography follows the next chapter. "To be 'poorly' is their aim & object as it ends in the house & spinning."[34]

Slave women could misplace or break tools and household items, or they could "slowdown"—what was the advantage of working hard? "Slave time," after all, was "slave time." Surely one reason for the high status of a cook was her opportunity (and willingness) to pilfer food. In one stroke, she put something over on the big house and nourished her family and friends in the slave community. Slave and owner engaged in a dynamic tension of sorts: she could not misbehave to the extent that she would be punished, sold, or have her family taken away; on the other hand, her owner could not push her so hard as to damage her health and adversely affect her fertility so she would no longer be a valuable worker.[35]

SLAVE WOMEN AND TEXTILES: "IN DE FIELD ALL DAY AN' PIECE AN' QUILT ALL NIGHT"

A fundamental household industry that depended on the labor of slave women was making cloth, especially homespun. Former female slaves remembered spinning, weaving, and quilting as important and meaningful activities in their lives. On the plantation near Garner where Hannah Crasson lived, her mother and grandmother "wove our clothes," which were called "homespun."[36] "De cardin' and' spinnin' room was full of niggers," remembered Temple Herndon Durham of Chatham County. "I can hear dem spinnin' wheels now turnin' roun' an' sayin' hum-m-m-m, hum-m-m-m, an' hear de slaves singin' while dey spin."[37] Although textiles had been generally men's work in Africa, plantation owners preferred the European division of labor in which women were the primary textile workers.[38]

On a few North Carolina plantations, depending on their level of self-sufficiency, certain women might be assigned full-time jobs of spinning, weaving, dyeing, and sewing. Ida Adkins of Durham County remembered her mother at the "big house helping Mis' Mary Jane. Mammy worked in de weavin' room. I can see her now settin' at de weavin' machine an' hear the pedals goin' plop, plop, plop as she treaded dem wid her feets."[39] Temple Herndon Durham's plantation had extensive textile facilities, including a weaving room, where blankets and winter clothing were woven, and a dyeing room. Linda Herndon and Milla Edwards were the "head weavers" who "looked after" the making of the "fancy blankets." In charge of the dyeing room was "Mammy Rachel," and according to Durham, Mammy Rachel "knew every kind of root, bark, leaf, an' berry that made red, blue, green, or whatever color she wanted."[40] Betty Cofer remembered that on the Forsyth County plantation where she was reared, "We raised our own flax an' cotton an' wool, spun the thread, wove the cloth, made all the clothes."[41]

On large plantations, cutting and sewing cloth might be a year-round activity, whereas on smaller ones, it was done in the slow season. In either instance, female slaves worked cloth at night after their day work had been completed. Jane Arrington of Nash County said that after working all day in the field, at night there was "a task of cotton to be picked an' spun" that amounted to "two onces of cotton" for each slave.[42] Fannie Moore, who moved to Asheville from South Carolina after freedom, recalled, "My mammy she work in de fiel' all day an' piece an' quilt all night. Den she hab to spin enough thread to make four cuts for de white fo'ks ebber night. . . . She hab to piece quilts for de white folks too."[43]

The division of labor varied from place to place. Slave women might work alone or with other slave women; the mistress might reserve special tasks for herself or work jointly with the slaves. Temple Herndon Durham's mistress, "Mis' Betsy," was a "good weaver" and spent considerable time at the looms herself, rather than simply supervising the slaves' work. "She weave de same as de niggers. She say she love de clackin' soun' of de loom an' de way de shuttles run in

FIGURE 5-7. *Cotton boy's coat*, Johnston County, 1860s. Slave seamstresses made the little cotton coat and pants for James Madison Lee. (Courtesy of the North Carolina Museum of History)

an' out carryin' a long tail of bright colored thread. Some days she sat at de loom all de mawnin' paddlin' wid her feets an' her white han's flitting over de bobbins."[44] Betty Cofer's mistress, Miss Julia, "cut out all the clothes an' then the colored girls sewed 'em up but she looked 'em all over and they better be sewed right!"[45]

If a large plantation had a full-time slave seamstress, she made garments (from either homespun cloth or purchased northern cloth) for both the slave community and the plantation household, possibly on a task system that stipulated a specific amount of work per day—for example, two pantaloons or three chemises (Fig. 5-7). On the Forsyth County plantation where Betty Cofer lived, slaves "made the mens' shirts an' pants an' coats. One woman knitted all the stockin's for the white folks an' colored folks too."[46]

Slaves quilted and sewed for their personal use, on their own time, or for the plantation mistress, who often supervised the work. Quilting is a classic example of slaves "making do." Africans brought to America already knew techniques of appliqué and patchwork piecing; so transforming bits and scraps of fabric into a bed covering was relatively easy.[47] Appliquéing and pieceworking could be done individually, but the quilting itself required several hands. Slave women could quilt in various ways—for example, four or five women going to each other's homes on successive winter evenings in a sort of round-robin to help each other finish their quilts. Or a large group (even men and children—though they were usually bystanders) could gather together for a quilting party or bee to finish off many quilts, with food, drink, and music. Occasionally, the plantation owner gave his slaves a quilting party as a reward for the harvest or to celebrate Christmas.[48]

Opinions differ among historians regarding an African American aesthetic in quilts (Fig. 5-8). Gladys-Marie Fry thinks that African American quilts are "eclectic"—some display a strong African influence of bold color, asymmetry, improvisation, and multiple patterning, and others merge almost completely with European American conventions of symmetry, careful stitching, and traditional patterns. Cuesta Benberry believes that too few examples of quilts that slaves made for themselves survive to define an African American aesthetic. According to her, the patchwork quilt may have developed in eighteenth-century America (rather than coming from Europe) and slave seamstresses may have partici-

FIGURE 5-8. *Tulip quilt* made and used at a plantation near Goldsboro, Wayne County, pre-1865. The unusual tulip pattern that an unidentified slave pieced for her mistress, Mary Peacock Atkinson, combines the bold color and large design elements of African textiles with the symmetry and balance of the European American tradition. (Collection of Mildred Guthrie, Snow Camp, North Carolina)

FIGURE 5-9. *Cotton Boll Quilt* made by Jennie Neville (Strowd), Orange County, ca. 1864. Several quilts, some rag rugs, and Strowd's sewing equipment were passed down through her daughter to her granddaughter and great-granddaughter, all of whom treated them as precious heirlooms. (Collection of Essie Hogan Leak, Chapel Hill; photograph courtesy of Roberson, *North Carolina Quilts*)

pated in its evolution; so a division between European and African aesthetics makes little sense. Benberry also rejects the notion that quilts displaying a high degree of technical skill are not "true African-American quilts" but merely reflect the white mistresses' aesthetic preferences: she believes that such judgments trivialize the expertise of the slave seamstress. Although slave-made textiles are difficult to document, and the exigencies of fire, theft, sale, in addition to frequent use, make documented slave quilts a rarity, some quilts have survived in the families of the original maker-owner.[49]

The largest collection of surviving slave quilts is by North Carolinian Jennie Neville Strowd (Fig. 5-9). Born a slave in Orange County in 1837, Jennie Neville spun, wove, knitted, made patterns, sewed, and quilted for her owner's family. She was especially valued by the Nevilles: she lived in the family residence; to save her eyes, she was permitted to quit her sewing at dusk; and each year she was allowed to make two new dresses for herself. When she married Joseph Strowd, her master's family presented her with some of the quilts she had made for them as a wedding present. Although the Strowds had hoped to leave the Neville household and strike out on their own after Emancipation, they fell on hard times, and Jennie Strowd continued to design and sew clothes for the Nevilles.[50]

Slaveholding Women's Household Work: "Making Others Work"

Mothers of the slaveholding class were advised to train their daughters in domestic skills, lest "they may be unhappy, unprofitable wives" and a "burden" to their husbands. Although women who had household help, slave or hired, were less directly involved than farmwives in the labor of housekeeping, their management skills and domestic capabilities were essential for their households to thrive.[51]

Phebe Caroline Jones Patterson, of Palmyra plantation in Caldwell County, took responsibility for the domestic production that sustained her family estate (see Fig. 4-5 above). Her granddaughter described her as a busy woman, "up hours before her guests, seeing that the house was put in order, the breakfast properly under way, fresh flowers gathered for the table, etc." Attentive to "her lawn, flower beds, and garden," Patterson was also a "beautiful seamstress . . . the most perfect darning I ever saw" (Fig. 5-10). She supervised the loom room where "pretty spreads and counterpanes" were made and was in charge of the "spinners, gardeners, dairy maids, house servants, cooks and nurses" who helped to create a self-sufficient way of life at Palmyra.[52]

Slaves had the hardest physical work, but running a plantation household required of the mistress abundant energy as well as management skills. She was in charge of domestic production in the "big house"—a term that signified the

FIGURE 5-10. *Wooden sewing box with accessories* used by Sarah Lenoir Jones, Caldwell County, ca. 1845. (Courtesy of the North Carolina Museum of History)

FIGURE 5-11. *Key basket* used by Isabella Barnhill Moore, Caroline Plantation, Pitt County, ca. 1850. A planter woman's authority in the household was delegated by her husband, but she held the keys that controlled access to the buildings and the food supplies, and those keys symbolized her domestic power. "I am up before sunrise to give out the keys," wrote Sara Frances Hicks Williams, who lived on Clifton Grove plantation in Greene County in the 1850s. (Courtesy of the North Carolina Museum of History)

planter's house regardless of its size—and the plantation complex of outbuildings, workshops, storehouses, dairy, and gardens. The storerooms were the center of the household and of her operations: she held the keys to the buildings and food supplies (Fig. 5-11). Her responsibilities extended to the slave quarters; so a planter woman looked after the well-being of everyone, black and white, who lived on the premises. Within the domestic landscape that underlay every plantation complex, white women saw that gardens were cultivated and their bounty preserved, eggs were gathered, cows were milked and butter was churned, pork was salted and sausage made. They supervised the domestic production of candles, soap, rugs, bedding, and clothing, and sometimes even the construction of buildings (Fig. 5-12).[53]

In Chapel Hill, Lucy Martin Battle managed a household consisting of her husband, eight children, and about thirty slaves (Fig. 5-13). Her domestic complex encompassed a dwelling house, outbuildings (including stables, a smokehouse, corncribs, and a bathhouse), slave cabins, numerous fruit and shade trees, a spring, a vegetable garden, and space for livestock. Even though the Battles lived in town, Lucy supervised the work of slaves to create what was close to a self-sufficient household. In addition to caring for her immediate family, she nursed the slaves when they were sick and supervised the birth of their babies, probably with the assistance of a black midwife.[54]

Lucy Battle was involved in every phase of food preparation—proud of her garden, hoping for the earliest peas in Chapel Hill but willing to settle for vegetables "as good as my neighbors have"; fretting over what a late frost would do to the fruit trees that provided apples, peaches, pears, plums, figs, and cherries; serving bread made from corn grown on her property; and getting dirty during hog slaughtering. A never-ending task was obtaining firewood, the sole fuel for cooking and heating—though she did purchase candles, the only source of light until 1854, when her husband bought some lamps in Raleigh.

In charge of providing most of the household clothing, as well as linens and bedcovers, she acquired the whole cloth in several ways. It could be woven by Louisa, the slave who was the family weaver, on looms at home; manufactured in the Battle family cotton mill; or purchased from a drygoods store. As mistress, she usually cut the cloth, and slave women,

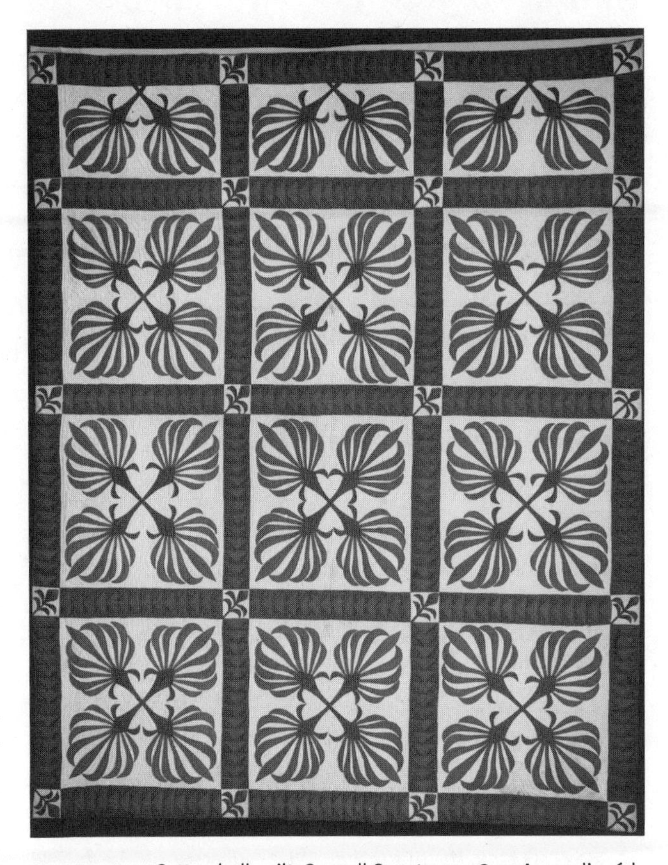

FIGURE 5-12. *Cotton boll quilt*, Caswell County, ca. 1855. An appliquéd quilt was often a best quilt, time-consuming to make, using fabric bought for a specific design, and intended for company use. A number of quilts in the green and red cotton boll design were made in the Piedmont before the Civil War. Frances Johnston made this quilt during the years she lived in her daughter Sarah Johnston Long's household and cared for her grandchildren after her daughter died in 1851 (Roberson, *North Carolina Quilts*, 92–96). (Courtesy of the North Carolina Museum of History)

FIGURE 5-13. William Garle Browne, *Lucy Martin Battle*, oil on canvas, Chapel Hill, ca. 1860. (Courtesy of the North Carolina Collection, University of North Carolina at Chapel Hill)

> Polly is getting on very well towards establishing a high reputation not only as a good wife and mother, but a choice housekeeper in all branches, house, kitchen, yard, garden, poultry, and the rest; and, withall, keeps her amiable manners, cheerful smiles, and social qualities, and genteel appearance.
> —Judge Thomas Ruffin, describing his daughter Polly, 1850. (Hamilton, *Papers of Thomas Ruffin*, 2:294, as cited in Guion G. Johnson, *Ante-Bellum North Carolina*, 237)

her two daughters, and a local seamstress named Matilda Williams did the hand sewing. Except for hats, gloves, and shoes, which could be obtained at the shops specializing in fancy goods, most women's clothing was made at home. Although men's coats were usually bought ready-made or sewn by a tailor, their shirts, pants, and underwear were made by the household women until the 1850s.

Mary Ann Bryan Mason's *The Young Housewife's Counsellor and Friend, Containing Directions in Every Department of Housekeeping including the Duties of Wife and Mother*, written in 1858 but not published until 1871, is a compendium of ideal housekeeping in slaveholding North Carolina (Fig. 5-14). Born to a prominent New Bern family, Mary Ann Mason was married to the rector of Christ Church in Raleigh, the mother of six, and renowned for her artistic talents and cooking skills. She warned that a "young and inexperienced housekeeper is always more or less in the power of her servants, especially of her cook." Moreover, "The eye of a kind but firm mistress is the great inspiration to produce efficiency and regularity in her subordinates." A mistress should show an interest in everything that concerns her servants, so that she will "win their esteem, love, and gratitude, and thus secure their faithfulness."[55]

Housekeeping, according to Mrs. Mason, required con-

FIGURE 5-14. *Mary Ann Bryan Mason*, Raleigh. The gentry housewife could use her taste, judgment, and fancy in selecting foods for the dinner table, but she should remember that "variety is the spice of life," according to Mason's *Young Housewife's Counsellor and Friend* (1871). (Courtesy of the North Carolina Division of Archives and History)

FIGURE 5-15. *Tea service*, coin silver, used by Ann Potter Kidder, Wilmington, 1836–65. The gentry, especially those living in town, often entertained one another with tea parties. Generally friends visited at 5:30 P.M., the hostess poured tea from a silver tea service set on a mahogany tea table, and a black servant passed around food such as muffins, biscuits, brandied peaches, preserves, and thinly sliced ham. (Courtesy of the North Carolina Museum of History)

stant vigilance (Fig. 5-15). Bedrooms should be aired daily, beds sunned twice a month, kitchen utensils scrubbed weekly, clothes mended and buttons replaced, hearths swept every day in the winter, cupboards and closets inspected and then locked, and lighting equipment put in good order for evening. The housewife should strain the milk herself and see that the churns were scalded and aired daily; check periodically to ensure that the proper amount of bluing and starch was added to the clothes, for "servants have little idea of proportion" and could get careless; and superintend the soap making, poultry yard, and garden. "Insist on all your wood-ashes being saved to make the family soap," she advised. "Let your servants understand at once that *you will not buy soap* when there are abundant materials at home for its manufacture."[56]

REBECCA BENNEHAN CAMERON AND "PORK": "AS YOU MAY JUDGE BEST"

Although the division of labor on a plantation meant that generally planter women supervised and slaves labored, even privileged women like Rebecca Bennehan Cameron, wife of one of the state's wealthiest planters, Duncan Cameron, at times participated in hard, dirty work. One of the most grueling jobs a mistress had to perform was in early winter, when she slogged through several exhausting weeks of bloody hog butchering, rendering lard, making sausage, and curing hams and bacon. In 1806 Rebecca asked her husband what she should do about the hogs at Eno, one of many units, each with its own land, slaves, and overseers, that comprised Fairntosh plantation. Duncan wrote back that she should handle "the pork at the Little River as you may judge best."

Thereafter, Rebecca took responsibility for the pork every winter for the rest of her life. In 1819 "We have been busily engaged since you left us taking care of our pork, we have I believe killed about 160 hogs," she told her husband. In 1835 her daughter wrote, "Mother has been suffering and she still suffers with a sty on her eye, [but she] has been in the kitchen engaged with her pork this week." In 1841, after thirty-five seasons, Rebecca noted, "I have gone through my business in the kitchen with the aid of my old faithful Hannah with very little trouble and I hope to be able to accomplish the job with as much ease and comfort to myself as in my younger days."[57]

PRIVATE AFFAIRS AND PUBLIC ROLES

Although men concerned themselves with the plantation's long-range affairs, the daily administration often fell to their wives. The dominance of planters, relative to their actual number, in state politics was facilitated by their being able to count on their wives to manage plantation affairs while they were gone. Half of North Carolina's planters held second occupations or served in the legislature. Under some circumstances, a wife was legally recognized as her husband's business agent, which gave her added authority—and him the freedom to enter public life.[58]

Planter John Steele, whose political career took him to Philadelphia, in 1796 wrote his wife Mary, "In respect to our private affairs, I need say nothing—You will do for the best and to your discretion I leave the management of everything." Rebecca Cameron stayed put at Fairntosh while her husband Duncan pursued a law career in Raleigh that financed the purchase of more land and slaves, served in the state legislature, and eventually established the state bank. Rebecca was expected to keep him informed of all the happenings on their growing plantation complex, though he was not compelled to keep her likewise apprised. While he was solidifying his political base in 1812, she wrote, "I see my dear by the papers that the Assembly has given you an appointment. I do not know what the duties are which will be required of you, but I fear they are such as will not add to my happiness." In 1829 Duncan was appointed president of the state bank, which left Rebecca "very much surprised and concerned."[59]

In town, also, a woman doing good at home could help her husband do well in public life. Lucy Martin Battle's exceptional management of her family's private affairs permitted her husband, William Horn Battle, to engage in the legal profession as attorney, legislator, and judge. He was absent for half a year annually during twenty-eight years of marriage. Although she gave birth in each of the two sessions that he served in the legislature (1833–34, 1834–35), she assumed much of the responsibility for his law practice and other business. Her son remembered "the neatly written copies by my mother, as amanuensis, of the opinions of Ruffin, Daniel and Gaston." When Lucy handled a particularly important piece of legal business from New York City, her husband observed: "I would do you an injustice were I merely to express a simple approval. I think you exhibited no little skill in the manner in which you disposed of the business." John H. Bryan, away from New Bern for extended periods while attending Congress in Washington, D.C., in 1829 wrote his wife Mary: "You had better endeavor to collect the notes of Wood and Bob Lisbon for the hire of the negroes, particularly the latter. . . . I am very well satisfied with your disposition of the negroes—you are my smartest as well as most trusted agent."[60]

Women's Work for Pay: "To Violate the Delicate Modesty"

Early nineteenth-century women who actually had to earn a wage found limited employment opportunities and meager earnings in North Carolina. They were even regarded as deviant in a society that viewed women's proper place (and work) to be in the home. The notion of a woman working outside her household was considered so unusual that the federal census did not begin to list women's occupations until 1860. Yet economic need required many women—particularly free black women, and poor, single, or widowed white women—to work for wages. For them, economic independence was hard to achieve.[61]

Throughout the 1800s the single largest occupation of women not working in agriculture was domestic service, including housekeeping, laundering, and sewing. Generally the most destitute women, obliged to be self-sufficient but with few job options, were employed as unskilled servants. Living at the margins of antebellum society, these free women, white and black, competed with slave labor, for hiring out slaves was a common practice in North Carolina.[62]

FREE BLACK WORKING WOMEN

Race determined how menial the domestic job might be: black women were always the washerwomen. Large numbers of free black washerwomen lived in Craven, Cumberland, Halifax, New Hanover, Pasquotank, Rutherford, and Wake Counties. Many free black women worked as household servants in Craven, Cumberland, Davidson, Greene, Hertford, Pasquotank, and Yadkin Counties. More than 170 of them were seamstresses, particularly in Craven, Halifax, and New Hanover Counties, although whether they did plain sewing or dressmaking is impossible to determine. In 1860 North Carolina counted 175 free black seamstresses and almost 300 free black spinners and weavers, the majority of whom were women. A few free black women could be identified as midwives (18) and nurses (66), occupations linked to domestic work but more skilled and specialized.[63]

As they went about their daily routines, black working women were visible in the public spaces of New Bern, Fayetteville, and Wilmington and in counties with substantial free black populations. Frederick Law Olmsted recounts riding in a stagecoach with a "free colored woman" who "was treated in no way differently from the white ladies" on his trip to North Carolina in the 1850s and learning, to his surprise, that this was "entirely customary."[64]

TEXTILES AND WHITE WOMEN

Both rural and urban white women who had to earn a living frequently turned to textiles. A survey of probate documents from the area prominent in North Carolina's early textile mill industry—Alamance and Orange Counties, including present-day Durham County—shows that women weavers earned money from home production. Included among the documents, for example, are the bills of "Miss Fanny Clark for weaving," account payable for 1£ (sterling) on October 1, 1800; Mary Williams, for "Weaving 50 yards of Cloth at 6 cents a yard $3.00" in 1821; and Nancy Sparrow, for 140 yards of cloth woven for 5 cents per yard, $7.00, in 1850. After weaving became established in the textile mills (spinning had begun in the late 1830s, weaving by 1852), no further bills exist. By midcentury, either women found it more profitable to work in the mills, or their home production could not compete with cheaper manufactured cloth and they lost their market.[65] In 1842 a Raleigh newspaper carried an account of a Tennessee woman who petitioned her state legislature, "In by gone days we could, by industry, not only provide clothing for our household, but we could make a sufficiency of domestic manufacture to spare to sell to the merchants to procure other necessaries for our families." No longer, she stated, could home production compete with the low price of manufactured cloth.[66]

Factory work became a viable option for women in the antebellum period, first in New England and later in the South, where workers were less educated and more apt to be compliant. U.S. wages were lower than those in the British textile industry, giving American textiles a competitive edge. Increasingly women were hired to work as operatives, comprising as much as 75 percent of the workforce in some textile factories (Fig. 5-16). Work in a textile mill was seen as a

FIGURE 5-16. *Women operatives outside original Alamance Mill*, built ca. 1839 in present-day Alamance County. The Alamance Mill was the first plant to manufacture colored cotton fabric in the South, and its owner, Edwin M. Holt [*inset*], was probably the most prosperous antebellum textile manufacturer in North Carolina. Holt's mill, like others in the Piedmont, was described as a "real blessing, present and prospective, for it gives enjoyment and comfort to many poor girls who might otherwise be wretched" (Benson J. Lossing, *Pictorial Field Book of the Revolution*, 2:388). (Courtesy of the North Carolina Museum of History)

natural extension of women's traditional household production, and most men considered it beneath them—by definition, textiles were "women's work." Yet the wages were higher than those paid in domestic service and other female occupations. Black women, as well as white, worked in textile factories, although the Lincoln Cotton Factory near Lincolnton evidently employed only white women. In 1860 the state's cotton mill industry was still relatively small—only thirty-nine mills in twenty counties, three mills employing more than 100 workers and 1,700 female millworkers. Yet, though the total numbers were smaller, North Carolina had a higher proportion of women in manufacturing than Pennsylvania at the start of the Civil War.[67]

Many millworkers were poor and young. About a third were between the ages of ten and fifteen. Many lived with their parents, supplementing the family income until they married and left home. "Respectable and intelligent girls" is how a Greensboro newspaper described the "Operatives" at the Franklinville mill in Randolph County in 1849. They were "tidy" in dress, "modest," and "healthy." The young women earned "12½ to 17½ cents per day, depending on the age, skill and experience of the hand," for working "twelve hours per day . . . except on Saturday when it is only nine hours." In 1856 Frederick Law Olmsted compared young Highland Scot girls employed in a cotton factory near Fayetteville favorably "in modesty, cleanliness, and neatness of apparel, though evidently poor" with girls employed in a cotton mill he had visited near Glasgow, Scotland. He noted that the young women eschewed their immigrant parents' "thrifty habits": the proprietor of the mill told him that "they very seldom laid up anything, and spent the greater part of their earnings very foolishly, as fast as they received them."[68]

Women who operated a tavern or boardinghouse enjoyed more status, more autonomy, and more money than those in domestic labor or textiles. Taverns had long been important landmarks along the North Carolina countryside, and boardinghouses served the commercial traffic that was a growing part of the more urban antebellum society—whether in Raleigh for legislators and businessmen or in county seats like Hillsborough or Tarboro for judges and lawyers, plaintiffs and defendants. Boardinghouses, with their facilities for an extended stay, home cooking, and a group of regulars, were an early instance of a home away from home.

As in colonial times, operating a boardinghouse was considered a respectable way for a widow to earn a living, because she still lived in her own home and remained firmly within the feminine sphere. Raleigh widow Eliza Haywood, who had a commodious house and a reputation for hospitality, was able to provide for her family when the default and death in 1827 of her husband, state treasurer John Haywood (who had embezzled nearly $70,000), deprived the family of most of its wealth. Eliza was a well-known hostess and gardener during her husband's lifetime, and after his death she turned the family home, Haywood Hall, into a boardinghouse and sold plants and herbs from her own garden (Fig. 5-17). In 1829 she advertised for "Travellers," "Gentlemen and their Families," "Boarders," and "Schoolchildren."[69]

A wife's prudent management of a boardinghouse might supplement her husband's income. For example, Edith Branson, the wife of educator, Methodist minister, and publisher Levi Branson, ran the Branson House in Raleigh for thirty years. Although most women's hospitality ventures tended to be on a small scale and marginal in prestige, a Mrs. Brown

FIGURE 5-17. *Haywood Hall, Raleigh*. (Courtesy of the Haywood Hall House Museum, Raleigh)

Buy your Butter at French's.
47
David Aaron.
Fred. Rheinstein.
OUR
MILLINERY DEPART'MT
Is under the charge of the experienced
Miss Lyons,
OF WILMINGTON.
Aaron & Rheinstein,
Wholesale and Retail Dealers in
DOMESTIC & FANCY DRY GOODS,
Carpets, Oil Cloths, Clothing,
HATS, CAPS, BOOTS, SHOES, TRUNKS, &c.,
No. 25 Market Street,
WILMINGTON, N. C.
This Stock is one of the most Complete and Beautiful in the City, and the most fastidious will be pleased with it.
No. 25
Is made doubly attractive by its new and tasteful
Millinery Department,
In which is kept a fine assortment of
HATS, BONNETS, TRIMMINGS,
Cloaks, Mantillas, &c.
Ladies, from the City and Country, are requested to call and examine our stock.
See A. Weill & Co's Advertisement, Page 33.

FIGURE 5-18. *Advertisement for Aaron & Rheinstein Domestic & Fancy Dry Goods*, engraving. Inviting ladies from the city and country to call, this notice asserted, "Our millinery department is under the charge of the experienced Miss Lyons of Wilmington." (From *Bernard's Wilmington and Fayetteville Directory and Handbook for Useful Information, 1866–1867* [New Hanover County, 1866])

operated the Fayetteville Hotel, praised by the *Fayetteville Observer* in 1849 as one of the handsomest in the state.[70]

Some women combined domestic industry with commercial endeavors, selling soap or dresses or hats. We know little about these early entrepreneurs, but based on advertisements for their goods and services in local newspapers, many appear to have been from the North or immigrants who relocated in North Carolina's growing towns. In contrast to most women, whose names never appeared in print, female shopkeepers depended on public advertisements to attract customers and thus stretched, ever so slightly, the boundaries of feminine space (Fig. 5-18).

By 1860 many women had ceased making soap at home. To them and others, Mrs. E. R. McGowan of Raleigh offered her own "mineral toilet soap," which "had a good effect upon the skin, relieving and curing eruptions." At fifty cents a bar, it was so popular that she increased production and sold it to merchants as well as to individuals. Similarly, Mrs. Joe Person sustained a brisk trade in the 1860s with her amazing skin care cream, its secrets known only to her.[71]

Women with sewing skills, business ability, and access to clientele opened millinery and dressmaking shops. They sold dresses and hats made on the premises and items of feminine fashion manufactured elsewhere, often in the North. Their "fancy goods" added a welcome variety to the wardrobes of women living in or near New Bern, Wilmington, Raleigh, Tarboro, Greensboro, Salisbury, Charlotte, and other towns.

These early businesswomen were often enterprising. Sarah Lane carried on a "Mantuamaking business in all its branches, making Ladies Dresses, Pelisses, and Great-Coats in the latest fashion and the neatest manner" in New Bern in 1811, but she supplemented her income by taking in boarders—four or five young ladies from the New Bern Academy—to whom she would also teach "Sewing and Marking."[72] The exotically named Madame Huau catered to New Bern's millinery needs in 1815, selling "elegant Silk, Satin & Striped Bonnets of the newest fashions," ribbons, and "a large assortment of Bandboxes." She could also make new bonnets or alter old ones "to any pattern" and bleach straw bonnets "to make them appear as handsome as when new."[73]

Along with silk and straw bonnets and "gipsey hats," "Mrs. NORMAN, Milliner" sold china tea sets, cut glass bowls, gilt-framed prints, fans, and wreaths in Raleigh in 1804. A "Miss Raley, from New York" opened a shop in Raleigh in 1817 to sell bonnets, gloves, perfumes—her millinery and dresses made "in the latest fashion, having . . . weekly correspondence from New York." Still in business two years later and still providing the latest "from New York," Miss Raley offered an even more extensive assortment of fancy goods, including "Plush and Ermine Trimmings," "Cassimere Shawls," and "Hair caps and Curls." In the 1840s Jane Henderson was the proprietor of another Raleigh millinery shop, which she subsequently sold to the Misses M. A. and S. Pulliam.[74]

Tarboro had Mrs. A. C. Howard, who in 1829 advertised millinery and dressmaking services "in the latest and most approved fashions" for the women in town and surrounding Edgecombe County. Mrs. Howard also offered "a handsome

FIGURE 5-19. Daniel Welfare, *Isaac and Elizabeth Boner*, Salem (present-day Forsyth County), portrait, ca. 1835. Hats were the business of the Boner family in the Moravian town of Salem. Although Elizabeth is depicted working on a hat, perhaps adding trim to the inside brim, no other evidence connects her with the family business. (Courtesy of the Collection of the Wachovia Historical Society, Winston-Salem)

assortment of FANCY GOODS, suitable for fall and winter wear" that had been purchased in "Northern cities" and reflected "the latest Northern fashions," including "Superior bobinett caps and capes," "Curls, caps, and turbans," "Beaded and spangled wreaths, flowers and sprigs, new and elegant articles," "Black and white ostrich feathers," and "Coral ear drops and necklaces."[75]

In the Moravian town of Salem, the Single Sisters operated a millinery business in the 1820s. By the mid-1840s, Louisa Sussdorf, Sarah Ann Fulkerson, and Catharina Stauber all sold hats (Fig. 5-19). The entrepreneurial Sister Catharina also sold baskets, shoes, perfume, and "sugar goods" to Salem Academy students—so irritating her fellow shopkeepers that she received a reprimand by town officials in 1846. She countered that it was impossible for her to "restrict" herself to "her own business" when local merchants also sold hats, "which actually should be her privilege."[76]

Needleworkers who could not afford to set themselves up in business often barely scraped by. One young woman described her plight in a letter to the *Southern Weekly Post* in 1851. The "elder of five sisters," her father dead and her mother sickly, she was responsible for supporting her entire family. She found work with a tailor, and for a week's labor of "pantaloons at seventy-five cents, vests at one dollar; three of the former, one of the latter, were the most I could do in a week; thus making seventeen dollars per month; no allowance made for sickness, &s five dollars of this must go for house rent, leaving twelve dollars for fuel, lights, food and clothing for a family of six." At this point, the "Sewing Girl" pleaded for a larger sphere of activity for young women who must support their families:

> Will our gentlemen merchants take our daughters as clerks? Will you, Mr. Post, and your brother editors, let our sisters set type at your stands, or must the next generation still be doomed to
>
> Stitch-stitch-stitch
> In poverty, hunger, and dirt
> Sewing at once with a double thread
> A *Shroud* as well as a shirt!

A year later "Mr. Post" replied, though indirectly, to the "Sewing Girl": "We doubt not our lady readers will pardon us for the opinion that their proper place is not in the full glare of public observation—not in the general practice of what are called the learned professions, nor in any employment which would compel them to violate the delicate modesty in which their virtue is enshrined."[77]

Virtue was not the commodity sold by women working in the "lewd houses" that could be found in the largest towns in the state and many smaller ones as well. Prostitutes were present at any large gathering, be they fairs, public celebrations, or trials. One man attending the Madison County Court in 1853 harrumphed: "Scores of women attend this court for the sole purpose of drinking and pandering to the lustful passions of dirty men." He regretted that "some men, I will not say gentlemen, are guilty of intercourse with these dirty, filthy strumpets, that ought to be, and one would think they are above doing such things."[78]

In 1821 "A Friend to Industry" wrote from the Forks of the Yadkin to warn readers of the *Western Carolinian* against "such characters as follow 'no honest calling' for a livelihood, but slink about from one place to another, alluring minors and heedless young men to the gaming table, and other scenes of vice and depravity." Dire warnings in newspapers, campaigns against "prostitute women" by state and local officials, and public outrage appeared intermittently throughout the early nineteenth century. Prostitution was the lot of the poorest women, white as well as black. Few owned property, and many were not even counted by the census. Their names appear in the court records, most often for violating laws intended to restrict miscegenation and black and white intermingling rather than for prostitution. It is an inescapable irony that the one business dominated by women was occupied by women at the bottom socially.[79]

WOMEN AND THE PROFESSIONS: "TO SUSTAIN HERSELF"

A handful of educated white women in antebellum North Carolina pursued teaching and writing careers that defied tradition and laid the groundwork for women's professions of the future. Both occupations were aided by changing attitudes toward educated women, but they also seemed to stay within the bounds of proper womanhood. Teaching was viewed as similar to a mother's role in rearing her children, and writing could be done within the privacy of the home.

The number of women who wrote never came close to those who taught, yet writers were important in articulating a woman's perspective. Between 1784 and 1860 more than one hundred magazines were founded in the United States, many devoted to women's interests. In the twenty years between 1830 and 1850, about 1,150 novels were published, perhaps a third written either by women or for women. There are many accounts of busy women taking time to read. As one example, on the Cool Spring plantation in Edgecombe County, Lavinia Bassett Daniel Battle and her family read magazines such as the *Eclectic*, *Littell's Living Age*, *Atlantic Monthly*, and *Harper's*; newspapers like the *Norfolk Virginian* and *Southern Churchman*; and novels by Thackeray, Dickens, Trollope, William Black, and other British and American writers.[80]

Educators and clergy claimed that novel reading had an adverse effect on young women's morals and that the Bible was all the reading a woman needed. Yet women loved novels, and when John Motley Morehead started his female seminary in Greensboro, he named it after the Irish novelist and essayist, Maria Edgeworth, who, with the possible exception of Sir Walter Scott, was North Carolinians' favorite novelist.[81]

Although writing was particularly suitable for women, few professionals could be found in rural North Carolina. Southern women generally wrote letters and journals, setting down private thoughts and daily activities for their family and friends. Writing was an important part of a girl's seminary training, and an adult woman was expected to keep in touch with family members with frequent letters. The surviving voluminous correspondence of southern gentry women is ample evidence that women took their letter-writing duties seriously. Federal era and antebellum North Carolina women who wrote and published books intended for a public audience can be counted on one hand, and they lived in Raleigh.

Winifred Marshall Gales, author of *Matilda Berkley, or Family Anecdotes* (1804), the first novel published in North Carolina by a resident of the state, was far more liberal than most North Carolinians. She and her husband Joseph were political refugees from England, lured from Philadelphia to Raleigh in late 1799 to publish the *Raleigh Register*, which promoted Jeffersonian Republicanism. The Galeses, active in organizing Unitarianism in Philadelphia, in Raleigh, and in the South, were out of step politically in North Carolina, and in 1831 they moved to Washington, D.C., where their oldest son edited the *National Intelligencer*.[82]

Mary Bayard Devereux Clarke was born to a prominent and wealthy North Carolina family, and she and her five sisters were educated by governesses on a level supposedly comparable to that of their only brother John, at Yale. Like many women of her class and education, she wrote for her own pleasure and, like her sister, Catherine Devereux Edmondston, kept a journal and wrote poetry. Mary Bayard, however, went public with her poems, compiling the first anthology of North Carolina poetry, *Wood Notes, or Carolina Carols*, published in Raleigh in 1854. She encouraged other poets to join her:

> "Come rouse you! ye poets of North Carolina
> My State is my theme and I seek not a finer."[83]

As author of the *Housewife's Counsellor and Friend* (written 1859, published 1871), Mary Ann Bryan Mason may have followed her own advice: her books are written from a sense of "duty" appropriate to a wife and mother. As a minister's wife, she may also have written to supplement her husband's salary. In 1859 she wrote the first book for children by a North Carolinian, *A Wreath from the Woods of North Carolina*—a Sunday school text of ten religious stories.[84]

The works of Clarke and Mason represent a dramatic shift in publishing, responding to the increased literacy of women and recognizing that they constituted a special audience.

In contrast to the small number of educated women who attempted writing as a professional activity, teaching attracted many. Teaching was a transitory profession, and a large number of female teachers moved in and out of it. Some taught for only a few months or a year or two between their own schooling and marriage. Some left teaching on marriage and returned because of family reverses or widowhood. Others, especially widows and spinsters, became governesses, teachers, or school administrators for their entire working lives. Mary A. Gash wrote of herself and two cousins

Mary A. Gash proposes to teach a school at Burn's Creek schoolhouse for the term of 3 months or 12 weeks commencing May 1857.

Spelling Reading Writing and Arithmetic $2.40
Geography English Grammar Philosophy & Composition 3.60
Astronomy Chemistry and Rhetoric 4.20

She obligates herself to preserve good order so far as is within her power, and those who are not willing to be governed by the rules of the school may expect to be expelled.

Twenty scholars are desired though she will commence with sixteen.

The subscribers are expected to pay their tuition at the close of the school.

—Advertisement, Gash Family Papers, 1857. (North Carolina Division of Archives and History, as cited in Clayton, *Close to the Land*, 39)

who were also teachers: "We all have an Old Maid's occupation and that is school teaching."[85]

Most women teachers were young, single, and mobile. They generally earned half the salary of men: a disparity that makes teaching an excellent example of men and women doing the same work but for different wages, an inequity not confined to the South. A popular advocate of female education, Catharine Beecher, who operated seminaries in Hartford, Connecticut, and Cincinnati, Ohio, believed that "women can afford to teach for one-half, or even less, the salary which men would ask, because the female teacher has only to sustain herself."[86]

Although teaching probably held little appeal for gentry women, hard times might necessitate that they use their education to earn a living by opening a select school—which meant that they taught in their own home. Betsy Haywood, whose inheritance had been lost by her father's financial dealings, his death in 1827, and her mother's soon after, started a day school in the family home, Haywood Hall, in Raleigh in 1832 to support herself and her younger sisters (Fig. 5-17 above). By 1841 Haywood Hall was a boarding school where Betsy taught the primary subjects and her sister Frances, the older girls.[87]

The majority of the early teachers worked at private schools—either female seminaries or female departments of coeducational academies—that proliferated in North Carolina (and elsewhere) in the early 1800s. Woman also taught in the public schools that opened during the 1840s, though not in large numbers. In 1849 only 19 women were public school teachers—1.25 percent of the total number statewide; on the eve of the Civil War, there were 156 female teachers, or 7.5 percent.[88]

The rapid growth of academies and seminaries in the early nineteenth century increased the demand for female teachers. Women normally taught music, drawing, painting, and fancy needlework, but they often taught academic subjects as well. Quaker Judith Mendenhall taught geography and the use of globes in addition to the usual curriculum in the boarding school she opened for boys and girls in 1815 in Jamestown, Guilford County. From 1815 to 1823 Susan Davis Nye of New York ran the female department at the Raleigh Academy, where she performed chemistry experiments.[89]

With few women qualified to teach school in North Carolina in the 1810s and 1820s, women educated in New York and elsewhere in the North were recruited for the state's schools.[90] Adventurous enough to relocate to another region, these middle-class teachers may have introduced new ideas and values to their students, who belonged to North Carolina's elite families. If financial need was the reason teachers worked for wages, many also had a mission. They had been trained in northern female seminaries that were an outgrowth of the Second Awakening, and they had come south imbued with the power of educating women.[91]

Teachers who had attended Emma Hart Willard's famous Troy Female Seminary in upstate New York were exposed to a curriculum comparable to that offered at men's colleges and to the forceful presence of Emma Willard herself—a woman of both intellectual vigor and female respectability. Willard was renowned for her "Plan for Improving Female Education" (presented to the New York State legislature and published in 1819) and for her efforts to train future teachers in her school. Envisioning teaching as a woman's profession, she prepared more than 12,000 young women between 1821 and 1871. Many of her students accepted positions in communities throughout the North, Midwest, and South. They constituted the first generation of professional teachers, in a field that was open, from the beginning, to women.[92]

It is possible to document both the Troy influence and the presence of Troy graduates in North Carolina. In 1835 the principal of the Greenville Female Academy, a Mrs. Saffrey, advertised that she had "adopted for her model, the justly esteemed and much celebrated system of Mrs. Willard." Throughout the 1830s schools in Chapel Hill, Scotland Neck, Northampton County, and other places were staffed by Troy teachers and administrators whose credentials were widely proclaimed.[93]

The majority of northern schoolteachers were young and single. In contrast to those who went west, found husbands on the frontier, and became pillars of the community, few who traveled south seem to have married local men and settled permanently. A study of 134 students from Mount Holyoke Seminary in Massachusetts who taught in the South puts the average length of their stay at just over three years.[94]

Possibly northern teachers returned home because the cultural differences and social adjustments were simply too great. The values of frugality and morality, hard work, and high seriousness that seminary training inculcated in them conflicted with the generally slower pace of southern life and a society in which slavery played a defining role. As Lydia Sigourney, the author of a popular book on etiquette, noted, "the northern youth, who engages in the business of instruction in the sunny south, perceives the necessity of conforming to new usages, in order to be in harmony with those around."[95]

Carrie Holt, a teacher at Warrenton Female Academy, found Warrenton a place that "nobody ever seemed to reach . . . from the outer world." Of her experience at the academy, she wrote: "It was my first meeting face to face with slavery, and though I am no Rabid Abolitionist, I could not help being struck with the Sleepy Hollow air which seemed to prevade the whole place in every department." Holt missed the stimulating activity of northern towns and "counted time by mail days, which were tri-weekly."[96]

Mary Young Cheyney, of Connecticut, who taught at Harriet J. Allen's school in Warrenton, was an outspoken abolitionist who returned north after she married Horace Greeley in the Episcopal church in Warrenton in 1836. Her views on slavery added to her discomfort in Warren, a major slaveholding county in the state, and her presence at Allen's school resulted in its closing shortly after her departure. Elizabeth Blackwell (who later became the first American woman doctor) was reluctant to be too candid in her views on slavery when she taught at a Presbyterian school in Asheville. Instead, she attempted "to slide in a little truth through the small aperture of their minds, for were I to come out broadly with my simple, honest opinions, I should shut them up tight, arm all their prejudices, and do ten times more harm than good."[97]

> A series of petty slights and annoyances aggravated my discomfort and a proposition on the part of the Principal to add to the number of my music pupils out of school hours, unaccompanied by any mention of remuneration for the extra labor, capped the climax. It was immediately answered by my resignation. . . . My three friends and fellow teachers seemed also to have reached the limit of their powers of endurance and very shortly after my departure, they returned together to the North.
>
> —Carrie Holt, "An Autobiographical Sketch of a Teacher's Life," 9. (Pope, "Preparation for Pedestals," 203–4)

Teaching institutions were modeled on the patriarchal family. Men held positions of authority as trustees, superintendents, and principals, and women served as teachers—moral, nurturing, and loving. The principal was the father, his wife was the mother and head of the female department, female teachers played the oldest daughter, and pupils were the younger children. Frequently the husband was a minister (often the most highly educated person in his rural community) who needed to supplement his modest salary, and a wife who could teach supported him in his calling. In an era of large families (where older daughters often played surrogate mother to younger siblings and stayed under their father's roof until marriage), teaching reflected familiar societal and economic patterns. "I feel very like Mother Goose's old woman who lived in a shoe some Saturdays when they all cluster around," wrote Emma Sue Gordon, a teacher at St. Mary's School in Raleigh. Like most female teachers, Gordon slept in the dormitory with her students, and her waking hours not spent in instructing her pupils were consumed by supervising them.[98]

After the 1840s, schools with denominational affiliations provided even more employment opportunities for clergymen and their wives. The Reverend Aldert Smedes and his wife Sarah Lyell Smedes moved to Raleigh from New York to start the Episcopal female academy, St. Mary's School, where they both taught classes, led students in prayers, and served as surrogate parents. In Murfreesboro, the Reverend Joseph H. Davis and his wife Anne Beale Davis had five children to educate and so accepted an offer in 1854 to serve the newly founded Methodist Wesleyan Female College as president and school matron respectively. Living in the same quarters as their students, the Davises were parents to their large "family," on call day and night. Anne Davis complained of "labouring like a galley slave" at everything from keeping the account books to making the pastry and from teaching the primary grades when a teacher was absent to being on her feet from daybreak until "8 or 9 O'clock at night." After five years of hard work, stress, and sacrifice, the Davises left schoolteaching.[99]

Many early schools netted barely enough to support the proprietor's family; not surprisingly, many educator couples appear to have been constantly on the move. A striking exception was the Institution for Female Improvement at Warrenton operated between 1809 and 1818 by Jacob Mordecai, who was unusual in being Jewish in overwhelmingly Protestant North Carolina. With thirteen children of his own, Mordecai had reason enough to be interested in education, and the involvement of his large family in every aspect of the school at no remuneration contributed to its success. Mordecai himself was head instructor, and nineteen-year-old Rachel, who had been educated at home, and fifteen-year-old Solomon, who left the Warrenton Male Academy, taught classes. The job of boarding and caring for the students fell to Jacob's wife Rebecca, their daughters Rachel and Ellen, and a slave named Mammy. The oldest Mordecai child, Samuel, already on his own in Richmond, served as the school's purchasing agent. Eventually, the younger daughters, Ellen and Caroline, began to teach as well. Despite their dislike for the job, Rachel and Ellen seem never to have considered disobeying their father.

The fifteen-hour workdays, course preparations, and constant supervision of "so many wild & apparently ungovernable children" became an intolerable burden for Rachel Mordecai. She found the repetition of lessons "irksome even to disgust" and the "daily instances of stupidity, obstinacy, & folly" tedious. Exhausted and frustrated, Rachel mused, "yet how can it be otherwise when our tranquility is dependent on a hundred children who feel no interest in promoting our interest." By 1817 the approach of another academic year filled her with "painful and rebellious feelings. . . . I can hardly imagine anything more uncomfortable than such a week of preparation, everything to be arranged, and the whole complicated machine to be set in motion with such a scrutinizing eye & well poised hand as that no part shall interfere with another and the whole be enabled to proceed with order, ease, and regularity."[100]

Jacob Mordecai also found the academy tiresome, but profitable. When he sold out, he was able to buy a plantation in Virginia, providing entry into the gentry class for him, his wife, and his children, some of whom later made auspicious marriages. The Warrenton school changed hands several times, and between 1822 and 1830 Jacob's daughter Caroline tried to revive it. She had married Achilles Plunkett, a planter forced to flee from Santo Domingo who had taught French, art, and dancing in her father's academy. Caroline lacked her father's resources, reputation, and large family from which to draw teachers. Her husband died in early 1824, and she and her stepson struggled for several years, but she could not keep the academy afloat.

By contrast, Hillsborough had three successful schools that were headed by women spanning the years from 1812 to 1890. Polly Burke, the daughter of Governor Thomas Burke and a single woman of considerable property, was the first. Starting in 1812, she began teaching neighborhood children grammar and manners, at first in her home and from 1818 to 1834 in a log schoolhouse (still standing on the John Graham Webb property in Hillsborough). She left in the latter year and moved to Alabama.[101]

Shortly afterward Burwell's Female School (1837–57) opened its doors. Margaret Anna Robertson Burwell's entry into education was typical of many of the early female teachers, but she expanded her domain by her enterprise, administrative capability, and intellectual energy. Described as a "veritable helpmate," Mrs. Burwell had moved to North Carolina from Virginia in 1835, when her husband Robert assumed the pastorate of the Hillsborough Presbyterian Church. She began by tutoring local girls to supplement his modest salary. In 1838 she opened a boarding and day school in her home and soon earned enough to erect a classroom and refectory on the grounds. By 1848 her school, which stressed rigorous academics and daily reading of the Bible, was prospering so well that her husband bought the property from his congregation and resigned his pastorate to help her run it.[102]

Margaret Burwell, as her former pupil Lavinia Cole recalled, "neglected no duty, kept the house beautifully, had the personal supervision of thirty boarders, attended to their manners and morals, saw that their beds were properly made—was particular about their health—kept house, made her own bread, washed the dishes, with our assistance—taught six hours a day—was the mother of twelve beautifully clean, healthy, and attractive children, dressed well always and entertained as much company as any other lady in the village."[103] Adhering to legal and social conventions of the day, Robert Burwell was the owner and titular head of the Burwell School, but Margaret Burwell was its heart and the real head. In 1857 she and her husband were called to the Charlotte Female Institute (later, Queens College), where they jointly served as "Principal."

Two years later, in 1859, the Nash and Kollock Select Boarding and Day School opened; it remained in operation until 1890. The organizers were two middle-aged sisters, Sally and Maria Nash, and their younger cousin, Sarah Kollock. The Nash sisters came from a prominent family—their Nash grandfather was an early governor and their Kollock grandfather a leader in American Presbyterianism. Maria had attended Polly Burke's school, and Sally had taught at Burwell. Their father, Frederick Nash, had been the chief justice of the North Carolina Supreme Court, but he died in debt in 1858 as a result of speculation in Chatham County coal fields, and the two sisters were forced to open a female seminary in their large residence. The social, religious, and political credentials of the Nash and Kollock families were impeccable, and the school was an immediate success.[104]

Women and work went hand in hand, and the labor of their hands was rewarded by a sense of sustaining and caring for their families. As education became available to more girls and women, their horizons broadened, and some of them began to carve out a woman's place in the schoolroom and church. Enslaved black women did not have the opportunities of their free black sisters or white women, and so within the limits of their circumstances they learned to cope with adversity and honed skills that one day would enable them to move beyond slavery. As the clouds of war came to North Carolina, women found themselves ready to step forward, but once more they would have to do what needed to be done in a time and a place that were about to undergo radical change.

CHAPTER 6

Women Entered the Struggle

War, Emancipation, and Reconstruction, 1860–1876

Although North Carolina women did not fight on the battlefields, they knew from their own experiences at home the truth of Northern general William T. Sherman's observation, "war is hell." The Civil War and the years of Reconstruction that followed were hard. But how each individual woman viewed the war and her experiences in it depended to a large extent on what she had to gain and what she had to lose.[1]

Many yeoman women, especially in the Piedmont and the Mountains, did not see much point in poor men fighting a "rich man's war." They resented North Carolina's commitment of troops—one-fifth of the state's approximately 630,000 white inhabitants—that took away their men, most of whom owned no slaves and worked their family farms by themselves. They even encouraged their husbands to come home where they were needed. These women were angry that planters responsible for twenty or more slaves were exempt from service, whereas their men, regardless of the number of dependents, received no exemptions. Viewing the conflict from their class interest, yeoman women felt that they not only sacrificed their men, but also bore the brunt of scarcities in salt, food, cloth, and other necessities. These women provided the most active resistance to the war and, in the process, redefined womanhood as assertive rather than deferential.[2]

Women of the Quaker faith and other dissenting sects also suffered shortages and wartime atrocities. But it was religious conviction that fed their opposition to the conflict, which they subverted with passive resistance, active defiance, and aid to deserters. They provided a moral stance against the war.

Black women who were slaves looked to the possibility of freedom at first with hope, then caution, and ultimately jubilation. Slaves had to stifle their joy and excitement over the prospect of the end of slavery, even as the bitterness of their masters increased as the war persisted. Female slaves assisted Union troops, joined the fugitive trek to liberated sites such as New Bern and Roanoke Island, and subverted the political and social system that denied them freedom. Although freedom had its risks as well as its opportunities, blacks who were already free saw that the end of slavery meant better times for all black people. Slaves of both sexes had the most to gain from a Union victory.

At first most elite white women were enthusiastically patriotic, eagerly forming Ladies Aid Societies, sewing and knitting for the soldiers, and wishing to be men so they could fight the Yankees. Some thought themselves sacrificing in giving up ice cream and cake for the Cause. Ultimately many of them suffered the loss of their husbands, sons, and brothers, realized that their privileged position did not protect them in a wartime society, and even resented their menfolks for not providing better for them. After the war, many joined Ladies Memorial Associations and commemorated the Lost Cause by honoring the dead, establishing cemeteries, and erecting monuments and memorials.

The years from 1861 to 1865 were a time of hardship, tremendous upheaval, dramatic social change, and violent civil disorder. With pro-Union and even antislavery sentiment in the state, North Carolina entered the war reluctantly, motivated by loyalty to the South rather than a desire for secession. Providing 140,000 soldiers, the largest number of any Southern state, North Carolina also sustained the greatest number of casualties—more than 40,000 men wounded or killed.[3]

Civilians at home—women, children, and those men not in service—had to contend with the pillaging, robbery, and violence perpetrated by soldiers on both sides and with the fighting between deserters and Confederate forces. They struggled with the inflation, speculation, hoarding, and shortages of food and manufactured items created by Union blockades and Confederate taxation in kind. Coping with scarcity became a harsh reality for just about everyone—rich and poor, black and white, rural and urban, on the Coast and in the Piedmont and Mountains. Discontent and opposition to the war rippled across the state's cultural and political landscape, especially among the yeomen. As the war persisted, deaths mounted, poverty became widespread, morale further deteriorated, and desertions increased.

Yet the Civil War years also brought challenge and opportunity for many women. With men gone, women became heads of households and obtained new, if temporary, sources of identity and power. White women appeared in public places previously off bounds—like railroad depots—and in new roles—some as patriotic canteen workers offering refreshments to the wounded soldiers, others as determined providers raiding stockpiled corn to feed their family. They traveled more, went longer distances, and often without a male escort, mainly to visit relatives in the military, but sometimes as refugees. White women mobilized in many ways—supplying textiles, clothing, and food to the troops, caring for the wounded, and mourning the dead while they sustained their families and kept their communities going with church work and teaching. How well each family and each community survived depended largely on women's resourcefulness.

Many women managed surprisingly well and felt a sense of accomplishment, although they never were free of what Mary Watson Smith of Guilford County called the "heartache that never lifted"—anxiety about the safety of their men. Mothers lost sons. Sally Nichols of Burke County sent seven sons to war, and Mrs. Reuben Jones of Robeson County, eleven sons. All seven of widow Polly Ray's sons died, and her neighbor Charity Boyles lost six out of seven. By 1862 Henderson County had "scarcely a family but mourns the loss of a member."[4]

Wives experienced the anguish of loneliness. Ella Harper of Lenoir told her husband, "Sometimes when I am writing to you my heart gets so full of love that if I was to follow its dictation, I fear you would think my letter very lovesick and foolish." Three months later, in August 1862, she wrote: "I have about finished your drawers. I love to sew for you. I have such sweet, loving thoughts about you. If your body is as warm when wearing the clothes as my heart is while making them, you will be very comfortable." And young women, like Sally Southall (Cotten), who graduated from Greensborough Female College in the midst of the war, had the "appalling fear" that they might never have "the opportunity to make good wives—or even *bad* wives—that they might miss "the great and only aim, and the divinely appointed mission of women" and never marry.[5]

Farm Women and War: "We Have Done till We Don't Know What to Do"

For the majority of white women who lived in self-sufficient independence on small farms, the Civil War made no sense. Why should their families be subjected to deprivation and starvation; their husbands, brothers, and sons exposed to danger, dismemberment, and death; and their way of life, community, and institutions shattered by war—all for slavery, from which few of them benefited? Under duress, they poured out their complaints about the inequities of the war in increasingly strident letters to North Carolina's newly elected governor, Zebulon Vance, and other Confederate officials. Suddenly these ordinary farm women—hitherto absent from written records—appear bold and center stage.

This class of women, concentrated in the Piedmont and western counties where the majority were small farmers who worked their own land without slaves, formed the state's major resistance to the war (Fig. 6-1). They suffered from the social upheaval caused by shortages and inflation as they tried to maintain some normalcy at home. As one woman wrote in 1865, "Slavery is doomed to dy out: god is agoing to liberate neggars and fighting any longer is against God." These women put the needs of their own family and community ahead of loyalty to the state—encouraging draft resistance or desertion, engaging in food riots and other acts of civil disobedience, and petitioning the government not to draft the blacksmiths, tanners, and other craftsmen essential for a self-sufficient community. With their disregard for authority, their lack of deference, and their acts of defiance, white farm women both resisted the war and redefined the behavior of women: "The Women is as Bad as the Men," reported one Southern official.[6]

Women's participation in North Carolina's "Inner Civil War" established a pattern of civil disobedience and military resistance that many historians believe contributed to the downfall of the Confederacy. The internal civil war flourished in what Paul Escott calls the "social and physical geography" of the Piedmont and Mountains—rural areas that provided sanctuary for dissidents, deserters, outlaws, and pacifists. In Chatham, Alamance, Moore, Randolph, Guilford, Forsyth, and Davidson Counties, Quakers, Moravians, and even Wesleyan Methodists were pacifists, and their presence encouraged tolerance for passive and sometimes active resistance. In mountain counties such as Henderson, Madison, Polk, and Wilkes, there was strong pro-Union sentiment. A number of mountain families were divided by sectional loyalties, and women and children were often caught in the crossfire of foraging raids, military forays, and personal vendettas. By 1864 and 1865 mountain women's lukewarm support for the war was badly eroded.[7]

Farm women tolerated the absence of their men, worked as best they could in the fields, tried to sustain their families, and faced down starvation. But they did not like it. They barraged Governor Vance with complaints. Vance conceded

> My husband he's been forced from me to the army . . . my request to you is that you will let my husband of[f] so he can come to my assistance . . . deny me not I come as a beging lazarus and as a weeping mary I come pleading for my husband myself and my child that we may not perish and die.
> —Elizabeth Chamberlain to Governor Zebulon Vance, 1862.
> (*North Carolina Women Making History* exhibition)

FIGURE 6-1. *William King White, Sarah Penelope Kitchin White, and their children, Emma and William Preston*, ca. 1865–66. The Whites were moderately prosperous Halifax County farmers who raised livestock, corn, and cotton and owned two slaves. William King White's local militia commission initially exempted him from active duty, but eventually he was conscripted into the Confederate army, although his North Carolina unit is unknown (Mast, *State Troops and Volunteers*, 219). (Courtesy of the North Carolina Division of Archives and History)

that conscription had taken "a large class whose labor was . . . absolutely necessary to the existence of the women and children left behind." Most of Orange County's enlistees were gone at harvest time in 1862, and by early 1863 food shortages were critical. One woman who had been widowed by the war wrote the governor that she had no meat, corn, or wheat to feed her six children, and that "We have done till we don't know what to do . . . i am thinking the worst is yet to come." Another Orange County mother of six was desperate to obtain cotton "to clothes [*sic*] my children." The state initiated relief efforts, but government help was too little and too scattered to alleviate the widespread poverty; its effectiveness was further undercut by wartime inflation.[8]

In January 1865 one who signed herself, "A Poor Woman and Children," implored Vance: "For the sake of suffering humanity . . . and especially for the sake of suffering women and children try and stop this cruel war, here I am without one mouthful to eat for myself and five children and God only knows where I will get som thing now you know as well as you have a head that it is impossible to whip the Yankees . . . my husband has been killed, and if they all stay til they are dead what in the name of God will become of us poor women."[9] From Fayetteville, O. Goddin, a private in the Fifty-first Regiment, North Carolina Troops, in 1863 began a letter to Vance, "Please pardon the liberty which a poor soldier takes in thus addressing you." He continued:

> When he *volunteered* he left a wife with four children to go fight for his country. He cheerfully made the sacrifices thinking that the Govt. would protect his family, and keep them from starvation. In this he has been disappointed for the Govt. has made a distinction between the rich man (who has something to fight for) and the poor man who fights for that he will never have. . . . Healthy and active

FIGURE 6-2. *Distributing Rations*. Shortly after Christmas 1862, Caroline Alligood wrote her soldier husband that the family's meat and bread were almost gone: "if it was not like it is an I did have the rite sort of mony I could fare very well. it is A bad chance for me for your wages is So low an every thing So high I dont See how I can live here much longer" (William Slade Papers, as cited in Yearns and Barrett, *North Carolina Civil War Documentary*, 266–67). (From J. T. Trowbridge, *The South: A Tour of Battlefields and Ruined Cities* [1866])

men who have furnished substitutes are grinding the poor by speculation. . . . By taking too many men from their farms they have not left enough to cultivate the land thus making a scarcity of provisions. . . . How can the poor live? I dread to see summer as I am fearful there will be much suffering and probably many deaths from starvation."[10]

Shortages, Inflation, and Speculation

Few women had more fortitude or endurance than those of the yeomanry, but they suffered most from the shortages, inflation, and speculation that plagued war-torn North Carolina (Fig. 6-2). A woman known only as "Mary" beseeched her husband to desert (the letter has been preserved only because it was used as evidence at a court-martial for desertion). Hundreds and thousands of other men receiving similar letters deserted in the last years of the war. Vance pleaded with the women to stop writing the men such depressing letters. But by late 1864 fully two-fifths of Confederate soldiers were absent without leave and the number of North Carolina soldiers who deserted was twice that of any other Confederate state.[11]

Many families of the farmers and artisans away at war probably had enough food and clothing to survive, but the high cost of everything made life bleak. Coffee, sugar, fresh meat, apparel, and other basic needs were out of reach for most. As Caroline Alligood informed her husband, the children "have had Shoos all along untill now but uncle Dick Daniel has promist to make the two girls Shoos. an Caleb Cleat was to make Charles Shoos but he broke his arm an if I cant get John to make them I dont know how I Shall get them." Hardly a day passed that local newspapers did not report the grim situation across the state. As the war continued, the combination of scarcity and speculation led to soaring prices. In Raleigh, a pound of bacon cost 33 cents in 1862 and $7.50 in 1865 and a bushel of corn, $1.10 in 1862 and $30.00 in 1865; in those years a barrel of flour skyrocketed from $18.00 to $500.00. Inflation around the state occurred at different rates. In 1863 a pound of sugar cost $1.00 in Raleigh and $1.50 in Greensboro, and a barrel of flour was $35.00 in Raleigh and $50.00 in Greensboro.[12]

Women blamed speculators for high prices. As the wife of a Confederate soldier living in the Mountains complained, "My husband has been taken away . . . by desyning men that

My dear Edward:—I have always been proud of you, and since your connection with the Confederate army, I have been prouder of you than ever before. I would not have you do anything wrong for the world, but before God, Edward, unless you come home, we must die. Last night I was aroused by little Eddies's crying. I called and said "What is the matter, Eddie?" and he said, "O Mamma! I am so hungry." and Lucy, Edward, your darling Lucy; she never complains, but she is growing thinner and thinner every day. And before God, Edward, unless you come home, we must die.

Your Mary.

—Letter from his wife, "Mary." (Lonn, *Desertion during the Civil War*, 13, as cited in Wiley, *Confederate Women*, 177)

wont go into the army themselves but prefer to stay at home & speculate by selling goods to the wifes of soldiers at 500 per cent[.]"[13]

In a number of public skirmishes and private encounters, women took matters into their own hands. Less than a year after North Carolina entered the war, a group of women from Newton in Catawba County assembled to issue a resolution to "STOP THE STILLS!—SAVE THE COUNTRY!! AND FEED THE POOR." The women opposed whiskey because it "demoralized" the troops and "sapped the courage of the people throughout the land." But more important, the making of whiskey—converting "corn into poison"—took bread away from their families. After giving the "sordid" whiskey makers fair warning that they intended to stop their enterprise, the women, "armed and equipped with short-range axes," marched to the depot where a supply of whiskey was on hand. They then began what was described in the *Greensborough Patriot* as "one of the most glorious battles fought in these days of wartime" in which the women showed courage, "cused" heroically, and demanded their rights. When the distillers claimed their "private right" to make whiskey, the women challenged a private right that contributed to public ruin. When the men complained that the "ladies" would "ruin" them, the women replied, "Well, when you put gold in your pocket, what shall we put in our children's mouths?" To protect the food supply, a law was passed in April 1862 against the distilling of grains, but lax enforcement prompted a group of irate Forsyth County women to write Governor Vance in January 1863 naming ten men from Forsyth, Yadkin, Davidson, and Davie Counties who persisted in distilling corn into liquor.[14]

The suspicion that food desperately needed by their families was being stockpiled by either speculators or government agents led a number of white women to defy government authority and initiate food riots. In Wilmington and Greensboro, and in Johnston County in the east and Yadkin County in the west, women angrily demanded food to feed their starving families.

In March 1863 a group of fifty to seventy-five wives of soldiers gathered in Salisbury "to make a dash on some flour." The women needed flour and believed that speculators were hoarding it. Armed with axes and hatchets, they marched from the depot to several stores, then to the government warehouse, and back to the depot. According to the newspaper account, everyone they met assured the women that they had no flour and were not speculating, but when the women found flour, storekeepers gave it to them rather than have them take it. The owner of the first store the women entered wrote Governor Vance that a "mob of females" had "cut away a portion of the door" with hatchets while city officials stood by and did nothing. When the women returned to the depot, the agent lied again about the flour and told them they would get in only over "his dead body." The women rushed inside anyway, found ten barrels of flour, and "rolled them out." In their search for food, the Salisbury women had been deceived, mocked, scorned, and patronized. At the end of their raid, however, they sat victoriously on the flour barrels and waited for a wagon to haul their treasure home. Less than a month later, Vance warned women that "broken laws will give you no bread, but much sorrow; and when forcible seizures have to be made to avert starvation, let it be done by your county or state agents."[15]

But many women no longer trusted their government. Margaret E. Love of Jackson County protested, "Our county agent the Rev Wm Hicks told the people at church last Sunday that he could not provide food for the wants of suffering familys. . . . and they must look out for themselves." In April 1864 about fifty women from Yancey County in western North Carolina marched "in a body" to a storehouse and "pressed about sixty bushels of Government wheat and carried it off." In coastal Bladen County, five women were sentenced to five months in jail for raiding a depot at Bladenboro and taking seven sacks of grain. The Newton, Salisbury, Yancey, and Bladen women made their raids in broad daylight, supported their action with reasoned arguments, and believed that they were redressing a public wrong. This unexpected behavior on the part of women gave added weight to their grievances.[16]

Nancy Mangum, of McLeansville, a soldier's wife and mother of six, was also willing to confront public officials. The Guilford County woman wrote Vance that she and a group of "Poor women went to Greensborough yesterday for

FIGURE 6-3. *Mary Elizabeth Holt and Lieutenant Nathanial Williamson*, wedding portraits, ambrotype, Alamance County, ca. 1865. The daughter of Alamance County textile magnate Edwin M. Holt married her Confederate suitor. (Courtesy of the Alamance County Historical Museum)

something to eat as we had not a mouthful meet nor bread in my house [and] what did they do but put us in gail." She rebuked her jailers and accused speculators of withholding needed thread from poor women while making it available to "big men" who can "git it withou aney trouble." She denounced "Harper Linsey," the man responsible for poor relief, for holding on to the money and not helping the "Poor women"—"I have not got one sent of it yet since my husband has bin gon he has bin gon most 2 years." Mangum warned that if things did not get better, "we wemen will write for our husbands to come . . . home and help us we cant stand it the way they are treating us they charge $11.00 Per bunch for their thread and $2.50 for their calico." She targeted "old Ed. Holt"—the Alamance County textile millowner—as a speculator and said that "if this war holds on 2 years longer he would own all of allamance county he has cloth and thread and wont let no body have it without wheat or Corn or meet what am I to do I cant get it to eat" (Fig. 6-3).[17]

Although the food shortage was the most serious, leather, salt, and textiles were also scarce. The state scrambled to obtain articles formerly imported from the North, but neither local tanneries nor a state-sponsored saltworks could be established quickly enough to meet people's needs. Before the war, each North Carolinian used about fifty pounds of salt a year for tanning hides, seasoning food, and preserving meat. Transportation in the Mountains was in such disarray—in 1863 many bridges between Asheville and Macon County were "entirely gone"—that what little salt there was seldom reached many mountain counties. Burke County was allocated only three pounds per person, not enough to cure bacon, and the Henderson County agent openly speculated in state-supplied salt. By 1862 a writer from Transylvania County reported that "not one-half" of the county had "the sign of a shoe on their feet," and "not one-third have shoes that will keep their feet dry, nor do I know how they will get them." There was "not one pound of salt to every white inhabitant in the county."[18]

Wartime Textile Production

Shortages produced by the war put women back in the business of textile production. Some women hoped to support themselves by supplying clothing to the troops. Others retrieved spinning wheels and looms that had been discarded when manufactured cloth had become cheap and available. Older women who remembered how to make cloth taught younger ones the intricacies of carding, spinning, and weaving and making dyes from natural ingredients like walnut

Sir, I wrote to Mr. Wilson to speake to you concerning a contract for making clothes. . . . I do not think the government work should be given to any particular parties and a few be allowed all the privileges accrued from government contracts. I did not expect to get a refusal merely because I am a woman.

—Mrs. M. E. Beasley, Old Town, February 8, 1862. (Quartermaster's Correspondence, Civil War Collection, NCDAH)

shells, roots, bark, and leaves. Hattie Deaver of Henderson County declared, "Mary Cansler is teaching me how to spin, but finds it rather a hard job."[19]

Cotton and wool cards—manufactured goods essential for home clothmaking—were scarce and fragile. Some 60,000 cotton and wool cards and the wire for repairing them were imported from England to aid home production. Cornelia Phillips Spencer of Chapel Hill saw "tears of thankfulness running down the cheeks of our soldiers' wives on receiving a pair of these cards by which alone they were able to clothe and procure bread for themselves and their children." In 1862 a reporter in Transylvania County observed that "cotton and wool cards can scarcely be had at all, the old ones being about worn out." A Fayetteville manufacturer told Governor Vance in 1863 that "our Country Women would have no difficulty in making a very desent living by their Labor if they could get Cards and Factory Thread."[20]

Manufacturers who speculated in thread and cloth sometimes drove desperate women to take action. In the early autumn of 1863 Eliza Armon and her cousin Nancy Vines traveled two days from their homes in Greene County to get some cotton from the "lowell factory." Despite Eliza's being a widow and mother of four children and Nancy having a husband "inn the Sirvis" and two children, the women were refused the cloth they needed to make clothing for their families. They fought with the person in charge, Ben Borden, over some cloth that he intended to sell to someone else and were told to get out. Eliza related, "I told him I should go when I got redy." When Borden told her he would have her put out, she replied, "no you wont," and again explained her situation and pleaded to buy some cloth. Borden said that "he did not car hoo was soldiurs wives and hoo wert not who was widows and hoo was not and hoo was nakd and hoo was not."[21]

Several wives of Alexander County volunteers complained to Governor Vance in May 1863 when Wilson Jones, the proprietor of a local cotton factory, refused to accept their Confederate notes in exchange for "thread to make clothing for themselves and their children." Jones claimed that he accepted only bacon or corn to feed his factory workers. Accusing him of speculation, the women wrote, "we do not believe that it Requires the Bacon and corn of Virginia & N. Carolina to support the hands of one Little Factory provided the like of this is allowed of the wives and children of volunteers must suffer for clothing."[22]

Mary Bell: "I Wish I Could Be Both Man and Woman"

Among those women who thrived in meeting the challenges of war was Mary Bell of Franklin in mountainous Macon County. She kept family, farm, and business going during the three-year absence of her husband Alfred, the captain of a company of county volunteers. Like many women in the Mountains, she was not particularly imbued with a sense of patriotic duty toward the South, though Macon County strongly supported the Confederacy. At first, she resented her husband's absence, chafed at the inequity of her sacrifice, hoped that other women's husbands would be drafted, and worried that men "staying at home and speculating" would become wealthy on the backs of those who served. Mary had heard rumors about her husband's behavior, which she confronted: "Reports are that you, Capt. Bell, a man in whom evry one had the utmost confidence as being a true devoted and virtuous husband, could play cards, drink whiskey, and —— as many women as any man in camps and by so doing had won the love and respect of nearly evry man in the regiment. . . . I should think that if by such acts I had to gain the love of my men, I should consider it dearly."[23]

Mary had a close-knit community of family and neighbors on whom to depend. As time passed, she became increasingly confident about her farm operations, boastful about her ability to "cheat" when bartering for corn and hogs or issuing credit, and proud that she had earned enough money to buy a slave family. In April 1864 her husband wrote: "I have nothing to say nor advice to give. Besides if I had, Caty [his nickname for Mary] takes no advice but acts for herself and her own judgement." Not a patriot, Mary Bell never became attracted to the Southern cause. When she proclaimed, "I wish I could be both man and woman until this war ends," she did not mean she wanted the opportunity to work harder for the Confederacy, but for herself and her family.[24]

Abuse and Violence toward Women

Civility wore thin as war dragged on, and the social order deteriorated. Country women often bore the brunt of frustrated public officials and hostile state militia. In 1863 Nancy

Mangum and the other women agitating for food in Greensboro were told by an agent that "he would feed . . . [us] poor woman on dog meet and Roten egges."[25] Women's willingness to help deserters frequently put them in danger when soldiers on missions against deserters resorted to cruelty and violence. A notorious incident in Randolph County during the last year of the war shows the brutality toward women by state troops, who too zealously followed the governor's orders to find deserters.

The state militia had tracked a deserter named Owens close to Asheboro, where they found his wife washing at "Owens spring" and "inquired" as to his whereabouts. She told them that her husband was "dead & buried." The soldiers insisted that she show them the grave, and she began to "curse and abuse" them "for every thing that was bad." When they ordered her to go with them, she picked up her baby and refused to budge. The colonel in charge, Alfred Pike, "slapped her jaws" until she put the baby down and went with the soldiers. They tied her two thumbs together and suspended her from a limb with her toes barely touching the ground until she admitted that her husband was not dead. Later in the questioning, Pike decided she was not telling the truth and "put her thumbs under a corner of a fence," after which she "soon became quiet and behaved very respectfully." During a subsequent official inquiry by Governor Vance, Pike asserted his "right to treat Bill Owens, his wife & the like in this manner."[26]

The judge investigating the woman's mistreatment reported other disturbing incidents of violence against women, such as the arrest in 1864 by the Home Guard of fifty women each in Chatham, Randolph, and Davidson Counties, "some of them in delicate health and five advanced in pregnancy." The women "were rudely (in some instances) dragged from their homes," put under guard, and left for some weeks with "shocking" consequences. The distressed judge found that the women were "frightened into abortions almost under the eyes of their terrifiers."

Women on the western North Carolina frontier often faced life-threatening situations. Lack of enthusiasm for the Confederate cause, strong pockets of Union support, foraging raids by troops on both sides, and guerrilla activity by bands of deserters created a climate of resistance, violence, and revenge that took its toll on the daily life of civilians. The number of violent encounters is unknown, but localized conflict and personal vendettas that characterized the war in the Mountains continually put women and children at risk.

In January 1863, for example, in the Laurel Valley of Madison County, Confederate soldiers "shot without trial or any hearing" thirteen males suspected of being Unionists, some of whom were old men and others, boys only thirteen or fourteen. An official reported that "several women" who had witnessed the atrocity "were severely whipped and ropes were tied around their necks." One of the women, Nancy Franklin, had seen three sons killed before her eyes. In Wilkes County, the Home Guard, along with "a kind of independent company, professing to put down robbery, were reported in 1865 to have hung women until nearly dead (some of them pregnant) to make them tell on deserters in the Country." In Cherokee County, a group of pro-Confederate women were threatened with death by Unionists and deserters fighting nearby in 1864. The wife of a prominent Unionist was told by Confederate soldiers that "if she didn't leave they would burn the house & her in it."[27]

Sarah Malinda Pritchard Blalock

Most women were unwilling participants in clashes with soldiers and outlaws, but a small minority, particularly Unionists, sought out military activity. Sarah Malinda Pritch-

FIGURE 6-4. *Sarah Malinda Pritchard Blalock (alias Private Samuel Blalock)*, Company F, Twenty-sixth North Carolina Troops, Watauga and Avery Counties, ca. 1875. (Courtesy of the Southern Historical Collection, University of North Carolina at Chapel Hill)

ard Blalock, who lived in Watauga County when the war started, had the distinction of being North Carolina's only known female soldier in the Civil War (Fig. 6-4).[28] Twenty-three-year-old Malinda cut her hair, disguised herself as a man named Sam, and joined Company F, Twenty-sixth Regiment, North Carolina Troops, in March 1862 in Kinston along with her husband Keith, a Unionist who intended to desert to the Federal lines. Within a month, her husband realized that desertion was unlikely, gave himself a self-inflicted rash, and received a medical discharge.

At that point, Sam revealed her identity, and she, too, was released from service. The Blalocks returned to the Mountains, joined with deserters, and spent the remainder of the war engaged in guerrilla raids and revenge sorties typical of the mountain warfare. In a vendetta with a staunchly Confederate family, Malinda was wounded in the shoulder in one encounter and Keith was shot in the eye in another. Despite her militancy, Blalock had at least four children (one born in 1863), lived a settled life in Avery County after the war, and died of natural causes in 1901.

Quaker Women and the War

Although most Quaker women probably held Unionist sentiments, believing that law-abiding citizens did not secede from the Union, their objection to the Confederate cause was based on their religious convictions against slavery and war. The Quaker Belt of Randolph, Guilford, Forsyth, and Davidson Counties provided widespread resistance to the conflict and sanctuary for deserters and draft resisters. Sixty percent of North Carolina Quakers left the state between 1860 and 1868, and those who remained continued to oppose the war.

In March 1862 peace rallies were held in Randolph and Davidson Counties, probably in response to North Carolina's attempt to draft men. Mary Hinshaw of Randolph County supported her husband Thomas when he refused to pay the $500 exemption fee because it would, in the end, support the war, even though his action caused him to be drafted. When Thomas was harshly apprehended by the Home Guard, Mary rebuked the soldiers, ignored their orders to leave her husband alone, and gave him a small sack of food and clothes.[29]

Black Women and War: "They Prayed for Freedom"

For slaves and for free blacks, faced with ever-tightening restrictions, the Civil War offered hope and the prospect of freedom. This epic struggle seemed the fulfillment of God's great plan to end slavery. As an oppressed people, blacks had to exist with relatively little control over their lives and to

FIGURE 6-5. *Freed slaves entering New Bern*, 1863. (*Harper's Weekly*, February 21, 1863; courtesy of the North Carolina Collection, University of North Carolina at Chapel Hill)

trust to God for justice. After four years of war, they saw that apparently those in power also had little control over events. In the early days of the war, wealthy whites had been optimistic, even boastful. Hannah Crasson, who had lived on a plantation about thirteen miles from Raleigh in Wake County, recalled that her owner thought that the Confederates "could eat breakfast at home, go and whup the North, and be back far dinner." But it was "four long years before he cum back to dinner. De table wuz shore set a long time for him. . . . Many of dem never did come back to dinner."[30]

Mary Anderson, who had lived on a plantation with more than 150 slaves near Franklinton, remembered that war news "went from plantation to plantation, and while the slaves acted natural and some even more polite than usual, they prayed for freedom." Of course, slaves knew "what all the fightin' was about," said W. L. Bost, who lived in the western Piedmont town of Newton, "but they didn't dare say anything. The man who owned the slaves was too mad as it was, and if the niggers say anything they get shot right then and thar." The Federal invasion in the eastern part of the state forced many white planters to flee and permitted slaves to express their real feelings toward their owners. As Josiah Collins's overseer reported to him, the slaves on his Somerset plantation "doo not cear for you at all." Collins's abandoned buildings were marauded by blacks and whites. Slaves could leave behind their servility and embrace freedom, and hundreds crossed into Union-held territory (Fig. 6-5).[31]

Cooks and seamstresses found the transition from slavery to freedom easier than field hands. Mary Jane Connor, who was freed by Union troops when they captured New Bern, was able to open a boardinghouse. A Union soldier who stayed there described Connor as "thoroughly capable" and "about the most remarkable colored woman I ever saw" (Fig. 6-6). Her sister-in-law, known as "Sylvia," was also freed during the war and worked as a seamstress in New Bern, where she was described by the same Union soldier as "a woman of very good sense & well developed reflective faculties" (Fig. 6-7).[32] In Union-occupied towns like New Bern and Beaufort and on Roanoke Island, African Americans organized a community life centered around their own churches, schools, and other institutions. By July 1862 black women in New Bern had started schools for freed slaves. A group of women founded the Colored Ladies Aid Association of North Carolina to assist the more than five thousand black Union soldiers who served in the state.[33]

Abraham Lincoln's Emancipation Proclamation that all slaves were "forever, free" after January 1, 1863, fanned their hope for freedom, but Emancipation was slow in coming, and their situation was still perilous. Slaves suffered from their owners' increasing hostility and depleted resources; they also had to endure mistreatment from the Union troops who liberated them. Many soldiers wantonly destroyed meager food supplies, killed livestock, and stole the slaves' few possessions. Sarah Debro remembered the Yankee soldiers "jumpin' over de palin's, 'tromplin' down de rose bushes an' messin' up de flower beds" at the Orange County plantation where she and her mother lived. "Dey stomped all over de house, in de kitchens, pantries, smoke house, an' everywhere." Debro refused to tell where her white owners' treasures were hidden. After liberation, she was often hungry and "had to keep fighting off dem Yankee mens." Soldiers raided the smokehouse on the plantation near Fayetteville where Sarah Augustus had worked as a slave, and then they "told us we were all free." Augustus remembered that slaves "began visiting each other in the cabins and became so excited they began to shout and pray." Although hard times and tough choices lay ahead, black men, women, and children rejoiced that slavery had ended—freedom was well worth the struggle and hardship of the war.[34]

FIGURE 6-7. *"Sylvia,"* tintype, New Bern, June 5, 1863, Craven County. (Courtesy of the Tryon Palace Restoration, New Bern)

FIGURE 6-6. *Mary Jane Connor*, tintype, New Bern, June 5, 1863, Craven County. (Courtesy of the Tryon Palace Restoration, New Bern)

Gentry Women and War: "We Are Still Ladies"

Traditionally guardians of their family's spiritual well-being, gentry women became custodians of public sentiment, patriotism, and morality during the Civil War. "Our hearts are filled with patriotic zeal," wrote Catherine Devereux Edmondston from Looking Glass plantation in Halifax County. The extraordinary circumstances of the war gave women visibility, at home and behind the lines, in critical and newly distinct ways. An English traveler questioned "whether ancient or modern history can furnish an example of a conflict which was so much of a 'woman's war' as this." Drew Gilpin Faust writes that the Confederate need for troops meant that women's traditional interest in protecting their family had to be redefined to a willingness to relinquish

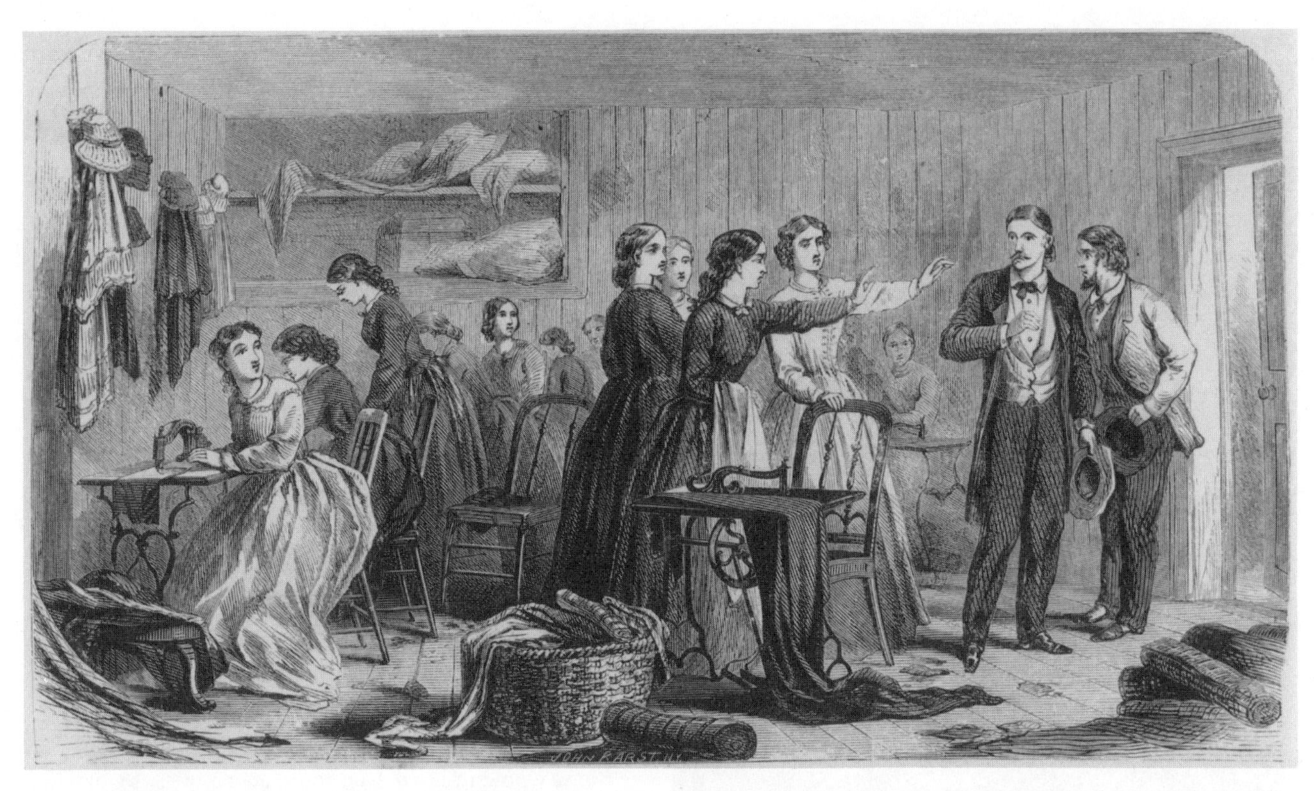

FIGURE 6-8. *Industry of Ladies in Clothing the Soldiers and Zeal in Urging Their Beaus to Go to War*. (From J. T. Trowbridge, *The South: A Tour of Battlefields and Ruined Cities* [1866])

their husbands, sons, and brothers to defend the Southern way of life—including slavery—without tears. Edmondston was "belligerently prosecession" yet felt that her husband Patrick was too old and too delicate to serve in the army.[35]

Most women of the slaveholding class agreed with the imperative of maintaining their privileged lifestyle based on slavery, especially early in the war. In 1861 Edmondston observed: "One thing struck me throughout the whole progress of the summer; the universality & the eagerness with which the women entered into the struggle! . . . "*The Soldiers*' excited an enthusiasm in the bosoms of all! Every thing must be given to them, every thing done *for* them."[36] Ladies Aid Societies, Soldiers Aid Societies, and Hospital Aid Societies sprang up in communities statewide. Patriotic women provided supplies and clothing for North Carolina troops that the state and Confederate governments could not. In Fayetteville, Wilmington, Edenton, New Bern, Hillsborough, Raleigh, Greensboro, Salisbury, Charlotte, and, in the only such alliance in the west, Asheville, they gathered in organized groups to sew, knit, roll bandages, and raise money for the soldiers.

Within two weeks of the shots on Fort Sumter, women in Washington, Beaufort County, formed a "Military Sewing Society," whose president, Mrs. M. M. Hoyt, sent word to the military companies in their vicinity: "Should there be members of your company not suitably provided for you will very much oblige the ladies by making known to them their wants and we will take great pleasure in giving them our prompt attention." Mrs. Hoyt even cut up her white satin wedding dress for the stripes in the flag that the women gave the departing soldiers. Catherine DeRosset helped organize the Soldiers Aid Society in Wilmington. Few records of the women's efforts survive, but the Eno Ladies Aid Society of Orange County alone sent its soldiers more than ninety shirts and one hundred pairs of stockings. In the spring of 1862, when a soldier wrote home for help in clothing the Alamance Regulators, the response was immediate—all the "Ladies were desirous of doing all that diligence and patriotism and admiration for the men could prompt or effect."[37]

These women encouraged their men to serve with honor (Fig. 6-8), expressed strong views on military matters, silenced their own fears, and wrote stirring patriotic prose and poems. They knitted socks wherever they went (Fig. 6-9), transformed their silk dresses into flags (Fig. 6-10), and collected food, bedding, blankets, and clothing for the soldiers. They established canteens at railroad depots to provide refreshments for the troops, rolled bandages from scraps of cloth, and nursed and fed the wounded in hospitals (quickly established in former schools, courthouses, churches, and homes). They kept law offices and businesses running, managed plantations, and looked after their slaves, who were becoming increasingly assertive as white male authority

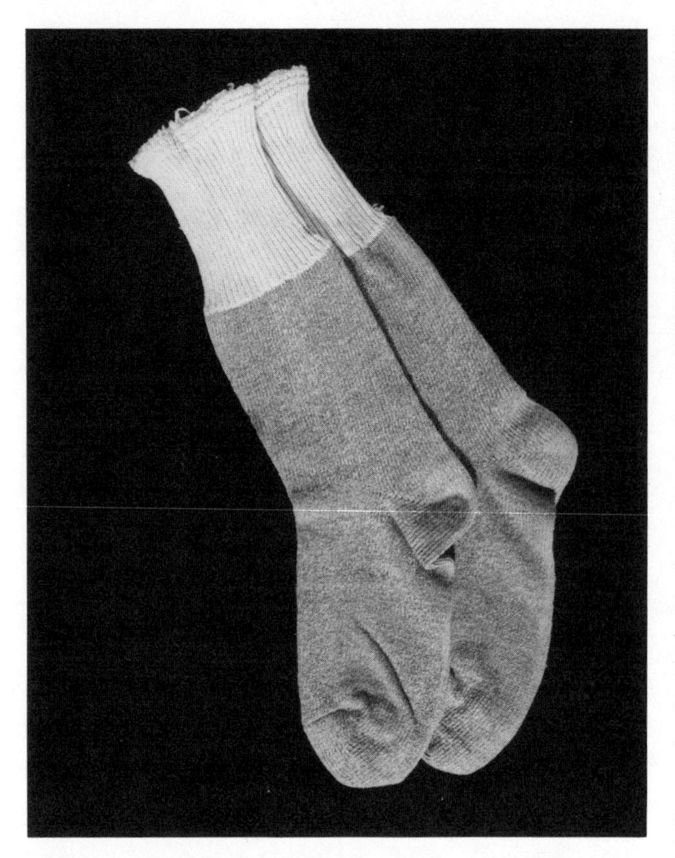

FIGURE 6-9. *Wool socks knitted by North Carolina women* for a Confederate soldier, ca. 1864. "Everybody was knitting socks for a soldier." Catherine Devereux Edmondston, in Crabtree and Patton, *"The Journal of a Secesh Lady."* (Courtesy of the North Carolina Museum of History)

The High School Knitting Society (of the Fayetteville Female High School) sends to you by the Raleigh stage today 79 pairs of socks, which the society desires the Govr. [governor] will cause to be sent to the 54th Regt. which lost its baggage at Fredericksburg.

—Emily Tillinghast, Fayetteville, January 12, 1863. (Quartermaster's Correspondence, Civil War Collection, NCDAH)

waned and freedom seemed possible. They invented substitutes for scarce familiar goods like tea and bread: wheat, rye, corn, sweet potatoes, peanuts, dandelion seed, melon seed, and okra seed were some of the (unsatisfactory) replacements for coffee.

Although women of the gentry rejected homespun, they did remake their old dresses in new combinations. Some women openly longed for the elegance of antebellum days. Mrs. J. G. Ramsay of Rowan County wrote to her husband, a member of the Confederate senate meeting in Richmond, that she had heard they "have Godey and harpers [ladies' magazines] in the [congressional] reading rooms. I wish you would get some and send me for I want to see the fashions."[38]

Women responded to the war in a variety of ways. Mary Anna Morrison Jackson spent the war years in North Carolina and wrote to her husband, General Thomas Jonathan "Stonewall" Jackson, every day, knit him socks, and made him pants and caps with broad gilt bands (for which Jackson scolded her, "Please, do not have so much gold braid about them"). She was with him when he died, later recounting the horror in her *Memoirs*. Phebe Caroline Jones Patterson opened up her house in Caldwell County for widows and orphans. Lavinia Bassett Daniel Battle took over the sole management of Cool Spring estate in Edgecombe County when her husband and both overseers left for service and devoted the plantation fields to raising supplies for the Confederate army. Mary Watson Smith of Greensboro ministered to the sick and wounded when her husband's church was converted to a hospital, survived the Union occupation of Greensboro in the spring of 1865, and later wrote an account of those years, "Women of Greensboro, N.C., 1861–1865."[39]

Some women played even more active roles. By day Elizabeth Carraway Hanland nursed Confederate prisoners in New Bern; by night she passed along messages about Union troops. Emeline Jamison Pigott of Carteret County carried medicine, food, and mail (under her hoop skirt) to leave in designated places for Confederate soldiers to pick up, was arrested, imprisoned (though never brought to trial—she probably would have been sentenced to death), and eventually released. She continued to help the Confederate cause in any way she could and later organized the Morehead City chapter of the United Daughters of the Confederacy, named in her honor.[40]

Abby House, who spent most of her adult life near Frank-

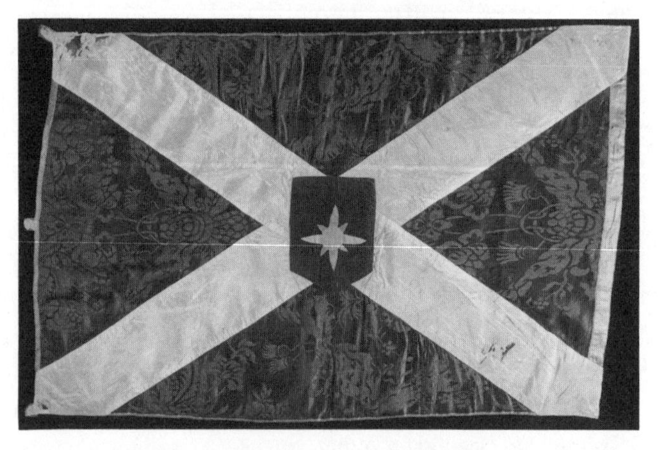

FIGURE 6-10. *Flag of Manley's Battery*, Company A, First Regiment, North Carolina Volunteer Artillery, Wake County, 1863. Raleigh women made this flag from their silk dresses. (Courtesy of the North Carolina Museum of History)

linton, was known as the Confederate "angel of mercy." "Aunt Abby" had promised her eight nephews that she would do whatever was necessary to help them if they became sick or wounded, and she spent much of the war traveling from North Carolina to Virginia (by train and even by foot), tirelessly extending aid, food, and clothing to Confederate soldiers. Called by Governor Vance "the ubiquitous, indefatigable, and inevitable Mrs. House" for her persistence in trying to obtain a furlough for one of her nephews, House personally visited Vance, General Robert E. Lee, and Confederate president Jefferson Davis to present her demands for the care of sick soldiers. She nursed troops on the battlefield at Petersburg and brought back to North Carolina for burial the bodies of five of her nephews who died in the war.[41]

The most notorious female patriot was a Confederate spy named Rose O'Neal Greenhow, who lived most of her life in Maryland and Washington, D.C., but died in North Carolina. In 1863 Greenhow had been sent by Jefferson Davis on a European mission; on her return to the blockaded Confederacy in the autumn of 1864, her ship, the *Condor*, was challenged and forced aground near the mouth of the Cape Fear River near Wilmington. She persuaded the captain to allow her to escape in a lifeboat, but the boat capsized, and she drowned, weighed down by two thousand dollars in gold intended for the Confederate cause. She was buried in Wilmington's Oakdale Cemetery.[42]

Some women became the war's refugees. Mary R. Anderson of Edenton was one of many who abandoned a coastal residence when Union troops arrived in 1862. Unlike Mary Riggs Collins, of Somerset plantation, who had inland plantations where she and her slaves could stay, Anderson was dependent on the kindness of her cousin, Paul Cameron, who lent her one of his houses in Hillsborough. Not that Anderson was ungrateful, but she found her new life difficult and her new neighbors "insolent." Although much had changed—"We are not as prosperous as we were before the war"—she took comfort in that "we are still ladies." As she wrote Cameron, "I trust the fortunes of war will never subject your wife & children to what we have borne from those people."[43]

As war dragged on, dislocation increased, deaths mounted, and hardships worsened, even gentry women's willingness to sacrifice grew thin. Plantation women resented their husbands' and sons' absence and found managing increasingly restive slaves a burden. Many women began to think that if their husbands could not protect them, then the state should provide. Sixty-year-old Harriet Stephenson, who had five sons in the army, wrote Secretary of War James Seddon, "I think I have did enough to you for you to take sum intrust in what I so mutch desrie of You"—the discharge of one of her sons so he could come home and help support her.[44]

Early in the war, an English traveler had observed that "the bitterest, most vengeful of politicians in this ensanguined controversy are the ladies." By war's end, the destruction, displacement, and defeat had intensified many "secesh" women's bitterness. Janie Smith hoped that Northern "widows and orphans [were] left naked and starving just as ours were left. . . . If I ever see a Yankee woman, I intend to whip her and take the clothes off her back." In 1865 Catherine DeRosset Meares of Wilmington found "the sense of captivity, of subjugation . . . so galling that I cannot see how a manly spirit could submit to it. . . . Oh, it is such degradation to see our men yield voluntary submission to those rascally Yankees. Better stand on the last plank and die in the last ditch."[45]

Women and Work during the War: "Noble in Itself and Befitting Their Sex"

As wartime shortages of male workers weakened Southern resistance to the idea of white women working outside the home, women in North Carolina and other Confederate states became employed as nurses, clerks, and teachers. White women volunteered as nurses in the makeshift hospitals established from Wilmington and Fayetteville to Goldsboro and Kinston. They attended to the soldiers' wounds, medical needs, and morale—and mortality rates dropped. Women filled positions as clerk copyists at the Fayetteville Arsenal when the men left for war. Although public sentiment argued against changes in women's behavior, the doors were opened to their entering nursing and clerical work in much larger numbers after the war.[46]

The most significant change in employment outside the home created by the Civil War was the demand for female

> After Christmas I applied to Dr. Fessington for a situation as assistant matron to the lower hospital. They were bringing the wounded from Fort Fisher, Wilmington, and other points. We already had one hospital and were establishing another. I shall never forget the doctor's look of amazement when I applied for the situation. My reply was: "Doctor, I don't want any pay but I must have constant occupation or I will lose my mind." I went every morning at nine o'clock and stayed until one and I always went late in the afternoon to see that the wants of the patients were attended to during the night. I always dressed the wounds every morning and I soon found that my grief and suffering were forgotten in administering to the wants of the sick.
>
> —Ann K. Kyle, Cumberland County, n.d. (Typescript, Women's History Project, North Carolina Museum of History)

teachers in the common schools. Public approval for this new role for women had to be shaped, and quickly. In November 1861, barely six months into the war, the North Carolina State Education Association offered a prize for the best essay on "the propriety and importance of employing more female teachers in our common schools." North Carolina's common school superintendent, Calvin Wiley, who had long campaigned for more women teachers, was concerned about staffing schools given the scarcity of men during wartime. In 1862 Wiley wrote, "many ladies are compelled, by the circumstances of the times, to labor for a living, and there is no employment better suited to the female nature, and none in which ladies can labor more usefully, than in the business of forming the hearts and minds of the young." The Reverend J. K. Kirkpatrick, president of Davidson College, urged the 1864 graduating class of Concord Female Academy to become teachers—"no occupation, to which the educated woman can have recourse, which is at once so respectable, so certainly remunerative, so congenial to her tastes, and so suitable to her sex." The crisis of wartime teacher shortages left no alternative. "*Our females must engage in the work of teaching*." Kirkpatrick told the young women's parents: "You have made your sons an offering on your country's altar. Would you withhold your daughters from a service, noble in itself and befitting their sex[?]" In North Carolina, the feminization of teaching had its origins in the Civil War.[47]

Textbooks as well as teachers were needed to replace the Northern books formerly used in North Carolina schoolrooms. Marinda Branson Moore, of Rockingham County, whose brother was Levi Branson (educator, Methodist minister, and publisher of textbooks especially designed for use in the Southern states), stepped forward and wrote *A Geographical Reader for Dixie Children* (1862). By the end of the war, the percentage of female teachers in North Carolina's public schools had increased from 7 percent to 50 percent, whereas the total number of public school teachers had decreased. In western North Carolina, for instance, the few women already teaching there could not replace the departed men in the almost three hundred schools; so many schools closed. All the public funds allocated to education in North Carolina would keep only two regiments in the field for one year, yet the state's delay in appropriating educational funds and the county courts' reluctance to collect taxes for schools created so much uncertainty that many schools closed or held only brief terms. North Carolina's fledgling public school system—before 1861 considered the best in the South—was one of the war's great casualties.[48]

Schools were an institution that women kept alive, though at diminished capacity, through the war. Churches, however, were another matter. Despite the evangelical fervor of the antebellum years, many churches lost their membership, financial support, and ministers and simply closed their doors. In the twenty western counties, only twenty-one ministers of the more than four hundred congregations were exempt from military service. From Wilkes County in 1862 came an urgent plea to Governor Vance, "The Churches in the county is left allmost without ministers so many of them has gone to volunteer in the service." Women were not recruited to take over the pulpits.[49]

Distributing religious tracts to soldiers became the churches' one great war effort, and, of course, women took up this task with great zeal. As religious literature was no longer available from the North, the General Tract Society was established in Raleigh to print Bibles and tracts for Southern troops. Operating under the joint supervision of the pastors of the city's Baptist, Episcopal, Methodist, and Presbyterian churches, the society printed titles like "A Mother's Parting Words to Her Soldier Boy," eight pages, by a Southern lady; "Are You Ready?" four pages; and "The Precious Blood of Christ, or How a Soldier Was Saved," four pages. After Salisbury's Rowan Bible Society was formed to buy religious literature for distribution, other communities followed suit.

White Women and the Aftermath

"In 1860 the South became a matriarchy," declared John Andrew Rice in 1942: women had managed farms and plantations without their husbands' "bungling hindrance," and when those husbands who escaped death returned home, "they found their surrogates in complete and competent charge and liking it." Whether Rice was expressing male anxiety about the increased authority held by women or was trying to inspire World War II women to similar feats, no doubt he overstated the gains made by women. About thirty years after Rice, in 1970, Anne Firor Scott published *The Southern Lady: From Pedestal to Politics, 1830–1930*, just as the women's movement was gaining momentum. Scott argued that the independence developed by Southern women in their demanding new roles during the war prepared them to be more confident and more assertive afterward.[50]

Some historians have tempered that heartening view. Suzanne Lebsock contends that in the postwar period Southern men could not handle independent women along with "defeat, freed slaves, and lost fortunes." Women were expected to revert to their submissive behavior, to preserve the illusion of Southern traditions, and to prop up the patriarchy. George Rable views the South's defeat as so overwhelming that women's immediate task was to heal men broken in spirit and to rebuild their self-confidence—not to challenge male authority with female independence. Sally

McMillen sees family survival, rather than "dreams of independence," as the goal of women struggling with "poverty, shattered husbands, and a changing social order."[51]

Certainly many white women embraced the Lost Cause. Almost immediately after the war they began erecting monuments to the Confederate war dead, consecrating graves, forming memorial associations, and providing assistance to veterans and their families (Plate 7). In 1866 Raleigh women formed the Wake County Memorial Association "to protect and care for the graves of our Confederate Soldiers" and mobilized efforts to remove 538 bodies from temporary graves and rebury them in a new Confederate cemetery (eventually reinterring bodies from other burial grounds and battlefields, for a total of 2,800). Conservative David Schenck

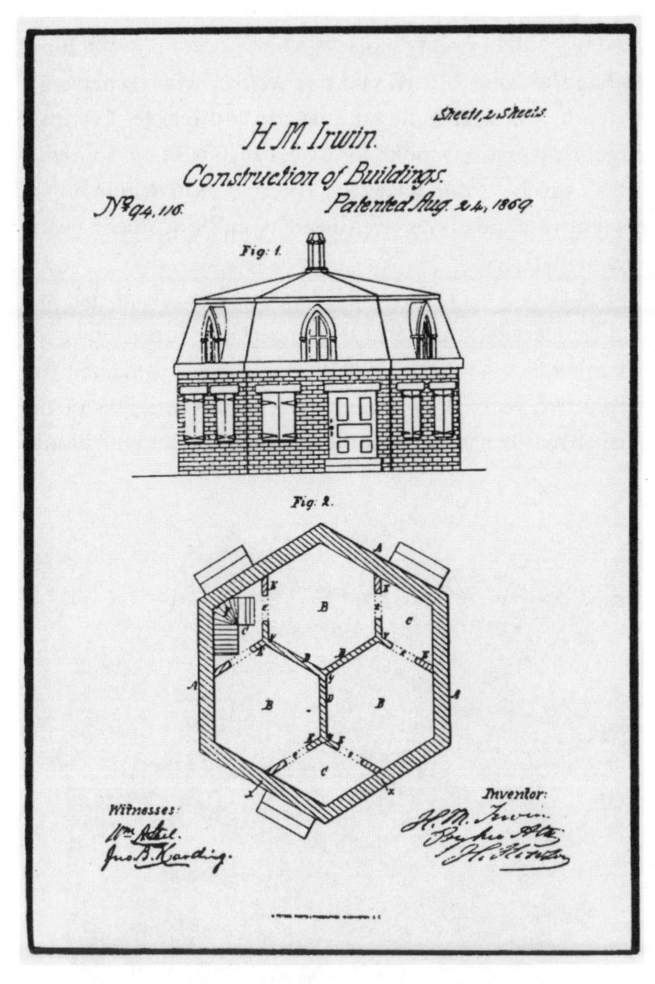

FIGURE 6-11. *Hexagon House*, designed and patented by Harriet Morrison Irwin, Mecklenburg County, 1869. Although Irwin claimed public space for her private designs, she was less famous in her own lifetime than her sister Mary Anna Jackson, whose renown rested on her status as Stonewall Jackson's widow. Irwin's obituary acknowledged that she was a "good and talented woman"—but "too fond of reading to be known and appreciated as she should have been." "Death of Mrs. Harriet Irwin," *Charlotte Observer*, January 26, 1897. (U.S. Patent Drawing 94, 116, August 4, 1869)

FIGURE 6-12. *Mary Bayard Devereux Clarke*. (Courtesy of the North Carolina Division of Archives and History)

exhorted the 1869 graduates of Lincolnton Female Seminary, "Now ladies, how shall we escape these pernicious influences, which are spreading like locusts and carpetbaggers among us. . . . God and Woman are our only hope." Many elite women did not take defeat lightly. A woman from Wilmington's wealthy DeRosset family wrote: "Think of Andy Johnson [as] the president. (I will not say *our*,) and Holden—governor. With such men, in such places, what will become of us—'the aristocrats of the South' as we are termed."[52]

And yet other women seemed to find a new life after the war. Cornelia Phillips Spencer, of Chapel Hill, whose biography follows this chapter, was propelled by early widowhood to earn money by her writing. Harriet Morrison Irwin of Charlotte designed an innovative (in the language of the day, "improved") hexagon dwelling and became in 1869 the first woman in America to patent an architectural design (Fig. 6-11). In 1870 she published a novel, *The Hermit of Petraea*, in which she explored her architectural ideas as well as other "speculative theories" on health, clothing, and vegetarian diets.[53] Mary Bayard Devereux Clarke had published her book of poetry, *Wood Notes, or Carolina Carols* (1854), before the war. Afterward, she supported herself and her husband with her earnings from her writing (Fig. 6-12): "I am busy

> Article 10, Section 6. Property of married women secured to them. The real and personal property of any female in North Carolina acquired before marriage, and all property, real and personal, to which she may after marriage become in any way entitled, shall be and remain the sole and separate estate and property of such female, and shall not be liable for any debts, obligation, and management of her husband. . . .
> —Married Women's Property Act, North Carolina State Constitution, 1868.

editing my paper, the *Literary Pastime*; corresponding with two others; contributing to two magazines; and translating a French novel; added to which I am composing a libretto for an opera; and writing Sunday-school hymns for five dollars a piece."[54] Also compelled to write for her livelihood after the war, Frances Fisher Tiernan of Salisbury took the pen name Christian Reid both to conceal her gender and identity and to convey the moral quality of her writing. One of the state's most prolific and popular novelists, she gave to the western highlands the nickname they have borne ever since her 1876 book, *The Land of the Sky*.[55]

Still another important legacy of the war was an improvement in property rights for women. Under Radical Reconstruction (1868–76), North Carolina had to write and ratify a new state constitution. A section of this legislation of 1868, known as the "Married Women's Property Act," provided the first significant advance in married women's legal rights. Under the new constitution, married women could own property and businesses, work for their own wages, sue in courts, sit on juries, make wills, and enter into contracts without their husband's consent.[56]

Reconstruction and Black Women: "After Freedom"

Although the war had freed African Americans, it had not changed a racist social system in which they were considered inferior and subordinate. The widow of a Piedmont Unionist who "lay out many a night" to evade the war declared that she did not "want nothin' to do with black ones." A Chatham County widow, who considered herself "the poorest of the whites," was concerned that freed slaves would surpass her: "We poor folks was about ekil to the niggers, about bein' hard put to it to live, I mean, and now's they's free they don't do nothin' but steal, and how we'll live I don't know. . . . I wish you'd tell me how poor folk is to live among these niggers." Anne Ruffin Cameron, whose father and husband had been among the state's largest slaveowners and who had no worries about where her next meal was coming from, supported her husband in his effort to force his slaves to leave their homes on the plantation. She advised: "drive [them] all off—get white tenants on any terms."[57]

For African American women, the war's end nevertheless brought an awareness of freedom, opportunity, and promise. Families were reunited, couples were legally married, and people could come and go at will. Temple Herndon of Chatham County "was glad when de war stopped" because then she and "Exter could be together all de time 'stead of Saturday an' Sunday." Mattie Curtis's parents wed and tried to find their fourteen oldest children who had been sold (they could locate only three). After freedom, Betty Cofer's father came "to get Muh and me" from the Forsyth County plantation where the two of them had lived. The state legislature required former slaves to register their marriages for a twenty-five-cent fee before the fall of 1866. "Me and my old man has lived more than twenty years together; I's proud my children all had the same father," said one woman who exchanged a quart of strawberries to get a license and register her marriage. Registration books for "Negro Cohabitation Certificates" survive from seventeen counties, where roughly 30 percent of adult slaves lived in 1860, and document nearly 19,000 marriages.[58]

For Lucy Ann Dunn of Neuse, freedom meant that she and her family could accept or reject her former owner's offer that they stay and work for wages. "Well," said Lucy, "we stayed two years" before they moved on to another of the former master's places and then returned. Josephine Smith,

FIGURE 6-13. *Estey Hall, Shaw University*, Raleigh, 1900. Completed in 1873, Estey Hall is considered to be the first building erected on an American college campus for the higher education of black women. (Courtesy of the North Carolina Division of Archives and History)

FIGURE 6-14. *Teaching the Freedmen*. (From J. T. Trowbridge, *The South: A Tour of Battlefields and Ruined Cities* [1866])

who had been a slave in Johnston County, moved to Raleigh and worked as a cook in several households and later in a hotel in Louisburg—her cooking skills facilitating her ability to change jobs.[59]

Less than three months after the Confederacy's surrender, on the Fourth of July 1865, blacks marched through Raleigh carrying banners that read, "Equal Rights before the law; the only equality we ask." According to Eric Foner, Reconstruction was a "Second American Revolution" in that it brought liberty to African Americans. In the autumn of 1865 a convention of more than one hundred black delegates, composed mostly of former slaves but also free black men representing about half of North Carolina's counties, met in Raleigh "to express the sentiments of the Freedmen." They asked for protection from punitive actions of former slaveholders, education for their children, legal protection of the black family, aid for orphans, support for the reunification of families broken up by slavery, and elimination from the state statutes of all the oppressive laws "which make unjust discrimination on account of race or color."[60]

Denominational institutions of higher education for blacks were immediately established—such as the Scotia Seminary, a Presbyterian school for women in Concord (1865) (renamed Scotia Women's College in 1916 and Barber-Scotia College in 1930), and two coeducational Raleigh schools, Shaw University (1865) founded by Baptists (Fig. 6-13) and St. Augustine's Episcopal College (1867). In 1874 coeducational Bennett College (reorganized as a women's college in 1926) was started in Greensboro, and in 1879 Zion Wesley Institute (renamed Livingstone College in 1885) opened in Salisbury. The young people educated at these institutions already had the rudiments of literacy and expected that with advanced training they would serve their race as teachers, physicians, preachers, and business and political leaders.

The priority of education is significant. Long denied the opportunity to learn to read and write, former slaves flocked to the schools operated by the Freedmen's Bureau, the American Missionary Association, and other Northern philanthropic organizations (Fig. 6-14). In Warren, Burke, and other counties, blacks raised money to build their own schools, buy textbooks, and hire teachers. In one of the Freedmen's Bureau schools, there were "*representatives of four generations* in a direct line. . . . a child of six years, her mother, grandmother, and great grandmother, the latter being more than seventy-five years of age." Henriette Pike, a white Northerner teaching in a Freedmen's Bureau school in Wilkes County, wrote that "Old and young are eager to learn" and described "mothers in the midst of their children trying to learn from *them* what *they* have learned during the day." Despite their enthusiasm for learning, it could not have been easy for North Carolina blacks, raised in a rural culture of oral tradition, manual labor, and communal experience, to relate to nineteenth-century pedagogy. The emphasis on correct spelling, precision, standardization, and individual learning, useful for a middle-class urban society, was alien to their agrarian world.[61]

White North Carolinians generally opposed education for blacks. A prominent Morganton woman explained: it "puts notions of equality into their heads that wholly unfits them for any kind of servitude." Rather than educate black students as well as white and risk the federal government's insisting on an integrated school system, the state was willing to abolish its common school program. During the two years of the presidential Reconstruction, from 1865 to 1867, black schools were established across the state, although not nearly enough to meet the need, and many white children were also deprived of a public education. Whites objected to blacks being taught by Northerners, because Northerners did not understand Southern ways. They reviled and ridiculed Northern missionary teachers. The *Wilmington Journal* warned against the "evil teaching" of New Englander Amy Morris Bradley, who intended to establish an integrated school in town shortly after the Civil War (she started, instead, a school for white children).[62]

African Americans faced other, more subtle, obstacles in their quest for an education. The American Missionary Association (AMA) was the first, and largest, of the benevolent groups to educate Southern blacks. Most of its female teachers were Northern—white, upper or middle class—and eager to serve. They worked for fifteen dollars a month, less pay than men; so employing them was economical. Yet according to one AMA official, despite the good hearts and "culture and refinement" of the white teachers, black students learned better from teachers of "their own race in a thousand and one ways." The AMA experimented with the employment of black teachers, who generally were not as prosperous as the white teachers but were strongly motivated by a sense of "racial uplift." As Sara G. Stanley, of Ohio, originally from New Bern and an Oberlin College student, wrote, "I have felt a strong conviction of duty. . . . I am bound to that ignorant, degraded long enslaved race, by ties of love and consanguinity; they are . . . my people." When she became a teacher, she was shocked that presumably race-sensitive white teachers referred "constantly to the alleged inferiority of blacks" and steadfastly maintained social distances from them. Although she could pass for white, Stanley identified with the black race, and her "motive" was "to utter a plea for those who have no voice to plead for themselves." Black students, she reported, preferred black teachers. They knew their friends not through "*word*, but *deed*." Even so, the AMA resisted using black teachers, who were evaluated by different, more rigorous standards, condescended to, and at times humiliated. As a result, the AMA undermined the efforts of independent black teachers and even black self-education. Traditional studies in educational history have suggested that blacks welcomed the Northern teachers with "open arms," but Jacqueline Jones and others have concluded that the patronizing attitude of the benevolent educators—pity, not justice, in Frederick Douglass's words—negatively affected black learning.[63]

During the years of Radical Reconstruction it seemed as though African Americans might be integrated into the political and economic life of the state. In 1868 Congress set two conditions for the Southern states' readmission to the Union, the establishment of a new state constitution and the guarantee of black men's right to vote and to participate in politics. African American men joined the North Carolina Republican Party, which was strong in the east where blacks were the majority in sixteen counties and in the west where there were few blacks but where many whites were ardent Unionists and opponents of secession. The Republicans captured 107 of the 120 seats for the constitutional convention of 1868, and

FIGURE 6-15. *Ku Klux Klan mask*, Person County, 1870. (Courtesy of the North Carolina Museum of History)

FIGURE 6-16. Willie Holt Ferguson, *The Burial of Radicalism in North Carolina, November 7, 1876*. This caricature celebrates the redemption of North Carolina in Zebulon Vance's winning the governorship over Judge Thomas Settle. As Vance tears off the state's shackles of Reconstruction, Abby House exclaims, "ZEB your setting CAROLINA free makes me feel like a gal again." (Courtesy of the North Carolina Collection, University of North Carolina at Chapel Hill)

of these, 15 were black delegates. The new constitution included a tax-supported, though racially segregated, educational system; elected, rather than appointed, local governments; senate representation based on population rather than on wealth; and more liberal property rights for married women. In short, the constitution granted some power and rights to the mass of people.[64]

Opposition was swift and violent. Between 1868 and 1872 the Ku Klux Klan, many of whose leaders were ousted Democratic officeholders, launched a campaign of terror against blacks to regain political power (Fig. 6-15). Mandy Coverson of Union County described the "heap of beatin' and chasin' folks out of the country" done by the Klan and termed the struggle for political power "mostly the cause of it." Newton's W. L. Bost recalled that the Klansmen's "long gowns, touch the ground.... Some time they put sticks in the top of the tall thing they wear and then put an extra head up there with scary eyes and great big mouth." Alamance and Caswell Counties, where Republicans were strongest, experienced the most violence. In addition, there were between one hundred and two hundred whippings of blacks in Rutherford County alone, and many others in Lincoln, Gaston, Cleveland, Mecklenburg, Guilford, Orange, Randolph, Chatham, Montgomery, and Moore Counties. Schoolhouses and churches were burned to the ground. Families were routed from their beds. Men were shot at, whipped, and lynched; one had his throat cut. Blacks were frightened out of their wits—and out of any notion of voting.[65]

By 1870 white Democrats regained political control, and by 1876 the federal government withdrew its support of Radical Republican policies. In November 1876 Zebulon B. Vance was reelected governor, thereby "redeeming" the state. Reconstruction was effectively over in North Carolina. According to tradition, Vance had the vote of "Aunt Abby" of Civil

War fame who had attended the Democratic convention in Raleigh. Because Clay County was unrepresented, Paul Cameron moved that Aunt Abby be permitted to vote, and, indeed, she cast her vote to return Zebulon B. Vance to office—possibly the first time that a woman had voted in North Carolina (Fig. 6-16).[66]

Civil War and Reconstruction had brought cataclysmic changes in everyone's lives, but one unescapable result was the increased visibility of women. War gave women new opportunities for responsibility and new, if temporary, sources of identity and power. They had displayed resourcefulness under trying circumstances, enlarged the boundaries of women's work, perhaps even altered the course of history with their resistance to the war, and demonstrated a willingness and an aptitude to take on new roles in the public life of the state. With 25,000 more women than men in North Carolina after the war, women continued to function in many areas of daily life that had been closed to them before the war.

Blacks believed that education was the key to their economic, social, and political progress, and optimism was high as Reconstruction ended, though hard times lay ahead. Slavery had been abolished, but law and custom still held blacks in their place. "Slavery was a bad thing," said Patsy Mitchner of Raleigh, who remembered that the slaves had "prayed for freedom." But freedom "of the kin' we got wid nothin' to live on wuz bad. De snake called slavery lay wid his head pointed south an' the snake called freedom lay wid his head pointed north. Both bit de nigger, an' dey wuz both bad."[67]

Harriet Jacobs

1813–1897

Harriet Jacobs. (From a drawing of a photograph, used in an exhibit sponsored by the North Carolina Division of Archives and History)

When *Incidents in the Life of a Slave Girl, Written by Herself* appeared in 1861, many readers doubted its authenticity as a true slave narrative. They thought it was impossible that the obviously educated author could have been a slave. More likely, the author was the abolitionist leader, Lydia Maria Child, who was listed on the title page as editor. The identity of the author was not the only problem. Her story of sexual encounters was disturbing, and her sober tone of voice to describe them seemed odd. All in all, *Incidents* was dismissed by some readers who knew nothing of the writer or her background.

Because the book was published after the Civil War had begun, the time had passed when it might have persuaded a greater number of educated Northern women to join the abolitionist movement. More than a century later, however, *Incidents* would be reconsidered on its own merits, in part due to a surge of interest in women's history. Working with other researchers, a contemporary scholar, Jean Fagan Yellin, established the author's real identity, the history of how the narrative had been written and published, and a carefully edited text. Now most readers regard *Incidents* as the best-known autobiography of a black woman in the antebellum South.

The author, called "Linda Brent" in the narrative, proved to be the fictive self of Harriet Jacobs, born in Edenton in 1813. The black woman from North Carolina whom Northern abolitionist leaders knew and befriended has been recognized in her home state. Although questions remain concerning whether historical personages actually did what their fictional counterparts were said to have done, the narrative of Linda Brent and the life history of Harriet Jacobs endure as representations of a slave woman's life.[1]

Evidence for what Jacobs's most recent editor calls the book's "radical feminist content" begins with the author's stated intention. In describing the story she was writing about her life in an 1857 letter to Amy Post, a white Quaker friend she had met in the abolitionist movement in Rochester, New York, Harriet explained, "I have placed myself before you to be judged as a woman." Then in the preface by "Linda Brent," she made another appeal: "I do earnestly desire to arouse the women of the North to a realizing sense of the condition of two millions of women at the South, still in bondage, suffering from what I suffered, and most of them far worse."[2]

Promising "to tell the truth, let it cost me what it may," the fictitious narrator then described her "headlong plunge" into a sexual affair with a white Edenton lawyer, called "Mr. Sands," whom Yellin identifies as Samuel Tredwell Sawyer. "I knew what I did," she wrote, "and I did it with deliberate calculation." She also confessed to feelings of terrible guilt. After she had entered into the relationship with Sands, she "wanted to confess to her [grandmother] that I was no longer worthy of her love; but I could not utter the dreaded words."

Jacobs's presentation of the narrator as a sexual woman was a dramatic departure from the silence of most eighteenth- and nineteenth-century women on this subject. Moreover, as the author of the book, Harriet assumed a public voice speaking in behalf of a woman's cause. As Lydia Maria Child wrote in the introduction to the first edition of the book, the "monstrous features" of slavery were presented "with the veil withdrawn." The narrator acknowledged her own sexual behavior and spoke of the liaisons that white masters had with other slave women. Although the subject matter is dramatic, the pace of Brent's story is slow, textured by rhetorical language and imagery characteristic of many other nineteenth-century narratives. The power of *Incidents*, Yellin observes, is that in making the narrator's sexual behavior a subject of public concern Jacobs projected "a new kind of female hero."

The twenty-nine years (1813–42) of her life in Edenton were years of enslavement, but they were also the years in which she discovered her own power. She escaped from North Carolina in 1842 and started her education in meetings with abolitionists in New York and Massachusetts. About a decade later she began writing the book that would bring her to the attention of more than a century of readers. In 1861 she published *Incidents* and promoted it among abolitionists. And in 1867, at age fifty-four, she returned to Edenton for a visit.

Harriet Jacobs was born in Edenton to Delilah and Daniel Jacobs. Her parents had one other child, John, born in 1815. Daniel was a skilled carpenter, often hired out by his owner for special work. Delilah was the daughter of Molly Horniblow, and Horniblow was the daughter of a South Carolina planter. Molly, along with her mother and two siblings, had been freed when the planter died. Apparently on a voyage to St. Augustine to visit relatives, they were captured, separated, and sold back into slavery. Molly, then about ten or eleven years old, became the property of John Horniblow, who operated the King's Arms tavern in Edenton. Delilah was given by her slave mistress, Elizabeth Horniblow, to her daughter, Margaret. Later, Molly Horniblow became Harriet's grandmother. The identification of these and other historic personages required some detective work on the part of a broad community of researchers consulted by Jean Yellin. The most recent edition makes possible a more appreciative reading of *Incidents* and provides a slave woman's perspective as historians try to complete the Southern narrative.

Narrator Linda Brent began her story at the moment of change in her "happy childhood" with her parents and brother, who "fondly shielded" her from the fact that they were all slaves. After her mother's death when Linda was six years old, she looked for comfort from her slave mistress. There, for a short while, she found another happy home; she was well-treated and taught to read, spell, and sew. "I loved her," Linda wrote of her mistress, "for she had been almost like a mother to me." Following the woman's early death, eleven-year-old Linda was sent to stay with her grandmother and to await the reading of the will.

Linda's grandmother, called "Aunt Martha," had been "an indispensable personage in the household, officiating in all capacities, from cook and wet nurse to seamstress." A person of intelligence, high expectations, and temper, she commanded respect. When Edenton neighbors wanted some of her famous crackers, her mistress agreed that she could offer them for sale. In this way she earned modest amounts of money that she put aside to buy her children. "Upon these terms," Linda wrote, "after working all day for her mistress, she began her midnight bakings, assisted by her two oldest children."

Linda believed that, because of her mother's "love and faithful service," the mistress would grant her freedom. But when the mistress died and her will was read, Linda had not been freed but had been bequeathed to the daughter of her mistress's sister, who was the wife of "Dr. Flint."

This unhappy turn of events was the first of many. Within the year Linda's father died, and Linda and her brother began talking in earnest about their desire to escape to freedom. Then, when she was no more than fifteen, Dr. Flint began his sexual advances. Flint was thirty-five years older than the slave girl. Yellin identifies him as Dr. James Norcom, a man of considerable power and wealth, who owned more than 1,700 acres in Chowan County, seven town lots, and nineteen slaves.

According to Yellin, in the years following the death of Harriet Jacobs's mistress, Jacobs's grandmother (Molly Horniblow) had been purchased by her mistress's sister and given her freedom. In 1828 she was a free woman of color living in Edenton, and in 1830 Congressman Alfred Gatlin helped her to buy her own house, near the center of town on King Street, in sight of the residence of James and Mary Norcom.

Linda charged that Dr. Flint was the father of eleven slave children, in addition to eight or nine children by his first and second wives. He thoroughly dominated his second wife, who was embittered by his suspected relationships with black women and afraid to confront him. She took her anger out on the slave girl. At first, Linda was no more than "the little Imp" to Mrs. Flint, who punished her for squeaky shoes, accused her of telling lies, and watched her closely for other mistakes. She demanded that Linda swear on a Bible that she would truthfully answer her questions about her husband's behavior. When Linda told her that Dr. Flint had made advances, his wife wept, and Linda was moved to sympathize with the poor woman whose husband was so filled with "evil." For a while, Mrs. Flint was kind to Linda. But the peace did not last, and she finally accused her husband of "crime," but he would confess to nothing. Linda testified to her readers, "I never wronged her, or wished to wrong her; and one word of kindness from her would have brought me to her feet." Elizabeth Fox-Genovese has argued that resisting the advances of her slave master would have been impossible, but whether Linda did or did not succumb to Dr. Flint's desires, the theme of her narrative is the threat that white masters imposed on slave women.[3] Linda Brent's narrative of rejection of Flint's advances was followed by her confession of a relationship with another white man, Sands, but first she provided the readers with reasons for her choice.

Earlier she had fallen in love with a "young colored carpenter, a free born man." Marriage between a free black and a slave required the consent of the owner. She went to talk with Flint, who demanded, "Do you love this nigger?" "Yes, sir," she answered. Enraged by her "insolence," he ordered her never to speak to the man again. Aware of his threats to whip them both, Linda urged the man she loved to go to the free states. "For *his* sake I felt that I ought not to link his fate with my own unhappy destiny."

Flint then contrived to build a small house for Linda in a secluded place outside of town, where no one in Edenton would see him come and go. Seeking to defeat him, Linda explained, "I thought and thought, till I became desperate, and made a plunge into the abyss."

She had decided to accept Sands as a sexual partner. "There is something akin to freedom," she argued, "in having a lover who has no control over you, except that which he gains by kindness and attachment. . . . There may be sophistry in all this; but the condition of a slave confuses all principles of morality, and, in fact, renders the practice of them impossible." Linda's description of kindness passing between lovers sounds like a passage from a nineteenth-century romance novel, but in attributing such feelings to a white man and a black woman she exploited the fictive model to raise the intensity of interest in the nature of slavery.

In identifying Sands as Samuel Tredwell Sawyer, Yellin claims that Linda's chosen lover was a man of distinction, a graduate of the University of North Carolina at Chapel Hill, practicing law in Edenton. He was unmarried. At the time they began the affair, she was about sixteen and he was about twenty-nine. Later when he married and wanted his wife to know about his children by Linda, purchased them, and promised to free them, Linda would feel vindicated by her choice.

In spite of the relief and satisfaction it gave Linda to have thwarted Flint by having chosen her own lover, she felt guilt over the liaison with Sands. Pregnant and ashamed, she faced her grandmother's wrath. As she wrote about confessing her guilt and receiving her grandmother's love, Linda played on the sympathies of her women readers, who would recognize the responsibility the older woman would have borne for her motherless granddaughter. In 1829 Linda gave birth to a son (identified as Joseph Jacobs) and in 1833 to a daughter (Louisa Matilda Jacobs). The births of the children brought her closer to her grandmother, who insisted that they be christened in the Episcopal church in Edenton where she attended services.

When Flint threatened her children's safety as well as her own, Linda began planning her escape from North Carolina so that she could secure their freedom. Yellin believes that in August 1835 she entered a hiding place in her grandmother's attic, only large enough to lie down in. In *Incidents* and in her brother's later written account, readers are told that she hid there for six years and eleven months, watching through a hole in the wall activities below on West King Street, hoping to catch glimpses of her children, and sometimes at night coming down to stretch her limbs in a darkened house.

Although the approximate seven years' travail may only be archetypal, accounts of slaves trying to escape their masters were known to Linda's readers, who recognized the truth of her desperation. Flint advertised her as a runaway, offered rewards, and traveled to the North in search of her. In whispered conversations with family members and friends, Linda made plans to escape to the North. Meanwhile, Sands, who had bought Linda's brother and her two children, allowed the children to live with her grandmother. But he did not live up to his promise to free the children, and in 1840 he sent "Ellen" (Harriet's daughter, Louisa Matilda) to live with members of his family in Washington, D.C., and then to Brooklyn, New York. Linda's tearful good-bye as the child was to leave is one of the most moving passages in her story. Linda's grandmother promised to keep "Bennie" (Harriet's son Joseph) until he could be sent north to safety. Now if she could escape, Linda could reunite the family. "Whatever slavery might do to me," she remembered, "it could not shackle my children." Her brother had already escaped to freedom while traveling as a servant to Sands and his new bride, and he was working with abolitionists in Massachusetts and New York. A new world awaited her.

About two years after her daughter left North Carolina (according to Yellin's research, June 1842) the day came for Linda to leave her hiding place. With the help of black and white friends along the way, she went by boat to Philadelphia and then by train to New York. After working in white residences in New York City, she moved to Rochester, where she lived for a time in the home of Amy and Isaac Post. Linda had learned to read as a slave in North Carolina, and as she continued to develop her skills she read abolitionist literature more widely in the Anti-Slavery Office and Reading Room, which her brother ran. She recovered a nucleus of her own family when she lived with her brother and was joined by her daughter, who had been sent by her father to live as a servant with his New York cousins. Linda enrolled her in a boarding school in Clinton, New York. Her son joined them, and she placed him as an apprentice in a print shop.

Earning modest wages to support herself and her children and traveling and working in the abolitionist movement, Linda Brent had a much happier life after leaving North Carolina; however, she continued to fear Flint's attempts to claim her as property and take her back to Edenton. After his death in 1850, his heirs tried but failed to find her. In 1852, when her employer insisted on securing her freedom, she was purchased from the Edenton family, but it was against her will, for she said that she was unwilling to be treated as property in order to be treated as free.

At the urging of Amy Post, Harriet Jacobs wrote her story as told by her narrator, Linda Brent. After unsuccessful attempts to have it published, she secured the editorial help and endorsement of Lydia Maria Child and published it herself in 1861. Harriet traveled and lectured to promote the book; she also worked with slaves behind the lines of the Union army and with freedmen to organize relief movements in Alexandria, Virginia; Washington, D.C.; and Savannah, Georgia. Louisa Matilda joined her in some of these activities—in 1868 they traveled to London to raise funds, and in 1885 they were living together in Washington. Harriet's son Joseph was residing in Australia in 1863, the last she heard from him.

Today—some seven editions later—*Incidents* is generally recognized as the most thoroughly documented female slave narrative and one of the most valuable slave narratives in American history.[4] As a woman's autobiography, it offers a number of roles for women: Harriet Jacobs as an agent of change, active in her own behalf and in behalf of other slave women; her grandmother as a source of judgment, forgiveness, and protection; and white women as having the power to accept or reject the evils of slavery.

The narrative of one slave woman's life as written by herself brings an original voice to this period in North Carolina history that property records and journals kept by plantation owners cannot provide. Factual evidence exists to document a great deal of Harriet Jacobs's life, and more evidence will likely be forthcoming when Yellin's biography of Jacobs is published. Even if some events in the life of "Linda Brent" can never be substantiated by factual records, the story's metaphors of resistance will continue to carry the power of truth.

In April 1867 Harriet Jacobs returned to Edenton to visit family members and friends, to distribute seeds for gardens, and to encourage schools for black children. She died on March 7, 1897, in Washington, D.C., and was buried in Mount Auburn Cemetery, Cambridge, Massachusetts. In a letter of April 25, 1867, to a Boston abolitionist friend, written from Edenton, North Carolina, Harriet left a final picture of her homeplace:

> I am sitting under the old roof twelve feet from the spot where I suffered all the crushing weight of slavery. thank God the bitter cup is drained of its last dreg. there is no more need of hiding places to conceal slave Mothers. yet it was little to purchase the blessings of freedom. I could have worn this poor life out there to save my Children from the misery and degradation of Slavery.
>
> I had long thought I had no attachment to my old home. as I often sit here and think of those I loved of their hard struggle in life—their unfaltering love and devotion toward myself and Children. I love to sit here and think of them. they have made the few sunny spots in that dark life sacred to me.
>
> I cannot tell you how I feel in this place. the change is so great I can hardly take it all in I was born here, and amid all these new born blessings, the old dark cloud comes over me, and I find it hard to have faith in rebels.[5]

Catherine Devereux Edmondston

1823–1875

Catherine Devereux Edmondston, photograph of a painting. (Courtesy of the North Carolina Division of Archives and History)

Catherine Devereux Edmondston belonged to the planter aristocracy of antebellum North Carolina. The Devereux-Pollock family owned many plantations and slaves, and she and her husband, Patrick Muir Edmondston, inherited some of them. She recorded her impressions of Civil War life in Halifax County in northeastern North Carolina. To read from the *"Journal of a Secesh Lady": The Diary of Catherine Ann Devereux Edmondston, 1860–1866*, published in a book of more than eight hundred pages, is to enter scenes wherein the familiar romance of the "southern lady" gives way to the realities of how such a "lady" lived.[1]

Although Edmondston wrote her journal mostly during the Civil War, she was not writing "war history" as such. It is one planter woman's perspective of her times and circumstances, and its themes are uniquely hers: rituals of domestic and social life, marriage and family, and the effects of the war on private lives. Thus, this discussion of one life in Halifax County in the first half of the nineteenth century focuses on the development of Catherine Edmondston rather than on the war itself.

Kate, as she was called, grew up in Raleigh, one of seven children. Their mother was Catherine Ann Johnson Devereux, of Connecticut, whose ancestors included distinguished English and American clergymen, educators, and jurists, and the famous Jonathan Edwards. Her father, Thomas Pollock Devereux, was born in New Bern and through the Pollock line acquired his properties. A Yale graduate and a trustee of the University of North Carolina, he practiced law before devoting himself to the management of his estate. His wife died of tuberculosis in 1836, when Kate was thirteen. The next year Thomas married Ann Maitland; the children found their stepmother to be "difficult and demanding," making their lives "sad and dreary."[2] Kate's father was a domineering man of energy (he danced the Highland fling at his fiftieth wedding anniversary) and authority (like most other men of wealth, he controlled the terms of his daughter's marriage settlement).

One of six daughters, Kate was tutored first at home and then at Belmont, a private academy for young women near Leesburg, Virginia. Her brother attended Yale.[3] Each year the family left Raleigh for their summer residence at Conneconara, on the Roanoke River in Halifax County. They enjoyed the pleasures of large houses (where much of the work was done by slaves), books, and visitors. In her earliest years Kate acquired her lifelong passion for reading and writing.

In 1846, at age twenty-three, Kate married Patrick Muir Edmondston, of Charleston, South Carolina, who was four years her senior. The wedding took place at Conneconara, and the rector of Christ Church in Raleigh performed the ceremony. Her husband, "Mr. E," as she calls him in her journal, was the son of a prominent Charleston family, whose commercial interests had probably brought him into contact with the Devereux family. After a few years in South Carolina, the couple accepted a $10,000 marriage settlement promised by her father and moved to Halifax County, North Carolina, to Looking Glass plantation and seasonally to the nearby summerhouse at Hascosea. Kate's father, his wife, and their daughter, Sue, lived on the adjacent plantation of Conneconara. Patrick managed Looking Glass and divided the profits of the farm with his father-in-law. Kate expected to enjoy the rural beauty of the Roanoke River valley for the rest of her life.

For the first fourteen years of marriage, she apparently spent little time writing in a journal. Then things began to change, though she had little sense of the defeat that lay ahead. Despite an overwhelming majority of antisecessionist voters in the state and presidential campaign of 1860, Unionist attitudes toward the slaveholding South were moving the state closer to war. "These troublous times" provoked Kate to begin a more faithful record of her life. Although her father and other family members were Unionists, Kate embraced her husband's views and became a secessionist or "secesh lady" with passionate disgust for "Mr. Lincoln" and threats to her idyllic life.

If the approaching war gave Kate sufficient material to make her journal readable, it also affected her on a more profoundly personal level: her husband was anxious to be part of the state's organizing efforts and had been given the task of training volunteers for the Home Guard.[4] They had seldom been apart, and Kate wondered if she could live without him—"my hope, my stay, my all." Their first critical separation, when Patrick attended a convention of militia companies in Goldsboro, inspired her to begin the journal to assuage "the loneliness of absence."

With the first entry on June 1, 1860—"Moved from Looking Glass to Hascosea for the summer"—readers enter her home. The June entries that follow—"Mama and Susan [Kate's stepmother and half sister] came," "Mr. E. all day drilling his troop," and "Made some Blackberry wine" are simple enough and introduce key elements of the narrative: a plantation house filled with guests, Patrick often away, and domestic life continuing. These simple-seeming references (typical of so many others like them) tell us a great deal about the contents of a day in her life.

Kate plaited straw, knitted undershirts, made honey and walnut pickles, sent packages to family and friends, decorated cakes, ordered groceries from New York, gave parties, wrote letters, nursed the sick, and supervised the house servants. She planted hyacinths, cut bores out of peach trees, boxed dahlias and tuberoses to send to her family in Raleigh, looked after the cotton, sowed eggplant and tomatoes, and watched the river rise:

> November 17, 1864
> This morning put up Jessie's 2 shirts to go by Express. Mr. McMahon (Express Agent) valued one of them at $75 (seventy five dollars)! Wrote her a letter, put up Mr. E's dinner, & a loaf of bread for Captain Cook, whom I am sorry to say is in very bad health, gave Mr. Walker, a soldier, his breakfast and hunted up a blanket for him, put up an undershirt which I had mended up for another soldier who has been separated from his baggage & caught in this severe weather with neither overcoat or Flannel & he a feeble man detailed on light duty—one Mr. Holmes. Weighed my butter & sent up to Halifax the first instalment of a payment in it for a block of cotton for my own wear & then set to work, & tho interrupted by my Vinegar manufacture & some trouble about a tight barrel, by constantly plying my fingers I finished the body of the second undershirt, got it washed & strained out on the table to dry & by four o'clock was ready for a walk over to Mr. John Lawrence's to call on Miss Ida Whitton, my maid Fanny attending me. I knit 5776 stitches & it took 140 pins, the positions of all of which had to be altered & tightened once & some of them twice before the shirt was properly strained to its full dimensions, so as it is not yet 7 o'clock I do not think I have been idle today.

In addition to performing household and garden tasks familiar to most women, during her husband's absences Kate Edmondston managed two houses, a large estate, and some eighty-eight slaves. For a woman who liked solitude, in which she read classical literature and history, as well as newspapers, and wrote a great deal—journals, letters, and poems—the external demands on her time and her interests conflicted: she yearned to be both a poet and a "useful everyday sympathizing woman."

Kate moved between the housework downstairs and her journal writing upstairs with only mild complaints—so long as she was in charge of the schedule. When the house was filled with children of visiting family, she was wary of "being used as a convenience" and expressed "a dread of having some neglected little child put off . . . to dry nurse!" "Why will not you who have no burden of that kind take one from your over burdened sister or brother?" she asked herself. "Simply because I wont!" came her answer. Kate and "Mr. E" often retreated to what they called the "Solitaire," a small house in the garden, simply furnished, where they sat quietly together "absolutely *alone*" and read and talked or left one another signs of having been there—a rose, an open book, a half-written letter. Such a retreat from "all the rest of the world" was remarkable in itself: running a large plantation and being a member of a large family were very demanding. Then, on the same day Kate described the Solitaire—August 22, 1864—she also reported, "the enemy have again cut the Petersburg & Weldon R R at Reams' Station, 9 miles from Petersburg. . . . a preliminary to an advance on Grant's part."

Scholars have differed about how much a planter wife generally knew about her husband's business. Kate's journal suggests that she knew a great deal. She learned how to inspect the drainage ditches, check the crops, and measure the flood damage. "I walk with him & enter into all his business as keenly as tho I were a farmer too," she wrote on July 15, 1860. She also had her own opinions of how things should be done: "It is a serious question with father & Mr. E whether they will put back the Looking Glass dams or not. I hope not. Make what corn we can & pasture the rest & by raising stock for the future fill up our income. The risk and loss is too great & our force too weak to put back the work."

Slaves—including her own "handmaidens," as she called them—worked both at Looking Glass and at the summerhouse at Hascosea. When the overseer was away, Kate portioned out the food allowance for each slave; she organized the women to spin, knit, and sew for the war effort, turning out uniforms, underclothes, tents, blankets, and bandages; she complained about needing to supervise their religious education but tended them when they were sick and concerned herself with a mother's feeding of a new baby. Her racial attitudes were those of most planter women of her time: she sometimes expressed her own affection toward servants ("Ah! Cuffee! Cuffee! you are no manager, & yet I love you. Faults & all"), but she objected to a white woman friend's calling a young black "a sweet child."

At both Looking Glass and Hascosea Kate recorded a steady coming and going of visitors: Father, Mama (both of them old and often unwell), and stepsister Sue, Kate's sisters and their children, her "despondent" brother who was always pessimistic about the war, members of her husband's family, and many people bearing war news. For all of them there were formal meals and extended visits. Even with a large staff of servants, every day was a full day's work.

Two years after beginning her journal, on June 1, 1862, Kate noted a dramatic change in her daily routine: "My garden, that great source of interest, passes unnoticed by & my housekeeping, which absorbed so large a portion, is now not deemed worthy of a single entry; but battles and seiges [*sic*], bloodshed, and the suffering of a mighty country occupy every thought." Thereafter, the entries are taken up with news of the war.

Kate worked hard keeping up with what was happening through newspapers, letters, and reports from travelers. On July 30, 1862, she asked herself, "How comes it that I can be so happy in the midst of such wide spread distress?" She answered, "God has mercifully protected me so far from it . . . and here I live quietly amid my groves & gardens . . . in short lead so delightful a 'dolce par niente' life that I could almost forget there was a war." As she became more intense about the Southern cause, Kate said that she would willingly give up having Patrick at home so that he could serve the war effort. But what this meant in terms of deprivation neither had to confront; he fought no battles, and when he went off to training camp for short periods, she sent him strawberries "in profusion." As she heard news of so many men she had known who were wounded or killed, her sister's plantation in Tennessee plundered, railroads and bridges destroyed in her own neighborhood, her fears deepened, and she filled the journal with reports of battles copied from newspapers, often analyzing the strengths and weaknesses of various military strategies.

In some instances Kate's concerns challenged the notion of "southern lady." She thought her stepsister Sue's behavior "uncertain & disappointing" when they went to see a gunboat launched: "the coy maiden had to be persuaded to venture upon the slippery ways that lead to the water." In the same entry, she boasted about having driven herself in the buggy. She was not vain. "Perhaps I prize [beauty] too much," she said, "as it has been denied me." She took interest in her sisters' children but admitted: "Not that I am inhospitable or annoyed by children, but they are not part and parcel of my enjoyment. They are a thing aside, as it were, to me & when they leave I fly back at once like a spring bent out of place & resume old habits & old modes of thought without once missing them; & yet I do thoroughly enjoy their prattle."

Perhaps nowhere were the complexities of Kate's interior life more apparent than in her references to her husband. "When he is away," she wrote, "I take strange liberties." Upstairs in her bedroom, she turned to her journal: "It would need no prophet to tell you, O Journal that Mr. Edmondston is from home." However much she failed to write (and she said that she did not tell her deepest feelings), she believed that the act of writing anything was an act of freedom. She called her writing both "chat" and "contraband."

An entry dated January 21, 1863, dramatizes her inner turmoil:

> Do you remember, Madam, how you wept & cried the first year of your marriage when your husband said, "that the first duty of woman was to attend to the cooking"? I do not mean to accuse you of neglecting it—that you had too high a sense of your duty as a wife ever to do. What pained & mortified you was the exaltation in which he placed it. . . . You were willing enough and happy in attending to domestic duties. You were too well brought up by your mother either to undervalue or feel them a burden to you, but the pedestal on which he placed them debased all else. You could not worship at such a shrine! and yet, Madam, have you not long years ago seen and confessed that your husband was right?; that a well ordered table, well cooked, well prepared food was the keynote to health, happiness, and usefulness?

On other occasions, she praised their marriage: "We have the same tastes, the same pleasures. He reads to me & gardens with me. . . . We are never long apart & our religious life is so bought up each in the other that I sometimes doubt whether he is not more to me than he should be." Again and again she declared, "How lonely it is without Mr. Edmondston!" When he failed to understand her, she wrote, "I was not expecting sympathy for myself—it was for him & his disappointments. I was not even thinking of how little I get outside of him."

The entries of the last two years of Kate's chronicle are marked by her recognition of the defeat of the Confederacy, and she made plans to hide her journal: "Think how [General Philip] Sheridan's bumming officers would seize upon the 'Journal of a Secesh Lady—a complete record of a daily life spent in the Southern Confederacy from July 1860–April 65' & how I would feel thus dragged from the recesses of private life & for aught I know published for the amusement of a censorious, curious and critical public?" Henceforth, she wrote on scraps of paper.

Kate's thoughts are caught up in the news of emancipation and scares of insurrection and the work of the Freedmen's Bureau, heavy debts, destruction of property, "hated troops stationed amongst us"—her center had not held. On June 26, 1865, she went to the Solitaire to write, "This Journal is now but a pain and greif [*sic*] to me. It is a transcript of disappointed hopes, of crushed expectations, which have all the bitterness of death without the lively hope of a Resurrection." Her father and her husband were required to take the oath of allegiance to the U.S. government. Kate's health faltered, and she was nursed by her maid, Fanny, until Fanny fled with other former slaves from Looking Glass plantation. On January 4, 1866, Kate wrote in her journal for the last time, "Terrible weather for ten days back. Incessant rain & mist."

On the death of Kate's father in 1869, his estate was encumbered with debt and litigation. Her newly widowed sister Nora and her four children moved to Hascosea, Kate's health drained away, and the house was "dull" and morbidly silent. Then, in 1871 Patrick died. Kate wrote to her nephew, "It requires one to be a widow & childless—who has hitherto enjoyed the elasticity of youth—& who has leaned on one person alone—to feel the utter desolation which seizes on her when that object is suddenly taken from her & with it the brightness of life—the visions of youth depart."[5]

Catherine Devereux Edmondston died on January 3, 1875, in Raleigh at the home of her sister, Frances Miller. She was fifty-one. More than a century would pass before her journal was published.

Cornelia Phillips Spencer

1825–1908

Cornelia Phillips Spencer, photograph of a painting. (Courtesy of the University of North Carolina Historic Properties Office)

Cornelia Phillips Spencer is the most famous woman in two centuries of history connected with the University of North Carolina at Chapel Hill. Growing up on the edge of the campus as the daughter of a professor allowed her access to books and teachers. This opportunity combined with her own intellectual strengths enabled her to become one of the best-educated thinkers of her generation. In two books—*The Last Ninety Days of the War in North Carolina* (1866) and *First Steps in North Carolina History* (1888)—and twenty-five years of newspaper articles and columns, she left a record of her timely observations and strong opinions. As a close friend and adviser to important men, she influenced the direction of the university and the state, although she never voted or held office or graduated from the university.

Among the eighty-four leaders of the University of North Carolina whose photographs appear in a volume of Kemp Battle's history (1868–1912), Cornelia Spencer is the only woman. She was the only woman among the twenty-eight incorporators of the Historical Society of North Carolina. In 1895, at the university's centennial commencement, she became the first woman in its history to receive an honorary degree; among the other recipients were the governor of North Carolina, a Confederate army colonel, a lawyer, and a congressman. At the university's bicentennial celebration in 1995, her name was woven into the texts of many public occasions.

Cornelia's greatest contributions were in behalf of education. One of the important twentieth-century men of the university, librarian Louis Round Wilson, observed, "Much of the State's educational development stems directly from her militancy."[1] She wrote letters and articles throughout the 1870s to raise public support for the common school. In 1877 she took particular pleasure in the opening of the University Normal School, the nation's first summer program for public school teachers, supported by the state legislature and the Peabody Fund. She joined several hundred teachers—men and women—in attending the school sessions and wrote daily reports for the press. Of her campaign to restore the University of North Carolina following years of decline, Wilson said: "No finer chapter of endeavor in behalf of the public good of North Carolina has been written by any other of the State's sons and daughters."[2]

Cornelia advanced the causes of public schools and the university on two fronts: for the public at large and their representatives in the legislature, she hammered away on her favorite themes in widely read columns and editorials; in private conversations and letters she advised—sometimes berated—important men. Nobody, it seems, ignored the opinion—or even the presence—of Cornelia Phillips Spencer. ("'There goes Spencer!' a student would almost whisper, and the entire group would stop and gaze respectfully, spellbound.")[3] She was, in her own words, a relentless "scold." Sometimes those with whom she differed hastened to explain themselves: in 1891 Judge E. G. Reade wrote her, "I now learn for the first time . . . that my address as the president of the State Reconstruction Convention made you very angry. I beg therefore to say a word as to that."[4] Her pen perhaps wielded more power than that of any other woman in North Carolina history. Had she not suffered from a severe deafness, beginning in her late thirties, perhaps she also would have been a great orator. As it was, her words still assert her authority on the printed page.[5]

Chapel Hill, North Carolina, is at the heart of Cornelia's story. She was brought there as a one-year-old child when her father, James Phillips, joined the university faculty, and there she remained for the greatest part of her long life. The years in which she was married to James Munroe Spencer and living away, mostly in his home state of Alabama (1855–61), would later seem like a dream. After her husband's death in 1861, she returned with their daughter Julia (June) to Chapel Hill and lived again with her parents. In later years when, because of failing health, she moved to be with her daughter and her daughter's family in Cambridge, Massachusetts (her son-in-law, James Love, was a Harvard professor), her thoughts often returned to Chapel Hill.

Cornelia loved the University of North Carolina with a passion most women reserve for personal relationships. From her earliest childhood, she knew the campus and its buildings, the books in the libraries, and presidents, professors, and students. As the years of the Civil War diminished the number of students and left the university financially destitute and as Reconstruction politics brought to the presidency a man Spencer loathed, Solomon Pool, who replaced her faculty friends with his own men, she was aroused from sorrow to fury. On February 1, 1871, when the trustees voted to close the university, its tragic decline suddenly gave way to a deathlike quiet. Resolutely, she began to work toward its recovery. As Louis R. Wilson described her efforts, "alone, and armed with only her pen, [she] formulated a plan of action and determinedly stuck to it until the nightmare was ended." In a letter-writing campaign to restore the university to its former glory, she challenged the attitude of defeatism that she felt was paralyzing the state's best leaders and citizenry. She aimed to drive the usurpers from Chapel Hill, which she called "the child of the state." She had promised, "There is nothing that a woman can do that I would not undertake for its redemption." And she did more than any woman of the nineteenth century was expected to do: she engaged in written public discussion of controversial political issues, launching attacks and dismissing those made against her. Doggedly, she and others persisted, and they were joyfully rewarded. On March 20, 1875, when Cornelia heard the news that the legislature had passed a bill to reopen the university, making possible the renewal of its traditions and reorganizing for its future, she climbed the stairs of South Building to ring the bell announcing the victory. It was her fiftieth birthday.[6]

This chapter in her life is the best known, but to understand how a woman could have played so important a role in the life of the university, readers need to know about her earlier years. From the beginning she had been encouraged to love learning. Both parents were bookish people. Her mother, Judith (Julia) Vermeule Phillips, of Plainfield, New Jersey, knew Latin, French, and Greek, wrote poetry, and read history and literature. Her father, James Phillips, was a self-taught mathematician who had emigrated from England to America in 1818 and had taught in a private academy for boys in New York. His research in mathematics was known in academic circles, and in 1826 he accepted a job as professor at the University of North Carolina. At that time the university comprised no more than a handful of buildings, faculty, and students. It had dirt roads, few imposing buildings, and no railroad. The Phillipses quickly became part of a community of faculty families. Professor and Mrs. Phillips tutored their three children at home, and then they did what others of similar resources were doing in towns across the state—they opened a private academy. Mrs. Phillips's School for Young Ladies—meeting in the Phillips house—offered instruction in English, Latin, Greek, and French; arithmetic, algebra, and geometry; natural history and natural philosophy; music, drawing, and needlework.

Cornelia was an early, enthusiastic reader, and in her teens, when her brothers entered the university, she continued her studies on her own; often she visited with professors in their homes, sometimes was allowed to sit in on lectures on campus, and borrowed books from the libraries of the literary societies. She delighted in learning. Later, recalling her education as compared to that of her brothers, she noted "this difference, that as they grew up [their education] was expanded" whereas hers "remained stationary on the lines of the earliest direction." She never lost her sense of having deficiencies, and she described what she did know as "the crumbs" she had gathered up from under the table. After the death of her husband (she was thirty years old), feeling bereft and in need of some means of supporting herself, she began tutoring children in her home. Apparently, she was very good at teaching as well as learning.

At an age (forty-one) when other women's work required long years of unrelieved domesticity, Cornelia wrote a book about North Carolina and the Civil War: *The Last Ninety Days of the War*. The most original parts are those in which she reported firsthand on the occupation of the Union army in Chapel Hill. It was the beginning of many publications, including "Pen and Ink Sketches of the University" (1869) in the *Raleigh Sentinel*, *First Steps in North Carolina History* (1888), and "Old Times in Chapel Hill" (1884–90) in the *University of North Carolina Magazine*. For almost three decades she wrote, published, and acquired a large following of readers, some of whom carried on a lively correspondence with her.

In her popular "Young Lady's Column" in the *North Carolina Presbyterian*, she tested her own ideas about suitable roles for women, sometimes reflecting traditional attitudes of most of her race and class and at other times raising provocative questions. Cornelia could sometimes be as honest with herself as with others: she confessed to being "blinded and bigoted" toward changes in what she regarded as "immutable" laws governing women. Because she remained faithful to Calvinist teachings about the subordination of women—"born to play second fiddle"—she was vexed by the issue of women's rights that was being raised mostly outside the South. Still, when she looked at the women's reform movement "dispassionately," she admitted with "inexpressible surprise and disgust" that they had "an argument or two on their side." However, the very next week in her column, she ridiculed "odious Yankee women"—Lucy Stone, Elizabeth Cady Stanton, Lucretia Mott, "and others of that ilk"—for their "sharp incisive chatter, their shrill treble, their feeble feminine gesture." "The wave," she predicted, "will subside."

In the home "there can be but one head," she wrote, "and the man is the head." Again, "A woman's first business is . . . to be womanly, and under the head of 'Forbidden Fruit' I class such work as would unsex her, and take her out of woman's plan." Such work included holding public office, preaching, practicing law, presiding as a judge, and speaking in public. Opposed to woman suffrage, coeducation, and women in public debate, Spencer nevertheless was a staunch supporter of the summer teacher institutes for women and men and an advocate for a state woman's college. She did not romanticize women's lives or think that all women should or would marry. Often addressing herself to single women, she cautioned against sitting around waiting for "Mr. Goggle-eyes" and urged them to become self-sufficient.

Cornelia rejected the image of the "southern lady" as ornamented and decorative. She preferred plain stitching over ruffles, sarcasm and attack over soft answers, and a vision of the future over dreaming of the past. Support for the state university, common schools, and women's colleges; for preservation of the university environment; and for services to the poor, the orphaned, the mentally ill, and the elderly—all of this placed her in the vanguard of the state's progressive leaders.

She regarded women as the great hope of North Carolina. She urged a unity of sisterhood—although she doubted it would happen—and believed that women had more intuitive wisdom, moral bearings, and common sense than men, whose province was knowledge and rhetoric. The burden of looking after the behavior of the young weighed heavily on her, however. She felt compelled to add, "Girls, I don't want any of you to run for public office, or to help in the public service in any way but this: don't any of you marry a man who says 't'aint no use.' "

In reminding women of their moral superiority, she admonished them to put their Christian principles to work. Cornelia herself tended the sick, ministered to the young and the elderly, took food to the poor, and befriended a few black families she knew in Chapel Hill. She visited the orphanage in Oxford and wrote the legislature for its support, and she walked down the rutted roads of Chapel Hill and into the countryside to enter the log cabins of both blacks and whites, to sit by the fire and hold the hands of the sick and the dying. As religion kept her subordinate to men, so it also led her to subordinate her own needs to those of others.

She believed that slavery was "evil," and although she was loyal to the South once the war began, she was never blind to its failures: "I believe the South sinned, sinned in her pride, her prosperity, her confidence." She looked to the future: the South must forgive and be forgiven. She urged "kindness" to the former slaves, whom she regarded as inferior to whites. In making a case for public education, she argued for education for black children and for black teachers to be trained to teach in their own schools. Yet she romanticized slaveholders and idealized relations between the races. Recent historians acknowledge her attitudes of white supremacy and Southern paternalism.[7]

Such a thinking woman of the nineteenth century who advised young ladies to be good—and important men to be great—inevitably was alone with her own conflicts and complexities. In 1876, just past her own half-century mark, as she read about new careers for women in business, law, and medicine in the publications of the Women's Centennial Exhibition in Philadelphia, she was both "melancholy" and "exultant." She could not deny her own regrets—or her pride in other women of achievement.

Many words have been written about Cornelia Phillips Spencer but none more often quoted that those by her friend, Governor Zebulon B. Vance, who said, "She is the smartest woman in the State, yes, and the smartest man too."[8]

Rhoda Strong Lowry

1849–1909

Rhoda Strong Lowry. (From an artist's impression by Karl Anthony Hunt, Pembroke, Robeson County)

As the wife of an Indian guerrilla fighter and declared outlaw, Rhoda Strong Lowry lived with more danger than most North Carolina women. In 1865, when Rhoda married Henry Berry Lowry, he was already committed to violence as a way to rectify wrongs against Native Americans, whose treatment by ruling whites as inferior people of color had been sharpened by the Civil War. Poverty and injustice isolated Indian communities living on small farms and in swampy byways. In one of these, Rhoda's home became a hiding place, and her survival depended on her canny and quick adaptation to whatever the day brought.

In 1872, when her husband died mysteriously or disappeared, after they had been married for only six years, Rhoda was interviewed by newspapermen searching for clues to the mystery. If she knew, she apparently said nothing. Her reputation for protecting her husband gave her a special place among the Lumbees of Robeson County, who preserve their history through an oral tradition in which Henry Berry Lowry is the central folk hero. To this day she is known as a "smart and gutsy" woman "who stood by her man." More recently, some have also seen her as a symbol of resistance to oppression. Contemporary accounts of the warfare between the Lowry Gang and whites sometimes record contradictions, factual errors, and exaggerations, but they vividly dramatize a chapter in history that informs the way Lumbees regard themselves. The stark facts of Rhoda's life must speak for her: she married the leader of the Lowry Gang, she shared the dangers of his life, and when he was gone, she was left with three children to care for as best she could.[1]

From the winter day in 1865 when sixteen-year-old Rhoda Strong married her twenty-year-old cousin, Henry Berry Lowry, her life was not her own. Their wedding party on his parents' farm in the Native American Lumbee community of Robeson County was interrupted by the arrival of the sheriff to arrest Henry Berry for murder. With Rhoda's help, it is said, he escaped from jail and continued to elude the law and bounty hunters during the most turbulent period in Southern history—Reconstruction. In 1872 Henry Berry disappeared, leaving Rhoda and their three young children. Regardless of whether she knew what happened to him, it is believed that she gave no help to journalists and bounty hunters, thereby confirming her reputation in the Indian community as having had the strength of character to withstand intimidation. For more than a century the adventures of Henry Berry Lowry have been repeated in the oral traditions of the Lumbee people, and in times of racial conflict in Robeson County, he has been used to inspire Lumbees.[2]

Accounts of Henry Berry's life are so layered with legend that it is sometimes impossible to distinguish between fact and fiction. Less is known about Rhoda because her story has been dominated by his. But Lumbee historians and oral history have supplied many of the missing pieces in her life.[3]

The group that claims Rhoda and Henry Lowry has been called different names—Croatans, Indians of Robeson County, and Cherokee Indians of North Carolina. In 1953 the first naming by people within the Indian community was accepted when the state legislature agreed to a tribal petition to call members "Lumbee," after the Lumber River, locally called the Lumbee, or simply the River. The origins of Robeson's Native Americans, however, are not as easily resolved. Where did they come from? Many Lumbees believe that they are descendants of the Lost Colony, the fate of which remains North Carolina's most popular unsolved mystery.[4] Although far from proved, the argument that Henry Berry Lowry was a descendant of the "Henry Berrye" listed on the roster of John White's settlement has powerful appeal. Other theories identify today's Lumbees as descendants of the Cherokee, the Tuscarora, and the Cheraw, reflecting a long history of migration and intermingling. In contemporary newspaper accounts, Henry and Rhoda were said to be "mulatto."

In 1835 the North Carolina legislature identified Indians as "free persons of color" and took away their rights to vote and carry firearms. The Civil War and Reconstruction only made life more difficult for them. Bereft of rights, opportunities, and legal redress, Henry Berry and the Lowry Gang conducted a guerrilla war of their own. For almost ten years they murdered and plundered and, according to legend, redistributed among Indians and blacks some of the white wealth. They challenged the local Home Guard and powerful white landowning families, mostly Scots. And although the Lowrys (and other Indian families) had been landowners for generations, Henry Berry had to find himself a hiding place in the dark cypress swamps, where among deserters and freed slaves and other men on the run, he and his gang became underground fighters. Escaping conscription as slave labor for Civil War fortifications on the coast, they were at risk of being accused of stealing hogs or harboring Union soldiers and could be hunted down and killed.

Rhoda had chances to hear about Henry Berry before she ever met him. For one thing, they were cousins, and her brother, Boss Strong, was his best friend. For another, everybody in Back Swamp, Burnt Swamp, Shoe Hill, Moss Neck, and other Indian places must have known that, in March 1865, members of the Home Guard had executed Henry Berry's father, Allen, and his brother William, who—among other things—had been accused of storing stolen hams in the barn on Lowry land. Henry Berry had watched the murders from the edge of some woods and, swearing revenge, became leader of the Lowry Gang.[5]

During this period Rhoda Strong was living with her father in Robeson County. Her father is thought to have been a white man named "John Gorman" who changed his name to "Strong" when he fled from Virginia (some accounts say western North Carolina) to escape the law because he had killed a man. Some historians believe that he married a Lowry in Robeson County. Rhoda's mother apparently had died young, and Rhoda was looking after her father. In these circumstances, she learned ways to live in secrecy.[6]

The attractive physicality of Henry and Rhoda is often emphasized in oral legends and in accounts by journalists who went to Robeson County in search of a good story about an Indian outlaw with a bounty on his head. The descriptions supplied by reporters tell us less about what they looked like than what the writers made of them—"He has straight black hair" and "can run like a deer." Rhoda was "Queen of Scuffletown," a place-name for the Indian community in Robeson County; reports often mention her "white beauty." A Wilmington newspaperman, in a story filed on March 25, 1872, tells of having been taken by some of the gang members to meet Rhoda Lowry. He found her "remarkably pretty; her face oval, of a very light color . . . large, dark, mournful-looking eyes . . . with profusion of straight jet black hair." He "felt compelled to add that this queen cannot write, that she smokes a pipe and rubs snuff."[7]

The six years of her marriage were fraught with adversity, beginning on their wedding day, December 7, 1865. The sheriff had come to arrest Henry Berry for the murder of James Barnes, a Confederate official in charge of conscription who had accused the Lowrys of stealing his hogs. About a year before, Barnes had been ambushed, and before he died, he had named Henry Berry Lowry and his brother William as his killers. Henry had reason to hate: he had seen a firing squad of the Home Guard execute his father and brother Allen on various charges—avoiding conscription, stealing property, and aiding Union soldiers. The Lowrys and other Indians had been in constant conflict with the Confederacy, having escaped slave labor by hiding out in the swamps. From there they conducted raids on the farms of white landowners, sometimes to secure food for survival, at other times to keep up harassment in return for being harassed. When the Civil War began, Henry Berry himself was said to have attempted to enlist as a Confederate soldier, but when he was turned down because of his race, his great pride was so wounded that he became an outlaw. Refused service with white Confederate soldiers and refusing conscription among blacks, he set out to make his own reputation. In many of his raids, he was said to be a gentleman, especially around women. Apparently when he was arrested on the day of his wedding, as he and Rhoda and family members were enjoying the feast, he went quietly. Perhaps he knew that he would not remain in the Whiteville jail for long (the Lumberton jail, where Lowry was first taken, was considered too risky because of damage to it from some of Sherman's troops).

A contemporary account by a white woman, Mary Norment, widow of a man who was killed by the Lowry Gang, has endured as a record of the gang's exploits. According to Norment, Henry Berry did not stay in jail very long because someone brought him a cake in which a file had been concealed. Perhaps it was a leap of the imagination to credit his wife with enabling him to escape. In any case Henry Berry escaped and in no time was back in Scuffletown. In another account, given in a contemporary newspaper, Rhoda was said to have gone to Whiteville with her brother, and that night she began to make friends in a local café. The woman proprietor hired her as a waitress and sent her to the jail across the street to carry lunch to her own husband, imprisoned for drunkenness. After Rhoda had seen her husband's cell, she returned to the café, borrowed a long dress from the proprietor, and again walked into the jail. The sheriff was overcome by her beauty and made a lunge toward her. Suggesting that she would return his advances, she watched as he took off his gunbelt. As he was taking off his boots, Rhoda reached under her dress and took out an iron pipe, knocked him unconscious, took his keys and guns, and unlocked the door to her husband's cell. The couple then joined her brother and returned to Scuffletown.[8]

Henry Berry's exploits continued. Reportedly, the more he stole, the more he gave away, earning his reputation as the Robin Hood of Robeson County. He sometimes appeared in a disguise, standing peacefully in the back of a public gathering. Once he knocked at a door and asked the white woman at home to prepare him breakfast, after which he played the piano. Rhoda was also alleged to be a trickster who knew how to play the game.

The wives, daughters, and sisters of the Lowry Gang lived in constant danger. Henry Berry's mother was tortured by armed men who threatened to kill her and Rhoda, and local authorities arrested Rhoda and wives of other gang members in hopes of drawing the men out. When Henry Berry threatened to seize local white women in retaliation, his wife and the other hostages were released.

After Rhoda had given birth to her third child, friends built the family a small frame house. Here Rhoda was often alone with her young children. When Henry Berry returned from his adventures, homecoming suppers with many guests were held in his honor. On receiving word of danger as it was passed along an intricate network by lookouts, he quickly departed through a passage concealed in the floor by the fireplace. Sometimes, Rhoda had to bundle up the three children and follow him into the tunnel, through which they crawled in the dark until they could emerge at some distance from the house near the swamp. The gang's hiding places were movable sites in the swamps, identified by cypress trees and pools of black water, indistinguishable except to Indian guides.

To imagine Rhoda Strong Lowry in these situations is to question the portrait of perfect beauty presented by reporters. A newspaper picture labeled "Mrs. Henry Lowery" that appears in the *Swamp Outlaws* does not seem to be that of a woman who lived in the woods and escaped with three clinging children through sixty yards of earthen tunnels. Dressed in a low-cut gown, a ribbon encircling her graceful neck, she rests one hand lightly on her breast.[9] Local Lumbee women today offer a more realistic picture of Rhoda. They suggest that, despite her reputation as a cunning trickster, she spent most days and nights looking after children, farming, and relying on her neighbors to relay messages to and from her husband. She knew how to do more than engineer a jailbreak. She no doubt pounded corn with a log mortar, scraped out gourds for dippers and pails, and winnowed corn in grass baskets. She could handle a boat and fish. She dressed in whatever homespun clothes she could make or borrow, and she probably wore a small bag around her neck, not a velvet ribbon. Such bags usually contained cedar, tobacco, sweet grass, and sage for healing, physical and spiritual. Perhaps she was one of those Lumbee woman said to have special powers, such as knowing when someone had died without being told. She certainly trusted her own instincts. Henry Berry came and went in the wink of an eye, and she adapted her rhythms to his.

After the Lowry Gang was accused of having murdered more than a dozen white people, rewards were posted for Henry Berry's capture, dead or alive. With as much as $10,000 riding on his head, bounty hunters arrived from near and far. Lowry made conciliatory public statements, offering to stop fighting if others would let him live in peace. But no assurances were forthcoming from the authorities. The fighting continued until, on February 16, 1872, the Lowry Gang robbed a general store and, finding the safe too heavy to carry, abandoned it in the middle of a Lumberton street. A few days later, Henry Berry Lowry was a missing person. Like the settlers of the Lost Colony, he simply disappeared. Stories in the press offered many explanations, but the one that has been most accepted is that he accidentally shot himself while cleaning or loading his gun. Of course, rumors circulated—someone had seen his body in a wagon, members of his gang had buried his body in the River, he had been helped to leave Robeson County by a federal officer, he had gone away, married, and raised another family. Once it was reported that he had returned to see Rhoda, and that she had recognized him as he got off the train. If she knew what happened to her husband, Rhoda was never heard to say.[10]

"Grandmother did not know," her granddaughter, Reedie Lowry Chavis, maintained in an interview in 1993. "They had to keep themselves secret, they didn't trust no one. If he could have been found, that reward would have been collected, and they would have probably killed him. The ones who . . . were with him came to the house and talked to my grandmother, and if they knew, they didn't tell it. The only thing she'd tell we children was our granddaddy was gone."

Rhoda Strong Lowry lived more than thirty-five years after her husband's disappearance and continued to speak of him as "the handsomest man" she had ever seen. She owned a little farm in the Sandcutt community of Red Banks, where she scraped out a living. She had a still and she sold whiskey to help support the family. Once a newspaper reported that she had been arrested for selling whiskey and taken to the jail in Lumberton. As there were no schools for Native Americans and they were prohibited by law from attending schools for whites, Rhoda's children attended school with black children. When they grew up, Henry Delany (or Delaware) went to Georgia to work on the turpentine circuit and then on to Mississippi. Neely Ann (Polly) married Bennie Chavis, and they followed her brother to Georgia, Florida, and Mississippi. Polly and Ben had four daughters; Reedie, the last, was born in Meridian, Mississippi, on Christmas Day, 1906. When Bennie abandoned the family, Polly and her children returned to Robeson County to live with Rhoda on the farm, only to leave again to follow farm work in the Carolinas.

Reedie Lowry Chavis explained that when her mother returned for good to Robeson County, she took over the housekeeping in their three-room house. Chavis remembered that Rhoda and Polly had a sense of humor and spoke openly to one another, but they "watched what they said" around children. They wore long dresses that hung to the floor. Grandmother Rhoda used a Singer sewing machine to make everything for the family. Except for memory, little remains to authenticate the life of Rhoda Strong Lowry, but Reedie Lowry Chavis has a treasured possession that she keeps in an old trunk: a small, darkened, almost deteriorated tintype of Grandmother Rhody, her hair pulled up under a cap. Chavis once heard the Methodist preacher tell the congregation that her grandmother was "the prettiest woman in our county."

Rhoda died when Reedie Lowry Chavis was about three years old. As an old woman, Reedie vividly recalled the funeral: "We were crossing the Lumbee River to Harpers Ferry Church, where she was funeralized. I could see the river though the bottom of the wagon, and I was frightened that we might fall through the floor and drown in the river. It was a safe trip, and a sad one. We children were standing around crying. They went ahead and buried her, and then we went on home."[11]

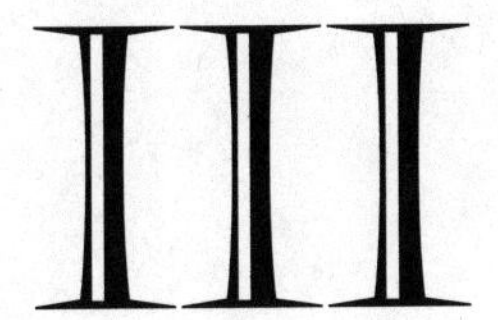

Reconstruction through World War II

CHAPTER 7

The Task That Is Ours

Women, Work, and Advocacy, 1877–1910

Between the end of Reconstruction and the beginning of the twentieth century, a changing rural economy and a growing industrial New South altered family life and work for North Carolina women. That is not to say that traditional ways vanished: on the contrary, the majority of women continued to live on farms and to rear large families. Yet the shift to cash crops of cotton and tobacco to feed the new factories springing up across the Piedmont in the late 1800s transformed rural life. Hard times forced some tenants and landowners to towns, where black women found jobs in domestic service or as stemmers in tobacco factories and white women worked as spinners in textile mills. By 1910 North Carolina, with its cheap labor and raw materials, was the most industrialized state in the South and the leading manufacturer of cotton goods and tobacco products. It became—and would remain—the state with the highest percentage of working women—more than 90 percent of whom labored on farms, in mills and factories, or in other women's homes.[1]

With industrialization came urbanization: five years after the war Durham and Winston (later to become Winston-Salem) barely existed, and Greensboro and Charlotte were but small trading centers. By the early 1900s all four were thriving cities, competing for the state's top spot in wealth, industry, population, and civic pride and supplanting the older coastal towns. Town women benefited from the emerging consumer culture and sought the modern amenities that were part of urban life—running water and electricity, automobiles and manufactured goods, department stores and picture shows. Indoor plumbing and washing machines became signs of class distinction.

In the 1890s a generation of "new women" attended newly created institutions of higher learning for white women, such as the State Normal and Industrial College in Greensboro, also known as the State Normal or the Woman's College (now the University of North Carolina at Greensboro), and the Baptist Female University in Raleigh (now Meredith College), where they were prepared to enter the professions and businesses. From the 1870s onward black women had opportunities for higher education at St. Augustine's College and Shaw University in Raleigh, Scotia Seminary in Concord, and other schools. After 1887 Croatan or Lumbee Indians attended the Indian Normal School in Pembroke (now the University of North Carolina at Pembroke); the Cherokee, on the other hand, had no such institutions, only the federal government or missionary schools teaching basics. The skills and attitudes that young women acquired in school transformed their private expectations and reshaped public life as they entered teaching and social service.

The high hopes of blacks in the Emancipation and Reconstruction eras that embracing values such as education, temperance, and hard work would create a place for them in North Carolina's economic and political life were dashed, however, by the reality that most whites had not relinquished their belief in Negro inferiority. Despite the growth of an educated and prospering African American "better class" by the 1880s and political success in the early 1890s, a backlash fueled the white supremacy movement. By 1900 a series of racial restrictions (Jim Crow laws) coalesced to ensure institutionalized inequality and segregation that lasted for more than fifty years.[2]

Across North Carolina, contrasts were intensified: between blacks and whites, between city and country, between men and women. In 1907 a Duplin County farm woman wrote: "We are not complaining about the task that is ours, though we do sometimes feel in our weary, worn-out hours that the good things in life are not equally divided."[3]

Women on the Farm

For most North Carolinians life was rural. Crops that had predominated before the war—tobacco, cotton, and corn—as well as backbreaking methods of cultivation, year-round family labor, and seasonal calendars for planting and harvesting, celebrating and resting continued well into the twentieth century (Fig. 7-1). Although their histories differ, landowning yeoman farmers statewide and the newly emancipated black farmers and white tenant farmers in the Coastal Plain and Piedmont had much in common. Whether they owned their land or worked someone else's, farm families had to be patient, resourceful, and sharing to survive. "Making do" and "getting by" were the lot of most. The nature of farming meant that there were good years and bad, and generally not much money, but many rural people felt the pride and satisfaction of working the land, growing their food, and living an independent life.[4]

In the years after the Civil War the farm economy had been restructured. Sharecropping was developed as a compromise: white landowners obtained the field labor they needed, and freed blacks were able to exert some control over

FIGURE 7-1. *Stemming Tobacco*, Pitt County, ca. 1909. (Courtesy of the North Carolina Collection, University of North Carolina at Chapel Hill)

the conditions under which they worked. Each family received a small plot of land, seed, rations, and supplies, and the landowner got a third or half of the crop. Although the accounting and credit systems heavily favored landowners, black tenants gained freedoms they had not known under slavery. They lived in their own quarters away from the "big house," decided who in the family would work and at what tempo, spent their money as they wanted, and participated in church, school, and community life (Fig. 7-2). At the heart of tenancy was family labor, and women worked in the house, their gardens, and the fields (Fig. 7-3).[5]

A second major change was the intensified shift to cash crops. With cotton mills and tobacco warehouses being built across the state, crops could be exchanged for cash in a day. Tenant and landowning farmers, white and black, replaced self-sufficient crop and livestock production with cotton and tobacco cultivation, often on credit, gambling that prices would be good.[6] But bad crops, overextended credit, and falling prices could mean losing the family farm. By 1890 three-quarters of North Carolina's black farmers and one-third of the white farmers were tenants or sharecroppers. The scientific agriculture being promoted by the newly established state agricultural college in Raleigh (now North Carolina State University) and the political actions of the Farmers' Alliance had little effect on farmers at the bottom of the economic and technological ladder who were struggling to eke out a living.[7]

Technology and Power in Farm Families

Lu Ann Jones analyzed women's letters of the early 1900s to the household section of the *Progressive Farmer*, the official organ of the North Carolina State Farmers' Alliance. The letters highlight a growing unease. Women felt that their traditional "partnership" role as unpaid domestic laborers was threatened by the monetary value of the men's cash crop. The discontent was exacerbated by the increasing availability of consumer goods. Although many women were proud to

FIGURE 7-2. *Tenant family in wagon in front of cabin*, New Bern. Tenant housing was often former "slavery-time" log cabins, with a few small window openings and wooden shutters to keep out the elements. (Courtesy of the North Carolina Division of Archives and History)

be farmers' wives, they often felt overworked and isolated. Their husbands went to town to buy farm supplies, negotiate credit, and sell crops. Women were stuck at home. In 1907 Maple's only break from her kitchen on a hot day was a "walk to the well for a fresh bucket of water, or to the chicken lot to care for the little biddies." Whenever she found time to visit a neighbor, her husband told her "the horses are all in the harrow or to the plows" and she must "wait until a more leisure time." "Farming folks should be the happiest of people," wrote Maple, "but I don't think they are."[8]

A major point of irritation was the different amounts of money spent for farm equipment and household technology (Fig. 7-4). "If only Mr. Husband would exchange places with Mrs. Wife, if only in imagination," wrote "Minnie" in 1904, and "humbly ask for a dime now and then to spend on some coveted article, and hear her say, 'I haven't got it to spare,' when he knows he has faithfully performed his part of the work, wouldn't there be a door slammed and wouldn't somebody go off mad?"[9]

Women's discontent with the division of power and allotment of technology within their families was both fueled and abated by various turn-of-the-century domestic and agrarian reform activities. Farmers' Institutes for Women began in 1906. Under the leadership of pioneer home extension worker Jane McKimmon, new equipment and products, all intended to upgrade homemaking skills—and all for sale—were demonstrated by women in the new profession of home economics. The institutes functioned for farm women as voluntary associations did for town women, providing an opportunity for women to socialize with one another and to be stimulated by new ideas. One woman was so determined to attend an institute that she overrode her husband's objec-

FIGURE 7-3. *Women picking cotton* near New Bern, 1900. Recently freed black women initially resisted working in the fields. It was a point of pride to stay home and care for their families. Economics won out, however, and eventually most rural black women ended up in agriculture. (Courtesy of the North Carolina Division of Archives and History)

tion that "it was all foolishness and I had my work to do in the field. . . . I got up before day and done my work with the crop so I could bring my little girl to the cooking school."[10]

Broadened in scope, the women's pages of the *Progressive Farmer* and *The Country Gentleman* addressed farm women's concerns. "How Can a Woman Earn Her Own Pin Money?" advised women to do so through their domestic production (in contrast to the traditional use of women's household surplus to supplement family income) (Fig. 7-5). "The Domineering Husband and the Remedy" indicates that attitudes toward the patriarchal husband were being challenged. Experts advised women to use domestic science and laborsaving technology to lighten their housework. But Lu Ann Jones comments that it is hard to know whether the reformers reflected or fostered women's grievances as they grappled with broad economic changes that undermined their traditional "partnership role" on the family farm.[11]

Electricity and other modern technology were slow to reach rural families from the Coast to the Mountains. Most farm women had to keep house the old-fashioned way, and washing clothes was a particularly laborious task (Fig. 7-6).[12] "We didn't know what galvanized tubs were then," said Nora C. Wagoner, of Allegheny County, who remembered her mother's washday in the 1880s when the clothes "had to be washed and brought out and boiled and battled and then washed again and then rinsed."[13]

The greatest technological leap for homemakers was the shift from open hearth cooking to the cast-iron woodstove (Fig. 7-7). The invention of glass containers with easily sealable lids both facilitated and increased housewives' work as

FIGURE 7-4. *Advertisement: "Greatest values ever known in washing machines."* Washing machines were coveted by women stuck with the laborious task of washing clothes. As a Watauga resident noted, "I ain't never seen no menfolks of no kind do no washing" (Arthur, *Watauga County*, 244). (*Sears, Roebuck & Co. Catalogue*, 1902)

> A farmer spends freely for this and for
> that if it lessens his toil a bit.
> The reaper, the mower, the new fangled sower,
> have each made with him quite a hit.
> But while he is riding at ease in his field
> 'neath skies that are calm and serene,
> His spouse has to rub all day at the
> tub for lack of a washing machine.
> —"The Farmer's Wife," "Our Social Chat" page, *Progressive Farmer*, November 5, 1908. (Lu Ann Jones, "'The Task That Is Ours,'" *Institute News*, 5)

they preserved hundreds of quarts of fruits and vegetables during the canning season, working at night after supper and in the morning before breakfast. Sewing machines cost more than cast-iron stoves, but they could be bought on credit, and treadle machines were widely available by 1900 (Figs. 7-8, 7-9). As a marketing ploy, feed and flour companies sold their products in colorful, printed cloth bags that could be used in a variety of other ways. Louise Phillips Kiser of Iredell County transformed flour sacks into tea towels, dish towels, and hand towels—"very, very nice" and "very durable." Other flour sacks were used to make curtains, quilts, blouses, aprons, and dresses (Plate 8). Still another new invention was a manually wound phonograph machine that provided entertainment for families who could afford one (Fig. 7-10).[14]

Mill Women: "Like a Family"

In the late 1800s crop failure, poverty, and debt forced thousands off the land and into mills and factories. In two broad waves, large numbers of white women and their families moved "from field to factory." In the first wave, in the 1870s, were women from female-headed households—those with least access to the land, labor, and capital necessary to survive in a cash-crop economy. The second wave began in the late 1880s as entire families lost their farms. Steam whistles and time clocks replaced the rhythms of the seasons and the daily patterns of rural life. In 1873 there were thirty-three cotton factories in all of North Carolina. Starting in the 1880s, unincorporated mill villages sprang up in the countryside and around the edges of such Piedmont towns as Greensboro and Durham. By 1904 three hundred textile mills were located within a one-hundred-mile radius of Charlotte alone; in fact, half the looms and spindles in the South were concentrated there. Millions of miles of cloth spewed from North Carolina mills as fine and coarse sheeting, shirting, gingham, and plaids.[15]

The former farm families—men, women, and children—were available at a pittance, exactly at the time when ring spinning frames and other new technology made using unskilled labor acceptable and profitable. Promoted as a "salvation" for poor white folks hoping for something better than

FIGURE 7-5. Margaret W. Morley, *Going Home*. Rural women usually stayed close to home. "Butter and egg" money supplied the "little extry" that was often the only source of family income until the annual crop was harvested and sold. Morley lived in Tryon, in southwestern Polk County, from 1900 to 1912; she published her writings and photographs in 1913. (From Morley, *The Carolina Mountains*, 1913. Courtesy of the North Carolina Museum of History)

hardscrabble farming, the mills offered ten-to-twelve-hour days and wages so low that an entire family had to work to eat. Yet workers stayed because the mills, although noisy and dangerous, were for many an improvement over the precarious existence of farming. The steady paychecks were welcome, and the fellowship of the mill village felt just "like a family."[16]

Women kept gardens and raised poultry, and outlying parcels of land owned by the mill company were used for communal pastures and hog lots. Familiar rituals of harvesting, hog killing, and quiltmaking linked their new life to their old, yet a mill village frequently offered amenities that were unavailable in rural settings. By 1900 about 90 percent of millworkers lived in mill villages. The textile companies frequently furnished subsidized housing, medical care, and social and recreational activities. In 1903 Proximity Mill in Greensboro provided the first mill village welfare worker in the state who involved both women and children in cooking, gardening, and sewing projects.[17] Company-owned housing was relatively cheap (in 1908 millhands paid an average monthly rent of $3.57 or 6 percent of their total monthly expenditures), and some even had electricity. Housing came at a price of at least one worker for each room occupied. In a typical four-room mill house, boys, girls, and parents slept in separate rooms and the fourth room was used as a kitchen.

Kin ties had been important in North Carolina's agrarian culture, and they were vital in easing the shift to factory life. Whole families often joined relatives working in the mills. Daughters learned job skills by working beside their mothers. Grandmothers and granddaughters worked in the same mill as did cousins, nieces, aunts, and in-laws.

The division of labor in textile mills was similar to the family labor system on the farm and reflected shared cultural assumptions of owners and workers about the position of men and women, adults and children, blacks and whites. White men supervised, performed the heavy labor and skilled work, and were paid the highest wages; white women carried out skilled but repetitive work and received about 60 percent of men's wages; and white children did routine tasks and were paid even less. Bobbin boys earned twenty cents a

FIGURE 7-6. *Woman washing clothes near New Bern*, 1900. For most rural women, clothes washing was a laborious task. Water had to be carried by hand and heated on a fire, clothes scrubbed on a washboard in a wooden tub. Black women often did the laundry for white families as well as their own. (Courtesy of the North Carolina Division of Archives and History)

FIGURE 7-7. *Mrs. Mattie Macon Lowe baking bread* in her wood-burning Majestic stove, Randolph County, ca. 1900. (Courtesy of the Randolph County Historical Society)

day, spinners fifty cents, and weavers seventy-five cents. Black men were relegated to the hardest, most bone-crushing menial labor and were paid the least; black women and children were not permitted to work in most textile mills.[18]

Black women had participated in antebellum textile production, but the postbellum emphasis on the mills as a salvation for poor whites all but eliminated them as potential workers. White women, on the other hand, were sought as mill operatives, especially for spinning and drawing-in. Women were considered particularly suited for the monotony of clothmaking. They and their children performed the jobs that required agile fingers rather than strong backs and hands (Fig. 7-11). Although weaving was generally men's work, the few women who became weavers were usually treated the same as male weavers (Fig. 7-12). Running a power loom was a high-status job, but it was noisy, hazardous work, and many weavers lost their hearing. Contemporary photographs that depict women standing in front of spinning frames—timeless, static, immobile, dignified, silent—are deceiving. As one woman remembered: "I had seen some women going all day in that miserable heat with their clothes stuck to their bodies like they had been dipped into a pail of water. Going up and down the alleys weeping, working all day."[19]

North Carolina millworkers were predominantly female and young (Fig. 7-13). In 1880 women and children comprised about 75 percent of the textile workforce. In 1910 approximately 90 percent of spinners in cotton mills were under twenty-one, and 50 percent were younger than fifteen. Flossie Moore Durham of Bynum was ten when she "stopped picking cotton and started spinning it." "They'd let you go in there seven, eight years old," remembered Alice Evitt. "I'd go in there and mess around with my sisters; they'd be spinning. I liked to put up the ends and spin a little bit, so when I got twelve years old, I wanted to quit school. So I just quit and went to work, and I was twelve years old." Durham earned twenty-five cents her first day at the mill in 1893; seventeen years later Evitt started at exactly the same wage. In 1889 millworkers in Lincoln and Gaston Counties, calling for

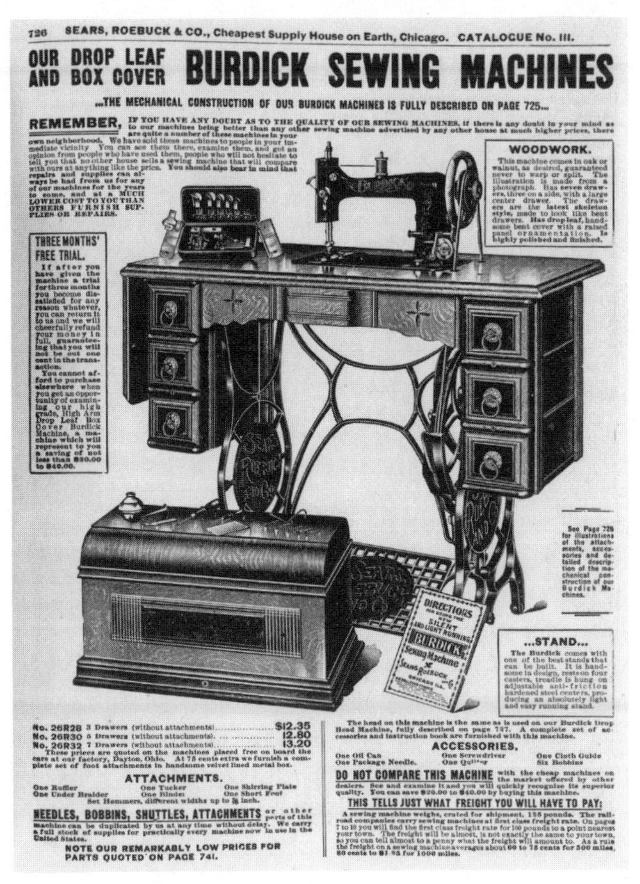

FIGURE 7-8. *Advertisement for sewing machines*. (*Sears, Roebuck & Co. Catalogue*, 1902)

FIGURE 7-9. *Maternity dress worn by Annie Cone Baines*, blue calico, Nash County, 1904–10. (Courtesy of the North Carolina Museum of History)

FIGURE 7-10. *Jenny and Maude Spivey posing with their phonograph*, Lee County, ca. 1900. (Courtesy of the North Carolina Collection, University of North Carolina at Chapel Hill)

FIGURE 7-11. *Women and men weaving* at White Oak Mill, Greensboro, 1909. (Courtesy of the Cone Mills Corporation)

shorter workdays of ten hours, argued that "twelve hours a day is too long to keep operatives at work, especially women and children." But not until 1913 were laws passed to restrict child labor. At that point women replaced children in the mills, and, coincidentally, birthrates dropped dramatically.[20]

Urban Women

In 1870 one in twenty-five North Carolinians lived in towns; in 1900 one in ten was a town dweller. North Carolina's

FIGURE 7-12. Lewis Hine, *Learning to Spin*, Newton, Catawba County, ca. 1908–9. Photographer Hine, representing the National Child Labor Committee, visited North Carolina in 1908–9. His widely publicized pictures of the exploitation of children were influential in the passage and enforcement of child labor laws. (Courtesy of the Edward L. Bradford Photograph Collection, University of Maryland, Baltimore County)

towns were small compared to those in the Northeast and Midwest—in 1900 only six had more than ten thousand people—but the rate of urbanization was rapid. In the Piedmont, Durham and Winston became tobacco manufacturing centers; Greensboro and Burlington, along with Charlotte and numerous smaller towns, the locus of the textile industry. The industrial towns started off rough and rowdy, with saloons commonplace, but the efforts of reformers such as the Woman's Christian Temperance Union forced many drinking establishments out of business or underground and allowed churches to become urban landmarks. Many smaller towns and hamlets such as Henderson, Oxford, Rocky Mount, and Tarboro experienced urban growth but maintained a rural ambiance. With the completion of the Western North Carolina Railroad, Asheville boomed as a resort town.[21]

Urban life drew the adventurous and ambitious as well as those forced off the land. Many who moved to the new industrial towns looking for work were young single women, living without male protection in unfamiliar circumstances. Class differences became more distinct in town, reinforced by one's occupation, residence, church, race, and even choice of recreation.

Urban women were the first to benefit from the changes in household technology like electricity, gas, and water and from new appliances, ready-made clothing, prepared foods, and factory-made furniture—though such benefits were not available to everyone. Winston-Salem got its first telephone line in 1879, electric streetlights in 1887, and electric streetcars in the spring of 1890. Greensboro went from kerosene lamps in 1875 to piped gas fixtures in 1880, to electric lights in the downtown in 1887, and then to some residential areas in 1890. By 1891 in Greensboro, if a family had electric light fixtures, an iron, and a small refrigerator, it was in "high cotton." By 1900 many towns had water and sewer systems, electricity, and telephones. Josephine Nunn, who grew up in Winston-Salem, described her childhood as a time of change—"with many new, wonderful, products and inventions" in addition to "running water and a bathroom."[22]

More exciting changes were in the air. Towns offered an array of stores and services, entertainment and sociability that country life simply could not match. Because people had neighbors, friends, and relatives living nearby, birthday parties, afternoon teas, Wednesday meetings of the literary club, and sleep-overs were possible (Figs. 7-14, 7-15, 7-16).

FIGURE 7-13. Lewis Hine, *Young Girl at Spinning Frame*, Cherryville, Gaston County, ca. 1908–9. The hair and clothing of the young girl operating the frame are covered with lint; millworkers were often denigrated by town people as "lintheads." (Courtesy of the Edward L. Bradford Photograph Collection, University of Maryland, Baltimore County)

FIGURE 7-14. *Seventeen women posing in a garden*, New Bern, 1890s. (Courtesy of the North Carolina Division of Archives and History)

So were concerts and lectures and myriad activities tied to school, church, and businesses. Greensboro had several movie houses, including the Crystal, the Lyric, the Ottoway, and the Amuzu. Electric streetcars connected business and residential districts and parks. Asheville had Riverside Park, Charlotte Latta Park, Durham Lakewood Park, Greensboro Lindley Park, Winston Nissen Park, and Raleigh Pullen Park, where families enjoyed picnic suppers from hampers filled with fried chicken, deviled eggs, pimento cheese sandwiches, ham biscuits, cakes and pies. The parks also offered baseball, amusement rides, horse shows, fireworks, and even movies. Younger children played games and rode on merry-go-rounds and miniature railroads; older ones went roller skating, bowling, boating, and swimming, while teenagers gathered at the pavilions for dancing. Wilmington families and visitors rode the streetcar to Wrightsville Beach.[23]

Schools, libraries, and hospitals marked a town as being up-to-date. As education became more obtainable, the number of young girls attending primary and secondary school rose. For example, Greensboro children attended school 120 days a year, in contrast to the state average of 59 days, because in 1880 the town supplemented state funds with local taxes (Fig. 7-17). In 1898 Lalla Ruth Carr and the Canterbury Club donated a building and raised money to establish in Durham the state's first library. In 1901 a local businessman donated the Olivia Raney Library to Raleigh in honor of his wife. A year later Greensboro installed a library in three rooms on the third floor of the city hall; in 1903 the town received a grant for a Carnegie Library, which opened in 1906. A group of Episcopal women, led by Jane Smedburg Wilkes of Charlotte, established the state's first hospital for civilians (rather than soldiers) in 1878 and founded Good Samaritan, the nation's first hospital for blacks, in 1888. Organized by Aurelia Bowman Gray, Winston-Salem women in 1887 helped found the city's first hospital (Fig. 7-18). More women, particularly middle-class white women, had their babies in hospitals attended by doctors.[24]

Courtship practices changed as well. Dances, bicycles, and automobiles provided opportunities for young couples to spend time together without parental supervision. Women

FIGURE 7-15. *Bessie White and nine friends at a slumber party*, Raleigh, ca. 1900. (Courtesy of the North Carolina Division of Archives and History)

joined men in playing vigorous new sports, swinging tennis rackets and whacking golf balls (Fig. 7-19). Urban women courted with more freedom than their rural sisters, tended to marry later, and had fewer children.[25]

Urban life varied depending on a woman's circumstances, but life was generally good for the middle-class women living in comfortable residences along shady main streets and in new suburban neighborhoods of such towns as Raleigh, Greensboro, Charlotte, and Winston-Salem. Because these women generally had laborsaving household devices and domestic help, they had more time to serve their communities and churches as volunteers, to join temperance crusades and women's clubs, to engage in hobbies such as china painting (Plate 9), and to read books and magazines. Many defined themselves outside the home through religious, civic, and cultural activities.

Popular national magazines such as the *Ladies' Home Journal* (Fig. 7-20) and *House and Garden*, as well as regional and state publications like the *Progressive Farmer* and *The Country Gentleman*, promoted the ideal of the home as women's sphere. Middle-class readers were told how to be a perfect wife and loving mother, to furnish the home with taste and elegance, and to provide a healthy and sanitary family environment. With their husbands away at work most of the day, these women played an important role in guiding their children's morals and development. Avoidance of motherhood was viewed by many as "immoral" and "race suicide."[26]

Urban women participated in the growing consumer society. They were delighted to "tote the pocketbook" as they rode the electric streetcar to the town center to shop in the grocery or dry goods store or millinery shop (Fig. 7-21). Department stores such as Belk's and Ivey's appeared in Charlotte between 1895 and 1900, and the Meyer Brothers of

FIGURE 7-16. *Birthday party*, Raleigh, 1906. Note the three black women holding babies. Black women and their charges frequently formed reciprocal bonds of lasting affection, but servants were careful not to cross the color line. (Courtesy of the North Carolina Division of Archives and History)

Richmond established a Greensboro store with "lunch counters and ladies parlors upstairs" in 1905. Drugstores opened on urban main streets, where young girls could buy a chocolate soda or other afternoon treat and women might purchase Lydia Pinkham's Vegetable Compound, touted as the "ultimate remedy for female complaints"—21 percent alcohol. Bars and brothels also populated the urban landscape, and middle-class women shoppers were occasionally irritated by the sight of them.[27]

Although North Carolina towns were racially segregated, initially boundaries were not sharply drawn. In the 1880s a thriving African American professional and business community developed in Wilmington and Charlotte, Durham and New Bern, along with a large class of laboring men and women. A decade later more than sixty black businesses, as well as doctors, lawyers, and funeral directors, served black workers who had moved to Winston to work for the R. J. Reynolds Tobacco Company. Black women and men of the "better classes," for whom education rather than money was the chief criterion, formed social and benevolent organizations. Reporters for black-owned newspapers wrote about women's literary clubs and other cultural and educational activities. Middle-class black women believed in the possibility of racial progress, interracial cooperation, and equality. Sarah Dudley Pettey and her husband, African Methodist Episcopal (AME) Zion bishop Charles Calvin Pettey, of New Bern had a conspicuous lifestyle: they rented reception rooms in the best "white" hotel, shopped in the best stores, and hosted white townspeople at the local AME Zion Church. Middle-class black suburbs—such as Columbia Heights in Winston-Salem, Idlewild in Raleigh, and University Heights and Maplewood in Durham—provided comfortable homes with modern conveniences.[28]

Sadie and Bessie Delany grew up in the 1890s on the campus of St. Augustine's College in Raleigh, where their father, a man "born in slavery" who became the first elected Negro bishop of the Episcopal Church USA, was the vice principal and their mother, the matron. They lived in a comfortable house with electricity and indoor plumbing. Mrs. Delany was a "working" mother with ten children who had the bene-

Shopping with my mother was a real pleasure. On those trips a person met old friends and picked up juicy bits of news; chatting with the sales ladies, all of them well known in the community, was fascinating. A choice between going to G. E. Rawles . . . or Kronheimers . . . was offered. These large, well-stocked "dry goods" stores had bolts of cloth mounting to the rafters. . . . Every small town of that era had hat stores. Durham had two—the Misses Albright's establishment and that of Mrs. Piper. Oh! What beautiful hats! Walking into those stores was like strolling through a flower garden. Nothing has ever surpassed them in beauty and grandeur. Each hat had its own pedestal and plenty of space for admirers to view it.

—Elsie Wallace Perkins, early 1900s (Elsie Wallace Perkins is a pseudonym for a longtime Durham resident). (Kostyu and Kostyu, *Durham*, 38–39)

fit of a "blessed childhood," reading books, learning Bible lessons, playing musical instruments, picking cotton on the college farm to earn spending money, and enjoying family outings (Fig. 7-22). The children never left the campus unchaperoned, for "things hadn't improved much since slavery days as far as the right of colored women and girls to be unmolested." Although the Delanys were perceived as an elite family because both parents were educated and held important jobs, money was tight and their clothes came from the mission store.[29]

My first introduction to sin occurred on Main Street. Durham had a famous prostitute, and I clearly recall her promenade down Main Street in the afternoon. I had been sent to the new Great Atlantic and Pacific Tea Company Store to buy two pounds of brown sugar, obtained from a big burlap bag, and a pound of coffee beans. . . . It was then that I first saw the notorious lady. I had been told she was an "evil" woman and that I was expected to scorn her. But how could one scorn such a gorgeous creature, quite tall, with a superb figure, dressed in the latest fashion! She strolled along with an assured, almost arrogant gait. Her eyes appeared to glitter with disdain as she looked at the dowdy women who shunned her as they passed. She could have blackballed half the men in town, and this knowledge gave her an air of assurance that manifested itself in her erect and haughty carriage. I was agog with excitement!

—Elsie Wallace Perkins, early 1900s. (Kostyu and Kostyu, *Durham*, 44)

FIGURE 7-17. *Greensboro Public Schools' float in the Fireman's Parade*, Guilford County, 1899. Young girls and women dressed in white grace the public school float that proudly announced that the city had "the first public school in North Carolina supported by a special tax." (Courtesy of the Greensboro Historical Museum)

FIGURE 7-18. *Twin City Hospital, Winston-Salem*, ca. 1895. In December 1887 the first hospital (for whites only) in Forsyth County opened its doors in Winston-Salem. By 1895 the Twin City Hospital occupied new quarters. Mollie Spach, one of the first licensed nurses in the state, was superintendent, and local doctors took turns giving a month's service. As hospitals became more familiar institutions in the state's urban centers, more nurses were trained to staff them and more patients came to rely on professional medical care. Eventually many women chose to deliver their babies in hospitals rather than at home. (Courtesy of the Forsyth County Public Library Photograph Collection)

FIGURE 7-19. *Twin City Golf Club, Winston-Salem*, ca. 1897. Young women and men from Winston-Salem's elite families avidly took up golf and established the first golf club in North Carolina in 1897. The young women did not let their cumbersome dresses keep them from wielding a golf club. The caddies were mostly black boys, who are seated in the front row. (Courtesy of Frank Tursi, Winston-Salem)

When Sadie was five and Bessie about seven, Jim Crow laws suddenly threatened the freedom they had taken for granted. As they boarded the trolley that would take them to Pullen Park for a picnic with their parents, the driver told them to go to the rear. The girls objected—for they liked to sit up front where the breeze would blow their hair, but their parents gently ushered them to the back without any fuss. Other indignities followed: at the park they had to drink water out of the "colored" side, though Bessie took the dipper from the white side when no one was looking. They were no longer served a limeade in a drugstore, as they had been hundreds of times before, and they had to enter the shoe store by the back door. In their words, "Jim Crow made it an even bigger stigma to be colored, and any hope of equality between the races came to a grinding halt." Thereafter drugstores, clothing stores, funeral parlors, and law offices served racially segregated clientele statewide.[30]

The shift to Jim Crow laws altered the behavior of both blacks and whites. White women of New Bern, Wilmington, and Winston-Salem reported that while they were shopping, strolling, or bicycling on public streets, they were laughed at, harassed, and forced to step aside by black women. In New Bern a black laundress allegedly poked one woman with an umbrella, shouting, "Oh, you think you are fine." Two women riding bicycles near the R. J. Reynolds stemmery in Winston-Salem when a shift ended became entangled in the crowd, and one cyclist was forced to dismount to the laughter and clapping of the black women. Black and white women had shared the streets since Emancipation, but Glenda Gilmore surmises that the virulence of the white supremacy campaign in the 1890s emboldened some white women to "put on airs" and encouraged black women, especially young women and workers, to become more militant as the political climate chilled.[31]

Black Working Women

Most urban black women worked either in the tobacco factories or in domestic service. In contrast to the textile industry, with its predominantly white millhands living in villages, tobacco manufacturing was located in towns and employed a workforce of both whites and blacks. Employers segregated workers by jobs, working conditions, spatial arrangements, and wages. Black men, women, and children worked during "the green season" to prepare the leaf—the "dustiest and more labor-intensive" work—for machines operated by white men and women. Black men pushed five-hundred-pound hogsheads of tobacco; white men operated and inspected machines. Black women, who constituted 75 percent of the female tobacco workers in 1900, sorted, cleaned, and stemmed tobacco, the dirty hand-labor jobs (Fig. 7-23). On other floors, white women inspected and packed the manufactured tobacco. Delores Janiewski found that 100 percent of all Durham female workers aged 20 to 24

FIGURE 7-20. *Gladys Coleman*. Dressed in wedding finery, Gladys Coleman of Asheville graces the cover of the popular woman's magazine. (Photograph from the Susan Robinson Anderson Collection. Courtesy of Susan C. Anderson, Amanda A. Klein, and Charles L. W. Anderson, as illustrated in Tessier, *Asheville* [1982])

who headed households were wage earners. About 80 percent of women aged 25 to 54 had jobs, as did 66 percent of those over 65.[32]

Many black women looking for paid work had little choice but to become domestics and clean the houses, care for the children, and wash the laundry of white families. They might have preferred the shorter hours and higher pay of factory work, but relatively few of those jobs were available to them. The great demand for household service in southern towns created almost unlimited work for black females. The term "domestic servant" became synonymous with a black woman. Black women greatly outnumbered black men in southern towns: approximately 20 to 25 percent were widows, many of whom relocated to town to find work after their husband's death.[33]

Household service provided the major point of contact among generations of North Carolina black and white women in which gender, class, and race relations were negotiated. During the Jim Crow years of ever-more stringent racial segregation, black women regularly entered the private space of the white home and participated in the intimacy of daily life. As Jacqueline Jones noted, the household-based interaction between black and white women repeated the mistress-slave relationship of antebellum times—but in a changed setting (Fig. 7-24).[34]

For domestic workers, a workday was sometimes twelve to fourteen hours long. They were often on call seven days a week and compelled to have their own Christmas and other holiday festivities after their paid work had been completed. They had to give attention first to their white charges rather than to their own children (see Fig. 7-16 above). Their pay was low, and employers often paid them with leftover food rather than financial wages. Black women were generally assigned the most burdensome housework, and if employed by middle- or working-class whites, they might work part-time in several households and do the heaviest work in each or do the washing for several families.[35] Although a chapter of the Wilmington Knights of Labor included domestic servants, and washerwomen in Atlanta actually went on strike in 1881, most North Carolina domestics had little opportunity to better either their situation or their wages. Efforts by black servants to organize, strike, or negotiate would have marked

FIGURE 7-21. *Women shopping* at Boylan-Pearce Co., Raleigh, ca. 1911. (Courtesy of the North Carolina Division of Archives and History)

FIGURE 7-22. *The Delany family*, Raleigh, ca. 1906. Educated and civic-minded, the Delanys represented the black middle class that strove for economic, political, and social parity in the 1880s and 1890s. They eventually had ten children, and when a friend suggested that she might prevent further births, Mrs. Delany declared, "I want all my children, every single one." (Courtesy of the North Carolina Division of Archives and History)

them as "uppity" and incurred retaliation. Most simply did not confront whites over wage and salary issues.[36]

Yet many domestic workers found ways to exercise some control over their lives. They resisted the middle-class work ethic by insisting on doing tasks at their own pace and taking days off at their own discretion—risking the displeasure of their employers. Generally they preferred day work over living in, a clear division between their jobs and their private lives. With day work, they could reside with their own family and participate in their church and community. When black women migrated north in large numbers, they carried this preference for day work with them and transformed the patterns of domestic service in Washington, D.C., and the Northeast.[37]

FIGURE 7-23. *Women stemming and redrying tobacco*, Kinston, Lenoir County, ca. 1915. (Courtesy of the North Carolina Collection, University of North Carolina at Chapel Hill)

FIGURE 7-24. *Fred Cross family*, Corinth, Chatham County, 1905. African American girls sometimes began tending white children when they themselves were still children. (Courtesy of the North Carolina Collection, University of North Carolina at Chapel Hill)

Other Working Women's Occupations

In the early twentieth century, both white and black women supported themselves as seamstresses, dressmakers, and boardinghouse operators. At a time when dry goods stores were stocked to the ceiling with bolts of cloth, seamstresses made women's and children's clothes at home or in their own dressmaking shop. In 1900 about eight hundred women ran boardinghouses across the state; probably the best known because of her son Tom's novel, *Look Homeward, Angel*, is Julia Wolfe, in Asheville, whose biography follows this chapter. These traditional women's home-based occupations were eventually eliminated by the availability of ready-made clothing and the growth of hotels and apartments. Seamstresses and boardinghouse operators, who worked in the privacy of their homes, were nonetheless known in every small town and were counted by federal census takers.[38]

As department stores, restaurants, and businesses opened in towns across the state, women moved ever more visibly into public space as retail clerks, waitresses, and clerical workers. These jobs were low paying but cleaner alternatives to the manual labor of farm, factory, or domestic work. Although fewer than 1 percent of women were employed in sales, service, and clerical jobs in 1900, the number in these new occupations was growing.[39]

Women and Office Work: "I Did the Work and They Drew the Pay"

"The prejudice against employing young ladies in office work is gradually dying out," proclaimed one female writer in 1893. Seven years later the *Ladies' Home Journal* warned women to stay home and avoid a nervous collapse, which working in a fast-paced modern office might induce. By 1916 the *Journal* had modified its earlier view; a secretary was a "competent mother-wife who sees to her employer's every need and desire." Developing government and business activities provided new jobs, and women with some education became typists, stenographers, bookkeepers, and telephone operators. The women who moved into office and clerical work in the government and business sectors expanded the boundaries of women's work. Many wore distinctive clothing suitable for the man's world they had invaded—a shirtwaist and tailored skirt in a modified Gibson girl look (Fig. 7-25).[40]

Several factors facilitated the movement of women into the new clerical and office positions. The typewriter, introduced in the 1890s, was considered gender neutral, so a female typist did not take away a man's job. Furthermore, typing and shorthand were "well suited to the finer nature and more delicate organization of womanhood" in addition to women's tolerance for daily routine, attention to detail, and manual dexterity. As schools to train women for business opened in towns across the state, the Durham Business School sought to lure prospective students with the assurance that commercial colleges furnished a "better education for practical purposes than either Princeton, Harvard, or Yale." In 1892 the State Normal and Industrial College for Women at Greensboro offered instruction in stenography, typewriting, bookkeeping, and telegraphy to prepare students "for high-class business work." Raleigh's Peace College and Baptist Female University had business programs as well.[41]

FIGURE 7-25. *Telephone switchboard operators*, Randolph County, 1900. The invention of the telephone in 1876 created another occupation for women. When the first telephone exchange in North Carolina opened in Raleigh in 1879, the operators were entirely male. By 1900 forty-four women worked as telephone operators, mostly young, white, and single. Telephone operators were expected to be unfailingly polite, unflappable, and knowledgeable. Like most other women's occupations, wages were low. (Courtesy of Randolph County Historical Society)

As businesses grew in scale and complexity, the specialization of office work and record keeping also increased, providing white-collar jobs for both men and women. After completing her college course, Katharine Smith, of Mount Airy, one of the early students at State Normal, took typing lessons so she could work as the only woman and one of three stenographers for her cousin, tobacco magnate Richard J. Reynolds, whom she later married. Black-owned businesses similarly hired African American women in secretarial and clerical jobs. Of twenty full-time employees in the Durham home office of the North Carolina Mutual and Provident Association in 1912, eleven were women, and nearly one-fourth of the agents were women. Susan Gille Norfleet, the official stenographer and secretary to the president of the prominent insurance company, had a degree from Wilberforce University in Ohio (Fig. 7-26).[42]

State government also hired women for clerical jobs. Elsie Riddick, who was born in Gates County and enrolled in the business program at State Normal in 1895, began working as a stenographer for the North Carolina Agricultural Commission in Raleigh in 1897. Two years later she said of her bosses, "I did the work and they drew the pay." Never married, Riddick became active in the North Carolina Federation of Business and Professional Women, worked for woman suffrage, and was the first woman in Raleigh to be a Democratic Party precinct chair. Riddick, who championed women doing "a common thing uncommonly well," believed that "nothing" was "beyond the scope of women's work." State government also gave Harriet Morehead Berry the opportunity to earn her living and to campaign for better roads. After she graduated from State Normal, Berry taught for two years at the Oxford Orphanage before returning to her alma mater to take the commercial program. In 1901 she became a clerk for the North Carolina Geological and Economic Survey, a position that eventually resulted in her leadership of the statewide good roads movement.[43]

Women and the Professions

Educated women had additional options. They could enter teaching, nursing, librarianship, and other service occupations. For middle-class white women, these emerging professional careers did not challenge traditional expectations of womanhood and could be defended on the basis of woman's historic interests, now expanded to a public arena. For middle-class black women, ambitious to take on the challenge of uplifting their race, education was essential to racial progress. Black or white, female professionals did not compete with men. Their work presumed a penchant for nurturing, compassion, and self-sacrifice and a willingness to work for modest wages. Few women entered the traditionally male domains of law, medicine, dentistry, and pharmacy. In 1900 fewer than 3 percent of the state's working women were in the professions; almost 90 percent of them were teachers and about 2 percent were trained nurses.[44]

Women's professions were tied to an increased opportunity for higher education and a sense of community responsibility. They reflected the new importance of "professionalism" with its emphasis on formal education, expertise, and credentials and a concurrent deemphasis on informally acquired skills. As North Carolina evolved from an agrarian culture based on kin relations and local networks to a more urban society embracing middle-class values, some women found an attractive place in that new world.

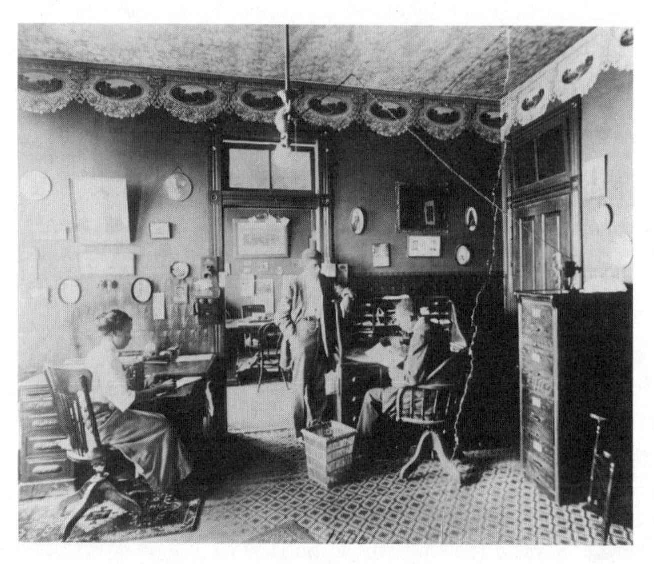

FIGURE 7-26. *The third headquarters of the North Carolina Mutual and Provident Association*, with Mrs. Susan Gille Norfleet, secretary, and C. C. Spaulding [*standing*] and John Merrick, officers, Durham, 1906. Black-owned businesses provided opportunities for black women to enter clerical and secretarial occupations. The North Carolina Mutual and Provident Association was organized in 1898 to provide "relief to the widows and orphans, of the sick, to those injured by accident, and for the burial of the dead." The oldest insurance company in continuous operation in the state, it is also the largest predominantly black-managed financial institution in the world. (Courtesy of the North Carolina Collection, University of North Carolina at Chapel Hill)

Professional Firsts

1878	Tabitha Ann Holton	Lawyer
1887	Annie Lowrie Alexander	Physician
1889	Mollie Spach and Adeline Orr	Licensed nurses
1898	Sallie Walker Stockard	University of North Carolina graduate
1902	Cara Collins Nance	Atlanta Dental College graduate
1922	Addie Pegram	Pharmacist

Women, Higher Education, and the Professions

Public higher education for women in North Carolina began at the end of Reconstruction in 1877, when the state legislature appropriated funds for teacher training (known as "normal" instruction) of both white and black students; in 1887 it did the same for Native Americans. A summer school was established for white teachers at the University of North Carolina in Chapel Hill. Although the legislation referred only to men, women were permitted to enroll. Cornelia Phillips Spencer, who as a faculty daughter had sometimes attended university lectures, wrote to the *Raleigh News and Observer*: "The lady teachers who contemplate attending may come feeling assured of welcome, encouragement, and protection. . . . Let no one stay away through want of courage and through want of faith." In the first year the student body consisted of 107 women and 128 men; in the seven years of the summer school's existence, women made up half of the enrollment. This was women's "entering wedge" into the state university.[45]

Black women also rode on men's coattails to gain access to public higher education. Governor Zebulon Vance was concerned that so much of black education was supported by the Freedmen's Bureau and northern charities. Despite strong white opposition, he urged the state to take responsibility for educating all citizens and for black people to stop looking "abroad for aids to their progress and civilization and turn to the state instead." He recommended that a $2,000 appropriation for training black teachers be used to establish a normal department at an already existing black college at Fayetteville (present-day Fayetteville State University). Black teachers would receive a three-year course of study—more comprehensive and longer training than was considered necessary for white teachers. The legislation specified "young men of the colored race," but black males were as reluctant as white males to enter a field with the prospect of only two to three months' employment annually, at a salary comparable to that of a common laborer. Women, who already represented a majority of the black elementary schoolteachers, received special permission to enroll. The first class had 42 students, 17 of them female. Eighteen months later, there were 114 students, 42 of them female. Although other normal schools for blacks were established at New Bern, Franklinton, Plymouth, Salisbury, and Elizabeth City, they received less funding, lacked trained faculties, and suffered from inadequate buildings, laboratories, and libraries.[46]

FIGURE 7-27. *President Charles McIver and faculty, State Normal and Industrial College*, Greensboro, 1893. McIver declared, "Educate a man, and you educate an individual; educate a woman and you educate a family." (Courtesy of the Archives, Jackson Library, University of North Carolina at Greensboro)

Public higher education for Native Americans received the least state support. Although the Eastern Band of Cherokee living in the Mountains paid state taxes, they were considered wards of the federal government, which provided only minimal schooling. In 1880, when the tribal common fund was used to send a few promising students to nearby academies and colleges, eleven women, ranging in age from eight to sixteen, enrolled in Asheville Female College, where they studied English, at least one learned arithmetic, and all took sewing and housework. One Cherokee father refused to allow his two daughters to return to the Asheville school because, he said, they were treated like servants: they had to wash clothes, pick up after the wife of a college official, clean up rooms, and "pack out pots full of excrement." The Indians of Robeson, Bladen, and Sampson Counties were citizens, but as institutionalized racial segregation began to emerge after Reconstruction, the General Assembly designated them as "Croatans" and established separate schools for them. The need for Native American teachers led the assembly to appropriate five hundred dollars in 1887 to establish near Pembroke the Croatan Normal School (now the University of North Carolina at Pembroke). Although no money was allocated for a building, the Croatans (later known as Lumbees) themselves erected a two-story wooden building in time for the opening of school, and in the fall of 1887 fifteen students enrolled. Much of the curriculum was elementary-level work, though some normal courses were taught. The first four-year degree-granting institution for Indians in the United States, Croatan Normal trained teachers for the Waccamaw Siouan, Coharie, Haliwa, and Lumbee communities.[47]

"Without educated women there can be no trained teachers. Without trained teachers there can be no effective schools. Without these schools, there can be no progress in North Carolina," declared Annie G. Randall in 1901. Randall was the registrar and English teacher at State Normal, which had been established in 1891–92 "to give young white girls such education as should fit them for teaching . . . and such industrial arts as might be suitable to their sex and conducive to their support and usefulness." Tuition was free, and the term was three months. Founding president Charles Duncan McIver and his faculty believed that public schools were essential to help North Carolina move from an illiterate Old South to an industrial New South; the success of the schools, in turn, depended on educated women who were willing to teach (Fig. 7-27). He thought that women should be "independent and self-supporting." So did North Carolina Baptists, who in 1891 chartered the Baptist Female University (renamed Meredith College in 1909) for Baptist women: "Too long our girls have been educated with little reference to gain a living independent of fathers, brothers, and husbands." In 1890, reflecting the new interest in higher education for women, a four-year college was established at Salem Academy. Other normal schools opened in Asheville, Boone, Cullowhee, and Greenville, and they trained hundreds of young women (Fig. 7-28).[48]

The first generation of women college students had a sense of privilege and responsibility in obtaining a higher education (Fig. 7-29). They led intellectually and physically active lives that reflected a new definition of womanhood (Fig. 7-30). Inspired by McIver and by their teachers, the students felt that they were "soldiers" who would battle illiteracy in the state, "crusaders" who would bring progress to towns. All of the members of State Normal's first graduating class became teachers.[49] Asheville graduate Alice Threatt Perry took further study at the Orange Memorial Hospital in New Jersey before volunteering for the U.S. Army Nurses

FIGURE 7-28. *Graduates of the Normal and Collegiate Institute*, Asheville, 1905. (Courtesy of the Warren Wilson College Archives)

Corps in Cuba and later becoming the first registered nurse in private practice in Charlotte.[50]

In the late 1890s a few white women who had attended other colleges were admitted to Chapel Hill as upperclasswomen. "We realized we were making history," said University of North Carolina graduate student Alice Jones in 1898. Guilford College graduate Sallie Stockard received the first University of North Carolina degree granted to a woman, in 1898, and two years later she earned a master's degree. These early women were "outsiders"; as one coed said, "you always have a creepy feeling that your hat is on crooked, or that your hair is coming down." But they redefined the roles of middle-class women, and a high percentage of them became physicians, lawyers, and leaders in education and social work. Many remained single. Stockard exhibited an independence unusual even for her generation of college women when she took back her maiden name after marriage and two children: "I have supported myself and brought up two children from birth without help. I am under no obligations to any man for the use of his name. . . . I do not hide behind any other name than my own. . . . Shall I have to be cremated to keep that man's name off my tombstone? Wooden headed tradition!"[51]

The new women's colleges quickly hired for their faculties outstanding women who had studied at leading universities, inspired their young students to accept the challenge of public life, and served as important role models. Many teachers at State Normal chose a career over marriage. Their lives, filled with work, travel, and study, must have impressed young women of rural and small-town North Carolina. Science professor Dixie Lee Bryant had degrees from the Massachusetts Institute of Technology (MIT) and a German university; school physician Anna M. Gove had graduated from MIT and the Women's Medical College of New York Infirmary and studied in Europe; Gertrude Mendenhall and Mary Petty, professors in mathematics and chemistry respectively, were Wellesley College graduates; Annie Petty was the state's first professional librarian, with a degree from the University of Pennsylvania. Meredith College alumnae remember college physician and physiology professor Delia Dixon Carroll as a "vigorous advocate of woman suffrage" and classics professor Helen Price, also a suffragist, as teaching them concern for "social and political struggles in the world" and giving them a global vision.[52]

These colleges also hired women for other important positions. In 1900, at a time when there were few female doctors in the state, the college physicians at State Normal, Baptist Female University, and Presbyterian Female College in Charlotte (renamed Queens College in 1913) all were women. In 1902 Lucy Henderson Owen Robertson, who had taught at State Normal, became the first woman president of the Greensboro Female College, established by Methodists in 1838. The college explained:

> The placing of a woman at the head of this long-established institution may be an innovation in this state, but it is no doubtful experiment. Some of the most prominent colleges for women, notably Wellesly [*sic*] and Bryn Mawr, in the North, the Wesleyan, at Macon, Ga., and others in the South, have been most successfully managed by women. . . . It seems eminently fitting that the College which was the pioneer in the State in the higher education of young women should thus be the first to give such a complete recognition of woman.[53]

Higher education also enabled black women to gain the skills to teach and to pursue even more advanced training (Fig. 7-31). During Reconstruction and after, recognition that education was essential if African Americans were to make any economic, political, or social progress led to the establishment of numerous institutions of higher learning. At Scotia Seminary, modeled on Mount Holyoke, a biracial faculty taught young women that the housekeeping skills they learned, along with their academic curriculum, were to be used for their own families, not in domestic service for white people. Mary McLeod, who attended Scotia in the mid-1880s, remembered that her northern white teachers had taught her

> Some would say that woman is good in her place. This reminds me of what some white people say of the Negro: that "He is good in his place."
>
> —Sarah Dudley Pettey, "Woman's Column," *Star of Zion*, August 6, 1896. (Gilmore, *Gender and Jim Crow*, 1)

FIGURE 7-29. *Students at the State Normal and Industrial College*, Greensboro, ca. 1899. The entire college community gathered for this photograph at the Brick Dormitory, which housed both students and female faculty members. (Courtesy of the Archives, Jackson Library, University of North Carolina at Greensboro)

that "the color of a person's skin has nothing to do with his brains, and that color, caste, or class distinctions are an evil thing."[54] A graduate of Scotia College in 1881, Lucy Hughes Brown entered the Women's Medical College of Philadelphia in 1890, returned to Wilmington after graduation in 1894, passed her medical examinations, and started a practice. Classmate Sarah Dudley returned home to New Bern after graduation, became the assistant principal of the black graded school, and wrote a women's column on a variety of social issues for the AME Zion Church.

When Sadie Delany graduated from St. Augustine's College in 1910, she began teaching in rural Wake County, but her father encouraged her to go on to a four-year college: "Daughter, you are college material. You owe it to your nation, your race, yourself to go. And if you don't, then shame on you." Both Sadie and her sister Bessie later graduated from Columbia University in New York City, Sadie from the Teachers College and Bessie from the Dental School. Another St. Augustine's graduate, Anna J. Hayward Cooper, whose biography follows this section, first taught in Chatham County, eventually obtained her Ph.D. from the Sorbonne in Paris, and dedicated her career to educating black children in Washington, D.C.[55]

Although North Carolina led the nation in the number of public black institutions, education for blacks largely depended on private liberal arts schools. For many whites, it did not seem "right" that a black man should be a successful businessman or a black woman a respected teacher, and they resisted spending tax dollars to educate blacks. The vocational training proposed in 1895 by Booker T. Washington gained currency as white supremacy attitudes hardened. Those African American colleges, both private and public, that resisted this approach, struggled mightily against financial, institutional, accreditation, and social barriers to provide black women with good college educations.[56]

Public School Teachers

Teaching was the most important profession for educated North Carolina women. From Reconstruction on, women—

FIGURE 7-30. *Basketball team, State Normal and Industrial College*, Greensboro, 1900. Team sports and camaraderie were part of the early college experience for many young women. (Courtesy of the Archives, Jackson Library, University of North Carolina at Greensboro)

white, black, and Native American—filled teaching positions in disproportionate numbers in the state's triracial school system. Women's entry into teaching paralleled the rise of public education. Slow to be reestablished after the Civil War, public schools were hampered by the state's poverty, by local communities' aversion to cede to state control, by white reluctance to pay taxes that could be used to educate black and Indian children, and by industrial leaders' economic interest in keeping child workers in the mills. In 1900 the average salary for a teacher in North Carolina was twenty-one dollars per month, less than 50 percent of the national norm, and terms lasted only four months. Most public schools were located in towns and cities, even though the state was predominantly rural. Many rural teachers taught in one-room schoolhouses, where they also chopped wood, fired the stove, and cleaned up.

Although women were considered particularly suited for teaching, their employment was initially thwarted by the concern that they could not maintain discipline. The justification for employing females, especially for the primary grades, was that they were more nurturing *and* more moral than males. Many towns offered contracts that forbade a female teacher to marry; consequently, many women left the field after only a few years. Yet of a group of "pioneer" white teachers whose biographies were compiled in 1955 by the North Carolina teachers' organization, Delta Kappa Gamma, about half were single and half were married or widowed.[57]

Three women's careers were typical. Margaret Hearne, of Wilson County, who had received her education in local private schools, started her own school in the town of Wilson at the age of seventeen and operated it for eleven years. When the town established a public school system in 1881, Hearne closed her school and became one of Wilson's first public school teachers. Two years later, when the public schools closed, she moved to a private institution. When the town schools reopened, she again joined that system and taught until retiring in 1927 at age seventy-five. Laura Lazenby, of Rowan County, who studied at private academies, started, at the request of her neighbors, a "subscription school," where she instructed pupils "taller and older" than she. In 1883

FIGURE 7-31. *Students at St. Augustine's College*, Raleigh, ca. 1900. (Courtesy of St. Augustine's College)

FIGURE 7-32. *Students at a rural school* near Lake Waccamaw, Columbus County, ca. 1900. (Courtesy of the North Carolina Collection, University of North Carolina at Chapel Hill)

Lazenby began teaching in the Statesville graded schools, where she remained for forty years. "Miss" Mollie Heath of New Bern had a long career primarily in the public schools, but she also taught in a private school when the New Bern public schools were closed because a citizen objected to "paying taxes to educate other people's children."[58]

African American teachers coped with substandard buildings, inadequate supplies, shorter terms, and tax monies grudgingly given (Fig. 7-32). Peabody, Rosenwald, Slater, and Jeanes philanthropic funds augmented meager state and local revenues to upgrade black education, despite whites' concerns about "outside" interference in the state's right to educate its citizens. Although the wages were little better than those of tobacco stemming and sometimes required having to engage in summer work as a laundress or domestic servant, teaching was a high-status position for black women.[59]

African American teachers believed in uplifting their race as well as earning a living (Fig. 7-33). Mary Burwell attended Raleigh primary schools, graduated from Shaw University, taught several years in public schools, and in 1890 began teaching at the Oxford Colored Orphanage Asylum, where she featured her students in concerts and used the proceeds to enhance the institution's facilities (Fig. 7-34). Mary Washington Howe of Wilmington received her normal training at a Quaker school in Philadelphia and returned home to teach at the Williston Grammar School. When the male principal left to go into medicine, Howe became its first and only woman principal, a position she held for twenty years—until her death in 1900. Howe was active in the civic, cultural, and religious life of her community, as was Willie Ann Smith, who taught in the Goldsboro schools, wrote poetry, and advocated temperance. Smith was described by a black male educator as "an ardent lover of her race" with "high hopes for its future glory."[60]

Native American schools in Robeson, Sampson, and Bladen Counties were especially hampered by the lack of money and teachers. Most white taxpayers believed that their taxes should be used only for white students, and the federal government refused to assume any responsibility for the Cro-

FIGURE 7-33. *Teachers at Myers Street School*, Charlotte, ca. 1900. (Courtesy of the Public Library of Charlotte and Mecklenburg County)

FIGURE 7-34. *Oxford Colored Orphanage*, Granville County, ca. 1900. (Courtesy of the North Carolina Division of Archives and History)

atan Indians. Thus elementary and secondary education for the Lumbees developed very slowly. Yet Bessie C. Brewington and Mary D. Maynor, both of the Coharie tribe, were pioneer teachers in Lumbee tribal schools in Sampson County (Fig. 7-35), and Lumbee Anna Mae Locklear served as an educator and Baptist missionary for more than forty years.[61]

The Eastern Cherokee generally followed a traditional way of life, speaking their native language (although fewer than half could read it) and teaching children at home (Fig. 7-36). In 1875 the federal Indian Office started a boarding school in Cheoah, central Graham County, with Mary A. Manney of Robbinsville in charge at a salary of thirty dollars a month for a five-month term. By early 1876 four other day schools were operating on the Qualla Boundary, but tribal factionalism and political disputes forced their closing. For three years responsibility for Cherokee education passed back and forth between state and federal agents. With no comprehensive state or federal program, it was left to Quaker missionaries to establish day schools in Big Cove, Macedonia (old Echota Mission), Bird Town, and Snowbird Gap in Graham County and a training school for both boarding and day students at Yellow Hill (later Cherokee) in the 1880s. The Quakers taught practical skills—domestic for females, mechanical and agricultural for boys—along with English, arithmetic, religion, and temperance, but, typical of missionary practice, they forced the children to abandon their traditional culture and to speak only English. In 1892 authority for Cherokee education shifted back to federal agents, who continued the Quaker training schools and instituted some extracurricular activities—baseball and football for boys, tennis and croquet for girls—and semimonthly "sociables" to encourage "gentility" (Fig. 7-37).[62]

Librarians

As elsewhere in the South, early librarians in North Carolina had to convince state and local officials that reading books was important, that a library was a sign of progress, and that education and literacy were as fundamental to an improved standard of living as public health and agricultural

FIGURE 7-35. *Herrings Township school*, erected 1911 by Coharie Indians, Sampson County, photograph ca. 1915. (Courtesy of the North Carolina Collection, University of North Carolina at Chapel Hill)

extension. By the early 1900s, when the public library movement started in North Carolina, its goals and objectives were well defined, but racism, rural isolation, and poverty affected its acceptance. Widespread illiteracy meant that many North Carolinians had limited or no reading ability and found little need for libraries. Librarians had to combine both professional and community leadership to foster the statewide growth of libraries.[63]

Like teachers, most early librarians were male. In the 1880s women were admitted to study library science in schools such as Columbia University and the University of Pennsylvania, and the new and growing field became an acceptable profession for educated women. Many of North Carolina's early female librarians attended the Atlanta Library School, the first library school in the South, which was established in 1903 with funds from the Andrew Carnegie Foundation. Its graduates had a shared identity as the first generation of professionally trained librarians in the state and were leaders in the public library movement.

Because North Carolina's rural population had difficulty getting to towns where libraries were located, librarians had to devise strategies to make books available to readers. The first travel library system (by which boxes of books were sent to rural areas) was formed in Durham in 1897, adopted as a local initiative by chapters of the North Carolina Federation of Women's Clubs after 1902, and taken over by the state Library Commission between 1905 and 1910.

Medical Professions

Before 1900 there were few hospitals in North Carolina and few nurses. In 1894 Rex Hospital Training School for Nurses, in Raleigh, had opened for whites, and soon St. Agnes of St. Augustine's College in Raleigh and Good Samaritan Hospital in Charlotte trained black nurses (Fig. 7-38).

Nursing was part of medicine's professionalization in that advanced training, specialization, registration, licensing, and formal nurses associations defined the occupation (see Fig. 7-18 above). In 1903 North Carolina became the first state

FIGURE 7-36. *Cherokee woman and baby*. (Courtesy of North Carolina Museum of History)

FIGURE 7-37. *Mrs. Emma J. Shelton Hampton Wike and her students* in front of the Cherokee Training School at Yellow Hill (present-day Cherokee), Swain County, Qualla Boundary, 1893. (Courtesy of the Museum of the Cherokee Indian)

to require compulsory registration and licensing of nurses. An important figure in this development was Mary Lewis Wyche. Born near Henderson in Vance County just prior to the Civil War, Wyche taught school and kept boarders so that her brothers could attend the state university at Chapel Hill. She considered becoming a doctor but opted instead to study nursing, which in the late nineteenth century was a new field for middle-class women. She was thirty-six years old when she finished nurse's training in Philadelphia and returned to North Carolina. For the next forty years, she was tireless in establishing professional standards and recognition for nursing. She directed the state's first two nursing schools—Rex Hospital, Raleigh, in 1894 and Watts Hospital, Durham, in 1903–13. She also supervised the infirmary of the State Normal and Industrial College in Greensboro and founded the Raleigh Nurses Association (later the North Carolina State Nurses Association).[64]

While Wyche and others struggled to obtain recognition for their profession, a few women challenged the boundaries of women's sphere to become physicians, dentists, and pharmacists (Fig. 7-39). Those who wanted a medical degree still had to leave the state (as had North Carolina's first female physician, Susan Dimock, in 1872, who never practiced in the state). Annie Lowrie Alexander, of Mecklenburg County, a graduate of the Women's Medical College of Pennsylvania in Philadelphia in 1884, was the first woman licensed to practice medicine in North Carolina and elsewhere in the South; in 1887 she established a practice in Charlotte. Alexander remembered the "hue and cry" when she left home to enter medical school, some of her relatives so outraged that "they asked her name not be mentioned in their presence." Elizabeth Delia Dixon-Carroll of Shelby graduated from Cornell University, received a medical degree in 1895 from Women's Medical College (later part of Columbia University) in New York City, ranked first among the two hundred doctors taking the New York medical examinations, and in the late 1890s became the first woman physician in Raleigh.[65]

By the turn of the century, dentistry had established a place in North Carolina's health care system, with particular concern for children. Although it is difficult to determine exactly when women entered this field, by 1910 there were ten female dentists in the state. Cara Collins Nance of Charlotte received her D.D.S. degree from Atlanta Dental College in 1902 and was North Carolina's first woman of record to graduate. Daisy Zachary McGuire began practicing dentistry in 1890, received her D.D.S. from Southern Dental College in

FIGURE 7-38. *St. Agnes School for Nurses*, Raleigh, ca. 1900. (Courtesy of the North Carolina Division of Archives and History)

1908, and four years later began a sixty-five-year practice with her husband, Wayne Patrick McGuire, in Sylva, Jackson County.[66]

Though few in number, women professionals made an impact on the health, education, and welfare of North Carolina. The turn-of-the-century establishment of schools, hospitals, libraries, and cultural organizations reflects both women's concerns and their growing influence in the state.

Women and Advocacy: "A Power for Good"

As North Carolina women staked out a woman's domain in public life, they used the rhetoric of religion and familiar gender relations to temper so revolutionary an act. Rural isolation, economic constraints, and male attitudes had prompted previous generations of women to focus their energies on their families and local benevolence. Starting in the 1870s, however, women joined secular voluntary associations to expand their sphere of influence in the civic realm. "Organized womanhood" is the formidable term used to describe this phenomenon, and it occurred throughout the United States. Women formed groups to provide mutual aid and self-education; to fight "King Alcohol" and crusade for (and against) woman suffrage; to establish schools, libraries, hospitals, orphanages, and homes for wayward girls; and to preserve, commemorate, and promote history and culture.

FIGURE 7-39. *Pharmacist Dorothy Sharpe* practicing from a log cabin, Henderson County, ca. 1910. Although pharmacology was not listed as a separate profession for women until 1950, Sharpe dispensed medicine in the Mountains. (Courtesy of the North Carolina Collection, University of North Carolina at Chapel Hill)

> I believe God is calling us by name to take the 'Sword of the Spirit' and go forth as brave soldiers battling for Him, our homes and our native state.
> —Laura Annie Ballinger Winston, North Carolina Woman's Christian Temperance Union, 1884. (Winston, "Duties of North Carolina Women," in WCTU Minutes, 1884, as cited in Sims, "Feminism and Femininity," 57)

The years between 1880 and 1910 were marked by political, social, and economic changes that were a source of pride for many—the New South was becoming a reality—and anathema for numerous conservative southerners. Urbanization, modernization, and industrialization were altering traditional ways of doing things. As Marjorie Spruill Wheeler has observed, women, excluded from direct participation in public life, played extremely useful roles in southern culture and politics. As women's voluntary associations gained momentum, African Americans hoped that full participation in civic life was possible, an aspiration that ended with the violence of white supremacy politics and Jim Crow legislation.[67]

Home and Foreign Missionary Work: "Women's Work for Women"

North Carolina women organized first for church-related benevolent and missionary work, both of which had roots in the early nineteenth century. As soon as freedom came, black women in New Bern, Wilmington, Charlotte, and other towns organized mutual aid societies and missions within their churches to care for the less fortunate in their communities. Native American women in Robeson County and elsewhere also joined mainstream denominations and participated in church work. By the 1870s and 1880s women's benevolence was linked to state and regional groups: all the major white and black Protestant denominations had ladies' auxiliaries to support mission programs at home and abroad. Church women believed that their fund-raising at home gave them the right to have some say in how the money was spent. They wanted women missionaries to serve the special needs of women and children in faraway places—"women's work for women." Frequently they clashed with male church leaders who preferred the old ways—women raising the money and men spending it.[68]

In organizations from the Household of Ruth to the AME Zion Women's Home and Foreign Missionary Society to the Baptist Women's Home Mission Convention to local Ladies Aid Societies, African Americans in the 1870s and 1880s sought to advance their race and to provide for those at the bottom. Unlike white women, they seem to have been less interested in imposing their values; they wanted to do what they could to help their people so recently freed from slavery. Their organizations built churches and paid off mortgages, supported the minister's family, and cared for orphans, the ill, and the aged.[69]

Along with charity, middle-class white women dispensed Protestant morals and values. They believed that women of Protestant America were destined to reshape the world into a moral Christian community. Methodist women were particularly effective. Their leaders were often ministers' wives or widows, many of whom had taken some college courses and, for at least part of their lives, pursued a career. Dedicating long years of service to church work, they were indefatigable organizers on the local, state, regional, and national levels, and often they were exposed to the ideas and strategies of women from other states. The first president of the North Carolina Women's Foreign Missionary Society was Mary Jane Wilson, of Greensboro, a minister's wife and mother of twelve; the second was Lucy Cunninggim, also a minister's wife from Greensboro, but childless. Lucy Robertson, a widowed educator who became the president of Methodist-affiliated Greensboro Female College, also served as president of the Western North Carolina Foreign Missionary Society and Women's Missionary Society for more than thirty years. Minnie Lee Hancock Hammer, a Salem College graduate and wife of a congressman, was for twenty-five years the president of the Women's Missionary Society of the North Carolina Annual Conference, and when the Foreign and Home Missionary Societies merged, she became national president. Hammer helped found two Methodist institutions in High Point, the Children's Home and High Point College.[70]

Methodist women helped lead the fight for temperance and were instrumental in obtaining statewide Prohibition in 1908. They worked to establish reformatories and a juvenile court system. And although many of them considered blacks their inferiors, they led other denominations in establishing black missions to improve the welfare of mothers and children.[71]

Baptist women held attitudes similar to those of the Methodists but had to contend with more entrenched male opposition. In the 1870s they wanted to create a women's organization to foster missionary causes, but that idea threatened many Southern Baptist churchmen, who feared that local church autonomy would be jeopardized by women diverting funds for their own programs and that women might even leave their homes for the pulpit. To men whose southern pride had been assailed by losing the war, the whole thing smacked of a northern plot—women's rights, public speaking, suffrage, even the women's missionary movement had started in the North. By 1888, however, the Southern Baptist Convention (SBC) authorized the Women's Missionary Union (WMU). North Carolina was not one of the ten states to vote for the new organization, but it joined two years later.[72]

Fannie Exile Scudder Heck, an active member of Raleigh's First Baptist Church, was committed to mission work. Heck was president of the state women's committee before and after it became formally affiliated with the WMU (she filled that position until her death in 1915) and president of the Southern WMU, for a total of fifteen years—1892–94, 1895–99, and 1906–15 (Fig. 7-40). Through her association with the WMU, the Raleigh Women's Club, the Associated Charities of Raleigh, and her personal missionary work among the Raleigh underprivileged, her benevolent activities were extensive. Heck thought that Chicago's Jane Addams had "left religion out of her plans." Heck promoted foreign missionary work, established a department of neighborhood missionary work for the state WMU, raised funds for the Baptist Female University, started a program in 1900 to send volunteer teachers to

FIGURE 7-40. *Gavel belonging to Fannie E. S. Heck*, Raleigh, Wake County. (Courtesy of the Baptist State Convention)

FIGURE 7-41. *Farewell party for Nina Troy* at Troy-Bumpass House, Greensboro, 1912. Troy's farewell party before her departure for Soochow was given by the Women's Society of Christian Service of the West Market Street Church, her sponsor for the mission field. She remained in China until 1943, when she was sent to a concentration camp. On her release, she returned home after World War II. (Courtesy of the Greensboro Historical Museum)

the Mountains in the summer months, and supported the recruitment of female missionaries through a fund named in honor of the first North Carolina woman appointed by the SBC Foreign Mission Board, Eliza Moring Yates.[73]

For missionary work abroad, North Carolina women educated themselves about foreign cultures; raised money for schools, orphanages, and hospitals; and recruited young women to serve as missionaries. In 1872 the Methodist Foreign Mission Board permitted unmarried women to act as auxiliaries to male missionaries and predicted that, "kept within her proper sphere," a woman would be a valuable ally in spreading the gospel. As the Methodist *Western Recorder* asked: "Why shouldn't she? Didn't she have much to do with bringing the curse upon the race? And ought she not do all she can to remove it?"[74]

Former publisher of the Methodist *Weekly Message* Frances Webb Bumpass turned her considerable energies to building a place for women within the Methodist Church. "Too long" have women "hesitated fearful, lest it be said they were stepping beyond their sphere." College-educated women, Bumpass argued, should be sent as missionaries throughout the world. She was instrumental in the 1878 organization of the Women's Foreign Mission Society of the Methodist Church and traveled extensively for the group, mobilizing women, until her death in 1898. Foreign missionary work became a viable career for idealistic young women such as Sophie Stevens Lanneau, a Meredith graduate and SBC educational missionary who directed a girls' school in Soochow, China, from 1907 to 1951, and Mrs. Bumpass's granddaughter, Nina Troy, a missionary schoolteacher in Soochow in 1912 (Fig. 7-41).[75]

Presbyterian Elizabeth Ann Harlee McNair MacRae of Robeson County embraced missionary work closer to home. Ignoring the opposition of local ministers, MacRae—twice widowed, middle-aged, and financially comfortable—began in the 1880s to organize the women of the Fayetteville Presbytery, which was spread over eight large, sparsely settled counties in the rural east. Like much of women's benevolence, MacRae's encompassed education and evangelicalism: she taught in her local community during the school year and spent her summers teaching in the Mountains, where she established a school for poor Mountain girls in Banner Elk, Avery County (now Lees-McRae College).[76]

Northern missionary women also found good works to do in the North Carolina highlands. In 1897 social worker Frances Louisa Goodrich of the Women's Board of Home Missions of the Presbyterian Church established Allanstand Industries in Madison County to encourage the revival of traditional crafts such as weaving and woodworking (Fig. 7-42). Handicraft industries provided needed work, especially in remote areas, and, at the same time, brought the cultural values of their promoters—the white, Protestant, educated, middle class—to people perceived as "folk" (Fig. 7-43). Goodrich, whose venerable New England family had a tradition of public service, had lived in France in her teens and studied art at the Yale Art School. Imbued by a mission similar to that of college-educated women working in the urban settlement movement, she joined her friend Florence Stephenson, a Presbyterian missionary who headed an in-

FIGURE 7-42. *Frances Louisa Goodrich*, Madison County, ca. 1900. Goodrich collected the products of Mountain craftspeople in a mule-drawn wagon and then sold them in such places as Ohio, Connecticut, and New Hampshire. (Courtesy of the Southern Highland Craft Guild, Asheville)

FIGURE 7-43. Margaret W. Morley, *A Mountaineer's Home*, 1900–1912. (From Morley, *The Carolina Mountains* [1913]. Courtesy of the North Carolina Division of Archives and History)

dustrial school for girls in Riceville, outside of Asheville, in 1890. Two years later Goodrich moved to Brittain's Cove, where she built herself a cottage and established a school and a church; five years later, she settled in Allanstand.

Goodrich believed that craft work, which could be done in "dodge times," was a way that people willing to change from being a farm family to a farm-and-craft family could stay on their homeplace instead of having to move to a textile mill town. Rather than preserve old ways of production, she distributed standardized patterns based on local coverlet weaving to women working in their homes who were paid by the piece—some to card, some to spin, and some to weave. She set up a guild to purchase materials, market the finished products, and serve as a social club. Although northern church women were Goodrich's initial market, she targeted a broader audience with an article in the December 1898 *House Beautiful* and with an exhibition of Allanstand crafts, with weaving demonstrations, at the spring Presbytery meeting in Asheville in 1900. Goodrich's goal for Allanstand was "the gain in habits of industry and thrift." With missionary certitude, she believed that the loss of industry and thrift—as well as the use of tobacco and alcohol—"caused the mountaineers to fall behind in the race."[77]

Woman's Christian Temperance Union: "Home Is to Women and Children Their Most Sacred Heritage, and the Saloon Its Blighting Curse"

As Anne Firor Scott observed, the "public life of nearly every southern woman leader for forty years began in a church society." Many women stepped easily from the women's culture and evangelical Christian values of church organizations to those of the Woman's Christian Temperance Union (WCTU) (Plate 10).[78]

Saloons were ubiquitous in North Carolina towns. In 1872 Rocky Mount reportedly had twenty-one saloons—and one church. Women, white and black, saw themselves as brave Christian soldiers fighting King Alcohol. Believing that it was a woman's duty to protect home and family from moral corruption, the Woman's Christian Temperance Union strove to legislate morality. "Our homes are in jeopardy. . . . The children . . . are in danger," declared a temperance crusader. Armed with righteous conviction and wearing white ribbons, these women left home to reform society. Temperance women entered into the rough-and-tumble of political life and even pulled off stunts like carrying WCTU banners across the state. Thus temperance thrust many women for the first time into the public arena, where they sought to exercise their moral authority and so-called feminine superiority.[79]

Temperance had few advocates in North Carolina's antebellum rural culture, but the growth of towns and industrialization after the Civil War made alcohol abuse a woman's issue. As North Carolina's WCTU president Mary Woody, a Quaker minister and teacher at Guilford College, explained in 1890: "All this improvement means . . . the increase in saloons, the growth of sin." In November 1883 WCTU national leader Frances Willard established the state's first chapter in Greensboro (Fig. 7-44). The next year saw the organization of eleven more chapters. By 1903 membership peaked at three thousand in the state's sixty-five chapters. In 1908, when statewide Prohibition was enacted, WCTU membership dwindled to about one thousand, a number that held firm through the 1930s.[80]

Black women also participated in the WCTU, and they adopted the issue of protecting the home from alcohol, but they were also aware that black drunkenness reflected on their race as a whole in a way that white drunkenness did not. They further hoped to create through the WCTU a model of interracial cooperation. White women recognized that they needed the support of black women who could influence their husbands, who had voting rights until 1900, and they envisioned a partnership with their "sisters in black," although with the black women as "junior" partners. When existing WCTU chapters were brought into a statewide organization, one of the departments was "Work amongst the Colored People," headed by Rosa Steele, the wife of the white president of Bennett College; all the black chapters were under her jurisdiction. In 1886, when Steele failed to attend the state meeting, the president of Greensboro's black chapter, Florence A. Garrett, delivered an extemporaneous speech—

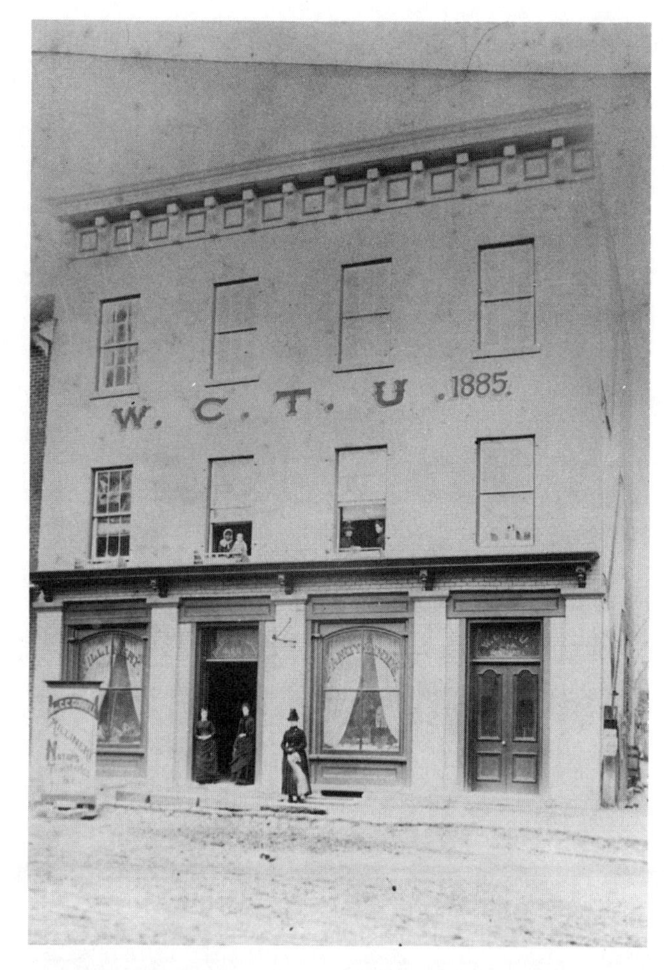

FIGURE 7-44. *State headquarters of the WCTU,* Greensboro, post-1884. The owner of the Gorrell Millinery Shop, which served as the headquarters, was WCTU activist Caroline Gorrell. The businesswoman, philanthropist, and civic leader was one of three women appearing in *Founders and Builders of Greensboro*, as cited in Fripp, *Greensboro*, 53. (Courtesy of the Greensboro Historical Museum)

which, Anastatia Sims notes, was "probably the first time a black woman had addressed a meeting of white women in North Carolina."[81]

African American women found the attitudes of their white colleagues patronizing and contradictory in an organization claiming "sisterhood" in God's work. In 1889 they seceded, forming WCTU No. 2, which reported directly to the national WCTU and had equal status with the white group. North Carolina was the only state to have a black women's temperance union, which by December 1891 had four hundred members and nineteen chapters. To the WCTU national newspaper, the *Union Signal*, WCTU No. 2 president Mrs. M. J. O'Connel reported: "We cautiously avoided using the word *colored*" because "that would exclude any white sisters who might wish to work with us; in other words, we wanted it distinctly understood that we had no prejudice, for we believe *all* men are equal."[82]

Temperance attracted women of many religious denominations. Although Methodists were especially active, Quaker women organized the state's first postbellum temperance union in Greensboro in 1884. Laura Annie Ballinger Winston, a native of Guilford County, who was widowed at twenty-three and remained single thereafter, combined missionary zeal and pragmatic altruism in her temperance activity and her life's work. She was a Quaker missionary to Mexico for five years, a longtime teacher of the deaf, and for more than thirty-eight years an effective advocate of legislation to require temperance instruction in the public schools. Mary Chawner Woody, a leader in the North Carolina and American Quaker community, became the first president of the state WCTU. Known for "sowing seeds of truth," she had studied both law and public speaking. Woody served for ten years—traveling, lecturing, preaching, and pressing the state legislature to pass temperance laws—and was vice president of the national organization when Frances Willard was president.[83]

In membership and mission the Woman's Christian Temperance Union was as closely identified with women's culture as were the church missionary societies. Temperance reform allowed North Carolina women to extend their feminine domestic perspective to a reformist, public realm; encouraged them to work with women from other denominations to achieve their goals; provided an opportunity for white and black middle-class women to cooperate and to affirm their class identity; and permitted them to participate for the first time in a national reform campaign that combined northern and southern women.

Women and Agrarian Reform: "The Equal of Her Brother"

Deteriorating farm conditions in the post–Civil War decades had led to an agrarian reform movement by the 1880s, and women joined along with men, acting on their solidarity as farmers rather than as women. Three groups, the white Farmers' Alliance, the biracial Knights of Labor, and the Colored Farmers' Alliance, encouraged desperate and isolated rural women and men to organize to exert some control over land, credit, and crops. Although the groups attracted different constituencies and sometimes clashed on race and class issues, Delores Janiewski notes that they all promoted unity among their members through rituals and agendas.[84]

In the Farmers' Alliance—the most widespread and successful of the farm organizations in North Carolina—women played a vital role. By 1890 the alliance, which first appeared in the state in 1887, had more than 2,000 local organizations and 90,000 members. More than half were landowners; about a third, tenants; and the rest, merchants and such.

> Let us all put our shoulders to this great wheel, the Alliance, and push with one purpose in view—independence and freedom. As sisters of this Alliance we may feel we are silent factors in this work; we know we constantly need something to lean upon, like the honeysuckle upon the tree or fence.
> —Katie D. Moore, North Carolina local of the Southern Farmers' Alliance, 1888. (*Progressive Farmer*, July 24, 1888, as cited in Lu Ann Jones, "'The Task That Is Ours,'" *Institute News*)

Some 25,000 women made up one-fourth of the state's alliance membership in 1891. They had "equal privileges to men," spoke up in discussions of political and economic issues, and learned "all the secret words and signs."[85] Their active participation reflects a reality of farm life: the hard labor of men and women working together. No women headed any of the North Carolina locals, however, and divisive issues such as woman suffrage were avoided, but women had the rare opportunity to make decisions with men—something denied them in political and church groups. To be sure, none of the agrarian groups threatened the separate spheres doctrine—alliance and Knights women were expected to play a helpmate role and exert a moral domestic presence.

The agrarian reform movement provided a brief "democratic moment" when farmers—landowners and laborers, white and black, men and women—had an opportunity to unite on the basis of economic interests. At first nonpolitical, the farm organizations became advocates for higher crop prices, railroad regulation, limited interest rates, better public schools, an agricultural college, and a state-supported college for females. In 1891 a group of "embattled farmers" was elected to the General Assembly and helped to enact legislation that increased tax rates for public schools; established a normal school for white females, one for African Americans, and an agricultural college; and somewhat curtailed railroad privileges. In 1892 a faction in the Farmers' Alliance formed the People's or Populist Party, and in 1894 the Populists joined with the Republicans in a Fusion Party to overcome the Democratic stronghold on state politics. By 1894, however, the alliance had declined in influence and membership, its effectiveness as a nonpolitical farmers' organization diminished. Despite women's political activities in the Farmers' Alliance, Knights of Labor, and later Populist Party, no movement for women's rights or woman suffrage emerged, and no lasting interracial cooperation developed. The 1898 defeat of the Fusion Party ended the attempt by southern farm women to play a major role in society and politics.[86]

Women and Organized Patriotism: "A Land without Monuments Is a Land without Memories"

Society and politics were the raison d'être of women's voluntary associations dedicated to celebrating history. In a scenario of the separate spheres doctrine enacted statewide, educated and privileged white women of leading families became guardians of history and bearers of culture while their husbands attended to the business and politics that moved North Carolina toward New South prosperity. In their efforts to interpret the past and influence the present, such women established boundaries between themselves and others, including blacks, whom they deemed less worthy, and became connected with a regional or national network of similar women and organizations. Unlike benevolent and reform associations, which attempted to attract members to swell their ranks, patriotic groups such as the Society of the Colonial Dames of America (Fig. 7-45), Daughters of the

FIGURE 7-45. *Dr. Annie Lowrie Alexander*, Charlotte. In addition to serving on the staffs of local hospitals and Queens College and maintaining her medical practice, Alexander was active in the Colonial Dames and other women's organizations. (Courtesy of the Robinson Spangler Carolina Room, Public Library of Charlotte and Mecklenburg County)

FIGURE 7-46. *Members of the United Daughters of the Confederacy*, Buncombe County, 1903. (Courtesy of the North Carolina Collection, University of North Carolina at Chapel Hill)

Revolution, Daughters of the American Revolution (DAR), and United Daughters of the Confederacy (UDC) (Fig. 7-46) had an exclusionary bent. Many members of their families had been prominent in the colonial era; had served in the Revolutionary War and the Confederacy; were linked by marriage, education (the University of North Carolina for men, St. Mary's for women), and religion (generally Episcopalian); and comprised the business, industrial, and agricultural elite of the state. Promoting a version of history that stressed continuity between past and present, they shaped public memory in ways that supported their own authority and ignored any competing views that blacks or working-class whites might hold. Thus they strengthened their families' old position in the South's new order.[87]

During the 1890s, the same decade that state Democrats engaged in a vicious white supremacy campaign to regain political control, all of the major women's patriotic associations emerged in North Carolina. In 1900 members of the hereditary and patriotic groups joined with those Democratic leaders who felt that the state needed a "historical awakening" and formed the North Carolina Literary and Historical Association in Raleigh to promote the state's history and, not incidentally, their own family histories. Although their numbers were small, their influence was considerable. As one member of the Daughters of the Revolution commented, "It must be remembered that it is the chosen few who bear the burden and heat of the day. From time immemorial quality, not quantity, has held the power of the world in the balance."[88]

Immediately after the Civil War North Carolina women had formed Ladies Memorial Associations to ensure that the Confederate dead received proper burials. This effort is what Catherine Bishir has termed the first step for many genteel women into "public roles as guardians of regional memory and history."[89] By the 1890s women's groups had shifted from commemorating graves in Confederate cemeteries to erecting civic monuments in prominent public spaces. A series of such memorials was placed in Union Square in Raleigh, the state's political and cultural center. First was the Confederate Monument, presented in 1895 by the North Carolina Monument Association, a group of well-connected women who organized a statewide fund-raising campaign because "a land without monuments is a land without memories." Then in 1912 the North Carolina UDC placed a monument in Union Square to Private Henry Lawson Wyatt, the "First Confederate Soldier to Fall in Battle in the War Between the States." Two years later, there appeared a memorial to North Carolina Women of the Confederacy, which was privately donated.[90]

The United Daughters of the Confederacy, established nationally in 1894, quickly attracted North Carolina women, who had formed thirty-three chapters by 1901. The Wilmington chapter in 1898 opened a Confederate museum (now the New Hanover County Museum of the Lower Cape Fear) and in 1910 erected a monument to George Davis, a local man who had served as attorney general of the Confederacy. In 1913 Fayetteville women (who in 1868 had erected in Cross Creek Cemetery the first Confederate monument in North Carolina) persuaded the General Assembly to fund the Confederate Women's Home for widows and daughters of veterans.[91]

Women in the hereditary groups were early pioneers of women's history. The state officers of the Daughters of the

American Revolution directed their members to search for information about women's contributions and to publicize their findings. Endurance, resourcefulness, loyalty, self-reliance, self-sacrifice, and southernness were admired qualities in women who kept things going in war and peace. As DAR historian Laura Orr proudly noted in 1912: "Southern housewives worked hard to keep in order their great households, and at the same time exercised their gracious hospitality, while New England women feared witches and discussed sermons as their only intellectual diversion."[92]

Virginia Dare and the Edenton Tea Party ladies were favorite subjects. "From the day when Virginia Dare was so wise and obliging to open her eyes on North Carolina soil," declared Laura Orr, "the women of North Carolina have helped to make history." Dare's birth was seen as the foreshadowing of a significant role for women in American history: "The first white child born in America of English parents *was a girl*, and her birth and baptism would seem to dedicate this land to Christianized womanhood."[93]

Memory of Edenton ladies' "patriotism and zeal" inspired the Daughters of the Revolution in 1908 to commission a bronze plaque for the rotunda of the state capitol (Fig. 7-47). Led by two Raleigh women, Mary Hilliard Hinton, who had planned the state's exhibit at the 1907 Jamestown tercentenary, and Elvira Worth Moffitt, who had helped obtain congressional funds to install in the state capitol a painting of Virginia Dare, the Daughters raised money for the plaque by publishing the *North Carolina Booklet*, a popular journal that helped to define the canon of the state's history.[94]

FIGURE 7-47. *Unveiling of Daughters of the Revolution's memorial* to "Fifty-one Ladies of Edenton," Raleigh, 1908. (Courtesy of the North Carolina Division of Archives and History)

Organized Women and Municipal Housekeeping: "The City Is the Next Thing to the Home"

"May be we'll be a power for good. We feel almost sure of doing no harm." With this cautious manifesto, Mina Weil of Goldsboro, in 1899, told her daughter Gertrude of plans to form a women's club for "self-improvement and social betterment."[95] Within a decade or so women, black and white, had formed women's clubs and service organizations in towns and cities across the state. The clubs differed depending on where they were located—Bryson City, Laurinburg, Manteo, Wilmington, Greensboro, or Asheville—and on the interests, education, and personalities of the members and leaders. But having a local women's club was considered a sign of progress and being up-to-date. Both black and white women joined the separate clubs in large numbers.

The white clubs, whose members were generally well-to-do and well connected, began as self-education groups. Most took on community projects like libraries and education, ventured into what was called "municipal housekeeping" and public welfare projects for people in a lower socioeconomic group, and sometimes embraced issues of social justice and labor reform. Generally their reform activities were tempered by the members' close ties with politicians and industrialists.[96]

Black women also were interested in literary and cultural topics, but the absence of social services for blacks motivated them to tackle broader community problems. Their organizations worked to improve life for their people—the motto of the National Association of Colored Women's Clubs (founded in 1896) was "Lifting as We Climb"—and to encourage interracial cooperation, challenge racial stereotypes, confront racial violence, and promote political and economic equality. The majority of members were professionals, mostly teachers, many with their own incomes, or were married to business and professional men who supported their reform efforts. For Sarah Dudley Petty of New Bern, taking part in club work was only one of many ways she sought to elevate her race. Petty represented the optimism of educated, middle-class blacks who participated in the economic, social, and religious life of their community. Black clubwomen had a different relationship with those they set out to help than

> To secure and enforce civil and political rights for ourselves and our group.
>
> To obtain for our colored women the opportunity of reaching the highest standard in all fields of human endeavor.
>
> To promote interracial understanding so that justice and goodwill may prevail among all people.
>
> —Motto, National Association of Colored Women's Clubs. (Scott, *Natural Allies*, 147)

did their white counterparts. They understood that race linked them to rural, poor, and uneducated blacks in a South where segregation, disfranchisement, and lynching were all too common.[97]

Southern women, black and white, lagged behind northern women in bringing clubs together into a more comprehensive organization. Not until 1902 was the North Carolina Federation of Women's Clubs (NCFWC), destined to become the largest statewide organization for white women, established (Fig. 7-48). Its founders, Lucy Bramlett Patterson and Sallie Southall Cotten, whose biography follows this chapter, had been impressed with the variety of women's accomplishments at the 1893 Chicago World's Fair. They hoped to inspire similar activity among women at home, though it took nearly a decade. Black women had formed literary and social associations in Raleigh, Charlotte, and other towns with middle-class black communities in the 1880s, but not until 1909 was the North Carolina Federation of Negro Women's Clubs (NCFNWC) founded by educator Charlotte Hawkins Brown, whose biography follows Chapter 8. The state, regional, and national organizations stimulated the growth of local clubs, which generally took their marching orders from the top. After federation, women's clubs grew steadily throughout the state.[98]

In the early 1900s women's clubs were considered radical. A Chapel Hill critic linked the high divorce rate in New England to women's participation in clubs. Another observer suggested that "women who have minds and ideas of their own, and those who have homes and loved ones to care for" should find their lives full enough without needing to join a club. Despite the assurances of clubwomen such as Mrs. Al Fairbrother that it "was not through lack of confidence in the masculine mind and heart that brought the Woman's Club into existence, but to cultivate a virgin soil rich in possibilities," the clubs made many southern men uneasy.[99]

The work of organized women was never intended to jeopardize home and family. Indeed, it was just the opposite. Both black and white clubwomen adhered to a belief in the importance of women's moral influence within the family as the cornerstone of society. It was women's domestic role that qualified them to tackle problems of social and public welfare that men had overlooked. "The organized women's club is to the community what the individual woman is to the home circle," declared NCFWC president Clara Swift Souther Lingle in 1915. "One woman alone can keep her house spotless, a hundred women acting together can make civic and moral righteousness not only a possibility but an actuality."[100]

Elvira Moffitt, who with Fannie Heck had founded the Raleigh Women's Club, considered municipal reform well within a woman's sphere—"As the City is the next thing to

FIGURE 7-48. *Members of the North Carolina Federation of Women's Clubs*, 1905. (Courtesy of the North Carolina Division of Archives and History)

the home it is but natural that she should feel a vital interest in its progress."[101] In 1904 Raleigh clubwomen, inspired by the monumental planning of the 1893 Chicago World's Fair and the City Beautiful movement that spread across America afterward, presented an ambitious plan to improve their city with wide streets, newly planted trees, and civic monuments.

Middle-class white women gained another foothold in public life with their activities in the Woman's Association for the Betterment of Public Schoolhouses (WABPS),

FIGURE 7-49. *The McIver family*: Charles, president of the State Normal and Industrial College, his wife Lula Martin, and their four children, Guilford County, 1890s. Lula McIver, an educated "New Woman," was active in numerous educational and community affairs and spearheaded a statewide campaign to improve schoolhouses. (Courtesy of the Archives, Jackson Library, University of North Carolina at Greensboro)

founded the same year as the NCFWC, in 1902. The impetus came from State Normal president Charles D. McIver and Governor Charles B. Aycock who, as members of the Southern Education Board, spearheaded a campaign to improve public schools, thereby improving the habits, behaviors, and lives of white working people. Lula Martin McIver, Charles's wife, enthusiastically mobilized WABPS women as an auxiliary group, charged with the "housekeeping" of the dilapidated schoolhouses (Fig. 7-49). The women were "schoolmothers" who would transform schoolhouses into neat and tidy "schoolhomes." They attacked the problem on two fronts—health and beautification—by installing sanitary privies and removing debris from school grounds, planting gardens and trees and establishing playgrounds, and hanging patriotic pictures and providing bookcases and comfortable furniture in schoolrooms. Elvira Moffitt and Lucy Patterson traveled the state spreading the WABPS message to a membership almost 90 percent of which consisted of either young teachers without children or middle-aged women whose children were grown. WABPS women concentrated their efforts on white schoolchildren. In 1905 Sue Tomlinson Hollowell, who had organized black women and children for temperance in the 1880s, attempted to recruit blacks for the WABPS group in Granville County. She was sharply reminded by Mrs. McIver and the state superintendent of education that WABPS members should never be involved directly in black school improvement. The belief in women's special understanding of the educational needs of children led the WABPS in 1912–13 to join with the North Carolina Teachers Association and the NCFWC to campaign for women on school boards.[102]

As white men promoted the economic development that fueled New South prosperity, women black and white coped with the social consequences. The women accomplished much, but they were bound by racial as well as class loyalties and limited by the degree of real power they had to shape North Carolina society. Volunteer activities gave women a place in that society, increased their self-confidence and sense of their own power, and encouraged some to think that women needed the same political rights as men if they were to influence public policy.[103]

Anna Julia Haywood Cooper

1858–1964

Anna J. Cooper, Oberlin College, 1884. (Courtesy of Oberlin College Archives, Oberlin, Ohio)

When Hannah Stanley Haywood, a slave woman living in Raleigh, gave birth to a daughter in the summer of 1858, prospects for the child's future were grim. That she grew up to become the now-celebrated Anna Julia Haywood Cooper, author, teacher, and race leader, is in part a testament to her mother's care. And although Anna (or "Annie," as she was first called) left home when she was twenty-three to fulfill her ambition for the best education available, she credited North Carolina with having given her "a goodly heritage."[1]

Anna was the third and last child and the only daughter of Hannah Stanley Haywood; her much older brothers, Rufus and Andrew, became musicians. Her father is believed to have been her mother's slave master, George Washington Haywood, a Raleigh lawyer.[2] Anna later alluded to her parentage in a way that suggests how much she wanted to belong to American history: "The part of my ancestors that did not come over in the Mayflower in 1620, arrived, I am sure, a year earlier in the fateful Dutch trader that put in at Jamestown in 1619. . . . I believe that the third source of my individual stream comes . . . from the vanishing Red Men, which ought . . . [to make me a] genuine F.F.A. (First Family of America)." In another account of her birth, she was more plainspoken: "My mother was a slave & the finest woman I have ever known. . . . Presumably my father was her master, if so I owe him not a sou & she was always too modest & shamefaced ever to mention him." This assertion was later repeated: "I owe nothing to my white father beyond the initial act of procreation."[3]

In 1858, the year of Anna's birth, Raleigh's black population consisted of 1,621 slaves and 466 free blacks. The name "Haywood" was prominent in capital city life. The Haywood family owned more than 200 slaves (most of them on outlying plantations) and had manumitted only one. Anna, her mother, and two brothers were freed only with the Emancipation Proclamation of 1863. Near the time of her daughter's birth, Hannah must have been "hired out" to work in the home of a Raleigh doctor, Charles Busbee, and his wife Annie, for whom Annie Julia may have been named. Although Hannah was learning to write when Anna was a child, the 1870 Raleigh census indicates that Hannah, her son Andrew, and her daughter-in-law were all illiterate. It is not clear how Anna learned to read at an early age, but by the time she was about eight she was prepared to enter a phase of her education that she remembered as "my world during . . . the most critical [period] in any girl's life."[4]

St. Augustine Normal and Collegiate Institute opened in Raleigh in 1868, under the sponsorship of the Protestant Episcopal Church and with assistance from the federal Freedmen's Bureau, only three years after General William T. Sherman's march through the city. The mission of the school was to prepare men for the ministry and teachers for the education of their own race. Officers of the Freedmen's Bureau reported that when black children were asked what they hoped to be when they grew up, the answer was almost always, "I'm going to be a teacher."[5] Anna could have been one of those who were asked; she enrolled and boarded in the home of the first principal, the Reverend J. Brinton Smith, former secretary and general agent of the Episcopal Freedmen's Commission, who awarded her a yearly stipend of one hundred dollars. Students were admitted tuition-free if they could demonstrate a degree of proficiency, and Anna's skills were sufficient for her to be designated as a "pupil-teacher." Within a few months, the number of pupils rose to twenty, and by the time Anna graduated in 1877, there were 127 students, many of them adult men enrolled in theology classes in preparation for the ministry. By then, 160 students from St. Augustine's were teaching in public schools.[6]

As Anna Cooper later recalled her years at St. Augustine's:

> I had devoured what was put before me, and, like Oliver Twist, was looking around to ask for more. I constantly felt (as I suppose many an ambitious girl has felt) a thumping from within unanswered by any beckoning from without. Class after class was organized for these ministerial candidates (many of them men who had been preaching before I was born). Into every one of these classes I was expected to go. . . .
>
> Finally a Greek class was to be formed. My inspiring preceptor informed me that Greek had never been taught in the school, but that he was going to form a class *for the candidates for the ministry*, and if I liked I might join it. I replied—humbly I hope, as became a female of the human species—that I would like very much to study Greek, and that I was thankful for the opportunity, and so it went on. A boy, however meager his equipment and shallow his pretentions, had only to declare a floating intention to study theology and he could get all the support, encouragement and stimulus he needed, be absolved from work and invested beforehand with all the dignity of his far away office. While a self-supporting girl had to struggle on by teaching in the summer and working after school hours to keep up with her board bills, and actually to fight her way against positive discouragements to the higher education.[7]

On June 27, 1877, she married George A. C. Cooper in the Episcopal church on the campus of St. Augustine's. Cooper, who was more than a decade older than Anna and from the British West Indies, was studying for the ministry at St. Augustine's. Each continued to take courses and to teach. Anna Cooper faced a sudden tragedy when her husband died two years later, leaving her a widow at age twenty-one.

After almost fourteen years at St. Augustine's, she "earnestly desired to take an advanced course in some superior Northern College," as she wrote in her application to Oberlin College. Oberlin, founded in 1833, was known to many African Americans as a station on the underground railroad. In 1862 at Oberlin, Mary Jane Patterson, also born in Raleigh, had been the first black woman in America to graduate from college; afterward, she became principal of the Preparatory School for Colored Youth in Washington, D.C. (the forerunner of the Dunbar School), a position that Cooper would hold about twenty years later.[8]

When Anna applied to Oberlin, she was able to say that she had read in Greek or Latin the works of Caesar, Virgil, Cicero, Plato, Thucydides, and Homer and was proficient in advanced courses in mathematics. The classical curriculum informed her tastes for the rest of her life and left a lasting example of the kind of program she believed the best schools should offer.

The class of 1884 at Oberlin College enrolled three black women who would become outstanding leaders. In addition to Anna Cooper, there were Mary Church and Ida Gibbs, who were roommates in Ladies Hall. All three chose the "Gentleman's" program, not the "Ladies literary degree." This decision meant, for example, that Anna was allowed to take Greek. At Oberlin, she, like many other students, boarded in a faculty home, and she felt herself fortunate to live for all three years of college with the Charles Henry Churchill family. Professor Churchill had founded the Physics Department, taught courses in many subjects, and was generally regarded as the "genius" of the faculty.

The Churchills, who often had student boarders, had had African Americans in their home before Anna. The family was large: seven sons and a daughter. Each Sunday afternoon the Churchills gathered for the most important family occasion of the week; music was at the center of their enjoyment. Almost everyone played an instrument, and they all sang. The large front lawn of their rambling home, set far back from the road, was a popular place for college parties. Lively discussions transpired at mealtime, and afterward the professor helped students with their lessons. Mrs. Churchill apparently had the capacity to make every person feel a part of the family, including Anna Cooper, who many years later would still ask after "Mother Churchill." In addition to domestic chores assigned in return for her room and board, Anna held other jobs to earn her way through college. One of these was reading to a student who had failing eyesight, and another was coaching students in third-term algebra.

One of the Churchill sons, Alfred, recalled that "two of the best scholars my father ever had" were "women of the Negro race." From the context of his remarks, it is likely that one of them was Anna Haywood Cooper. Alfred also described having heard Cooper read a paper at her commencement: she "delivered it mannishly, not pretending to read an 'essay' as a lady properly should."[9]

After graduating in 1884, Anna taught at Wilberforce University. In 1885, when she returned to Raleigh and St. Augustine's College, her mother was nearly seventy years old, and Anna assumed responsibility for her care. In addition to teaching mathematics, Latin, and Greek, she established a Sabbath School and was active in community organizations. She bought property in Raleigh and began building a house. At that point Oberlin officials were asked to recommend a graduate of that school for the faculty of the Preparatory School for Colored Youth in Washington, D.C., and Cooper's name was put forward; she applied and was offered the position. In 1887 she joined the faculty as a teacher of Latin; in 1901 she was named principal of the M Street School (later the Paul Laurence Dunbar High School).

As school principal, Cooper had to satisfy many different factions in a city rife with political conflicts. Among some blacks, Booker T. Washington's Tuskegee plan for vocational education was growing in popularity; others endorsed the more academic course of W. E. B. Du Bois. In an address at M Street School, Du Bois urged blacks to develop their intellect. He gave the speech during the second year of Cooper's tenure as principal, and no one could have heard it more sympathetically than she. She was particularly proud of her success in having graduates admitted, without qualification, to such Ivy League schools as Harvard, Yale, Cornell, and Brown. During the debate about which kind of education would prevail, a handful of powerful blacks charged that Cooper lacked firm discipline over students and even raised questions about her own conduct. In a move that a friend called "outrageous" and "a plot for the undoing of Mrs. Cooper," a case was made for her removal. Had she been able to hold out until the emerging power of Du Bois solidified or had she been more skilled politically, she might have remained. But in her words, "the industrializing wave" swamped her. In 1906 she was removed by the Board of Education as principal of the M Street School. She left Washington and for the next four years taught at Jefferson University in St. Louis, Missouri. When the M Street's leadership changed, she was reinstated on the faculty in 1910 and remained there until 1929. Back among Washington friends, she made her own home a place of intellectual, social, and cultural life.[10]

From the time she first moved to Washington, Cooper was absorbed in the life of close friends. They included Dr. Alexander Crummell, rector of St. Luke's Episcopal Church, where Cooper was a member (she regarded him as "the Moses of the race"), and the Reverend and Mrs. Francis Grimké. Grimké, the son of a slave woman and a wealthy Charleston, South Carolina, planter, was pastor of the Fifteenth Street Presbyterian Church. His father's sisters, Sarah and Angelina, were well-known abolitionists. Grimké's wife, Charlotte L. Forten, Cooper's devoted friend until Charlotte's death in 1914, was the granddaughter of the well-known Philadelphia abolitionist leader, James Forten, and had herself done important work with freed blacks in Port Royal, South Carolina.[11] The Grimké and Cooper homes, much like the Churchill residence in Oberlin, were filled with family and friends and sustained by musical afternoons and lively conversations. Anna shared with these friends the belief that where one lives is "not merely a house to shelter the body, but a home to sustain and refresh the mind, a home where friends foregather for interchange of ideas and agreeable association of spirits." For some thirty years they met regularly on Friday evenings at the Grimké house for discussions of art and on Sunday evenings at the Cooper home for music.[12]

In addition to her work at the M Street School, Cooper was involved in forming and sustaining other groups for the advancement of her race, especially women. She helped to charter the Colored Women's League of Washington, the Colored Settlement School (the first of its kind in the city), and the Phillis Wheatley YWCA, which was founded before the white YWCA. She attended conferences far and wide—among them, the first National Conference of Colored Women in Boston (1895) and a Pan-African Conference in London (1900), where she delivered, along with W. E. B. Du Bois, one of the major addresses. She was the only woman among the original forty members of the prestigious American Negro Academy, founded in 1897 by Alexander Crummell; indeed, she was chosen to give the inaugural address to this group of distinguished scholars.

These activities suggest the magnitude of Cooper's work, but there was another side to her life. The year after she arrived in Washington for her first teaching assignment, Anna opened her home to the two adolescent children of a North Carolina friend who had died. With the same capacity to adapt to sudden change that she had revealed when widowed after only two years of marriage, she adjusted her life to accommodate the needs of fifteen-year-old Lula Love and her younger brother John, establishing what she lovingly called her "North Carolina colony." If motherhood and a new job posed a challenge early in Cooper's career, she faced an even greater one several years following her reinstatement at the M Street School when she assumed responsibility for her brother Andrew's five grandchildren on the death of his son; the youngsters ranged in age from six months (a girl named Anna Cooper Haywood) to twelve years. At the time, she was fifty-six years old. One might have echoed the words of the judge speaking in the children's court as Cooper accepted the guardianship: "My, but you are a brave woman!" To make a place for the children, she purchased an old spacious house in LeDroit Park, which, she recalled, "in the historic past had been forbidden ground for colored people except as servants." Despite the burden of a substantial mortgage, Cooper restored the house to much of its former glory, over the years filling it with art objects and friends. The children went on to preparatory schools and colleges (her namesake attended St. Augustine's).[13]

Child care interrupted the academic work Cooper was undertaking toward an advanced degree. From 1911 to 1913 she had used her summer vacations from teaching to study in Paris, and in 1914 she began doctoral studies in summer courses at Columbia University. In 1924, she returned to Europe, apparently with considerable opposition from the high school. After two summers of study and having transferred her credits, she received a doctorate in philosophy from the Sorbonne. She was sixty-five years old.[14]

Dr. Anna J. Cooper returned to teach at the Dunbar School and to write and lecture. In 1929, at age seventy-one, she was required by school authorities to retire after more than forty years of teaching. Her involvement in civic activities was still extensive, however. A new opportunity came when she accepted the presidency of Washington's Frelinghuysen University, an unorthodox collection of "schools" founded in 1906 "for colored working people." At Frelinghuysen innovative education had been overshadowed by burdening financial costs and the conflicting needs of black people. For twelve years Cooper operated the school out of her home, directing, teaching, and presiding over formal occasions. An old woman of aristocratic bearing was attempting to reach out to the "masses." Her career ended as it had begun—among people of her own race struggling to raise themselves through education.

After retiring in 1940, Cooper devoted herself to the task of writing a Grimké family history, requested of her by her old friend, the Reverend Francis Grimké.[15] For the last two decades of her life, she continued to live in the home she dearly loved, often visited by friends and former students. She died on February 27, 1964, at the age of 105, and was buried in Raleigh following a service at St. Augustine's Chapel. There in the chapel, where she had donated a stained-glass window in memory of her husband, Anna Cooper and St. Augustine's College are honored together.

Beyond the study of her life, what remains for students of history are her texts. In addition to uncollected letters, poems, speeches, and essays, there are two notable publications. One is her doctoral thesis, "The Attitude of France toward Slavery during the Revolution," which one critic calls her most important work. The other is *A Voice from the South*, which establishes Cooper as an important feminist writer. For her race she claimed the urgent need for universal education, to lift blacks out of their history of chattel slavery into the mainstream of American life. For her gender she claimed the right to equality, challenging especially the men of her race to examine their own negative attitudes toward women's advancement. Moreover, she saw women as leaders of the race: she believed that only the black woman can say "when and where I enter, in the quiet, undisputed dignity of my womanhood, without violence and without suing or special patronage, then and there the whole *Negro race enters with me*."[16]

Sallie Southall Cotten

1846–1929

Sallie Southall Cotten. (Courtesy of the North Carolina Division of Archives and History)

In the summer of 1893, as if looking into a kaleidoscope, Sallie Southall Cotten saw a new world made up of changing colors and patterns. The old world was the farm in eastern North Carolina, and the new was the architectural splendor of the Chicago World's Fair. Back home, Cottendale filled with shadows when lamps were lit at sundown, the field work over for the day, but when night came to Chicago the exposition site suddenly was illuminated by thousands of electric lights. Visitors would remember it as the "White City." From the Tar River of Pitt County to the shores of Lake Michigan, Sallie Southall Cotten, North Carolina educator and women's leader, had come a long way. "It is like a dream," she confided to her journal, "like an Arabian Nights tale, this wonderful city of all nations—with its buildings grand within and without—glittering in the sun and holding veritably the treasures of the earth."[1]

Sallie had arrived at the fair by the sort of chance that often marked her life, and with pluck and determination she seized every opportunity to learn new things. Anne Firor Scott, writing about the "transforming power" that the 1893 exposition had on women, cites Cotten as a case study. "After a summer in Chicago," Scott observes, "Cotten came home to launch a career that would last the rest of her life."[2] When there were disappointments, she dealt with them in her stalwart fashion.

Sallie Southall was born on June 13, 1846, to Susannah Sims Southall and Thomas J. Southall in Lawrenceville, Virginia, the last of five daughters. A younger brother, John Richard, became a successful lawyer, but throughout her life, for unexplained reasons, Sallie seldom mentioned his name. There were other family matters that must have troubled her—her father's inability to support his family, and her separation from her mother when Sallie was an adolescent—but she always adjusted. Difficult challenges often helped to determine her course, rather than to deter her.[3]

In 1859, when her father's brother, John Wesley Southall, offered to take one of the girls to live with his family and attend school where he was a trustee, thirteen-year-old Sallie was ready to go. Life with her cousins in Murfreesboro, North Carolina, provided security, an impressive home, and good times. Three years of public school and studies at Wesleyan Female College (established by Methodists in 1853) gave Sallie her first sustained intellectual challenge. But the Civil War forced the closing of the school, and three years after she had settled in she was uprooted again. This time she crossed the state by train to the central Piedmont and enrolled at Greensboro Female College, also founded by Methodists with the help of her uncle. Despite the turmoil in Greensboro, a Confederate railroad depot, the students and faculty stuck to their tasks, and in 1863 Sallie Southall graduated at age seventeen. For the next several years she moved about, supporting herself by tutoring and looking after young children. In one of those homes, that of the Johnson family with eight children in Edgecombe County, she met Robert Randolph Cotten, a Confederate cavalryman.

The next year Sallie and Robert were engaged, and the year after that they were married, on March 13, 1866. She was twenty and he was twenty-seven. They were better off than many young couples. Robert had a friend in Baltimore who lent him money to start a mercantile business. Sallie had enthusiasm and energy. Self-reliance was sorely needed in the defeated South, and, where it was found, things began to take root again. Robert Cotten struggled in his business enterprises, but every move—and there were many in the first ten years of their marriage—brought him closer to his dream of owning a plantation. During those years Sallie had her hands full with six children. Then, in 1878, Robert moved the family to a place they would soon call Cottendale, a thousand acres on which sat a rambling, comfortable farmhouse. Although his successes were often offset by crop failures and economic depressions that plagued the South, he set a good example—he was a hardworking farmer who attended agricultural conventions and served in the state legislature.

For half a century Cottendale was the much-beloved home of Sallie and Robert and their family, and the house parties and dinners for their children and guests, as well as corn shuckings and log rollings with neighbors, would be long remembered. To find so much good talk, food, games, dances, and visitors down a country road was evidence of Sallie's ability to make things happen; their friends exalted the Cottens' southern hospitality.[4] Sallie was an efficient homemaker. She had help for certain tasks, such as sewing, when Sarah Blount, "a middle-aged spinster of good family," went to live with the Cottens, but apparently it was only late in life that she turned over the main responsibilities to a housekeeper.[5] Sallie recognized that she had more than most farmwives—her home included a piano, a sewing machine, an upholstered rocker, a bathroom on the back porch, and good books and magazines.

But the lives of less fortunate families were among her concerns. Housekeeping also meant keeping a community house: she invited neighborhood children to a school she organized at Cottendale, she worked through her Episcopal Church to help families in need, and she tried to give special attention to tenants living on the farm. For a woman who loved travel and cities and conversation and culture, rural life with a large family and many responsibilities required cheerfulness and initiative. Sallie and Robert had both qualities.

In 1883 a tragedy shattered their happiness when their oldest son, Robbie, on his fifteenth birthday, drowned while swimming in the Tar River, a favorite sporting place of the Cottens. Perhaps the months following Robbie's death were the ones her son Bruce remembered when he noted in his memoirs that his mother's usual cheerful countenance could give way to "gloomy broodings." Her recourse was to take on more work at home and in the community, to read more—she enrolled in a kind of correspondence book club with readers in Chapel Hill—and to write. Always a busy letter writer, she often corresponded with her most intimate woman friend, Kate Connor. Sallie and Kate had become companions when Kate, younger by nine years, had been engaged to teach the Cotten children at home; after she left, Sallie continued to write her until Kate's sudden death only three years after Robbie's. When Sallie was most discouraged about doing the best thing for her children, she would pour out her sense of failure to Kate.

Something new came Cotten's way in 1890, when Governor Elias Carr, friend and neighbor, appointed her as an alternate lady manager for the Chicago World's Fair to be held in 1893—the fair's first official role for women, largely brought about through the efforts of Susan B. Anthony. Because the two regular North Carolina delegates could not attend many meetings, the main duties fell to Sallie Cotten, who would become the most familiar presence at the North Carolina exhibit. The assignment was a stroke of good luck, and Cotten made it the turning point of her public life.

A campaign was under way to raise funds for a North Carolina building at the fair; she determined that women should participate and traveled across the state to enlist their support. Although the proceeds from bake sales and community programs fell far short of the goal ($4,000 of $10,000 was raised) and the legislature refused to make up the difference, Cotten succeeded in getting the attention of women. Wherever she went, she made and kept friends. Her enthusiasm and energy especially captivated women and inspired them to work together on behalf of the project; it was only a matter of time before they decided to do something more than meet for social gatherings (on occasion, she felt the need to remind her friends not to spend so much time preparing the refreshment table).

Cotten also collected materials for the North Carolina exhibit, including books written by North Carolina women. Her display of these treasures went on to win her a medal at the fair. She tracked down the original image of the Edenton Tea Party and had a copy made to take to Chicago. But she was proudest of the tribute she secured for Virginia Dare, the first white child born in America. It was an impressive desk, carved out of wood from Roanoke Island by Kate Cheshire of Tarboro; later it was used in the boardroom of the lady managers at the fair. Cotten's delight and tenacity in recounting the legend of Virginia Dare would be the signature of her Chicago experiences.

After an initial meeting with the board in 1890 in Chicago, Cotten returned when the fair opened in 1893; for four months she lived in a hotel and went to the fairgrounds almost every day. When she remained in her room, it was usually to write to her children, reminding Agnes, at school in Washington, D.C., to brush her teeth, and to express concern to her husband about the health of various farm families at home. Beginning on

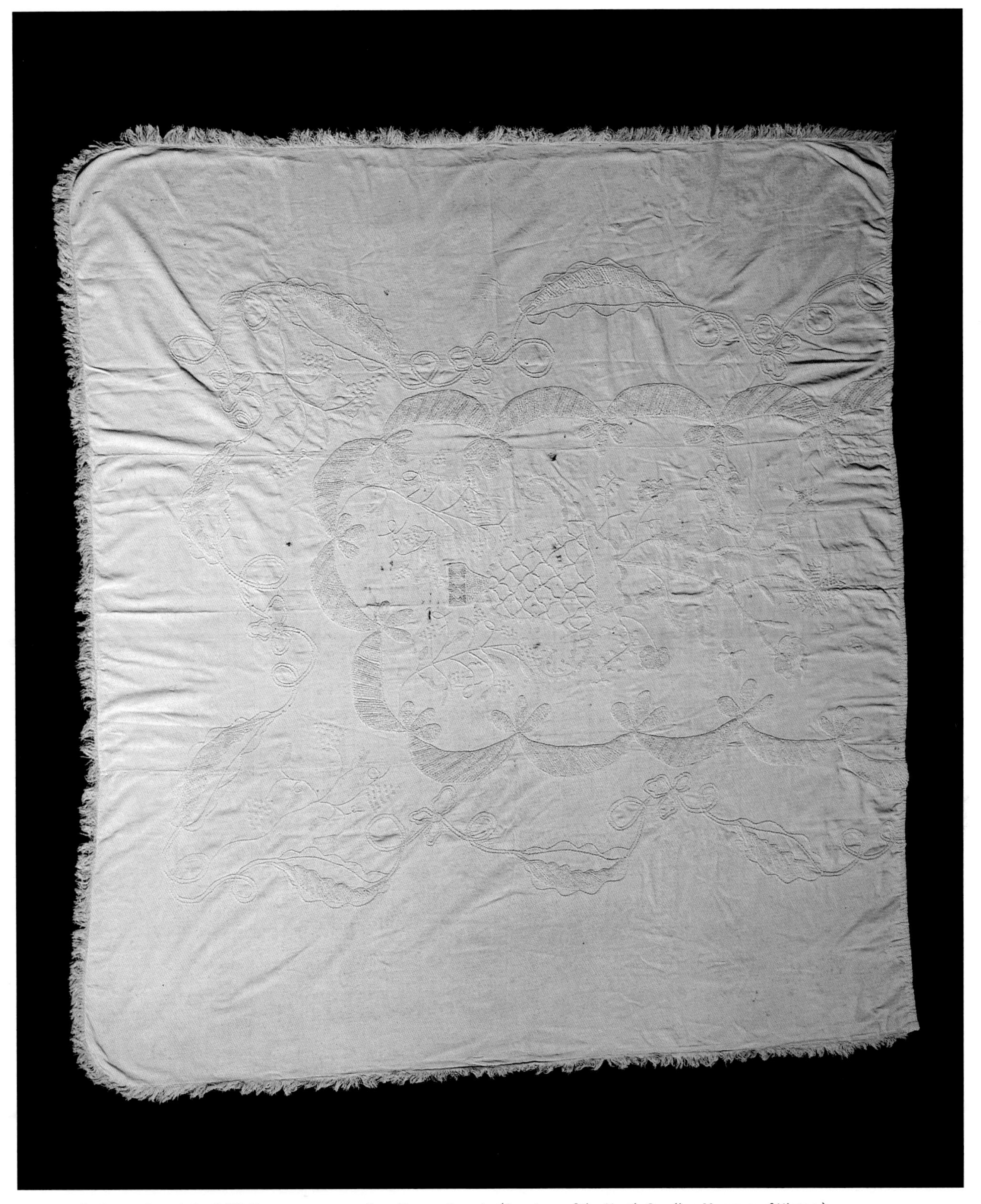

PLATE 1. *Bedspread made by Edith Bruner,* ca. 1750–1800, Rowan County. (Courtesy of the North Carolina Museum of History)

PLATE 2. *Mourning brooch*, Lenoir County, 1800. Anna Caswell White received this brooch from her husband to commemorate their son John, who died at four years old. The urn-topped plinth is inscribed "In Maternal Sorrow," and on the back is a glass-covered oval that contains a blond hair and the initials "JAW"—John and Anna White, a son's memory and mother's love, linked forever in a keepsake. (Courtesy of the North Carolina Museum of History)

PLATE 3. Guilford Limner, *Elizabeth Dick Lindsay and Daughter Susanna Julia Lindsay*, watercolor, Guilford County, ca. 1825. Elizabeth Dick married Andrew Lindsay of Reedy Fork Plantation on the Haw River in 1812. During the first twenty-six years of their marriage, Elizabeth—Betsy—had nine children, three of whom probably died in their first year. The couple was painted by an itinerant artist in two matching portraits. Here, Betsy Lindsay sits beside her sixth child and fifth daughter, Susanna Julia Emmaline. The knitting needles, handiwork, and flower-filled vase signify her domestic role in the family. (Private collection)

PLATE 4. *Gold medal awarded to Jane E. Stanback*, Euphradian Academy, Richmond County, 1826. Medals were tangible reminders that the young scholar had successfully completed her courses in literature, music, and painting. Many schools awarded prizes, medals, and certificates for the "bests" in different subjects at commencement. St. Mary's School, by contrast, offered "no medal, or prizes, or stimulants of any kind to rivalry or emulation." Instead, the school expected and received from its pupils "zeal in their studies and order in their conduct, from motives of duty to their school, to themselves, to their parents, and to their God." (Courtesy of the North Carolina Museum of History)

PLATE 5. Harriet W. Higgs, *Sampler*, embroidery, Halifax County, 1841. Although female education was more academically rigorous in the nineteenth century than in the eighteenth, girls still were expected to be capable with the needle, to sew for themselves, and to direct the work of others. Harriet Higgs learned both patience and platitudes as she laboriously embroidered her ABCs and various proverbs on a sampler at the Vine Hill Academy, Scotland Neck, in 1841. (Courtesy of the North Carolina Museum of History)

ABCDEFGHIJKLMNOPQRSTUVW-
XYZ. abcdefghijklmnopqrstuvwxyz. 123456789

123456789101112131415161718192021.

ABCDEFGHIJKLMN
OPQRSTUVWXYZ.

Remember now thy Creator in the days of thy youth.

If good we plant not vice will fill the place
And rankest weeds the richest soils deface

The piety of a child is sweeter than the incense of Persia offered to the sun

Harriet W Higgs
Vine Hill Academy
Scotland Neck
Aug't 1841

yea more delicious than odours wafted from a field of Arabian spices by the western gales.

Honour and shame from no condition rise.
Act well your part there all the honour lies.

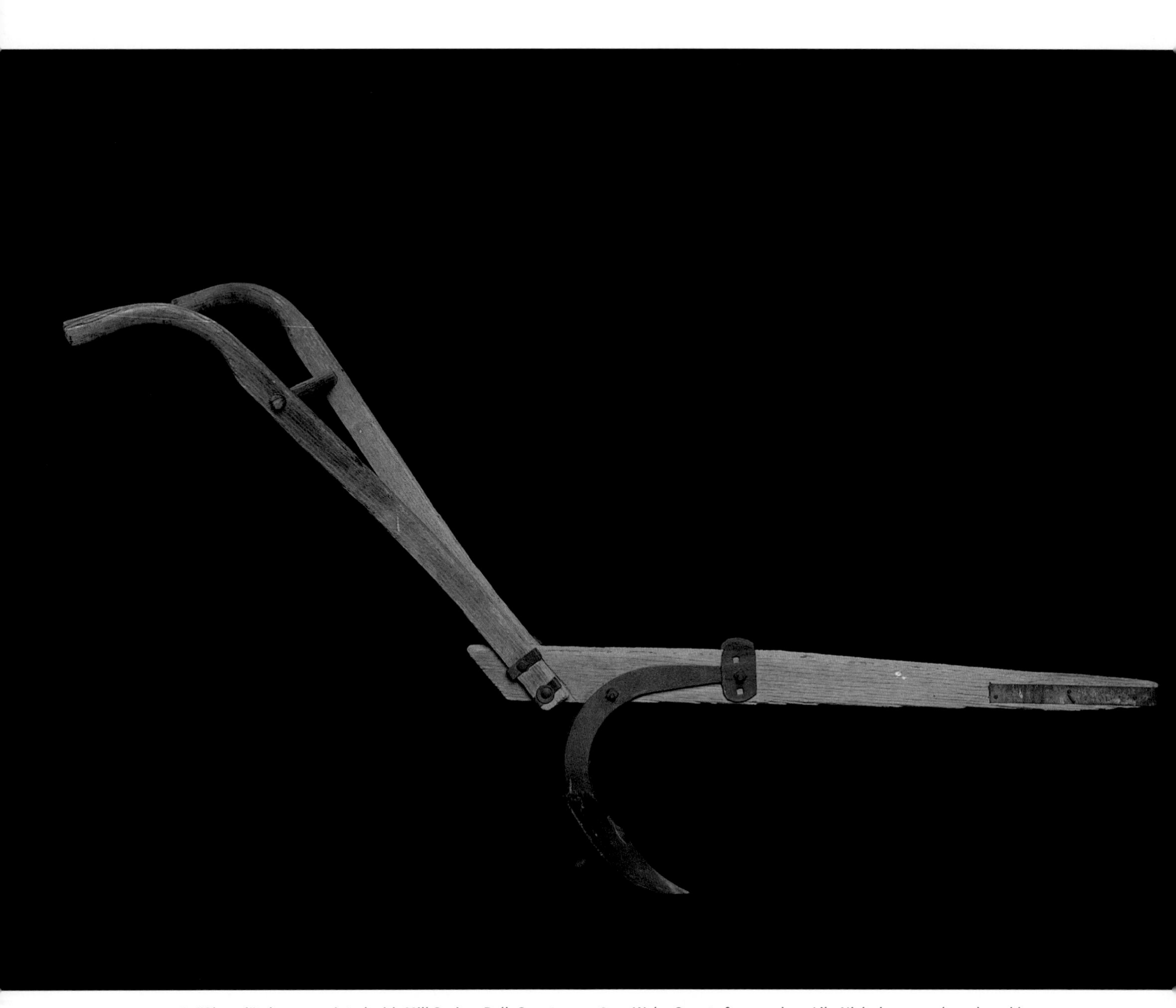

PLATE 6. *"Shovel" plow associated with Mill Spring*, Polk County, ca. 1850. Wake County former slave Lila Nichols remembered working all week and her "mammy plowin' wid a two-horse plow all de year when she warn't clearin' new ground or diggin' ditches" (Rawick, *American Slave*, 15:149). (Courtesy of the North Carolina Museum of History)

PLATE 7. *Confederate Monument quilt*, made by the ladies of Fayetteville, silk, 1865. This quilt was made as a raffle prize to raise funds for the Confederate Monument at Old Cross Creek Cemetery and then given to Jefferson Davis. The first Civil War monument in North Carolina and the second in the South, the Cross Creek monument was erected in Fayetteville through the cooperative efforts of the women of that city, led by Maria Spear and Jessie Kyle. (Courtesy of the Museum of the Confederacy, Richmond, Virginia)

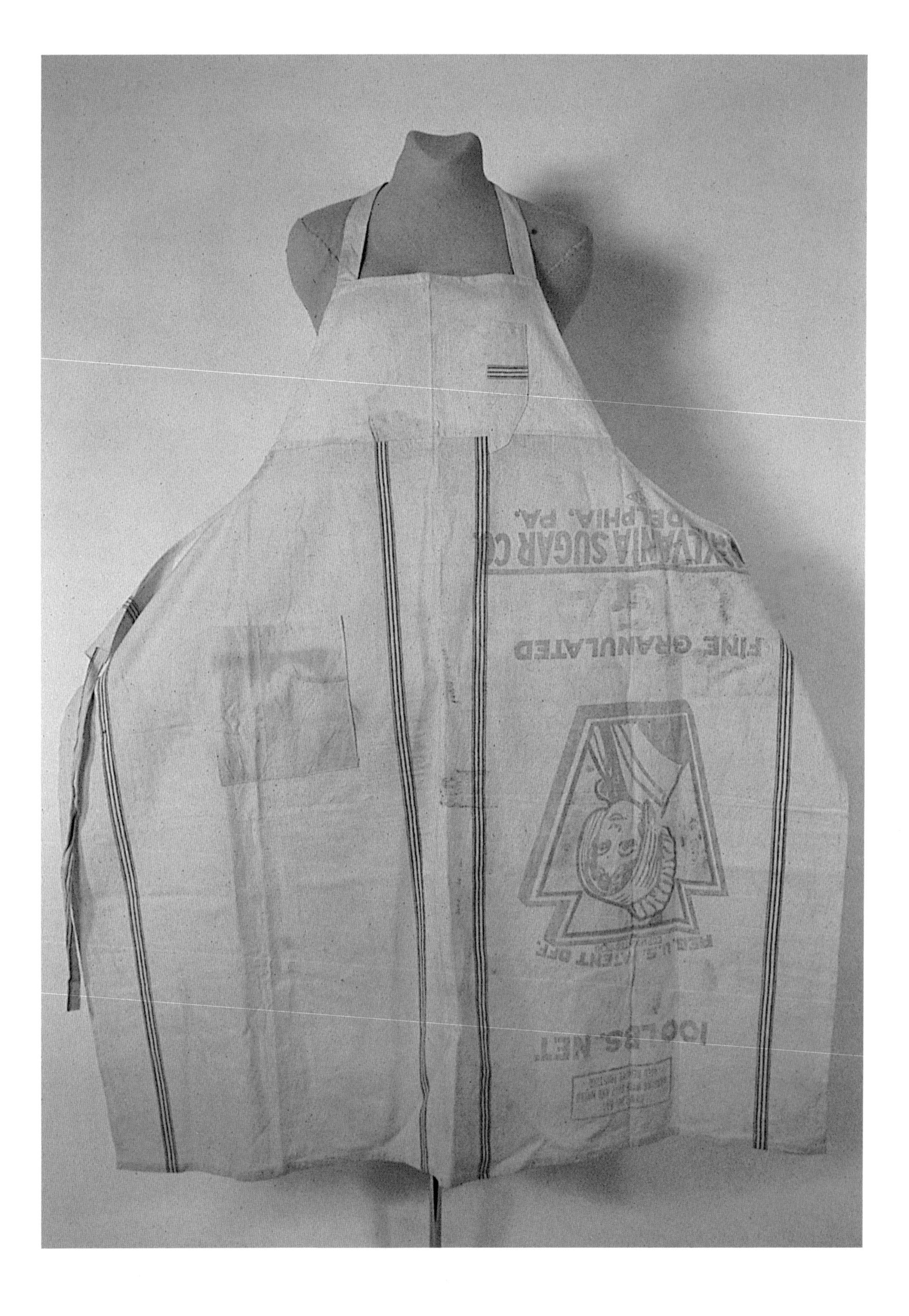
SUGAR CO.
FINE GRANULATED
100 LBS. NET

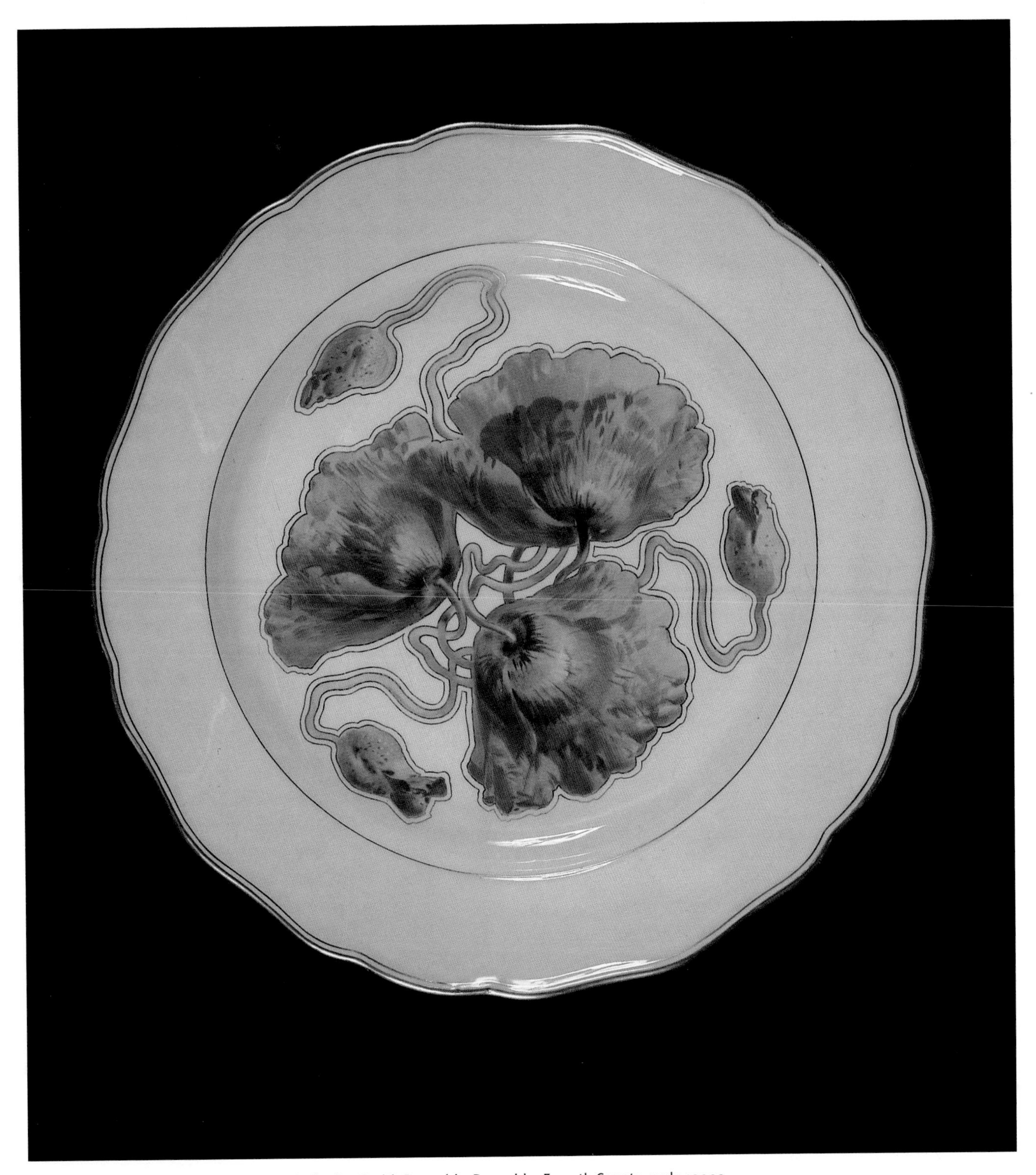

PLATE 9. *China painting belonging to Katharine Smith Reynolds*, Reynolda, Forsyth County, early 1900s.
(Courtesy of the Reynolda House, Museum of American Art, Winston-Salem; photograph by Jackson Smith)

PLATE 8. *Feed sack apron*, ca. 1900–1930.
(Courtesy of the North Carolina Museum of History)

PLATE 10. *Temperance medal* awarded by North Carolina Woman's Christian Temperance Union, 1908. (Courtesy of the North Carolina Museum of History)

PLATE 11. J. Howard Miller, "We Can Do It!" Produced by Westinghouse for the War Production Co-Ordinating Commission. (Courtesy of the National Archives and Records Administration, Washington, D.C.)

6001 *We Can Do It* was printed for the War Production Coordinating Committee during World War II. National Archives and Records Administration, Washington, DC.

PLATE 12. Minnie Evans, Pender and New Hanover Counties, *Untitled*, 1980. (Private collection; photograph by Jackson Smith)

July 7, 1893—"Here I am!"—she kept a journal of her adventures and observations in Chicago. Her last entry, on Friday, November 3, reads: "Goodbye Chicago! Goodbye white city! The World's Fair is dead, but memory will keep it bright, and the future results will be its real lustre."[6]

Cotten had been a receptive learner. The exhibits and buildings, the "stormy" debates, the erudite speeches, the opportunities to meet women from other nations, and the responsibility for representing North Carolina and meeting important visitors—the U.S. secretaries of the navy and Treasury, the governor of North Carolina—were not wasted on her. The frequent arguments that arose in the women's meetings and the attempts of suffragists to take over the leadership (they failed) annoyed her. She was on the side of tradition, but the seeds for change had been planted.

In Chicago, Cotten took as her own special cause the promotion of an idea that had been brewing in her imagination: a North Carolina vocational training school for girls, to be called the Virginia Dare School. At the fair she seized every opportunity to press her case, distributing a paper she had written on the subject to anyone who might give her encouragement. Often, it was returned unread or with perfunctory praise, and she would record her hurt feelings in her journal. Yet she could not admit that such a notion seemed provincial to visitors to a world's fair. When the exposition ended, she was eager to return to North Carolina and work for the Virginia Dare School. She also took home another idea: she would tell women what she had seen and encourage them to organize the kinds of clubs and activities already established in other states.

By 1902 the concept of women's clubs had taken shape, and Cotten was one of the conveners of a meeting to form a statewide organization. On the campus of Salem Academy, celebrating its centennial, women met to form the North Carolina Federation of Women's Clubs. In communities large and small across the state, white women—mostly middle-class with some formal education, mostly married—established committees and organized programs around art, history, literature, and civic responsibility.

When Cotten wrote the history of the federation in 1925, at age seventy-nine, her enthusiasm was still boundless: "The Club Movement has more nearly brought a realization of the dream of a united womanhood than anything yet known to the world."[7] Although her rhetoric was extravagant, there were solid gains to be had. Out of the club movement came many leaders; Gertrude Weil, North Carolina's best-known suffragist, was one of Sallie's protégés. Opportunities to read and to think, to intellectualize as well as to socialize, raised the sights of many women from the home to the community. Cotten's reputation extended beyond North Carolina: she became a leader in the National Congress of Mothers, served on the boards of expositions in Atlanta and Charleston, and was a popular speaker at meetings regionwide.

She also tried to keep her dream of the Virginia Dare School alive by writing about Virginia Dare in an entertaining fashion. Imitating the familiar cadences of Longfellow's poem about Hiawatha, Cotten wrote a verse drama called *The White Doe*, which she based on a legend about how a beautiful white maiden (Virginia Dare) was transformed into a white doe. It was a literary novelty, and the author herself recognized its poetic limitations. But she had learned how to perform for an audience. Dressed in a fringed white dress, she made the circuit of women's clubs, and everywhere she went her recitation captivated audiences. She also sold her publication; sometimes on the road she wrote home to ask one of the children to get a clean copy of her book out of the box and send it to a buyer. Newspaper reporters acclaimed her as a modest southern lady, a pointed comparison with what they thought of northern suffragists.

As World War I aroused women to work at home for the war effort, a change in the roles of women was also registered in the position taken by the federated clubs regarding voting rights. Cotten described the meeting in Raleigh in May 1918:

> The committee on Resolutions reported and the long delayed storm burst. For many years the expediency of adopting a resolution in favor of Suffrage for women had been discussed at each Convention but in respect to many, who believed in it but thought the time for action had not come, it had not been brought before the Convention until the Raleigh meeting. It was the thirteenth Resolution, and the last one to be read. Again superstition was defied, and after some discussion the Resolution endorsing Suffrage for women was passed amidst great applause. The Corresponding Secretary was instructed to send a telegram to Senators Overman and Simmons, announcing the action of the Convention, as the Suffrage Amendment to the United States Constitution was at that time being discussed in the Senate. It was considered a good day's work and the meeting was adjourned to discuss the victory.[8]

When Sallie Southall Cotten was past seventy—on her way to speak to the graduates at Greensboro College, she told a reporter, "I believe these girls [at the college] will make better mothers than their mothers and grandmothers did."[9] It is not surprising that she worded her praise in maternal terms, for she had always said that her greatest pleasure was as a wife and mother. After the death of her husband in 1928, she went to live with her daughter Sallie and family in Massachusetts. Invited to a convention of women in Boston, she was introduced as "the Julia Ward Howe of the South" and made a speech that was broadcast over national radio. "Mother Cotten," as she was called in the press, was eighty-two years old.

From her birth in 1846 until her death on May 4, 1929, the kaleidoscope shifted many times, one century turned into the next. Throughout those years Cotten never lost interest in life and all its changing patterns.[10]

Julia Westall Wolfe

1860–1945

Julia Westall Wolfe and son Tom, seated on the porch of her boardinghouse, Old Kentucky Home, 1937. (Courtesy of the North Carolina Collection, University of North Carolina at Chapel Hill)

Julia Westall Wolfe opened a boardinghouse at the turn of the century in Asheville, made money speculating in real estate, lost it during the Great Depression, and was immortalized by her son, novelist Thomas Wolfe. Whoever she was, she is now a character named Eliza Gant in his first book, *Look Homeward, Angel*. The controversies raised in Asheville when a native son hung all the family and town linen out for the world to see have pretty much been forgotten in the years since the book appeared in 1929. But the reputation of Julia Wolfe as Eliza Gant endures.

Many characters in *Look Homeward, Angel* resemble real people in Tom Wolfe's Asheville family and in his mother's boardinghouse. No protest on Tom's part that fiction is an act of the imagination and not strictly true to life could satisfy his hometown critics or his readers. As the fictive Eliza Gant, Julia was given a larger-than-life role that defined her place in literary history.

Readers meet Eliza early in the novel. She has given up teaching school in a rural township and is trying to make a living selling books door-to-door in the mountain town of Altamont, which "enjoyed the summer patronage of fashionable people." When she calls on one of the shopkeepers, a stonecutter named Oliver—W. O. Gant—she meets the man she is going to marry:

> He looked appreciatively at her trim erect figure, noting her milky white skin, her black-brown eyes, with their quaint child's stare, and her jet black hair drawn back tightly from her high white forehead. She had a curious trick of pursing her lips reflectively before she spoke; she liked to take her time, and came to the point after interminable divagations down all the land-ends of memory and overtone, feasting upon the golden pageant of all she had ever said, done, felt, thought, seen, or replied, with egocentric delight.

Soon into the conversation—she is a talker—she begins to speculate about what she would do if she had money: buy property. She knows land is going to be worth money, she sees progress coming to a scenic mountain town. He abhors the thought. Property "is nothing but a curse and a care."

They marry, and the curse is upon them. She had been a temperance reformer. He loves drink, she loves money. Their lives and the lives of their seven children will be dramatically affected by her "insatiate love of property" and his alcoholic binges. She is a penny-pincher, a money-grubber, rough, sometimes vulgar, an embarrassment to the seven children: a mother who breaks up their home to attend to the needs of paying strangers. She takes one child to live in the boardinghouse with her—Eugene; her husband and the other children go there only when they have to. The boardinghouse, the real estate investments, the fortune made and lost, are based on Tom Wolfe's flood of memories of his mother. Eugene is his fictitious self.

The publication of *Look Homeward, Angel* kicked up a storm back home in Asheville, where townspeople were outraged by its familiarity—they found too many characters they thought they recognized. Even Tom's beloved schoolteacher, Mrs. Roberts, said that he had "crucified" his family. Julia herself was hurt, though she was too proud to say so publicly. Tom sought to reassure her that Eliza Gant was "a very strong, resourceful, and courageous woman who showed great character and determination in her struggle against the odds of life."[1] Julia Wolfe was ambitious enough to look beyond furor erupting over a book. Her attitude was, if he could make money with his books—and they were selling—let him write them.

Julia Wolfe earned the money that sent Tom Wolfe to the Harvard Graduate School and supported him often in the years afterward when he was traveling or writing. She was the real family provider, willing, eager to make money, and she was proud that she did it.

Julia Westall was born in 1860 in Swannanoa, a small and somewhat remote mountain community. She attended Asheville Female College and Judson College in Hendersonville, and although she did not stay to graduate, she did not lack for hard work. After a few years' stint of teaching, she left for a place where things were happening—the town of Asheville—and took a job selling books.

Julia was an exceptional mountain woman. Few such women left home, and most kept house the way their grandmothers had. Few had any education beyond the graded schools, and few would ever go much beyond the next cove. Julia was tough, independent, and devoid of social pretensions, like many mountain women, but she was far more adventuresome than most in what she set out to do.

Soon after arriving in Asheville in 1884, she met and married W. O. Wolfe. Once divorced and once widowed, he was living alone in a house on Woodfin Street, near the center of the town. Julia began her married life in the house that he had built for his second wife. Julia hated it, but apparently she was willing to own it. By the next year she had saved two thousand dollars and bought the house from her husband. She took in a few boarders that summer, but her more successful efforts to operate a boardinghouse came eighteen years later when she went to St. Louis, rented a house for the summer, and took in boarders attending the World's Fair, many of them from North Carolina. She took most of the children with her, and while they were there, one of them, Grover, became ill with typhoid fever and died.

This association of tragedy with Julia's boardinghouse perhaps fixed the family's dread in a way never to be forgotten. In 1906, when she bought the Asheville boardinghouse that would figure so dramatically in Tom's imagination, Mr. Wolfe and all the children hated it. About thirteen years after Grover's death, his twin brother, Ben, died of influenza in a room there, after refusing to let his mother come up the stairs to be with him. Ben's death is the subject of one of the most moving scenes in *Look Homeward, Angel*.

Boardinghouses and women boardinghouse operators (and earlier, tavernkeepers) had a long tradition in commercial trade and women's work when Julia took over the house, named "Old Kentucky Home." Asheville—with its tuberculosis sanatorium, growing number of summer people, and new rail connections—was about to become a boomtown of sorts. Julia's brothers were already getting rich in lumber and timber. She saw an opportunity to live up to the Westall interest in moneymaking, even though her customers paid less than ten dollars a night. She printed up some flyers and hustled her trade, even though it embarrassed the family. When she visited Tom during his student years at the University of North Carolina in Chapel Hill, he was mortified to hear her urge his friends to come and stay at Old Kentucky Home.

The boardinghouse, located at 48 Spruce Street, just a block and a half from the Wolfe home, had been erected in 1883 by an early Asheville businessman and had gone through a number of owners.[2] The purchase price was $6,500, and Julia made a $2,000 down payment, borrowed the balance from her husband, and paid the debt off monthly. At first she lived in their home on Woodfin Street, where all the children had been born and which they always thought of as home, and walked over to Spruce Street to operate the boardinghouse. This arrangement did not last long—it was not only inconvenient, but she enjoyed getting away from her abusive husband (he drank and swore a lot) and demanding children. She also needed to look after her business. In 1906 she moved to the boardinghouse, taking six-year-old Tom with her and leaving behind Effie, age nineteen; Frank, eighteen, who was mostly living away; Mabel, sixteen; Ben, fourteen; Fred, twelve; and, of course, her husband.

Although the family profited from Julia's financial success, her leaving destroyed the household. Julia thrived on the opportunity to talk to her guests, many of them somewhat marginal travelers, but Tom bore the burden of growing up in a noisy, alien environment (he would use many of the guests as characters in his stories). His mother was less interested in respectability than in earning money and owning property.

Julia made money. After she paid off the debt, she added more rooms. Although rooms often went unrented, she continued to make enough money to buy more property, and when she saw the opportunity to follow speculators, she went to Miami, Florida, to buy land. In 1925 she wrote a personal check for $26,000, "the first payment on 400 ft. ocean front, Ormond Beach, Florida."[3] In 1926 her name (and sometimes her husband's) appeared on more than 150 registered deeds in Asheville.

Then came the crash. Asheville real estate and the wildly speculative market in Florida collapsed. In 1929 the whole country went bust, and banks failed. Julia Wolfe lost a small fortune. Tom had money to send her; she asked for none. She was proud and resourceful. But the glory days were over. She was a widow who had only an unhappy marriage to remember. W. O. had died in 1920 after years of decline, and her children were gone. By 1931 she had few boarders and the house badly needed repair; at best, it lacked the amenities, such as steam heat, that guests could find in other places. Spruce Street was no longer the best part of town. By 1933 Julia was charging only fifty cents a night and accepting boarders she might have scorned in better days. By the winter of 1938, she wrote Tom, "I feel the cold, but I dress like an Eskimo, to keep from suffering, and can't get any work done for I have to stay close to the fire here in the living room, even sleep here." Financial and legal problems mounted. She had bought more property during the real estate boom than she could make payments on. Taxes and mortgage went unpaid. Ultimately, in a tangle of claims and counterclaims, Julia Wolfe lost; she could not pay her debts. On Monday, October 2, 1939, Old Kentucky Home was sold at auction to Wachovia Bank and Trust Company for $32,876.65. She was allowed to continue living there.[4]

In 1938, during the midst of litigation over the ownership of the house, Julia Wolfe's misfortunes had deepened. While on a western trip, Tom, who drank and smoked and lived carelessly, became very sick, and doctors advised that he immediately be sent to Johns Hopkins in Baltimore for treatment. When his mother met his train in Chicago, he greeted her as "Mrs. Julia E. Wolfe of the Old Kentucky Home," which was the way she always introduced herself. He died of tuberculosis of the brain a few weeks later. His body was returned home, and the coffin was placed in the boardinghouse parlor, visited by mourners and curiosity seekers.

Tom's death inadvertently gave Julia Wolfe a public role to play as his mother. Now she was sought out for interviews, for tours of Old Kentucky Home, and, occasionally, for speech making.[5] She relished meeting his friends and going where he had gone: for example, she gave a lecture to a class at New York University, where he had taught. She traveled to Florida and California, spending a month in Hollywood. In 1944, with proceeds from Tom's estate, sales from his posthumous publications, and shares in the house given to her by two of her children, she regained ownership of Old Kentucky Home. Frank, whose wife had died, lived there with her. While in New York to promote one of Tom's unpublished plays, she had a heart attack and died on December 7, 1945.

Old Kentucky Home later was sold by the family to the Thomas Wolfe Memorial Association, restored, and opened as a memorial site in the summer of 1949. Some 1,300 visitors arrived the first year to see the house where Julia Westall Wolfe began with nineteen boarders. In 1990, at the first Thomas Wolfe Festival, a marker was placed at the site of her house on Woodfin Street.

Her son had made Julia and her boardinghouse famous. Perhaps only a woman as ambitious, tenacious, and independent as Julia Wolfe could have weathered—and often enjoyed—the notoriety.

CHAPTER 8

More Was Expected of Us

Women Making a Difference, 1910–1941

The progressive impulses that led North Carolina women to organize to make the public world more homelike continued in the early twentieth century. Women worked to establish libraries, schools, and parks and public health and social welfare programs throughout the state. White women attempted to alleviate social injustice and instigate labor reform, rehabilitate prostitutes, and end juvenile delinquency. Black women worked through their churches and women's clubs to provide social services for their communities. Women black and white mobilized to support the war effort, and some women, though not all, thought that they should be rewarded by having the right to vote. But North Carolina, the last state to ratify the U.S. Constitution and the last to enter the Confederacy, tabled the Nineteenth Amendment granting woman suffrage. Through new kinds of women's organizations, urban middle-class white women tried to help working women, but generally they overlooked rural women and black women, and female solidarity across racial and class lines was elusive and fragile. Native Americans were not recognized as American citizens until after 1924, and Jim Crow laws mandating racial segregation between blacks and whites remained in effect until well after World War II.

On the economic side of life, rising farm prices and increased textile production tied to the outbreak of war in Europe fueled a brief semblance of prosperity. In 1920 more women were employed in textiles and tobacco in North Carolina than in any other southern state. Starting in the 1920s and increasingly in the 1930s, women coped with speedups and stretch-outs in the factories and poor crops and low prices on the farms. Making do or doing without—a time-honored North Carolina tradition—became a way of life as the Great Depression settled across the state in the 1930s. As always, women had the primary responsibility for their household and family, and their numbers in the workforce steadily rose. By 1940, one in four women worked outside the home. Many women were in essentially the same agricultural, industrial, and service occupations as in 1900, although more women worked in clerical jobs or retail sales or became teachers, nurses, or librarians. As social welfare programs expanded on the local, state, and federal levels, women participated in the public development of organized reform. Women with missionary backgrounds led the social and cultural programs that revived mountain crafts and helped to define a new relationship between twentieth-century change and traditional women's work.[1]

The interest in ordinary people's lives as part of the depression-era federal work projects and the development of sociological studies at the University of North Carolina in Chapel Hill meant that, for the first time, the voices of poor and middling women and men, black and white, former slaves and current sharecroppers were heard and preserved. Earnest caseworkers appeared on country lanes and backroads to collect the accounts of "ordinary" people, and such books as Margaret Jarman Hagood's *Mothers of the South* (1939), Arthur F. Raper and Ira De A. Reid's *Sharecroppers All* (1941), and the multivolume *American Slave* (1972), edited by George P. Rawick, are based on oral histories gathered in the 1930s.

Just what was "women's place" was debated in the state as well as the nation. There was an alarming 100 percent national increase in divorce between 1900 and 1920. Critics claimed that women's embracing civic activity and paid work was diverting their attention from home and family and undermining society.[2] The national birthrate, which had decreased by half between 1800 and 1900, continued to decline. When births fell dramatically across the nation as people adjusted to depression-era economics, North Carolina's women had fewer children than previously but still had larger-than-average families.[3]

The values of the larger modern, urban, commercial society competed with tradition. Movie theaters, radios, and magazines provided new images of womanhood that emphasized pleasure, consumerism, and sexuality. Advertising and technology generated a demand for products with national brand names and created new expectations of what constituted a good life. For many North Carolinians, however, rural isolation, poverty, and the Great Depression restrained a growing consumerism.

Civic Maternity and Women's Service

Between 1910 and 1941 women's collective power, which had been building throughout the 1800s, continued to exert influence in North Carolina's public world. Women—black, white, and Native American—carried on their traditional roles as mainstays of church and missionary work (Fig. 8-1). Black women worked through their churches and women's clubs to create a network of social services, invisible and therefore unthreatening to whites, for their own communities in what Glenda Gilmore describes as a "para-political" strat-

FIGURE 8-1. *Lumbee women grooming the grounds of the First Methodist Church*, Pembroke, Robeson County, 1929. (Courtesy of Jane Smith, Cary)

egy.[4] White women found countless opportunities to gather in groups for sociability or social good—civic leagues and Junior Leagues; women's clubs; hospital auxiliaries; garden, book, and home demonstration clubs; hereditary groups.

By 1910 "King Alcohol" was defeated, due in large part to organized women's efforts, and Prohibition was the law in North Carolina. Membership in the Woman's Christian Temperance Union declined, while that in the United Daughters of the Confederacy (UDC) and other statewide women's groups increased. In 1923 the North Carolina Federation of Women's Clubs (NCFWC) experienced a huge jump in membership when the home demonstration clubs for rural women joined it; by 1924, 50,000 members tackled such issues as education, libraries, public health, and children's welfare. For example, in 1914 the Greensboro Women's Club pushed for more sanitary conditions in local grocery stores. Raleigh clubwomen established the city's first day-care center for black children. Members of the state Federation of Women's Clubs joined with women from other groups to advocate compulsory education and promote public health. In Winston-Salem the Monday Afternoon Book Club met regularly, although always on Tuesday![5]

In this era of growing professionalism, wives and daughters of the state's elite joined women's clubs and civic groups. Their volunteer activities can be understood as an attempt to balance their husbands' industrial and business endeavors. For many women, volunteering *was* their profession, and they rose through the ranks to leadership positions at state and national levels. Enterprising women used their work in voluntary associations as a means to do good in their community and as an opportunity for personal growth. In a variety of church, community, cultural, political, and social activities, they learned organizational skills, personnel management, strategic planning, and political lobbying. They traveled frequently, became public speakers, and were much admired. According to Anne Firor Scott, these clubs "provided a support system for virtually every woman of professional or political or even literary ambition."[6]

Young Women's Christian Association

The YWCA was formed in the North in the 1860s to protect women who had left home to work in urban factories and were virtually alone in the city. In 1903 two recent college graduates, Martha Dozier (later Flagg) of Greensboro College and Alma Pittman (later Pinnix) of the State Normal and Industrial College gathered together other college students and local leaders to found a Greensboro branch of the

YWCA. Lucy Henderson Owen Robertson, president of Greensboro College, was the temporary chair, and State Normal women such as the president's wife Lula Martin McIver, librarian Mary T. Petty, and history instructor Harriet Elliott were early members. The group sponsored a summer camp for girls and a cottage for unwed mothers; through its District Nurse and Relief Committee, it provided nursing services for poor families stricken with typhoid, diphtheria, and other contagious diseases. In 1915 the Greensboro "Y" started a Traveler's Aid Society. For many years, its secretary, Julia Yopp, occupied an office in the Southern Railway Station and met up to thirty trains a day to assist handicapped or inexperienced travelers and children traveling alone. She was particularly alert to young women arriving late at night without arrangements for shelter or employment who might be prey for "runners," young men who worked the trains to lure unsuspecting women into prostitution. For several years the society operated in rented quarters, but by 1920 members had established a building fund and erected a temporary "hut" as offices and boardinghouse for "industrial girls."[7]

Thirty miles away in Winston, local church women established another branch of the YWCA in 1908. They wanted to ease the transition for single white girls coming off farms to work for the R. J. Reynolds Tobacco Company, the Hanes Knitting Company, and other local factories. In the Y building, centrally located near the factories, young women took courses in stenography, typing, arithmetic, English grammar, cooking, sewing, and millinery—and perhaps learned skills to move beyond industrial labor to clerical or sales positions. After 1917 they could eat in a Y lunchroom, sleep in the dormitory, or exercise in the new pool or gymnasium. In 1918 a branch was established on Chestnut Street for young black women, who outnumbered the white women working at Reynolds Tobacco. The Chestnut Y served as the first community center for African Americans in Winston-Salem and housed a number of organizations through the years, including the Better Homes and Gardens Clubs, the Work Projects Administration, the Well Baby Clinic, the Carolina Fair Association, and the first library for blacks.[8]

FIGURE 8-2. *The Reynolds family*: Richard Joshua, Katharine Smith, and children Richard Jr., Mary, Nancy, and Zachary, Winston-Salem, ca. 1912. (Courtesy of the Reynolda House, Museum of American Art, Winston-Salem)

Two Women Who Believed in Service

KATHARINE SMITH REYNOLDS

Katharine Smith Reynolds represented white upper-middle-class women active in their community, though her financial resources were greater than those of almost anyone in the state (Fig. 8-2). Kate Smith had grown up in the Surry County seat of Mount Airy, and her family had been "tobacco" for generations. One of North Carolina's first generation of college women, she attended State Normal. Her roommate described her as having "an active social conscience and a penchant for service." Reynolds evidently also had "a bit of a tendency to persuade people to do things for their own good."[9] After college she married her cousin, tobacco magnate Richard Joshua Reynolds, and soon was planning Reynolda, her Forsyth County estate, as a community resource, a model farm, and an experimental station where local farmers could learn the benefits of diversified agriculture—no cotton or tobacco—and country women the merits of nutritious and sanitary food preparation.

Imbued with Progressive Era spirit to better the welfare of people whose lives were affected by the economic transformation in the New South, Kate Reynolds was a founding member of the YWCA and the Junior League in Winston, encouraged her husband to provide a cafeteria and nursery for his workers, and served on a statewide committee to improve rural life (Fig. 8-3).[10]

LULA SPAULDING KELSEY

Lula Spaulding Kelsey, a cousin of C. C. Spaulding, founder of the prominent Durham black-owned North Carolina

FIGURE 8-3. *Edith Sturtevant Vanderbilt* on a tractor, Buncombe County, ca. 1920. When George Washington Vanderbilt died in 1914, his widow Edith, a native New Yorker, remained in Asheville and continued the farm and forestry work begun at Biltmore Estate by her husband. She participated in the statewide movement to improve rural life and, for three years, chaired the agricultural committee of the State Fair in Raleigh. Here she gamely posed on a Fordsen tractor, one of the first manufactured, at an agricultural show. She was also interested in traditional crafts of the Blue Ridge and Great Smoky Mountains. (Courtesy of the Biltmore Estate, Asheville)

Mutual Insurance Company, established the Salisbury Colored Women's Civic League in 1913 and presided over the group for at least two decades, during which she had eight children and managed her businesses (Fig. 8-4). Her mother, Lucy Sampson, was a Lumbee Indian who had met Lula's father, John Spaulding, when he taught Lucy's class at the State Croatan Normal School at Pembroke. Both came from families that were "freeish," an eastern North Carolina term for blacks and mixed-race people who had never been slaves. Lula Kelsey and her husband William, a barber who also had a funeral business, were important people in their community, and in their occupations they functioned independently of whites. From her stint as an agent for the insurance company and her practice as a mortician (one of the first licensed women in the state), Kelsey understood the needs of her community and set about to improve black civic life.[11]

Women from a variety of backgrounds—rich and poor, teacher and laundress—joined the civic league, although the officers tended to be educated. Many of the league's projects involved interaction with whites. For example, cleanup days had been initiated statewide by white clubwomen interested in eliminating germs in black neighborhoods, but until they recruited Kelsey to organize plans for a joint endeavor, nothing much happened. Salisbury officials later reflected that "without a Negro leader it is probable that the movement would have been a flat failure." Through a united front and Kelsey's leadership, the Salisbury African American community was able to effect positive change in its community and to influence public officials.[12]

World War I:
"War Work Might Be of Permanent Benefit"

In countless North Carolina towns, women had organized to serve their communities. Once the United States entered World War I in the spring of 1917, these women were ready to serve their nation. North Carolina women, like women throughout the country, moved quickly. Their work fell into two categories: traditional support of the war effort on the homefront and abroad, and reform activities using wartime measures to improve social conditions.[13]

The most visible work of the women on the homefront was through local chapters of the American Red Cross (Fig. 8-5). From Pamlico to Buncombe Counties, women collected articles for the soldiers, conducted War Fund Drives, provided war relief, operated canteens (serving a million men),

FIGURE 8-4. *Lula Spaulding Kelsey*, Salisbury, Rowan County. (Courtesy of the family of the late Lula Spaulding Kelsey, Salisbury)

FIGURE 8-5. *Have You Answered the Red Cross Christmas Roll Call?*, poster, ca. 1917. (Courtesy of the North Carolina Museum of History)

visited more than twenty thousand families between October 1917 and August 1919 (through the Home Services Sections of mostly volunteers), and took up "knitting, knitting, knitting" (Fig. 8-6). In January 1917 Greensboro started a chapter in response to the war emergency, quickly recruited 193 charter members, and established sixteen all-volunteer committees to assemble comfort bags for soldiers and layettes for French and Belgian babies; they made tens of thousands of hospital gowns and surgical dressings and hosted in the local canteen more than 166,000 servicemen passing through town (Fig. 8-7). Women in Raleigh, Wilmington, Fayetteville, Southport, and Charlotte invited soldiers from nearby army camps for home-cooked Sunday dinners. In the autumn of 1917 between 3,000 and 4,000 soldiers from nearby Camp Greene were treated to Charlotte hospitality. The War Camp Community Service, a precursor to United Service Organizations of World War II, entertained the servicemen. Almost 200 women from North Carolina, most of them single and white, served as military nurses stateside and overseas. Cherokee Lula Owl Gloyne, an army nurse, was the only Native American officer in World War I.[14]

National women's organizations also rushed forward to support the war effort, and the federal government quickly established a special Women's Committee of the National Council of Defense to provide a central clearinghouse for the women's activities. The one in North Carolina was headed by a prominent Charlotte clubwoman and suffragist, Laura Holmes Reilley. Honorary chairs were Sallie Southall Cotten, the "mother" of the North Carolina Federation of Women's Clubs, and Fannie Yarborough Bickett, the governor's wife and a member of the UDC. Reilley embraced her new challenge with organizational verve. What seemed to be the most difficult task of all was to define a role for the women's committee beyond simply coordinating the efforts of other groups. Women's clubs and civic groups provided a pool of experienced leaders who were able and willing to apply their organizational skills during a wartime crisis.

Reilley recruited for her board prominent women who represented practically every white woman's organization in the state: Mrs. John S. Cunningham of the Equal Suffrage League; Gabrielle De Rosset Waddell of the Colonial Dames; Jacksie Daniel Thrash of the UDC; Lucy Owen Robertson of the Women's Missionary Society, Methodist Episcopal Church, South; Mary Hilliard Hinton of the Daughters of the Revolution; Mrs. Ralph Van Landingham of the Daughters of the American Revolution; Delia Dixon-Carroll, Cornelia Petty Jerman, Kate Burr Johnson, Jane Simpson McKimmon, Lucy Bramlett Patterson, and Gertrude Weil of the North Carolina Federation of Women's Clubs. The Women's Committee envisioned a more expansive role than simply administrative, hoping that "war work might be of permanent benefit to the community." Their contributions were not welcomed by state political and industrial leaders, who sensed that woman suffrage might be a subtext to their public patriotism and who resented their addressing social welfare issues under the umbrella of the war effort.[15]

The most successful endeavors of the Women's Committee were its food departments, which met immediate food needs and represented Progressive Era concerns for better long-term dietary practices. Statewide women were encouraged to pledge to conserve food, to plant victory gardens, and to preserve their produce by canning (Fig. 8-8). Lucy Bramlett Patterson, pioneer clubwoman and avid gardener, headed the Food Production Department, the slogan of which was "A Garden for Every Home the Year Around." Jane Simpson McKimmon, whose biography follows this chapter, was well known for her home demonstration leadership and chaired the Food Administration Department. Katharine Smith Reynolds opened Reynolda, sponsoring demonstrations in canning, cheese making, and dairying and encouraging the establishment of boys' corn clubs and girls' canning clubs. Food demonstrations increased and canning clubs multiplied—forty-two in all with 12,000 women and girls learning up-to-date canning techniques in congenial and sociable settings (Fig. 8-9). When the war ended in November 1918, food production was four times greater than it had been in 1917.[16]

FIGURE 8-6. *Knitting Club of the Red Cross*, Rocky Mount, Edgecombe County, 1918. (Courtesy of Mrs. Tom Suter, Rocky Mount)

The most controversial work was that of the Child Welfare Department, headed by Lucy Robertson of the Methodist Women's Missionary Society. Allied with the national Children's Bureau of the U.S. Department of Labor, the program had three objectives: to weigh and measure infants (targeting poor, largely black communities where infant mortality was as high as one in three), to provide wholesome recreation (such as summer vacations) for older children, and to encourage school attendance for children affected by the new federal Child Labor Law that went into effect in September 1917. The child welfare initiatives angered powerful industrialists and politicians who charged that the women were involving themselves in child labor issues and overstepping their wartime mandate.[17]

Other committees challenged the status quo. Gertrude Weil, whose biography follows this chapter, chaired the Department for the Maintenance of Existing Social Service Agencies to ensure that hard-won social welfare gains would not fall by the wayside because of war emergencies. The work of the Committee on Women in Industry, chaired by Harriet Morehead Berry, encouraged educated women to return to school to study "chemistry, biology, pharmacy, medicine, and allied sciences" so they could replace men who were in military service (the war ended before their work got under way).[18]

Southern black women also responded patriotically to the war, yet hopes that women of both races would work together in a common effort and that black women's organizations would be officially recognized were unrealistic. Despite pressure from the federal Women's Committee for state groups to include blacks in their organizational structure, the southerners rejected any recognition of black women that implied social equality. Black women felt so aggrieved at their shabby treatment that the federal committee hired Alice Dunbar-Nelson, the widow of poet Paul Dunbar and a high school English teacher in Wilmington, Delaware, to work as a field representative among black women in the summer of 1918. North Carolina's Laura Reilley was one of the few white southern state chairwomen willing to meet with Dunbar-Nelson. Reilley, eager to mobilize the black community, commented, "I decidedly approve of a woman coming to work and talk to our colored population and each community can decide how they prefer to work." Dunbar-Nelson also met with Mamie McCullough, chair of black war workers in Charlotte, who believed that "a separate state organization among colored people, that is, a colored state chairman, with county chairmen, and local chairmen, would accomplish the best good for the colored people of the state, since it would throw them all on their own responsibility and at the

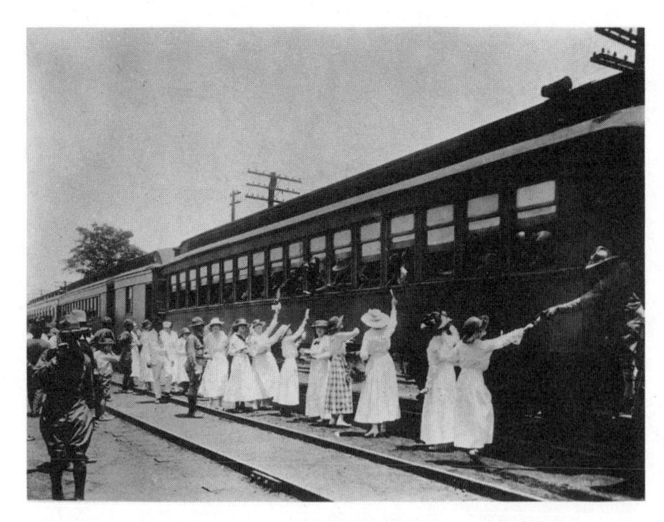

FIGURE 8-7. *Red Cross volunteers give refreshments* to African American troops passing through Raleigh at the railroad station, Wake County, 1917. (Courtesy of the North Carolina Division of Archives and History)

same time enable them to reach down to all classes." The "colored people were simply aching to be put into touch in an official way with the situation"; however, the North Carolina Women's Committee viewed the existence of a separate, officially designated black women's group as "fatal to good policy" and insisted that blacks should be incorporated into existing county organizations. Reilley took the food demonstration and canning club message to black women and found an "attentive audience."[19]

Although the war ended before any significant social or racial change occurred in North Carolina, the markers were clear. Women were ready to assume power for the good of the people, but racial and class divisions remained in place.

Women also mobilized to care for the sick during the influenza epidemics in 1918–20. The scale of the epidemics was so great that public health officials were overwhelmed. Although more than 13,000 North Carolinians died, women's nursing is credited with saving the lives of many others. Because trained nurses black or white could not begin to meet the situation, countless volunteers filled in. The Greensboro Red Cross chapter alone supplied more than a hundred nurses. Rocky Mount's Red Cross volunteers ran an emergency hospital in the First Methodist Church when existing hospital facilities became overtaxed.[20]

Efficient organization and domestic science expertise were brought to bear on the influenza crisis. North Carolina home demonstration leader Jane McKimmon immediately organized county agents (who were not trained nurses but had taken courses in home nursing), who, in turn, organized farm women and girls into nursing squads to care for the sick and to prepare and distribute food. Volunteer cooks received from the county agents recipes and methods for making quantities of soup. In Whiteville, Columbus County, home agent Lucille Clark turned the courthouse into an emergency hospital; the local domestic science teacher operated the soup kitchen. A Stanly County cotton mill closed for fifteen days when nearly two thousand people were ill; the school building was turned into a temporary hospital and the mill day nursery into a kitchen staffed by volunteers under the direction of the local agent. In Buncombe County, about twenty volunteer women washed and sterilized food containers, and a long line of volunteer automobiles stood ready to carry the food baskets: to the very sick, chicken or beef broth, buttermilk and eggs; and for the convalescing, heavier soups, baked potatoes, baked apples, custards, Spanish cream, jelly, and bread. In Harnett County, agent Rachel Martin orga-

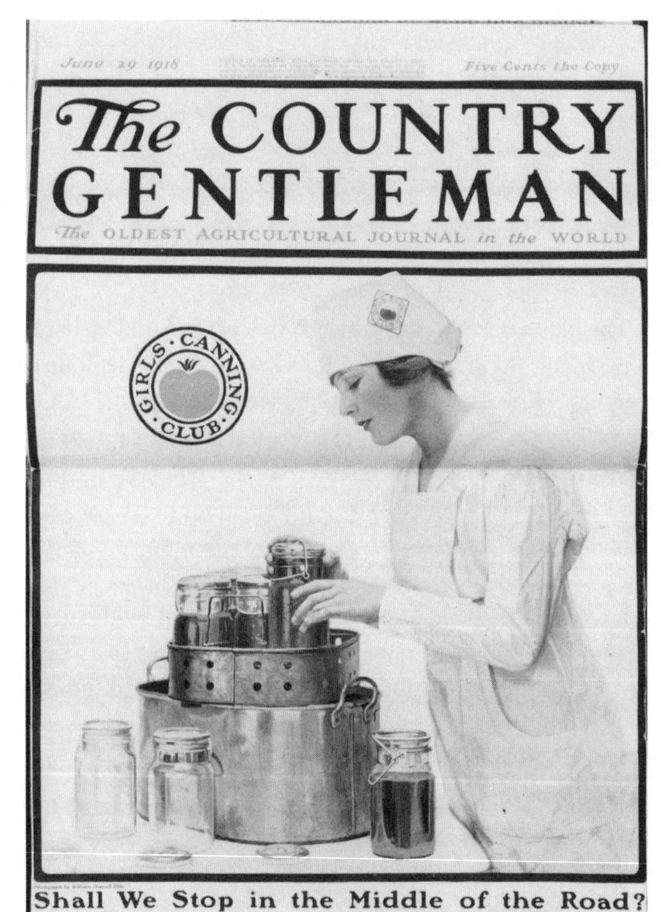

FIGURE 8-8. *The Country Gentleman*, the oldest agricultural journal in the world, 1918. Girls' canning clubs and boys' corn clubs were Progressive Era attempts to train farm children in good farming and housekeeping habits. By 1916 more than 6,500 women and girls in forty-four counties were enrolled in 412 clubs (some in Mother-Daughter Canning Clubs) across the state. (Courtesy of the North Carolina Division of Archives and History)

FIGURE 8-9. *Community canning*, Asheville, 1917. Home demonstration agents taught local women sanitary and efficient canning techniques to help meet the World War I demand for increased food production and preservation on the homefront. (Courtesy of the North Carolina Division of Archives and History)

nized a committee of housewives to make soup in their own kitchens, placed volunteer nurses in homes where they were most needed, and herself visited the homes of stricken African Americans.[21]

Indirectly, the war also gave impetus to the good roads movement in North Carolina. In 1918 Harriet Morehead Berry, who had worked for the State Geological and Economic Survey since 1901, was appointed head of the Roads Commission when her boss left for military service. The need for better roads had been a long-standing concern, dating to the 1880s, but even with the advent of the automobile, local communities were reluctant to turn over to the state the authority to create a network of roads. Berry believed that the health of a society lay in the well-being of all its members, and that good roads would help farmers get their crops to market, children to schools and libraries, and rural folk to towns. The *Raleigh News and Observer* considered her "the best woman politician in the state." The tireless Berry understood politics and people. She spoke in eighty-nine of the state's one hundred counties, emphasizing how good roads benefited every single county. In 1919 the North Carolina Good Roads Association had 272 members; by 1921 the number had risen to 5,500. And a bill creating a highway commission with both authority and funds to build a statewide system of roads passed the 1921 General Assembly (Fig. 8-10). Harriet Morehead Berry was labeled the "Mother of Good Roads in North Carolina."[22]

Woman Suffrage in North Carolina: "Reason and Fair Play"

Once the war ended and women's highly visible contributions to the popular war were widely acknowledged, the national government could no longer deny women the vote. In June 1919 a Republican Congress passed the Nineteenth Amendment granting woman suffrage and sent it on to the states for ratification. On that occasion North Carolina senator Lee Overman stated that "the Woman Suffrage Amendment just adopted by the Congress is a reaffirmation of the Fifteenth Amendment. . . . The language is not identical, but it is evident that the Woman Suffrage resolution is a postscript to the former amendment, which we have always opposed in the South." National suffrage leader Carrie Chapman Catt called Overman's remarks "the keynote of the opposition." Although thirty-five of the required thirty-six states had ratified the amendment by April 1920, North Carolina had not, for a majority of the General Assembly re-

FIGURE 8-10. *Ribbon worn by North Carolina Good Roads delegates*, Wake County. (Courtesy of the North Carolina Division of Archives and History)

> Mr. Hyatt, by unanimous consent, introduced S.B. 676, an act to provide for woman suffrage in North Carolina. Referred to Committee on Insane Asylums.
> —Entry, Senate journal, 1879. (H. G. Jones, *North Carolina Illustrated*, 9–198)

garded the amendment as one more instance of federal-mandated change being forced on the South.[23]

North Carolina's opposition to woman suffrage was strong and abiding. The "peculiar social and political conditions" of the region and the state created what Marjorie Spruill Wheeler calls a very "different playing field" for women activists who thought that women should have political rights equal to those of men. Of the ten states that failed to ratify the suffrage amendment, nine were in the South. The fate of the first petition to the North Carolina General Assembly for woman suffrage in 1897 is telling: the bill was referred to the committee on insane asylums. A flurry of suffrage activity in the 1890s led by Helen Morris Lewis, a South Carolinian living in Asheville, failed to ignite much interest in the rest of the state.[24]

The nascent suffrage activity had occurred as the white supremacy campaigns of 1898 and 1900 were disfranchising black men and frightening white voters with images of white women needing protection from rapacious black men. Many historians believe that the racial and political events of those years had a "chilling effect" on woman suffrage in the state. The women's movement for suffrage threatened white supremacy in several ways: it was thought that more black women than black men could pass the literacy tests; it was feared—incorrectly—that because women's rights evolved from the abolition movement, southern white women would want their black sisters to have the right to vote; and it seemed as if woman suffrage was a wedge for the federal government (and northern ideas) to interfere with southern business. And business was a concern. If women, given their affinity with morality and interest in protecting women and children, had the power to advance protective legislation on the federal level, how would that affect the North Carolina textile industry? David Clark, an apologist for southern textile manufacturers, tried to nullify any reform inclinations by sending women's club members newsletters featuring paternalistic, caring industrialists. His outraged father, the pro-suffragist Walter Clark, chief justice of the state supreme court, charged that "cotton men" and whiskey interests were allied as the "real opposition" to woman suffrage.[25]

Woman suffrage resurfaced in North Carolina in 1913, largely through the efforts of Anna Forbes Liddell of Charlotte and Suzanne Bynum of Asheville, who organized in Charlotte the first meeting of the Equal Suffrage League of North Carolina. Barbara Bynum Henderson of Chapel Hill was elected president and Laura Reilley of Charlotte, vice president. Liddell, a twenty-two-year-old college student and free-lance writer at the time, publicized the issue. She was an editor of a special suffrage edition of the *Charlotte Observer* and one of eight winners of a *Life* magazine contest on the best original article on "Feminism." In the same year women in Morganton, Greenville, Charlotte, Bakersville, Raleigh, and Goldsboro gathered to discuss suffrage. Woman suffrage also was the statewide high school debating issue, with students from ninety schools arguing its pros and cons all that year. Newspapers across the state carried serious articles on the topic.[26]

By November 1914 the state had fifteen suffrage chapters: in Asheville, Chapel Hill, Charlotte, Goldsboro, Greenville, Henderson, Hickory, High Point, Kinston, Morganton, New Bern, Raleigh, Reidsville, Salisbury, and Washington (Fig. 8-11). Men as well as women were members, and people who lived in places where there were no clubs joined the state or-

FIGURE 8-11. *Poster: "Women Bring All Voters into the World,"* ca. 1920. (Courtesy of the North Carolina Museum of History)

It seems very difficult to get the women of Winston-Salem to take an active part in the movement. I do not understand why there is so much conservativism in this matter. I am personally greatly interested but am held back by our Board of Trustees and their general attitude, not wishing me to appear publicly in committee work on account of the College.
—Katharine B. Rondthaler, wife of Salem College president Bishop Edward Rondthaler, to Mary Henderson, November 7, 1914, Mary Henderson Papers. (Southern Historical Collection, University of North Carolina at Chapel Hill, as cited in E. Taylor, "Woman Suffrage Movement," 51–52)

ganization. By 1917, however, the state had only 175 members in some twenty suffrage clubs: Equal Suffrage League president Mrs. Charles Platt of Asheville suggested that women's apathy was a greater obstacle than male opposition. Women's campaigning for the vote was interrupted briefly by their participation in World War I on the home front but reinvigorated afterward. As suffragist leader Mrs. John Cunningham said: "To my mind every stroke given for war work by North Carolina women strengthened our cause in the State just that much." In 1920 there were twenty-four local groups.[27]

For many women, the campaign for the right to vote grew out of three factors: successful participation in clubs and organizations, advocacy for public schools and service on local school boards, and frustration with just how far indirect influence actually went in political and business circles. Not all clubwomen supported suffrage, however. Although the national General Federation of Women's Clubs endorsed it in 1914, the state federation (NCFWC) declined to do so until 1918. *Raleigh News and Observer* reporter Nell Battle Lewis observed that if the NCFWC endorsement had come sooner, it would have confirmed many a husband's fears about women's clubs and perhaps kept away women who needed the clubs' broadening experiences.

Even women who supported suffrage moved cautiously. At the first meeting of the North Carolina Equal Suffrage League in 1914, members voted to oppose "any form of militancy." Perhaps they were trying to distance themselves from the controversial English suffragists, the Pankhursts, mother Emmeline and daughters Christabel and Sylvia, who after 1903 had harassed British officials with heckling, violence, and riots, or from the National American Woman Suffrage Association (NAWSA), which had five thousand women march in their own parade to overshadow Woodrow Wilson's inaugural procession on March 3, 1913. North Carolina women preferred to gain the vote through "reason and fair play." In the first annual report, Suffrage League president Barbara Henderson stated, "The chief work of the year has been the effort to arouse interest throughout the state without arousing opposition." Under Henderson and her successors, the suffragists used clubwomen's standard operating methods: setting up letter-writing campaigns, distributing brochures, traveling and giving public talks, marshaling local chapters, gathering names on petitions, and lobbying legislators (Fig. 8-12). National suffrage leader Madeline McDowell Breckinridge of Kentucky found them excessively low-key; she later commented that North Carolina suffragists seemed to think they could get the vote without anyone realizing they wanted it.[28]

State Normal students, on the other hand, enthusiastically supported suffrage with parades, bands, and speeches. Student leader Gladys Avery (later Tillett) of Morganton reported that every member of her class of 1915 favored the vote. When antisuffrage legislators appeared on campus and spoke against the amendment, the young women refused to applaud. Thanks to the influence and contacts of Harriet Elliott, a popular professor since 1913, students were able to hear the persuasive arguments of national suffrage leaders Jeanette Rankin, the first woman to serve in the U.S. House of Representatives, and Dr. Anna Howard Shaw, president of the National American Woman Suffrage Association. Louise Brevard Alexander, Elliott's friend and a Greensboro high school teacher who went on to study law at the University of North Carolina in 1919–20, became a spokeswoman for suffrage in the state. "Raise fewer dahlias and a lot more hell," Alexander urged. "The place is here. The time is now. The opportunity is yours. It is not the time for women to be alone. They must work together."[29]

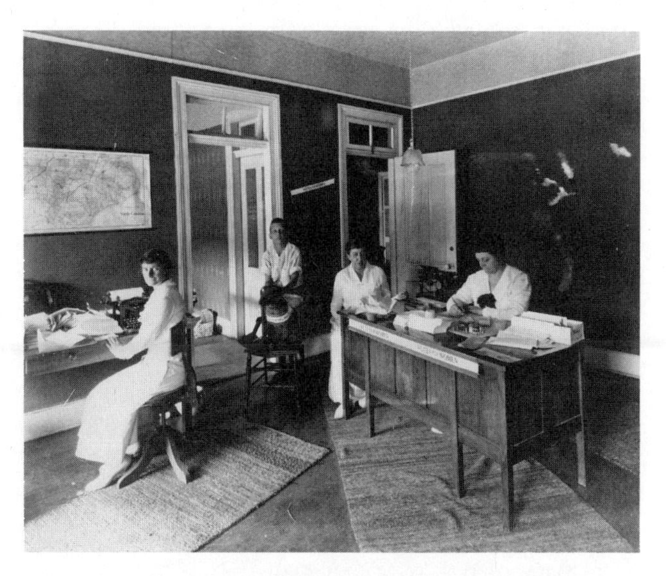

FIGURE 8-12. *Headquarters of the North Carolina Equal Suffrage League*, Raleigh, ca. 1919. (Courtesy of the North Carolina Division of Archives and History)

FIGURE 8-13. *Headquarters of the North Carolina Equal Suffrage League and the Antisuffrage States Rights Defense League*, Raleigh, 1920. The headquarters of these organizations were practically next door to one another on Fayetteville Street. (Courtesy of the North Carolina Division of Archives and History)

Antisuffragists were slow to enter the fray in North Carolina but powerful when they did. Organized resistance to the amendment did not appear until the spring of 1920, late in the campaign, when only one more state was needed for ratification. Tennessee and North Carolina were targeted by both suffrage and antisuffrage groups as states that might take the amendment over the top. The antisuffragists set up headquarters down the street from the Suffrage League in Raleigh (Fig. 8-13). Their motto was, "Politics are bad for women and women are bad for politics." The Southern League for the Rejection of the Susan B. Anthony Amendment was chaired by Mary Hilliard Hinton of Midway Plantation in Wake County. Hinton came from a family of prominent planters, her uncle was Governor Elias Carr, and she was a leader in patriotic and school betterment groups and the World War I Women's Committee. The Southern Rejection League had two boards, male and female, composed of members from prestigious families with overlapping ties to state legislators and to one another. It drew particular strength from eastern North Carolina, where the black population was largest; from textile and agricultural interests; and from members of the Episcopal Church. Its links to white supremacy interests were clear.[30]

Although public opinion generally favored woman suffrage and the suffragists engaged in a fevered campaign to "THINK RATIFICATION, TALK RATIFICATION, WORK FOR RATIFICATION, Make North Carolina the PERFECT THIRTY-SIX," the antisuffragists won over the politicians. On August 11, 1920, 63 of the 120 members of the North Carolina House of Representatives sent a "round robin" to Nashville urging Tennessee to join them in resisting ratification. On August 13 Governor Thomas W. Bickett, accompanied by his wife Fanny and several suffrage leaders, appeared before a joint session of both houses, the galleries packed with suffragists wearing white flowers and antisuffragists, pink ones. Bickett stated that he had "never been impressed with the wisdom of, or the necessity for woman suffrage in North Carolina" but felt ratification was "inevitable." Four days later, however, after debating the issue, the senate voted, 25 to 23, to postpone consideration of the amendment until the regular 1921 legislative session. The close vote and betrayal by some supposedly staunch allies were bitter blows for North Carolina suffragists. Reporter Nell Battle Lewis later commented: "It was quite a sensation to be a young southern woman just slapped in the face by her state." The next day Tennessee became the thirty-sixth and final state to ratify the amendment, and woman suffrage became the law of the land. Women from both sides of the issue came together and urged women to register and vote, and in the November 1920 election many did. But not until 1971 did the North Carolina General Assembly ratify the suffrage amendment.[31]

Women, Politics, and Labor Reform: "Our Responsibilities Are Especially for Women"

In October 1920 Equal Suffrage president Gertrude Weil and other suffragists gathered in Greensboro and made plans to use the right to vote to focus on issues affecting women. As Carrie Chapman Catt had done at the national level, they transformed the North Carolina Equal Suffrage League into a new organization, the North Carolina League of Women Voters (NCLWV). The group had two main objectives: to encourage women to be responsible voters by educating them on political issues in "citizenship schools" and to pass reform legislation that reflected women's social, moral, and humanitarian concerns. These white middle-class urban women practiced what Kathryn Nasstrom terms an "ideology of assistance." Although generally ignoring the plight of rural women and black women, they envisioned woman suffrage as a tool to help the less fortunate—to establish reformatories for delinquent girls, improve prisons, champion better working conditions for white working-class women, and curb child labor.[32]

As North Carolina was one of only nine states that had no protective legislation for women in 1917, the reformers had their work cut out for them. The women's center of progressive ideas was the Legislative Council of North Carolina Women, a new statewide clearinghouse for the legislative activities of seven major women's organizations, including the NCLWV and the NCFWC. Throughout the 1920s and 1930s the Legislative Council and members of the NCLWV (especially Gertrude Weil, NCLWV founder and then president; Mary Cowper, NCLWV executive secretary and editor of its influential newsletter; and Cornelia Petty Jerman, president of the Legislative Council, 1922–33) fought the fight for working women.

Next to woman suffrage, nothing aroused opponents to women's efforts to extend their sphere of influence so much as the issue of labor reform. The large number of women and children in factories, the nature of the work in textiles and tobacco, the alliances between government and business, and the public stance of David Clark, a vitriolic critic of child labor reform, all earned North Carolina a reputation that was greatly at odds with its standing as a progressive state in other realms.

In the 1910s and 1920s North Carolina was still a farming state, with rural underpinnings of every kind—geographic, social, philosophic, and spiritual. As it seemed impossible to reverse the collapse of the farm economy, one of the ways reformers could get a handle on coping with change was to focus on a single issue. The reliance on women and children in the expanding textile and tobacco industries was a compelling cause with which women reformers identified. Reformers saw working-class women and children as needing protection in an urbanizing South. Industrialists saw them as providing economic resources and cheap labor. So the reformers needed to document actual conditions and then implement protective legislation to limit hours, control child labor, and improve working conditions. Critics of reform argued that government had no business telling families what they could and could not do.

As early as 1916 Gertrude Weil of Goldsboro had spoken publicly of the need for North Carolina to follow other states in at least surveying women's labor conditions. About ten years later North Carolina Federation of Women's Clubs president Gertrude Dills McKee persuaded a reluctant Governor Angus McLean to authorize a survey of industrial working conditions of women, a controversial promise he later reneged on. During these years opposition rained down on the women's organizations that pushed for the survey. Factory owners and state government used ploy after ploy to avoid a survey of working conditions, and North Carolina remained one of a handful of states that did not permit inspection of its factories.

A critical event was the violent death of Ella May Wiggins, one of the most outspoken union activists in North Carolina's best-known labor disputes, the Loray strike in Gastonia (Fig. 8-14). The strike began in March 1929 at the Loray Mill, which produced fabric for automobile tires, when workers organized by the communist-led National Textile Workers Union protested a workload increase. In September Wiggins was killed when a truck in which she was riding was attacked by union opponents (Fig. 8-15). Nine people were accused of her murder but all were released by the grand jury, and the strike was broken shortly afterward. Antiunionists thought she got what she deserved. But many reformers, including Weil and journalist Lewis, publicly expressed outrage over her death, and middle-class women in the NCLWV openly supported unionizing through their monthly newsletter. (A biography of Ella May Wiggins follows this chapter.)

FIGURE 8-14. *Women strikers confronting the National Guard at Loray Mill*, Gastonia, Gaston County, 1929. (Courtesy of the Archives of Labor and Urban Affairs, Wayne State University)

Yet league women from families of millowners were often forbidden by their husbands and fathers to lobby for labor reform, and financial support for women's organizations such as the YWCA and NCLWV depended on the goodwill of businessmen and industrialists. Furthermore, the long labor discussions were costly to women's support groups. They were accused of being "radical" or a "menace to the Democratic party" or, even worse, "soft on communism." Membership in the league declined from a high of 800 in 1927 to 100 in 1931, two years after the 1929 strikes.

THE WEATHER

The News and Observer

THE ONLY DAILY PAPER IN THE WORLD HAVING MORE SUBSCRIBERS THAN POPULATION OF CITY IN WHICH PUBLISHED

Yesterday's Paid Circulation 40,715

VOL. CXXX. NO. 81. SIXTEEN PAGES TODAY. RALEIGH, N. C., THURSDAY MORNING, SEPTEMBER 19, 1929 SIXTEEN PAGES TODAY.

SENATOR SIMMONS CALLS ATTENTION OF PRESIDENT TO TOBACCO BELT CRISIS

Senate Reveals Names of Tax Returns Corporations

Involve More Than 300 Concerns and Individuals Whose Tax Returns Democrats Seek in Considering Need of Tariff Increases; McMaster Wants Tariff Commission Data

GARDNER ACTS TO PROBE KIDNAPPING AT OWN DOORSTEP

Shocked By Lawlessness in Home County, Governor Puts Machinery in Motion

CONFIDENT GUILTY WILL BE PROSECUTED

TERRORISTS SWOOP DOWN ON MILL TOWN, CARRY OFF AND FLOG UNION ORGANIZER

ORPHANED BY MOB THAT MURDERED MOTHER

Here are the five children of Mrs. Ella May Wiggins, of Bessemer City, standing by the grave of their mother who was buried Tuesday after having been shot to death Saturday by a mob that drove her and a number of companions away from South Gastonia where they went to attend a meeting of the National Textile Workers Union.

Fresh Outbreak of Animosity Against Communistic Union Forces Occurs at Kings Mountain

CLEO TESSNER LATEST VICTIM OF WRATH OF ENEMIES OF UNIONISM

Taken Half Naked From His Bed at Kings Mountain and Carried To Cherokee County, South Carolina, Where He Is Severely Beaten; Borrows Overalls From One Farmer and Shoes From Another and Leaves For Headquarters of International Labor Defense In Charlotte, Where He Tells of The Attack Made Upon Him; Little Clue To Identity of Attackers Except That They Were From Gastonia; Tessner Freshly Come To State From Baltimore; Communist Center Issues

FIGURE 8-15. *Children "Orphaned by Mob That Murdered Mother."* (*Raleigh News and Observer*, September 19, 1929; courtesy of the North Carolina Collection, University of North Carolina at Chapel Hill)

The league's first real victory came in the 1931 legislative session in the form of a compromise: children under age sixteen could only work an 8-hour day and a 48-hour week. The league was less successful in getting protective legislation for women, who were held to an 11-hour day and a 55-hour week. Meanwhile, league executive secretary Mary Cowper began working for national labor legislation, while Weil and others opposed the National Child Labor amendment and concentrated on reforming state laws.[33]

Then, a new element began to surface in the women's movement. As Alice Kessler-Harris notes, two assumptions underlie the notion of women needing special protection in the workplace—their proper place is domestic rather than public and their childbearing and childrearing render a service to the state. Therefore if women have to work outside the home, regulations should help them preserve mind, body, and morals. The reformers had a dilemma in arguing for both equality and different treatment for women workers. League secretary Cowper realized that by exposing the rhetoric and logic of male protection, they had played into the hands of labor reform opponents. National women's rights leader Alice Paul also rejected the arguments for women's weaknesses and their need for protective legislation, stating, "If you demand equality, you must accept equality." With a few legislative victories in hand (and no survey), women reformers and their reform-minded organizations had difficulties to surmount—the difficulties within their own ranks.[34]

Labor reform had brought to the fore a recognition of what Nasstrom calls "differences among women." Answering the question, What do women need?, very much depended on how rich or how poor they were. The labor reform movement had deep class differences. And the two leading female occupations—agricultural and domestic services—remained untouched by protective legislation. The question of "equal but different" continued to divide the women's movement for many years.

Adelaide Daniels, a prominent Raleigh clubwoman who was an officer in the North Carolina League of Women Voters, expressed disappointment. If asked, " 'What have women accomplished with the ballot?' our answer would be that we are forced to say that we have not done much better than our brothers. And yet more was expected of us." Nonetheless, the list of legislative initiatives advanced by women is impressive: age at which a girl could marry without parental consent raised from fourteen to sixteen, improved prisons for women, juvenile justice, the Australian or secret ballot to curb election fraud, and federal programs for maternity and infancy.[35]

Evidence does not support a widespread perception that women left public life after getting the vote. Some younger women may have embraced the "flapper" quest for fun, but many North Carolinians continued through the twenties to bring a woman's agenda to politics and to participate in party

FIGURE 8-16. *Eleanor Roosevelt with members of the Greensboro Junior League*, Guilford County, ca. 1933. (Courtesy of the Greensboro Historical Museum)

politics. Morganton native Kate Burr Johnson, for example, promoted woman suffrage and child welfare from her various official positions in the women's club movement, both in Raleigh and as president of the state Federation of Women's Clubs (1917–19) before the vote. She combined advocacy of women's rights with her interest in penal reform, child welfare, and social justice and in 1921 became the first woman in the nation to serve as state commissioner of public welfare and the first North Carolina woman to head a major state department, a position she held until 1930, when she became superintendent of the New Jersey State Home for Girls in Trenton.[36] Salisbury's Annie Kizer Bost, women's club leader and Democratic Party stalwart, was then appointed commissioner by Governor O. Max Gardner. During the years of the New Deal transition Bost converted North Carolina's welfare program into a major welfare organization.[37]

The election of Franklin Delano Roosevelt in 1932 and the implementation of his New Deal programs provided an arena in which women could continue working on behalf of the less fortunate (Fig. 8-16). Record numbers of women—45 percent in North Carolina—had supported FDR, and politically active women expected to be rewarded with political appointments.

Sarah Wilkerson-Freeman has traced the careers of women who honed their political skills in women's organizations in the 1920s and went on to play important roles in government programs of the Democratic Party in the 1930s. Cornelia Petty Jerman of Raleigh had worked "without a cent of pay, night and day, month in and month out" to help elect Roosevelt. Dedicated to advancing women's causes and active in the Raleigh Women's Club, the North Carolina Federation of Women's Clubs (president, 1923–35), the Legislative Council (president, 1922–33), the North Carolina League of Women Voters, and the Democratic Party (national convention committeewoman, 1928), Jerman received a federal appointment as assistant state collector of internal revenue.[38] Frances Blount Renfrow Doak, who had extended family ties in eastern North Carolina, experience in the state Democratic Party (she had been former governor Charles B. Aycock's assistant until his death in 1912), and celebrity (she was

North Carolina Women [should] be given just reward for their part in polling the tremendous vote, particularly the large woman vote, in this State in the last election. It was due principally to the efforts of these able workers that women who left the party in 1928 were brought back in 1932. It has been expected as certain and fair that North Carolina women would be given adequate recognition in the matter of appointments in office.
—Petition to Franklin D. Roosevelt (carbon copy), n.d. (Records of Democratic National Committee, Women's Division, FDR Library, as cited in Wilkerson-Freeman, "From Clubs to Parties," 329)

North Carolina's first woman radio announcer in 1928 and had the first hourly woman's program on radio), was an executive secretary in the Farm Debt Adjustment Section of the Farm Security Administration from 1934 to 1941.[39]

Annie O'Berry, who had campaigned extensively for Roosevelt, was appointed by Governor J. C. B. Ehringhaus as state director of the Federal Emergency Relief Administration (FERA)—to the surprise of national FERA director Harry Hopkins, who conceded that although her appointment was "political," she had "qualifications for the job." Her administrative experience as state Federation of Women's Clubs president, legislative activist, and party organizer, as well as her having taken courses at the New York School of Social Work and in social work at the University of North Carolina at Chapel Hill, had prepared her well for this post. One of only two women in the country to hold such a position, O'Berry set up relief offices in every North Carolina county and administered the distribution of $40 million of FERA funds to the 11 percent of the state's population on relief between 1933 and 1935. Reflecting her idealistic women's club commitment to "good government" principles, she insisted on a nonpartisan approach, keeping Republicans as well as Democrats on the payroll, and resisted local politicians who viewed relief work as an opportunity for patronage. Politicians saw that her strength derived from federal power and that her nonpartisan style of politics challenged not only them but states' rights. She had to go.[40]

While O'Berry tangled with disgruntled state politicians, Harriet Elliott, who also campaigned for Roosevelt, moved onto the national political scene. In 1935 she accepted an offer from one of FDR's top women, Molly Dewson, to organize the Institute for Democratic Women. Taking a leave of absence from her teaching and her new duties as dean of women at the Woman's College in Greensboro, Elliott traveled around the country to meet with women's organizations and to promote the New Deal.[41]

Only two North Carolina women were elected to state office before World War II, and both were from mountain counties. In 1920 Lillian Exum Clement of Asheville was recruited by local Democrats to represent Buncombe County, defeated her opponent by the largest landslide victory the state had ever seen, and became the first woman elected to the North Carolina legislature. Although she was not a suffragist, during her one term of office she advanced such women's issues as tuberculin testing of dairy herds and reducing the number of years of abandonment from ten to five in order for a woman to get a divorce (Fig. 8-17).[42] In 1930 Democrat Gertrude Dills McKee of Jackson County parlayed her active career as a clubwoman, including terms as president of the North Carolina Federation of Women's Clubs

FIGURE 8-17. *Lillian Exum Clement*, Buncombe County, 1920. The same year that women got the vote, Clement became the first woman elected to the North Carolina House of Representatives. The woman also known as "Brother Exum" had studied law at night, passed the bar examination in 1916, and was the first woman in North Carolina to begin a law practice without male partners. She married Asheville newspaperman E. Eller Stafford during the session and died in 1924. (Courtesy of the North Carolina Division of Archives and History)

(1925–27) and of the state United Daughters of the Confederacy (1928–30), to become the first woman elected to the state senate. She served three (nonconsecutive) terms to 1943. A veteran of the 1920s crusade to survey mill conditions, Senator McKee advocated welfare programs and succeeded in ensuring compulsory education through the sixth grade—over considerable opposition from industrialists who resisted any regulation affecting the cheap labor supplied by school-age children.[43] Twenty-eight women held national office between 1918 and 1940, but no North Carolina woman was elected to Congress until Eva Clayton in 1992.[44]

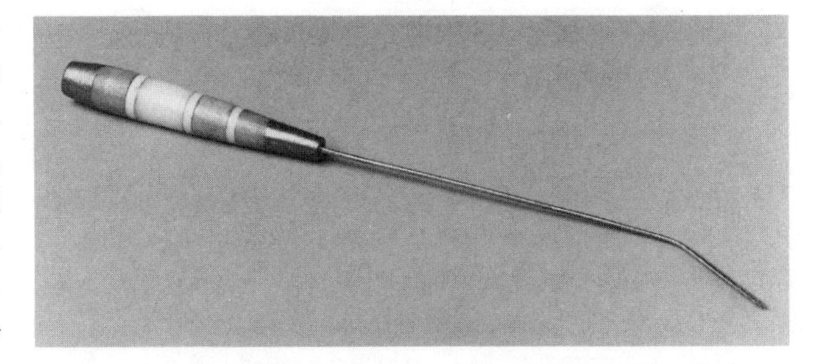

FIGURE 8-18. *Reed hook used by Ina Coward* (b. 1920) at Randolph Mills, Inc., Franklinton, Franklin County, 1930–50. (Courtesy of the North Carolina Museum of History)

Women and Work

The number of North Carolina women working outside the home increased steadily, although the proportion of women declined from one in three to one in four, which was closer to the national average. In 1910 more than one of every two black women and one in four white women were employed; by 1940 the proportion had dropped for both races to a little more than one in three black women and one in five white women. In 1900 almost 95 percent of women's jobs in the state were in farming, factory work, domestic service, and teaching; fewer than 1 percent of the state's female workers were employed in sales, service, and clerical jobs. By 1940 that proportion increased to 15 percent, and clerical, retail sales, and nursing were among the top ten occupations. Most women worked out of economic need, but there were also rising expectations about "necessities" that sent married women increasingly into the workforce.[45]

Textile Work

One result of labor reform legislation was that women replaced children in the mills. In 1910 fewer than 15 percent of spinners were over twenty-one. In 1930 almost half of North Carolina's female textile workers were married, and by 1940 more than 70 percent were married.[46] A 1926 bulletin from the U.S. Women's Bureau concluded that, in addition to their paid work, mill operatives spent more than three hours daily on their housework. (In 1916 about 50 percent of mill houses had electricity, but almost 80 percent had no indoor plumbing.) Exhaustion took its toll, and women in the childbearing years 20–40 missed nearly a third more work than younger or older women.[47]

For most millworkers, their job and family life were inextricably bound together. Women met their future husbands in the mills, typically moved back and forth between paid work and home work (depending on family circumstances and economic needs), and lived in company housing. "We met, and it must have been love at first sight, because it wasn't very long after we met that we married," remembered Alice Hardin's husband Grover, a millworker in Guilford County. "She was a spinning room person, and I would go, when I could, up to the spinning room, and we'd lay in the window and court a little." After marriage, mill couples might have a small celebration, but usually not a honeymoon. As Charlotte millworker Edna Hargett put it, "They went on back to work right after they were married."[48]

Millworkers interviewed by Jacquelyn Hall, Victoria Byerly, and others expressed pride in their work, both the mastery involved and its value to their families. Mary Thompson of Greenville started working during the summer when she was fourteen, married at sixteen, quit school, and became a draw-in hand. Her work required skill: lacing each warp thread—finer than your hair—through individual metal eyes in the harness that raised and lowered the threads in the warp, then separating them for the weft (Fig. 8-18).[49] Although Alice Copeland found tying weaver's knots "tedious work," and the din of the spinning room contributed to her deafness, she asserted that "there never was a time that I wasn't proud of my job, because I knew that instead of my children having to stop school and go to work, that by me and their daddy both working they could go to school."[50]

> I loved drawing in [piecework]. I enjoyed it more than anything I've done. I tell you lots of people would complain about the work, but honest to goodness, I'd rather draw in than eat when I was hungry. I liked piecework the best. That gives you more incentive to get interested in your work, to see how much you can do.
>
> —Mary Thompson, Greenville. (Hall et al., *Like a Family*, 74–75)

> We worked 13 hours a day, and we were so stretched out that lots of times we didn't stop for anything. Sometimes we took sandwiches to work, and ate them as we worked. Sometimes we didn't get to eat them. If we couldn't keep our work up like they wanted us to, they would curse us and threaten to fire us. Some of us made $12 a week, and some a little more. One day some textile organizers came to Gastonia. . . . This was the first time I'd ever thought that things could be better. I thought that I would just keep working all my life for 13 hours a day.
>
> —Bertha Hendrix, 1928 Southern Summer School Scrapbook. (Frederickson, "Southern Summer School for Women Workers," 74)

In the 1920s, however, conditions in the mills "just kept getting worse and worse." Edna Hargett, who was employed by the Chadwick-Hoskins Mill in Charlotte, described the pressure she felt as production demands increased, the work pace accelerated, and workers had to tend more and more machines: "There's many a times I dreamt about it. . . . Sometimes you'd be up on your job and other times you'd be behind. So I just sweated it out in my dreams like I did when I was on the job, wanting to quit, and I knew I couldn't afford to."[51]

Women typically were concentrated in the least skilled and lowest-paying occupations. Their workloads could be increased, their wages cut, their labor replaced by machines, and they and their families displaced. Generally they were not welcome in the unions, which began organizing in North Carolina in the 1920s. A woman who worked for Hanes Hosiery in Winston-Salem reported that the men in her plant were well paid and did not work more than eight hours a day, but women were excluded from the unions and worked only every other day. Women did not have much power, but there was a limit to their patience, and as their expectations and dissatisfactions increased, they became a force to be reckoned with. Bertha Hendrix, who had worked from the age of fourteen at the Manville-Jenkes Mill in Loray, near Gastonia, was one of the women who participated in the Gastonia Strike.[52]

During the Great Depression the federal government became increasingly involved with the textile industry. For instance, in 1933 the National Recovery Administration (NRA) established minimum standards for wages and hours. Workers like Mrs. B. M. Miller, a Chadwick-Hoskins millhand, appealed to Secretary of Labor Frances Perkins: "We have just lots of good citizens in Textile Plants, but we cant come out of bondage alone. We must have help. We must have someone to break the shackles. We need action now. If we don't get it, it will lead to strikes."[53]

Tobacco Factory Work: "Little Pay Each Week"

Whereas labor unrest in textiles in the 1920s and 1930s eventually resulted in strikes, tobacco workers, most of them black and powerless, chose not to strike but instead to change jobs frequently. Black women who worked in unskilled jobs in tobacco factories were particularly affected by mechanization, as machines either replaced them or speeded up production. But white women were also vulnerable. C. D. Whittier, a Liggett and Myers worker in Durham, said that the pressure of faster work speed made the white female packers so nervous that if spoken to, "they jump all to pieces."[54]

All of the Durham female tobacco laborers interviewed by Beverly W. Jones had started working between 1920 and 1940 because of family obligations. As Margaret Turner remarked, "That's what a family is all about, when we—the children—can help out our parents." But the women resented their meager wages and dirty work. Receiving the lowest wages of all adult tobacco workers, black women felt little common cause with white women who had "cleaner" jobs and were better paid. Annie Barbee put it succinctly: "You're over here doing the nasty dirty work. And over there on the cigarette side white women over there wore white uniforms. . . . You're over here handling all the old sweaty tobacco. There is a large difference. It ain't right."[55]

Barbee was one of many black women who were "pushed" by deteriorating farm conditions and "pulled" by better-paying jobs to find work in town (Fig. 8-19). Annie Foster Jones, who was born in Wendell in rural tobacco-growing Wake County, moved to Durham in 1928 and worked as a stemmer and dropleaf picker at the American Tobacco Company for twenty years. Jones preferred the tobacco factory over the farm—she got a "little pay each week. . . . you know, on the farm, sometimes you didn't clear nothing; it was just a gambling life."[56]

Tobacco factory work was hard and dirty. Annie Barbee's sister, Pansy Cheatham, found the Georgia leaf tobacco "so dusty that I had to go to the tub every night after work." Working in the sweltering rooms preparing tobacco leaf was often harmful to women's health. Cheatham remembered, "There was only one window and it got so hot that some women just fainted. The heat and smell was quite potent." According to Mary Dove, a "salt dispenser" was located on the factory floor to revive workers who fainted. When Dove

FIGURE 8-19. *Shift change at Liggett and Myers* on Morgan Street, Durham, ca. 1930. (Courtesy of the Durham Historic Photographic Archives, Durham Public Library)

herself fainted, she woke up in the dispensary, "soaking wet from my head to my feet." Blanche Scott recalled that the burley tobacco from Georgia was so disgusting with its dust, fumes, chicken feathers, and even manure, that she sometimes kept an orange in her mouth to keep from throwing up. After she stopped working, she had "difficulty" breathing, and she knew women who died of tuberculosis. Others miscarried. One woman declared, "I felt that all that standing while I stemmed tobacco was the reason I lost [miscarried] my two children."[57]

Other Occupations

Far more North Carolina black women worked in domestic service than in the tobacco factories, and the proportion increased from about 32 percent in 1910 to almost 60 percent in 1940. When commercial laundries opened in towns, black women dominated that service as well (Fig. 8-20). Mattie Sparks Shaw, who grew up in LaGrange in Lenoir County, remembered that "there were a lot of women then, who get up every morning and leave their husbands in the bed and go cook breakfast for white people." Child care was generally one of the domestic's tasks. Billy Parks Douglas, who was born in 1928 in Cabarrus County, started baby-sitting for millworkers who were on second and third shifts: "See that was all that you knew, so it was okay. I mean, that was what you did. We didn't have any other choices. We didn't harbor any ill feelings because we didn't know anything else, and we'd fall in love with those kids and they would love you. You'd raise those children . . . and sometimes they'd cry to come home with you. The mother would be just a little jealous of your relationship with that child." Douglas would have liked to work in the Kannapolis mills but "they didn't 'low no black women in there. I remember we used to walk by the mill and we'd think, you know, if I was in there, we could get well. If I could bring a check like that home we could all get well."[58]

On the increase for both white and black women in the

FIGURE 8-20. *Women washing and ironing clothes in sweatshop laundry*, Raleigh, 1913–19. (Courtesy of the North Carolina Division of Archives and History)

1920s and 1930s was beauty service, considered, along with waitressing, clerical, and retail sales, to be a pink-collar occupation. Beauty shops appeared in North Carolina towns after World War I when the short bob cuts associated with the flapper look became popular. These required skilled cutting and sometimes perming and coloring and created a demand for trained beauticians. In 1921 Winston-Salem listed its first beauty parlor in the city directory. By 1930 there were fourteen, with three designated for "colored" clientele, and by 1940, sixty-three establishments, forty-five for white women and eighteen for black women.[59] For tenant farmwife Mollie Goodwin, interviewed by Margaret Jarman Hagood in the 1930s, a trip to the beauty shop represented the good life. When hard times persisted and Goodwin no longer expected to attain her dreams, she transferred them to her daughter, who she hoped would attend school regularly, leave behind the "hardships" of farming, and get "maybe a beauty parlor job."[60]

Statewide the number of female barbers and beauticians rose from 9 in 1900, to 861 in 1930, and to nearly 3,500 by 1940. This growth was paralleled by a movement to professionalize. Initially, women operated beauty shops in their homes. By 1943 they had to take a thousand hours of training in an accredited school and pass an examination to obtain a beautician's license, requirements that gave beauticians higher status than waitressing. Throughout the 1920s and 1930s the number of women employed in pink-collar jobs continued to rise steadily.

By contrast, midwifery, an occupation long associated with women, especially black women, was all but eliminated in the 1920s and 1930s. The midwife was one of the best-known members of a North Carolina rural community, and her skills, often learned from her mother, were as essential as a man's knowing how to plow and plant. Payment for her services was sometimes a few eggs, a mess of fish, two dollars, or simply a verbal thanks, but when a woman needed her, she went. Midwifery and healing have a long but separate history from that of professionalized medical care. In the twentieth century the medical profession with its science and what Paul Starr terms "power hierarchies" systematically attacked the role of midwives and healers.[61]

The public health movement that gained momentum in North Carolina in the 1920s brought to light the state's alarming infant and maternal mortality rate: in 1929 the rates of only three states were higher. Although midwives and physicians had similar mortality rates, reformers saw control over midwives as a way of rectifying those statistics

FIGURE 8-21. *First class of trained and certified midwives*, Washington, Beaufort County, 1925. (Courtesy of the North Carolina Collection, University of North Carolina at Chapel Hill)

(Fig. 8-21). Training and licensing for midwives became ever more stringent during the 1920s and 1930s (after 1935 it was illegal to practice without a license), and the number of midwives declined dramatically. Consequently, large numbers of black and white women, especially in rural areas, went without natal medical care. In 1920 midwives guided approximately 34,000 deliveries, 80 percent of which were black. In the mid-1930s midwives delivered about 21,000 infants, almost 68 percent of all nonwhite births and more than 11 percent of all white births.[62]

Even when physicians had all but taken over childbirth, they seldom went to outlying rural areas. On Goose Creek Island (now Lowland) in coastal Pamlico County, Nancy Elizabeth Jefferson, a white woman, taught herself medicine from books and delivered more than five hundred babies before her death in 1927. Sallie Clyde Carroll Triplett began working as a midwife in 1928, walking over the mountains above Elk Creek, just south of Boone, to reach her clients in Watauga County. She carried a few simple tools, eyedrops, and a blank birth certificate, and in a career lasting into the 1970s, she delivered all of the babies born along Elk Creek—also over five hundred. Triplett's grandmother, Lottie Watson of Deep Gap, had been a midwife who had delivered Triplett and her brothers and sisters and taught her the correct midwife practices. After seeing how skilled she was in easing the labor of a first-time mother, a doctor from Boone recommended Mrs. Triplett for state certification in 1927. There was only one death among all of her deliveries—a woman stood up just at the moment the baby came, and the baby fell to the floor and hit its head. "She had no business of getting up," said Triplett. "But there's people—you can't tell them nothing." Carrie McDonnell Stewart of mountainous Macon County was fifty-six years old when she took midwifery classes offered in the mid-1930s in Franklin. She learned "everything from the time the child was conceived until it was born, all about it, every way, shape, form, and fashion" and became a certified "Midwife Permit Grade A from the North Carolina Board of Health" (Fig. 8-22).[63]

Women workers as a group were not necessarily devastated by the Great Depression, and the trend toward their increased participation in the workforce continued. Because the economy was segregated into "women's jobs" and "men's jobs," women's occupations were generally protected even during the depression. Few men were willing to work as beauticians, waitresses, or midwives. Furthermore, women's clerical, retail, and service occupations did not shrink as much as others did. Alice Kessler-Harris believes that the Great Depression affected men and women differently, and that it both accelerated women's movement into the workforce and confirmed job segregation by gender. Ruth Milkman points out that it was not just that women worked for less money but that they worked in jobs so specifically women's work that men could not envision doing them. Because

FIGURE 8-22. Susan Mullally Clark, *Midwife Carrie McDonnell Stewart*, Macon County. The mother of ten children—a few born with a doctor, others with a midwife, all born at home—Carrie Stewart of Franklin in the western mountains was fifty-six years old when she delivered her first baby in 1934. (From E. H. Wilson, *Hope and Dignity*; photograph courtesy of Susan Mullally Clark)

most women were positioned at the bottom of the wage scale, they also benefited from minimum standards for wages and hours set by the National Industrial Recovery Act. Such federal programs made the need for the protective legislation promoted by middle-class reformers in the 1920s less compelling. At the same time New Deal protective laws targeted industrial production. Agriculture and domestic services, two of the major occupations for women, especially black women, and clerical jobs were exempt from this legislation.[64]

Helping Professions

The number of North Carolina women working as teachers, nurses, librarians, missionaries, and social workers was proportionately small, but although they rarely challenged racial or gender attitudes of the time, their impact on the public welfare was significant. Fewer than 3 percent of the state's working women were in these professions in 1900; by 1940 the proportion had risen to 10 percent. The rapid expansion of hospital facilities, the development of public health programs, and the establishment of nurses' training combined to make nursing the second largest female profession in 1940, surpassed only by teaching. Women rarely entered traditionally male professions: in 1940 there were eighty-eight physicians; thirty-three dentists, pharmacists, and veterinarians; and twenty lawyers or judges.[65]

The middle-class values of education, industry, and morality implicit in these professions allied them with many of the reform efforts initiated by progressive women across the state in the early 1900s, and the lines between professional work and advocacy frequently overlapped. To cite only a few examples, all of whom are the subjects of biographies following this chapter, Charlotte Hawkins Brown, a missionary teacher, founded the Palmer Memorial Institute in Guilford County to educate black children; Jane Simpson McKimmon, a Raleigh home demonstration worker, established a statewide network of extension programs to educate and better the lives of countless rural women; and Mary Martin Sloop, with her husband, practiced medicine in Avery County and started a boarding school for mountain children in Crossnore.[66]

An exceptional woman whose profession as a teacher intersected with her advocacy for black education was Annie Wealthy Holland (Fig. 8-23). One of the first teachers hired

FIGURE 8-23. *Annie Wealthy Holland*, 1939. (From Newbold, *Five North Carolina Negro Educators*)

through the Jeanes Fund, a national philanthropy to improve the education of rural blacks, Holland worked behind the scenes because she felt that recognition of her efforts could bring criticism and limit her usefulness. As she stated, she wanted "publicity from neither friend nor foe." Holland began teaching in 1888 in a country school in Franklin in southeastern Virginia and succeeded her husband as principal in 1897. In 1911 she became the Jeanes supervisor in Gates County, and by 1915 she was the North Carolina home demonstration agent responsible for supervising forty-four county Jeanes supervisors. Her success led to her appointment as North Carolina state supervisor for Negro elementary education, a position that she held until her death and that she used to improve the education of rural blacks statewide. In 1928 she founded the North Carolina Congress of Colored Parents and Teachers.[67]

Medicine, rather than teaching, became Lula Disosway's profession, and the world, rather than North Carolina, was her field of mission. Born in New Bern, Disosway was about eleven years old and a tomboy when she heard a missionary from Japan speak about her work at the local Episcopal church. She made a promise to herself that she would have a life of service, and she went on to State Normal, in Greensboro, where evangelicalism and education were closely linked in the minds of students and teachers. Founding president Charles McIver urged the students to do "the work which God has given us to do." After graduation in 1918, Disosway served one year as a principal in a small high school in Moyock, Currituck County, before entering the premed program at Johns Hopkins University, in Baltimore, which admitted women medical students on the same basis as men. She then attended the Women's Medical College of Pennsylvania, where Mary Martin Sloop had graduated in 1906; there she got the best medical education available to women and established her independence in a place far from home. After working at the James Walker Hospital in Wilmington, North Carolina, where she was the first woman intern, in 1925, Disosway was sponsored by the Episcopal Church for service in Shanghai. For fifteen years she directed a 150-bed hospital, assisted by a Chinese doctor, and she delivered about ten thousand babies, twenty in one twenty-four-hour period. World War II ended her China mission, and she returned to New Bern in 1940. Years of service to those people, black and white, who had the least access to good medical care still lay ahead of her.[68]

Many educated white women who came of age in the 1920s generally abandoned what Nancy Cott calls the "civic maternity" of the early reformers and embraced the youth culture for which the twenties are known. In 1919 the State Normal and Industrial College in Greensboro was renamed North Carolina College for Women and, in 1935, the Woman's College of the University of North Carolina (known as the Woman's College). From a normal school of fewer than 500 students and 23 faculty members in 1900, it had become by 1930 the second largest women's college in the nation with nearly 1,900 students and 170 faculty members. Inevitably the close teacher-student bonds that characterized the college's early years were weakened by this growth, the aging of the pioneer faculty, and the tendency of newer faculty to live off campus. And in contrast to the women-centered "homosocial" world, a more "heterosocial" one of parties, dating, rituals, and social organizations dominated campus life. Reflecting a concern that competitive sports might make the "girls" too masculine, "play days" with no "stars" and no unwomanly behavior were instituted. By the 1920s it was accepted for the daughters of middle- and upper-class families to attend college, but compared to students of previous generations, they may have had a different focus. In the 1930s the emphasis on women fulfilling their destiny through marriage and family was strong, although many women continued to combine marriage and careers.[69]

Teachers and Librarians

Schoolhouses and libraries were two public spaces where women took charge of activities and values formerly the province of the home. As the public school and public library systems expanded throughout the state, so did opportunities for women. Teaching was the major professional endeavor for educated women, black, white, and Native American—and an important occupation in terms of the number of women employed (Figs. 8-24, 8-25). In 1930, 80 percent of North Carolina teachers were women, many of them graduates of the state's normal schools. In 1940 only mills employed more white women than did the public schools. Teaching was the fourth largest employer of black women, after domestic service, agriculture, and mills.

Many teachers were young women who were expected to be paragons of virtue and to resist the trappings of the emerging youth culture such as rouge and mascara or flashy clothes. They were also expected to remain single, for public opinion still opposed married women working outside the home, especially as teachers (but yet accepting of married women working in mills and domestic service).

The hostility toward married teachers intensified during the Great Depression, when it was believed that women were taking jobs that men could hold. However, Bessie Kelvin, a black schoolteacher in the Cape Fear region, was teaching when she married in 1911, and her husband told the Federal

FIGURE 8-24. *Croatan Normal School, Pembroke* (now the University of North Carolina at Pembroke), Robeson County, 1920. (Courtesy of the North Carolina Division of Archives and History)

Works Project interviewer in the 1930s, "she's still teachin'." With only a fifth-grade education, he could read, write, spell, and figure. As he said, "My wife teachin' he'ps us out a lot 'cause it's ready cash in a season when de crop has all been sold. It gives us money to run on through de spring an' summer months."[70]

Female professors were welcomed only reluctantly at the University of North Carolina in Chapel Hill. Assistant Professor Sallie Marks, the supervising principal of the elementary school on campus in 1927–28, had the distinction of being the first woman professor at the state university. Women had an even harder time being accepted in academic disciplines. Guion Griffis Johnson, author of the classic *Ante-Bellum North Carolina* (1937), overheard Dr. J. G. de Roulhac Hamilton, chairman of the history department and founder of the Southern Historical Collection, declare: "No woman is competent to teach a class in history. No matter how qualified, no woman is competent to teach courses except on the public school level—elementary or high school. But in the university, no." Johnson had been recruited with her husband Guy Benton Johnson by Howard Odum in 1924 for the newly established Institute for Research in Social Science, but while Guy Johnson pursued his career in the university, Guion Johnson was active in numerous women's organizations and wrote extensively on social issues—outside of the academy. Julia Cherry Spruill, who received the William Jennings Bryan Prize in history in 1923 and wrote the important *Women's Life and Work in the Southern Colonies* (1938), also remained on the margins of academic life. In 1949 Spruill described herself as "a housewife" who does "a little research in history and writing." The majority of female professors were employed by women's colleges such as Meredith College and Salem College, and even there the number of male faculty members began to rise in the 1930s, threatening, in the words of Susan Ware, academic women's "one safe haven."[71]

There were far fewer librarians than teachers—in North Carolina, only five women in 1900 and about five hundred in 1940—but women also dominated that profession. Many of North Carolina's early female librarians had been educated at the Carnegie Library School in Atlanta, but in 1927 the state's first library school opened at the North Carolina College for

FIGURE 8-25. *Simon Green Atkins, Oleona Pegram Atkins, and the 1916–17 class at Slater Industrial and State Normal School, Winston-Salem*, ca. 1916–17. Scotia-educated Oleona Atkins assisted her husband at Slater Industrial, which he founded in 1892; it became a state school in 1895 and Winston-Salem State University in 1969. (Courtesy of the Archives, Winston-Salem State University)

Miss   agrees:

1. Not to get married. This contract becomes null and void immediately if the teacher marries.
2. Not to have company with men.
3. To be at home between the hours of 8:00 P.M. and 6:00 A.M. unless in attendance at a school function.
4. Not to loiter downtown in ice cream stores.
5. Not to leave town at any time without the permission of the Chairman of the Trustees.
6. Not to smoke cigarettes. This contract becomes null and void immediately if the teacher is found smoking.
7. Not to drink beer, wine, or whiskey. This contract becomes null and void immediately if the teacher is found drinking beer, wine or whiskey.
8. Not to ride in a carriage or automobile with any man except her brother or father.
9. Not to dress in bright colors.
10. Not to dye her hair.
11. To wear at least two petticoats.
12. Not to wear dresses more than two inches above the ankles.
13. To keep the schoolroom clean:
    (a) to sweep the classroom floor at least once daily.
    (b) to scrub the classroom floor at least once weekly with soap and hot water.
    (c) to clean the blackboard at least once daily.
    (d) to start the fire at 7:00 A.M. so that the room will be warm at 8:00 A.M. when the children arrive.
14. Not to wear face powder, mascara, or to paint the lips.

—1922 contract for teachers. (The Eagle Express, "Junior Tar Heels" of C. C. Erwin Junior High School, Salisbury, n.d.)

Women in Greensboro. Similar schools were instituted at the University of North Carolina in Chapel Hill in 1931 and at the North Carolina College for Negroes (present-day North Carolina Central University) in 1941.[72]

The expansion of the statewide public library system opened up more opportunities for women. With little state or local governmental support, cooperation between volunteers and professionals was essential in establishing libraries. Libraries became a major civic project for many local women's clubs and the North Carolina Federation of Women's Clubs, which gathered small collections of books and placed them in churches, schools, homes, and other places (Fig. 8-26). The Rocky Mount Women's Club started the town's first library in a room in the local department store in 1915. By 1924 women's clubs had initiated more than 90 percent of North Carolina's libraries, and in 1927 the first citizens' library movement in the nation began in North Carolina. At that time almost half of the state's ninety-six counties had no library facilities, and North Carolina ranked last in the United States in libraries.[73]

The collective efforts of professionals and volunteers led to the appointment in 1918 of Carrie L. Broughton of Raleigh as state librarian; she was the first woman to head a department of state government in North Carolina. Despite opposition to her assignment as "unconstitutional," she was endorsed by many professional librarians, the citizens' North Carolina Library Association, and the president of the state Federation of Women's Clubs. Chief Justice Walter Clark of the state supreme court answered her opponents: "It is true, as someone has said, she is guilty of the atrocious crime of being a woman, but she is a taxpayer, a good citizen, experienced and thoroughly competent. I have found nothing in the constitution of this State which forbids a woman to be appointed to any office."[74]

A sense of mission informs the careers of many pioneer librarians. In 1923 Durham public librarian Lillian Baker Griggs, a 1911 Carnegie Library School graduate, started the first bookmobile in the state. She also organized a branch

FIGURE 8-26. *Lending library at the Jamestown Post Office*, Guilford County. Turn-of-the-century women's organizations encouraged lending libraries and often operated small libraries in borrowed spaces like this corner of the post office. (Courtesy of the North Carolina Collection, University of North Carolina at Chapel Hill)

FIGURE 8-27. *A branch office "on wheels" of Guilford County's Public Library Service*. (*Progressive Farmer*, July 28, 1928. Courtesy of the North Carolina Collection, University of North Carolina at Chapel Hill)

library in Durham's mill district, developed a high school library, and helped start a branch library for African Americans. Griggs went on to become director of the North Carolina Library Commission (1924–30) and librarian of Duke University's newly created Woman's College (1930–49). Greensboro librarian Nellie Rowe Jones, a 1915 Carnegie Library School graduate, spearheaded the state's second bookmobile service in 1926 with substantial support from the Greensboro Council of Jewish Women (Fig. 8-27).[75] Helen Marjorie Beal, a New York native who was secretary and director of the North Carolina Library Commission from 1930 to 1947, extended public library service to rural North Carolina with more bookmobiles and helped plan the Home Demonstration Reading Program for agricultural extension clubs.[76] Women also promoted school libraries, and in 1930 Mary Peacock Douglas, North Carolina's first state school library adviser, traveled the state helping teachers and school librarians to set up collections of books that appealed to young people.

Generally, African Americans had less access to library books than whites. Separate libraries for blacks were established in Charlotte in 1903, in Durham in 1914, and in Greensboro in 1916. In 1934 Shaw University librarian Mollie Huston Lee, the first African American to receive a scholarship to study at the Columbia University Library School, formed a statewide association of African American librarians (Fig. 8-28). The first of its kind in the nation, the North Carolina Negro Library Association strove to improve library services and literacy for blacks statewide.[77]

Culture, Altruism, and Exceptionalism

At the same time that many educated women were prodding state and local leaders to improving educational and social services, other women, influenced by the arts and crafts movement and by Protestant missionary activity, were establishing craft workshops and cottage industries in the Highlands and Sandhills of North Carolina. Similar to Frances Goodrich's Allanstand and Biltmore Industries at the turn of the century, these craft programs, which multiplied in the 1920s, attempted both to revive domestic "folk" arts and to create well-executed, marketable products. In 1915 Charlotte Yale and Eleanor Vance, who from 1901 to 1914 had run Biltmore Industries, moved to Polk County and opened their own enterprise in mountain crafts, the Tryon Toy-Makers and Weavers (Fig. 8-29). Engaged in a sort of settlement house endeavor, they taught wood carving and weaving to local boys and girls: about twenty years later, Eleanor Roosevelt visited their shop to demonstrate her support for the handicraft industry. In 1925 Olive Dame Campbell, whose biography follows this chapter, founded the John C. Campbell Folk School in Brasstown, Cherokee County, based on Danish models.[78]

Lucy Morgan, a Macon County native, moved to Mitchell

FIGURE 8-28. *Mollie Huston Lee* (seated at desk on left) at Harrison Library, Raleigh, 1935. (Courtesy of Raleigh Historic Properties Commission)

FIGURE 8-29. *Eleanor P. Vance and Charlotte Yale of the Tryon Toy-Makers with artisans from Biltmore Industries*, Asheville, ca. 1901–14. (Courtesy of the North Carolina Division of Archives and History)

County in 1920 to help her brother Rufus run the Appalachian School, a day and boarding school for mountain children in Penland operated by the Episcopal Church. When that school closed in 1924, she started a community crafts program, which became the Penland School of Handicrafts. Morgan had studied weaving for nine weeks at Berea College in Kentucky, and she was inspired by that program in which local women learned to weave—or relearned the craft of their heritage—and then sold their work to the school for resale. Like her handicraft counterparts, Morgan sought to instill pride in mountain people in their traditional crafts; to train them in weaving, metal working, wood carving, and pottery; and to find a market for these products. Initially the women wove at home, but a "Weaving Cabin" of logs was built by the weavers' families, and on the eve of World War II, more than sixty looms were clicking away at Penland. Interested in Scandinavian craft traditions, Morgan traveled to that region and arranged exchange programs with similar schools in Finland. She also brought renowned artisans, such as Edward F. Worst, an authority on hand weaving, to teach at Penland, transforming the school into a cultural arts center that attracted students beyond Mitchell and Yancey Counties (Fig. 8-30).[79]

Juliana Royster Busbee, a Raleigh woman and an alumna of St. Mary's, championed the traditional pottery from the North Carolina Sandhills. Both she and her husband James (later Jacques) Busbee had prepared for artistic careers in New York City, she as a photographer and he as a portrait and landscape painter. After marrying in 1910, their shared interest in the traditional pottery of Moore County (where English Staffordshire potters had settled in the 1740s, and whose descendants had continued to make pottery) led them to collect as many old pieces as they could find. In 1915, as the fine arts chairman of the North Carolina Federation of Women's Clubs, Busbee traveled the state promoting folk crafts that seemed to be languishing. After convincing local potters to make traditional ware rather than imitating cheap commercial designs, the Busbees developed a market for authentic "Jugtown" pottery (the original purpose of the most marketable product had been undercut by Prohibition). While Jacques stayed in Moore County working directly with the potters, Juliana opened a tearoom in New York's Greenwich Village featuring southern cooking and Jugtown pottery.[80]

Back in the mountains of Madison County, Jane Hicks Gentry, a Watauga County native who operated a boardinghouse with her husband in Hot Springs, was a well-known singer of traditional mountain ballads. In 1916 she sang sixty-four songs to English folk song collector Cecil Sharp, contributing more songs than anyone else to his authoritative *English Folk Songs of the Southern Appalachians*.[81]

Women were instrumental in preserving North Carolina's traditional folk culture, although inevitably they transformed it. As members of such hereditary groups as the Colonial Dames, the Daughters of the American Revolution,

FIGURE 8-30. *Lucy Morgan and Howard C. Ford*, Mitchell County, 1933. Morgan and Ford were about to leave for the 1933 Chicago World's Fair, where they exhibited Penland crafts in this small cabin. (Courtesy of the Penland School, Penland)

FIGURE 8-31. *Participants at the dedication of the Mint Museum of Art,* Charlotte, October 22, 1936. Mary Myers (Mrs. Harold C.) Dwelle, the principal mover and shaker to save the Mint and establish the state's first art museum, stands in the center. Left to right are Charles W. Tillett, Gladys's husband; Frank Porter Graham, president of the University of North Carolina; Dwelle; Leila Mechlin, advisory director; and Philip N. Youtz, president of the American Federation of Arts and Brooklyn Museum director. (Courtesy of the Archives, Mint Museum of Art, Charlotte)

and the United Daughters of the Confederacy, as well as local historical and cultural associations, many middle- and upper-class white women took on the task of interpreting the past. One DAR member, Mrs. E. L. Shuford, complained in 1926 that one could read "thousands and thousands of pages of history" about great men and find no mention of a "single great woman." Shuford issued a challenge: "Ladies, let not history repeat itself, lay false pride aside, consider the coming generations, and see to it history is written." These women preserved records, collected documents, compiled histories, started museums, donated artifacts, built monuments, erected plaques, designated landmarks, restored battlegrounds, saved birthplaces, refurbished courthouses, and lobbied legislators—and helped to create the professions of historic preservation, restoration architecture, museum education, and women's history. In Charlotte, Mary Myers Dwelle mobilized local women's groups—including the women's club, the garden club, the Colonial Dames, and the Junior League—to save the old U.S. Mint building, have it relocated, rebuilt, and refurbished. The Mint opened in 1936 as the first art museum in North Carolina (Fig. 8-31).[82]

Two New Bern natives, newspaperwoman and patriot Gertrude Carraway and philanthropist and clubwoman Maude Moore Latham, spearheaded the North Carolina Garden Club's campaign to rebuild Tryon Palace (the residence of the last royal governor Josiah Martin), which burned in 1798—a project that started in 1934 and was completed in 1959. Carraway marshaled public opinion and lobbied politicians: she arranged a tour of New Bern for the Sir Walter Cabinet (composed of state legislators' wives) and told them to "go home and convince their husbands." Latham, who funded the Garden Club's *Old Homes and Gardens of North Carolina* (1939), established a trust fund for the palace (in exchange for the state's purchase of land), financed the endeavor, and in 1951 bequeathed her entire estate valued at more than $1 million to the Tryon Palace Commission.[83]

Creative professionals, drawing on their own education and class perspective, also interpreted the state's history. Playwright Paul Green, who conceived the idea of outdoor drama, drew on the legend of Virginia Dare to create *The Lost Colony* in 1937. Much of the music for *The Lost Colony* was composed by Adeline Denham McCall, a founder of the North Carolina Symphony. Novelist Inglis Fletcher went to Edenton in 1938 and began working on the first of her "Carolina Series," awakening interest in the colony's early history. Her *Raleigh's Eden* was published in 1940, *Men of the Albemarle* two years later, and eventually ten books in all, which sold millions of copies. Bernice Kelly Harris, an interviewer in the Federal Writers' Project, went on to write folk plays dramatizing the interaction between whites and blacks. Photographer Frances Benjamin Johnston documented the state's colonial and antebellum houses in the 1930s; in 1941 the North Carolina Society for the Preservation of Antiquities published her photographs in *Early Architecture of North Carolina*, with a text written by Thomas Waterman.[84]

Photographer and artist Bayard Wootten of New Bern came from a family long prominent in North Carolina, but she was an enterprising and modern woman who, as a single mother, supported herself and two sons with a variety of endeavors. Self-taught, she became the photographer for the North Carolina National Guard, which trained at nearby Camp Glenn, being designated an official member with a uniform and the title of chief of publicity (Fig. 8-32). She later held a similar position for the U.S. Army at Fort Bragg during World War I. In 1914 she persuaded a pilot to take her up in a Wright Brothers' airplane and photographed New Bern and the Neuse River in what is possibly the first aerial photograph by a woman. In 1918 she bought her first car, a Ford touring model, and began a statewide photographic portrait business. From the Coast to the Mountains she posed her subjects in their own environments, and she took scenic pictures all over the state. She moved her studio from New Bern to Chapel Hill, and in the 1920s and 1930s became known for her genre and architectural photographs. Her

FIGURE 8-32. *Bayard Wootten in army uniform*, Camp Glenn, Carteret County, ca. 1910–15. (Courtesy of the North Carolina Collection, University of North Carolina at Chapel Hill)

work appeared in many books, including *Old Homes and Gardens of North Carolina* and *Cabins in the Laurel* (1935) by Muriel Earley Sheppard (Fig. 8-33).[85]

The Lure of Town Life

Annie Barbee, whose family had left the uncertainties of farming to become tobacco workers in the 1920s, lived in a rented two-room house in a black section of Durham that had few urban services or conveniences to facilitate housekeeping. Although there were paved streets in the white sections of town, Barbee's street was unpaved, muddy when it rained and dusty the rest of the time. There were no private family toilets. But according to Barbee, "It was an exciting life. . . . In the county, things were dull—no movie house."[86]

East Hargett Street was Raleigh's "Negro Main Street," where black doctors, lawyers, tailors, beauticians, dentists, barbers, and undertakers worked, and insurance companies, a theater, hotel, banks, and retail stores were concentrated and convenient to black neighborhoods. East Hargett Street provided a place for the rural poor, arriving in wagons, to sell their eggs and butter and buy secondhand clothes and furniture. Although it was also where the annual Black Debutante Ball had started and where professional and social clubs met, the street had an easy informality. Neighborhoods around St. Augustine's College were known as "Culture Town" because middle-class educated African Americans lived there (Fig. 8-34).[87]

Only 10 percent of North Carolina was considered urban in 1910, 20 percent in 1920, and almost 30 percent in 1940.[88] But even though more people were living in town, the towns were not all that large. In most cases black and white business districts were surrounded by a residential fringe of black and white neighborhoods segregated by race and income. Only a tiny minority of North Carolinians were very rich, and they

FIGURE 8-33. *Bayard Wootten*. "Under a tree by the side of a branch an iron kettle steams over a pile of ashes," Mitchell or Yancey County. (From M. E. Sheppard, *Cabins in the Laurel* [1935]; courtesy of the North Carolina Collection, University of North Carolina at Chapel Hill)

FIGURE 8-34. *Sunrise Breakfast at Bishop and Mrs. Delany's home*, St. Augustine's College, Wake County, ca. 1920. (Courtesy of Raleigh Historic Properties Commission)

lived in exclusive residential enclaves marked by large Georgian Revival or Tudor Revival houses, expansive lawns, and wide streets. The majority were neither rich nor poor, and they lived closer to the central business districts in modest neighborhoods filled with bungalows and cottages. Depending on their circumstances, women could get downtown to market and shop by electric street cars, the family car, or walking.

In the twenties, a mass culture that accentuated pleasure, entertainment, and consumption reflecting urban and national interests existed alongside traditional agrarian values emphasizing family and religion. North Carolinians read about movie stars' romances in mass-circulation magazines, listened to *Amos 'n' Andy* and the *Grand Ole Op'ry* on the radio, and received Sears and Roebuck and Montgomery "Monkey" Ward catalogs. They admired Henderson native Georgia "Tiny" Broadwick, the first woman to parachute from an airplane, in Los Angeles in 1913, who then barnstormed across the country and became an early celebrity endorser for Coca-Cola (Fig. 8-35). Movies and magazines taught young women how to dress fashionably, apply the latest makeup or hairdo, "catch" a husband, and have the whitest teeth and the freshest breath (Fig. 8-36). Movie theaters and other popular diversions, city parks, streetcars, department stores, drugstores, and beauty parlors offered variety and excitement that urban dwellers, black and white, took for granted, and country people looked forward to when they took trips into town. Department stores, such as Belk's (modeled after Wanamaker's in Philadelphia), which began in Monroe and soon appeared across the state, provided a friendly environment and offered a variety of manufactured products, fixed prices, cash sales, and returnable merchandise (Fig. 8-37).[89] Mostly female customers were served by mostly female retail clerks in a commercial transaction where personal assistance and sociability were important.[90] Men formerly had handled the money and made the major purchases; increasingly women did this (Fig. 8-38).

Since the turn of the century, advertisers had targeted middle-class women; home economics experts taught them how to shop; and interrelated products, each encouraging the use of another, such as washing machines and soap or refrigerators and processed food, came on the market (Fig. 8-39). Women were alerted to the dangers of germs lurking in every corner. They were told that a sanitary house was healthier for their families and cleanliness a sign of their good housewifery (buy that vacuum cleaner!). Ruth Schwartz Cowan, who has studied the impact of household technology on women's roles, observes: "The mystique makers of the 20's and 30's believed that women were purely domestic creatures, that the goal of a normal woman's life was the acquisition of a husband, a family, and a home." Influenced by popular culture, a woman could regard housework as worth the effort because it was an expression of her "personality and her affection for her family." The Great Depression delayed the full expression of these consumer trends, and many women temporarily returned to home canning, sewing, and baking to get by: however, the real task of the housewife was no longer home production, but home consumption.[91]

FIGURE 8-35. *Georgia "Tiny" Broadwick in parachute gear*, ca. 1913, Henderson, Vance County. (Courtesy of the North Carolina Division of Archives and History)

It appears that white women got both the message and some help. From 1920 to 1930 the number of black women employed in domestic service in North Carolina grew from 33,537 to 56,062, a 67 percent increase; from 1920 to 1940 there was an 83 percent increase. In 1920 one out of every three black female workers was in service; in 1930 and 1940 the proportion increased to one out of two.[92]

Rural families also were exposed to movies and radio, and they too came to believe that electricity, running water, and modern appliances comprised a good life (Fig. 8-40). Yet technological change came slowly. North Carolina, one of two southern states with electrical cooperatives organized by farmers, had only two such cooperatives before the Rural Electrification Administration (REA) was established by federal mandate in 1935. Not until after World War II did many rural families have indoor plumbing, electricity, and telephone service.[93]

Other changes affecting women's lives in the twenties and thirties were more personal. Courtship practices continued the century-long pattern of romantic attraction between two young people as the rationale for marriage, and parental control further loosened. Magazine articles advised women on how to have a "companionate" marriage in which romantic love and sexual pleasure were central; a husband should fulfill a wife's emotional as well as financial needs. Birth control information, illegal since the Comstock Law of 1873, became legal and available in 1936. The notion of family planning moved into mainstream acceptance, and family size decreased, a pattern that continued during the Great Depression, when many people also delayed marriage and avoided divorce because of economic uncertainty.[94]

Contrasted with the poverty and despair of the depression was the glittering world portrayed in 1930s films, in which movie stars like Joan Crawford, Claudette Colbert, Bette Davis, Myrna Loy, Carole Lombard, and Katharine Hepburn lived in elegant penthouses, wore tailored suits by day and beautiful gowns at night, outquipped their boss, and got the handsome leading man. Against all odds, a North Carolina woman, whose family was engaged in tenant farming and

FIGURE 8-36. *Listerine advertisement*. (*Progressive Farmer*, August 1928. Courtesy of the North Carolina Collection, University of North Carolina at Chapel Hill)

FIGURE 8-37. *Employees gathered outside Belk Brothers' East Trade Street Store, Charlotte*, ca. 1915. The establishment of department stores in North Carolina towns provided white-collar jobs for a mostly female workforce. Sales demanded long hours of standing and a commitment to service, but because goods were sold in clean, attractive surroundings, it was considered a step up from dirty factory work. (Courtesy of the Robinson Spangler Carolina Room, Public Library of Charlotte and Mecklenburg County)

whose skills were typing and stenography learned at Atlantic Christian College (present-day Barton College), was discovered in 1937 by a Metro-Goldwyn-Mayer agent and whisked to Hollywood to take a screen test. Louis B. Mayer exulted, "She can't act. She can't talk. She's terrific." And Ava Gardner of Smithfield became a movie star (Fig. 8-41).[95]

Women on the Farm and the Great Depression: "Making Do"

For many North Carolinians, the hard times of the Great Depression did not seem so different from normal. Generations of rural families, black and white, in the east and the Piedmont had long been trapped in a downward spiral of tenancy as cash crop economics kept them in debt to landowners, creditors, and merchants. Mountain farming had always been a precarious enterprise. The lives of many rural women had continuities—poverty, isolation, high fertility, meager incomes, overdependence on cash crops, and lack of modern conveniences—that transcended the economic disruptions of the 1930s.[96]

Margaret Jarman Hagood determined that the lives of white tenant women were characterized by the hard work demanded by farming, obligations to their large families, little opportunity to gain an economic foothold, a marginal standard of living marked by deprivation, and powerlessness in a traditional patriarchal family. Tenant men held little power in the public world, but within their household they were the boss. They directed their wife's and children's work on the farm and controlled decisions about church attendance, political activity, and socializing. They agreed to the tenancy or sharecropping terms, settled accounts each December, and purchased food and other supplies at the local store. The wife does not " 'tote the pocketbook,' " Hagood found, "and neither she nor her husband thinks it right for a woman to do so."[97] Most of these women did not participate in the growing consumer society.

In cash crop farming, women's labor was essential to family survival (Fig. 8-42). More than 75 percent of the white tenant women interviewed by Hagood worked in the field. Seven out of eight favored fieldwork over housework. One woman stated, "I used to tell my mother, 'Don't tell me to do anything in the house; let me work in the field.' " A woman might leave the field when she felt she had given birth to enough children to replace her labor and let "the house take her." But many women prided themselves on working "like a man."[98] "Men ain't no good in 'bacco," one tenant woman said. "They can't sit still and work steady. They's always got to be going outdoors to see about somp'n—even if they ain't got no excuse better than the dog." A Durham County black women stated, "Men's work is for men. Women crossed over more doing whatever was needed. They worked in the field when necessary but that was men's work." Bertie Loman, who came from black landowners in Durham County, remembered that she and others did "women's work, men's work, and more than their share of both."[99]

In contrast to women living in town, poor rural women generally stayed close to home. Their houses were small, their possessions few. Almost all disliked housework. A common attitude was, "In the house you never get through." One woman said, "In the field there's just one thing and you can finish it up; but here in the house there's cooking, cleaning, washing, milking, churning, mending, sewing, canning, and always the children." Without gas or electricity, running water, or indoor plumbing, these farm women kept house the way their grandmothers had—firing up and cooking on wood stoves, filling kerosene lamps, emptying slop jars, and laundering by hand. The women without indoor plumbing hauled every drop of water they used for cooking, dishwashing, bathing, laundry, and housecleaning.[100] Cooking on wood stoves for large families took an enormous amount of time. Hungry farmworkers wanted hot bread at every meal, as well as cakes and pies and vegetables seasoned with fat meat and simmered for many hours. With "before light" breakfasts, noon dinners, and "after dark" suppers, cooking and cleaning up spanned women's entire day.[101]

FIGURE 8-38. *Opening of the Mother-Daughter Store, Winston-Salem*, March 14, 1940. (Courtesy of the Forsyth County Public Library Photograph Collection)

Although tenant houses varied, Hagood described a composite tenant house as an "unpainted, one-story weatherboard structure of four rooms," the front porch and steps needing repair (Fig. 8-43). The typical 1930s family had "a [treadle] sewing machine and inadequate screens," curtains in the front sitting room, and "calendars on the wall and photographs on the mantel."[102]

Rural families were larger than the norm (Fig. 8-44). Even as birthrates declined nationally in the 1930s, North Carolina's remained high. Hagood found fertility rates for the Piedmont women she interviewed similar to those of the colonial era. Early motherhood and numerous pregnancies are evidence that birth control was limited to "hoping," either from ignorance or lack of money. (One study of southern rural white men found that although some had used condoms before marriage, almost none did afterward). Even though both black and white rural women had numerous children, black fertility was lower than that of whites. Yet fear that the black population was growing proportionately larger during the hard times of the Great Depression led North Carolina in 1937 to become the first state to use tax dollars to implement a state-sponsored birth control program.[103]

"They say children is shore nuff riches," said Jessie Jeffcoat, wife of a Durham County tobacco farmer and mother of five children. "But if you mean money and things, we ain't got 'em."[104] Hagood's women were ambivalent about the large size of their families. Mary Mathews, a black woman from Pleasant Hill, expressed a common sentiment: "I never had a child or grandchild I felt I could do without. Course sometimes 'fore dey got here I felt like I didn't want to own

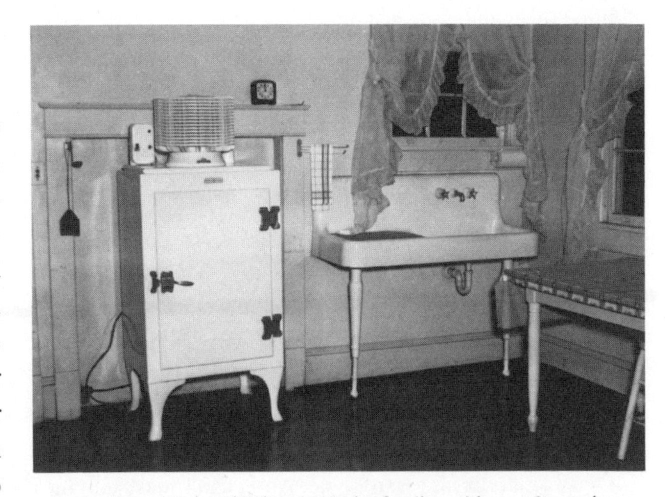

FIGURE 8-39. *Modern kitchen in Marley family residence*, Greensboro, 1922. This kitchen had the latest modern appliances, and the house had electric lights and wall sockets. (Courtesy of the Greensboro Historical Museum)

FIGURE 8-40. *Poster: "I AM ELECTRICITY,"* the Farmwife's Handy Annie. (Courtesy of the North Carolina Museum of History)

no more, but when dey come dey was welcome. I ain't never had nary one I was willin' to spare." Yet the women worried about providing for so many offspring and knew that childbirth and child care took a toll on their own physical and emotional well-being: "Eleven. I done my share, didn't I?" or "I hope this will be the last one."[105]

In the following narratives of two tenant women, interviewed as part of the Federal Writers' Project, one hears resignation to a woman's reproductive cycle and a man's control. Gracie Turner was black and Sarah Easton white, yet the accounts of their lives depict the inevitable deepening in both races of the poverty cycle of tenancy.[106]

GRACIE TURNER

For Gracie Turner, life as a landless farmer "been nothin' but hard work . . . and de boss man gettin' it all." One year she and her family cleared $179, but most years, $50 or $60 was all they had after settling their accounts. "Farmin's all I ever done, all I can do, all I want to do. And I can't make a livin' at it." One of her daughters would "soon farm as anything else," but another was ready to go into service as a cook or maid for white people. Gracie tried to keep track of the charges against her family's account, even got a book where she wrote them all down and added them up on an adding machine. Her initiative made the landowner, Mr. Anderson, mad—he said "we'ed settle by his figgers or get off'n de place." In their last year with Anderson, the Turners made eleven bales of cotton and three hundred bags of peas. They received five dollars for their share and took the only course open to them—they left.[107]

At the time she was interviewed, Gracie and her family—which included her husband, ninety-one-year-old father, and enough children, her own and her children's children, to make nine in the household—were about to move again. They already had lived several places in Virginia and in North Carolina, where they had sharecropped for thirteen years on Anderson's farm. This continual packing of meager belongings and starting over took its toll, yet the typical cotton tenant family moved frequently—about every three years—in the hope of finding a "better place."

FIGURE 8-41. *Ava Gardner*, Smithfield, Johnston County, 1937. This is the "discovery" photograph in the window of a New York photography studio that attracted the attention of a Hollywood agent. (Courtesy of the Ava Gardner Museum, The Neuse Art Center, Smithfield)

FIGURE 8-42. Bayard Wootten, *Handers and Loopers*. "Give me the field every time and tobacco growing," declared one North Carolina woman. Tobacco demanded hand labor of the entire family. After it was harvested, women usually had the task of stringing, or looping, ripe tobacco leaves onto sticks, held in place by a wooden looping horse, and men hung the tobacco-laden sticks in a log barn for curing. The final stage was stripping—taking the cured tobacco off the sticks, men sorting and grading it for quality, and women tying it up into bundles to be taken to market, usually by men: "Women didn't go to town much" (Janiewski, *Sisterhood Denied*, 30). (Courtesy of the North Carolina Collection, University of North Carolina at Chapel Hill)

SARAH EASTON

Sarah Easton, a tenant woman who lived near Wilson, was interviewed in the late 1930s. She and her husband John had begun farming ten acres, working "early and late." They raised a "money crop" of tobacco, cotton, and corn, and, for themselves, vegetables, hogs, and chickens, but "we ain't never had nothing and we won't ever have nothing." By the 1930s they had stopped farming for themselves and "worked out" for other people, receiving food but no wages because they were hired on credit. "If you know anything about tenant farming," said Sarah Easton, "you know they [tenants] do without everything all year hoping to have something in the fall."[108]

Her account is replete with the tribulations of pregnancy, returning to field work too soon, and her husband's being "mighty disappointed" at four daughters and only one son. When John began to get drunk—"like a hog in a bucket of slops"—they would fight and make up, and Sarah "got big again" with another child. During her third pregnancy, she sought the help of an old granny in the neighborhood to induce an abortion. The cotton root tea must have worked because the pregnancy ended. Easton "liked to of died": she had to deal with her own damaged health along with John's remorse. He thought that the abortion was "his sin" more than hers. Sarah noted, "He didn't think it was wrong to cuss, drink, and work me to death, but he thought it was awful to get rid of a baby or to impose on a dumb animal." When she got her tubes tied, her childbearing days ended.

Illiterate themselves, the Eastons wanted education for their children. They felt that the indignities of illiteracy had kept them from "'sociating with good people." But their three oldest children had only five or six years each of schooling before they left to help with the farm and housework, and the two youngest stopped after eighth grade because the family could not afford to buy schoolbooks.

Despite the meagerness of their means, the Eastons owned a car, which they bought new in 1924 after a good crop. A decade later, they could not afford gasoline. Sarah Easton had attempted to fix up her home, a weather-beaten, one-room filling station with a patched tin roof and crumbling brick chimney. She painted one of the beds sky blue. They had an eight-day clock, a cracked blue pitcher "too pretty to throw away," and wildflowers in the "Sunday vase." Although the house was wired for electricity, they could not afford lights and owned no radio. Sarah cooked on a wood-burning stove and pumped water from the backyard, where the privy was located. Her husband would have liked to give her some lace curtains, but at this point in their lives, they were "without half enough to eat."

Sarah Easton belonged to the Baptist Church but had stopped going because she had nothing to wear or to dress the children in. Besides, the church was "a good ways to go and John wouldn't go with me nor keep the younguns" for her to go. She never voted because her husband forbade it. She appreciated the irony that he expected her to defend herself with a shotgun, laughing that "taking a man's place at home is all right but [taking] a man's place in voting is all wrong."

Notwithstanding its hardships, rural life offered the traditional values of generations caring for one another (Figs. 8-45, 8-46), of attending church and socializing with food

FIGURE 8-43. *Rural family on front porch*, probably Edgecombe or Nash County, 1936. (Photographed by Carl McGowan for the Emergency Relief Administration. Courtesy of the North Carolina Division of Archives and History)

FIGURE 8-44. *Mountain woman and family from Hickory Nut Gap*, Rutherford County. (Courtesy of the North Carolina Museum of History)

and music (Fig. 8-47), and, for some, hard work rewarded. Although most rural blacks were landless, others, such as Maude Lee Bryant of Moncure and her husband Gade, prospered as farmers. Maude Lee would "chop cotton, wheat, tobacco, and we'd plant the corn, just whatever there was to do, I did, except to plow. Always come in about ten o'clock and get dinner ready. We had dinner together every day while they were growing up. Everyday I'd do the dishes and go back to the field and work until time to have supper, just before sundown." After laboring in the field ("just made a regular hand"), cooking for her family, and getting her children clean and ready for bed, Bryant toiled into the night. "I'd patch, wash, iron, starch," work she "enjoyed."[109]

Fifty years after Hagood and the federal interviewers documented the lives of southern farm families during the Great Depression, Anne Radford Phillips talked to black and white farm women born at the turn of the century in Stokes and Surry Counties.[110] Now in their eighties and nineties, the women remembered farm life with pride and pleasure. These Piedmont women centered their lives and work on home and on the production of a single cash crop—flue-cured tobacco. Money was scarce, and life was close to the bone. They grew cotton to make quilts, gathered broom sedge for brooms and mattresses, and used corn shucks and cotton for mattress filling. With few automobiles, paved roads, or telephones

> When we first married, we rented on halves from a man, and whatever we made, well, half of it was his. Well, that year we made five bales of cotton, and nobody but Gade [her husband] and I, it didn't take much for us to eat, and after he laid by the crop he went to work out at the brickyard, just a few weeks, but we saved out a hundred dollars then had a little money left. Soon that winter we bought a mule, paid cash. The next year we was able to buy this land and begin farming without on halves, straight on ourselves. And in about forty years we added to our land. Me and my husband, we own about five hundred and thirty acres, I believe.
>
> —Maude Lee Bryant of Moncure. (E. H. Wilson, *Hope and Dignity*, 42)

FIGURE 8-45. Doris Ulmann, *Marian Johnson and Grandchild*. (Courtesy of the North Carolina Division of Archives and History)

FIGURE 8-46. *Delphia and Elais Locklear* with their grandson, Erbert, Robeson County, ca. 1940. (Courtesy of Darlene Jacobs, Raleigh)

until the mid-1940s, travel and communication were difficult, reinforcing insularity and self-sufficiency. Neighbors helped one another with work swaps, barn raisings, wheat threshings, corn shuckings, and apple peelings. These occasions combined work and sociability, and customarily ended with music, for almost every family had members who sang and played violins, banjos, and mandolins. When the Great Depression hit, they had many survival strategies already in place. Even though cash poor, they grew their own food, swapped work, bartered for goods, and paid doctors and merchants with farm products.

Part of the women's pride came from living in a culture in which holding on to land was an important value. They derived a strong sense of identity, autonomy, and pride from working their own land and making do. Men did the heavier outdoor farmwork, but women were proud of their physical stamina and ability to do manual labor. Nevada Jane Hall always wished that she had "been a man: all I wanted to do was get out in the fields."[111]

"Everybody was a farmer," said Magdaleine Robertson Tilley Compton, who was born on a tobacco farm in the

FIGURE 8-47. Bayard Wootten, *"Mothers and daughters unpack the lunch*, and people crowd up to the tables," Mitchell County. Muriel Earley Sheppard describes a singing convention at the Bear Creek Baptist Church: "A long table extended more than the length of the building on the shady side, piled high with boxes and baskets." Three hundred dinners were served—"platters of fried chicken and roast meat, soda biscuits, cold sweet potatoes, cake, pickles, canned peaches, and stacked pies." Each family had its own section of the table, but mountain hospitality included Sheppard, who was invited to eat with four families. (From Sheppard, *Cabins in the Laurel*; courtesy of the North Carolina Collection, University of North Carolina at Chapel Hill)

Snow Hill community near Lawsonville north of Sauratown Mountain. "They growed everything to eat," only buying "a little sugar and maybe a little coffee." "They didn't buy new stuff like they do now. If you wore out a shirt or something, and it had a hole or two in it, and it was ragged, and you didn't want to wear it, you'd cut the good parts out and make you a cotton top or two or a quilt and fix it." Compton was strongly attached to her homeplace, her family, her neighbors—"I grew up on this hillside and my husband grew up on the other."[112]

With the historic challenges of World War I and the Great Depression and the more routine, although no less trying tests of earning a living, rearing a family, and nursing children and loved ones, the years from 1910 to 1940 brought hardship and struggle to many women. They were also times of great excitement, from getting the vote to enjoying the freedom provided by automobiles, to the array of goods and images tantalizingly presented by movies and media, to new professional and occupational opportunities. Modern commercial values existed side by side with traditional ones, and the range of possibilities for women's lives continued to expand. During the depression women had clear roles to play, as housewives conserving their family's meager resources, as workers helping to support their families, and as social workers providing relief. When World War II arrived on everyone's doorstep and men mobilized for battle, North Carolina women, as they had in the past, took up the slack.

Charlotte Hawkins Brown

1883–1961

Charlotte Hawkins Brown (center) with teachers at Palmer Memorial Institute, Sedalia. (Courtesy of the North Carolina Division of Archives and History)

In 1901, when Charlotte Hawkins left Cambridge, Massachusetts, to teach in Sedalia in her native North Carolina, she moved from a northern urban center that had become a mecca for southern blacks to a rural southern state where education for her race had only begun. Thirteen years earlier, she, her mother, and other relatives had left North Carolina to live in Massachusetts, returning only for summer visits. In a sense, Charlotte was now coming home, and she took up her assignment from the American Missionary Association (AMA) with a zeal for education that would last for over half a century.

Lottie (her childhood name) had been born near Henderson in Vance County, where her mother's family owned land. When she was five, her mother, Caroline Frances Willis, and a large number of family members moved north to join other relatives already living in Cambridge. There her mother, who was a laundress and cared for foster children, immediately enrolled her daughter in school. By age twelve Lottie had organized a kindergarten in their church, and by age fourteen she had made her first public speech, in the presence of the governor of the state. In her own words written many years later, she thrilled to "the plaudits of the great throng."[1]

By the time she graduated from Cambridge English High School in 1900, Charlotte Eugenia (as she now called herself) had been exposed to more educational opportunities than most seventeen-year-old girls and boys in North Carolina, some of whom had had no more than a few months' schooling a year. There were only two black public high schools in the state.

In addition to acquiring a good education, Charlotte also had learned the value of knowing the "right people." According to a story that she loved to tell in later years, one day while reading Virgil as she pushed the stroller of a white baby she had been hired to tend, she was noticed by Alice Freeman Palmer, who had retired as the first woman president of Wellesley College and was serving as a member of the Board of Education that governed normal schools in the Commonwealth of Massachusetts. When Palmer learned that Charlotte was ready for college and offered to pay her fees, Charlotte enrolled at the State Normal School in Salem, Massachusetts, living at home and commuting by train. She had completed the first of two years when she accepted a request from the AMA to teach in one of several southern states, and she chose North Carolina.

Since about 1861, the American Missionary Association had been sending mostly white New England women to establish schools for black children in the South, but by the end of Reconstruction it was assigning more black teachers. Young Charlotte Hawkins was going on a mission to assist in the educational advancement of her race. She traveled to McLeansville by train and from the station set out on foot to find her schoolhouse in a small community about eight miles east of Greensboro, soon to be called "Sedalia."

The four or five miles of country landscape seemed to her forsaken. Along the way, there were scattered small houses and fields of some fifty black families. When she finally reached her new home, she discovered a post office, a general store, and Bethany Normal and Industrial Institute, housed in Bethany Congregational Church. Hawkins settled in and went to work.

After her first year, in which she and Manual Liston Baldwin, the church minister, taught classes for children of different ages, the AMA determined that a number of its schools must be closed, including the Bethany school. While Charlotte was considering another assignment from the association, some people in the area asked her to stay, promising to help her if she would start her own school. This support was a victory for an outsider who, on her arrival in Sedalia, had been called a "Yankee hussy." She agreed to stay and spent the summer in Massachusetts raising money for a new school from a list of possible benefactors earlier recommended by Alice Freeman Palmer, who had recently died. At the end of the summer she returned to Sedalia with several hundred dollars to fix up an old blacksmith shop as a classroom for about twenty students, with sleeping and living space for two teachers and for the several girls who boarded there (the boys were day students). Charlotte named the school for Alice Freeman Palmer and asked two church members to serve with her on the first board of trustees. Manual Baldwin and his wife deeded fifteen acres to the school, and on October 12, 1902, Palmer Memorial Institute (PMI) was established to prepare students for jobs in agriculture and industry.[2] It became Charlotte's family, her home, her work, and her community. The Bethany church continued to play an important role: students and faculty attended Sunday services and sang in the choir, and in later years students helped build a house on campus for the minister, John Brice, who also taught them classes in religion. Charlotte was always one to remember where she came from on the way to where she was going.

With no public school for blacks in the community, the need for a private school was obvious, but Charlotte intended to make her school different by offering instruction in the liberal arts and in personal development and appearance. Like other educators of the period, she also emphasized vocational learning as a character-building experience as well as a way to provide essential labor for the campus: boys were given work assignments on the farm, and girls were trained in the domestic arts. Local farmers guided her in setting up the agricultural program, and an interdependence developed between school and community. As this alliance grew, she organized a Home Ownership Association to encourage families who had been tenant farmers to buy land from a tract that was bought and given to Palmer by Helen F. Kimball of Brookline, Massachusetts. The slow process of building trust worked for Charlotte, who was able to introduce a landownership program practiced in other AMA schools and a system promoted by one of her heroes, Booker T. Washington.

The Palmer Memorial Institute became a focal point for community activities; it also became both a workplace and a home for teachers, often single women. When the local Congregational minister stopped teaching after the first year, Charlotte hired Lelia Ireland, a graduate of Scotia Seminary in Concord. Lelia became a close friend, one with whom to share a home, a school, and a vision. A pattern developed whereby other Palmer women kept house for Charlotte, freeing her to direct the school and raise funds. In 1911 she married Edward S. Brown, who had boarded with her mother while a student in Cambridge. Brown taught for at least a year at Palmer, but the marriage lasted only briefly, and he left. Most students would not remember that Charlotte had ever been married, except to PMI. As she and Lelia spent evenings writing letters asking for contributions, then kneeling and praying for a favorable response, Charlotte gathered confidence to travel the lonely road to build public support.

In the first decade, the school grew in land, buildings, students, teachers, and reputation. By 1915 about two hundred boys and girls had been graduated. Moreover, Brown had begun to attract some of the country's leading educators and philanthropists, and their visits and gifts to the school were evidence of her growing ability to raise money. In one year—1925—she raised more than $300,000. In 1922 PMI became one of the nine black high schools in North Carolina accredited by the Southern Association of Colleges and Secondary Schools.

Funds for additional facilities and teachers came from the Julius Rosenwald Fund, the Jeanes Fund, and individuals in Cambridge, Boston, New York City, and North Carolina. Women constituted the largest number of individual donors, and the largest contributions were made by businessmen. By the mid-1900s Palmer's greatest benefactor was Galen Stone, a Boston financier, who, with his wife Carrie and son, gave over $500,000.[3] In Brookline, Massachusetts, Helen F.

Kimball organized the Sedalia Club, and Charles W. Eliot, president of Harvard College, led a capital and endowment campaign. In her letters and summer visits to the North, Brown learned to hold her tongue when contributors cautioned her to be more modest in her expectations for her race. Kimball urged her to be "practical," and another white friend, Francis A. Guthrie, argued against teaching more to African American children "than at present their natures are ready to perceive."[4] Such responses often evoked periods of despair and rage in Brown, whose role as what Glenda Gilmore calls "a double agent" was difficult to maintain.[5]

The need to win the support of black and white southerners at home and white benefactors in New England required her to be pragmatic and tenacious, and she became adept at tailoring her appeals to her audiences. Stone advised her to keep better records and to secure more benefactors from her own region. She agreed. But to her women friends, she expressed fatigue with the endless process and anger over efforts "to tie my hands so I can't speak out when I'm being crushed. Just what are they going to ask me to submit to as a Negro woman to get their interests?"[6] She relished supplying the personal touch in fund-raising efforts, jealously guarding the leadership role that she had every right to claim. Often in letters she argued with her advisers, but she was willing to receive advice as long as it was attached to a check. She had an ally in Galen Stone, who reflected a philosophy very much like her own, quoting him as having said, "I am not interested in educating and advancing Negroes, but in making American citizens, and I feel that they should be given the highest and best there is."[7]

At Stone's insistence she also began to collect her own white patrons at home: E. P. Wharton, a Greensboro banker, who agreed to become chairman of the board of trustees; Lula Martin McIver, a leading advocate for public education and the wife of Charles D. McIver, founder and first president of the State Normal School for Women in Greensboro; Ceasar Cone, a local textile industrialist; and Dr. Frank Porter Graham, of the University of North Carolina.[8] The encouragement of leaders in her own race gave her deep personal confirmation. Among them, Nannie Helen Burroughs and Mary McLeod Bethune were correspondents and visitors to the Palmer campus, and Brown often measured her success by theirs. Bethune, Brown, and Burroughs became known as the "three B's" of African American education.

In 1917, after a fire destroyed three of the school's wooden buildings, Greensboro banker Wharton urged Brown not to go north for the money; he said that he would help her raise it at home. The fund-raiser they organized became a model for success: a concert for white audiences by the Sedalia Singers, made up of Palmer students; a rousing speech by Charlotte; and her request for pledges. Afterward, laudatory editorials appeared in the local newspaper. In 1922 with the construction of the first brick building—the Alice F. Palmer Building—Brown embarked on a campaign to replace the wooden structures, and the school began to acquire the look of a permanent campus.

By the 1930s the school had more than a dozen buildings and about 350 acres of campus and farmland. But there were constant problems: there was never enough money, and the public school movement for blacks was taking students away from Palmer. To stay afloat, the trustees and Brown at various times attempted to ally PMI with a secure partner: during the 1920s the institute had been associated with the American Missionary Association, but the partnership was dissolved by 1934. Subsequently Brown sought alliances with Durham's North Carolina College for Negroes (present-day North Carolina Central University) and Greensboro's Bennett College and present-day North Carolina A&T State University. All such arrangements ultimately failed because PMI had become the lengthened shadow of one person and operated under special circumstances that only Charlotte Hawkins Brown could define. Other measures had to be taken to save it.

Brown had worked to obtain from the state a per capita payment for local students attending Palmer. In 1937 she helped to secure a public elementary school for the community. No longer needing to offer the elementary grades, PMI now attracted students from across the nation. After seven years (1932–39), a junior college curriculum was dropped because of low enrollments and costly instruction. Finally, Palmer completed its move away from vocational education toward the traditional liberal arts and in the early 1940s embarked on a path that would make it one of the most prestigious private black academies in the country. By the 1940s the campus of PMI began to represent what Charlotte had earlier envisioned—"a little bit of New England" in North Carolina.

An attempt to make Palmer more self-supporting through tuition proved successful. The transformation from a vocational school for local farm children to a boarding school for children from what Brown liked to describe as the "best" families created striking changes. In 1943, for example, 178 students were from twenty-three states; only 4 were from the local community. Often Brown was off campus speaking, recruiting, and fund-raising, her magnetic presence and the audience's standing ovation reported in national publications. In 1947 a photograph in *Ebony* magazine showed young boys and girls in evening clothes against the romantic backdrop of lighted columns on Galen Stone Hall. By contrast, the central image of PMI's first brochure had been a barefoot boy in overalls.

In 1919 Brown had written *Mammy: An Appeal to the Heart of the South*, an emotional tribute to the black woman stereotyped in southern literature and folklore as the "mammy" to white children, admonishing white families to take care of mammy in her old age. Twenty years later, however, she addressed a black audience and prescribed the kind of behavior that she espoused for her students: *The Correct Thing to Do, to Say, and to Wear* (1941), which Brown admittedly patterned on etiquette books by prominent white authorities such as Emily Post while using examples from her own school.

With the publication of *The Correct Thing*, Brown in part reflected her own upbringing in Cambridge, where as one of a small number of black students among whites she had begun to believe in the advantages of education and good manners. But in instructing PMI students how to behave at the theater, travel on the train, or treat servants in their homes, she seemed far removed from the reality of racial inequality in the South. Her philosophy of finding a place through knowing "the correct thing to do, to say, and to act" provoked W. E. B. Du Bois to say that Brown represented the white South and led to her reputation as the "first lady of social graces."[9]

Whether she turned to paying families as the only means to keep her school going or to establishing the kind of cultural and class standards she had admired among New Englanders, the fact is that from the 1940s until 1971, Brown made Palmer Memorial Institute a place for children of the state's, the region's, and sometimes the nation's most successful black families. Parents usually chose the school because it offered their children a better education than was available in their own communities. Ahead of other schools, PMI required students to take a course in black history. The school motto defined Brown's values: "educationally efficient, religiously sincere, and culturally secure."

Although a strict disciplinarian at home, she was recognized as an advocate for change in her many travels as an activist for women and for interracial cooperation. In 1909 she helped organize the North Carolina Association of Colored Women's Clubs and later served more than two decades as its president. She became cofounder with Mary McLeod Bethune of the National Council of Negro Women. She was a charter member of the Southern Commission on Interracial Cooperation and the Southern Regional Council. In 1940 Governor Clyde R. Hoey appointed her to the State Council of Defense. She became the first black woman elected to serve on the national board of the YWCA. A popular and powerful speaker, she flew some two thousand miles in 1940 to deliver almost a score of commencement addresses and spoke to a national audience on a CBS broadcast called "Wings over Jordan." In 1945 in Paris she was well received when she addressed the International Congress of Women.

Of all her travels, one of the most dramatic moments came early in her career on the way to a meeting of the White Woman's Missionary Convention in Memphis. On October 8, 1920, as her train pulled into Anniston, Alabama, she was confronted by a group of angry white men who demanded that she leave her sleeper and sit in the day coach designated for black passengers. Brown had no choice except to comply, but she arrived in Memphis seething with indignation. The next day, to an audience of mostly white women, she delivered a fiery lecture entitled "Where We Are in Race Relations." Declaring herself "a little different" from the "most conservative" speaker who had preceded her—Margaret Murray Washington, the wife of Booker T. Washington—Charlotte described her experience on the train. Decrying the absence of any dissenting voices from white women in the Pullman car, she charged those in her audience with the responsibility for controlling white men. Lynching, she argued, would stop if southern white women took action.[10] It was one thing to be lectured in a letter from a friend, but it was quite another to be humiliated on a public train among strangers, and Brown was a proud defender of her public image and the public space she had come to occupy. She was also courageous when, during World War II, she suggested that blacks should not serve their country until they were treated equally under the law. At such moments the anger that she had contained at home for the protection of her "family" spilled out in a larger arena.

Another issue was awaiting the women returning from Memphis: voter registration. Passage of the Nineteenth Amendment had been a long time coming, but the controversy was not over. Race once more loomed large in the attempt by some whites to limit black registration. Most white suffragists had backed away from efforts to educate black citizens to vote, but Charlotte Hawkins Brown, in her role as state president of the Association of Colored Women's Clubs, encouraged black women. Despite a smear campaign against her, Brown directed a statewide offensive, working through the NAACP and women's organizations.[11] But she had much to endure, from black men who opposed black women's taking the spotlight and from some of her own compatriots at interracial meetings. In the year after they had been together in Memphis, Charlotte chose to suffer silently as Frances Bickett, the wife of the former governor of North Carolina, introduced her as a friend "as fine as my Negro mammy."[12] Brown had worked too hard for PMI to risk losing support.

She retired as president of Palmer in 1952 and as treasurer in 1955. Generations of students remembered her as one of the most formative influences in their lives, and in later years they worked to preserve the campus at PMI as a tribute to her. A woman who had graduated in 1937 observed, "She was the moving force, a stern disciplinarian, and we loved her in a respectful way. She spoke her mind."[13] Glenda Gilmore calls Brown a "political genius" and a "consummate pragmatist."[14] At her death at age seventy-seven, she was widely known as Dr. Charlotte Hawkins Brown, the recipient of honorary degrees from Wilberforce, Lincoln, and Howard Universities.

Palmer Memorial Institute continued under three succeeding presidents for a decade longer. In 1971 the Alice Palmer Building was destroyed by fire, the school was financially strapped, and trustees voted to close PMI.[15] Ironically, school integration and the civil rights movement had undermined many historically black institutions as school choices were giving parents and students more options. In 1987 the Palmer campus reclaimed its history when it was designated a state historic site, opening to visitors the Carrie Stone Cottage, where single women faculty members had lived, and the Charlotte Hawkins Brown grave site and Canary Cottage, where she had lived and often entertained students, faculty, and visitors.

The legacy of Charlotte Hawkins Brown can be measured in several ways: in the lives of graduates (and of their children) who became successful leaders and productive citizens, in the campus that now serves as a state historic site, and in the example of one black woman's leadership. In successfully negotiating the difficult southern landscape in the first half of the twentieth century, she educated others who would help to change it forever.

Jane Simpson McKimmon

1867–1957

Jane McKimmon. (Courtesy of North Carolina State University, Raleigh)

Jane Simpson McKimmon and her home demonstration agents were true "mothers of invention." In the early 1900s while farmers were learning new principles of scientific agriculture to improve their crop production and increase their profits, McKimmon was training home demonstration agents to work with farm women. Sometimes their suggestions for home improvements were as simple as bringing the pump inside to the sink and putting the wood box up on legs. Flowers in the yard and curtains at the window prettied up the place. Organized competitions, public recognition, and prize money were rewards for housework, and Jane and her agents—so cheerful, so tireless—brought a good deal of fun and fellowship. At the beginning of her career as a home demonstration agent in 1911, Jane McKimmon—affectionately called "Miss Jenny"—was hailed as a friend coming down a country road. By the end of her long life in 1957 she had become a legend.[1]

Jane was the first of nine children born to Anne and William Simpson, Presbyterian Scots who believed in God, frugality, and hard work. Both sets of Jane's grandparents were Scottish immigrants. William was born in 1839 in New York City; Anne was born in Glasgow, Scotland, and emigrated with her family to Virginia when she was eight years old. After Anne and William married in 1860, they moved to Raleigh, where Simpson was a retail druggist for thirty-eight years. He gave lectures at the School of Pharmacy at present-day Shaw University, which had been founded to educate African Americans, and in 1894 he was president of the National Pharmaceutical Association. Jane often cited her father's influence in shaping her own career. Anne Simpson, an observant Christian especially interested in the arts, was in charge of the care of a very large family. Jane, the oldest child, came to embody her parents' values. Her father's brother, who was blind, became an important person in her life. As a young woman she would go to his house to read to him; thus she developed an interest in books and acquired a personal understanding of people with special needs.

After attending public school for four years, Jane went to Peace Institute in Raleigh (now Peace College). The state capital was a place where agriculture was a frequent theme of conversation and government business. Raleigh was becoming a city, but it still had a "country" feel to it. Many farm people went there to buy or sell or sightsee and took a good deal of the life of the land with them—mules and wagons, produce, and curiosity about the "city." On her way to school, young Jane might see the governor on his way to his office as well as a farm mother loaded down with store purchases and tired children.

Three years after becoming the youngest student to graduate from Peace, nineteen-year-old Jane Simpson married forty-year-old Charles McKimmon. Not much is known about him except that he was a Raleigh businessman. They had four children (Charles, Anne, William, and Hugh), and Jane and Charles brought them up in a house on Blount Street, right in the heart of Raleigh.

Jane's community was a good place for a woman with her ability to take advantage of an early opportunity to extend her "homemaking." A casual conversation with a neighbor while they worked in their vegetable gardens started her on a career that would change McKimmon's life and the lives of a great many women in the state. McKimmon's neighbor was I. O. Schaub, director of the North Carolina Agricultural Extension Service. Schaub told McKimmon about the success other states were having in getting farm girls and boys involved in projects, and he outlined his own work with North Carolina boys' corn clubs—each boy raised and sold an acre of corn and had a great time doing it. He also said that Marie Cromer in South Carolina had started tomato clubs for girls, who were growing, harvesting, canning, and selling tomatoes. Jane McKimmon must have heard a door opening: her interest was keen. And so when Schaub asked her to start tomato clubs in North Carolina, she agreed.

In 1908 Jane had begun work as lecturer for women's programs sponsored by the Farmers' Institute; two years later she became director of the women's division. She traveled all over the state recruiting farm girls to join "tomato clubs." These clubs became so popular that mothers and daughters asked that she give them information about their other interests—baking, sewing, and gardening. McKimmon, in turn, urged the women to talk with their local commissioners about helping to pay for a home agent's salary. The women spoke; the men listened. Thus was the home demonstration movement launched, and Miss Jenny, the agent, was on the move from Macon County to Roanoke Island, finding women waiting in their yards to greet her.

McKimmon's quick adaptation to her job suggests that she loved what she was doing, but there was an even more compelling reason to work: her family needed the income. Letters from Jane and Charles to their adult children indicate that her salary was often the couple's main means of support and that sometimes she lent money to the children. They had moved from their house on Blount Street into an apartment in downtown Raleigh, and life now seemed comfortable and rewarding. In January 1918 she wrote to her son Billy, "I think God is very good to make it possible for me to earn enough to keep father and me in such comfort."[2]

Nationally, what many people came to think of as "home economics" burst upon the scene as a recognized profession, given impetus in 1914, when home demonstration services were institutionalized by the passage of the Smith-Lever Act. McKimmon entered the field at a time when both state and federal programs were beginning. Her contributions increased in importance. In 1917 she was appointed by Governor Thomas W. Bickett to help direct the food conservation program established during World War I. In 1935 Governor J. C. B. Ehringhaus named her to the Rural Electrification Authority. During World War II Governor J. Melville Broughton appointed her to the State Council for National Defense. In a career that spanned about thirty years, she made women's work both personal and public: women cared for the family and for the state and nation.

In the beginning, providing instruction and recognition for time-honored traditions of house and garden was plain and simple: teaching girls to raise, process, and can tomatoes to sell had its immediate appeals, even if it took some trials to learn how to do it. Seasons of drought and a few unacceptable cans with bulging lids doomed some efforts, but members of the clubs were undaunted. In 1912 McKimmon reported that a ten-year-old girl in Guilford County had canned 250 quarts and sold $20 worth of fresh tomatoes. The money these girls made provided spending money for extras and also paid for such necessities as school clothes. In 1915 more than one hundred girls went to college by paying part of their tuition with products they had canned and sold to the college dining hall. At the state woman's college many majored in home economics and on graduation became demonstration agents.

Miss Jenny's agents spread out across North Carolina like water bearers to the fields, traveling on foot and horseback, by wagon and model-T, bus and train. Farm women eagerly awaited them in homes, yards, schools, courthouses, churches, curb markets, and fairgrounds. The women came to learn how to do better the work they had to do and sometimes also to enjoy it more. Moreover, home demonstration agents were models for women who had hope of becoming paid workers themselves. Jane McKimmon recruited, trained, assigned, inspired, counseled, and *paid* women who became her home demonstration agents. Such opportunities promoted furthering one's education. And after she had hired them, she encouraged them to work for promotions.

But finding new ways to do old tasks did not always meet with approval. Often housewives would confess to the home demonstration agents that their husbands simply refused to take seriously any "nonsense" about the need for a better-equipped kitchen. Sometimes the agent showing the housewife how to do her work more effectively first had to gain the husband's permission. Jane understood that men often controlled options for women at home and in public places. She would help them find a way to take care of the home and family and do something for themselves.

When local funding for programs was at risk, as it usually was, Jane, an excellent speaker and a tireless persuader, trained her agents and club members to lobby their county commissioners. Funding often depended on the good reputation that each agent had established in the official's community. Success was partly due to the traditional comportment and training of the women and also to the needs of a state with a rural economy.

Some of her projects—like the women's exhibit hall at the State Fair—had wide public appeal. In other ways, her work was simply indispensable. During two world wars and the Great Depression, she adapted demonstration work to the acute needs of people—feeding, clothing, sewing, caring for the sick, sustaining family unity. During flu epidemics, her agents took on the duties of nurses. During the depression, when money and food were scarce, gardens saved families, and good nutritional guidance helped mothers in trying to prevent such common diseases of malnourishment as pellagra and scurvy. By the 1920s and 1930s, poorer women were receiving many of the same services that middle-class women had enjoyed for the last decade. Blacks and whites had their own agents, their own demonstration sites, and their own advocates in the local community. Almost three times as many women in the club movement were from landowning families as from tenant families, but benefits to tenant farm women were often more dramatically felt because their circumstances were more meager.

Race divisions were as obvious in the home demonstration movement as in other places, but when war increased the need for food production, the state had to find a way to enlist the help of black farm families. In 1915 Annie Wealthy Holland, an African American woman who supervised the Jeanes teachers in public schools, became a home demonstration agent in a program operated under the Negro Rural School Fund and kept separate from that for whites. As demands grew, McKimmon looked for ways to reach most farm women, and with federal funding she was able to hire part-time black demonstration agents—often Jeanes teachers—in forty-one counties and in Wilmington and New Bern.[3]

In trying to meet the needs of many black farm women, she focused on counties with the largest black populations, and successes were regularly reported in Columbus, Johnston, Beaufort, Richmond, Davidson, Anson, Wayne, and Wake. Jane was enthusiastic about the extent to which black women helped increase farm production. Reports emphasized the strong links between the black church and the home demonstration movement. Emma McDougald wrote: "It is proved to the church folks that it is a part of their religion to take good care of the Master's dwelling place which is their bodies and their children's bodies, and to show them how impossible it is to do this without a garden behind each home."[4]

Educated and more secure than her country sisters (although two world wars, a depression, and widowhood were great equalizers), Jane McKimmon worked as hard as any farm woman to formalize the oldest women's network in history—women helping women. When she started in 1911, there were 400 girls enrolled in home extension programs. When she retired in 1937, there were 75,000.

McKimmon's life as we know it was more public than private. She was the kind of go-getter who must have waked up in the morning with her hat on. But there was a private life we do not know much about. The first years of marriage between a nineteen-year-old "girl" and a forty-year-old man must have required adjustments on both sides. When, after forty-two years of marriage, Charles McKimmon died in 1928, Jane had completed the requirements for a master's degree at present-day North Carolina State University. These school years undoubtedly made many demands—to attend class, to get along with students younger than she, to complete assignments, to meet her husband's needs. In 1944 her only daughter died of cancer at age forty-one, and McKimmon moved in with her son-in-law to look after her three grandchildren. After her career ended with full retirement, her life was still busy and satisfying. She was a soloist at Christ Episcopal Church, she was a mother and a grandmother, she walked the four miles to the North Carolina State campus, and she played golf almost every week with women friends. Her desks and cabinets spilling over with files, she turned her attention to writing the history of the home demonstration movement. Her book, *When We're Green We Grow*, the motto of the 4-H club, was published in 1945. It records a busy woman's calendar, more reconstructed out of collected scrapbooks and letters than narrated, but it is an impressive indicator of what she did and the results that followed.

Hot school lunches, milk and juice for undernourished children, balanced meals at home, painted porches, vegetable gardens near the kitchen door, a new dress made from feed sacks, a spring bonnet to make a woman feel pretty, pride in products made in North Carolina, help during medical crises, and thrifty ways of feeding a family—these were the achievements. "We hope to still live on the farm in spite of the boll weevil," one white woman wrote after she had prepared soups for the pantry and sold jams and jellies for cash. In Beaufort County Sarah Williams, the state's first full-time home demonstration agent for African Americans, and Violet Alexander, the white home agent, sometimes worked together. When the county commissioners and school board did not pay Williams enough to cover her travel expenses, Alexander asked Williams to ride with her. Alexander found it "mutually helpful" because Williams knew the roads and people who could assist them in almost every county. In Wayne County another African American, Emma McDougald, was allowed to speak in black churches and introduced by the ministers. When the "Negro family folk" heard about the home demonstration programs, they began to feel that government was "a real friend." Although the number of black agents increased dramatically in emergencies created during World War I, their salaries lagged behind those of most white agents, and when McKimmon retired in 1937, many counties still did not have African American agents.[5]

In 1947, when McKimmon's portrait was presented by the North Carolina Agricultural Extension workers at State College, she was a widely recognized woman. She had earned degrees (and received an honorary doctorate from the University of North Carolina), held a professional job, served on gubernatorial commissions, and was a national speaker and adviser. Before her death at age ninety (for most of her life she had seemed "youthful" to family and friends), she saw the fruits of her labors: housework had become an "art" and the housewife a Master Farm Homemaker. She would have been at home in a computerized kitchen. Indeed, Jane McKimmon was a nineteenth-century romantic who saw things a little better than they were and a twentieth-century scientist who believed that they could be made still better.

Olive Dame Campbell

1882–1954

Olive Dame Campbell (at left) and colleague-friend Marguerite Butler visiting folks schools in Copenhagen. (Courtesy of the Southern Historical Collection, University of North Carolina at Chapel Hill)

Olive Arnold Dame was born in Medford, Massachusetts, and grew up in a home especially interested in education and travel. Her father was a school principal, and the family spent summers on Nantucket Island. In 1903, after graduating from Tufts College, she and her sister Ruth taught in public schools in Medford and saved their money for an adventure: three years later they and their mother sailed for the British Isles. On the Atlantic crossing, the youthful sisters were observed by a solitary older gentleman, John Campbell, a New Englander and a Scotsman. He was recovering from the recent loss of his wife and exhaustion from his work as president of a small mountain school in northern Georgia. The sea voyage and the Dames were just what the doctor had ordered. During the voyage Ruth found John Campbell "a terrible wag," "inspiring" and "humorous," but apparently it was Olive who fell in love with him.[1]

Landing in Glasgow, John and the women traveled together to Edinburgh, and later in the summer met again to tour Cornwall and Devonshire and to take a boat trip on the Thames. After their return to Glasgow, John visited his relatives and then sailed home with the Dames. By this time—it had been a remarkable summer—Olive Dame, who was twenty-four, and John Campbell, who was forty, were practically engaged.

The following March they married and set sail for Italy at the suggestion of John's doctor, who thought another trip would do his patient more good than returning immediately to work. They had a nine-month honeymoon, and the time they spent in Sicily, in a small apartment overlooking a pleasant orchard, was the most uninterrupted period of their twelve years together. They had much to tell one another. John had already spent a decade traveling in the southern highlands, teaching, and getting to know the mountaineers. He had not gone, he would later write, "to uplift anybody." Rather, "The pioneer call was irresistible as it came in striking contrast to the call of the conventional."[2] As they talked about his work, John wanted to find a way to get back to it. He thought that he could locate a sponsor in a new organization he had read about, the Russell Sage Foundation in New York. He wished to make a systematic study of the conditions that affected the lives of the highlanders. After he and Olive talked it over, he wrote in his proposal, "It has been in my thought to make such a study with my wife, for a woman may often learn many essential facts from the women teachers and from the women of the mountains which would not otherwise be available."[3] The foundation was interested in developing his ideas, and Olive and John were filled with anticipation as they packed for home. They returned to Demorest, Georgia, so John could finish his work at Piedmont College. In 1908 they began their travels through the southern Appalachian Mountains.

John Campbell and his first wife Grace (who had died in 1904) had spent a decade getting to know the southern highlands, first in a school in Joppa, Alabama, supported by the American Missionary Association, and later at Piedmont College. Although John had been missionary-minded as a student at Andover Seminary, his interests increasingly had become those of the humanist and social scientist. Olive knew from the first that she had an interest in the culture of people and places. In 1909 with a grant of $3,000 from the Russell Sage Foundation, recently incorporated as a philanthropic organization, they began to collect data on the health, education, and social and economic conditions of the region.

Olive kept a detailed journal of their journey through the mountains of

Tennessee, Kentucky, Georgia, West Virginia, and North Carolina—by train and wagon, surrey, hack, buckboard, buggy, horseback, mule, and on foot and in all kinds of weather. After two years of marriage the Campbells had traveled 1,500 miles and visited more than seventy schools. They met with state and federal officials; they talked with teachers, ministers, and school superintendents; and they visited many isolated homes in the mountains. John collected data for population studies; Olive liked to see how families actually lived, sometimes setting off alone on horseback to visit a mountain woman. Both Campbells might be asked to speak or to teach. Sometimes they rose before 4:00 A.M. to catch a train. Invited to stay in a mountain cabin, they slept under worn and dirty homespun covers on a hard tick mattress in a cold room. The next morning, when they had dressed, warmed themselves before a fire, and eaten rabbit prepared by their hosts, they paid for their bed and breakfast and the horse's feed: it came on one such occasion to $2.30. Many nights neither slept. John worried about the highlanders, and Olive, aware of her husband's frail health, worried about John.[4]

Olive's journal tells of children with hacking coughs and paralysis and typhoid. In one home where there were thirteen children, six had died. She saw "illegitimacy in almost every family." In North Carolina the streets of Blowing Rock were free of drunks, an improvement Olive attributed to "the good results of [state] Prohibition." The new hospital at Banner Elk "will have to grow slowly, as people are suspicious and slow to convince"; Dr. Reid "does not see $5 in a month." John had interviewed the superintendent of a mine who complained that his workers did not know how to keep time records.[5]

On March 11, 1909, Olive's twenty-seventh birthday, she visited a home for "factory girls," where a matron described how they must be "made-over from scalp to toenails" and put to bed. A doctor working out of a church was "quite belligerent in defense of the people" and resented outsiders seeing "peculiar cases" as typical. At the next stop, near Asheville, Olive went with a local woman to interview the Episcopal rector at "the Vanderbilts' church." The rector's wife "rolled in in elaborate silk and exchanged a few condescending words before sailing out again." Olive learned that mountain boys who went to the mills found themselves hampered by their lack of education and were "determined to learn." Asked if she did not "find it depressing to study these peculiar people," Olive replied, "I would perhaps if at the bottom they were not pretty much like the rest of us."[6]

During these early years Olive demonstrated her ability to live in the highlands. A local man noticed how she kept up with the party and was especially impressed with her determination on a snowy winter day to climb a mountain. He told of having heard that "up thar in Massachusetts" there was "nary woman ever sot her afoot out of the house to do a lick of work."[7]

Olive's attention, almost from the first day of her mountain travels, had been drawn to "all things native & fine" exemplified in the handicrafts she saw and the "ballets" she heard sung and played. At the Hindman Settlement School in Kentucky, Katherine Pettit and Mary Stone had shown her handmade "kivvers" and woolen rugs. While visiting a home up a cove, she bought for seven dollars a beautiful old indigo cover. But it was an evening at the Hindman School that became a defining moment:

> Shall I ever forget it. The blazing fire, the young girl on her low stool before it, the soft strange strumming of the banjo—different from anything I had ever heard before—and then the song! I had been used to singing "Barbara Allen" as a child, but how far from that gentle tune was this—so strange, so remote, so thrilling. I was lost almost from the first note, and the peasant room faded from sight; the singer only a voice. I saw again the long road over which we had come, the dark hills, the rocky streams bordered by tall hemlocks and hollies, the lonely cabins distinguishable at night only by the firelight flaring from their chimneys. Then these, too, faded, and I seemed to be borne along into a still more dim and distant past, of which I myself was a part.[8]

No truer romantic spirit ever spoke, but she was practical enough to make a plan. In her visits to mountain homes, she concentrated her attention on the ballads she heard, putting performers at their ease by her sincere and quiet interest, until they played and sang half the night. In the morning she had scribbled sheets of words and music. When she realized that she was hearing very old ballads of British and Scottish origin, she sought the help of British ballad collector Cecil J. Sharp. In the summer of 1915, she traveled to meet him in Lincoln, Massachusetts, during one of his visits to America. When she told him about the wealth of new materials to be collected in the southern mountain states, he was at once interested. The next year he visited the Campbells in Asheville and examined her ballad collection. He was impressed with what he saw, and they became collaborators.

Olive's work was distinctive in two ways: she felt that she and the people who had given her their songs were "friends," and she did not exploit them or seek to keep other ballad collectors from having access to the materials. David Whisnant observes, "For the time, Mrs. Campbell's collection was almost unique in the United States in according major importance to the ballad tunes, instead of solely to the texts so prized by most American ballad scholars, still tied to the primarily literary origins of their enterprise."[9] When *English Folk Songs of the Southern Appalachians* was published in 1917, Olive Dame Campbell and Cecil Sharp were listed as coauthors. Early in their work together, Sharp observed that Olive's "high standard" was remarkable in view of the fact that she had no contact with ballad collecting being done in other places. He praised her for having "just the combination of scientific and artistic spirit which work of this kind needs if it is to be of any use to posterity."[10]

"These people" were more to Olive Campbell than a subject to be studied. The Campbells, as early as 1911, had felt it "imperative" to establish a permanent home in the South. Two years later, when the Russell Sage Foundation asked John to head up the new Southern Division office in Asheville, they moved into a house on St. Dunstan's Road. John ran the office, and Olive, with the help of female students from the nearby Presbyterian Home School, looked after the house and helped with a good deal of John's work. Blythewood, a low, rambling house, "overflowed with guests." The toll of long hours, arduous travel, and a frail constitution created recurring periods of exhaustion and sickness for John.[11]

Olive was in good health and active, enjoying playing tennis. On April 1, 1912, she gave birth to a daughter, Jane, who "was everything [John] ever wanted except strong." Three months later the baby still had a "food problem." In December, her condition was "precarious." "I do not like to think of that Christmas," Olive later wrote, "and the days that followed, when we alternated between hope and despair." Then, Jane's "heart failed, and she was gone." Except for these brief passages, Olive's diary gives no further account of their grief. Another girl, Barbara, perhaps named for John's sister, was born on February 5, 1915. During her second year, Barbara suffered from bronchial pneumonia. On October 24, 1917, Cecil Sharp wrote Olive to say how sorry he was to hear about the death of their second child, adding, "I am glad you have your sisters with you."[12]

The sorrow of losing their second child perhaps took the last life out of John Campbell, who was already a semi-invalid. He died in 1919 at age fifty-one. After his death, Olive determined to continue their work. As she later observed, in "the hard years that followed . . . I had to learn to find my way, alone in a new world."[13] She began by completing things that John had planned to do. For instance, he had left materials for the book that he had been working on for many years in conjunction with his survey for the Sage Foundation, and Olive went to the family home at Nantucket to finish it. Although she did most of the writing, in 1921 she published *The Southern Highlander and His Homeland* in his name.

With the book completed, she began to think more seriously about the plans John had made for their visit to Denmark to study folk schools, which they had had to cancel with the advent of World War I. After receiving a grant from an American-Scandinavian foundation, she, her sister Daisy, and a friend, Marguerite Butler, sailed for Europe. During their fourteen-month visit, Olive had opportunities to hear more about Marguerite's teaching at the Pine Mountain Settlement School in Kentucky. They rode their bicycles or went by rail from one Danish city and town to another gathering ideas to use the Danish Folk School as a model for an "out of doors" school to build community and economic stability in the Appalachians.

When Olive and Marguerite returned from Scandinavia, Olive began looking in the highlands for a suitable location for a school. Meanwhile, Marguerite had left Kentucky and was working in Cherokee County when "Uncle Luce" Scroggs of the Brasstown community asked her to help build support for a school there. Marguerite arranged for Olive to visit Brasstown, where in 1925, with a commitment from local people of land, labor, lumber, stone, and cash, the John C. Campbell Folk School was founded. Other gifts came from churches and from the Carnegie Corporation. One of Olive's first decisions was to hire Marguerite as her assistant, formalizing a partnership that lasted twenty-five years.

From the beginning, the people of Brasstown liked Campbell. One person who had been present in the farmhouse the first winter after the school was founded recalled that when no one else volunteered to sing, Olive herself sang "Barbara Allen" and then blushed. The native highlander exclaimed, "I'd have walked ten miles to hear that." It was in that sort of informal setting that she was at her best. Gathering around her small groups of students, she stimulated their interest in music, and she sat at the piano and played the folk songs they brought from home. The annual performance of a nativity play brought many community members together.[14]

Campbell was determined to help mountaineers make a living by marketing crafts made at the school and by establishing cooperatives. With help from local farmers she got a dairy cooperative started, planted and harvested crops, and developed a program in forestry. A credit cooperative was opened, and modest gains were made in helping local people to get loans for land and farming needs. Profits were never high during the fifteen-year period (1928–43) in which the school operated its agricultural programs, but, observes David Whisnant, Olive Dame Campbell was more successful than most organizers in developing agricultural cooperatives. The Brasstown Savings and Loan Association was one of the credit unions that gave North Carolina the reputation for having some of the best credit legislation in the nation. Crafts also became a moneymaking enterprise. Early on, Campbell had been fascinated by the group of men who carved with pocketknives as they sat on a bench outside Scroggs's store in Brasstown, and it gave her the idea of teaching wood carving at the school. By the early 1930s the distinctive highland carved figures of animals had found a market.

In 1928 Campbell finished almost a decade's work as executive secretary of the Conference of Southern Mountain Workers, which John had founded. She next focused on helping to create a new organization to market highland crafts. At a meeting held in Penland, she worked with Lucy Morgan and others to organize the Southern Highland Handicraft Guild and helped another New Englander, Frances Goodrich, to move her Allanstand Cottage Industries into the newly formed guild and work out guidelines for a sales cooperative. When Doris Ulmann went to the mountains to make photographs and Allen Eaton was conducting field studies for a book on handicrafts, they enlisted Olive Dame Campbell's assistance. The people who worked with her would remember her gentleness, understanding, wisdom, dependability, and generosity. They also recalled her beautiful smile.

In 1946, as retirement approached, she took pleasure in walking from one new farmhouse to another, greeting some of her former students who had bought land and built their homes, furnishing them with chairs, hearth brooms, metal work, and weaving that they had made at the school. She recognized that she had finished her work, that it had been shaped by her personality, and that she would be in the way of a new director. She returned to Medford and summers on Nantucket but continued to hear from friends who were concerned about change. She shared their hope that the "old" school could survive, but her own energies had waned. She died on June 14, 1954, in her seventy-second year.

More than a half century later, almost every week of the year, the John C. Campbell Folk School offered students of all ages and places hundreds of noncredit, nongraded classes lively with discussion and "hands-on" experience, whether in making baskets or playing the dulcimer or studying nature. And the Craft Shop sold crafts made by more than three hundred regional artists. Anyone who seeks evidence of Olive's legacy need only visit Brasstown. It is remarkable that a nineteenth-century New England school woman who collected English folk ballads and taught Danish dances introduced cultural studies—likely to be one of the major themes of the twenty-first century—into the landscape of western North Carolina.

Gertrude Weil

1879–1971

Gertrude Weil (at left) and suffragists, ca. 1910. (Courtesy of the North Carolina Division of Archives and History)

Gertrude Weil belonged to a small number of prominent North Carolinians who happily wore the label "liberal." As a Jew, she was among a small minority of southerners; as a single woman of wealth, she was independent; and as a learned and witty public speaker, she made friends easily and held the rapt attention of audiences. She lived well, laughed often, and left a legacy of good causes. Her place in history exceeds any one description, but to call her a citizen activist seems logical and appropriate.

There was always something exceptional in the life of Gertrude Weil. At twenty-two, she was already far ahead of most other North Carolinians in education, a graduate of the Horace Mann School of Columbia Teachers College and Smith College, two of the finest schools in the country. When she received her degree from Smith in 1901, she returned to North Carolina because her parents wanted her home. What she might have done with her life had she joined some of her classmates in law or medical school, in business or journalism, or in work in the settlement houses, or if she had lived in Boston or New York or even Baltimore, where women had more freedom and opportunity—well, Gertrude seemed never to have brooded about what might have been. She looked ahead.

As the train from New York pulled into the Goldsboro station, Gertrude could have reassured herself that this was where she belonged simply by walking through town. Her mother and grandmother had helped establish the temple where Gertrude worshipped every Friday night. Her father, Henry, and his brothers, Herman and Solomon, were prominent business leaders. For their families Henry and Solomon had built houses—side by side—near the center of town. These German-Jewish immigrant brothers and their capable wives always gave something back to their community, for they were the builders of Goldsboro. Following their example, Gertrude would lay a few cornerstones of her own.[1]

Weil was one of a small number of well-educated, affluent, politically active North Carolina women born in the latter half of the nineteenth century. She had friends among national women's organizations with whom she corresponded and attended many meetings. Throughout her life she and other family members actively supported Jewish causes; they gave generously to help rescue Jews, some of them their relatives, from the death camps of Nazi Germany. Gertrude and other family members visited the newly created state of Israel. The activist phrase of the 1990s—"Think globally and act locally"—was made to order for Gertrude Weil.

Her graduation from Smith College in 1901 was also the year in which Charles Aycock, who had practiced law in Goldsboro, took office as governor. Although he supported universal education, Aycock opposed the vote for women. If Weil, already an "avowed suffragist," read a local newspaper on January 1, 1901, her usual optimism may have faltered. The front-page news was not promising for a young woman who had been exposed to some of the most liberal ideas of the day. Two separate columns, positioned midpage in the *Goldsboro Argus*, might have caught her attention. On the right she would have seen an advertisement for Dr. Pierce's Favorite Prescription for women "troubled with female weakness" and in the column to the left, a message from "His Eminence Cardinal Gibbons," who was quoted as saying: "I regard women rights women and society leaders in the higher walks of life as the worst enemies of the female sex. They rob women of all that is amiable and gentle . . . and give her nothing in return but masculine boldness and brazen effrontery."

Such a declaration would not have set well with Weil, who was a southern lady and a thinking woman. She was a suffragist. Later, she campaigned for Al Smith, a Catholic, and for Frank Porter Graham, a liberal. She became more liberal as she grew older—a union sympathizer and an integrationist. In her eighties, she convened biracial committee meetings in her Goldsboro home; in conversations and interviews she called herself a "socialist" and sometimes a "radical." The family biographer, Moses Rountree, who interviewed her when she was eighty-eight, observed, "Her blue eyes sparkle with fun and mischief; her mind is razor-sharp."[2]

For more than a century, the Weil name signified civic responsibility in North Carolina, and perhaps Gertrude was the family's best-known member. Although she was born in the nineteenth century, the public opinions she expressed still seem relevant for the twentieth and twenty-first centuries.

The migration of European Jews down the American eastern seaboard into southern towns brought North Carolina a number of civic-minded citizens who were active in business and cultural affairs. It was a stroke of good luck when the Weil brothers settled in Goldsboro—other family members emigrating from Germany stayed in Baltimore—as Goldsboro proved to be very hospitable. It was the county seat, with four newspapers and a woman's college. Goldsboro Female College opened in 1854, was used as a hospital during the Civil War, and closed in 1871. Here north-south and east-west railroads intersected. In 1881 the town had a model public school, initiated by the Weils, after the German system. The Weil brothers were civic as well as business leaders, often serving as aldermen and members of the school board. They advertised their department store in the local newspaper as "H. Weil and Brothers—Who Do What they Say."

Nothing was more characteristic of the Weil brothers than that they had married smart women. Henry Weil had to talk Mina Rosenthal out of studying medicine so they could marry as soon as she graduated from the Wilson Collegiate Seminary for Young Ladies. Mina was sixteen, Henry twenty-eight. Solomon Weil married Sarah Einstein, of Boston, who was never satisfied with southern life in Goldsboro, although she worked hard to make it better. It was Sarah who encouraged Gertrude to apply to Smith College. While other North Carolina clubs were reading ancient history, the Goldsboro Ladies' Benevolent Society, which Sarah had started, invited Charlotte Perkins Gilman as a speaker. Gilman had just published *Women and Economics*, and Goldsboro men stood on the street corner and wondered what the ladies were up to when they went to hear Gilman give four lectures on the economic oppression of women. They feared that the next thing Goldsboro women might want was the vote. Soon Mina Weil, Gertrude's mother, organized the Goldsboro Women's Club (1899) and dedicated it to Charlotte Perkins Gilman. These progressive women were the mothering spirits of Gertrude Weil.

Gertrude herself attended Goldsboro Graded School and, at age thirteen, was sent to the Horace Mann preparatory school of Columbia University. Her physical education teacher was Margaret Stanton Lawrence, the daughter of Elizabeth Cady Stanton. She introduced Gertrude to physical exercise, which became a lifelong interest. After graduation from Horace Mann, Weil was the first student from North Carolina to attend Smith College, joining more than a thousand women in liberal, often experimental learning. A series of lectures at Smith on the economic status of women, poverty, and social injustice may have encouraged her to become a suffragist.[3]

In the first several years after leaving Smith, Weil seemed restless, traveling abroad, considering first one thing and then another. Like many young people returning home, she might have felt as if she would be sacrificing a good deal of her own independence. She may not even have thought of the return to Goldsboro as a permanent move, but as the months passed and she became more and more involved in organizations, the die was cast. Gertrude was too important a part of the family and the town for bonds to loosen. She stayed.

Her main anchors in Goldsboro and North Carolina generally were women's organizations. The club movement that Sallie Southall Cotten had helped turn into a statewide federation in 1902 was one in which Gertrude's mother and aunt were active. Mina Weil had sought Gertrude's suggestions regarding the formation of the women's club in Goldsboro while her daughter was at Smith. Sallie Cotten very much admired the older Weil women, and when Gertrude began to take part in club work, Sallie quickly recognized her talents and invited her to join the inner circle of Sallie's protégés. Gertrude was chosen for one office or another on federation committees on both local and state levels, and her attendance at the annual meetings was cause for great pleasure among her many friends. Letters exchanged back and forth concerning upcoming meetings were filled with anticipation. She was a popular speaker, witty, modest, well organized, and persuasive.

"Federation Gertie" turned down the presidency of the North Carolina Federation of Women's Clubs, but during the meeting her name brought an ovation from the large audience. Instead, she served two terms as president of the North Carolina Equal Suffrage League, leading support for passage of the Nineteenth Amendment. Weil had been clear on the need for voting rights for a long time. "When I came home [from Smith College]," she said, "I wondered why people made speeches in favor of something so obviously right. Women breathed the same air, got the same education; it was ridiculous, spending so much energy and elocution on something rightfully theirs."[4]

But when energy and elocution were called for, Weil responded. She was the state's best organizer, and following strategies set forth in letters and telegrams from Carrie Chapman Catt, president of the National American Woman Suffrage Association, Weil marshaled her forces—gathering thousands of names on petitions, securing letters of endorsement from prominent North Carolina men, traveling to communities to help local leaders organize, and keeping her foot soldiers informed about the timing for the next lobbying effort directed to state legislators. From her office in Raleigh's Yarborough Hotel, she took charge like a "seasoned veteran." She knew the state too well to count on an easy victory, however. At best, she thought suffrage had about a fifty-fifty chance of winning, which turned out to be a pretty good guess.[5]

But the amendment did not pass. The North Carolina legislature, in one of those southern political dramas in which race and gender were as entangled as a Gordian knot, voted it down and urged Tennessee to do the same. Tennessee resisted North Carolina legislators telling them what to do. The affirmative carried by one vote, and Tennessee became the final state necessary to make the amendment a part of the Constitution.

It was a great victory nationally and could have been a bitter pill for the tireless North Carolina suffragists, but Gertrude apparently did not waste tears on having lost one battle while helping to win the war. She immediately moved to the next step—following Carrie Chapman Catt's national leadership—and founded the state's League of Women Voters and served as its first president. Now that women could vote, an organization was needed for citizen education.

North Carolina was even more inhospitable to labor reform than it had been to woman suffrage. It took a lot of courage—then and now—to stand up for workers' rights. Weil's participation in the labor reform movement in North Carolina followed that of her mother, who had worked for child labor legislation. But Gertrude became a more visible and vocal statewide leader. Marion Roydhouse refers to a speech made by Gertrude Weil in 1916 as the first call for a survey of the "social and economic condition of women and girls in North Carolina." Such a survey, endorsed by women's groups but fiercely opposed by textile leaders, would be debated throughout the 1920s. Weil was also a leader in the Legislative Council of North Carolina Women, organized to advance progressive reforms. According to Roydhouse, Weil and her close friend, Laura Cone of Greensboro, provided "the crucial financial underpinning of the Council work." Kate Burr Johnson, the state commissioner of public welfare and a friend of Weil's, urged special legislation protecting women. Meanwhile, the call for a survey of working conditions affecting women remained stalled. Modest victories were achieved when a child labor bill passed, but the powerful textile lobbyists overwhelmed the small group of women reformers. Recognizing that the survey would not be supported, Weil urged the League of Women Voters to turn its attention to the strikers in Marion, North Carolina, led by the United Textile Workers. Some members did; most did not.[6]

Outbreaks of violence between union strikers and management had deepened the statewide antagonism toward organized labor. In 1929 in Gaston County, union organizer and ballad singer Ella May Wiggins was murdered. Weil had followed the news day by day; in her papers there are many clippings about the strikes, including one from the *Raleigh News and Observer* that carried a picture of Ella May's five orphaned children in front of her grave. Enormous antiunion sentiment—and fear—was erupting around the state when Frank Porter Graham asked his good friend Gertrude Weil to sign a proposal in support of collective bargaining and another appeal for a survey of conditions in the mills. Weil and Graham were loved and esteemed by many people, but some of their own friends could not go along with their views. More than four hundred people, however, signed the petition, including most members of the women's Legislative Council. When the General Assembly met in 1931, it passed a measure shortening women's workweek but once again rejected the survey.

Programs spawned by the New Deal were made to order for the next step in Weil's education. As director of public relief in Goldsboro, she began to see firsthand inequities in the education and standard of living for many local black citizens. Unlike most moneyed people, Weil thought that wealth and power should be more evenly distributed among the masses. "There should be more collaboration among citizens for the benefit of the whole community," she said. "People are wrong in thinking that the best incentive is competition. Competition is good, but only as an instrument for the common good."[7]

White women and black women, although separated, had worked in the club movement for many of the same causes. Gertrude Weil was a friend and an ally of Charlotte Hawkins Brown, who had established and for many years led the federated club movement for blacks in North Carolina. Weil refused to be drawn into the divisive arguments many suffragists waged against race advocates and avoided rhetoric that exploited prejudice. Later she was active in organizations working to improve race relations. In 1932 Governor O. Max Gardner asked her to serve on the North Carolina Commission on Interracial Cooperation (later the North Carolina Council on Human Relations). Her work for the council for almost twenty-five years put her in touch with some of the most critical race issues of the period, and time and again her leadership gave full expression to her beliefs.

Weil worked in Frank Porter Graham's losing senatorial campaign of 1950, a textbook case on the use of racism to defeat a candidate. Her contributions to society were also generous in countless private ways—giving checks, for example, to community organizations and to individuals petitioning her for help. During the 1960s she was always willing to put her name to causes supporting equal justice and bettering race relations. She continued to live in downtown Goldsboro long after most other white families had moved out, to be friendly with her black neighbors, to invite them to her home, and to go with them to public meetings.[8]

Weil had most of what she needed—education, money, intelligence, wit, courage, and energy. For about seventy years she was recognized as one of the state's most progressive leaders, a rather startling reputation for a woman. She received public accolades to "Miss Gertrude" with modesty and humor. When Anne Firor Scott first met Weil, she was eighty-four, and she seemed to Scott the rarest of individuals—one who had grown old gracefully.[9] In May 1971 the North Carolina General Assembly perfunctorily ratified the woman suffrage amendment, by which time it did not matter, perhaps even to Weil. It was to be the last month of her life, and after spending it with family and friends, she died at age ninety-one in the room where she was born. She did not live to follow the 1975 debate over the Equal Rights Amendment (ERA), which opponents defeated with arguments like those raised over voting rights for women. Weil, who had witnessed the packed and noisy galleries in the North Carolina legislature when the Anthony Amendment was defeated, would certainly have recognized in the ERA debates how little had changed. But she would have listened to the arguments with good humor and good sense. She knew that a good laugh saves many a day from disaster, and she returned and returned to address the next day's needs.

Ella May Wiggins

1900–1929

LABOR DEFENDER
Oct.1929
10¢
ELLA MAY
MARTYR FOR AN ORGANIZED SOUTH

Ella May Wiggins. (From a drawing on the cover of *Labor Defender*, October 1919; courtesy of the North Carolina Division of Archives and History)

Ella May Wiggins was born on September 17, 1900, near the town of Sevierville, Tennessee, southwest of Knoxville. Today it is still a small foothills town built around a courthouse. The great defining character of the region is the mountain ranges: the Great Smokies, the Appalachians, the Blue Ridge. In the early 1900s migrants leaving the timbered-out mountains to reach the textile mills of the Carolinas were desperately searching for jobs. By the late 1900s the economy had changed: jobs had been created by tens of thousands of tourists jamming the roads to Gatlinburg, Tennessee, and other mountain communities. How far away seems the story of Ella May Wiggins, a mountain-born woman and self-taught ballad singer, who had been a nomadic millhand in the Carolinas for almost a decade and was on her way to a union meeting in Gastonia, North Carolina, when she was murdered by an armed mob in the labor unrest of 1929.

Ella was the daughter of Catherine Maples May and James May. A brother, Wesley, was born in 1907, and she had an older half brother and half sister. By the time she was ten years old, her father had given up farming and was working in logging camps in Tennessee. The family moved from camp to camp, living in shanties. Her mother took in washing for loggers, and her brother hauled water and helped James cut trees. Ella herself was a popular girl in the camps, regarded as a "purty young'un" with a fine singing voice. When she was eighteen, her mother died, and the next year her father was killed in a logging accident. Ella married handsome John Wiggins—ten years her senior—who was known as "a ne'er-do-well" and "a sweet-talking charmer."[1] They soon had a child.

Ella's parents, who had provided for their family, however meagerly, were gone, and in their place were John Wiggins and a mill recruiter. When the recruiter stood around the camp and pitched his promises, he implied that working in the mill could change a family's life. There would be hourly wages, for example. Because of that promise Ella rousted out her sweet-talking husband, bundled her young child, and headed down the mountain. The recruiter paid the fare, and the three Wigginses kept going until they settled near Cowpens, South Carolina. It is likely that they both got jobs in the mill, but it was Ella who became the main support for the family.

"Hillbillies" from the Mountains could become "lintheads" in the Piedmont about as quickly as it took a mill recruiter to sign them up, but probably no employer gave much thought to the adjustments such a change in their lives might require. Isolated mountain areas with few jobs, deep poverty, and workers accustomed to physical labor were worth a recruiter's visiting. But what he was really offering was inside work as hard as cutting and hauling timber on the mountain—and without fresh air and sky. For some of these mountain recruits, the mill village, where houses rented at rates lower than any place the workers could find outside the village and where there might be a school and a company store, did seem a better place than a logging camp. Indeed, many mill workers came to describe their relationship to the mill, to the mill village, and to one another as being "like a family."[2]

Ella was from a different mold. She never spoke of herself as belonging to the mill family. She was unwilling to live in a village where owners made the rules. She had carried down off the mountain a sense of pride, a fierce independence, and a lasting certainty that she was an outsider. She found out quickly enough that the recruiter's promises of steady wages and good work were false. Why would she trust her life to a mill that exploited workers? Where would she belong?

Ella and her family left Cowpens and moved to another mill town. At one point they were evicted from company housing, either because John refused to work and the mill required that each family living in one of its houses to supply a certain quota of workers, or because Ella stayed out of work to be home with her children. They just moved on.

Marriage was as hard as work for Ella May Wiggins. Apparently John spent more time talking and loving than working. During the approximately nine years that they were together (1918–26), Ella had eight babies. She likely worked in the mill on a twelve-hour shift during most of her pregnancies, and she was pregnant most of the time. She may have had some prenatal care when a mill clinic was available, but it would have been irregular at best. It is a safe assumption that all of her children were born at home, perhaps with a midwife, but not with a doctor.

Her babies had tenuous lives. Four of them died, one from pellagra when he was sixteen months old and the others probably from similar diseases associated with malnourishment. How healthy they were at birth, what medical attention they received during their first months, if and how long she was able to breast-feed them, what kinds of food they were given, what kind of rest Ella had after working, what threats the boss made if she slacked off—these are sobering questions that suggest only the bleakest of speculations.

Not only was Ella working and having babies, but by age twenty-five she was the sole parent as well. Sometime between 1925 and 1927 she and her children had moved to Gaston County, North Carolina, and John had abandoned them. Soon afterward, Ella began living with her cousin, Charley Shope (also spelled Shoop), who fathered her ninth and last child. She rented a shack in a black district outside Bessemer City called Stumptown, where her neighbors helped look after the children while she was at the mill.

Many poor people at this time were leaving farm labor and looking for factory work in Gaston, the third largest textile county in the nation. Many of them hired on at the big Loray operation in Gastonia, the City of Spindles, but Wiggins had taken a job at American Mill No. 2 in nearby Bessemer City. American was undercapitalized and was known for paying the lowest wages. By then Ella believed that mills were "all the same." So probably the location made a difference; she likely did not want to live in a mill village and in a place as big as Gastonia.

At American Mill No. 2 she worked as a spinner—twelve hours a day, six days a week, for about nine dollars a week. During this period conditions in southern textile mills worsened. The recruiters were not saying anything about "stretch-outs," that is, longer hours for no additional pay. Nor were they saying that North Carolina government and business leaders fiercely opposed interference from "outsiders" —those who wanted to survey mill conditions and those who wanted to organize workers for collective bargaining. In Gaston County millowners and local government officials shared power. Union organizers in the North who studied southern mills believed that Gaston County was the place where a big battle could be fought and won.

Unions had already gained a foothold in the South, especially in the Loray mills. Then, in April 1929 the communist-sponsored National Textile Workers Union (NTWU) moved in, and Loray workers struck to increase their pay, to end the stretch-out, and to win collective bargaining. The presence of communists was immediately reported in headlines across North Carolina and the nation, and the reaction of most local citizens—and state government leaders—bordered on hysteria. The words "union" and "communism" were linked in the North Carolina public mind in a way that unions could never overcome. Moreover, antiunion sentiments were as passionate as anticommunist ones. Violence was inevitable.

Ella had already made her reputation as a hard woman who would not back off a fight. From the beginning, women comprised at least half of the strikers, a larger number proportionately than they represented in the workforce. Women were often the ones stepping forward, the ones most vocal in their comments to the press. Ella found her voice and her place on the front lines. She said that the union was "the first bright spot in my life. . . . It is the first thing I can stick to."

Ella had received her education in the union, attended union meetings to learn organizational and strike tactics, become a union bookkeeper (she was more literate than many millworkers), and traveled with delegations to Washington, D.C., to testify about labor practices in the South. She had learned to hold the attention of a large, restless audience, whether she spoke or sang, on the back of a truck or platform or on the edge of the woods. Her ballads were popular. Someone at a union rally would call on her to sing, and she would come forward. When she sang, making up words to well-known tunes, the audience joined in the refrain, and she would add verse after verse, until often they led into hymn singing. All-day meetings ended in sports for the men and a picnic prepared by the women. In no time at all, union meetings were like family reunions.

What most distinguished Ella's leadership was her personal story. By citing her own desperate life, she dramatized the role of mill mothers. "I'm the mother of nine," she began her speech. "Four died with the whooping cough, all at once. I was working nights, and I asked the super to put me on days, so's I could tend 'em when they had their bad spells. But he wouldn't. I don't know why. He's the sorriest man alive, I reckon. So I had to quit, and then there wasn't no money for medicine, and they just died." Directly addressing the large numbers of women in her audiences, she said, "I couldn't do for my children anymore than you women on the money we git. That's why I came out for the union, and why we all got to stand for the union, so's we can do better for our children, and they won't have lives like we got."

Her testimony carried a powerful message. After she spoke, she sang. Her best-known song was sung to the tune of a 1913 ballad, "Little Mary Phagan," based on the murder of a child in an Atlanta factory. It later was called "A Mill Mother's Lament." The first verse aroused her listeners:

> We leave our homes in the morning
> We kiss our children goodbye
> While we slave for the bosses
> Our children scream and cry.

Verse after verse followed, until she reached the last one:

> But understand all, workers,
> Our union they do fear,
> Let's stand together, workers,
> And have a union here.

The other focus that she gave her presentations was of the boss man, who "rides in a big fine car" and "sleeps in a big fine bed," in contrast to the worker, who "sleep[s] in a old straw bed and shivers from the cold." (In her shack in Stumptown, there were two beds for two adults and five children.)

What Wiggins called her "song ballets" attracted the attention of Margaret Larkin, a journalist and ballad collector who was in North Carolina to cover the strike. About Ella May Wiggins she wrote, "She had a clear, true tone in her untaught voice. She sang from the chest. Full throated, unmodulated, her voice rang out in the simple monotonous tunes. . . . she observed the conventions of each tune carefully." At the end of some lines, she added a "yip," "an indescribable upward lift of the note."[3]

The deaths of Ella's four children had not occurred at the same time, but one had followed another so quickly—two in one year—that it must have seemed as if they had died all at once. Perhaps she was an insightful student of ballads, recognizing that dramatization and exaggeration were the ballad singer's stock-in-trade. A line that began "four died" and ended with "all at once" was immediate, compelling. We do not know how often she told her story; it is quoted just this way by Larkin, who met Ella at a union meeting three weeks before her death. Larkin recalled, "She held the smallest of her five children in her arms, and told me about herself."[4]

Whereas union work was energizing for Wiggins, life at home was desperate. Apparently soon after she began working at Mill No. 2, she had moved her family to Stumptown. It is likely that she had made friends with some of the black men and women working at the mill, which, atypically, employed a large number of blacks (nearly 50 percent), and some of them may have been her neighbors in the remote settlement. Segregation in Gaston County, as elsewhere in North Carolina, was so tight that even a black man's look at a white woman or a black woman's look at her white employer held the potential for conflict. A white woman living among blacks was exposing herself to outbreaks of race violence.

Ella's black neighbors helped look after the children, whom she left alone in the house when she went to work the night shift. The children went barefoot and stayed out of school. They hated Charley Shope, who argued and fought with Ella and with them. By day, she foraged for food, cooking opossums she trapped in the woods. She would not steal, and she refused charity, although she might entice a neighbor's chicken with bread crumbs. One of her children, Millie, said that her mother "was short and dark and starved to death." She held her chin high. Then tragedy struck with a terrifying reality. One day Ella came home from the mill to find her daughter Myrtle holding the baby, not knowing that the baby was dead.

Wiggins, grieving and desperate, threw herself into union work to fight for her family's survival. According to one reporter who covered the strike, "Meetings, speeches, picket lines, and that strange mass power we call solidarity, developed [her] latent talents. . . . She learned to speak; she worked on committees; she helped give out relief; she organized for the defense of imprisoned strikers. She was proud that she could keep neat and accurate account books." Another remembered her as "a person of unusual intelligence who grasped every feature of the strike and could explain it in her own words." A union organizer declared that she was among the best union leaders in the South.

Wiggins had the courage to talk back to authority. When someone in Washington told her delegation that children ought to be in school, she spoke up. "How can I send my children to school when I can't make enough to clothe them decently? When I go to the mill at night I have to lock them up at night all by their lone selves. I can't hire anyone to look after them. Last winter when two of them were sick with the flu, I had to leave them at home in bed when I went to work. I can't get them good enough clothes to send them to Sunday School."

She was bold in another way: the job that she took for herself, and one that others shunned, was organizing black workers. When a rope was tied to separate blacks and whites at a union meeting, Ella alone crossed the rope and walked on the side with blacks. "I know the colored don't like us," she said. "But if they see you're poor and humble like themselves, they'll listen to you." In a close vote, the local NTWU voted to admit blacks to the union.

In the spring of 1929 trouble escalated. Workers protested in the streets, and in a raid on a tent city that had been set up for evicted families, the Gastonia police chief was killed. Sixteen unionists were charged with the killing.

The atmosphere was tense, and Ella's brother urged her to stay away from union meetings, but she refused. Her association with blacks in particular had made her a target of personal threats. She was afraid in her own house and no longer would sit near a window or door. On one occasion, someone poisoned the water in her spring. Toward evening on September 14, 1929, she and other union members climbed into the back of a truck headed for Gastonia for a meeting of the NTWU. Wiggins herself had insisted that no one go armed, and apparently no one did. As they arrived in Gastonia, an armed mob turned them back. They had driven about five miles toward home, when a car blocked the road, and men with guns jumped out of the car that had been following them and began shooting. Wiggins was struck in the chest by a bullet. She reportedly cried, "They have killed me." The banner headline the next morning in the *Raleigh News and Observer* read: "Gastonia Mob Slays Woman/Unionists Headed For Rally, Halted, Chased And Then Fired Upon."

Ella May Wiggins died three days shy of her twenty-ninth birthday. Workers arrived for the funeral in battered old cars and on foot through the cotton fields. Three union organizers spoke, and six union members carried her coffin. As red earth was shoveled over the casket, one of her friends began to sing "A Mill Mother's Lament." The *News and Observer*, which had waged a vigorous editorial battle against the mobs, ran a picture of her five children standing before the grave. Myrtle is holding the baby, Charlotte, and beside them three small bewildered children stare into the camera. A local jury acquitted Ella's accused killers after less than thirty minutes' deliberation.[5]

Ministers placed Ella's children in a Presbyterian orphanage. Millie remembered, "They called us 'the unkempt.' It was like they drew straws. The Presbyterian orphanage got stuck with us." From time to time, when possible, Ella's brother Wesley and his family and other relatives would take the children. In her *News and Observer* column, "Incidentally," Nell Battle Lewis wrote a long piece entitled "Ella May: A Triumph of North Carolina's Industrialism." Writing with anger and passion, Lewis concluded, "For Ella May the union was a light in a dark sky. In it she saw hope for herself and her children, the possibility of a fuller life. . . . Who in her own State had ever tried to help her?"[6]

In a letter to Lewis that she published in her column, President Frank Porter Graham of the University of North Carolina wrote, "The sheer power of the figure of this woman shining out from the facts is simple, beautiful, terrible!" The writer of an editorial, entitled "Ella May Wiggins Doesn't Count," took the Gaston grand jury to task: "Ella May is rotting in a cheap coffin in a neglected graveyard. Her five children are in an orphanage, where they will be taught to love their State, to obey its laws, to honor justice who stands with a keen sword to protect the rights of the weak as well as the strong, the poor as well as the rich, the weary cotton mill hand as well as the mighty mill barons."[7]

Journalists who had been in Gastonia to report on the strike returned to New York vowing to keep Ella's story alive. Articles appeared in various national publications, including the *Nation* and *New Masses*. Novelist Mary Heaton Vorse made Wiggins the main character in her book *Strike!*, published within months of the Bessemer City murder. Margaret Larkin performed some of Ella's songs at gatherings in Greenwich Village.

The words of Ella May Wiggins had proved prophetic: "They'll have to kill me to make me give up the union." They did.

At least one critic finds "mythic proportions" in the history of the 1929 Gastonia strikes, but myth has not changed fact: unions still have a bad name among many North Carolinians, and Wiggins's death is but a tragic reminder of an era in which fear—of communists, of blacks, of protesters—prevailed. Her story is well known to historians of the southern labor movement. Jacquelyn Hall and others, in *Like A Family: The Making of a Southern Cotton Mill World*, described her as "perhaps the best known of the militant women who graced the 1929 strikes." In rallies and protest movements, balladeers still sing her songs. And in history, she represents a woman who moved out of poverty to become a courageous leader of the underprivileged and forgotten.[8]

Mary Martin Sloop

1873–1962

Mary Martin Sloop and Eustace Sloop, at Crossnore School, ca. 1957. (Courtesy of Emma S. Fink, Crossnore)

Mary Martin Sloop began life with advantages, which seemed to motivate her to help children less fortunate. In the early 1900s her school in Crossnore, in western North Carolina, was a model of education that took an interest in everything—from the homes students came from, to the subjects taught in the classroom, to the futures of the students after they graduated. Sloop was a dynamic woman, and her story is different from that of many dedicated educators: she was trained as a medical doctor, started her own school, and made it the center of a mountain community.

Born on March 9, 1873, in Davidson, Mary was one of ten children. She was the daughter of Letitia Costin Martin and William Joseph Martin, a member of the faculty of Davidson College. Late in life, she still spoke of her pleasure in having grown up on the edge of the men's campus. As a child she enjoyed stories of faith, hardship, and service told by many a Presbyterian missionary, and when she was five years old she promised God that she would be one, too. As it turned out, she did become a missionary of sorts but not in foreign fields. She recalled that her most satisfying years were in the 1920s and 1930s, when she was building Crossnore School and was one of North Carolina's most progressive reformers. Better medical care, better schools, and better roads—advances needed to be made, and Mary Martin Sloop was determined to help make them. As Legette Blythe said in the introduction to Sloop's autobiography, *Miracle in the Hills*, "There was about her an air of unquenchable energy, a contagious vitality."[1]

Davidson College was the center of life for Mary's parents.[2] Her mother was one of the earliest members of the Presbyterian Ladies Benevolent Society, and the family attended the College Presbyterian Church. Her father, a committed scientist who built the chemistry program at Davidson, was a stern disciplinarian. His contemporaries would remember his capacity for quickly distinguishing between essential and nonessential matters. Mary took him for her mentor.[3]

When she was fifteen, after Mary had finished the program at Miss Lucy Jurney's private School for Boys and Girls in Davidson (which she described as "a little one-teacher school"), her father determined that she would go to college. He had been impressed that the daughters of Professor Elisha Mitchell of the University of North Carolina faculty could read the Bible in Greek and had attended Statesville Female College, a Presbyterian school twenty miles from Davidson. Mary protested—she did not know anything about the school, and she considered "female" "one of the most horrible words in the English language." But Professor Martin had made up his mind, and Mary went to Statesville.[4]

Following graduation in 1891, Mary reentered the familiar community at Davidson, where town and school were growing up together. Her sister Lucy was teaching in the new public school, and her brother William—recently graduated from the University of Virginia—was a town commissioner and a new member of the Davidson faculty. Students were frequent visitors in faculty homes; faculty wives, noted for gracious hospitality, were almost as important to the well-being of students as the men who were their teachers. The wives helped students over their shyness or homesickness, and while they served refreshments the wives listened to the men talk about their studies.

On the margin of college life, women organized their own alternative education in the form of club activities. Mary became a member of the Book Lovers Club. She still had not told her mother that she intended to become a medical missionary, but she enrolled in classes for medical students at Davidson. Now was no time to confront her mother with her alarming ambitions. Letitia Martin's health had failed, and she was practically an invalid when Mary arrived home from college and became her caretaker.[5]

After her mother's death in 1901—her father had died a few years earlier—Mary was released from her home duties and enrolled in the Women's Medical College of Pennsylvania, in Philadelphia, the only women's medical school in the country. She—and no doubt many other students—had to make up academic deficiencies. Although she had not been allowed to study anatomy at Davidson, she had learned to make her own way in an unfamiliar environment. She had made friends with the men in her classes, one of whom was Eustace Sloop, a young man from a neighboring farm, a good athlete, and a resourceful student who worked his way through Davidson. Mary first met him when he was a freshman attending a class party at her home, and he had returned to complete the two-year medical course at the college, rooming next door to the Martins. He was a tall, slender, handsome fellow, and Mary was interested in him. Furthermore, her long years at home had heightened her determination to do something else. At age twenty-nine, she was already considered a spinster. Moreover, the Presbyterian Church had informed her that she was too old to be a candidate for a foreign mission.

Mary and "the Doctor," as she always referred to Sloop, had a lot in common: they had both wanted to be medical missionaries. She felt completely comfortable with him. After Mary went off to Philadelphia, they wrote one another often, and before she graduated in 1906, they became engaged. She never seemed to lose a certain adoration for him. She was talkative; he listened well. She had a vision; he fixed things with his hands. They were a good pair.[6]

After graduation from the Women's Medical College and an internship at the New England Hospital for Women and Children in Boston, Mary took a position for a year as the first resident physician at Agnes Scott College in Atlanta. When Eustace, who had gone to Jefferson Medical College, had finished his education, they were married at the Martin summer home at Blowing Rock on July 2, 1908. They left the ceremony on horseback, tin cans and cowbells tied by children to their saddles. During their journey Eustace led Mary up hollows to meet some of his patients in the practice he had recently established; at night they stayed in a nearby inn. By the end of the week they had arrived at Plumtree, where Eustace had opened an office. Plumtree was in mica mining country, providing a small wage industry, and most of his patients were scattered near and far.

The Sloops wanted to practice medicine together. There were no roads, only a few muddied paths and creekbeds, but they rode horseback to deliver babies and to take care of the sick and the dying. Anxious parents could look down the mountain and watch the two physicians pick their way up, sometimes through seemingly pathless woods. In the time it took for the strangers to reach the top, the mountaineers had put aside their distrust—at least enough to let the doctors examine a feverish child.

It was a hard life. In Mary's words: "I had left a cultured home in a friendly little college town, a home of books and music and newspapers and magazines and evenings of good talk and the companionship of interesting people.... The Doctor and I could have assured ourselves of such a life by establishing a joint practice in some town or city in our own part of the country. Yet we were leaving this sort of life for one I knew little about, for a life that I was quite certain would be hard most of the time, primitive, often lonely, always challenging." By the time Mary wrote her memoirs at the age of eighty, she had mastered the challenge so long and had made the telling of it so engaging that nothing ever seemed to have stopped her in her tracks. "Life was daring us. Life was dealing out the cards. I would pick up my hand and play it. And I'd have fun, too, doing it."[7]

In Plumtree, Eustace often rode off alone to treat patients in their mountain cabins while Mary saw those who could walk or ride to their office. Many children suffered from malnutrition because of the absence of fresh fruit and other vitamin-producing foods in their diets, and antibiotics for curing diseases were yet unknown. Parents waited too long to consult the doctor, trusting that a poultice of leaves would cure pneumonia; when they did bring the sick child wrapped in a blanket, often the doctor could only watch the child die in their arms.

When a young blacksmith was brought groaning in pain, Mary diagnosed a ruptured appendix and went into action. She asked for a fifty-pound lard can from the storekeeper, made it into a sterilizer, and set it on the two-burner oilstove. Her husband helped with the preparations. She got out their medical school gowns and masks and set up an operating room. She filled the kerosene lamps. As daybreak approached, the blacksmith's friends gathered around with shotguns, trying to convince the boy's father that he was a fool to let the young strangers cut into his son. ("They'll kill him. He won't never wake up.") The Sloops operated, and the patient survived. Later, they would decide that operating outdoors, under an apple tree usually, was the safest, cleanest place. (Once, inside a cabin with only a dirt floor, a rooster jumped up on the makeshift operating table and stared into the patient's open belly.)[8]

The Sloops worked together. On a bitter winter's night boots could freeze in the stirrups—Eustace's did once, and Mary had to get the hammer to knock him loose. When they rode out at night to treat a desperate case at Grassy Ridge, Mary had to remember the number of times she had crossed the creek—thirteen—to find her way back home, her horse whirling around, refusing to face the wind. Nothing seemed to stop her. She noted, "Perhaps we were beginning to fulfill our mission."[9]

With the birth of their first child, Emma, Mary needed to be at home as much as possible, and she saw patients in the office. Increasingly, Eustace's patients were east of Plumtree, in the Linville Valley, and when residents of Crossnore appealed to the Sloops to move there, they agreed. On Friday, December 11, 1911—a dreary, cold afternoon in winter—they reached the place that would be their permanent home.

Their decision in 1908 to live in the mountains had set this life in motion. For three years they had been tested by the elements and the mountaineers' distrust of strangers. They had been useful and generous, true to their native North Carolina, and they were now viewed as such by the mountaineers. The match between the Sloops and Crossnore was going to work.

When Mary—like her father, able to size up a situation quickly and to lose no time taking action—went down to church on the first Sunday and found a crowd of people huddled in the gloom of a dilapidated building that served as both church and school, she took it all in: the earnestness of the Sunday school teacher, the eagerness of his listeners, and the curiosity about her Oxford teacher's Bible. At that moment a new challenge was forming: the need to establish a school in Crossnore. Later, the Sloops also built a Presbyterian church. Eustace would dam Linville River with his own hands and construct a generator to bring the first electricity to Avery County. Mary would raise money for a hospital.

A community with a school was especially important to families who lived in the region west of Morganton. The hills are steep, and the roads are winding. It takes a long time, even today, to get there, but the views are often more beautiful than anything visitors see coming from the Piedmont. In the first decade of the 1900s districts were served by many scattered one-room schoolhouses, and children had to start out before daylight to reach them. The schoolhouse usually had a potbelly stove and crude desks, and the teacher often taught thirty or more students of all ages. The children arrived home so late from school that they had to do their chores in the dark. In the four-month sessions, students learned numbers and letters, and many came to love books, pencils, and papers. Some felt a hunger for more learning.

Mary went to work. When she heard that twelve-year-old Hepsy would not be returning to the sewing class for girls Sloop held every Thursday afternoon in her home because the youngster had finished all the grades at the school and so it was time to get married, Mary intervened. She wrote to old friends in Davidson asking for money and clothes to help send Hepsy to school at Banner Elk, about thirty miles away, where she could board and complete her education. The money and the clothes arrived—all of the dresses black. Mary despaired. She hung the dresses on the front porch. Women came along, looked them over, asked to buy them. Never one to turn down a good idea, she sold them all; then she had brighter dresses made for Hepsy and sent her off to school.

From that legendary beginning came the time-honored tradition of selling secondhand items donated to Crossnore School from near and far. Mary wrote to all of her friends again and again, and the clothes kept coming. Then, Aunt Pop and Uncle Gilmer (unrelated to one another but called "Aunt" and "Uncle" in the mountain fashion) took charge of the selling. If Uncle Gilmer did not get up at daybreak to open the "store," the women were knocking on his door. Families shopped for what they needed, money from the sales went toward Mrs. Sloop's school, and the community came together. She would build a residential campus around the public Crossnore School so that children could continue their education. She presented her plan to the town, and in a community meeting in 1916 bylaws and a board of trustees were chosen for a school that required public tax support. The plan lit a fire as quickly as a good pine knot.

While churches and patrons were supporting denominational private schools of every kind, public schools were struggling to garner support from local communities and meet the state's new regulations governing attendance and teacher certification. Sloop was both a relentless fund-raiser and an effective lobbyist for passage of a compulsory school law. Trained teachers were streaming forth from the State Normal College in Greensboro, transforming schools throughout the state; members of the Woman's Association for the Betterment of Public Schoolhouses were dramatically improving the places in which white children learned. It was a heady time for women, and progressive change was in the air they breathed. Sloop was a traditionalist who embraced progress. Crossnore School was well into its first growth by 1920, and Mary was having the time of her life as a pioneer.

In the small village of Crossnore, she had to figure out ways to get the local community behind her, especially when it meant trying to change a way of life. She waged a determined and usually good-natured campaign to shut down moonshiners. On one occasion she confiscated a still herself, rolling it away in a wheelbarrow. The owner of the still later gave her the vote she needed to secure support for a high school. As school reforms required the community's agreement to a local tax, Sloop's opposition could be formidable. And so could she. She knew when to stand her ground—facing a moonshiner in court or ordering the arrest of a father who refused to comply with the new compulsory school attendance law—and when to keep her mouth shut—remaining silent as tight-lipped voters left the polling place.

Little by little and building by building, Mary Martin Sloop and the students, teachers, staff, and people of Crossnore built themselves a campus they regarded as "the miracle in the hills." Sloop did it by accommodating the geography and the mountaineers themselves, having first determined what she thought they needed. She did it by insisting that everyone work and work hard: even young children carried rocks up from creek beds for the foundations of new buildings. And she did it by calling on friends and women's organizations. "Some one said," Sloop reported, "if all the letters I had written for old clothes were laid in a row, they would reach from the Atlantic to the Pacific. Perhaps that's true but I shall keep on writing them."[10] Friends did respond, especially women of Davidson—who sent checks and boxes of clothes. Sloop started a school newsletter in which she often described a need that pulled at the heartstrings: for instance, a boy who hoped that she would find twenty-five dollars so he could have a hernia operation. She asked for someone to help out with a check, and then she listed other things: sewing machines, scholarships, sheets, sewing supplies and scraps, shoes and stockings, sweaters—and pianos and trousers.[11] In the direst of times, a gift would arrive.

To guarantee these gifts in a timely and regular fashion, Mary had turned to the Daughters of the American Revolution (DAR). A young woman visiting Crossnore knew about the "Approved List" of schools supported by the Daughters because she was herself from a DAR family, as was Mary Martin Sloop, and was going to work in the national office. She suggested that Sloop tell the "nationals" about Crossnore. Never one to let grass grow under her feet, Mary was off to Washington. Traveling was difficult because she did not drive; Eustace had to drive her in the Model-T, later the Model-A, to the train station in Morganton or Marion, or she would take the bus. Mary made an effective presentation at a local meeting, and Crossnore School was placed on the Approved List to receive funds. A DAR dormitory was built for girls, and a house was built for the newly organized DAR chapter in Crossnore. "D.A.R." was talked all over the campus.[12]

Crossnore began to receive annual checks from various DAR chapters. In addition, individual members sent personal checks and remembered Crossnore in their wills. Each year a tour of the DAR–Approved Schools originated in Washington at the national headquarters. Gertrude Carraway, of New Bern, a national DAR leader, especially enjoyed showing members her own home state. When the bus pulled into Crossnore, everything was ready—a special lunch, student assemblies in the dining hall and gymnasium, American flags, the singing of patriotic songs, and special plays. Even when she was old and ill, Sloop still conducted business (from a bed set up in her office in the administration building) and had her address to the DAR visitors broadcast over the microphone in the dining hall. It all worked. Mary described the checks that arrived as a "miracle" and thanked her children for having made it happen by their prayers.[13]

In 1951, when Mary Martin Sloop was seventy-eight years old, she was named both North Carolina and National Mother of the Year. When she went to New York to accept the national recognition, her husband Eustace had to stay behind as he could not leave his patients and the supervision of Crossnore Hospital, which he had established. In New York Mary was accompanied by their daughter, Emma Fink, whose own medical career had brought her home to join her father in practice. Emma's brother Will had also returned to Crossnore to practice dentistry. The children had grown up in a large "extended" family in which their mother was usually so busy with work at the school that she had had to call upon other women—for a time, Eustace's widowed sister—to help look after her own two children at home. And yet "Mother of the Year" was a title that perfectly suited Mary Martin Sloop, for she cared for all the children of Crossnore with a deep maternal love, reinforced by women—often widows who brought their children with them—whom she hired to serve as house-mothers in the dormitories. She often stayed up at night to cook supper for her husband, who returned late from seeing his patients.

Eustace died in February 1961, and Mary, who became bedridden after a heart attack, died the next year. All their marriage years had been spent in the mountains, where they had first gone to find their life's work.

At Crossnore Mary Sloop would sweep into the dining room when the children had finished supper and teach them just one more thing. "Noblesse oblige"—she would begin—slowly spelling out each word and translating the phrase: "Rank imposes obligation. Be an *example*, Rise to the *challenge*. Make yourselves *proud*. Nearby Grandfather Mountain is the oldest mountain in the world. There's something *lasting* about the mountains."[14]

CHAPTER 9

Turning Point or Temporary Gain

Women and World War II, 1941–1945

We must never forget "what this war was really like," Eleanor Roosevelt warned in June 1945—"the dirt, the hardships, the horror of death and the sorrow." A half century later, Martin Gilbert looked back to World War II as a "prolonged and horrifying cruelty" for 46 million soldiers and civilians who died. The experiences of American women back home were at once less traumatic and more difficult to recall. Their beautiful faces appeared on recruitment posters, urging men to join the fighting forces. As poet and airman Randall Jarrell wrote, pilots flew deadly raids "in bombers named for girls." In reality, women showed the strain of worry and fatigue from work.[1]

What happened to American women during World War II has been the focus of several studies over the last two decades. Some historians have argued that the war marked a "turning point for women workers"; others contend that the position of women was only "modified," that gains were "temporary" and that attitudes about women's place remained the same.[2] But the numbers are indisputable: job opportunities for women increased dramatically because of the war. Six million women entered the workforce for the first time, and for the first time large numbers of married women and older women took jobs. Many women were paid more and were employed in higher-skilled jobs. One of the most dramatic increases occurred when the federal government added nearly a million women to its roster of employees. Although job inequities remained greatest for black women, they too made gains. Many were able to leave domestic service and find better wages in manufacturing and white-collar jobs. In southern agriculture, one of the region's major contributions to the war effort, both black and white women had to work harder in the field to help meet the demand for increased cotton and food production.

At the beginning of the war, the government waged a vigorous campaign to recruit women for work. Traditional attitudes about working women varied according to race, class, and marital status, and resistance to a woman's doing a "man's job" continued in many workplaces. But in the final analysis, Americans would do what they had to do to win the war.

There were some exceptions, as there had always been. Quakers remained pacifists, and women like Helen Binford and Miriam Levering served the nation in different ways. Helen and her husband, Raymond Binford, directed a Civilian Public Service camp in Marion. After the war Miriam and Sam Levering, members of Mount Airy Friends Meeting, worked to organize the American branch of United World Federalists, to try to bring about a peaceful union of countries worldwide.

As the nation prepared for war, however, polls indicated strong support for drafting women, but opposition from Congress and the War Department kept this from happening. Nationally about 350,000 women enlisted in branches of the military. Women were not sent into combat, but many nurses who often worked just behind the front lines saw "what this war was really like." After a college commencement, a small number of enthusiastic graduates would volunteer for military service, often ending up in the same officer candidate school. Even women in the military who worked in offices often found themselves in new, sometimes critical situations and were on their own to earn a living and fit into a massive operation. Many developed strong alliances with one another, especially when they felt unwelcome in what remained a man's domain. In North Carolina, as in other states, the news that someone's daughter had joined the service was announced in the paper, her photograph in uniform went up on the mantel at home, and her letters were passed among family members and friends. Some local critics had their own opinions, of course—more than one young woman was said to have joined the military simply to find a husband.

Even as the things women did were changing, the way women were perceived often remained almost the same. The popularized image of a woman defense worker—Rosie the Riveter—came complete with muscles but also ruby-red lips on Norman Rockwell's classic cover of the *Saturday Evening Post* and numerous government-sponsored posters (Plate 11). The recruitment for both military and civilian jobs appealed to a woman's ability to tend, mend, stitch, and make do. Still, World War II was giving a dramatic shake to the kaleidoscope of women's history, and the pieces would never fit back together in the way they had in the previous decades.

North Carolina Women and the War: "Keeping the Home Fires Burning"

Much of the North Carolina story of World War II remains undiscovered and thus untold. The majority of women fought the war at home: as farmers in the fields, as blue-collar workers in textile factories, as civilian office workers on military bases, as volunteers in community centers, and as mothers who "kept the home fires burning." About seven thousand of them joined the women's branches of the military. This chapter relies in part on the memories of the survivors from these groups.

During World War II more servicemen were trained in North Carolina than anywhere else in the nation.[3] With its Atlantic location, climate, large, sparsely populated areas, and cheaper land, the state was well suited for both new and expanded military bases.[4] Fort Bragg in Fayetteville was already an established army post; large marine bases were created at Cherry Point, near New Bern, and Camp Lejeune near Jacksonville, and many temporary installations opened in other parts of the state. This expansion in the military led to the almost-overnight creation of government jobs for civilians. It also affected North Carolina communities, because every military installation meant that nearby towns were flooded with service personnel and their families.

Indeed, the North Carolina home front became intimately related to events occurring across the oceans. Residents of Fayetteville or Morehead City or Jacksonville or Goldsboro knew the war in personal ways: they saw it in the faces of men and women in uniform who came to church or wandered downtown looking for something to do; they read the newspaper with special anxiety for what troop assignments meant to Fort Bragg or Camp Lejeune; they rented rooms to lonely war brides, in town to see their husbands before the troops shipped out. And North Carolina military bases began to change the makeup of a mostly rural Anglo-Saxon and African American population. A retired schoolteacher in Goldsboro who rented rooms to military families recalled that the names in her guest book included Desjardins, P'Simer, Sobieski, Chew, and Zadowsky; she exclaimed, "I never dreamed there were so many different kinds of people living right here in our United States."[5]

Camp Lejeune, built during World War I, became the largest artillery post in the world during World War II, changing the rural landscape along the main roads leading into Jacksonville. On family farms near Kenansville and Beulaville, women hanging out wash and children waiting for the school bus counted convoys of men and supplies headed toward Camp Lejeune. In New Bern fifteen-year-old Janet Latham saw jeeploads of American sailors whose ship had been sunk offshore by German U-boats. "All of a sudden we were on the front line."[6]

In 1942, when Seymour Johnson Field was being built two or three miles south of Goldsboro, townspeople opened their homes to some of the hundreds of electricians, carpenters, and foremen brought in to do the work. And when soldiers and their families began to arrive, the pattern was repeated to supply housing for relatives of service personnel, some for only a weekend, others for longer periods. Blanche Egerton Baker and her husband George S. Baker converted every inch of available space to provide room for workers and later family members coming to see their sons or husbands. Often arriving frightened and weary, strangers were directed to the housing desks set up in the railroad station, the bus station, the USO building, and the lobby of Goldsboro's largest hotel. There women volunteers telephoned around town to find vacant rooms. Many visitors ended up with the Bakers, who gave up still more of their privacy and space; soon everyone used the kitchen. Sometimes a visiting wife was able to get a job in a store in downtown Goldsboro so she could remain near her husband. Other women did housework in exchange for rent. For the most part, the women had little money, and when there was a USO dance at the school gym a few blocks from the Bakers' house, they borrowed scarves and earrings from one another and crowded into one room to dress together. The theme that ran through most of their stories was romance—courtships, marriages, and broken hearts. Blanche Baker seemed to know them all. She was mother, grandmother, housemother, and, on occasion, disciplinarian. When her own son was sent overseas, she was comforted by her "girls." Many years later, they continued to write to her about their lives and to send pictures of their children.[7]

Fighting the War at Home: "The Call to Arms"

In the summer of 1941 counties throughout the state began setting up civil defense programs to train volunteers to protect the civilian population and to build morale; a year later North Carolinians constituted the largest number of volunteers in the Southeast.[8] Negro women in Durham were among the first to become members of the interracial American Women's Volunteer Services, encouraging the purchase of war bonds and participating in Red Cross projects.[9] Women learning to be airplane spotters and ambulance drivers had a sense of urgency to their work, but perhaps nothing was more exciting—and frightening—than "blackout" procedures when mothers taught their children to draw shades and turn off lights at night to protect towns from possible air raids. "Block Mothers" were instructed how, in an emergency, they should ensure that every child was cared for by an adult. "The safest place in an air raid is at home," a civil defense pamphlet cautioned.[10] As meat, butter, sugar, coffee, and other food were rationed, women had to conserve their stamps and modify their meals. By 1943 three-fourths of America's housewives were putting up their own food. One North Carolina woman declared, "I was canning until midnight, night after night, and I frequently said, 'I wish I had Hitler in that pressure cooker!' "[11]

Public school teachers and children raised $43 million in bond drives. The Elizabeth City Junior Women's Club was proud to have raised enough money to pay for a bomber. In Red Cross meeting rooms women knitted gloves and sweaters and rolled bandages for the soldiers. Near military bases, there were dances at USOs and open houses at YWCAs. Busloads of servicemen—racially segregated—were taken to recreation centers and parish halls, where local women were waiting to meet them. At an armory dance, New Bern women met Tyrone Power, who was stationed at Cherry Point. Aberdeen women met Glenn Miller. Kitty Van Mullineaux of New Bern met someone less famous, but ultimately more important in her life—George Van Buskirk, a Marine from Cherry Point. They were married in 1946. She later reflected, "If it weren't for the Marine Corps, all my age group would have been old maids, because all the guys had left."[12] But for every happy ending, there was a sad one. Any family that rented out rooms during the war heard young women crying at night, alone in strange towns a long way from home.

The war years loosened traditions and sometimes severed ties in homes and communities. The effect of separation was especially dramatic in communities that had been close-knit. Adolph Dial described the effects that military bases in Robeson County had on the Lumbee Indian community. Before the war facilitated the movement of people in and out of Robeson, most Lumbees did not marry whites. During the 1940s some Lumbee women married soldiers stationed at nearby Laurinburg-Maxton Air Base and Fort Bragg, and some Lumbee men serving in the military married women from other countries and, when the war was over, took them home to live. The war created new opportunities for intermarriage and that "helped bring the Lumbee community out of its relative isolation," but also threatened to weaken its traditional customs and networks.[13]

Even before marriage, some Lumbee women moved out on their own. In 1944 Ressie Sampson responded to the call for women workers and obtained a civil service job in Washington, D.C. In 1944 she was transferred to Laurinburg-Maxton Air Force Base near Harpers Ferry and Moss Neck, where she and her eleven older siblings had grown up. Once back in North Carolina she chose to live on base. "I was making my own money," she remembered, "and it gave me a real sense of accomplishment." She met Charles Larson, a Swedish American from Wisconsin stationed at the base, at a party on V-E Day (May 8, 1945), and they were married a few months later. When Larson received his discharge the next October, he and Ressie moved to Wisconsin, but she continued to keep in touch with family and friends in North Carolina.[14]

Although the war necessitated many changes, the daily lives of many women continued in traditional ways. In Raleigh a reporter for the *News and Observer* noted on April 1, 1942, that the officers of the Junior League would be installed at a meeting at the hotel, a program on "Annuals for Your Garden" was being offered at the YWCA, the Readers Club was meeting, and there were bridge clubs and wedding parties. Yet even these customary activities could take on new meaning in wartime. The YWCA offered classes in nutrition and first aid, both seen anew in the context of military emergencies. Isabelle Bowen Henderson of Raleigh was photographed at work in her victory garden prior to her lecture, "Our Gardens in War Time," at the Women's Club. The War Production Board, in attempting to make an estimated one hundred million yards of cloth available for war purposes, asked that women not wear their skirts below knee length (the style of that period). Mrs. E. L. Daughtridge's poem appeared on the editorial page: "The call to arms, 'tis yours, 'tis mine, Speed up production, fall in line."

Despite the efforts of mothers to reassure children, the horror of war could suddenly disrupt an ordinary day and put it "right in our lap," as Isabel Eggers Zuber remembered her childhood in Boone. The *Life* magazine picture showing a man in a gas mask carrying a dead child was horrifying, but other horrors were closer and familial: one uncle had his thumb shot off in the Battle of the Bulge; a cousin, who was a pilot, was reported missing in action and later declared dead; another uncle was killed. In Boone, where Zuber grew up, neighbors checked the large honor roll in the campus gym at present-day Appalachian State University that listed the names of alumni who were in service: when one was injured, a blue star was placed by his name; when one died, a gold star appeared.[15] War and youth were irrevocably joined. In photographs in local newspapers shone the youthful faces of men and women in service in some faraway place on the map. Further to the west, even the relative isolation of the Cherokee Qualla Boundary was altered: Cherokee mothers and fathers reportedly did not hesitate to give their underage sons permission to volunteer for service.[16] African American children in Durham's Burton Elementary School made scrapbooks to show off their successes in bond drives, first-aid classes, and victory gardens, honoring their fathers and brothers who

OUR
BOND
STAND
VICTORY
We observe Bond Day once a month by putting
dimes in Uncle Sam's hat to buy bonds.

FIGURE 9-1. *Pupils contributing money to the war effort*, Burton Elementary School, Durham County. (Courtesy of the North Carolina Division of Archives and History)

served in the armed forces (Figs. 9-1, 9-2). In her African American community in New Bern, Carolyn Bland felt close to the center of excitement—and tragedy—because her father's grocery store had the only phone in the neighborhood. "When the Western Union messenger boy arrived on his bicycle, all community activity came to a screeching halt because relatives were usually notified of emergencies by [telegram]. I remember, if a red star was on the outside of the envelope, it usually meant a death notice."[17]

Jobs to Be Done: "Free a Man to Fight"

In the realms of defense, construction, textiles, cigarettes, and agriculture, North Carolina's stature increased during the war. The state had more large-scale construction projects, which tended not to hire women, than defense plants, where women were being hired in large numbers in cities like Detroit and Los Angeles. Women were employed in the Fairchild Aircraft Plant in Burlington and in the North Carolina Shipbuilding Company in Wilmington. Although some women helped build Liberty ships, often the largest number of female government employees worked as clerical staff or nurses.[18] Taking to heart the patriotic posters and slogans urging women to go to work "to free a man to fight," many women employed in a Hendersonville textile factory lined up at the U.S. Employment Services office to obtain jobs that would help win the war. Factory owners and civic leaders scrambled to convince the women that making cloth was an "essential industry." They placed window displays in downtown stores exhibiting yarn and cloth next to uniforms and other war clothing. Success was reported, but whether women returned to their jobs because they had been persuaded of their importance or because in western North Carolina the higher-paying jobs of the defense industry were out of reach is unclear.[19]

War jobs also created greater movement in and out of the state and gave many women their first opportunities for travel away from farms and small towns. Richard Lingeman described the changing landscape as "Everyone, on the move."[20] Gains for black women were dramatic. Fifty percent of rural black women migrated to cities, where job opportunities were the best that most of them had ever known. Between 1940 and 1945 two in five black women were employed, compared to one in three white women.[21] Although many black North Carolina women remained in low-paying jobs, often as tenant farmers and domestic workers in white homes, some of them found opportunities elsewhere. At the end of the term Theresa and Irwin Bland left their teaching jobs in the Goldsboro city schools and went with their children to New London, Connecticut, to work in the Naval Yard. Theresa supervised eight women in setting up valves in submarines and worked as a machinist on the *Trident*. Irwin

FIGURE 9-2. *First graders showing off radishes grown in the school victory garden*, Forsyth County. (Courtesy of the North Carolina Division of Archives and History)

worked in the foundry, and their oldest daughter, Harriet, was a welder. In the fall, they returned to their home in Goldsboro, where they later retired after forty-five years in public education.[22]

Perhaps the greatest contribution North Carolina made to the war effort was in agriculture. All across America women helped the country become "the bread basket of democracy" by working on farms. The percentage of women in agriculture rose from 8 percent in 1940 to 22.4 percent in 1945.[23] As Sarah M. Lemmon has shown, the war made staggering demands for increased production. North Carolina ranked fourth in the nation in the value and the volume of its crops. Despite the shortage of farm labor (a consequence of drafting many North Carolina men into military service), the state dramatically increased wheat, peanut, and potato production.[24] Photographs in state bulletins touting wartime agricultural production showed women—and their children—picking cotton. Tobacco factories, which employed large numbers of black women, made cigarettes that were bought by the government and shipped to service men and women overseas. Ernie Pyle reported that nothing improved a soldier's morale like a letter from home and a free carton of cigarettes. Thus the 1943 strike by workers at Winston-Salem's R. J. Reynolds Tobacco Company, the largest tobacco factory in the world, took courage because not only were workers in a staunch antiunion state but also in shutting down the plants they could be accused of being unpatriotic. Reynolds had been pushing workers to meet production deadlines on its large government contract. The strike leader was Theodosia Simpson, a stemmer, and 80 percent of the workforce was composed of black women. The protest led to improvements in wages and benefits and ultimately to increased black voter registration. At the time Simpson and other black women showed considerable enterprise in focusing attention on conditions at home in the midst of a world war.[25]

Women recruited to do certain kinds of skilled work needed special training. Within four months of the time America entered the war, the proportion of women to men enrolled in vocational courses sponsored by the federal government increased from 1 percent to 13 percent. Goldsboro High School offered vocational classes in airplane riveting and sheet metal work, and women were given the same training as men. One instructor reported that women had shown "excellent aptitude in precision work." A female student explained that "In helping to build planes. . . . I am helping the men to keep the enemies from dropping bombs on my children, and other children like them." A forty-year-old woman talked the instructor into believing that she was not too old for the program. Another boasted, "We aren't sissies. We'll do a man-sized job anywhere we are placed." The state director of the Works Progress Administration's women's division, Kathleen Young, reported: "We shall extend our efforts and see that North Carolina helps as many women as possible to attain the needed skills so that they can take over men's jobs so the men can do the only 'he-man' job which women cannot do, that of actually fighting to win the war." Young urged employers to consider local women before trying to recruit men from outside the area.[26]

Dixie King Kennedy of Rockingham County grew up in a family where her father was overseas serving in the army and her mother was working in the defense industry in Baltimore. Dixie was left in the care of grandparents, who lived near Leaksville (part of present-day Eden). Every other weekend her mother went home, catching the Friday night train from Baltimore to Danville, Virginia, then the bus to Leaksville, and finally a cab to her parents' farm, arriving early on Saturday morning. When Dixie awoke, her mother was there. She would spend all day Saturday with her daughter, and on Sunday she would take the cab to catch the bus to catch the train to Maryland in time to shower in her apartment, put on her coveralls, and go to work.[27]

North Carolina Women in the Military: "We Are in It to Stay"

Because women were not drafted, they had to volunteer to serve. When the recruitment campaign began, most volunteers were motivated by patriotic fervor. Later in the war, new recruits were attracted by the promise of better jobs and wages. The branch of service that drew the largest number of North Carolina women—four thousand—was the Women's Army Auxiliary Corps (WAAC, later changed to WAC), which was proposed in legislation by congressional representative Edith Nourse Rogers of Massachusetts and signed into law by President Franklin D. Roosevelt on May 15, 1942. Thereafter, other branches were added: WAVES (Women Appointed for Volunteer Emergency Service), SPARS (the acronym for the Coast Guard's motto—*Semper Paratus*—Always Ready), WASPs (Women's Air Force Service Pilots), and a women's division of the Marines (called simply Marines). In addition, many women served as nurses and medical technicians in the Army and Navy Nurse Corps (Fig. 9-3).

Although joining the military provided many women with opportunities to go to new places and meet new people, discrimination continued to exist as it did in civilian life. Women were usually given clerical jobs on American bases, women with children could not enlist, and black women were segregated.[28]

In spite of racial segregation in the armed forces, black Americans supported the war effort. In June 1941 black

FIGURE 9-3. *Recruitment campaign for women volunteers*, Marion, McDowell County, ca. 1943. (Courtesy of the North Carolina Division of Archives and History)

women were called to Washington by the leadership of Alpha Kappa Alpha Sorority and the National Council of Negro Women to discuss ways to encourage black women to participate in the national defense program. As the conflict wore on, protests met with some success: WAVES and SPARS were integrated, but black women were not accepted in the women Marines or the Women's Air Force Service Pilots. Black women in the WAAC and WAC were racially segregated throughout the war, and at peak strength only 4 percent of the corps was African American. Nevertheless, in July 1942 thirty-nine black women were the first students to attend officer candidate training for the WAAC in Fort Des Moines, Iowa (Fig. 9-4).[29]

The 7,000 North Carolina women who enlisted during World War II were a small percentage of the more than 350,000 North Carolinians in military service, but they volunteered—sometimes against the wishes and prayers of their families. The notion of women in the military met with hostility in some quarters, including military men, and led to protests from politicians. One congressman groused, "Who will do the cooking, the washing, the mending, the humble homey tasks to which every woman has devoted herself?" (Fig. 9-5).[30] In 1942 *Time* reported that army recruitment officers gave pink application blanks to women and told them not to "fib" about their age. Recruitment was described in this way: "The staccato questions and treble chatter in the 440 recruiting stations got on officers' nerves . . . Said [an] officer: 'They're just as tough to handle in this recruiting office as they are in civilian life.' "[31]

Nonetheless, independent-minded women stepped for-

FIGURE 9-4. *Women dancing with servicemen*, Chapel Hill, 1943. (Courtesy of the North Carolina Division of Archives and History)

ward, some of them, like Salem College graduate Emma Grantham, "joining the fight for recognition of a new branch of the Service and a new field of endeavor for women."[32] In the autumn of 1943 a mass induction of WACs, the state's first contingent of recruits, was held on Capitol Square in Raleigh, where Governor J. Melville Broughton presented a North Carolina flag to each WAC. The women trained as a unit and came to wear the state insignia on the sleeves of their uniforms. Among them was forty-year-old Lona Hanna Johnson, of Hendersonville, the mother of three sons, all serving in the war, and the wife of a disabled World War I veteran. Another WAC was Dorothy Goforth (later Jordan), then eighteen years old. She had been working in a defense plant in Spartanburg, South Carolina, but obtained her father's permission (parental consent was required for women under twenty-one) to join the corps. "I just had a mind to explore," she remembered. She spent two years working in the officer candidate school at the Eastern Signal Corps Training Center in Monmouth, New Jersey. After her discharge, she joined up again and became one of the seventeen thousand WACs sent overseas. She worked in the code room at the headquarters of the European Command, where women were treated as well as men, "but a lot of women were a lot smarter than men who were doing the same job."[33]

Mary Webb Nicholson, of Greensboro, "the first aviatrix of the Carolinas," was one of twenty-five women pilots who, as members of the Air Transport Auxiliary of the Royal Air Force (RAF), ferried fighter planes from English factories to battle stations. "It is not too much to imagine that women will be given an even greater part in protecting the freedom of our democracy," Nicholson claimed as she took on her new responsibilities, "and if they are called upon to give this service, the women of America will not be found wanting. . . . We are in it to stay." While serving with the RAF command, Nicholson was killed over Berkshire, England, as she ferried planes to the front, on May 22, 1943 (Fig. 9-6).[34]

In 1942 Westray Battle Boyce, a native of Rocky Mount, was a working mother living in Washington, D.C. She enlisted in the WAAC and became a member of the first officer candidate class at Fort Des Moines, Iowa, the "woman's West Point." (Although Boyce was divorced in 1941, the army always stated that she was a widow.) She, like other women in the corps, was better educated and had scored higher in army tests than most men. After completing officer training, she remained at Fort

FIGURE 9-5. Idealized image of a woman "keeping the homefires burning." (Cover, *Progressive Farmer*, February 1944; courtesy of the North Carolina Museum of History)

FIGURE 9-6. *Service personnel check engine of a warplane*. (Courtesy of the North Carolina Division of Archives and History)

Des Moines as a training officer. Later, she was sent to Atlanta to become WAAC staff director of the Fourth Service Command, the first time a woman had served on a command military staff. The urgent need for a woman who could take charge is revealed in the fact that after only one year in the corps, Captain Boyce supervised military activities in seven southeastern states, including North Carolina. The press, which saw a good story in her career, described a "gentle-voice, quiet-mannered lady from the Fighting South." Five-foot-two with curly blonde hair, Boyce overcame opposition to women in the military by displaying "charm and femininity." Promoted to lieutenant colonel, she directed more than two thousand women in the North African theater of operations, working closely under Generals Mark Clark and Dwight D. Eisenhower. The WACs who followed the advancing battle soldiers into the Mediterranean theater were the first women soldiers based in Europe. Although women were usually sheltered from battle, Boyce's "up-forwardest WACs" moved close to the front lines; they included a large number of women from North Carolina, among them Sergeant Ann Fenner of Southern Pines and Sergeant Ruby Stroup of Cherryville. In a letter to her aunt in Rocky Mount, Boyce wrote, "WACs are of the cut and caliber of the great pioneer women of America. . . . They are worthy of the new chapter they are writing in the saga of American women."[35]

When Boyce returned to the United States in 1944 for her next assignment, she received the Legion of Merit, the first WAC so honored. In Washington she joined the War Department and became deputy director of the corps under WAC director Colonel Oveta Culp Hobby. Later, she succeeded Hobby and was promoted to colonel, the highest rank available in the Women's Army Corps (Fig. 9-7). As the war ended, she had to deal with the question of what would become of the corps. Many of the one hundred thousand WACs wanted to return to civilian life and urged that the corps be disbanded. Boyce favored demobilization but also believed that an inactive reserve unit should be retained. General Eisenhower had come to value the WAC and believed that it should become a permanent part of the army. In 1948 President Harry Truman signed legislation to accomplish that objective.[36]

Women's Air Force Service Pilots flew nearly sixty million miles for the U.S. Army Air Force (Fig. 9-8). They were the nation's first military women pilots, although the federal government did not acknowledge them as such until 1977. As a rule, WASPs were assigned domestic missions to free men for overseas duty. They ferried planes, hauled gunnery targets, transported cargo, served as instructors, and tested overhauled aircraft. They flew trainers, and they flew bombers. At Camp Davis, near Topsail Beach, WASPs were members of a target-towing squadron, training air-to-air and ground-to-air gunners. "What people like the WASPs did is [that] they

FIGURE 9-7. *Colonel Westray Battle Boyce tours WAC facilities* around the world at the end of the war. (Courtesy of the North Carolina Division of Archives and History)

FIGURE 9-8. *Viola Thompson, Mary Clifford, and Lydia Linder, WASPs,* target-towing squadron, Camp Davis, N.C., November 1943. (Courtesy of the North Carolina Division of Archives and History)

laid the groundwork, showing the capability that women could do things in aviation," observed Linda DuMoulin, a retired lieutenant colonel from Alexandria, Virginia.[37]

Women Marines received six weeks of basic training at Camp Lejeune under the command of Major Ruth Cheney Streeter. Eugenia Lejeune, daughter of Lieutenant General Archer Lejeune, for whom the camp was named, received her commission there in 1943. Women received instruction and engaged in exercises comparable to those given men to perform, including firing antiaircraft guns and dropping from parachute towers. An all-woman crew at the Marine camp at New River also became carpenters, electricians, and plumbers. Esther Holcomb (later Crisanti), a sergeant in the Women's Reserves at the Marine Corps Air Station in Edenton, wryly noted in a letter home: "Most of the men are rather sullen. They seem put out because women have invaded their secluded station."[38] Rosie Katz of Bloomfield, New Jersey, wrote home from Cherry Point about how much she admired her "buddies" in the South Pacific. "I'm glad I'm a Marine," she insisted, "but I only wish I were a male Marine instead of a female Marine." Still, she was happy to be a radio operator, realizing that it would be her job to contact the planes if there was an attack.[39]

Because women were not allowed in combat, they had different experiences from men who were on the front lines, but those who served as military nurses came to know well the injury and death inflicted by war. More than 76,000 women served as war nurses, and they were assigned to every theater. For the women nursing in hospitals at Manila, Bataan, and Corregidor, "Days and nights were an endless nightmare. . . . Patients came in by the hundreds, and the doctors and nurses worked continuously under the tents amid the flies and heat and dust." Army and navy nurses waded ashore at Oran and Normandy to set up hospitals and help bury the dead. One nurse said, "It meant a great deal to the wounded and sick men to have American women to give them the expert care their mothers and wives would have wanted for them." But the "official" statement was somewhat different: according to the army's surgeon general, "They have conducted themselves as coolly as the most hardened veterans." Newsman Ernie Pyle encountered a group of fifty doctors and nurses from Charlotte working in a tent hospital pitched in an oat field in northern Africa. He reported that in the "first rush of casualties [women] were calmer than the men."[40]

The Aftermath: "Getting Rid of the Women"

In August 1945 parades and speeches marked the end of the war, but in homes across America this celebration was tempered by grief for the dead. In North Carolina 4,088 men and women had been killed in action. Some came home with medals, but many arrived with terrible injuries. Fathers and children seeing each other for the first time felt like strangers. When Alice Patterson met her husband Joe in Chapel Hill on his safe return from service as an army surgeon and introduced him to their eighteen-month-old daughter, born while he was overseas, the baby kicked him. The lives of families had been dramatically disrupted by the war. In 1946 divorces —and marriages—peaked. Although many wartime marriages did not last, most divorced people quickly remarried. As the war economy shifted to a consumer economy, the image of marriage and family was promoted everywhere, especially in advertisements for modern household appliances for the "dream" home.

The rush to celebrate the peace was complicated by what the nation had endured. Public opinion polls indicated that many people thought that a woman should stay at home and look after the family while the man earned the living—an idealized image that had not existed in many households before the war. Some business and civic leaders called for women to give up their jobs, and one headline put it bluntly—"Getting Rid of the Women." But in fact, two-thirds of the women who went to work during the war continued to work, though often in lower-paid jobs. One of them was Rose Will Monroe, who had played "Rosie the Riveter" in a promotional film about the war effort and was featured in posters. Monroe drove a taxi, operated a beauty shop, and started her own construction firm in Indiana.[41]

As postwar cutbacks began with the cancellation of defense contracts and a return to normalcy, women were twice as likely as men to find themselves unemployed (Fig. 9-9).[42] Their status in the job market returned to just about what it

FIGURE 9-9. *Sports writer Mary Garber*. Garber took over the sports desk of the *Winston-Salem Journal* when all the men went off to war—and kept her job when they returned. (Courtesy of the Forsyth County Public Library Photograph Collection)

had been before the war. At the same time, the number of women enrolled in colleges and universities declined in many places. In 1945 Dr. Benjamin Spock published an article in the *Journal of Pediatrics* advising mothers on how to deal with behavioral problems in children. Two years later the U.S. Government Printing Office republished Spock's article, and Spock's name was on the way to becoming the most recognized authority among Moms. By 1957 his *Baby and Child Care* was the parenting Bible, and prescriptive guidelines for taking care of children made motherhood seem like a full-time profession. Women themselves were "not of one mind" about what they should be doing: some wanted to fulfill a husband's need for "a wife, not a career woman"; others had enjoyed working out of the home and wanted to keep their jobs. Most wished to continue working because they needed the income.[43]

World War II as a Catalyst for Change: "Turning Point" or "Temporary Phenomenon"?

The war produced some immediate gains for women: higher wages, more kinds of jobs, and job security, at least for the duration of the conflict. Some concessions were wrung out of necessity: to solve the teacher shortage, the North Carolina General Assembly equalized pay for white and black teachers, initiated a retirement program, and in 1943 gave teachers the highest increase in annual salary ever provided.[44] Although the more than three thousand federally funded programs for child care for working mothers were accepted only as a temporary necessity and federal support for child-care facilities ended in 1946, the wartime Child-Care Project had introduced a useful model: the first project opened in August 1942 for kindergarten and school-age children in New Haven, Connecticut, setting its hours from 6:30 A.M. to 6:30 P.M.[45] More women had acquired new skills—from typing to electrical engineering—through courses in vocational education and had learned to manage offices and materials.

In 1948 Congress passed legislation to give women permanent status in the military establishment, although other inequalities remained: units were limited to 2 percent of total strength, female officers could not advance higher than the rank of colonel or commander, and married women could not enlist unless they were veterans. The WACs were so angered over the way they were treated that only 126 of the 8,000 stationed in Europe accepted the army's offer to reenlist. As D'Ann Campbell puts it, "The military remained this man's army."[46]

Although women who had served in the armed forces were seldom recognized as having made anything close to the contribution of men, some left with advantages. Black women had found skilled jobs with higher wages and had lived outside the segregated South; military women had learned administrative skills, which helped them find civilian jobs; and many women had earned money and acquired self-confidence and independence. Sixty-five thousand women used their veterans' benefits to go to college or graduate school. Laura Anderton, who had been an officer in the WAVES, went to graduate school on the GI Bill, her interest in medical research stimulated by her wartime experience at the Naval Medical Center in Bethesda, Maryland. On receiving her doctoral degree, she joined Salisbury native Katherine Taylor at the present-day University of North Carolina at Greensboro. At war's end, Taylor, who had also been an officer in the WAVES, returned to her alma mater as a faculty member in Romance languages and later became dean.[47]

William Chafe argued in 1972 that World War II was a "turning point in the history of American women," for it, "temporarily at least, caused a greater change in women's economic status than a half century of feminist rhetoric and agitation had been able to achieve." His bright picture began to fade as more academics studied the emerging field of women's history. Almost twenty years later, in a substantially revised edition of *The American Woman* entitled *Paradox of Change*, he considered the ensuing years of new scholarship and his own changed understanding of women's history. Chafe concluded that "the war had brought *no progress* toward economic equality between the sexes, but it had created a social legitimacy about the practice of married women working that carried over into the postwar years within the traditional framework of sex segregation and second-class jobs." In 1989 Sara Evans observed, "What the war had accomplished, with a reinvigorated economy and pent-up consumer demand, was a new expectation that most Americans could enjoy the material standard of living promised by the consumer economy in peace." The legacy of the war years lay in the "contradictory and illusion-filled decade of the 1950s." Some years earlier Leila Rupp (*Mobilizing Women for War*, 1978) had argued that "little had changed in the public definition of sex roles. . . . The image of Rosie the Riveter . . . was a temporary phenomenon." And D'Ann Campbell (*Women at War with America*) in 1984 made the case that World War II was liberating only for the women who lived through it. Their sons and daughters had little sense of history. Indeed, even when the war necessitated hiring women in jobs traditionally held by men, Nancy A. Hewitt found, politicians and manufacturers "were less interested in transforming traditional gender roles than in reassuring society that traditional roles could be maintained in the midst of war."[48]

Although World War II changed life for every family in North Carolina and thrust women into new roles, individual preferences were still maintained in many households. In the biographies that follow this chapter, Minnie Evans, a self-taught artist in Wilmington who began painting in the 1940s, and Elizabeth Lawrence, a Raleigh, then Charlotte, gardener and garden writer who published her first book in 1942, are examples of women whose private lives informed their timeless achievements (Plate 12). In contrast, two other women achieved extraordinary public lives as restrictions on race and gender began to loosen in the decades following the war. Pauli Murray, who grew up in Durham, became a national leader in the civil rights movement, in women's rights, and in the ordination of Episcopal women priests. Gladys Avery Tillett was a political activist in Charlotte and nationwide; at the end of her career, she traveled abroad to support issues and undertakings promoting the status of women.

Whether America's participation in World War II helped to bring about permanent changes in the lives of women is a question that historians continue to address. Asking the question in itself has led to important studies of American women's history. Perhaps the most significant shift was not in the way society thought about women but in the way women thought about themselves. In this sense the war prepared women for a battle that was yet to be fought, for public recognition of "women's worth." When the war ended, Governor R. Gregg Cherry praised communities for the sacrifices they had endured and the victory they had helped to achieve. "In short," he said, "home life was strengthened."[49] The end of a terrible war was not a time for society to accept changes in American "home life." That understanding would have to come later.

Minnie Evans

1892–1987

Minnie Evans.
(Courtesy of Susan Mullally Clark)

When Minnie Eva Jones was born on December 12, 1892, her mother was fourteen years old and living in a log cabin in Long Creek, Pender County. Anyone stopping there—midwife or hunter or distant neighbor—might have had some fear for the survival of the very young mother and baby, but the mother lived to be one hundred and two and the child to be ninety-five. The life of the child assumes historic importance when we realize that she grew up to become one of North Carolina's acclaimed artists without having advanced beyond the sixth grade. Her success gives credence to the theory that artists are born, not made.[1]

In 1979 Minnie was eighty-seven years old and living in Wilmington with her son George, his wife Martha, and her mother "Honey" Jones (who was one hundred) in a small apartment filled with noisy activities and conversations generated by grandchildren, great-grandchildren, and other visitors coming in and out. Almost totally deaf, Minnie fixed listeners with her eyes, eager to talk about her pictures. At times, she sounded like a whimpering child; then suddenly, she would boom forth in the thunderous voice of a bass-throated preacher:[2]

> I was born in Long Creek, in the county. My grandmother [Mary Croom Jones] had left her husband, [and] left my mother [Ella Jones], up in the country with my aunt [Meg]; had left her husband because he was a disagreeable man. She was too intelligent for him. When she was little, Mama, she got that way, and Mary found it out. She told Aunt Meg to "keep her [the baby], take care of her, till they bring her to me." I was three months old before she seen me. Then she brought me to Wilmington. Then they reared me up. My mama went to Fayetteville and stayed there and then when she come from Fayetteville, then my grandmother carried me to Norfolk, Virginia, and I went to school. Then when I came to be fifteen years old, my mother moved to Wrightsville. That's when she carried me, and that's where I came up, in Wrightsville. I got my great-grandmother's picture, Rachel.

Her narrative is as intricate as one of her drawings, but like a drawing it has the clarity of a central image: a cohesive circle of women. Minnie knew family women of four different generations. She often said that when she was young her mother seemed like her sister. Because of the closeness of their ages, the women in her family all seemed "mothering" to the young child, and each could have moved in and out of her life without interrupting her sense of belonging to someone.

Grandmother Mary Jones assumed responsibility for Minnie because Ella was so young a mother, and she had a formative influence on her life. Sometime between 1903 and 1908, the women—Mary, Ella, and Minnie Jones—moved to Wrightsville Sound, near Wilmington. The grandmother worked as a seamstress for white Wilmington families, making by hand "the most beautifulest clothes." Minnie dropped out of school in the sixth grade to work as a sounder, selling oysters and clams house to house. When she was sixteen, she married Julius Evans, who was nineteen and working for Pembroke Jones, the owner of Pembroke Park, a large estate near Wrightsville Beach. After their marriage, Minnie stayed at home to begin a family. Following the infant death of their first son, she gave birth to Elisha Dyer in 1910. Another son, David Barnes, was born in 1913 and George Sheldon in 1915. Minnie and Julius had named their children after three of Pembroke Jones's friends who came down from New York City to go hunting with him.

When the boys were still under six or seven years of age, Minnie Evans also went to work as a domestic at Pembroke Park. There, in the house of a wealthy family, she became familiar with elaborate furnishings and art. Outside there were lush plantings, ponds, and creeks. The house interiors and the natural setting would figure in her paintings some years later.

During Minnie's childhood, the Wilmington race riot of November 10, 1898, threatened the stability that many of the 17,000 blacks had found in a city of 8,000 whites. Blacks had done well in Wilmington, owning cafés, drugstores, law offices, clothing shops, and a newspaper. When violence erupted, many blacks left for northern cities, including Minnie's great-grandmother Rachel Williams.[3] If Evans's own memory of when she was taken to Norfolk, Virginia, is accurate, she was not living in Wilmington during the race riot. Her grandmother may have moved with her to Norfolk because the family wanted to get the child away. In later years, after Minnie and Julius were both employed at Pembroke Park and enjoying relative economic security, perhaps they were removed from the daily reminders of troubled race relations that hung over Wilmington. Either because she was not asked directly or because the subject was her paintings, Evans seemingly did not talk about race during interviews. Maybe she lived in her dream gardens and the immediate life around her had been translated into images of another world.

Minnie Evans came into the world dreaming dreams. "I couldn't sleep when I was a child," she remembered. "I couldn't sleep for dreams." One of her favorite dreams was about old men dressed as prophets, who tossed her so playfully into the air that the next morning she woke up tired and was chided by her teacher for falling asleep in class. But when she told listeners about seeing as a child green elephants going around the moon, she insisted, "This is natural. What I'm telling you now is not a dream." From a very young age she did not make clear distinctions between fact and fantasy, and she was mocked by other children and admonished by adults. Finally, a neighbor told her mother to leave her alone, that God had shown her visions He had not shown others.

In her heavenly visions, Evans moved outside the segregated community of black southern women.[4] She was able to remain a visionary even when she spent most of her time in the outside world. Her own needs were modest and realistic. She liked to remind her listeners that "even John D. Rockefeller can only eat one meal at the time." From years of collecting fees as a gatekeeper at Airlie Gardens, she could say with some literal truth, "Money is dirty. Money is *dirty*!" And she laughed heartily when she told her dream of dollar bills marching together, shaking their tails.

For Minnie Evans, things of the spirit were more valuable than material wealth. She and her husband and their young children were ardent churchgoers. She attended St. Matthew's African Methodist Episcopal Church in Wrightsville Beach and visited Pilgrim's Rest Baptist Church, where she had many opportunities to learn oratory from listening to preachers. Like orators, she enjoyed asking questions, and she loved to think about the answers. When she talked about her religious beliefs, she quoted by heart some of her favorite Bible passages and applied them to her daily living. "Ezekiel and the wheel," she might murmur, and her voice would drift away. Then she would straighten up and address her listeners, "What would the world be today without wheels?"

In the Bible Evans found images that she transformed over and over in her art. Beasts with wings and wheels with eyes seem to have leaped from the pages of Revelation and Ezekiel into her pictures. Like British visionary William Blake, she saw the Chariot of God and the New Jerusalem. "Whatever it is that has happened to Minnie Evans," observed a literary critic, "it is surely the same thing that happened to Blake."[5]

In writing about her pictures for a retrospective at the North Carolina Museum of Art in 1986, Mitchell Kahan considered her religious beliefs as "the original impetus to this art" and "its major theme." Noting that her pictures are more symbolic than narrative, he also observed that Evans was more visionary than illustrator. Religious and nature imagery was "spiritually replenishing."[6] Art gave expression to her visions and lifted her out of her particular time and place.

The story of how Minnie Evans became an artist whose work is analyzed by critics is singular and dramatic. At home one day she began to make pictures after she heard a voice command, "Paint, or die!" So she took an old board from a trash pile and began to draw, for hours. "I never did nothing as hard and as terrible as that in all of my life. Oh, what a terrible condition I was in. My husband said, 'Minnie, how you feel? I want to know, what ails you?' The children say they didn't know I was their mother. I had changed in looks of some kind of thing."[7]

Her family began to complain that she was always working on her pictures and acting strangely. When we look at her work today, it is almost impossible to imagine that she was also cooking, washing, doing the usual household chores, yet we know that she always lived in the midst of many people—

whether her own family or the family and guests of Pembroke Jones. We can also see that she lived in "the real world" in another sense—her drawings were made on the back of grocery lists, paintings on discarded boards. Clearly, those around her could *see* pieces of their own world in hers. Still, their objections persisted. One night she dreamed that an angel said, "Tell Julius to let you alone. If he don't, he going to die." She woke up and said to her husband, "Julius, don't say anymore to me." After that, nobody interfered.

As this story, often repeated, is undated, we do not know if her confidence in asserting authority over her life signaled a new stage of development as an artist. After beginning to draw in 1935, she made no more art for the next five years. When she began again, she steadily advanced, enlarging her drawing surface, adding color, shape, and design. Romare Bearden and Harry Henderson, in writing about African American self-taught artists (including Minnie Evans), observe that most led "ordinary, hard-working lives until, around the age of fifty years, they begin to follow with stubborn persistence their artistic vision."[8] By 1942, when she was fifty, Evans had begun to make more elaborate pictures, which would be exhibited, and she continued her work until almost the end of her life.

Between 1948 and 1974 Evans was a gatekeeper at Airlie Gardens, collecting admission fees from visitors. All around her the world was colorful, green lawns and leaves, reds and pinks of brilliantly flowering bushes, silver moss, and the textured surfaces of dark tree bark. Artistic designs were formalized in walks, a pond, and statuary.

Although her surroundings influenced her art, Evans's main source of inspiration was the Bible. She often quoted Scripture, her voice trailing off at the end to rise again in a breathless expression of wonder and delight in her own free associations. When asked to talk about some of her paintings, she explained them in biblical terms: "This big picture is The Ark of the Covenent. Moses. That's it! This is Ezekiel saw the wheel, in the middle of the air. God told Moses to make the covenant and paint it with gold. The Tree of Life, the Tree of Life, my! Is in the Garden of Eden, it's there!"[9]

As she began to paint more and talk more, others began to hear about her art. Encouraged by visitors who took an interest in the pictures (and sometimes bought one) and by George Rountree Jr., a Wilmington lawyer (her grandmother had worked for the Rountrees), Evans began to think of her pictures as things to show. In 1961 arrangements were made for the Little Gallery in Wilmington to exhibit some of them. In 1962 Nina Howell Starr, a photographer from New York, went to Wilmington to meet the artist. In 1966 Starr arranged for Evans's work to be shown in New York at the Church of the Epiphany and at St. Clement's Episcopal Church. At that time, Evans visited the Metropolitan Museum of Art and was Starr's guest at a private dinner party in her New York apartment.

This New York debut was followed several years later by exhibits at the Art Image in New York, then at the Davison Art Center at Wesleyan University in Middletown, Connecticut. In 1970 the artist was celebrated at home when St. John's Art Gallery in Wilmington staged a major exhibition. In the same year, some of her paintings were shown at the Portal Gallery in London.

The world of Minnie Evans was enlarging in a social and geographic sense, but at the same time, although some images of modernity were in her pictures (airplanes and bombs, for example), she seemed to have renewed confidence in her own dream-works. With Starr's help, her work was brought to the attention of more art curators, and in the next decade her pictures were included in many exhibits. In 1975 she gave a one-woman show at the Whitney Museum of American Art in New York. Her pictures were accepted for group exhibitions at the Los Angeles County Museum of Art and the High Museum of Art in Atlanta, among others. In 1986 the North Carolina Museum of Art presented a retrospective of her work, entitled "Heavenly Visions: The Art of Minnie Evans." In 1993 a traveling retrospective exhibit was organized by the Wellington B. Gray Gallery of East Carolina University. St. John's Gallery in Wilmington now has more than four hundred paintings from Evans's estate.

The art of Minnie Evans has been considered as belonging to different schools—folk, visionary, surrealist. Her influences have been said to be Caribbean (the family traces its roots back to her great-grandmother's great-grandmother in Trinidad, who was brought as a slave to Charleston, South Carolina), African, and Asian. Sharon F. Patton observes "a feminine presence" in images of women's faces with long eyelashes, red lips, and flowers woven into long hair. Estelle Lauter's study of women as mythmakers gives us a way of seeing Evans's use of nature "remythologized in female forms."[10] Although Evans often told visitors that they could read about her "in a book," she always seemed to regard comments about her pictures as existing apart from the pictures themselves. Even at the end of her life, she said her paintings were still a mystery to her.

Evans belonged to no institution. She always said that she had no teacher. "Who can teach me?" she asked in a booming voice. "I have *made* pictures, nobody else's pictures." Even a person without knowledge of art history and criticism can recognize a picture by Minnie Evans: the colors are basic and vibrant—red, orange, yellow, green, blue—and the images of wheels, angels, animals, statuary, vines, and eyes—many eyes—are recognizable, but also strange. We have seen these things before, but everything is freshly dislocated. Elephants circle the moon, eyes stare from the folds of leaves, wheels have no place to turn, figures in white float into a blue sky. We are comforted at the same time we are unsettled: something extraordinary is going on. The pictures of Minnie Evans resonate with dreams in our own unexpressed lives.

Elizabeth Lawrence

1904–1985

Elizabeth Lawrence, on the steps of her garden in Raleigh. (Photograph by Bayard Wootten; courtesy of the North Carolina Collection, University of North Carolina at Chapel Hill)

One of America's finest garden writers was an artist and a scientist whose garden was her life and her laboratory. Elizabeth Lawrence wrote about what was blooming in her garden, first in Raleigh and later in Charlotte. She also wrote about what was blooming in Hannah Withers's formal walled garden in Charlotte, which Elizabeth helped design, and in Caroline Dormon's wildflower garden at Briarwood in Natchitoches Parish, Louisiana, and on Carl Krippendorf's woodland estate near Cincinnati, Ohio, and in Rosa Hicks's mountain garden in Rocky Knob, near Banner Elk in Avery County, and in the gardens of so many others who became familiar characters to readers of her continuous narrative.

Moreover, she wrote about gardens she knew from having read about them—the nineteenth-century gardens of Gertrude Jekyll and E. A. Bowles in England and Countess Elizabeth Von Arnim in Germany—as well as the gardens described in hundreds of weekly letters sometimes addressed to "Kind Flower Lady" from "a friend" in rural Mississippi or Seattle or Baltimore.[1] She wrote about the history of plants from all over the world, their Latin and their country names, allusions to flowers in literature, the success and failure of plants growing in her own garden that had been sent as seeds in envelopes or dug up from gardens of friends, and personal remembrances, such as a lavender stick from Greece, a gift from a traveling cousin who knew it would give her pleasant memories of the garden of their Georgia grandmother. In these ways Elizabeth connected time, people, and places and taught readers to keep their senses alive to the beauty in their own backyards.

Her first book, *A Southern Garden*, published in 1942 and reprinted several times over a half century, has become a classic. She published two more major gardening books and for many years wrote a literary gardening column for the *Charlotte Observer* but was unable to finish all that she had wanted to write. It vexed her—toward the end of her life, perhaps even frightened her—that she could never get all of her work done. She left boxes of materials and half-finished manuscripts, which admirers edited and published after her death.[2]

Friends were as essential to Elizabeth's life as flowers. She often invited neighbors to "elevenses" in the garden, an old English—and southern—custom of having morning refreshments (in her case, sherry), and she, her mother, and her sister had lunch outdoors in the "sun-catch" in winter. She visited often with her near neighbors in Charlotte, Elizabeth and Eddie Clarkson, in their garden and bird sanctuary (which is now opened to the public as Wing Haven). She enjoyed conversations, especially with one person at a time. She spoke quietly, and her silences were like the hush just before something was about to happen. "Even if something is left undone," she said, "everyone must take time to sit still and watch the leaves turn."[3]

A passionate reader, her favorite book was *The Secret Garden* by Frances Hodgson Burnett (1911), and with the same kind of belief in the magic and mystery of gardens that she found in the book, she loved to engage the imaginations of children, especially her sister Ann's children, Elizabeth and Warren. Her niece and nephew encouraged the mischief—and the wisdom—in her to write: "As long as nothing is accomplished, children love to join in whatever is being done—especially out of doors. They love to clip anything that doesn't need clipping, to rake up leaves and then scatter them, and above all they love water . . . the way to hold their interest is to give them gardens of their own, and to allow them to care for or neglect the plants in their own way."[4]

In 1948, when Lawrence and her mother left Raleigh for Charlotte, they moved into the stately Myers Park neighborhood, but the house Lawrence had designed for them on Ridgewood Road was relatively small. Inside, the elegance of hardwood floors and china plates and the inviting warmth of a roaring fire in winter had the same expansive, romantic effect as her enclosed half-acre garden behind the house. She occasionally wore long silky dresses or artful caftans in the evenings when entertaining poet-friends and visiting artists from nearby Queens College, but except for a hint of lipstick for the Clarksons' Christmas party, she did not "make up." She ordered her groceries over the phone and did not pay much attention to food, but she admired the skills of the cook who prepared the evening meal as much as she did the skills of her assistant gardener who helped her dig and weed. She called herself "a dirt gardener." When she worked she wore jeans, and she crawled on her hands and knees in every season to discover (sometimes with William Hunt of Chapel Hill or other gardening friends) the smallest blooming flower. Between the two images of elegance and earth, Elizabeth conveyed an aura of mystery and particularity.[5]

Born in 1904 in Marietta, Georgia, Elizabeth was the first of two daughters of Samuel Lawrence, a civil engineer, and Elizabeth Brandenbaugh Lawrence. When Mr. Lawrence bought a quarry in northeastern North Carolina, he moved the family to nearby Garysburg in Northampton County. Elizabeth and Ann attended public school and enjoyed church and social activities in the small town built around a railroad. Elizabeth's diary, written in 1915 when she was eleven, is filled with the pleasures of riding her "wheel," playing jacks and paper dolls, and on a June morning picking ninety-six poppies.[6] The next year her parents moved to Raleigh so the girls could attend St. Mary's Academy. Afterward, the sisters chose different paths: Ann went to the University of North Carolina at Chapel Hill, married, had children, and worked in her community as a volunteer. Elizabeth did not marry, nor did she join anything, except for a few horticultural societies and the Episcopal Church. Still, the sisters were as close as they were different, and when Ann moved to Charlotte, Elizabeth and their mother, called "Bessie" by family and friends, moved from Raleigh to be near Ann and her family. The two sisters built houses next door to one another.

If St. Mary's in Raleigh was a conservative choice made by her parents, New York City's Barnard College, one of the most prestigious women's colleges of the period, represented Lawrence's willingness to venture away from home. In 1922, at the age of eighteen, she enrolled and majored in English. Apparently it was a happy experience; she made friends (especially Ellen Flood, whom she met in a class they both were taking at Columbia), and she acquired a very good background in classical literature. After graduating in 1926, she returned to Raleigh to live with her parents in a large frame house on Hillsborough Street. When she arrived, the garden was in bloom; she later said that she had never seen a more beautiful spring: her life and her life's work were to be at home. She enrolled in the state's land grant college, present-day North Carolina State University, where she was the first woman to receive a degree in landscape architecture. When her formal studies were over, the real work began. She determined, "I would have to grow the plants in my garden, and learn about them for myself."[7]

After her father's death in 1936, Elizabeth and her mother were alone to share the house and garden. Together they forged a close, lifelong relationship. Her mother introduced her to gardening, and it was through female relatives that Elizabeth had received her earliest memories of gardens—the old tea rose that grew under her grandmother's window in Georgia, the primrose jasmine in her great-aunt's garden, plantain lilies in her great-grandmother's. In remembering family gardens and in moving old family plants to new gardens in North Carolina (the jasmine, the coral tree), she and her mother continued a tradition that bound them to the past, to women in their family, and to one another. They checked each other's daily garden records to confirm their own observations. Bessie—who had "an opinion on every subject"—was a great favorite with Elizabeth's friends.[8] She died at the end of the summer in 1964 after a long illness, during which she was cared for by nurses at home. For a time Lawrence seemed lost. When she wrote about herself for a gardener's magazine in 1944, she had explained the role her mother had played in her life as a gardener:

> When I was a little girl, my mother took great pains to interest me in learning to know the birds and wild flowers and in planting a garden. I thought that roots and bulbs and seeds were as wonderful as flowers, and the Latin names on seed packages as full of enchantment as the counting-out rhymes that children chant in the spring. I remember the first time I planted seeds. My mother asked me if I knew the Parable of the Sower. I said I did not, and she took me into the house and read it to me. Once the relation between poetry and the soil is established in the mind, all growing things are endowed with more than material beauty.[9]

A Southern Garden is perhaps the best introduction to Elizabeth Lawrence as a garden writer. She had submitted the manuscript to the editor of the University of North Carolina Press with a letter that began: "Dear Mr. Couch, I have written a garden book for the Middle South based on my own records which I have been keeping for a number of years with a book in my mind, for there is no book for gardeners in our section, and there is need of one."[10] The editor agreed, and the book was published in 1942. With this straightforward letter, she staked out a geographic space for herself—the states of Virginia, North Carolina, South Carolina, Georgia, Alabama, Tennessee, and parts of the Southwest. She described her philosophy, also no-nonsense, in a foreword to the book, "An Apology for Myself as a Gardener": "I have no green or growing hand. Nor do I believe what old-timey people say, that flowers grow for those who love them. On the contrary, I believe that gazing upon them too fondly and too intently is the death of many. . . . Although I have gathered as much information as I can from all sources reliable and unreliable, which 'I git ter you as gun ter me,' one learns about gardens from gardening."[11]

With the first book, Lawrence gave notice of her confidence, her intelligence, and her originality: "I do not believe in pampering plants. If they are miffy, let them go." "Pampering," "miffy"—her words came from the common vernacular. But not far into the book Latin terms like *campanula garganica* appeared, and the reader was told that one of her chief delights was the gnarled rosemary, treasured "for the charm of its irregular outline, for the pale blue of its flowers in very early spring, and for the refreshing odor of its foliage as I brush against it in passing" (adding that it needs a poor light soil and lime).[12] She began her lifelong practice of writing about gardens and their gardeners, near and far. And whether they were her neighbors or the authors of gardening books or famous people (she corresponded with Vita Sackville-West, Katharine White, and Eudora Welty) or farm ladies who sold plants through the mail, Lawrence wrote of them as friends. Her comprehensive knowledge of horticulture, her careful observations about what was growing (or not growing) in her garden, her perfect pitch for sentences and words, and her understanding of people who garden—all come together in *A Southern Garden*.

When a new edition appeared in 1967, Katharine White reviewed it in her *New Yorker* column. "*A Southern Garden* is far more than a regional book," she observed; "it is civilized literature by a writer with a pure and lively style and a deep sense of beauty." White, herself a gardener, acknowledged that she had "learned more about horticulture, plants, and garden history and literature from Elizabeth Lawrence than from any other person."[13]

Fifteen years later Lawrence published her second book, *The Little Bulbs: A Tale of Two Gardens*. She described her own "small city back yard laid out in flower beds and gravel walks, with a scrap of pine woods in the background" and the hundreds of woodland acres belonging to Carl Krippendorf, near Cincinnati. Lawrence met Mr. Krippendorf, as she called him in the book, when he wrote to her regarding an article she had published on amaryllis in North Carolina, and their correspondence continued for "ten springs, and ten summers and falls and winters as well." "Sometimes I am not sure," she wrote, "which is more real to me: finding an early flower in my own garden, or following Mr. Krippendorf's solitary ramblings across his wooded hills." She made several trips to see him and his wife—but she knew the woods and the gardener even before she actually saw the man in "his leaf-colored jacket, with a red bandanna about his neck."[14] The personal was always present in her friendship with nature. Even as a scientifically trained landscape architect, she never lost the intrinsic belief that what determines the design of a garden "is more a matter of emotion than of forethought."[15]

Lawrence made many friends through letters and devoted a great deal of time to correspondence, responding to requests for information, ordering plants, and seeking to know more about other gardeners as well as their gardens. She was approaching eighty when she had to give up her dream of writing a book based on letters from her "farm ladies," and friends helped her to box up the materials and send them to the Duke University Press. After her death in 1985, Allen Lacy, a nationally recognized garden writer and editor, agreed to take on the task of putting together *Gardening for Love: The Market Bulletin*, published in 1987. It reads like a book of stories about women who advertised their seeds and plants in the state market bulletins, first recommended to Lawrence by her friend, Eudora Welty. Welty's fictional references to gardening ladies may have inspired Lawrence to take more liberties with her own prose style as she wrote about them.

Through the *North Carolina Agricultural Review*, she met Rosa Violet Hicks, who sent Lawrence "a handwritten list of more than sixty native species that she grows on her place." A correspondence followed, Elizabeth bought and swapped plants, and a friendship was forged through letters. They met when Elizabeth drove to western North Carolina along Shawneehaw Creek to Blueberry Farm onto Gwaltney Road and on through Pisgah National Forest. Mr. Hicks and his two sons were standing by the mail box, "waiting for us to pull up." She met Granny, "who was cheerful, loving, and wheezing like a kettle about to boil," and Rosa herself: "Quick to sorrow, quick to mirth, she has a light in her dark eyes." Though the steep banks of flowers were too much for Lawrence to climb, even with her cane, she saw the musk mallow for the first time. Later, she noted that it was a European and North African perennial, and seldom written about, except by Gertrude Jekyll.[16]

Lawrence's decline began in 1980 with the death of her sister, who died of cancer at the age of seventy-two. Four years older, Elizabeth had expected to spend the rest of her life near Ann; suddenly, she was alone. The next years took their toll, and, though she continued to see friends and to work over her papers, her fear grew that she would not live to finish another book. As she approached her eightieth birthday, suffering from heart disease, she required the care of her niece, Elizabeth Rogers. Lawrence sold her house in Charlotte, left her garden with everything in place—including the sculpted frog spouting water in the pond—and moved with her namesake to Maryland. She seemed to accept having to leave the garden behind, but her health was failing, and she died the next year, on June 11, 1985, at age eighty-one. She was buried in the St. James's Episcopal Churchyard in Lothian, Maryland.

For Lawrence, the world of gardening had been wide and deep. It was "a world as old as the history of man, and as new as the latest contribution of science; a world of mystery, adventure and romance; a world of poetry and philosophy; a world of beauty; and a world of work."[17]

Pauli Murray

1910–1985

The Reverend Pauli Murray, 1979.
(Courtesy of Susan Mullally Clark)

Pauli Murray personalized history. A passionate activist and a meticulous scholar, she entered some of the most historic battles of her time. In civil rights and in women's rights, she left her mark. That so much fire could erupt from one so impish delighted her friends, and surprised her opponents. In the end, at age seventy-five, the Reverend Pauli Murray had simply worn herself out on what she always thought of as her journey.

Her books are the place to begin to know her. The titles center her stories on a national experience: *Proud Shoes: The Story of an American Family* and *Song in a Weary Throat: An American Pilgrimage*. In writing about her own family and life, she discovered meaning in her personal successes and failures and meaning in her country's. Her most frequently cited book is the first comprehensive study of segregation statutes and civil rights laws, *States' Laws on Race and Color*, which Justice Thurgood Marshall said he and other young NAACP lawyers used as a "bible" in the early days of preparing cases. *States' Laws on Race and Color* represents the scholarly side of Murray; *Proud Shoes* and *Song in a Weary Throat*, the personal.[1]

Murray was an accomplished broken-field runner—she could scramble and scrap. "I grew up," she wrote, "a thin, wiry, ravenous child, overly active and eager to please but strong-willed and irrepressible."[2] At the time of her death, the description still held true. Anyone who ever met her would remember her sparkle, her pluck, and her courage.

A distinction that appeared in her obituary—the first black woman to be ordained a priest in the Episcopal Church—secured her a unique place in history, and, in a way, she would be pleased with the notice because she always had great respect for "firsts." At the same time, such a single biographical note also limits her place. Murray was ordained in 1977, when she was sixty-seven years old. By the time she had answered what she experienced as a call to God, she had answered many other calls to service as social activist and teacher. She was a restless spirit who always wanted to be where the action was, and the decades from the 1940s to the 1970s were filled with clarion calls to right some of America's wrongs.

She began her personal journey thinking about race, and in later years she spoke and wrote more often about gender issues. In 1976 she said, "I have reached that point in my conviction where being a woman is perhaps a more complex and more difficult status than being a black." As a person with a mixed racial heritage—Negro (the term she preferred), Anglo-Irish, and Cherokee—she embraced wholeness and never seemed to waver in her belief that people of all races belong together. Her training as a lawyer prepared her to confront laws of separation. The church brought her into direct conflict with a theology that held that an exclusively male priesthood was "ordained by almighty God" and "carried the weight of centuries of custom."[3]

Pauli Murray's public struggles were America's. Beginning in the 1930s, when she challenged segregation (in public transportation and in admission to the University of North Carolina at Chapel Hill), society was not ready to accept her kind. But ever an inquiring student, she was willing to study the matter, as well as to protest. When McCarthyism raised questions about patriotism, she noted, "I found it imperative to declare my American heritage." To do so she began the research for the book *Proud Shoes*, first published in 1956.[4]

Proud Shoes describes Murray's maternal ancestry in the years 1808 to 1919 and introduces readers to the family in

Durham that reared her after the death of her mother. The family tree included great-grandmother Sarah Ann Burton Fitzgerald, a white woman married to a mulatto, Thomas Fitzgerald, who proudly claimed "noble blood" in ancestry with Lord Fitzgerald of County Kildare, Ireland; Robert George Fitzgerald, her grandfather, whose pride was in having been a black soldier in the Union army; Cornelia Smith Fitzgerald, her grandmother, who knew almost nothing of her own mother Harriet, a half-Cherokee slave, but revered her white father, Sydney Smith, a trustee of the University of North Carolina; and Aunt Pauline, who adopted Murray after the early death of her mother, Agnes Fitzgerald Murray. In the house in Durham to which Pauli was brought as a child, Aunt Pauline supported the extended family on her earnings as a teacher.

When Grandfather Robert Fitzgerald went south to establish and to teach in schools for the newly freed blacks, married the beautiful and high-tempered Cornelia Smith, and arranged for his family in Pennsylvania to join him, he both enriched and complicated his own life and the life that became his granddaughter's. In the home there was a volatile mixture of pride: Robert's pride in his race and the Union, and Cornelia's pride in the landed Smith family of North Carolina. This racial heritage gave Pauli the first problem to be resolved: "It was a confusing world to me because I was both related to white people and alienated from them."[5]

From her earliest years, Murray sought to be a courageous soldier, like her grandfather; a high-spirited woman, like her grandmother; and an achiever, like her Aunt Pauline. As a girl she had a conflicted sense of her own gender: on the one hand, she was a soldier; on the other hand, girls were supposed to do girl-things. In learning to be both manly and womanly, she would have to invent herself. In writing her own story, she would "exploit a rhetoric of *uncertainty*," which, as a contemporary feminist writer observes, is the struggle for many women autobiographers.[6]

After her mother's death from a cerebral hemorrhage, the three-year-old Pauli went to live in her grandparents' house in the Maplewood section of Durham. At the time, her grandparents were elderly, and her mother's sisters—Aunts Pauline and Sallie—mostly looked after things. Each was unmarried, and Sallie, like her sister, taught in public schools. Pauline took her namesake with her to the West End school when the child was only four or five and where the older students adopted her as their "class mascot." When America entered World War I, Grandmother Fitzgerald took Pauli to see the Negro soldiers march in a parade to Union Station.

Murray's grandmother owned a hundred-acre farm near Chapel Hill, but she was hard-pressed to pay the taxes and rented it. Orange County and the seat of the state's first university held a special place in Grandmother Fitzgerald's proud heritage—she had been christened as a child in the Episcopal Chapel of the Cross. But Orange County had also been a place of terror when Cornelia Fitzgerald heard marauding Ku Klux Klansmen in her woods, and even after she moved to the Durham house that her husband had built, the nightmares continued. The Durham homesite—where Cornelia held sway with her broom and her fiery temper—had many of the markings of a rural life—chickens, a garden, a grape arbor—but roads and businesses were encroaching. When she was eight, Pauli had a paper route that took her through the West End and the Bottoms, where Negro families lived.

Although they lived modestly and sometimes meagerly, the Fitzgeralds were well known, and Pauline had friends among many of Durham's prominent black families—as a child Pauli dined at the home of Dr. Charles Shepard, president of present-day North Carolina Central University. Pauli's great-uncle, Richard Fitzgerald, was one of the leading businessmen. Pauli went with her family to the Episcopal church, where the new Negro suffragan bishop of North Carolina, the Right Reverend Henry B. Delany, regarded as a member of the family, confirmed her when she was nine years old.

After finishing at the West End school, Murray was enrolled at Hillside High School, a three-mile walk or bike ride every day. High school gave her more outlets for her energy: she excelled at sports, edited the school newspaper, and was a member of the debating team. When she was thirteen, her beloved grandmother died, and Murray threw herself into school activities with even more intensity, carrying both academic and commercial class loads. She graduated in 1926 as "most studious," and she already knew that she wanted to leave North Carolina. The segregated South was no place for her. The wave of southern blacks migrating toward greater freedom and opportunities caught Pauli Murray and carried her north.

What legacy did she take with her? As a three-year-old deprived of her mother, she had been left with a sense of abandonment, overcome by the nurturing of other women who were her caretakers, but not forgotten. Pauli was fortunate in having been adopted by her Aunt Pauline (when Pauli was three, Pauline was forty-three) and taken into a home where she was loved and taught. But her earliest remembrance of having clung to her mother's skirts, of being enfolded in the "warm fragrance" and movements of her mother's body, remained with her for a lifetime. After her mother's death in 1914, when Pauli was taken from her parents' home in Baltimore to live in Durham, her father was a shadowy figure. He had once been a public school teacher and a handsome man, but his mind and body had been affected by a near-fatal case of typhoid fever. His increasingly violent behavior and depressions led the family to commit him to a state hospital. Although Pauli was living securely in Durham when he was committed, she would hear from her brothers and sisters in Baltimore the taunts of the neighborhood children: "Your daddy went crazy and your mother killed herself!" (neither of which was true). Later as an eight-year-old taken by her aunt to Baltimore to visit her father, she was appalled that the disheveled old man who shuffled into the visitors' room could be William Murray. When in 1923 he was brutally murdered by a guard who Pauli believed was racially motivated, she insisted on looking at the body and bludgeoned skull. Her reaction was one of personal horror mixed with old fears of lynching and her grandmother's dreams of the Ku Klux Klan. The cruelty of children and the uncertainty of the cause of her father's behavior gave rise to what Murray described as her lifelong fear of family insanity. Perhaps it is one clue to the tenacity with which she disciplined her mind for multiple kinds of work. And certainly the evidence of violent racial crime fueled her anger.[7]

Durham was a city where blacks were gaining status. Both Booker T. Washington and W. E. B. Du Bois publicly recognized the southern tobacco town as the black capital of the South. Yet, Pauli Murray tells readers in *Proud Shoes*, Durham was also a place where blacks "were bottled up and labeled and set aside—sent to the Jim Crow car, the back of the bus, the side door of the theater, the side window of a restaurant." In the black children's school—dilapidated and swaying in the wind, in contrast to the beautiful brick school with an expansive lawn for white children—Pauli was eager to learn and did. After the family homeplace was sold in 1946 and her aunts went to live with her in New York City, she often returned to Durham. Her visits gave rise to stories told by old-timers—how she bobbed her hair, smoked cigarettes, rode in box cars, protested in the streets—until she became something of a hometown legend.[8]

Although as a sixteen-year-old Murray had already achieved a good measure of feistiness, when she left North Carolina in 1926 she was still naive about the world she so eagerly entered. She did not want to attend segregated schools in North Carolina, or anywhere else for that matter (she turned down a scholarship to Wilberforce University), and so she set her sights on New York City, where she sought admission to Columbia University. Rejected, she was told to repeat her senior year in high school and then to apply for admission to Hunter College. She followed the advice and in 1933 was graduated from Hunter, one of 4 blacks among 247 women. Free admission to college was one of her rewards for having chosen to leave the South, but nothing was easy. She had almost no money, and she had made-do by living cheaply and working many jobs. But study at a woman's college gave her a greater awareness of her strengths, and she was better prepared to deal with America's growing social conflicts. Her record of involvement over the next four decades is studded with activities, which can only be highlighted here.

In 1936 Murray was hired by the Works Progress Administration's Workers' Education Project, a job that provided her first contact with labor organizing. It gave her a sense of "an almost religious fervor" she would recognize later in the civil rights and women's movements.[9] In 1938 her application to the University of North Carolina Law School was rejected on racial grounds. Two years later she had her first meeting with Eleanor Roosevelt, whom she asked to speak during National Sharecroppers Week, which Murray was directing. The first lady agreed, and a friendship was forged that lasted until Roosevelt's death in 1962. Also in 1940, after testing segregation laws on interstate transportation, Murray spent a night in a Virginia jail. The next year she enrolled at Howard University Law School. In 1943 she joined a protest in Washington, D.C., for equal service in public restaurants, the first of many protests over segregation in the nation's capital. In 1944 her application for graduate study at Harvard University was rejected because of her sex. She then was accepted for master's work at the Boalt Hall of Law at the University of California at Berkeley.

In 1948, under the sponsorship of the Women's Division of the Methodist Church, she began the arduous research that would lead to her book on state laws on segregation. Soon after publication of *States' Laws*, she began *Proud Shoes*. In 1959 she traveled to Ghana to become a faculty member at the law school in Accra. Sixteen months later, she returned to do graduate work at the law school of Yale University, where in 1965 she received the doctor of juridical science degree. In the early sixties she became a women's rights activist and in 1966 was one of the founders of the National Organization for Women. In 1968, at age fifty-seven, she joined the faculty of Brandeis University. In 1970 she published *Dark Testament and Other*

Poems. Finally, she took part in the challenge to Episcopal Church practices that resulted in the ordination of women as priests in 1977.

Murray's public engagements were demanding. At Brandeis in the late 1960s, as one of two black professors, both of them women, she felt helpless to confront "the bid of black males to share power with white males in a continuing patriarchal society, in which both black and white females are relegated to a secondary status."[10] Her interest in women's issues intensified.

Although she had intended to study constitutional issues for the emerging African states, she now chose to concentrate on women's rights in America. The President's Commission on the Status of Women, created by John F. Kennedy in 1961 and chaired by Eleanor Roosevelt until her death the next year, was for Murray "the most significant and exciting development affecting women in decades." She accepted an assignment to study civil rights, property rights, and family relations. During the eighteen months that she met with other members of the President's Commission, she became part of a feminist network that gave her some of her most satisfying experiences in life. When members of the commission took up the question of the Equal Rights Amendment, they were looking for a way to avoid the bitter divisions that had prevented passage in every session of Congress since the ERA had first been introduced in 1923. Protective labor laws for women were at the center of the opposition of groups that believed passage of the ERA would eliminate protective labor legislation.[11] When the President's Commission on the Status of Women made its final report, Murray's was the guiding hand for the argument that state laws discriminating against women violated the Fourteenth Amendment. Discrimination could now be addressed through the courts. This was the first time that the acrimonious debates between opposing women's groups had led to any significant agreement, and most participants gave Pauli Murray credit for this achievement.

Three months after the commission presented its report to President Kennedy, another historic event took place—the formation of the National Organization for Women. Pauli Murray was an insider now, a member of what Betty Friedan would later describe as the "feminist underground" in Washington, D.C. Murray took a great deal of pride in having been at the luncheon when Friedan "hastily scribbled" the purpose of a new women's organization on a paper napkin—"to take the actions needed to bring women into the mainstream of American society *now* . . . in fully equal partnership with men."[12]

Buoyed by her success in the women's political movement, Murray applied her feminist thinking to the church when, on a Sunday morning in 1966, she felt "an uncontrollable anger." She left the service and wrote a letter to the minister protesting the absence of women in the service. This protest set in motion her last journey: in 1973 she entered the General Theological Seminary in New York. About four years later, on January 8, 1977, sixty-seven-year-old Pauli Murray was ordained a priest at Washington National Cathedral, where she felt "the spirit of love and reconciliation" as she had never felt it before.[13]

At home in North Carolina on February 13, 1977, in the same Chapel of the Cross in Chapel Hill where her Grandmother Cornelia had been baptized a century earlier as one of "five servant children belonging to Miss Mary Ruffin Smith," the Reverend Pauli Murray celebrated her first Holy Eucharist. It was also the first Eucharist to be celebrated by a woman in North Carolina. Crowds of old friends and the media were on hand. Murray believed her role that day "to be a symbol of healing. All the strands of my life had come together."[14]

In the last years of her life, Murray served as a priest in the St. Stephen Incarnation Church and the Episcopal Church of the Atonement in Washington, D.C.; the Holy Nativity Church in Baltimore; and the Holy Cross Church in Pittsburgh. She was a frequent speaker at church meetings and on university campuses, and she worked on her autobiography, *Song in a Weary Throat*. She died while completing revisions. In a foreword to the posthumous publication, Washington activist and legal scholar Eleanor Holmes Norton, who as a young woman had taken Murray as one of her mentors, described her as "a civil rights activist before there was activism, and a feminist when feminists could not be found."[15] Pauli Murray often said, "I've lived to see my lost causes found."

Gladys Avery Tillett

1893–1984

Gladys Avery Tillett with Eleanor Roosevelt. (Courtesy of Charles Tillett Jr. and Sara Tillett Thomas)

"I was reared in a family which had an interest in public affairs." In the straightforward manner that distinguished her, eighty-two-year-old Gladys Avery Tillett thus acknowledged the roots of her lifetime of political activism.[1] Her paternal great-grandfather, Colonel Waightstill Avery, attended the meeting that drafted the Mecklenburg Resolves in 1775 and was the first attorney general in North Carolina. Her maternal great-grandfather was a state senator. Her father was a judge in Morganton and later an associate justice of the North Carolina Supreme Court, and her mother, a graduate of Asheville Female Institute, was keen on politics. Gladys Tillett herself became a leader in her city, state, and nation, and in her last leadership role she traveled worldwide.

If Gladys's home seeded her life with public interest, her education helped it grow. In 1911 she and her only sibling, her sister Edith, entered the State Normal and Industrial School in Greensboro. When their father died suddenly, their mother would not hear of their dropping out and going home to be with her. The education available in the first state-supported institution of higher education for women was too important.

Gladys's history and political science teacher became her mentor: Harriet Elliott, an independent-minded Midwesterner who later worked in the Roosevelt administration. One of Elliott's own mentors was the prominent suffragist, Dr. Anna Howard Shaw, whom she invited to speak on the Greensboro campus. When a male speaker of a different persuasion told the students that he was sure that they were not interested in voting, they snickered into their handkerchiefs (embroidered at the corners with "Votes for Women"); after the assembly, they marched and burned him in effigy.[2] College president Walter Jackson, another progressive, sent Gladys and two other student leaders to New York City to participate in a form of settlement work. Before they left, Jackson called them in to have a talk. A lifetime later, Tillett still remembered his charge: " 'Girls, you're going up north, and they may be more assertive than you are, and whatever you are asked to do, show them how well you can do it. You are all good executives.' And so we arrived. No matter what they asked us to do, we did it. All ready to push forward." In 1914 Gladys organized the college Student Government Association and served as its first president. The life and times of Gladys Avery Tillett had been launched. In later years she often singled out for praise her "marvelous teacher," Harriet Elliott, and her school, "as progressive as any college in the country on suffrage."

While in college, Gladys fell in love with Charles W. Tillett, who recently had set up a law practice in Charlotte. After graduation she enrolled as a day student at his school, the University of North Carolina in Chapel Hill, where she received another bachelor's degree in 1917. A month later, on the eve of his entering the armed forces as the nation prepared for World War I, they married. Thereafter Gladys moved from army camp to army camp, following her husband. As it happened, he was not sent overseas, and before he left the service Gladys returned to Charlotte to prepare for the birth of their first child, a girl named Gladys, in 1919.

With Charles's law practice and Gladys's maternal responsibilities, they still made time for public interests: they loved politics and the Democratic Party. Gladys soon plunged into "the woman question," working to organize suffragists. After ratification of the Nineteenth Amendment, she cast her first vote in the presidential election of 1920, believing that with the vote women had what they needed to be on equal footing with men. It was her first lesson in political naïveté.

Meanwhile, the family continued to grow—Charles Jr. was born in 1920 and Sara in 1925—and Gladys seemed to thrive on a busy life. The Tilletts lived in a big, comfortable house in Charlotte's Myers Park, where a meeting was always being planned or taking place and the phone was always ringing. No sooner had suffrage been achieved than Gertrude Weil, former president of the North Carolina Suffrage League, urged Gladys and other suffragists to move quickly ahead to educate voters. Gladys helped found the Mecklenburg County League of Women Voters, became its president, and then president of the state league. She was a joiner, and what she joined, she organized and led.

Gladys went with Miss Elliott and Miss Weil to her first national meeting of the League of Women Voters, held in Baltimore, where Carrie Chapman Catt was the main speaker. Later she could still recall the words of a large banner that had been strung up in the hotel to welcome the women: "Get in the political party of your choice and work for the things you believe in." She went home and signed up with the Democratic chair to work in her precinct, going door-to-door to encourage women to register to vote. League workshops in Baltimore had taught her how to put on public meetings in which political candidates presented their views, and she organized the first candidates' meeting around the campaign for mayor of Charlotte.

By the end of the twenties, Tillett had held many offices and served on many committees in the county and state League of Women Voters. There was no question in anyone's mind that she, like many seasoned league members everywhere, wanted to work for a political party. And her party was Democratic, from birth to death. Beginning at home, she was elected vice chair of the local Democratic Party; she then helped to write a new rule that there had to be men and women in equal numbers for party positions. She persuaded the Mecklenburg county chairman to appoint fifteen other women as members of precinct committees. She was proud that North Carolina was one of the earliest states to have equal party representation and regarded it as a sign that the state was "progressive."

In the 1928 election, Tillett campaigned door-to-door and hers was the only precinct in Mecklenburg County that went for Al Smith, whose Catholicism was feared by many southern Protestants. She soon became a member of the party's state executive committee. Her first big break came in 1932, when she was chosen as one of four women delegates to the Democratic National Convention. Another of the delegates was her old friend, Harriet Elliott. They all voted for Franklin Roosevelt. Soon afterward, Eleanor Roosevelt's friend Molly Dewson recruited Gladys to promote New Deal policies and programs around the country. Travel was as second nature to Tillett as politics. She and Dewson took to the road, and by the time the trip was over they were lifetime friends as well as political allies: Dewson asked Tillett to direct the Speakers Bureau for the Women's Division of the National Democratic Committee. It was 1936, and opposition to the New Deal was growing. Gladys remembered, "She said that she wanted somebody that [could] take it and . . . get it done." Apparently Gladys did the job, as she was reappointed in 1940.

As director of the Speakers Bureau, Gladys trained and sent women out to speak for the Democratic Party. They had a great unifying presence in Eleanor Roosevelt. Tillett, Elliott, Dewson, and thousands of Democratic women in Washington and across the country admired the first lady. She invited them to Hyde Park and the White House to tell the president what their views were. She carried their issues to him herself; she worked through many of his staff members and heads of federal agencies. Most of all, women loved Eleanor Roosevelt. They caught the spirit of her deep commitment to people who had been left out of the system, and Gladys Tillett was thrilled to be her friend.

In 1940 Tillett got a call from the National Democratic Party that surprised her—she had been asked to serve as national party vice chair. It was a major opportunity for her. She and Charlie and the children talked it over, and of course no one could resist Gladys's persuasive causes. The first summer that she went to New York, she sent Sara to camp and young Charles worked in his father's office. The younger Gladys was a teenager, and her mother felt that she should not be left at home alone. Molly Dewson told Tillett to bring her along, and they would find something for her to do. Young Gladys went, and mother and daughter had a wonderful time.

What Gladys had learned from her father—be pleasant, be patient, and be persistent—she taught others. She and women like her could organize thousands of meetings in every state at a week's notice. She set up training sessions, and no detail was too small. Speakers learned how to use the stepladder in speaking on street corners. They learned to use the telephone as men never had. Women callers were willing to listen and would not let anyone hang up without having promised to do something for the party. They became seasoned travelers, able to pack quickly, travel light, and sleep sitting up while a train carried them through the small towns and big cities of America. The next morning, they would meet a cadre of women party workers who held out cups of coffee and a printed agenda. Gladys Tillett—whose folksy approach belied her careful preparation—stood up to speak, and even when she did not persuade, she charmed.

As the national party's vice chair with new authority to dispense patronage, Gladys found that her work took on added meaning. She stayed in touch with her national women's network to get women's names in the pipeline for federal appointments, both in paid positions and in volunteer service on national boards. She was a letter writer. "My dear Mr. President," one letter began, "It gives us such a feeling of hope and faith in the future to know that we have as our leader a man who understands so well the contribution women can make in the international field." Although busy, she was always approachable on a personal level. One of the letters sent to her begins, "Aunt Mary has asked me to send you a copy of her recommendation of Arthur White for the position as Secretary of Labor."[3]

And there were personal rewards. When she returned from lunch with Eleanor Roosevelt at the Val-Kill cottage at Hyde Park, she wrote Charles about everything—including the menu. There were tables on the lawn for about fifteen guests for a lunch "as informal as one of Mother's Sunday dinners." Among the guests was Frances Perkins, the secretary of labor and the first woman to hold a cabinet post. After lunch, they went to see the big house at Hyde Park, where they met FDR's mother, and then greeted the president himself. There were many family members and friends, party workers, and staff. Molly Dewson introduced Gladys as chair of the Speakers Bureau, saying, "Mr. President, I want to tell you what her husband said—that when you listed the campaign contributors and put them down, Mrs. Casper Whitney, $2,000, etc. he wanted you to put down, Charles W. Tillett, his wife." It worked. "The President laughed heartily."[4]

By 1944, the year of Roosevelt's campaign for a fourth term, Gladys was an experienced and trusted party leader. In planning their national conventions, both parties chose women to give major addresses at the evening sessions, and Gladys Tillett of North Carolina was one of those speaking for the Democrats.

When Roosevelt died and Harry S. Truman became president, Truman brought in his own appointees. In 1950 Gladys headed home to North Carolina to help direct the senatorial campaign of Frank Porter Graham, her husband's college roommate and their dear friend. Graham was a known liberal, and the primary issue used against him was his friendly relations with blacks; wherever Gladys traveled, she met a vehement opposition. She went to work, calling up her own network and organizing a Committee of Two Thousand with the slogan, "Women Will Win This Election." Charles Tillett wrote letters to friends, answered attacks with letters to the editor, helped raise campaign money and contributed his own, and advised Graham.[5]

As cochair of the Graham team, Gladys threw herself into the campaign, and when he came out ahead in the primary, his passionate supporters rejoiced. None were more elated than Gladys and Charlie. But the war had not been won. Graham's major opponent, Raleigh lawyer Willis Smith, called for a second primary. Between the first and the second primaries, the campaign intensified in response to a dramatic announcement: the U.S. Supreme Court in three cases brought by blacks handed down rulings that challenged segregation. The issue of race inflamed the campaign; Smith beat Graham in the runoff, and the state was left bitterly divided.[6]

Everybody who had worked in the effort was worn out. One of the weariest was Charles Tillett, who had struggled to keep his law practice going while he worked for Graham. Then tragedy struck the Tilletts. Charles had severe clinical depression; although he was in treatment and seemed to be recovering, he committed suicide. The family was plunged into grief. No expression of sympathy to Gladys was more poignant than that of a woman who herself had lost her husband, Eleanor Roosevelt. She wrote, "I am so convinced that work is the best way to live through this kind of period in your life that I beg of you to go on with some of your many interests." Gladys wrote back, "I shall endeavor to set my face to the future." She had been prepared since childhood to do just that, but it took grim determination now.[7]

One of the projects that Gladys and Charles had worked on together involved the United Nations. They had gone as observers to the international meeting in San Francisco in 1945 to draft the charter, and they wrote and spoke in support of America's role in the organization. After Charles's death, the work of the United Nations was Gladys's most deeply felt connection to her husband's public interests. Her golden opportunity to be a part of that international body came in 1961, when President John F. Kennedy appointed her to the American delegation. From 1961 to 1965 she was a U.S. representative on the Commission on the Status of Women and served in many other U.N.-related roles, including acting as a consultant to UNESCO (U.N. Educational, Scientific, and Cultural Organization) on the development of women's programs. In these capacities she traveled all over the world, meeting government officials, touring new countries, conversing with women, and sharing agendas for the improvement of women's lives. In three years and traveling fifty thousand miles, she moved from Africa to Asia to Europe. She was excited "to be alive in such a revolutionary period in the progress of women." In Tehran she observed five thousand women marching on the second anniversary of their having been granted the vote. In meetings of the U.N. Commission on the Status of Women, Gladys, chief of the U.S. delegation, cited gains made in securing political rights for women worldwide. Seminars in political and civic responsibility sponsored by the commission were like those she and many other members of the League of Women Voters had first organized at home after suffrage had been won in 1920.[8]

Tillett returned from her work with the United Nations to live alone in the family home in Charlotte. But she was still in touch with many of her old friends. Young women sought her help as they entered some of the battles she had fought for more than a half century. In the early 1970s active support was growing for passage of the Equal Rights Amendment. In 1974, as ERA proponents geared up for another try, they hoped to avoid the divisiveness that had helped defeat every effort to get the amendment passed since its introduction in Congress in 1923. North Carolina women decided to unify support by choosing Gladys Avery Tillett as "titular head" and what historians of the ERA in North Carolina called "the proponents' icon of legitimacy." She was now eighty-two, but she could not turn down the appeal from younger women, who promised that if she would serve they would take on the arduous work of the day-by-day campaign. Organizer Beth McAllister recalled going with Tillett to sit in the gallery of the legislature to follow the debates on the amendment. As soon as lawmakers down on the floor recognized Tillett, they set up such a show of shouting and waving that business was disrupted. When they entered the senate, the same spontaneous display of affection occurred.[9]

The ERA failed to win enough states for ratification. North Carolina, as it had done in the suffrage campaign, cast a negative vote. Tillett became reflective, noting that women on opposite sides of the question needed to understand the others' point of view. But in looking back on her own campaigns, she admitted that she had learned to accept the harsh realities of public life: "After all those years of struggle, after all that work, there were still plenty of women who weren't interested, who thought women participating in a political process that affected daily lives was still some kind of modern notion. I expect there will always be people who feel that way, men and women, but it's a mystery to me."[10]

Gladys Tillett lived to be ninety-two. When she died, North Carolina women in politics felt bereft. She had been, one woman reflected, a "role model for every female politician throughout the state." The myth that southern women were only homemakers, Tillett once remarked, was "all nonsense." Her long and productive life as a wife, mother, and political leader demonstrates how right she was—and how much had changed in almost a century of North Carolina women's history.[11]

Epilogue

The history of American life after World War II, as we noted in our introduction, requires a book all of its own. What happened to North Carolina women in the second half of the twentieth century is an exciting question that will invite new generations of historians. They will want to consider how North Carolina kept up with progressive changes undertaken across the nation, moved ahead, or lagged behind, and which changes in women's lives caused by the war proved to be temporary and which became permanent. Statistical data, demographic studies, new scholarly approaches, and unprecedented media coverage will provide more extensive materials for study than would previously have seemed possible.

To end with World War II, as we do here, leaves the generation of readers born afterward without a chapter about their own lives. Before a new century begins, we would like to record in this epilogue some observations about the period in which we have lived. In doing this, we will take a more personal and discursive approach, framing our observations in terms of the thematic structure laid out in earlier chapters.

Women's lives, we now know in great detail, varied according to race and class. Native American women, white European settlers, and enslaved African Americans lived differently from one another. Land-owning families lived differently from tenant farmers. Life for mill spinners was different from life for schoolteachers. Women who stayed at home did not face the same demands as women who also worked outside the home. Lives of people in the Mountains, the Piedmont, and the Coastal Plain were affected differently by geography. And rural families lived differently from urban families. Moreover, many individual personalities, attitudes, and circumstances distinguished women within the larger context of their own race and class. Despite the influences of time, place, and circumstances, it is not a foregone conclusion how lives are lived.

As we see when inquiry is focused on women rather than men, history has a different look from earlier histories in which women mostly were excluded. In many ways women lived differently from men, even the men in their own families. Women's lives were more private; their moves into public life had to be justified as "good works" benefiting society or, in emergencies, as paid work because the family needed the money or the society needed the labor. Achievement for women recognizes a different set of goals to be reached and of obstacles to be overcome.

As we moved through the research that led us to these and other observations, we recognized themes in the second half of the twentieth century that we found in the past: a woman's primary responsibility for home and family; a sense of belonging to a larger community of women; participation in women's volunteer organizations; a growing awareness of a consumer culture; slow, incremental, and cumulative changes that improved women's opportunities; and, despite the significant emergence of marginally represented groups, continued dominance by white men in government and commerce. When we came to the end of World War II, we had a new perspective through which to see this half century. Here are some of our observations.

In the 1950s a nation that had played the major role in winning a world war sought to emphasize the common bond that Americans shared at home. All citizens were to be patriots, and they were all to enjoy the peace and prosperity that followed. Everyone had *pulled* together during the war; now everyone needed to *be* together. And home was the place to be together. After years of separation—massive numbers of men in the war, women in the labor force—"coming home" for many people was a prayer answered. Expectations were high, and they rested on the ability of women to fulfill the dream: the making of the "perfect" home.

And there were encouraging signs. War had given a great boost to production, and after helping to win the conflict, producers could turn their attention to the American family. At the same time that production could continue to stimulate the economy, production for the home suited the nation's moral purpose. Citizens as consumers and a consumer economy shaped the postwar years. A shining white new electric stove was easier to use and faster than the old cast-iron cookstove with an oven that a farm woman had filled with pans of biscuits for the family and the "hands." Something magical—a new piece of furniture with a small round screen, the first television set—would displace the radio for family entertainment. In 1950 fewer than 2 percent of North Carolina homes had a television, but by 1970 television was watched in 95 percent of homes. The house itself needed modernizing. For many people that meant getting away from the old downtown neighborhoods and early "suburbs" and going out past the town limits to live in suburban developments on an unprecedented scale. There, the houses and the families who lived in them, mostly middle-class and white, looked very much alike.

At home, in farm or factory, in apartments or suburbs, women were essential to success in the ways they had always been: in establishing permanent roots, in bearing and caring for children. Although many marriages ended in the aftermath of separation during the crisis-driven war years, people tended to remarry quickly. With the increase in marriages, the birthrate rose. In the late 1940s Dr. Benjamin Spock and other child care experts urged mothers to avoid establishing rigid "rules" and to adapt to the needs of their new infants. While the mother was supposed to be at home engaged in time-consuming family and household tasks, the husband was expected to earn the living and be the head of the house, the latter role, many church members believed, to be in accordance with God's law. The woman was the wife and mother; she would take care of the children and keep the family happy. This image had been imagined in earlier periods of women's history, but now it was enforced by a shift in the economy to consumer goods.

What we have just described is the way it was "supposed" to be. But history, as we have seen it, is full of contradictions and differences. In fact, the female workforce continued to grow. Although consumer products, child rearing, and women as homemakers were the central images of the 1950s, in reality there were layers of difference. In 1950 there were women who agreed with Dr. Spock that they should stay at home and women who did not know who Dr. Spock was. Many women did not have time to read, nor did they put their faith in books. Like farm women who went to work in the war factories, women of the fifties continued working to help support their families. Others worked, as they had worked during the Great Depression and the war years, to survive, often in low-wage jobs—usually in textiles or tobacco. As more consumer goods flooded the market, priced for the people who could buy them, many North Carolina working women had reason to feel bitter. Tenant farm women interviewed in the 1930s had spoken plaintively of their wish to have a Sunday dress. In the 1950s, as high school girls from the middle class starched their crinolines and rolled their socks, blue-collar, working-class women still had lint in their hair from the mills, and women, who comprised the largest number of employees in the tobacco industry, did much of the dirtiest work on the floor. In fact, not everybody was doing well in those "fabulous fifties."

In addition to stimulating the economy and creating a new national image, the war had left another legacy: it had given women and southern blacks a different way of seeing themselves. North Carolina's reputation as a progressive state was nowhere more contradicted than in its discrimination against blacks and women, enforced by both laws and customs. Fortunately, there were strengths for resistance. The centrality of the church in the black community provided a base of support for its members as they began to confront racism in public places. A network of white women active in community service and political organizing produced leaders who were willing to confront sexism. Each group created what came to be called a "movement" and sometimes a "revolution." Although blacks took the leadership role in the civil rights movement and whites became leaders of the women's movement, the movements were connected in complex ways that remain fertile areas for research and discovery. The importance of issues affecting blacks and women throughout this half century is so stark that at least a brief review is called for here.

During the war years, when southern blacks migrated to northern cities for better jobs or were sent on military assignments to distant places, the geographic, social, and psychic landscape of their lives changed. When they returned to visit or to live, they brought with them a sense of a better life than the segregated South permitted them. Blacks expected things at home to change.

The most striking evidence that history would change came in 1954, when the Supreme Court decision in *Brown v. Board of Education* challenged racial segregation in America. North Carolina's reputation as a progressive southern state largely had depended on the cooperative relationship between government and business and on the leadership of a few citizens like Frank Porter Graham, who had been president of the University of North Carolina in Chapel Hill. Graham's deep liberal convictions influenced generations of Chapel Hill students and were often accepted by North Carolina conservatives as being humanitarian rather than political. But when Graham entered politics, appointed in 1949 by Governor Kerr Scott to fill an unexpired term in the U.S. Senate, the state became divided dramatically. The next year racial attitudes inflamed political rhetoric and defeated Graham's candidacy for a full term. Moreover, the 1950 senatorial campaign cast an ominous cloud over the next half century in North Carolina.

When school boards and school systems began to draw up various plans to meet desegregation orders, responses took different forms, but all were characterized by a slowness to change. In Greensboro, with its culturally rich community of Jewish families and the Quaker tradition of religious tolerance, community groups formed across race lines to discuss how racial cooperation could be achieved. In many ways, it was a model of the kind of community "dialogue" that needed to take place in other towns and cities. When men in government and business agreed that it was necessary for the good image of the community to bring groups together, women often set up meetings in churches and community organizations like the YWCA and led the discussions. Greensboro—and North Carolina generally—despite serious racial tensions and extremist groups like the Ku Klux Klan and the Black Panthers, somehow managed to avoid the violence taking place in other southern cities. But it was not until 1971—seventeen years after the *Brown* decision—that Greensboro fully complied with the federal desegregation order.[1]

As responses to the 1954 court decision developed across the state, momentum was building for something other than efforts behind closed doors by whites to put together school desegregation plans and by blacks to instigate lawsuits against local school systems not in compliance. In February 1960 the civil rights movement experienced a defining event when four black college students sat down at Woolworth's segregated lunch counter in downtown Greensboro. They were refused service but continued to sit. Such a simple act had immediate and lasting consequences. The four young men were joined by other black citizens, including many students, and they marched in the streets. The sit-in and the marches were replicated in other North Carolina towns and cities and across America. Often behind the scenes were black women, feeding and housing protesters, staffing offices, and supporting the movement.

Women played many roles in the civil rights movement that contemporary journalists and historians continue to examine. In this short reflection, we want to mention one woman whose role was critical to the success of black students. She was Ella Baker, a native of Virginia, who grew up in North Carolina, where she was graduated from Shaw University, founded by Baptists for the education of African Americans. In 1958 Baker was asked by the Reverend Martin Luther King Jr. to set up the national office of the Southern Christian Leadership Conference (SCLC) in Atlanta. In 1960 Baker, taking note of the large numbers of black students who were following the example of the four young men in Greensboro, proposed a conference of the "sit-inners" to be held in Raleigh. When adults took over the conference and told students what they must do, an outraged Baker "walked out." She recognized "from the beginning that having a woman be an executive of SCLC was not something that could go over with the male-dominated leadership. And then, of course, my personality wasn't right, in the sense I was not afraid to disagree with the higher authorities." Baker's answer was to help found the Student Nonviolent Coordinating Committee (SNCC), where furious debates took place. Baker let students think and talk for themselves. She later said, "You didn't see me on television, you didn't see news stories about me. The kind of role that I tried to play was to pick up pieces or put together pieces out of which I hoped an organization might come."[2]

The role of race in North Carolina has continued to be played out in many of the life histories of women we hear across the years. One brief example suggests the lasting implications of the 1960s civil rights protests. In 1994 an eighty-year-old black woman who had picked crabs all of her life in eastern North Carolina spoke of the effects of the civil rights sit-ins on her own behavior:

> Those demonstrations made a little change in me. I go into the crab house and my grand baby don't have boots and the bossman drives a nice car and it was working on my nerves in my stomach, and I *quit*. [When I returned to the job] it was different. I had got mad and got away with it. When I went back I still put in a good day's work, but I didn't want no pat on the back. Used to be I would be waiting for somebody to say something nice to me, but now I was doing it for myself and my children. I put supper on the table, and I'm glad I could do it and proud I could do it.[3]

Another dominant theme since midcentury has been the role of women in public life. In the national media, as the image of making happy homes was displaced by images of protest, a shift from private lives to public history occurred. The home did not remain static, however, and issues between men and women, both private and public in nature, often remained unnamed—and unresolved. These generalizations must serve as an introduction to the complex issues that dominated discussions of "women's liberation."

Although many North Carolina women were affected in one way or another by the heightened attention given the national women's movement, most did not join demonstrations. Indeed, many southern women, in keeping with traditional attitudes, were wary of public discussions, especially those in which conflict and anger were likely to arise. The movement also failed to appeal to most of the state's large group of low-wage working women and to the conservative households of religious believers. Women like Crystal Lee Sutton, who in 1973 was fired from her textile job in Graham because of union activity (her story was made into the Hollywood movie *Norma Rae*), had their working lives controlled by the factory "Boss." At home, many women faithfully acknowledged their husbands to be the head of the house, usually adding, "in all things."

It had been obvious that laws affecting segregation needed to be changed for blacks to gain equal rights. It was less clear what changes needed to take place for women, because no single obstacle to their success could be readily identified or agreed upon. In that uncertain context, the new women's movement came alive. Not since North Carolina women had packed the gallery when legislators considered the Nineteenth Amendment had women been as visible and vocal as they suddenly became in the 1960s. What happened? Who made it happen? Were the changes temporary or permanent? What were the differences among women? Was there any common bond?

On the basis of past history, we can expect certain answers: some single event triggered a reaction, perhaps larger than expected; a few women took the lead, others countered; some things changed and others did not; groups of women felt differently. The search for a common bond among women, like a common theme in history, remains elusive.

The "status of women" became an issue for consideration in 1961, when President John F. Kennedy asked Eleanor Roosevelt to serve as chair of the Presidential Commission on the Status of Women, with a mandate to study women's place in the economy, the legal system, and the family. In 1963 North Carolina governor Terry Sanford appointed the Governor's Commission on the Status of Women, with Duke historian, civic leader, and wife and mother Anne Firor Scott as chair. Out of the North Carolina commission came a relatively short report (vis-à-vis later studies) documenting that between 1940 and 1960 the number of women in the state's workforce had increased by 80 percent. Many worked in low-wage jobs and lacked benefits at home and at work: many did not qualify for social security or have health care and pension plans provided on the job. Most women were primarily responsible for housework and the care of the family, and few had access to paid child care. The recommendations of the report placed pay equity and child care at the top of the list of those matters requiring action.[4]

These were some of the issues being identified and defined through statistics and studies in the 1960s. But it was a book, more than any other single thing, that epitomized and helped to create what came to be called the women's liberation movement. In 1963 Betty Friedan published *The Feminine Mystique*, the title of which referred to her sense of a false and destructive ideal of womanhood. Arguing that Friedan's generation had been slaves to the home and had languished intellectually, socially, and psychologically, *The Feminine Mystique* became the touchstone for a mostly white, mostly middle-class audience of women—political activists, community volunteers, career women, as well as stay-at-home wives and mothers for whom the words "stay-at-home" had never represented the reality of their busy lives. "The problem that has no name" was a malaise that many white middle-class women recognized.[5]

The message of discontent resonated with millions of American women who came together and found that they had a lot in common. They shared the same frustrations—the tedium of housework, the never-ending demands of families, the limited opportunities to be paid for their skills—and they talked about themselves in discussions that came to be called "consciousness-raising." The self-styled "sisterhood" launched a "revolution" for "women's liberation." The movement became defined in part by language invented as events took place. In 1964 a victory was registered when Congress added—to Title VII provisions against discrimination in employment on the basis of race, creed, and national origin—the word "sex."[6] In concrete terms, the legal basis for economic parity between the sexes had been laid.

In 1966 another event defined the movement. One day when Betty Friedan and others, including civil rights activist and legal scholar Pauli Murray and various women working on Status of Women reports, got together over lunch, Friedan wrote on the back of a napkin the name of a new organization, the National Organization for Women (NOW). Its purpose was "To take action to bring women into full participation in the mainstream of American society now, assuming all the privileges and responsibilities thereof in truly equal partnership with men." Local NOW chapters, which subsequently flourished all over America, turned their attention to the Equal Rights Amendment.

One of the issues that had divided women since it was first introduced in the U.S. Congress in 1923 was the passage of an Equal Rights Amendment. Even in the 1960s, members of NOW and of committees working on Status of Women surveys still disagreed about whether passage of ERA would help or hurt women. In North Carolina a group of women organized to support ERA. Most were longtime political activists, and they chose for their "titular" leader Gladys Tillett. They organized across the state for the purpose of lobbying legislators in the General Assembly; leaders included Martha McKay and Betty Ray McCain (later secretary of cultural resources), both savvy political activists; Beth McAllister, president of North Carolinians United for ERA; and Nancy Dawson-Sauser (formerly Drum), a NOW member who became a salaried coordinator. The language of the proposed amendment was straightforward: Equality of rights under the law shall not be denied or abridged by the United States or by any State on account of sex. Some advocates hoped for specific gains, such as pay equity; others hoped that a constitutional amendment would result in general equality in the way women were treated in society and in the home.

In the decade after 1972, by which time the ERA had passed Congress and had been submitted to the states for ratification, it was introduced six times in the North Carolina General Assembly. Six times it failed for the same reason it had failed in certain other states: legislation governing women's place was loaded with meaning far beyond anything the words actually said.

The most powerful North Carolina opponent of the Equal

Rights Amendment was the U.S. senator from Morganton, Sam Ervin Jr. After the ERA passed in the Congress, he turned his attention to helping defeat it in the states. Nowhere was his influence more directly felt than in North Carolina. With the weight of his legal knowledge and his popularity, Ervin said the things that many North Carolina legislators already believed: there were enough laws to protect women, the ERA was against God's law, and women did not want it. Opponents of ERA loved what he said. A mother wrote to Senator Ervin expressing fears that her three little girls would grow up to be drafted. "Oh, God! I can't stand it," she exclaimed. "I just can't stand it." The proposed amendment was "immoral" and "filthy" and would lead to "vast sexual chaos."[7] From whether or not women and men would have to use the same public bathrooms (no) to whether or not women could be drafted and sent into military combat (even those favoring women in the military expected some exceptions), questions of what exactly would be changed by passage of the amendment were never satisfactorily answered. Amid this uncertainty, fears were more powerful than any facts that could be given.

Another anti-ERA leader was Phyllis Schlafly, who organized a powerful STOP ERA movement. She alleged that ERA supporters were "the unkempt, the lesbians, the radicals, the socialists" and that homemakers and mothers who stayed at home would be forced to take jobs and put their children in state day care programs. Ervin's legal arguments that ERA was unnecessary and Schlafly's moral arguments that ERA would destroy "normal" relationships between men and women were difficult to counter. Thus, when a vote for or against ratifying the ERA came down to a simple yes or no, by voting "no" legislators could appear to be voting "yes" for protection of "the home" and "the family."

The *Raleigh News and Observer*, whose support for the Nineteenth Amendment had not helped secure its passage in 1920, pointed out that Schlafly had "left her fashionable house in Alton, Illinois, her six children, lawyer husband, and two secretaries to tell North Carolina women that their place is in the home." In 1982 North Carolina was one of four states that would determine whether the Equal Rights Amendment would succeed or fail. As national attention focused on Raleigh, proponents in the General Assembly conceded that they did not have the votes. By June 30, 1982, the deadline had passed for securing enough states for ratification.

Women who had been active in NOW and the pro-ERA movement made some gains in spite of the amendment's failure. They had learned some valuable lessons for promoting their causes in the future: women differed among themselves—there was not a single "sisterhood," women needed to have more of a public presence in bodies like the General Assembly, and changes in women's history are slow and are subject to setbacks and losses.

Relationships between men and women were the subject of another set of issues that affected private lives and became matters of public concern: marriage and divorce. Significant changes in marital and divorce laws brought about equality between marriage partners and thereby altered centuries-old common law in which the husband was regarded as head of the house and responsible for the support of his wife and dependents. In 1968 a new law said that either the husband or the wife has a legal obligation to support a dependent spouse. By 1981 divorce settlements provided for the equitable distribution of marital property between the husband and the wife. With gender no longer an issue, women acquired equitable status with men; at the same time they lost the sort of "favored" settlements in which the man was directed to pay alimony and the woman claimed most of the household property.

Other gains for women and children received legislative support. For example, in 1997 the General Assembly appropriated about $11 million to address the causes of the state's high infant mortality rates and also funded Governor James B. Hunt's program, Smart Start, in all one hundred North Carolina counties so working mothers could find affordable child care. In recent years more women have been elected to the legislature, to school boards, to city councils, to boards of county commissioners, and to the office of mayor. In 1996, 68 out of 524 mayors were women; in the Piedmont Triad women were mayors of Greensboro, High Point, and Winston-Salem. In 1992 Eva M. Clayton, a former commissioner in Warren County, became the first woman (and the first African American since Reconstruction) elected to the U.S. Congress from North Carolina and the first woman elected president of the Democratic freshman class. Joyce Conseen Dugan was voted the first female principal chief of the Eastern Band of Cherokee Indians. When a Cherokee man insisted, "Men should be head of all things," a Cherokee woman answered, "In our traditional society, women have always held the tribe together."[8]

Another group of women emerged from the margins to claim a place in the public mind: lesbians. Although Phyllis Schlafly had called attention to them during the ERA debates at a time when public discussion was relatively infrequent, research has not yet been done to document the impact of her stance on North Carolina voters. Although many people agreed with her opposition to the ERA, many did not like her attempts to discredit groups of supporters. A few lesbians, such as Mab Segrest, became effective public advocates for exposing hate campaigns based on sexual preference (and race). Segrest, the author of *My Mama's Dead Squirrel: Les-*

bian Essay on Southern Culture (1985), was frequently invited to give readings and lectures on tolerance issues in North Carolina. The general effect of lesbians organizing statewide was to make sexual preference a topic for public discussion. Educational institutions began to state in their catalogs and admission application forms that they did not discriminate on the basis of race, gender, or sexual preference. Decisions affecting workplace security and insurance benefits for same-sex partners began to make their way slowly through some offices, and the "don't ask, don't tell" posture concerning acceptance of gays and lesbians in the military was increasingly followed in civilian circles.

In North Carolina progress in recognizing lesbians has perhaps been most significant in college and university communities, where students have created gay/lesbian organizations and faculty members have taught courses in gay/lesbian studies. Another front on which some gains have been made is churches. Although many denominations have taken stands against recognizing gay/lesbian couples, some individual congregations have welcomed them into their faith communities. Quakers, as in earlier times, seem to have been the most tolerant. Increasingly, as images of gays and lesbians have become acceptable among large national audiences, partly due to the popularity of some movies and television shows, it can be expected that communities generally will broaden their understanding.

Economically, many women have continued to be marginalized. Although by the 1990s more women occupied positions at the top in government and business, a larger number of women in North Carolina still held low-paying jobs. Nothing made this reality clearer than a 1991 report from NC Equity, Inc., an advocacy group for low- and middle-income women organized in 1985. Once more, women asked for a study of pay equity, noting that the General Assembly, the largest employer in the state, had yet to conduct pay equity studies in state government. In 1980, the report pointed out, North Carolina ranked first among states in the percentage of mothers in the labor force. With the decline in real wages in the seventies and eighties and because of already-existing low earnings, a family needed the income of both husband and wife or their equivalent. Only one in eight households fit the traditional image of breadwinner husband and homemaker mother. Large numbers of women were still in part-time, low-wage jobs without benefits. In 1987 half of all working white women earned less than $10,000, just above the poverty level for a family of three. Half of all black women earned less than $8,000, barely enough to raise them above the poverty line for a family of two. Native American and Hispanic women had earnings comparable to or below those of blacks. North Carolina reflected national trends in two significant ways: in the rising number of women of all ages who never married and in the dramatic rise in the number of families with children headed by a single women.

In the last decade of the twentieth century, a shocking number of women and children still lived in poverty. The language of the 1991 study by NC Equity, Inc., was harsher than that of the 1964 study of the Status of Women. NC Equity described "the economic caste system in which most of our state's women live out their lives. And [the report] details the bitter consequences not only for women themselves, but for their children and families."[9]

Dramatic differences continue to exist among women in the workforce. At one end of the scale a small number of women were employed in executive positions in banking, government, and higher education with substantial salaries and benefits. For example, in 1990 Nan Keohane was appointed president of Duke University, and in 1997 Molly Broad became president of the University of North Carolina system, which included sixteen member campuses. Recruited from outside North Carolina, Presidents Keohane and Broad gave evidence that the top leadership in the state no longer belonged exclusively to men. In the middle of the scale, women enjoyed more job options as banking, technology, and management industries recruited more workers with the sort of adaptability to change and ambition for advancement that women often represented. On the other hand, women were more likely than men to work as "temps" in temporary employment and in part-time jobs.

Thus, North Carolina remained at the end of the century what it was at midcentury: a state divided between progressive and conservative attitudes and between wealth and poverty. But if numbers are any predictors of change, the facts are significant: women constituted 52 percent of North Carolina's population and approached 50 percent of the workforce; more women than men made up the student enrollment of the state's public universities. The possibility is becoming clearer that North Carolina women increasingly will define the look of the state in the twenty-first century.

And what is the common bond that unites women? We have learned in this history that all kinds of differences between women have always existed. The bond that we, as authors, have discovered repeatedly during our many years of research and writing is that we learn more about our own lives as we learn women's history. Studying the lives of countless women, we were impressed by their great diversity. And as we traveled throughout North Carolina, we also began to appreciate what a truly big state we live in. In the Mountains, we learned to be patient and to appreciate the landscape: it takes longer to get places, the way is often circuitous, but the views can be spectacular. We thought about how mountain women have lived: more self-sufficient, more isolated, and perhaps more suspicious of outsiders. As we drove across North Carolina to Elizabeth City, we considered the necessities that living there has imposed on families: to get from "here" to "there" one must drive around waterways. En route, small towns with scenic waterfronts and women with fishing poles walking across country bridges made us aware of coastal life in new ways. In Edenton, as we looked for the house of Penelope Barker, leader of the so-called Edenton Tea Party, and the street where Harriet Jacobs lived in her grandmother's attic while hiding from the slave master, we felt a sense of gratitude for historic preservation and for the courage of a black woman who overcame white, patriarchal authority. In Raleigh, where we went to examine state archives (often sitting in lanes of traffic); in Chapel Hill, to work in the Southern Historical Collection; and in colleges and universities in Durham, Greensboro, Winston-Salem, and Charlotte—in all of these places we appreciated the institutional resources of the Piedmont, especially those with historic commitments to women: the University of North Carolina at Greensboro, Bennett, Meredith, Salem, and Queens. Conferences, readings, and meetings devoted to women's studies drew us back again and again. And our journey continues.

And so—in that expression popular during the heyday of the current women's movement—we have "come a long way." We hope that readers have enjoyed learning more about women in North Carolina and that this knowledge enriches the way they think about history. We hope that we have learned ways to locate our own personal histories within the larger picture. The making of history is, after all, a bond that unites us.

And we hope that women's history will be used as a barometer for recognizing the conditions that affect the health and happiness of North Carolina. One truth has not changed in all these hundreds of years: in most homes, women are the primary housekeepers and caregivers in addition to being workers outside the home. The future state of the home and of the community will depend on whether we can provide women with the support necessary for the success of both.

Notes

ABBREVIATIONS

AANC
Jeffrey J. Crow, Paul D. Escott, and Flora J. Hatley, *A History of African Americans in North Carolina* (Raleigh: NCDAH, 1992).

CRNC
William L. Saunders, ed., *The Colonial Records of North Carolina*, 10 vols. (Raleigh: State of North Carolina, 1886–90). Second series, vols. 1–3, edited by Mattie Erma Edwards Parker (Raleigh: NCDAH, 1968–71); vols. 4–5, edited by William S. Price Jr. (Raleigh: NCDAH, 1974).

DAR
Daughters of the American Revolution

DNCB
William S. Powell, ed., *Dictionary of North Carolina Biography*, 6 vols. (Chapel Hill: University of North Carolina Press, 1979–96).

DU
Duke University, Durham

FHC
Friends Historical Collection, Greensboro

MESDA
Museum of Early Southern Decorative Arts Archives, Winston-Salem

MOR
Archives of the Moravian Church in America, Southern Province, Winston-Salem

NCC
North Carolina Collection, University of North Carolina at Chapel Hill

NCDAH
North Carolina Division of Archives and History, Raleigh

NCMOH
North Carolina Museum of History, Raleigh

OCA
Oberlin College Archives, Ohio

PJI
Don Higginbotham, ed., *The Papers of James Iredell*. 2 vols. (Raleigh: NCDAH, 1976).

SHC
Southern Historical Collection, University of North Carolina at Chapel Hill

SS
Secretary of State Papers, NCDAH

TN
Tennessee State Archives

UDC
United Daughters of the Confederacy

INTRODUCTION

1. Redford, *Somerset Homecoming*, 235, 171.

CHAPTER 1.
THE FIRST SETTLERS OF THIS LAND

1. Fladmark, "Times and Places," 40–41; Silver, *New Face on the Countryside*, 35. Many archaeologists now believe that Native Americans lived in North America 20,000 years ago, and sites like Williams Island near Chattanooga confirm southern Appalachian settlement at least 10,000 years old with continuous occupation. North Carolina's western mountains have been occupied by the Cherokee and their ancestors for at least 10,000 years. We are indebted to Barbara R. Duncan of the Museum of the Cherokee Indian for the preceding observations.

2. Fenn and Wood, *Natives and Newcomers*, 1–2.

3. Wetmore, *First on the Land*, 134–39; Harriot, "A briefe and true report," 68–69; Lederer, *Discoveries*, 13–14. The Tuscarora creation myth is similar to that of the Iroquois, with whom the Tuscarora aligned.

4. Scarberry, "Grandmother Spider's Lifeline," 101; Mooney, *Myths*, 242–49; Rights, *American Indian in North Carolina*, 224–25.

5. Coe, *Formative Culture*, 25, 57. Archaeologists have divided prehistoric culture in the southeastern United States into four stages—Paleo-Indian, Archaic, Woodland, and Mississippian. The first two phases are based on subsistence strategies, the latter two on cultural evidences of pottery and farming.

6. Watson and Kennedy, "Development of Horticulture," 260; Ward, "Review of Archaeology," 61.

7. Bonvillain, *Women and Men*, 4–5; Slocum, "Woman the Gatherer"; Martin and Voorhies, *Female of the Species*, 181–82, 189–90; Yarnell and Black, "Temporal Trends," 93; Watson and Kennedy, "Development of Horticulture," 267. Anthropologists believe that subsistence groups tend to be more egalitarian because they recognize the contributions of both men and women as essential to survival.

8. Burials at Woodland settlements like the Parker (Davidson County) and Donnaha (Yadkin County) sites show a high mortality among infants and children, common among hunter-gatherers and horticulturists. The Donnaha burials also have a high percentage of adult men and women. See Newkirk, "Parker Site," 145, and Hancock, "Skeletal Analysis," 248.

9. Watson and Kennedy, "Development of Horticulture," 261, 257.

10. Archaeologists discovered that an early "primitive" type of maize, about two thousand years old, had been grown in the Dismal Swamp. Other early maize, found in the Mountains, dates from around 1,800 to 2,300 years ago. Another variety, found in the Piedmont, dates from 1,000 to 1,400 years ago. (Northern Flint maize, the type of corn familiar today, did not appear until considerably later.) See Watson and Kennedy, "Development of Horticulture," 266–68. For the Coast, see Phelps, "Archaeology," 35; for the Mountains, aka Middle Woodland period, Pigeon Phase, see Purrington, "Ancient Mountaineers," 135–36; for the Piedmont, see Ward, "Review of Archaeology,"

72. See also South, *Indians in North Carolina*, 10–11; Perdue, *Native Carolinians*, 8, 10; and Wetmore, *First on the Land*, 107–8.

11. Two different ceramic traditions in which the pottery shards are four to five thousand years old have been identified from prehistoric North Carolina: fiber-tempered pottery, probably using palmetto fiber, was found in the southeastern coastal area, and sand-tempered pottery has been excavated throughout the Piedmont and the Mountains. See Phelps, "Archaeology," 26; R. J. Rogers, "E. Davis Site"; Purrington, "Ancient Mountaineers," 131; and R. P. Wright, "Women's Labor and Pottery."

12. Claggett, "First Colonists."

13. Perdue, *Native Carolinians*, 15. The Algonquians appear in the 1580s Roanoke chronicles of Arthur Barlowe and Thomas Harriot and the drawings of John White. Because the Tuscarora, Siouan-speaking, and Cherokee tribes survived longer, observations about them extend over a longer period of time in the reports of German trader and explorer John Lederer in 1669–70, English explorer John Lawson in the early 1700s, Edenton doctor John Brickell and English traveler and naturalist Mark Catesby in the 1730s, Philadelphia naturalist William Bartram in the 1760s, and Irish trader James Adair in the 1770s.

14. Wood, "Changing Population," 38.

15. Hatley, "Three Lives of Keowee," 240–41 (Bartram).

16. Perdue, "Traditional Status of Cherokee Women," 20. Many anthropologists observe that women's status in matrilineal societies is almost universally high and that women enjoy a dignity and respect often lacking in patrilineal groups. See Martin and Voorhies, *Female of the Species*, 225.

17. Lederer, *Discoveries*, 13.

18. Lawson, *New Voyage to Carolina*, 192.

19. Reid, *Law of Blood*, 37–39; Hudson, *Southeastern Indians*, 187.

20. Perdue, "Cherokee Women," 152 (Bartram); Martin and Voorhies, *Female of the Species*, 274.

21. Lawson, *New Voyage to Carolina*, 193, 40–41. Kelly-Gadol ("Did Women Have a Renaissance?") argues that sexual control is a measure of women's status within their society—generally the more patriarchal the society, the more women's sexuality is regulated.

22. Lawson, *New Voyage to Carolina*, 41; Brickell, *Natural History*, 291.

23. Adair, *History of the American Indians*, 45–46.

24. Martin and Voorhies, *Female of the Species*, 215; Harriot, "A briefe and true report," 56.

25. Hatley, "Three Lives of Keowee," 228 (Adair, Bartram).

26. Hudson, *Southeastern Indians*, 285.

27. Claassen, "Gender, Shellfishing."

28. Vogel, *American Indian Medicine*, 238–45; Lawson, *New Voyage to Carolina*, 195, 210.

29. Lawson, *New Voyage to Carolina*, 215; Henry Spelman quoted in Swanton, *Indians of the Southeastern United States*, 414, as cited in Lebsock, *Share of Honor*, 13, n. 5; Hatley, "Three Lives of Keowee," 235.

30. Perdue, *Slavery*, 52.

31. Martin and Voorhies, *Female of the Species*, 266; Reid, *Law of Blood*, 129; Lawson, *New Voyage to Carolina*, 217, 174.

32. Grumet, "Sunksquaws, Shamans"; Barlowe, "Narrative of the 1584 Voyage," 5.

33. Merrell, " 'Our Bonds of Peace,' " 202, 199, and " 'This Western World,' " *Season II*, 24.

34. Price Hughes to Duchess of Ormonde, October 13, 1715, quoted in Crane, *Southern Frontier*, 103, n. 101, as cited in Hatley, "Three Lives of Keowee," 241, n. 69. See also Hatley, 232–35.

35. Hatley, "Three Lives of Keowee," 232–35.

36. Peterson and Druke, "American Indian Women and Religion," 6; Hudson, *Southeastern Indians*, 366–75.

37. Grumet, "Sunksquaws, Shamans," 53–54; Hudson, *Southeastern Indians*, 310.

38. McCartney, "Cockacoeske: Queen of Pamunkey," 173; Lawson, *New Voyage to Carolina*, 57; Grumet, "Sunksquaws, Shamans," 46; R. J. Rogers, "Clans of Passage"; Hudson, *Juan Pardo Expeditions*.

39. Rogers, "Clans of Passage."

40. Navey, "Mortuary Practices," 85–87.

41. Perdue, "Cherokee Women," 152; R. Green, "Native American Women."

42. Barlowe, "Narrative of the 1584 Voyage," 5.

43. Merrell, "Natives in a New World," 597–605 (quotation, 598).

44. Perdue, "Cherokee Women," 151.

45. Perdue, "Southern Indians." See also Perdue, *Slavery*.

46. Perdue, "Cherokee Women," 154–55.

47. Grumet, "Sunksquaws, Shamans," 49.

48. Perdue, *Slavery*, 53–55.

49. Perdue, "Cherokee Women," 156.

50. Ibid., 153–54, 156.

51. Ibid., 157.

NANYE'HI/NANCY WARD

1. This biography is based primarily on Perdue, "Nancy Ward." See also McClary, "Nancy Ward: Last Beloved Woman."

2. See, e.g., Adams, *Nancy Ward*; Alderman, *Nancy Ward*; Felton, *Nancy Ward*; and Foreman, *Indian Women Chiefs*. A fictionalized account is King, *Wild Rose of the Cherokee*. The "longer study of her life" is Perdue's "Nancy Ward."

3. Timberlake, *Memoirs*, 64, 88. Timberlake noted that both old warriors and old war women were often called "Beloved" in recognition of their achievements in earlier years.

4. T. Roosevelt, *Winning of the West*, 303.

5. Rayna Green ("Native American Women," 266) urges historians to consider the role of Native American women as "cultural brokers, working to create, manage, and minimize the negative effects of change on their people."

6. Perdue, "Nancy Ward," 91–92.

7. Ibid., 94.

8. Ibid., 85, 94.

9. In response to the Little Carpenter's remarks, the American leader is said to have answered days later that "the white men do place confidence in their women and share their coun-

cils with them when they know their hearts are good." Corkran, *Cherokee Frontier*, 110–11. See also Perdue, "Nancy Ward," 94.

10. Williams, *Early Travels*, 489–90. Perdue ("Nancy Ward," 95) observes that a class system began to replace the clans as wealthy Anglo-Cherokee married whites or each other. Nannie Martin, the daughter of Elizabeth Ward Martin and her husband Joseph, married Michael Hildebrand, the son of a white miller and a Cherokee woman.

11. Perdue, "Nancy Ward," 97.

12. McClary, "Nancy Ward: Last Beloved Woman," 541–43.

CHAPTER 2. THE MOST INDUSTRIOUS SEX IN THAT PLACE

1. Spruill, *Women's Life and Work*, 19.

2. Kolodny, *The Land before Her*, 3 (Hakluyt), 17–54; Horne, *Brief Description* (recruitment promise), 9–10.

3. Fox, *Journal*, 136; Lawson, *New Voyage to Carolina*, 91.

4. Many works document the Roanoke voyages. See Powell, "Elizabethan Experiment" and "Roanoke Colonists"; Quinn, *Set Fair for Roanoke*; Stick, *Roanoke Island*; Kupperman, *Roanoke*; Quinn and Quinn, *The First Colonists*.

5. "White's (John) Narrative," 107–9, 94; Powell, "Roanoke Colonists."

6. Powell, "Roanoke Colonists"; "White's (John) Narrative, 102, 108.

7. Lefler and Powell, *Colonial North Carolina*, 21–25.

8. Spruill, *Women's Life and Work*, 19.

9. L. S. Butler, "Life in Albemarle County," 12, and *North Carolina Genesis*, 6; Lounsbury, "Plague of Building," 12–13. Five families held large tracts of land that comprised 17 percent of the total acreage granted in the Proprietary period. See Wolf, "Patents and Tithables," 268.

10. Lounsbury, "Plague of Building," 12; Brinn, "Blacks in Colonial North Carolina," 30 (Urmstone); Anna Sothel to Hazelelpony Wood, March 12, 1694, in L. S. Butler, *North Carolina Genesis*, 2. For similarly gloomy feelings on the part of New England female settlers, see Kolodny, *The Land before Her*, chap. 1, "Captives in Paradise," 17–34.

11. The province of Carolina extended from Florida to the Virginia border and from the Atlantic to the Pacific Oceans. All free persons were eligible for a land grant, for which they had to erect a habitable shelter and to clear, fence, and plant at least one acre. See Lefler and Powell, *Colonial North Carolina*, 29–55; Wolf, "Patents and Tithables," 264; Parramore, "Tuscarora Ascendancy"; and Haley and Winslow, *Historic Architecture*, 3.

12. See Horne, *Brief Description*.

13. Will of Mary Fortsen, recorded November 15, 1665, NCDAH. The three female indenture bonds for North Carolina were discovered in the British Record Office, Higher Court Records, County Court, December 1686, 375–76, and are in the NCDAH. Valentine Bird's inventory lists Ann Farmer, an indentured servant with four years still owed when he died in 1680, eleven black servants, and a Native American servant. See Grimes, *Wills and Inventories*, 472–74. For indentured servants, see M. Campbell, "Social Origins"; Horn, "Servant Emigration"; Carr and Menard, "Immigration and Opportunity"; and Lefler, *North Carolina History*, 41–42. For the different migration pattern in Maryland, see Carr and Walsh, "The Planter's Wife."

14. Stone, *Family, Sex, and Marriage*, 216, as cited in Shammas, "Domestic Environment," 4.

15. As cited in Evans, Hodsdon, and Barger, *America's 400th Anniversary Handbook*, 60.

16. *AANC*, 3. Records are scarce, but extant inventories indicate that Native American slavery was as common as African slavery in this early period.

17. Mattie Erma E. Parker, "Ann Marwood Durant (Durand, Duren)," *DNCB* 2:122–23.

18. Bjorkman, "Hannah (Baskel) Phelps Phelps Hill"; McCall, "Mystery Woman's Life"; Grimes, *Wills and Inventories*, 421–23; Lefler and Powell, *Colonial North Carolina*, 54, 56.

19. Mattie Erma E. Parker, "Diana Harris Foster (Forster)," *DNCB* 2:227–28; Walsh, " 'Till Death Us Do Part,' " 132.

20. In Maryland, widows remarried three times more often than widowers. See Carr and Walsh, "The Planter's Wife," 560. Not all North Carolina women were dutiful and faithful wives. "Margaret the Wife of Hanaball Haskins" and Edward Murrell of Chowan Precinct "wickedly and adulterously consented together" so that Edward had "Carnall Knowledge" of Margaret. *CRNC*, 2d ser., 2:328 (October 1, 1696), 2:220–21 (November 28, 1695). According to court records of October 1, 1695, Sarah Meakins "is a woman of evill life." *CRNC*, 2d ser., 2:180.

21. Lawson, *New Voyage to Carolina*, 91; Gallman, "Determinants of Age at Marriage." According to Rutman and Rutman (" 'Now-Wives and Sons-in-Law,' " 158), Virginia women typically married at age twenty.

22. The few North Carolina second-generation brides were not as young as those in Maryland, who married at sixteen and a half years, but the pattern is similar. See Carr and Walsh, "The Planter's Wife," 564.

23. Lawson, *New Voyage to Carolina*, 91.

24. Brinn, "Blacks in Colonial North Carolina," 68, 94.

25. Ibid., 94–97; Wolf, "Patents and Tithables," 267–68.

26. Brinn, "Blacks in Colonial North Carolina," 94–96. Handlin and Handlin ("Origins of the Southern Labor System") argue that slavery in its earliest beginnings in colonial America was not the rigid institution that it became in the 1700s, when it denoted lifelong servitude based solely on race.

27. Brinn, "Blacks in Colonial North Carolina," 99–100; C. W. Rountree, "Quaker Meeting," 65.

28. Brinn, "Blacks in Colonial North Carolina," 95–98.

29. Ibid., 38, 70, 69.

30. *CRNC*, 2d ser., lxvii-lxviii, December 1679 (quotation); L. S. Butler, *North Carolina Genesis*, 22; Correspondence with Raymond A. Winslow Jr., December 6, 1993. Anthropologists have observed that women's status is higher when they live in a society in which they are not isolated from public events. See Rosaldo and Lamphere, *Women, Culture, and Society*.

31. Mattie Erma E. Parker, "Diane Harris Foster (Forster)," *DNCB* 2:227–28. L. S. Butler (*North Carolina Genesis*, 55) cites a big bar bill at the Harrises' inn. See also Lefler and Powell, *Colonial North Carolina*, 49–54.

32. Mattie Erma E. Parker, "Ann Marwood Durant (Durand, Duren)," *DNCB* 2:122–23.

33. Angle, "Women in the . . . Courts," 38–40; *CRNC*, 2d ser., 5:359–60; Brinn, "Blacks in Colonial North Carolina," 60, n. 44 (Pollock).

34. Angle, "Women in the . . . Courts," 38–39, 58–65; *CRNC*, 2d ser., 2:20–21 (September 24, 1694—Heartley), 2:39 (September 27, 1694—Stuart), 2:43–44 (September 28, 1694—Ros), 2:208, 220, 223, 226 (November 27–28, 1695; February 25, 1695/96—Moline), 2:57 (October 7, 1689—Laker). We are grateful to Terrell Crow for alerting us to these *CRNC* references to women.

35. Bjorkman, "Hannah (Baskel) Phelps Phelps Hill," 294 (quotation); C. W. Rountree, "Quaker Meeting"; Haley and Winslow, *Historic Architecture*, 9. In 1704 the Reverend John Blair classified four religious groups in North Carolina: Quakers, who were "enemies" of the established church; people who had no religion but would be Quaker if they were not obliged to lead a more moral life than they were willing to; those who were somewhat like Presbyterians, preaching and baptizing, but without orders from any church; and people zealous about the Anglican Church, few in number but of the "better sort." For Blair's quotation and the established church in Proprietary North Carolina, see Lefler, *North Carolina History*, 45–46.

36. Fitzherbert, *Book of Husbandry*, 95, cited in Shammas, "Domestic Environment," 5–6; Tusser, *Five Hundred Points of Good Husbandrie*, 156, cited in Cowan, *More Work for Mother*, 16–17 (quotation).

37. Lounsbury, "Plague of Building," 12–14; Boyd, *William Byrd's Histories*, 54; Lawson, *New Voyage to Carolina*, 90.

38. Lawson, *New Voyage to Carolina*, 91.

39. Lounsbury, "Plague of Building," 18 (Byrd), 20 (Godfrey). For Chesapeake, see Carson et al., "Impermanent Architecture." For the Albemarle discussion, we are indebted to Raymond A. Winslow Jr. in a personal communication dated December 6, 1993, and Lounsbury. Tobacco cultivation depleted the soil rapidly, so Albemarle planters (like their Chesapeake counterparts) directed their energies at accumulating more land and more servants or slaves to work the land, not houses.

40. Grimes, *Wills and Inventories*, 472–76 (Bird inventory), 560–61 (Sothel inventory); L. S. Butler, *North Carolina Genesis*, 53–54 (Godfrey inventory). Sothel's priority seems to have been trading, in which he invested twenty times more than he did in furnishing his household—furnishings were worth 14 pounds out of a 266-pound estate—although he may have died in Virginia, which would have affected the extent of his estate holdings in North Carolina. For seventeenth-century inventories in Plymouth, Mass., see Demos, *A Little Commonwealth*, chap. 2, "Furnishings," 36–51.

41. Cowan, *More Work for Mother*, 20, 38; Strasser, *Never Done*, 12; Demos, *A Little Commonwealth*, 39–41.

42. See Bird, Godfrey, and Sothel inventories, cited in n. 40 above.

43. Will of James Tooke, February 1, 1659, Isle of Wight County Records, Isle of Wight, Will Book 1, p. 590, SHC; L. S. Butler, *North Carolina Genesis*, 55.

44. Lawson, *New Voyage to Carolina*, 90; L. S. Butler, *North Carolina Genesis*, 46.

45. Many historians believe that the yeoman households were places in which to work and sleep, perhaps to pray, but generally not to relax and play in. See Shammas, "Domestic Environment."

46. See Will of James Tooke, n. 43 above, and Bird, Godfrey, and Sothel inventories, n. 40 above. See also Shammas, "Domestic Environment," and Spruill, *Women's Life and Work*, 24.

47. Mattie Erma E. Parker, "Ann Marwood Durant (Durand, Duren)," *DNCB* 2:122–23.

48. North Carolina genealogist and legal writer Helen Leary ("Marriage, Divorce," 131) explains that common law derived from ancient English principles and practices that were manifested, confirmed, or amended by successive judicial decisions—as opposed to statutes, which must be written down before they can be enacted by a legislature. Salmon (*Women and the Law of Property*, 3–5) points out the wide diversity in colonial laws regarding property, despite their derivation from common law.

49. Leary, "Marriage, Divorce"; Salmon, *Women and the Law of Property*, 44–56.

50. Mattie Erma E. Parker, "Diane Harris Foster (Forster)," *DNCB* 2:227–28; *CRNC*, 2d ser., 2:429, as cited in Angle, "Women in the . . . Courts," 45; *CRNC*, 2d ser., 2:326, October 1, 1696 (Hannah Wood petition). We are grateful to Terrell Crow for the Wood reference.

51. Will of Mary Fortsen, SS 848, recorded November 15, 1665, NCDAH; Mattie Erma E. Parker, "Mary Fortsen (Fortson)," *DNCB* 2:225–26. See also T. Crow, " 'The Task That Is Ours,' " 9–10.

CHAPTER 3. A PATTERN OF INDUSTRY

1. Spruill, *Women's Life and Work*, 81 (Byrd). When the Proprietary period ended in 1729, North Carolina was the most sparsely populated English colony in America, with about 36,000 inhabitants, five-sixths of them white. On the eve of the American Revolution, the population was almost 300,000, and by the time of the first national census in 1790, almost 400,000—288,204 whites, 100,572 enslaved blacks, 5,041 free blacks, and about 7,800 Native Americans. In the 1770s Germans comprised about 10–30 percent of the backcountry population (8,000–15,000 people), and Scots-Irish, English, and Scots made up the rest. See Fenn and Wood, *Natives and Newcomers*, 69–75; Lefler and Powell, *Colonial North Carolina*, 89; Wood, "Changing Population," 38; and A. D. Watson, "Women in Colonial North Carolina."

2. More than 7,000 Native Americans are estimated to have lived in North Carolina's Coastal Plain and Piedmont at the beginning of the 1700s; by 1790 there were only 300. In the Mountains, the Cherokee decreased from 16,000 in 1700 to 7,500 in 1790. See Wood, "Changing Population," 38. The number of Africans increased dramatically. In 1712 there were about 800 blacks in North Carolina (Virginia had 6,000–10,000 blacks out

of a total population of 63,000 in 1700, and South Carolina—with 4,100 African American inhabitants—was 50 percent black in 1708). North Carolina had 6,000 slaves in 1730, nearly 20,000 in 1755, and more than 40,000 in 1767; by 1790 it had more than 100,000 slaves. Only nine households—eight located in New Hanover and Brunswick Counties—had more than fifty slaves. For colonial African Americans, see Kay and Cary, "Demographic Analysis," and *AANC*, 1–11.

3. Lefler and Powell, *Colonial North Carolina*, 89–97; Otto, "Migration of Southern Plain Folk."

4. Henretta ("Families and Farms") discusses the importance of lineal families in agrarian societies. Degler (*At Odds*) traces the conflict between women as individuals and as caretakers of their families in terms of female nurturing, sacrificing, subservience, and just plain hard work.

5. Grimes, *Wills and Inventories*, 16.

6. Apprentice and Indenture Bonds, Chowan County, folder 1740–49, NCDAH; K. R. Jones, "That Also These Children May Become Useful People," 41, 35. Apprenticed children were also supposed to learn basic reading, writing, and ciphering, though fewer than 10 percent of apprenticeship bonds in Rowan County between 1753 and 1795 contained an educational clause.

7. Grimes, *Wills and Inventories*, 273–76 (Jones); Butler and Watson, *North Carolina Experience*, 96 (Robertson); Lynda J. Morgan, "Status of Women," 84–85 (Swann).

8. E. W. Andrews, *Journal of a Lady*, 161; de Miranda, *New Democracy*, 5–6.

9. See H. L. Watson, *Independent People*, 17–18; Allen Family Files, Alamance Battleground State Historic Site; and Allen Family Papers, NCDAH. The Allen House was moved from its original location in Snow Camp to the Alamance historic site and restored to the late 1700s–early 1800s period of the family's residence.

10. The discussion on backcountry housewifery is drawn from Cowan, *More Work for Mother*; Strasser, *Never Done*; and Moss and Hoffman, *Backcountry Housewife*. A. H. Jones (*American Colonial Wealth*, 1404–71) lists inventories for Halifax and Orange Counties on the eve of the American Revolution. Robert Whaples, Department of Economics, Wake Forest University, did the statistical analysis of household items in the North Carolina counties. There was no statistically significant link between households with female slaves, mostly in Halifax County, and those with few or no female slaves, generally in Orange County, and textiles and spinning equipment. Comparable studies of Massachusetts show about the same number of spinning wheels, almost 50 percent, but far less linen and flax equipment (5.7 percent) than North Carolina's 75 percent. It is unknown whether the looms are large or small tape looms. See Shammas, "How Self-Sufficient Was Early America?," and J. M. Lewis, "Women Artisans," 227 (quotation).

11. Governor Tryon's Report, January 30, 1767, in *CRNC* 7:429; Jensen, "Cloth, Butter, and Boarders." In her survey of Rowan County wills prior to 1790, J. M. Lewis ("Women Artisans") found that approximately 35 percent contained specific references to spinning equipment.

12. In 1759, for example, Edenton women could buy brass kettles, card tables, dish covers, frying pans, looking glasses, pewter plates, tin canisters, women's saddles, and all kinds of cloth, including Negro cloth and osnaburg, at George Blair's store. See McCall, *Business as Usual*.

13. Shammas, "Domestic Environment"; Grimes, *Wills and Inventories*, 134, 482–84 (Corbin); *CRNC* 4:305 (Burrington, October 13, 1735); Spruill, *Women's Life and Work*, 65.

14. E. W. Andrews, *Journal of a Lady*, 204; Helen "Nelly" Blair to James Iredell, April 20, 1789, Iredell Papers, DU, as cited in Norton, " 'Alarming Crisis,' " 208.

15. *AANC*, 16 (Brickell and Schaw).

16. Brickell, *Natural History*, 254; E. W. Andrews, *Journal of a Lady*, 204.

17. Swan, *Plain and Fancy*; Spruill, *Women's Life and Work*, 67–70; Grimes, *Wills and Inventories*, 482–84 (Corbin); *North Carolina Magazine*, July 6, 1764 (poem).

18. Shammas, "Domestic Environment," 15; Roth, "Tea Drinking." For the Stanly "tea room," see Rodman, *Journal of a Tour*, 20–21. "Mrs. Skinner is still with her mother[;] they all drank tea with me last evening & desired me to mention them affect[ionate]ly to you when I wrote," Hannah Iredell informed her son James, April 13, 1805, Samuel Johnston Papers, NCDAH, as cited in Sykes, "James Iredell House," 28. The John Wright Stanly Estate Papers (NCDAH) lists the family's many possessions, including 7 teapots (2 of silver), plus a tea urn, sugar dish, slop bowl, milk pot, 2 sugar tongs, and 18 teaspoons, all of silver; a silver-plated tea urn, sugar dish, and cream pail; a tin sugar box, large and small tea boards, and 4 tin tea canisters, all "japanned" with a hard lacquered finish; 1 small painted paper tea chest; 1 set of "black pencill'd" china for the tea table consisting of 12 cups for tea, 6 cups for coffee, 10 saucers, 1 cream pot, 1 tea canister, 1 sugar dish, 1 slop bowl, 1 plate for bread and butter; many other cups and saucers; and a mahogany tea board, tea table, and many chairs.

19. Brickell, *Natural History*, 272; Spindel, *Crime and Society*, 133–34; *AANC*, 2–11.

20. Brickell, *Natural History*, 275; D. G. White, *Ar'n't I a Woman?*, 88–89.

21. *AANC*, 17–18; Brickell, *Natural History*, 272.

22. *AANC*, 16; Brickell, *Natural History*, 275. Faust ("Slavery") suggests that the sexual imbalance may reflect the economic reality that women were regarded as the more productive workers in Africa, whereas men were more valued in the plantation economy of the New World.

23. Brickell, *Natural History*, 274; *AANC*, 16–17. Brickell's astonishment at slave women's autonomy—if they returned the "Present," at any time, the marriage contract was no longer binding—sounds similar to that of other European Americans describing the independence of Native American women in sexual matters, marriage, and divorce. Not all North Carolina blacks were enslaved, and there are examples of free black married women. George Anderson and his wife, son, and daughter appear on the Granville County tax lists of 1755, and John Driggott and his wife on Beaufort County lists in 1764, indicating that the mistresses Anderson and Driggott must have been free black married women for two reasons: white females would not

have been listed as taxable, and slave marriages were not recognized by law. See A. D. Watson, "Household Size," 560.

24. Marriage contract between Jean Innes and Francis Corbin, October 28, 1761, New Hanover County Deeds, 1752–1872, in Alexander Young File, NCDAH; John Wright Stanly Estate Papers, NCDAH; *AANC*, 17.

25. *AANC*, 18 (Tryon), 14 (Watson).

26. *Spectator*, no. 254, as cited in Spruill, *Women's Life and Work*, 164; for ladies' libraries, 208–31. Although published in England in the early 1700s, the *Spectator* was popular among literate readers throughout the eighteenth century. Helen "Nelly" Blair Tredwell received many books and all volumes of the *Spectator* under the will of her mother, Jean Johnston Blair. See James Iredell Papers, August 20, 1784, DU.

27. *North Carolina Gazette*, July 14, 1775 ("her Wit must never be display'd"); *North Carolina Magazine*, August 7, 1764 ("The CHOICE of a HUSBAND); *Wilmington Centinel and General Advertiser*, June 18, 1788 ("Hints for Young MARRIED WOMEN"). See also Spruill, *Women's Life and Work*, 164–65.

28. de Miranda, *New Democracy*, 6; Kerber, *Women of the Republic*, chap. 8, "The Republican Mother," 165–88.

29. DePauw and Hunt, *Remember the Ladies*, 12; Alexander McAllister Papers, 1779, DU, as cited in Norton, *Liberty's Daughters*, 59; Mary Jones to Edward Jones, 1793, Wilmington, Eccles Family Papers, SHC, as cited in Lynda J. Morgan, "Status of Women," 39.

30. Ekirch, *"Poor Carolina,"* 37; William S. Price Jr., "Edward Moseley," *DNCB* 4:332–33 (first quotation, p. 332); James M. Clifton, "Alexander Lillington," *DNCB* 4:65–66; Genealogy of the Swann Family from the year A.D. 1580, Elizabeth Moore Collection, NCDAH; J. Battle, letter (January 24, 1801), in Battle et al., *The Battle Book*, 75.

31. James Iredell to Francis Iredell Sr., July 20, 1772, *PJI* 1:104–11; James Iredell to Hannah Johnston, April 1773, *PJI* 1:148–49.

32. Norton, *Liberty's Daughters*, 51; D. S. Smith, "Parental Power."

33. James Iredell to Hannah Johnston, ca. April 1, 1772 (1:94–95), February 15, 1773 (1:131–32), and July 7, 1773 (1:158), *PJI*.

34. Wellman, *County of Warren*, 60, 65.

35. ——— to Sally Pomfret, June 7, 1782; John Wallace to Pomfret, May 28, 1783, and Thomas Grafton to Pomfret, March 2, 1784, Samuel Smith Downey Papers, DU; as cited in Norton, *Liberty's Daughters*, 53.

36. Norton (*Liberty's Daughters*, 71–72) thinks that five to seven children was the norm and that fewer women died in childbirth than formerly thought. A. D. Watson ("Household Size," 555) estimates that most households consisted of three to nine people and that more than 90 percent had fewer than fifteen members. See Perquimans County Births, Deaths, Marriages, Brands and Flesh Marks, 1770–1820, NCDAH; Lemmon, *Pettigrew Papers* 1:xv.

37. Mordecai Family Papers, SHC; as cited in Norton, *Liberty's Daughters*, 83.

38. *AANC*, 8 (Quincy). Janet Schaw (E. W. Andrews, *Journal of a Lady*, 178) characterized industrious housewife Mary Harnett's husband, Cornelius, as a "brute" probably because she disagreed with his politics but possibly because she disapproved of his fathering an illegitimate child. Other public figures, such as Francis Nash and Matthew Rowan, also had illegitimate children. John Wright Stanly had a mulatto son named John Carruthers Stanly. Women, not men, were penalized for adultery or having a child out of wedlock. Margaret Doyles wrote a will in 1783 to protect her daughter Elizabeth, fathered by Harnett. Doyles requested Harnett's executors "to do justice and be friendly to my unfortunate daughter as much for her father's sake as for her own sake." Andrews, *Journal*, 154; Lynda J. Morgan, "Status of Women," 50–51 (Doyle will); Schweninger, "James Carruthers Stanly."

39. Snow Separation Agreement, Book A Real Estate Conveyances, Brunswick County, 67–70, NCDAH. The contract between Joseph and Mary M'Gehe of New Bern was published in the [New Bern] *North Carolina Gazette*, April 7, 1775, and illustrated in H. G. Jones, *North Carolina Illustrated*, 121. Mary admitted eloping with a man not her husband, by whom she was then pregnant, and announced her intention never to live with Joseph or to claim any support from him in consideration of personal "effects" worth 120 pounds. Joseph agreed to allow Mary full and free use of the effects she requested and not to claim her as his wife. See Spruill, *Women's Life and Work*, 183.

40. J. M. Lewis, "Women Artisans," 224; Will of John Allen, November 17, 1825, Orange County, NCDAH. Orphaned children were sometimes taken from their mothers, who, as widows, had little means to support them. See Frazier, "Nobody's Children." For the legal status of widows, see Leary, "Marriage, Divorce."

41. A. D. Watson, "Household Size," 561; *PJI*, 1:100. A survey of the *Wilmington Town Book* of the fifty-eight taxable houses in 1755 shows that eight buildings or 14 percent—ranging in value from Rose Long's, worth 5 pounds, to Ann Wright's, valued at 225 pounds—were owned by women. See Lynda J. Morgan, "Status of Women," 57–58, for reference to Lennon and Kellam, *Wilmington Town Book*, 77.

42. Grimes, *Wills and Inventories*, 428; Will of John Wright Stanly, January 22, 1788, probated June 1789, Craven County Clerk's Book A, NCDAH; Will of Patrick Campbell, 1775, Cumberland County Collection, NCDAH, cited in Meyer, *Highland Scots*, 123; J. M. Lewis, "Women Artisans," 224.

43. Leary, "Marriage, Divorce"; Kerber, *Women of the Republic*, 146–47; *Laws of North Carolina, 1784*, chap. 22, "An Act to regulate the descent of Real Estates, to do away Entails, to make provision for Widows, and prevent frauds in the Execution of last Wills and Testaments," in Clark, *State Records*, 24:572–77.

44. Dower petitions cited in Lynda J. Morgan, "Status of Women," 40–43; Jones quoted in W. C. Allen, *History of Halifax County*, 156, as cited in Spruill, *Women's Life and Work*, 167–68.

45. Lynda J. Morgan, "Status of Women," 104 (Wilmington domestic workers). For "deputy husband" as part of a good wife's duties, see Ulrich, *Good Wives*, 9. B. J. Harris (*Beyond Her Sphere*, 19) observes that a woman who had a "live, healthy, competent" husband did not work outside the home.

46. A. D. Watson, "Ordinaries in Colonial Eastern Carolina";

McCain, "Women Tavernkeepers." Lynda J. Morgan ("Status of Women," 42–43) states that there were thirty-five instances of women inheriting taverns before the Revolution and three afterward. Other examples include Elizabeth Horniblow, who ran Edenton's King's Arm Tavern—later Horniblow's—for about twenty years after her husband's death. According to the *Edenton Gazette* of July 7, 1808, she supplied an "excellent dinner" as part of the 1808 Fourth of July festivities at the Chowan County Courthouse, just next door to her tavern. Sarah Moore Delano Decrow had helped her second husband Robert operate his Hertford ordinary, and after his death in 1784 she applied for a license in her own name. Decrow became the first woman postmaster in the United States after the adoption of the Constitution. See Esther Evans, "Sarah Moore Delano Decrow," *DNCB* 2:48–49.

47. A. D. Watson ("Ordinaries in Colonial Eastern Carolina," 69, 71–72) cites instances of women keeping ordinaries for long periods of time. Dorothy Sherwin, Elizabeth Wallace, and Mary Wallace operated their establishments in Edenton for twelve years each, and Mrs. Fielder Powell of Craven County was in business for twenty years.

48. *CRNC* 4:1190, 7:57 (ferry quotations), as cited in Spruill, *Women's Life and Work*, 302–3; Payment invoice to Mary Taylor, Salaries and Contingent Expenses, Treasurers' and Comptrollers' Papers, NCDAH; *CRNC* 2:184. See also A. D. Watson, "Women in Colonial North Carolina," 20, and "The Ferry in Colonial North Carolina."

49. Miller, "My Daily Bread Depends upon My Labor"; John Steele Papers, SHC (King and Crosby receipts); MESDA (Moravian references); J. M. Lewis, "Women Artisans," 214–36 (Rowan County references).

50. See Rachel Allen Home Remedy book, Allen Family Papers, NCDAH.

51. Tamers receipt, John Gray Blount Papers, NCDAH. For Anna Brendel Bonn, see Fries et al., *Records of the Moravians*, 2:675, 680, 731, 825; 3:1221; 4:1539, 1735, 1703, 1802, 1830, 1814; 5:2038, 2161, 2331. For MacKinley's and Austin's advertisements, see *Hall's Wilmington Gazette*, March 8, 1798, and the *Wilmington Gazette*, October, 30, 1800, both cited in Lynda J. Morgan, "Status of Women," 105–6. North Carolina doctor John Eustace's 1769 inventory included *Burton's Midwifery* and *Councill's Midwifry* among its many books; see Grimes, *Wills and Inventories*, 490–94.

52. Norton, *Liberty's Daughters*, 155–64, 171 (Anne Hooper); *PJI* 2:258 (William Hooper).

53. Poem in *Massachusetts Gazette*, November 9, 1767, and quotations as cited in Norton, *Liberty's Daughters*, 164.

54. Norton, *Liberty's Daughters*, 155–64; Spruill, *Women's Life and Work*, 244–45; E. W. Andrews, *Journal of a Lady*, 155. Mecklenburg quotation is from *South Carolina and American General Gazette* (Charleston), February 2, 1776, as cited in Spruill, *Women's Life and Work*, 245.

55. Michael C. Martin Jr., "Penelope Barker," *DNCB* 1:95–96; Cumming, "Edenton Ladies' Tea Party"; Davis, "Another Echo of the Tea Party"; Arthur Iredell to James Iredell, January 31, 1775, *PJI* 1:282.

56. Henderson, "Elizabeth Maxwell Steel"; William S. West, "Elizabeth Maxwell Steel," *DNCB* 5:432.

57. Joseph R. Suggs, "Martha McFarlane McGee Bell," *DNCB* 1:132; Paula S. Jordan, "Hannah Millikan Blair," *DNCB* 1:171; Jordan, *Women of Guilford County*, 9–19; "DAR to Honor Woman's Fight against the British," *Winston-Salem Journal*, October 26, 1991.

58. *James Sprunt Historical Monograph*, 27 (DeRosset letter); Norton, *Liberty's Daughters*, 214 (Tory quotation). See also Troxler (*The Loyalist Experience*, esp. 32–35, 40), who cites the trials of Mary Dowd in attempting to collect the debts owed her Tory husband after the war.

59. Meyer, *Highland Scots*, 15, 126; Maud Thomas Smith, "Flora MacDonald," *DNCB* 4:138–39; Belton, "Legendary Women," 13–14.

60. William Dickson to Robert Dickson, November 30, 1784, William Dickson Papers, NCDAH ("rings" quotation); Jean Johnston Blair to James Iredell, March 27, 1778, *PJI* 2:12; Blair to Hannah Iredell, May 10, 18, 24, 1781, *PJI* 2:239, 244–46; Terrell Crow, " 'The Task That Is Ours,' " October 1987.

61. *AANC*, 37–40; Blair to Hannah Iredell, May 19, 1781, *PJI* 2:246.

62. Spruill, *Women's Life and Work*, 245; Norton, *Liberty's Daughters*, 155–56; Kerber, *Women of the Republic*, 283–84; J. H. Wilson, "The Illusion of Change."

63. Clinton, "Equally Their Due," 40. Rebecca and Duncan Cameron's family read the works of Hannah More; see Rankin, *Ambivalent Churchmen*, 72.

64. Straub, "Benjamin Rush's Views"; Kerber, "Daughters of Columbia" and *Women of the Republic*; Clinton, "Equally Their Due," 40–43; Norton, *Liberty's Daughters*; Cox, "Good Wives."

65. Potts, *Asbury's Letters*, 3:103, as cited in A. E. Mathews, " 'A Plain Lively Methodist,' " 70.

66. Spruill, *Women's Life and Work*, 241.

67. Angle, "Women in the . . . Courts," 19–24, 73, 76; Spindel, *Crime and Society*, 89.

68. Spruill, *Women's Life and Work*, 243–44; Clark, *State Records*, 26:389–90, as cited in Lynda J. Morgan, "Status of Women," 115. E. Watson (*Men and Times*, 250–51) described Delia Martin Hawkins of Warrenton as a "sensible, spirited old lady" and a "great politician."

69. See Bacon, *Mothers of Feminism*, 44.

70. Stearns quotation is from Semple, *Baptists in Virginia*, 374, as cited in [Author unknown], "Women in Late-Eighteenth-Century North Carolina," 15.

71. Burkitt et al., *Kehukee Baptist Association*; North Creek Primitive Baptist Church, Minutes of Conference, 1790–1890, DU, as cited in "Women in Late-Eighteenth-Century North Carolina," 15–17. See also D. G. Mathews, *Religion*, 105.

72. Clark, *State Records*, 24:572–77 (1784 Act); Kerber, *Women of the Republic*, 146–47.

73. Norton, " 'Alarming Crisis,' " 205; Helen Blair to William Blair, August 20, 1784, as cited in "Women in Late-Eighteenth-Century North Carolina," 10; Norton, *Liberty's*

Daughters, 194 (Ann Steele). John Steele added the "e" to the family name.

REBECCA BRYAN BOONE

1. Faragher's *Daniel Boone* is the main source for this biography. The quotation is from p. 91.

2. Ibid., 89–92. For the meaning of Kanta-ke, see pp. 68–69.

3. Ibid., 92–97.

4. Ibid., 40–43.

5. Ibid., 47.

6. Ibid., 43, 49–50. In " 'White People That Live Like Savages,' " Faragher focuses on the similarities between Indians and backwoods American settlers in the gender division of labor.

7. Faragher, *Daniel Boone*, 67.

8. Ibid., 48.

9. Ibid., 58–59. In 1939 John Edwin Bakeless, in what was then called "the definitive biography," *Daniel Boone: Master of the Wilderness*, dismissed the story that Rebecca had a baby by Daniel's brother Ned.

10. Faragher, *Daniel Boone*, 138.

11. Ibid., 261.

12. Ibid., 307.

ANN MATTHEWS FLOYD JESSOP

1. New Garden Meeting got its name when members of the New Garden Meeting in Chester County, Pa., moved to North Carolina and used the name for their new meeting. Prior to that, it had been the name of a meeting in Ireland. Subsequently, there was a New Garden Meeting in Indiana.

2. For the role of Quaker women as changemakers in America, see Bacon, *Mothers of Feminism*.

3. Ann Matthews Floyd Jessop was the great-great-great-great-grandmother of Emily Herring Wilson. Although the name is spelled "Jessup" in some records, the family spelling is "Jessop." Wilson is indebted to her mother's sister, Margery Allen Stoltz, who has spent many years compiling the family history and who saved personal papers used in this study.

4. One signature on the marriage certificate is that of Mary Payne, the mother of Dolley Payne Madison, the wife of President James Madison. Friends Historical Collection, Guilford College.

5. According to Jessop family letters, the covered wagon that brought Ann Jessop and her children to York was for many years kept in the barn at Jonathan Jessop's house in York. Jessop Family Papers, Private Collection.

6. Sue Chalfant, granddaughter of Jonathan Jessop, to her cousin Alfred Jessop, February 18, 1881, ibid.

7. *The American Friend*, March 28, 1895, 307.

8. Ibid.

9. Coffin, *Guilford Collegian* 3 (1890–91): 174–76.

10. Beach, *The Apples of New York*, 1:386.

MORAVIAN WOMEN

1. Primary materials related to Moravian women are available in a number of references, especially Fries et al., *Records of the Moravians in North Carolina*. Church diaries, usually kept by the minister, and individual memoirs, written by church members, are housed in the Archives of the Moravian Church in America, Southern Province, Winston-Salem. Publications of the Moravian Archives and Old Salem, Inc. are always useful. An important source for this biography is Griffin, *Less Time for Meddling*.

2. For Salem gardening, see D. Spencer, *Gardens of Salem*.

3. Capps, "References to Women at Work." Among a sampling of references to approximately one hundred occupations, twenty-six related to some kind of housekeeping, twenty-one to teaching, twelve to nursing, and six to laundry work.

4. Thorp, *Moravian Community*, 48.

5. Griffin, *Less Time for Meddling*, 144.

6. Moravians had turned down John Ridge's petition to have Sally admitted to Salem "on the grounds that it spoiled Indians to educate them away from home." However, when Susanna Ridge applied for her daughter, they accepted her, perhaps because they felt that they could not deny a member of the faith. Griffin, *Less Time for Meddling*, 166–69.

7. Fries, *The Road to Salem*; Memoir of Anna Catharina Ernst, Archives of the Moravian Church in America, Southern Province, Winston-Salem.

8. Sensbach, *A Separate Canaan*, 136–37, 173.

9. This discussion is based on Sensbach, *A Separate Canaan*.

10. Capps, "Demographic Studies of Moravian Women."

11. In 1991 Julianne Still Thrift became the first woman president of Salem Academy and College.

THE BONDSWOMEN OF SOMERSET PLACE

1. The sources for Somerset include Lemmon, *Pettigrew Papers*; extracts from manuscript collections associated with the Pettigrew and Bryan families, compiled by Sykes; Durrill, "Origins of a Kinship Structure" and *War of Another Kind*; and Tarlton, *Somerset Place and Its Restoration*. Dorothy Spruill Redford is credited with bringing Somerset Place to its largest audience of visitors and students of history. In her book, *Somerset Homecoming*, Redford describes how the search for her own roots in the slave community at Somerset led her to organize the first homecoming on August 30, 1986. That day more than three thousand descendants of the slaves who worked and lived there returned, a tradition that has continued. Somerset Place, located near Creswell in Washington County, is now a North Carolina Historic Site, and Redford became site manager. The plantation manor house, a number of outbuildings, and lawns and gardens have been restored. Archaeological research and design are under way for the reconstruction of two slave houses, a hospital, a chapel, and a kitchen for field hands.

2. These names, other details, and an understanding of life at Somerset have been provided by Dorothy Spruill Redford.

3. Collins was first in partnership with John Allen and Dr. Samuel Dickinson of Edenton in the Lake Company, but when that failed Collins ultimately assumed sole ownership of the land and slaves.

4. Durrill's study of kinship among blacks at Somerset includes information about their health. Doctors' reports indicate that many bondswomen suffered serious injuries from

their heavy labors and that pregnant women were especially endangered.

5. Durrill ("Origins of a Kinship Structure") states that "the slave community achieved an astonishing level of affiliation by marriage or descent before 1839." He found that most of the 284 blacks had connections to someone else on the plantation.

6. The John Koonering and other activities observed by the Collins family doctor are reported in "Dr. Edward Warren's Account of Life at Somerset Place," included in Tarlton, *Somerset Place and Its Restoration*.

7. In 1982 Peter Wood ("Digging Up Slave History"), professor of history at Duke University, led an excavation team to uncover archaeological evidence of the slave quarters at Somerset.

8. For the Somerset slaves removed to Alabama, see C. L. Montgomery, "Charity Signs for Herself."

9. The term "refugees" is Durrill's.

10. The illness and death of Charlotte Cabarrus and Somerset as "a perfect graveyard" are described in Sykes, "1805–1860: Extracts concerning Somerset Place," 78–79.

CHAPTER 4. A HARDIER MOLD

1. Lefler and Newsome (*North Carolina*, 419) state that early-nineteenth-century North Carolina society was characterized by provincialism, conservativism, sectionalism, excessive individualism, impatience with the orderly process of legal and social control, superstition, and social stratification. Chapter 20 (p. 314), entitled "The 'Rip Van Winkle' State,'" refers to North Carolina's reputation for being backward, undeveloped, and indifferent to its conditions. Powell, *North Carolina through Four Centuries*, characterizes North Carolina in the first half of the nineteenth century as "A State Asleep," 245–52.

2. *State v. Mann* (1829), as cited in Bynum, *Unruly Women*, 7; (Ruffin); *Joyner v. Joyner* (1862) (Pearson), and *North Carolina Standard*, October 22, 1845, as cited in Guion G. Johnson, *Ante-Bellum North Carolina*, 241–43. The *Standard* further editorialized, "We have only to add the hope that the article . . . may not cause a 'rebellion' among the married ladies." For women's status, see McMillen, *Southern Women*, 9, and *Motherhood*, 35. From 1800 to 1860, the state's slave population increased more than 2½ times—from 140,000 to 361,522. Almost 95 percent of black North Carolinians were slaves, and the 5 percent who were free found their rights and movements increasingly restricted by law because of whites' fears that free blacks would ignite rebellion among slaves. See *AANC*, 51.

3. McMillen, *Southern Women*, 1.

4. Edenton slave Harriet Jacobs (1813–97), who had been sexually assaulted by her owner when she was fifteen years old, escaped to the North in 1842, and later wrote an account of her life, *Incidents in the Life of a Slave Girl* (1861), contended that "slavery is terrible for men, but far more terrible for women."

5. D. G. White, *Ar'n't I a Woman?*; Scott, *Southern Lady*. For North Carolina law, see Bassett, *Anti-Slavery Leaders*, 28. So prevalent was the sexual abuse of slave women that it was one of three basic indictments against the institution of slavery brought by the Manumission Society of Guilford County, which urged that statutes be established "for the protection of the female slaves in their rights to chastity." Parish, "Slavery in Guilford County," Guilford College Quaker Room, Greensboro, as cited in Jordan, *Women of Guilford County*, 46.

6. McMillen, *Southern Women*, 101; Rawick, *American Slave*, 14:190.

7. Ibid., 15:96.

8. Ibid., 15:97–98. For the sexual exploitation of slave women, see D. G. White, *Ar'n't I a Woman?*, 31–40; McMillen, *Southern Women*, 17, 26; Gutman, *The Black Family*, 182–83; and Blassingame, *The Slave Community*, 82. Orange County slave Harriet Smith, who had been purchased when she was fifteen years old by Dr. James Strudwick Smith for his daughter, Mary, endured years of rape and impregnation by his sons. Even after Harriet married a respected free black man, Reuben Day Jr., her marriage had no legal status because she was a slave and she still was abused by her owner's sons. Her story is known partly because she was the grandmother of civil rights and religious activist Pauli Murray. See Bynum, *Unruly Women*, 17, 38.

9. Rawick, *American Slave*, 14:218.

10. Ibid., 14:139.

11. Ibid., 15:193.

12. Ibid., 14:218.

13. Ibid., 14:248, 252; Escott, *Slavery Remembered*, 22, 24.

14. D. G. White, *Ar'n't I a Woman?*, 105.

15. Rawick, *American Slave*, 14:288.

16. Ibid., 15:131. Two of North Carolina's largest plantations kept records from which family histories can be constructed. On the Bennehan-Cameron plantations in Orange County slave women born between 1780 and 1801 usually had their first child around age seventeen, and every woman, except for one, was a mother before her nineteenth birthday. More than 80 percent of their children had at least four siblings, and more than half had at least eight. At Somerset plantation in Washington County, slave women typically had their first child at age nineteen. See D. G. White, *Ar'n't I a Woman?*, 98, 100; Gutman, *The Black Family*, 171–80; and Durrill, "Origins of a Kinship Structure," 52. According to Phifer, "Slavery in Microcosm: Burke County," 146, slave breeding made slavery an attractive long-term investment.

17. *AANC*, 59.

18. Rawick, *American Slave*, 15:218–19.

19. Ibid., 15:98. Scholars have long noted that much of the strength of the slave family lay in the kinship network that involved mutual obligations and responsibilities, especially in regard to child care but also to illness and other family troubles. Although about 70 percent lived in a household of father, mother, and children, there were also aunts, uncles, and grandparents to whom the children could turn. Should a slave need a place to hide, food to eat, or simply emotional support, there was a large group of people on whom to call. See Collins, "The Meaning of Motherhood," and Reed, *Research on the African American Family*.

20. *AANC*, 60; Will of Isaac Wright, Bladen County Wills, as cited in Censer, *North Carolina Planters*, 140–41; Thomas

Turner to Ebenezer Pettigrew, November 20, 1841, in Lemmon, *Pettigrew Papers*, 2:490–91.

21. Rawick, *American Slave*, 14:79.

22. Ibid., 15:119. One in five families recorded in the slave narratives, which includes former slaves from all the southern states, lost a family member who was sold or moved to another plantation. See Escott, *Slavery Remembered*, 44, 46.

23. Rawick, *American Slave*, 14:71.

24. See D. G. White, *Ar'n't I a Woman?*, 153; Blassingame, *The Slave Community*, 88.

25. Gutman, *The Black Family*, 262; Blassingame, *The Slave Community*, 78–79; Escott, *Slavery Remembered*, 49.

26. Rawick, *American Slave*, 14:185.

27. Ibid., 14:286–88. See also Joyner, "World of the Plantation Slaves," 60; D. G. White, *Ar'n't I a Woman?*, 142, 158; Genovese, *Roll, Jordan, Roll*, 50; and Gutman, *The Black Family*, 273. Like the owners of Exter Durham, sometimes the slaveholder made the slave wedding festive, especially at Christmas and particularly if the slaves were house servants. Anson County former slave Julius Nelson recalled, "We also had regular weddin's wid a preacher an' all de fixin's an' de marster usually give us a big supper case he knowed dat he wuz gwine ter soon habe more slaves from de union." Rawick, *American Slave*, 15:146. Sarah Louise Augustus, who lived on a plantation near Fayetteville, wed a man who was a "fireman on the Cape Fear River boats," whom she characterized as "a white man's Negro." Wearing her "missus' graduating dress," she married in "the white folk's church" in a "wedding attended mostly by white folks" (Rawick, 14:56). Alice Baugh, a former Wake County slave, told of her parents being married by a Methodist preacher. Her mother wore "Miss Mary's weddin' dress, all of white lace," and her father wore "Mr. Charlie's weddin' suit wid a flower in the button hole." The newly married couple were given a "big dance" after supper, and "Marster Charlie dance de first set" with the new bride (Rawick, 14:84).

28. There was a numerical balance between slave men and women on Somerset plantation in 1839, yet more than 30 percent of the black women were married to men who lived somewhere else, generally the nearby Pettigrew plantation, Bonarva. See Durrill, "Origins of a Kinship Structure," 22–23; Escott, *Slavery Remembered*, 61. John Blassingame (*The Slave Community*, 86) argues that male slaves preferred to marry someone from another plantation so they would not have to watch their wives being beaten, raped, or otherwise mistreated, a conclusion that underscores the greater mobility and marital choices men had. Sometimes the distance between the farms was great; Mary Barbour's father lived in the hills of Avery County and her mother in McDowell County. Rawick, *American Slave*, 14:79. Betty Cofer and her mother resided on Dr. Beverly Jones's plantation in Forsyth County, whereas her father lived "yonder." Cofer's mother and father "could visit back and forth sometimes but they never lived together 'till after freedom." As the "young'uns" went with their mothers, Betty belonged to the Jones family. Rawick, *American Slave*, 14:167.

Slavery limited the marital choices of free black women. They had few potential partners among the small population of free black men in any community, and, as a consequence, some of them married slaves or broke with custom and married their cousins, uncles, and other relatives. See Bynum, *Unruly Women*, 95, 17.

29. Rawick, *American Slave*, 14:190–91.

30. Quotation from Starobin, *Blacks in Bondage*, 91–92, as cited in Degler, *At Odds*, 121–22; Bynum, *Unruly Women*, 95 (Sarah Boon to James Boon, 1850). Orange County slave Harriet Smith had to remain on her plantation while her free husband, Reuben Day, was often chased away by the jealous sons of her owner. See n. 8 above and Bynum, *Unruly Women*, 95.

31. Franklin, *Free Negro*, 45; Bynum, *Unruly Women*, 78.

32. North Carolina statistics on runaway slaves are from Genovese, *Roll, Jordan, Roll*, 798. The attention to black men was partly in reaction to the Moynihan Senate Committee Report's conclusion in the 1970s that black women as single heads of households contributed to the pathology of their race, had too much power in the modern family, and emasculated black men. See Blassingame, *The Slave Community*; Genovese, *Roll, Jordan, Roll*; and Gutman, *The Black Family*.

33. McMillen, *Southern Women*, 12; Bynum, *Unruly Women*, 10; Censer, *North Carolina Planters*, 52 (quotation). Sisters often found such separations difficult. When Phebe Caroline Jones married, her sister Sarah Lenoir Jones gave her a beaded band inscribed, "Absent but not Forgotten" (NCMOH).

34. Hickerson, *Happy Valley*, 117

35. Correspondence from Rebecca Haywood Hall to her sister Elizabeth Haywood, 1836–41, Ernest Haywood Collection, SHC. See also McMillen, *Motherhood*, 140–41.

36. Bynum, *Unruly Women*, 61, 44–46 (letter). In Granville County, however, between 11 and 17 percent of the households were headed by unmarried women.

37. Censer (*North Carolina Planters*, 70, 86) found that one in ten planter marriages were between first and second cousins.

38. Stowe, *Intimacy and Power*, 109–14 (Skinner quotations, 110); Ebenezer Pettigrew to Ann Blount Shepard, April 14, 1815, and Shepard to Pettigrew, April 17, 1815, in Lemmon, *Pettigrew Papers*, 1:480, 483. Ann also noted that the almanac forecast for "cloudy disagreeable weather" on May 10 might bring "very bad luck."

39. Sarah Polk to Mary Polk, March 17, 1842, in Polk and Yeatman Family Papers, SHC, as cited in Censer, *North Carolina Planters*, 77. Eighteenth-century ideals of the compliant and obedient wife were updated in the nineteenth century in "the cult of true womanhood," in which the exemplary woman embodied the virtues of piety, purity, submissiveness, and domesticity, as defined in Welter, "The Cult of True Womanhood." Southern white women rarely challenged those views publicly, and they ridiculed northern women who tried to move beyond women's prescribed place. See Censer, *North Carolina Planters*, 78; Stowe, *Intimacy and Power*, 57; and McMillen, *Southern Women*, 9–10, 19.

40. Stowe, *Intimacy and Power*, 50–51; James Norcum to Elizabeth Norcum, 19 August 1846, James Norcum Papers, NCDAH; Censer, *North Carolina Planters*, 90–91, 94. Even though most parents wanted their oldest daughter to marry

first, approximately 30 percent of daughters from planter families bucked that tradition.

41. Skinner's courtship is drawn from Stowe, *Intimacy and Power*, 109–14.

42. This biography is based on Paula S. Jordan, "Frances Webb Bumpass," *DNCB* 1:268, and *Women of Guilford County*, 36–39 (quotation).

43. Bessie Lacy's courtship is drawn from Stowe, *Intimacy and Power*, chap. 5, "The Lacys: The Thing, Not Its Vision," 192–223 (quotations, 213). Bessie's close friend, Maggie Morgan, viewed her own impending marriage as a "great event," and although Maggie feared losing her "identity," she maintained that she probably would not be unhappy because "I am not looking for bliss." Ibid., 215.

44. McMillen, *Southern Women*, 20; Ebenezer Pettigrew to Ann Pettigrew, October 10, 1815, and Ann Pettigrew to Ebenezer Pettigrew, November 5, 1815, in Lemmon, *Pettigrew Papers*, 1:490, 493.

45. MS in John H. Bryan Papers, May 6, 1820, as cited in Guion G. Johnson, *Ante-Bellum North Carolina*, 243; Julia P. Miner to Mary W. Shepard, 1 November 1621, John H. Bryan Papers, NCDAH, as cited in Rankin, *Ambivalent Churchmen*, 105–6.

46. The changing nature of marriage among the southern gentry is debated among scholars. Stowe (*Intimacy and Power*, 124) cites some of the various positions. Censer found reciprocity, respect, and compatibility in most of the planter couples she studied; Wyatt-Brown and other historians saw the many conflicts caused by the trend toward a companionate marriage and the tradition of male dominance. Rankin believes that Episcopal husbands reinforced their control within their families by restoring the Episcopal Church in North Carolina as an institution that upheld hierarchy, patriarchy, and slavery and, in the process, co-opted their wives' evangelical leanings. Scott and Clinton emphasize the gulf between the romantic expectations and the reality of marriage for many women. Most historians seem to agree, however, that whatever the opportunity for intimacy and affection, these southern gentry marriages were characterized by what Wyatt-Brown calls "conflicting emotional maps" between husbands and wives. Stowe warns that to characterize most planter marriages as "affectionate" and "companionate," and therefore, "modern," is only partially true.

Even so, the trend toward companionate marriages in North Carolina and the South generally is an important topic for women's history. The assumption is, as Degler asserts, if a husband and wife are in a mutually satisfying relationship, then the woman's rights, status, and power in the family will increase. But Lebsock and McMillen argue that even companionate marriages were fundamentally asymmetrical relationships because husbands had economic, legal, and social control over their wives. In the more industrialized Northeast, where middle-class men and women were increasingly occupying two separate spheres—work and home—the lowered birthrate is taken as evidence of women's growing power within the home and family. That indicator of women's status is less applicable for the agrarian culture of the South, where women and men worked and lived together in rural households, their traditional roles different but overlapping—and, significantly, where fertility rates remained high. See Degler, *At Odds*, chap. 2; Lebsock, *Free Women*, chap. 2; McMillen, *Southern Women*, 20, 29, 39; and Censer, *North Carolina Planters*, 91.

47. Stowe, *Intimacy and Power*, 221.

48. Mary Sawyer to Mary Shepard, November 22, 1821, John H. Bryan Papers, SHC. Degler (*At Odds*, 174) attributes the rise in the divorce rate, in part, to the increasing individualization of women within the family.

49. Husbands' right to corporal punishment in *Raleigh Register*, August 26, 1825, as cited in Guion G. Johnson, *Ante-Bellum North Carolina*, 241–42; Bynum, *Unruly Women*, 61.

50. McMillen, *Southern Women*, 46; Guion G. Johnson, *Ante-Bellum North Carolina*, 217–23 (generally); Bynum, *Unruly Women*, 68. A divorced woman had no legally defined position until 1819, when the courts gave her *feme sole* status and allowed her to take back her maiden name. In Granville, Orange, and Montgomery Counties between 1830 and 1861, more than half of the fifty-seven divorce petitions were initiated by women, and about half of these were granted a divorce—although no wife received a divorce solely on the grounds of having been beaten by her husband. Women cited a variety of reasons for the divorce—adultery, drunkenness, physical and mental cruelty, abandonment, and wasting of property. Men almost always cited adultery. See Bynum, *Unruly Women*, 77.

51. Paul Cameron to Margaret Cameron, April 23, 1853, Cameron Family Papers, SHC, as cited in Censer, *North Carolina Planters*, 75.

52. *Bryan v. Bryan*, 16 NC 47 (1827), as cited in Guion G. Johnson, *Ante-Bellum North Carolina*, 239 (Taylor); Leary, "Marriage, Divorce."

53. According to Bynum (*Unruly Women*, 64, 67–68), the attention given to property laws in antebellum North Carolina indicates less an interest in protecting women's rights than in demonstrating the family's "central position" in the state's economy, to which divorce was a direct threat. See also Leary, "Marriage, Divorce."

54. J. De Hart Mathews, "Status of Women in North Carolina," 429–32.

55. See Bynum, *Unruly Women*, chap. 4, "Punishing Deviant Women: The State as Patriarch," 88–110.

56. *Star*, January 4, 1810, as cited in Guion G. Johnson, *Ante-Bellum North Carolina*, 212; Bynum, *Unruly Women*, 104 (Nash).

57. McMillen, *Southern Women*, 48; Temperance Williams to Rebecca Hilliard, August 3, 1853, John Buxton Williams Papers, DU, as cited in Censer, *North Carolina Planters*, 26.

58. Large numbers of children and infant mortality are traditional indicators of families described more as "functional" than "affectionate," but North Carolina gentry families display the characteristics of families bound by affection as well as economics. See Censer, *North Carolina Planters*, 24.

59. McMillen, *Motherhood*, 6; Frances Bumpass Journal, February 6, 1844, SHC, as cited in ibid., 56; Censer, *North Car-*

olina Planters, 24, 26 (Henderson). See also McMillen, *Southern Women*, 48, 50.

60. Laura Norwood to Julia Pickens Howe, March 1843, Chiliab Smith Howe Papers, SHC, as cited in McMillen, *Motherhood*, 108. In the early nineteenth century the number of children declined nationally from seven to five, but not in the South. Some historians have viewed large southern families as a reflection of the husband's power and the smaller northern families as women's growing power at home. See ibid., 35. In large families, another pregnancy did not always excite "as much sympathy or apprehension as it ought," wrote Isaac Avery of Morganton of his wife Harriet's twelfth. Cited in McMillen, *Motherhood*, 31.

61. William Dorsey Pender to Fanny Pender, March 6, 1862, in Hassler, *The General to His Lady*, 118–19.

62. Elizabeth Haywood to Rebecca Haywood, February 28, 1835, Ernest Haywood Collection, SHC, as cited in McMillen, *Motherhood*, 108; Eliza Haywood to Jane Williams, December 20, 1803, Jane Williams to Rebecca Moore, December 11, 1804, and Jane Williams to Eliza Haywood, 1805, Ernest Haywood Collection, SHC. John Haywood was annoyed when his young wife Eliza chose to visit her family in New Hanover County after she discovered she was first pregnant. He was further irritated when she announced that she planned to stay there and have her baby delivered by Mary, an excellent local black midwife, and confessed that he "should feel greater love and affection for your Mother if she did not so completely rival me in the affections of her Daughter." John Haywood to Eliza Haywood, June 26, 1798, Ernest Haywood Collection, SHC. We are grateful to Terrell Crow for the Haywood references.

63. Ebenezer Pettigrew, June 30, 1830, Pettigrew Papers, SHC, in Lemmon, *Pettigrew Papers*, 2:142–43, and as cited in McMillen, *Motherhood*, 88. Probably fewer than half of gentry women had physicians deliver their babies. See McMillen, *Motherhood*, 9, 68, 94–95, 81. After Ann Pettigrew's death on June 30, 1830, her older sons remained in boarding school, and the younger sons went to live with their grandmother and unmarried brothers in New Bern. Four-year-old daughter Mary and the infant, Ann, whose birth caused her mother's death, were taken by Ann's sister and brother-in-law, Mary Williams Shepard Bryan and John Herritage Bryan, leaving their father alone at Bonarva. Embraced by the "large and interesting" Bryan family of fourteen children, Mary came to call her aunt and uncle, "Mother" and "Father," and her father, "Pa." Lemmon, *Pettigrew Papers*, 2:xviii.

64. Anne Cameron to Paul Cameron, December 26, 1845, Cameron Family Papers, SHC, and Laura Norwood to her mother, Selina Lenoir, June 3, 1841, Lenoir Family Papers, SHC, both as cited in McMillen, *Motherhood*, 177–78 (Cameron), 47–48 (Norwood). Sophia Devereux Turner, who had four sons and a daughter, also became addicted to morphine, causing her husband such "deep felt mortification" that he committed her to the newly opened state insane asylum in Raleigh. Crabtree and Patton, *"The Journal of a Secesh Lady"*, 161.

65. U.S. Federal Census, *Mortality Statistics*, as cited in McMillen, *Motherhood*, 196, 167; Censer, *North Carolina Planters*, 28.

66. For gratitude in surviving childbirth, see Mary Jeffreys Bethell Diary, 1844, SHC, and Frances Bumpass Journal, May 14, 1844, SHC, both as cited in McMillen, *Motherhood*, 75–77. For the dead children, see Bethell Diary, April 1, 1849, and M. S. Henderson Diary, July 1, 1859, SHC, both cited in Censer, *North Carolina Planters*, 30–31.

67. Bynum, *Unruly Women*, 55–56; Paula S. Jordan, "Frances Webb Bumpass," *DNCB* 1:268.

68. For Johnson and Marling, see E. R. Murray, *Wake, Capital County*, 156–60, 203. Women's historic vested interest in textile production was recognized in 1823, when the legislature passed an act designating a spinning wheel and carders (also bed and furniture) a widow's due portion rather than her deceased husband's property. See Wilson and Franck, " 'She Had a Web of Cloth.' " For Madame Huau, see *Carolina Federal Republican*, January 3, 1818, MESDA.

69. Stowe, *Intimacy and Power*, 193–96.

70. A description of *The Crowning of Flora* (Fig. 4-14) appeared in the *Lynchburg Echo*, 10 July 1816. Since 1943, this painting has been identified as a "Young Ladies Seminary in Virginia, Artist Unknown." Old Print Shop *Portfolio*, October 1943, 36–37. The discovery of the *Echo* article plus the identification of the weathervane and cupola of North Carolina's first statehouse to the far right documents the painting as the "large painting called 'The May Queen' " in Louisa Marling's possession at her death. See Haywood, "Jacob Marling," 199, and Deutsch, *The Luminary*, 3–4, and "The Polite Lady."

71. See Straub, "Benjamin Rush's Views on Women's Education"; Kerber, "Daughters of Columbia"; Norton, *Liberty's Daughters*; Cox, "Good Wives," 1, 3–4; and Guion G. Johnson, *Ante-Bellum North Carolina*, 260 (Edgecombe County example).

72. Maria H. Campbell to Mary Hume, September 21, 1819, Campbell Collection, DU, as cited in Clinton, "Equally Their Due," 39.

73. Three years before the founding of Salem, North Carolina congressman John Steele enrolled his daughter Ann in the Moravian Seminary in Pennsylvania, explaining that he was "of the opinion that Bethlehem is unrivalled in the United States as a place for female education." John Steele to Ann Steele, July 27, 1799, John Steele Papers, SHC; Griffin, *Less Time for Meddling*; Milton Academy advertisement in Coon, *North Carolina Schools*, 301, as cited in Cox, "Good Wives," 26.

74. Annabelle Norwood to her father, January 18, 1847, Styron Collection, Hillsborough, as cited in Cox, "Good Wives," 27; see also ibid., 32–34. Greensborough Female College (1838) was the third formally chartered college for women in the United States (after Mount Holyoke in Massachusetts and Wesleyan in Georgia). Guion G. Johnson, *Ante-Bellum North Carolina*, 285; Pope, "Preparation for Pedestals," 8–9, 52; Stoops, *The Heritage*, 14–15.

75. Cox, "Good Wives," 37; Advertisement, Edgeworth Female Seminary Scrapbook, SHC.

76. William Polk to Mary Polk, July 25, 1823, in Polk, Badger,

and McGehee Family Papers, SHC, as cited in Censer, *North Carolina Planters*, 46; M. C. Stephens to Mary Ann Primrose, November 7, 1841, Marcus Cicero Stephens Papers, SHC.

77. Mary W. Bryan to Charlotte Bryan, November 26, 1857, December 14, 1859, January 18, 1860, J. Bryan Grimes Papers, NCDAH.

78. Cox, "Good Wives," 35. Such male behavior was encouraged by many parents. In fact, discipline problems contributed to the closing of the Episcopal School for Boys in Raleigh in the early 1830s only a few years after it opened. See Rankin, *Ambivalent Churchmen*, 91, and Griffin, *Less Time for Meddling*, 91.

79. Griffin, *Less Time for Meddling*, 91 (Salem Academy); Margaret Burwell to Fanny Burwell, 1848, Styron Collection, Hillsborough, as cited in Cox, "Good Wives," 40; Salley, *Life at Saint Mary's*, 15–16.

80. For critical discussion of female academies, see Melder, "Mask of Oppression."

81. U.S. Census Office, *Seventh Census, Sixth Census*, as cited in Vinovskis and Bernard, "Beyond Catharine Beecher," 859; Stoops, *The Heritage*, 14.

82. Guion G. Johnson, *Ante-Bellum North Carolina*, 278 (Wiley), 419–22; Knight, *Public Education in North Carolina*, 85. According to the 1850 census, half as many southerners attended school as New Englanders and two-thirds as many as in the Middle Atlantic States. That more southern students enrolled in private schools than students in other regions may indicate that southerners, particularly those with means, were less willing to support public schools. See Vinovskis and Bernard, "Beyond Catharine Beecher," 461.

83. Guion G. Johnson, *Ante-Bellum North Carolina*, 213; "Farmers' Daughters," *Farmer and Planter* 11 (June 1860): 189, as cited in Hagler, "Ideal Woman," 406.

84. "Eight Things That Do Not Look Well," *Southern Cultivator* 1 (November 22, 1843): 191–22, as cited in Hagler, "Ideal Woman," 407.

85. Franklin, *Free Negro*, 164–69.

86. "der [*sic*] Fremden Diener"; Henle and Merrill, "Antebellum Black Coeds." Most of the 140 black women who attended Oberlin between 1833 and 1865 were in the preparatory school; however, more than fifty were enrolled either in the four-year ladies' literary course, which did not require the study of ancient languages or higher mathematics, or, like Patterson, in the four-year bachelor of arts program, which taught a full curriculum. After graduation Patterson and her two sisters taught school in Washington, D.C. For another North Carolina black woman attending Oberlin, see William S. Powell, "Sara Griffith Stanley Woodward," *DNCB* 6:264–65.

87. D. G. Mathews, *Religion*, 103; A. E. Mathews, " 'A Plain Lively Methodist,' " 70; Lebsock, *Free Women*, 115–16, 87; D. Dickerson to Margaret Silar, 17 November 1821, Mary A. Gash and Gash Family Papers, NCDAH (quotation). Three historians explain women's attraction to religion within the poles of self and community. Donald Mathews believes that part of women's attraction to religious conversion and commitment was the space—psychological and social—that it provided. Once women claimed their personal space by speaking out in camp meetings, they moved rather quickly to organize prayer groups and missionary, education, and aid societies. By 1830 they were firmly in charge of the young churches' benevolent outreach. According to Alice Mathews, Methodist beliefs allowed women some space to operate independently and to achieve a public voice in the church, as they gave testimony and sought other converts. Those actions encouraged autonomous behavior, which threatened one of the basic supports of the social order: the subordination of a wife to her husband. Now she could admonish him, though in a "mild and sweet manner." Women's new status gave them some emotional and psychological independence, breathing space in their domestic lives. Finally, in her Petersburg study Suzanne Lebsock found that religion served the particular needs of women as members of a subordinate group who took advantage of the psychological distance from men and created a respectable space in which they could be effective.

88. Rawick, *American Slave*, 14:143.

89. Escott, *Slavery Remembered*, 112, 179. Slaveowners might hope that their slaves heeded the preacher's message to accept their bondage, obey their masters, and work hard, but many slaves heard the evangelical promise of spiritual equality rather than their master's Christianity of piety and obedience. Eventually, many masters came to fear the consequences of evangelical Christianity's emphasis on religious justice and fraternalism with free blacks. In 1831 laws were passed that prohibited public preaching by blacks for fear that black preachers might incite rebellion. See Franklin, *Free Negro*, 176.

90. Jean B. Anderson, *Piedmont Plantation*, xvi–xvii, 45; Esther Lowry, June 19, 1831, Mary A. Gash and Gash Family Papers, NCDAH; Catherine DeRosset, 1819, in Moses Ashley Curtis Papers, SHC.

91. Guion G. Johnson, *Ante-Bellum North Carolina*, 425. Johnson cites numerous examples of North Carolina churchmen acknowledging the women's contributions. By contrast, Lebsock (*Free Women*, 225) notes that Virginia ministers coped with the predominance of women in religion by magnifying their own efforts and minimizing the women's collective endeavors.

92. "Questions of Importance," in H. Green, *The Light of the Home*, 173.

93. Franklin, *Free Negro*, 177; McMillen, *Southern Women*, 95–97. The Baptist faith especially attracted blacks because its practice of total immersion was similar to familiar African ritual.

94. D. G. Mathews, *Religion*, 101–20; A. E. Mathews, " 'A Plain Lively Methodist,' " 65–66; Rankin, *Ambivalent Churchmen*, 27–28; Guion G. Johnson, *Ante-Bellum North Carolina*, 369.

95. A. E. Mathews, " 'A Plain Lively Methodist,' " 74; D. G. Mathews, *Religion*, 105–8.

96. D. G. Mathews, *Religion*, 103–5.

97. Mary Jeffreys Bethel Diary, SHC; MS in Gash Family Papers, August 9, 1819, and Asbury Journal 1:296, both cited in Guion G. Johnson, *Ante-Bellum North Carolina*, 408, 442. Just before Mary Jeffreys was finally saved at a Methodist meeting in

Leesburg, Va., she wrote: "I felt awful, thought I had sinned away my day of grace, I would have given anything for religion, I felt pressed down with a weight of guilt, I was afraid I would drop into hell, I seemed just between an angry God and an awful Hell." See also D. G. Mathews, *Religion*, 107.

98. Ann B. Pettigrew to Mary B. Bryan, September 30, 1829, John H. Bryan Papers, SHC, as cited in Guion G. Johnson, *Ante-Bellum North Carolina*, 345–46. Mathews (*Religion*, 101–20) states that women made the evangelical movement possible and the early preachers appreciated them.

99. A. E. Mathews, " 'A Plain Lively Methodist.' " Countless journal entries of itinerant Baptist and Methodist preachers describe the hospitality and kindness of the many women who provided for them on their circuit ministries throughout North Carolina. The ministers' papers are filled with references to women living a "Godly" life. One woman was called "a pattern of piety," another a "plain, lively Methodist."

100. In 1870 at age seventy-two, Chipman was reaccepted into the Quaker meeting at Deep River, and in 1877 she published her second work (only twenty-three pages) entitled *A Wonderful Revelation of Heaven by an Angel Sent from God to Luzene Chipman*.

101. The granddaughters of Hannah and James Iredell went to hear the new Methodist preacher in Edenton; Catherine DeRosset of the prominent Wilmington family joined the new Methodist Church in her town; and Frances Bowen, a schoolteacher in Raleigh, Richmond, and Fayetteville for twenty-five years, became a member of the Methodist Church of the free black preacher, Henry Evans, in Fayetteville. See Rankin, *Ambivalent Churchmen*, 32, 38–40.

102. Jane Williams to Elizabeth E. Haywood, 4 January 1817, Ernest Haywood Collection, SHC, as cited in ibid., 43; Rankin's observation, 48. Rankin (p. 63) notes that there was a pattern of "spiritually less-committed Episcopal men" founding churches for "more devout women." The men supplied the money and served as vestrymen for the newly restored churches. Their wives and daughters composed the membership, especially the members who were confirmed and thus able to take communion. In the late 1820s, 53 of 61 at Christ's Church in New Bern were women. In 1840, 36 of the 38 at Christ Church Episcopal in Elizabeth City were women. At St. James Episcopal in Wilmington, women outnumbered men more than four to one (167 of 204), whereas only 6 of the 123 male benefactors were eligible to receive communion.

103. [Mrs. William Hooper, undated], John DeBerniere Hooper Papers, SHC, as cited in Rankin, *Ambivalent Churchmen*, 67. See ibid., chap. 2.

104. See Greenwood, *Bittersweet Legacy*, 15–16; Friedman, *Enclosed Garden*, xi–xii, 19; Guion G. Johnson, *Ante-Bellum North Carolina*, 424–26. According to Boylan ("Evangelical Womanhood"), most women moved from the conversion experience to benevolent work in two stages: first, they redefined feminine piety—more activist and rooted in evangelical Protestantism—combining what it meant to be a Christian and to be a woman. In this process, they affirmed females' inherent religious nature but also incorporated the church into women's sphere. Second, they formed organizations by which they could carry out their benevolent goals. Evangelicalism redefined appropriate social activity for genteel women, moving away from "worldly" or fashionable pursuits to organized benevolence. As an acquaintance (the wife of the Presbyterian minister and former head of the Raleigh Academy) wrote to socially prominent Eliza Eagles Haywood, a convert to Presbyterianism, "Why should we not be friends, we are both I hope aspiring after higher enjoyments than the World can bestow[.] We profess to be followers of the same Devine [*sic*] Savior." Ann A. Turner to [Eliza E. Haywood], 23 November 1811, Ernest Haywood Collection, SHC, as cited in Rankin, *Ambivalent Churchmen*, 44.

105. Guion G. Johnson, *Ante-Bellum North Carolina*, 425, 163; *Fayetteville Observer*, April 22, 1830, as cited in ibid., 164.

106. "Ecclesiastical Intelligence," in *Catawba Journal*, November 23, 1824, as cited in Guion G. Johnson, *Ante-Bellum North Carolina*, 423–25.

107. *Raleigh Register*, September 4, 1818, as cited in Guion G. Johnson, *Ante-Bellum North Carolina*, 418, 426; Greenwood, *Bittersweet Legacy*, 16.

108. Guion G. Johnson, *Ante-Bellum North Carolina*, 419; Jordan, *Women of Guilford County*, 34.

109. *North Carolina Presbyterian*, December 10, 1859, as cited in Guion G. Johnson, *Ante-Bellum North Carolina*, 426; Paula S. Jordan, "Frances Webb Bumpass," *DNCB* 1:268.

110. Bishir, *North Carolina Architecture*, 78–81; *Swain's Early Times*, 36–37. Within two years, the Presbyterians began constructing an edifice that resembled a New England meeting house and could seat eight hundred people, a quarter of the town's population. Reflecting its evangelical mission, the church's interior featured a raised pulpit set against the front wall, so the preacher would be seen and heard by all.

111. Jaquelin Drane Nash, "Mary ('Jackie') Sumner Blount," *DNCB* 1:179–80; E. R. Murray, *Wake, Capital County*, 380. Born to a wealthy Warren County family, Mary Sumner in 1796 became the second wife of General Thomas Blount of Edgecombe County, North Carolina's representative in Congress at the time of their marriage and until his death sixteen years later. In her long and detailed will, Blount left a bequest for the "Building of a Protestant Episcopal church in the City of Raleigh" to be funded by "a large sum of money now due me by virtue of the will of my late husband," estimated to be between $10,000 and $15,000. Her executors were Duncan Cameron, Moses Mordecai, and William Hooper. The wooden church was built in the 1820s and served until the late 1840s, when a stone Gothic Revival church designed by New York architect Richard Upjohn was erected. Today Blount's legacy exists in fragments, its interiors at Stagville in Durham County and its altar in Charlotte in Mecklenburg County.

112. Guion G. Johnson, *Ante-Bellum North Carolina*, 422.

113. Sims, "Feminism and Femininity," 16.

114. Jordan, *Women of Guilford County*, 42. Despite the hostility of their proslavery neighbors, Friends kept up a steady stream of antislavery letters, tracts, and petitions to the General Assembly throughout the first half of the century.

115. Bynum, *Unruly Women*, 52–53; Franklin, *Free Negro*, 23–26; Jordan, *Women of Guilford County*, 43.

116. Jordan, *Women of Guilford County*, 46–49; Hinshaw and Hinshaw, *Carolina Quakers*, 32.

117. Bynum, *Unruly Women*, 25; Jordan, *Women of Guilford County*, 47, 49–51.

118. Jordan, *Women of Guilford County*, 43.

119. Bessie Dewey to Mary Rice Lacy, February 15, 1855, Drury Lacy Collection, SHC, as cited in Greenwood, *Bittersweet Legacy*, 19. Women also organized for causes other than temperance—to eliminate prostitution, enact "age of consent" laws for statutory rape, and enforce a single standard of sexual conduct. See Sims, "Feminism and Femininity," 14.

120. Jordan, *Women of Guilford County*, 44.

121. Seven years passed before a site was chosen, funds were raised, and a structure was built, but on March 5, 1856, the new state hospital for the insane opened on "Dix Hill" (which Dorothea Dix insisted was an honor for her grandfather, Dr. Elijah Dix) and received its first forty patients. Dix did for North Carolina what she did for many other states: she forced legislators to adopt laws for the mentally ill. She helped open thirty-two of the seventy-five state hospitals. See McCulloch, "Founding the North Carolina Asylum for the Insane"; H. Marshall, *Dorothea Dix*, 119; and Gollaher, *Voice for the Mad*. See also Bynum, *Unruly Women*, 54–55.

122. *North Carolina Standard*, November 2, 1850, as cited in Guion G. Johnson, *Ante-Bellum North Carolina*, 250; Bynum, *Unruly Women*, 56.

123. Raleigh *Register*, November 2, 1850, as cited in Guion G. Johnson, *Ante-Bellum North Carolina*, 249–50; Bynum, *Unruly Women*, 56. According to Jordan, *Women of Guilford County*, 44, there is evidence that a "lecture on Women's Rights" was held in Greensboro in 1860, but what position was espoused and who attended are unknown.

CHAPTER 5. THE LABOR OF HER OWN HANDS

1. Calvin H. Wiley Papers, February 1, 1854, NCDAH.

2. Bynum, *Unruly Women*, 8; Pattishall, "Plantation Voices," esp. 19 (Fox-Genovese quotation).

3. Guion G. Johnson, *Ante-Bellum North Carolina*, 65. Lefler and Newsome (*North Carolina*, 420) list the percentage of slaveholding families: 1790, 31 percent; 1850, 26.8 percent; 1860, 27.7 percent.

4. Hagler, "Ideal Woman"; Bynum, *Unruly Women*, 8, 49; *M. Lewis Recipe Book*, 1832, NCDAH.

5. *Miner's and Farmer's Journal*, October 11, 1830, as cited in Guion G. Johnson, *Ante-Bellum North Carolina*, 88. L. W. Montgomery (*Sketches of Old Warrenton*, 51) cites examples of farm women selling homewoven cloth for 25 cents a yard on the streets of Warrenton. By the 1840s homespun was generally relegated to slaves and poor whites, but some home cloth production continued, especially in the mountains. "I have been quite busy for the last week or two," mused Louisa [Gash?] of Buncombe County in 1852. "I made some 8 pare of breeches and 2 shirts[.] I expect I will have to spool after dinner and I must be in a hurry and get to weaving." Gash Family Papers, NCDAH.

6. "Farmer's Daughters," *Farmer and Planter* 11 (1860): 189, as cited in Hagler, "Ideal Woman," 406.

7. U.S. Census Office, *Sixth Census*, 41–42.

8. Rawick, *American Slave*, 14:4.

9. Ibid., 14:352–53.

10. Ibid., 14:3; D. G. White, *Ar'n't I a Woman?*, 114; J. Jones, *Labor of Love*; McMillen, *Southern Women*, 101 (Powers).

11. *AANC*, 51, 56. Of the 67,022 farms in North Carolina in 1860, only 311 were plantations of 1,000 or more acres, and 46,307 had 50 or fewer acres. In a total population of more than 360,000 slaves in 1860, only 2.6 percent—or about 9,400 slaves—lived on plantations with 50 or more slaves. Fifty-three percent of the slaveholders owned 5 or fewer slaves, and 18 percent—or 6,440 out of 34,658 total slaveholders—owned only 1 slave. See Guion G. Johnson, *Ante-Bellum North Carolina*, 54–55. According to the 1860 census, only 133 planters owned 100 or more slaves, 15 owned 200 or more, 4 owned 300 or more, and no one owned as many as 500. See Lefler and Newsome, *North Carolina*, 421. In Burke County, 16 percent of the slaveholders owned only one slave. See Phifer, "Slavery in Microcosm: Burke County."

12. Sykes, "The Women of Somerset Place"; D. G. White, *Ar'n't I a Woman?*, 120; Burgwyn Diary, March 8, 10, 1847, "Activities on the Plantation, 1840–48," NCDAH. For Burgwyn's plantation activities, see also Guion G. Johnson, *Ante-Bellum North Carolina*, 485–86.

13. Rawick, *American Slave*, 15:98.

14. Ibid., 15:364.

15. McMillen, *Southern Women*, 101–2 (Olmsted), 104. See also D. G. White, *Ar'n't I a Woman?*, 119–20.

16. Guion G. Johnson, *Ante-Bellum North Carolina*, 53, 478–79, 485; *AANC*, 53.

17. Ibid., 53; Wellman, *County of Warren*, 98, 163; Joyner, "World of the Plantation Slaves"; *AANC*, 53.

18. Vlach, "Plantation Landscapes"; Joyner, "World of the Plantation Slaves"; *AANC*, 53–54. Rice planters especially valued slaves from Upper Guinea and the Niger Delta for their knowledge of rice cultivation. See Faust, "Slavery in the American Experience."

19. Joyner, "World of the Plantation Slaves"; *AANC*, 53–54; McMillen, *Southern Women*, 105. During Reconstruction female rice workers objected to earning less than men, insisting that *they* were *the* skilled rice cultivators.

20. Rawick, *American Slave*, 14:248–49.

21. Ibid., 14:4.

22. Lemmon, *Pettigrew Papers*, 1:612 (Ann Pettigrew); Jean B. Anderson, *Piedmont Plantation*, 53 (Anne Cameron); Pattishall, "Plantation Voices" (Fox-Genovese observation), 19.

23. Rawick, *American Slave*, 14:168.

24. Escott, *Slavery Remembered*; McMillen, *Southern Women*, 101–2; Pattishall, "Plantation Voices" (Fox-Genovese interview), 20.

25. Mordecai, *Gleanings from Long Ago*, 33, as cited in Harper, "House Servants and Field Hands," 48.

26. Rawick, *American Slave*, 14:9.

27. Ibid., 14:168.

28. Ibid., 14:218.

29. Fry, *Slave Quilts*, 16; Lemmon, *Pettigrew Papers*, 1:325 (September 12, 1803); Rawick, *American Slave*, 14:54.

30. Anonymous, *Aunt Sally*. For 1840, the U.S. Census Office (*Sixth Census*) lists 71,576 slave women between 10 to 55 years by county residence and 2,284 slave women between 10 to 55 years living in four towns.

31. Lemmon, *Pettigrew Papers*, 2:5 (January 13, 1819).

32. Rawick, *American Slave*, 14:219–20.

33. Ibid., 15:98.

34. McMillen, *Southern Women*, 10; Escott, *Slavery Remembered*, 89; Edmondston quoted in Crabtree and Patton, *"The Journal of a Secesh Lady"*, 20, as cited in D. G. White, *Ar'n't I a Woman?*, 114.

35. McMillen, *Southern Women*, 105–7.

36. Rawick, *American Slave*, 14:189.

37. Ibid., 14:286.

38. Fry, *Slave Quilts*, 14–15; Stachiw, *"Negro Cloth."* When manufactured cloth became cheaper and more available in the 1840s and 1850s, it was more economical to buy ready-made clothing from Northern mills for slaves than to use slave labor for homespun production. Even so, the women usually engaged in some textile activity.

39. Rawick, *American Slave*, 14:9.

40. Ibid., 14:285–86.

41. Ibid., 14:168–69.

42. Ibid., 14:47.

43. Ibid., 15:129–30.

44. Ibid., 14:285.

45. Ibid., 14:170.

46. Fry, *Slave Quilts*, 17; Stachiw, *"Negro Cloth"*; Rawick, *American Slave*, 14:168–69 (quotation).

47. Benberry, *Always There*, 23.

48. Fry, *Slave Quilts*, 69–82.

49. Ibid., 10; Benberry, *Always There*, 28, 23.

50. Roberson, *North Carolina Quilts*, 108, 111.

51. Mason, *Young Housewife's Counsellor*, 120, as cited in Guion G. Johnson, *Ante-Bellum North Carolina*, 234–37.

52. Hickerson, *Happy Valley*, 64. Elizabeth Dick Lindsay (*Diary*), of Deep River, Guilford County, wrote about planting 195 cabbage plants, molding 40 to 50 candles at a time, weaving a dozen sheets, raising silkworms, and supervising the butchering of 53 hogs on a single day.

53. Clinton, *Plantation Mistress*, 16–35. John Croker, a planter in Northampton County, permitted his wife to keep "what money she could make by the use of her needle (she being a good tailoress), and the sale of fowls, eggs, butter, and vegetables from their garden." Unusual for the time, the Crokers kept separate accounts, and Mrs. Croker lent money on her own recognizance, even to her husband. See *Croker v. Vasser*, 37 NC 553, as cited in Guion G. Johnson, *Ante-Bellum North Carolina*, 246.

54. Gass, "Felicitous Life."

55. Guion G. Johnson, *Ante-Bellum North Carolina*, 231–35; Mason, *Young Housewife's Counsellor*, 10–12. See Richard Walser, "Mary Ann Bryan Mason," *DNCB* 4:233–34.

56. Guion G. Johnson, *Ante-Bellum North Carolina*, 231–35; Mason, *Young Housewife's Counsellor*, 20, 36, 28–29, 27. More household advice from Mason: In February, as "vermin begin to lose their torpor about this time," beds should be moved outside, inspected, dusted, wiped over "with cold soapsuds," and "every crack, seam, and screw-hole" sealed with "hard turpentine soap." Spring cleaning started in May, and housewives should have all the furniture removed from the house, the carpets taken up, walls whitewashed, and woodwork scrubbed.

57. Duncan Cameron to Rebecca Cameron, December 11, 1806, Rebecca Cameron to Duncan Cameron, December 8, 1819, December 5, 1841, and Mary Anne Cameron to Duncan Cameron, December 17, 1835, Cameron Family Papers, SHC, as cited in Winfree, "Cameron Women," 17–18.

58. Stowe, *Intimacy and Power*, 127; Clinton, *Plantation Mistress*, 30–31; Censer, *North Carolina Planters*, 7–8. For women as their spouses' agents, see *Cox v. Hoffman*, 20 NC 319, as cited in Guion G. Johnson, *Ante-Bellum North Carolina*, 243. In 1860, 85 percent of state legislators were slaveholders, although less than 30 percent of free families actually owned slaves; 36 percent of the legislators were of the planter class, although planters comprised only 3 percent of the population. See Bynum, *Unruly Women*, 18.

59. John Steele to Mary Steele, July 3, 1796, John Steele Papers, SHC, as cited in Clinton, *Plantation Mistress*, 29; Rebecca Cameron to Duncan Cameron, September 13, 1812, December 7, 1829, Cameron Family Papers, SHC, as cited in Winfree, "Cameron Women," 24.

60. Gass, "Felicitous Life," 370; MS in John H. Bryan Papers, SHC, January 7, 1829, as cited in Guion G. Johnson, *Ante-Bellum North Carolina*, 243. No doubt other wives played equally crucial roles in their husbands' businesses; however, documentation for the Battles survives because his regular and lengthy absences encouraged a sustained correspondence in which both of them discussed family business.

61. Lebsock, *Free Women*, 164; Bynum, *Unruly Women*, 79–80.

62. Franklin, *Free Negro*, 134–35. Traditional women's occupations, as listed in the 1860 census for North Carolina, included boardinghouse keepers (57), housekeepers (2,675), lace manufacturers (12), laundresses (612), librarians (2), mantuamakers (106), midwives (72), milliners (66), nurses (39), patternmakers (4), seamstresses (5,019), and servants (21,082), though the race and gender of the employees are unspecified. There were 85,198 farmers. U.S. Census Office, *Eighth Census*.

63. Franklin, *Free Negro*, 134–35, 143. According to Franklin, in 1860 there were 412 free black washerwomen and 413 free black servants. The number of free black girls apprenticed in spinning, weaving, and dressmaking indicates that they worked in those occupations as adults.

64. Bynum, *Unruly Women*, 79; Olmsted, *Our Slave States*, 315.

65. Wilson and Franck, " 'She Had a Web of Cloth.' "

66. *Raleigh Register*, February 1, 1842, as cited in Guion G. Johnson, *Ante-Bellum North Carolina*, 245–46.

67. Degler, *At Odds*, 369; *North Carolina Standard*, October 31, 1849, as cited in Guion G. Johnson, *Ante-Bellum North Carolina*, 247.

68. *Greensborough Patriot*, 1849; Olmsted, *Our Slave States*, 356–57. Thirteen-year-old Martha Jenkins worked for the Richmond Manufacturing Co. in Richmond County up to two days before her death in 1847. Timesheet, September 1847, Richmond Manufacturing Co., Records, NCDAH.

69. *Raleigh Register*, May 15, 1829.

70. Charles R. Holloman, "Levi Branson," *DNCB* 1:213–14; *Fayetteville Observer*, May 8, 1849, as cited in Guion G. Johnson, *Ante-Bellum North Carolina*, 246.

71. *North Carolina Standard*, March 31, 1860; Alice Morgan Person Autobiography, SHC.

72. *Carolina Federal Republican*, March 5, 1811, MESDA.

73. *The Carolinian*, August 19, 1816, and *Carolina Federal Republican*, January 3, 1818, MESDA.

74. *Raleigh Register*, December 12, 1817, October 22, 1819, MESDA; Guion G. Johnson, *Ante-Bellum North Carolina*, 247.

75. *Tarborough Free Press*, March 13, 1829, as cited in H. G. Jones, *North Carolina Illustrated*, 165.

76. MOR, April 1, 1833, November 22, 1841, June 4, 1846; Boner Files, MESDA; Batson, "Daniel Welfare," 105. All of the tradespeople—from blacksmiths to weavers, female and male—were subject to the authority of Salem's governing body, the Collegium, which was responsible for ensuring the town's self-sufficiency. Women were sometimes granted permission to fill a vacancy if a man could not be recruited. In 1824, for instance, Single Sister Maria Rosina Gambold worked as a dyer. Male weavers were in perpetual shortage, and in 1828 Sisters Johanna Dorothea and Christina Elizabeth Broessing carried on an active business in weaving, just as Sarah Butner, Mary Elrod, and Elizabeth Hauser Eldridge had earlier. Catherine Transou Reich, with her son Jacob, continued after her husband's death to carry on his business of coppersmithing—a highly unusual activity for a woman. See MOR, March 22, April 26, 1824, November 10, 1828, June 7, 1837, November 22, 1841, MESDA.

77. *Southern Weekly Post*, December 13, 1851, December 11, 1852, as cited in Guion G. Johnson, *Ante-Bellum North Carolina*, 247–48. The four lines of verse in the extract are from a poem by Englishman Thomas Hood entitled "The Song of the Shirt."

78. Cited in Guion G. Johnson, *Ante-Bellum North Carolina*, 216.

79. *Western Carolinian*, April 3, 1821, as cited in Guion G. Johnson, *Ante-Bellum North Carolina*, 215–16 (quotations); Bynum, *Unruly Women*, 93–94. Lebsock's (*Free Women*, 176, 179) observation that the only early nineteenth-century businesses in which women were represented at the top economically were those in which men did not compete, such as prostitution, was based on her Petersburg, Va., research. But the same could probably be said of North Carolina. The 1860 census lists several Raleigh prostitutes—all mulatto—as heads of households and owning real estate property variously valued at $500 and $800. We are grateful to Catherine Bishir for alerting us to the Raleigh prostitutes.

80. Battle, Yelverton, and Battle, *The Battle Book*, 91.

81. Pope, "Preparation for Pedestals," 124.

82. Robert N. Elliot, "Winifred Marshall Gales," *DNCB* 2:270.

83. Beth Crabtree, "Mary Bayard Devereux Clarke," *DNCB* 1:380–81; *Tar Heel Authors*, 11.

84. *Tar Heel Authors*, 5; Richard Walser, "Mary Ann Bryan Mason," *DNCB* 4:233–34.

85. McMillen, *Southern Women*, 113–14; Mary A. Gash Papers, April 14, 1865, NCDAH. Two examples of ephemeral teaching stints are those of Miranda Pitt, of Raleigh, who offered to teach "Young Ladies and Misses, in Reading, Writing, Needlework, Tambouring, Drawing, &c." in her home in 1813, and a Mrs. Mumford, a "recluse" in Rowan County, who intended to follow her husband's advice to instruct two or three young ladies in her home to ease her loneliness. See *Raleigh Star*, February 12, 1813, and *Raleigh Register*, 30 June 1815, MESDA. An extended teaching career is that of Frances Bowen, who headed the "female department" of the Fayetteville Academy (1804–6) and taught at the Raleigh Academy (1807–10), Fayetteville Academy (1811–14), and Euphradian Academy in Richmond County (1826). Again in Fayetteville in 1831, she subsequently returned to Raleigh and opened her own private school. Pope, "Preparation for Pedestals," 90.

86. Degler, *At Odds*, 380; Beecher, *Godey's Lady's Magazine* (January 1853, 176), as cited in Pope, "Preparation for Pedestals," 201–2.

87. For Haywood Hall, see Ernest Haywood Collection, SHC.

88. Noble, *History of Public Schools*, 245. The total number of public school teachers in 1849 was 1,487; in 1859, 2,066; and in 1863, 875.

89. *Raleigh Register*, December 1, 1815, MESDA (Mendenhall); Susan Davis Nye Hutchison Diary, SHC; Pope, "Preparation for Pedestals," 90 (chemistry experiments). Susan Davis Nye was the preceptress at the Raleigh Female Academy from 1815 to 1823. After a hiatus in which she married and became Mrs. Hutchison, widowhood may have thrust her back into teaching. In January 1835 she opened her own academy for young ladies in Raleigh; the advertisement noted that she had traveled to "one of the first Female Seminaries in the United States, for the express purpose of still better qualifying herself for employment she is about to resume among us." *Raleigh Star*, December 4, 1834, as cited in Coon, *North Carolina Schools*, 504. In 1838 Hutchison became principal of the Salisbury Female Academy, and from 1839 to 1845 she headed the female college that was the forerunner of Queens College in Charlotte.

90. Two teachers at the Hillsborough Female Seminary in 1825—Lavinia Brainerd and Maria L. Spear—were educated "in the best schools for women in the North." Later Spear declared that she "followed the methods of the Common School Union," thus aligning herself with other graduates of northern seminar-

ies who took active roles in the common school movement of the 1830s. Mariah Allen, Harriet Allen, and Amelia Thompson—"all from the North"—taught successively at Lincolnton Female Academy from 1825 to 1836. Martha E. Richardson, who taught at Pleasant Grove Academy, was described in 1839 as "a young lady from the north." By the 1850s, however, the subject of northern teachers was more sensitive and might have to be defended to prospective patrons. Pope, "Preparation for Pedestals," 189, 195; Coon, *North Carolina Schools.* For many examples of schoolteachers' transience, see these works of Pope and Coon as well as the MESDA files.

91. Scott, "Ever-Widening Circle."

92. The Troy curriculum included mathematics, science, modern languages, Latin, history, philosophy, geography, and literature, as well as moral and mental philosophy. See Pope, "Preparation for Pedestals," 12, 16, 195, 197; Scott, "Ever-Widening Circle."

93. *Raleigh Register*, April 28, 1835 (Mrs. Saffrey), as cited in Coon, *North Carolina Schools*, 335. In 1836 an assistant "from Mrs. WILLARD'S Seminary at Troy" taught at Phillip's Boarding School in Chapel Hill, operated by Julia Phillips and her husband James, a professor at the university (the parents of Cornelia Phillips Spencer). In 1837 Matilda B. Rowan, from "the female seminary at Schenectady, New York" was appointed the principal of Scotland Neck Female Seminary. Eugenia Hanks, Rowan's assistant who followed her as Scotland Neck's principal, "finished her education at Mrs. Willard's celebrated school." Harriet A. Dellay, an assistant at the Jackson School in Northampton County, "was recommended to the Trustees by Mrs. Emma Willard, of the distinguished Female Seminary at Troy, N.Y." In 1838 Louise Mooar, "a lady from the North . . . from the well known and highly approved Seminary of Mrs. Willard," was recruited "at great cost and expense" to teach at Wood's Female Academy in Northampton County. Willard recommended Mooar as "a Lady of most exemplary character, and amiable disposition, qualified to instruct in all the English branches, French, Musick, Drawing and Painting." Willard's recommendations, according to Scott, are considered by some to be the earliest form of teacher certification in the country. *Raleigh Register*, November 22, 1836 (assistant "from Mrs. WILLARD'S), March 12, 1838 (Dellay), December 26, 1838 (Mooar), and *Raleigh Star*, January 12, 1837 (Rowan), June 2, 1837 (Hanks), all as cited in Coon, *North Carolina Schools*, 315, 277, 279; *Raleigh Star*. See also Scott, "Ever-Widening Circle."

94. Pope, "Preparation for Pedestals," 204–5.

95. Sigourney, *Letters to Young Ladies*, 132, as cited in Pope, "Preparation for Pedestals," 205–6.

96. Holt, *Autobiographical Sketch*, 7–9, as cited in Pope, "Preparation for Pedestals," 207–8.

97. L. W. Montgomery, *Sketches of Old Warrenton*, 146–48 (Cheyney), and Ross, *Child of Destiny*, 75 (Blackwell), both cited in Pope, "Preparation for Pedestals," 206.

98. Spring, *American School*, 112; Emma Sue Gordan to John Kimberly, 29 April 1858, Kimberly Papers, SHC, as cited in Pope, "Preparation for Pedestals," 209–10.

Examples of husband-and-wife teams at educational institutions include Sarah De Rippe Falkener and her husband William, who emigrated from England and "pioneered" in female education; they managed the first boarding school for girls in Warrenton—the Falkener Academy for Young Ladies—from 1801 until their deaths in 1819. Julia Edmonds, who had taught "English and French Literature, Plain and Ornamental Needlework" in her own schools in Alexandria and Norfolk, in 1819 took charge of the Female Department at Wadesboro Academy, in Anson County, where her husband Robert, a graduate of the University of Glasgow, was superintendent. In 1812 Mr. and Mrs. Burton ran the Williamsborough Female Academy in Vance County. In 1830 Mr. and Mrs. Daniel Kerr were at Pleasant Grove Academy in Wake Forest, and a year later they operated a male and female school in Raleigh. In 1835 Mr. and Mrs. Jewett managed male and female schools in Wilmington. In 1837 Mr. and Mrs. Hall ran the Wilkesboro Seminary, and Mr. and Mrs. Crook had Crook's Grammar School in Wilmington. For the Falkeners, see Coon, *North Carolina Schools*, and *Raleigh Register*, March 26, 1819, as cited in L. W. Montgomery, *Sketches of Old Warrenton*, 133. All others are from Coon, *North Carolina Schools*.

99. Stoops, *The Heritage*, 2–4; Stephenson, "The Davises, the Southalls" (quotation, 275).

100. Mordecai letters and Ellen Mordecai journal, as cited in Pope, "Preparation for Pedestals," 66–70; Falk, "Warrenton Female Academy." Lucy Martin Battle was a student at Mordecai's academy.

101. Mary Claire Engstrom, "Mary ('Polly') Williams Burke," *DNBC* 1:279–80.

102. H. L. Watson, *Independent People*, 68–71; "A Brief Sketch of the Life of Mrs. M. A. Burwell"; Mary Claire Engstrom, "Robert Armistead Burwell," *DNCB* 1:286–87.

103. H. L. Watson, *Independent People*," 70–71 (quotation).

104. Mary Claire Engstrom, "Sally (Sarah) Kollock Nash and Maria Jane Nash," *DNCB* 4:360–61.

CHAPTER 6. WOMEN ENTERED THE STRUGGLE

1. This introductory discussion is based on Bynum, *Unruly Women*, chap. 6, " 'The Women Is as Bad as the Men': Women's Participation in the Inner Civil War," 130–50; McKinney, "Women's Role"; Escott, *Many Excellent People*, chap. 2, "An Unpopular War and Poverty," esp. 32, 52, 54, and chap. 3, "Internal War"; Faust, "Altars of Sacrifice"; Jordan, *Women of Guilford County*, 52; Yearns and Barrett, *Civil War Documentary*, 166, 213, 233; and Wiley, *Confederate Women*, 155; Campbell and Rice, *A Woman's War*.

2. According to Lefler and Newsome (*North Carolina*, 419), the state's population in 1860 was 992,622 (968,068 rural and 24,554 urban), including 629,932 whites, 331,059 black slaves, 30,463 free blacks, and 1,168 Native Americans.

3. Ongoing research with the Civil War Roster Project now puts the number of troops at 140,000 rather than the long-accepted figure of 125,000, as cited in Lefler and Newsome, *North Carolina*, 456, and Powell, *North Carolina through Four Centuries*, 356.

4. Jordan, *Women of Guilford County*, 52 (Smith); Wiley, *Confederate Women*, 155; McKinney, "Women's Role," 53 (Henderson County quotation).

5. Ella Harper to her husband, July 15, 1862, as cited in Wiley, *Confederate Women*, 170–71; Stephenson, *Sallie Southall Cotten*, 20.

6. Bynum, *Unruly Women*, 132, 134, 142–50.

7. Rable, *Civil Wars*; Escott, *Many Excellent People*, 70–71; McKinney, "Women's Role," 38, 42, 45, 49–51.

8. Escott, *Many Excellent People*, 39, 56–58; Kenzer, *Kinship and Neighborhood*, 85. The state bought enough corn to feed almost 20 percent of the women and 85 percent of the children in Orange County, more than 34 percent of the women and children in Randolph County, and more than 32 percent of the women in Duplin County. Counties spent $6 million on poor relief. Escott argues that although the suffering of many soldiers' families in the Piedmont and Mountains was mitigated, their resentment against the war increased because the yeomanry's sense of self-sufficiency was offended by dependence on charity; therefore the tenuous social and economic balance between the classes was violated.

9. Wiley, *Confederate Women*, 176.

10. O. Goddin to Vance, February 27, 1863, Governors' Papers, in Yearns and Barrett, *Civil War Documentary*, 97–99.

11. McKinney, "Women's Role," 48; Bynum, *Unruly Women*, 130; Yearns and Barrett, *Civil War Documentary*, 94; Bardolph, "Inconstant Rebels," 165. General Robert E. Lee wrote Vance in February 1865 that complaints from home were hurting the soldiers' morale and encouraging desertion.

12. Yearns and Barrett, *Civil War Documentary*, 265–67, 221; Prices compiled for Women's History Exhibit, NCMOH.

13. H. T. McLelland to Vance, February 22, [18]63, reel 16, McKinney and McMurry, *Vance Papers*, as cited in McKinney, "Women's Role," 49.

14. *Greensborough Patriot*, 27 March 1862, taken from the *Charlotte Bulletin*, as cited in Yearns and Barrett, *Civil War Documentary*, 176–78; Bynum, *Unruly Women*, 126.

15. *Salisbury Daily Carolina Watchman*, March 23, 1863; Michael Brown to Vance, March 18, 1863, Governors' Papers, as cited in Yearns and Barrett, *Civil War Documentary*, 219–20; Escott, *Many Excellent People*, 65; Bynum, *Unruly Women*, 126 (Vance).

16. Margaret E. Love to Vance, May 10, 1864, reel 23, McKinney and McMurry, *Vance Papers*, 51–52; J. W. McElroy, Brigadier General, North Carolina Home Guards, to Vance, April 12, 1864, as cited in Yearns and Barrett, *Civil War Documentary*, 106–7 (Yancey County quotation), 219–20; McKinney, "Women's Role," 47; Escott, *Many Excellent People*, 66.

17. Nancy Mangum to Vance, April 9, 1863, Governors' Papers, as cited in Yearns and Barrett, *Civil War Documentary*, 220–21.

18. *North Carolina Standard*, November 18, 1862, as cited in ibid., 215, 185 (writer from Transylvania County); S. H. Miller to Vance, March 23, 1863, reel 16, S. C. Wilson and others to Vance, December 4, 1862, reel 15, McKinney and McMurry, *Vance Papers*, and L. S. Gash to Eli Patton, Private Collection, Gash Family Papers, NCDAH, all as cited in McKinney, "Women's Role," 47.

19. Wiley, *Confederate Women*, 168; Letter from Hattie Deaver, March 30, 1863, in Gash Family Papers, NCDAH, as cited in McKinney, "Women's Role," 49.

20. C. P. Spencer, *Last Ninety Days of the War*, 20, *Raleigh Standard*, November 18, 1862, and A. A. McKethan to Vance, August 10, 1863, Governors' Papers, all as cited in Yearns and Barrett, *Civil War Documentary*, 184, 214–15.

21. B. Eliza Armon to Vance, September 6, 1863, Governors' Papers, as cited in Yearns and Barrett, *Civil War Documentary*, 216.

22. C. Mary Reed and others to Vance, May 21, 1863, ibid., 216–17.

23. Inscoe, "Coping in Confederate Appalachia," 395, 397. North Carolina men went off to fight in companies organized locally, and the wives at home were often very involved in their husbands' military life, partly because men from the same locality served together and so the women knew everyone, had opinions, and took sides, and partly because the petty disputes and rivalries spilled over from home to camp and were intensified by war. Alfred Bell blamed "my good lady friends at home who have been writing their husbands" for problems he encountered in his regiment, which he had raised of men from Macon County. Ibid., 400.

24. Ibid., 403, 405, 404.

25. Nancy Mangum to Vance, April 9, 1863, Governors' Papers, as cited in Yearns and Barrett, *Civil War Documentary*, 221.

26. This story is taken from Thomas Settle to Vance, October 4, 1864, H. L. Carson Papers, as cited in Yearns and Barrett, *Civil War Documentary*, 103–5.

27. *North Carolina Standard*, February 10, 1865, and Claim of Thomas Runnion, Southern Claims Commission Papers, both in McKinney, "Women's Role," 43–45; A. S. Merrimon [Solicitor for the Western District] to Vance, February 24, 1863, U.S. War Department, *The War of the Rebellion: A Compilation of the Official Records of the Union and Confederate Armies*, 128 vols. (Washington, D.C.: GPO, 1880–1901), ser. 1, 18:893, as cited in Yearns and Barrett, *Civil War Documentary*, 108–9.

28. This discussion is based on W. T. Jordan Jr., "Sarah Malinda Pritchard Blalock," *DNCB* 1:174–75; Company Front, December–January 1988–89, Twenty-sixth Regiment, North Carolina Troops, Incorporated Newsletter, 18–20, copy in authors' possession; and McKinney, "Women's Role," 43. According to McKinney (43–45), in mid-1864 Wilkes County women took part in organized raiding parties with deserters and Unionists. Other women acted as scouts and guides for Federal soldiers who had escaped from the Confederate prison at Salisbury.

29. Zuber, "Conscientious Objectors in the Confederacy"; Hinshaw and Hinshaw, *Carolina Quakers*, 34; Escott, *Many Excellent People*, 71, 60; Bynum, *Unruly Women*, 149.

30. Rawick, *American Slave*, 14:192; *AANC*, 70–71.

31. Ibid., 14:24, as cited in *AANC*, 72; Ibid., 14:144; Escott, *Many Excellent People*, 62.

32. *AANC*, inside front cover.

33. Escott, *Many Excellent People*, 42.

34. Powell, *North Carolina through Four Centuries*, 360–61; Rawick, *American Slave*, 14:250, 253, as cited in *AANC*, 75, and 14:55.

35. Crabtree and Patton, *"The Journal of a Secesh Lady"*; Sims, "Feminism and Femininity," 20–23; Wiley, *Confederate Women*, 140 (English traveler); Faust, "Altars of Sacrifice," 1209–11; Escott, *Many Excellent People*, 39 (characterization of Edmondston).

36. Crabtree and Patton, *"The Journal of a Secesh Lady,"* 87.

37. Kenzer, *Kinship and Neighborhood*, 75–76; Thomas Ruffin to his son, May 21, 1862, in Hamilton, *Papers of Thomas Ruffin*, 3:237–38.

38. Mrs. J. G. Ramsay to her husband, November 18, 1854, in Wiley, *Confederate Women*, 169.

39. Jackson, "High Hopes Waning," 218 (Mary Anna Jackson); Hickerson, *Happy Valley* (Phebe Patterson); Battle, Yelverton, and Battle, *The Battle Book*, 93 (Lavinia Battle); Jordan, *Women of Guilford County*, 52–53 (Mary Watson Smith).

40. Ruth Royal Barnes, "Emeline Jamison Pigott," *DNCB* 5:99.

41. Maury York, "Abby House," *DNCB* 3:210.

42. L. T. Moore, *Stories Old and New*, 174–79.

43. Mary R. Anderson to Paul Cameron, October 1862, Cameron Family Papers, SHC, as cited in Yearns and Barrett, *Civil War Documentary*, 247.

44. Faust, "Altars of Sacrifice," 1223.

45. Wiley, *Confederate Women*, 140; Janie Smith to Janie Robeson, April 12, 1865 (Lenoir Family Papers, SHC), and Mrs [Catherine Douglas DeRosset] Meares to her mother, March 28, 1865 (Meares–DeRosset Papers, SHC), both as cited in Escott, *Many Excellent People*, 52.

46. McMillen, *Southern Women*, 133–34; Faust, "Altars of Sacrifice," 1215–17.

47. Faust, "Altars of Sacrifice," 216; "Report of the Superintendent of Common Schools of North Carolina for the Year 1862" (Public Documents of North Carolina, 1862–63, 12) and J. K. Kirkpatrick, "The Duty of Females in Relation to the Future Educational Interests of Our Country" (85–94), both as cited in Yearns and Barrett, *Civil War Documentary*, 231–32.

48. Charles R. Holloman, "Levi Branson," *DNCB* 1:213–14; *Fayetteville Observer*, April 9, 1863, as cited in McKinney, "Women's Role," 51; Marinda Branson Moore, *Excerpts from Geographical Reader*, as cited in Yearns and Barrett, *Civil War Documentary*, 235–37; Zuber, *North Carolina during Reconstruction*, 59.

49. J. K. Baldwin and others to Vance, September 27, 1862, reel 15, McKinney and McMurry, *Vance Papers*, as cited in McKinney, "Women's Role," 49.

50. Rice, "I Came Out of the Eighteenth Century," 116, as cited in Scott, *Southern Lady*, 100.

51. McMillen, *Southern Women*, 135–36 (all quotations).

52. Foster, *Ghosts of the Confederacy*, 38–45; E. R. Murray, *Wake, Capital County*, 586–87; Bynum, *Unruly Women*, 154 (Schenck); Lossie[?] to Louis DeRosset, June 30, 1865, DeRosset Family Papers, SHC, as cited in Escott, *Many Excellent People*, 91.

53. One of six daughters of Robert Hall Morrison, a Presbyterian minister and the first president of Davidson College, and Mary Graham Morrison, Harriet studied two years at Salem Female Academy, married James P. Irwin, a planter and cotton factor, and had nine children. She was mentioned as a female architect in the February 3, 1870, issue of *Revolution*, a weekly magazine edited by Elizabeth Cady Stanton and owned by Susan B. Anthony. The article "Woman as Architect" asks: "Who knows so well as she how a house should be constructed? Men may build barns and bridges; but women know best . . . how to plan a dwelling in which they live, move, and have their being." See "Woman as Architect," as cited in Heisner, "Irwin's Hexagonal House," 116–17. See also Stern, *We the Women*, 55–61.

54. Quoted in *Tar Heel Authors*, 11. Clarke wrote patriotic verses, book reviews for *Harper's*, *Appleton's*, and *Scribner's* magazines, novelettes published in *Peterson's Magazine*, poems, articles, travel accounts, reminiscences of prominent North Carolinians for *The Land We Love*, and translations of works like Victor Hugo's poems. Her patriotic pieces and other writings were collected in *Mosses from a Rolling Stone, or Idle Moments of a Busy Woman*, sold to benefit the Stonewall Cemetery in Winchester, Va. In 1865 she edited *Southern Field and Fireside*, a periodical devoted to "Polite Literature, [a] gem for the fireside, an ornament for the parlour, and an indispensable companion to the housewife and agriculturalist." Beth Crabtree, "Mary Bayard Devereux Clarke," *DNCB* 1:380–81.

Crabtree emphasizes the background of inherited wealth and family tradition of education as important for Mary Bayard's accomplishments.

Other Devereux sisters were writers, but not so public or prolific as Mary Bayard. Catherine Devereux Edmondston kept a journal during the Civil War that has been published as *"The Journal of a Secesh Lady"* (Crabtree and Patton, eds.). Nora Devereux Cannon, reduced to poverty after the war, wrote: "I wish I *could* get something with either my pen or my needle by which I might make a little money. I feel so *useless* and *dependent*." Cannon wanted her work published and did "not care a straw for fame, glory, or anything except the Almighty Dollar." Cannon to Willie Clarke, December 25, 1870, March 23, 1873, Clarke-Devereux Letters, NCDAH. Still another sister, Sophia Devereux Turner, who became a morphine addict and was committed by her husband to Dix Hill Hospital for the Insane, also wrote poetry. See Clayton, *Close to the Land*, 86.

55. *Tar Heel Authors*, 10.

56. Guion G. Johnson, *Ante-Bellum North Carolina*, 241; Leary, "Marriage, Divorce," 134. The new constitution also gave voting privileges to Cherokee and Lumbee Indian as well as to African American men and a public school education of four months a year to all children, regardless of race. See Finger, *Eastern Band of Cherokees*, 150, and Dial and Eliades, *The Only Land I Know*, 89–90.

57. Escott, *Many Excellent People*, 118, 121.

58. *AANC*, 79, 76; Rawick, *American Slave*, 14:289, 221, 172. In a sample of a few county records for the Negro Cohabitation Certificates, Gutman found that more than 60 percent of the slave couples registered as married. One-fourth of the married

couples had lived together for ten to nineteen years and one-fifth, for more than twenty years. In short, stable slave marriages existed in all types of settings—small farms, plantations, and in town. See Gutman, *The Black Family*, 14–17, 415, 417, and Degler, *At Odds*, 112–15.

59. *AANC*, 76; Rawick, *American Slave*, 15:282.

60. *AANC*, 77–79; Bynum, *Unruly Women*, 151.

61. *AANC*, 81 (first quotation); Alexander, *North Carolina Faces the Freedmen*, 152 (second quotation); Wyatt-Brown, "Black Schooling"; James Anderson, *Education of Blacks*, 4–32.

62. Mrs. McAvery to Mrs. R. L. Patterson, February 1866, Patterson Family Papers, SHC, as cited in Alexander, *North Carolina Faces the Freedmen*, 152 (see also Alexander, pp. 153–68); *AANC*, 80.

63. Perkins, "Black Female American Missionary Association Teacher" (all quotations); J. Jones, *Soldiers of Light*, 42; William S. Powell, "Sara Griffith Stanley Woodward," *DNCB* 6:264–65.

64. *AANC*, 84–88. Zuber, *North Carolina during Reconstruction*, 28.

65. Coverson and Bost quoted in *AANC*, 89–92.

66. Maury York, "Abby House," *DNCB* 3:210.

67. Rawick, *American Slave*, 15:123.

HARRIET JACOBS

1. This biography is based on Jean Fagan Yellin's 1987 edition of Jacobs's *Incidents*. All the quotations and factual data are from Yellin's edited text and notes, unless otherwise indicated. In 1997 Harriet Jacobs joined a select number of writers in being named to the North Carolina Literary Hall of Fame. We are indebted to Judith White for our understanding of the questions that have concerned readers about *Incidents*.

2. Jacobs, *Incidents*, xiii, 1.

3. Fox-Genovese, *Within the Plantation Household*, 392. Though expressing doubt that Jacobs actually remained hidden in her grandmother's attic for almost seven years, Fox-Genovese believes that Jacobs's account was "true in its essentials."

4. *Incidents* and Harriet Jacobs are examined in a number of recent studies, including Fox-Genovese, *Within the Plantation Household*; W. L. Andrews, *To Tell a Free Story*; Braxton, *Black Women Writing Autobiography*; and Carby, *Reconstructing Womanhood*. A useful bibliography is Davis and Gates, *The Slave's Narrative*. In 1987 a special exhibit on Harriet Jacobs's Edenton years (1813–42) was created for the lobby of the Department of Cultural Resources by the North Carolina Museum of History, North Carolina Division of Archives and History.

5. The letter, included in the appendix of the Yellin edition, was written to Ednah Dow Littlehale Cheney, Boston philanthropist, writer, and abolitionist.

CATHERINE DEVEREUX EDMONDSTON

1. Crabtree and Patton's *"Journal of a Secesh Lady"* is the main source for this biography. All quotations and other materials are from this publication unless otherwise indicated.

2. Barden, " 'Tenella.' "

3. Catherine's sisters were Frances Devereux Miller, Elizabeth Devereux Jones, Mary Bayard Devereux Clarke, Honoria (Nora) Devereux Cannon, and Sophia Chester Devereux Turner. Their brother was John Devereux Jr. Their half sister, Susan (Sue) Harrison Devereux, was the only child of their father and his second wife, Ann Mary Maitland Devereux. The best known of the Devereux sisters was Mary Bayard Clarke, a published poet and journalist and editor of the first anthology of poems by North Carolina writers, *Wood Notes, or Carolina Carols* (1854).

4. In 1859 Edmondston helped organize the Scotland Neck Mounted Riflemen, one of the first North Carolina cavalry troops to volunteer for service at the start of the war, but in 1861 Edmondston, hoping to obtain a better position in the army, resigned before the riflemen were mustered into Confederate service. In 1860 Edmondston was elected president of a convention representing militia companies and commanded local volunteers, often assigned to construct military defenses. Information on Edmondston's military service is provided by the editors in footnotes to Catherine Edmondston's published journal.

5. Mary Moulton Barden, Epilogue to *"The Journal of a Secesh Lady,"* 731.

CORNELIA PHILLIPS SPENCER

1. Louis R. Wilson, *Selected Papers*, 211.

2. Ibid., 601.

3. Quoted in Russell, *The Woman Who Rang the Bell*, frontispiece.

4. Ibid., 286.

5. Unless otherwise noted, quotations attributed to Spencer are from Louis R. Wilson, *Selected Papers*.

6. The history of Spencer's efforts to help the university is told in Russell's biography, *The Woman Who Rang the Bell*, and in Spencer's own words in Louis R. Wilson, *Selected Papers*, 599–728.

7. A. C. Wright, " 'The Grown-Up Daughter,' " 261–62. Wright makes the case that rather than "critique the region's societal norms" concerning race, Spencer reflected them. For a closer examination of her attitudes on race, see Wright's article.

8. Russell, *The Woman Who Rang the Bell*, 20.

RHODA STRONG LOWRY

1. Interviews conducted by Emily Herring Wilson in Robeson County, December 13–14, 1994. "Lowrie" and "Lowery" are variant spellings of her name.

2. On the Lowry Gang, see W. McKee Evans, *To Die Game*, and Blu, *The Lumbee Problem*. Blu is especially useful in looking at the history of Native Americans in Robeson County, past to present, and the ways in which Lumbees have rallied around the legend of Henry Berry Lowry.

3. The authors are indebted to Barbara Braveboy-Locklear for introducing us to her native Lumbee community in Pembroke. Among other meetings, she arranged for Emily Herring Wilson to interview the noted Lumbee historian, Adolph L. Dial, and Reedie Lowry Chavis, granddaughter of Rhoda Strong Lowry and Henry Berry Lowry. Linda Oxendine, direc-

tor of Indian Studies at the University of North Carolina at Pembroke, has added to our understanding of Lumbee history.

4. The theory that the Lumbees are descendants of the Lost Colony is discussed in many places. See, e.g., Blu, *The Lumbee Problem*; Dial and Eliades, *The Only Land I Know*; H. McMillan, *Sir Walter Raleigh's Lost Colony*; and Norment, *Lowrie History*.

5. For the execution of Allen and William Lowry and the activities of the Lowry Gang, see the report of a woman whose husband had been killed by members of the gang in Norment, *Lowrie History*, and contemporary newspaper accounts in Townsend, *Swamp Outlaws*.

6. Sources differ regarding Rhoda's parents. Adolph L. Dial (interview) believed that her father was a white man named Gorman and her mother an Indian named Lowry, and that Rhoda and Henry Berry were cousins.

7. Townsend, *Swamp Outlaws*, 12–13, 73–74. A novel, Lucas and Groome's *King of Scuffletown: A Croatan Romance* (1940), is said to have been based on stories told Groome, "a frequent visitor among the Indians" (p. vii), by Sinclair Lowry, brother of Henry Berry Lowry.

8. Norment, *Lowrie History*, as cited in Barton, *Life and Times of Henry Berry Lowry*, 59; see also 46–47.

9. Townsend, *Swamp Outlaws*, 13.

10. Dial, *The Lumbee*, 55.

11. All quotations from Reedie Lowry Chavis are from Chavis, interview.

CHAPTER 7. THE TASK THAT IS OURS

1. In 1880 about one in six females over age ten was employed outside the home; in 1900 the number increased to about one in five; and by 1910, to one in three. In 1880, 17.6 percent (86,976 out of 494,683) of North Carolina females over ten years old were considered "employed." By 1900 the number of employed females almost doubled at 160,161 (out of 685,003 total women, or 22.9 percent) and by 1910, 272,990 women worked outside the home (34.2 percent of 797,161). From 1880 to 1910 almost half were in agriculture; the other half were in domestic service or in mills and factories. Although the number of women in the workforce increased, their jobs remained essentially the same. A comparison of the top ten female occupations in the state in 1880 and 1910 shows that women's occupations did not change much over the years. See Flowers, Population Statistics, 1880, 1910, Women's History Exhibit, NCMOH, and Degler, *At Odds*, 415, comparing 1900 and 1940 censuses.

Because so many white women were employed in the textile industry, more North Carolina white women continued to work after they married and had children than was typical nationally. Their employment, in addition to that of many black women who worked their entire lives, means that the state historically has had a large proportion of married women in its workforce. In 1890 more than 42 percent of black women worked, whereas less than 15 percent of white women did. In urban centers at the turn of the century, between 50 and 70 percent of black women worked, in proportions three times greater than that for single white women and six times greater than that for married white women. Nationally, black and white participation in the workforce was 25 percent to 4 percent. See Degler, *At Odds*, 415; Goldin, "Female Labor Force Participation," esp. 94; J. Jones, *Labor of Love*, 113; and Flowers, Employment Statistics, Women's History Exhibit, NCMOH.

2. Gilmore, *Gender and Jim Crow*, 1–3. Institutionalized inequality and segregation lasted until the Supreme Court decision (*Brown v. Board of Education*) of 1954 declaring school segregation unconstitutional, Civil Rights Act of 1964, 1965 Voting Rights Act, and 1968 Fair Housing Act.

3. *Progressive Farmer*, October 3, 1907, as cited in Lu Ann Jones, " 'The Task That Is Ours,' " *Institute News*, 5.

4. Nathans, *Quest for Progress*, 5–6.

5. J. Jones, *Labor of Love*, 58–61, and " 'Tore Up and A-Moving.' "

6. Most rural blacks were poor and landless, but some accumulated large acreage, especially in Halifax, Warren, Nash, Wilson, Edgecombe, Wake, Franklin, Granville, Craven, Wayne, and Northampton Counties. See *AANC*, 105; J. Jones, " 'Tore Up and A-Moving,' " 17; and Nathans, *Quest for Progress*, 10–11.

7. Of the almost 55,000 North Carolina women classified as farmers in the 1900 census, 70 percent were agricultural laborers, 67 percent of them black and 33 percent white. Of the 30 percent designated as farmers or planters, 27 percent of them were black and 73 percent white, statistics that underscore the racial distinction among sharecroppers, tenants, and landowners. See Janiewski, *Sisterhood Denied*, 27–54.

8. *Progressive Farmer*, August 1, 1907, as cited in Lu Ann Jones, " 'The Task That Is Ours,' " *Institute News*, 3.

9. *Progressive Farmer*, March 29, 1904, as cited in ibid., 5.

10. Dixon, "Work Which the Women's Institutes May Do," 51; McKimmon, *When We're Green We Grow*, 9–10 (quotation), both cited in Lu Ann Jones, " 'The Task That Is Ours,' " *Institute News*, 5–6.

11. Lu Ann Jones, " 'The Task That Is Ours,' " *Institute News*, 6.

12. In the 1880s a recruiter for the Farmers' Alliance thought that "indoor plumbing" was an issue that might attract women as "honorary members." To make his case, he calculated one woman's mileage, which was published in the *Progressive Farmer*, December 3, 1886. The farm woman and her husband (who had appeared at the alliance meeting in a faultlessly clean white linen suit) had a good spring on their property about sixty yards from the house in which they had lived for forty-one years, and water was brought to the house eight or ten times daily. "Well, suppose we figure a little, and we will put it at six instead of eight or ten times a day. Sixty yards at six times a day (round trip) is 720 yards—in one year it amounts to 148 miles and during the forty-one years you have been living there it amounts to 6,068 miles—don't you think we could get up a question that would interest the farmers' wives and daughters? Remember too that half that distance is up hill without water."

13. Ginns, *Rough Weather*, 26.

14. Strasser, *Never Done*, 138–39; Cowan, *More Work for Mother*, 94; Ginns, *Rough Weather*, 23 (Kiser).

15. Janiewski, *Sisterhood Denied*, 8, 57–60; Kratt, *Charlotte*,

105, 108. Our discussion of mill women is based on Hall et al., *Like a Family*.

16. Hall et al., *Like a Family*, 52, 66.

17. Pearl Wyche, a Vance County native who majored in domestic science at the State Normal, was Proximity Village's welfare worker. See Jordan, *Women of Guilford County*, 88–89.

18. Hall et al., *Like a Family*, 66–69; Nathans, *Quest for Progress*, 28–38.

19. Roydhouse, "'Universal Sisterhood,'" 51; Nathans, *Quest for Progress*, 34; Hall et al., *Like a Family*, 72.

20. Flowers, "Census of U.S. Manufacturers" chart (showing ages of females employed as spinners, 1910), Employment Statistics, Women's History Exhibit, NCMOH; Byerly, *Hard Times Cotton Mill Girls*, 62–64; Kratt, *Charlotte*, 111; Janiewski, *Sisterhood Denied*, 35–36; Hall et al., *Like a Family*, 34, 63, 78, 110.

21. Nathans, *Quest for Progress*, 45; Kostyu and Kostyu, *Durham*, 36. According to Lefler and Newsome (*North Carolina*, 512–13, 576–77) and Powell, *North Carolina through Four Centuries* (415), the population figures were as follows:

Year	No. Urban	No. Rural	% Urban
1880	55,000	1,345,000	4.0
1890	116,000	1,502,000	8.0
1900	187,000	1,707,000	10.0
1910	318,474	1,887,813	14.5

22. G. S. Taylor, *Frontier to Factory*, 35, 37; Fripp, *Greensboro*, 56; Exhibition label, Women's History Exhibit, NCMOH (Nunn); Logan, *Negro in North Carolina*, 201–8; *AANC*, 97.

23. B. W. Jones, "Race, Sex, and Class."

24. Fripp, *Greensboro*, 71, 76; Kostyu and Kostyu, *Durham*, 42; Brownlee, *Winston-Salem*, 90; Kratt, *Charlotte*, 77–78; Bishir, "Landmarks of Power," 5.

25. S. M. Evans, *Born for Liberty*, 147. The Comstock Law of 1873 prohibited the circulation of contraceptive information and devices through the U.S. mail. Condoms, douching, male withdrawal, and diaphragms were methods of birth control. The use of diaphragms, considered most effective by birth control advocates like Margaret Sanger, increased by the 1930s. See D'Emilio and Freedman, *Intimate Matters*, 60–61, 246.

26. Jennie Buford to Katharine Smith Reynolds, November 23, 1911, Reynolds Family Papers, Reynolda House Museum of American Art, Winston-Salem.

27. Nathans, *Quest for Progress*, 49, 51–52; Fripp, *Greensboro*, 79; Kratt, *Charlotte*, 91–92. Charlotte had fifteen saloons in the 1880s, and Durham, Greensboro, and Winston, almost as many.

28. Greenwood, *Bittersweet Legacy*, 5, 111; Gilmore, *Gender and Jim Crow*, 13; G. S. Taylor, *Frontier to Factory*, 36.

29. Delany and Delany, *Having Our Say*, 23, 49, 43, 51–52. Sadie (Sarah Louise) was named for her two grandmothers, and Bessie (Annie Elizabeth) was named for Dr. Anna J. Cooper, whose biography follows this chapter.

30. Ibid., 66–67.

31. Gilmore, *Gender and Jim Crow*, 102–5.

32. B. W. Jones, "Race, Sex, and Class," 443–44; B. Jones and Egelhoff, *Working in Tobacco*, 4; Janiewski, *Sisterhood Denied*, 109–110. According to the 1900 census, 1,395 blacks and 502 white women worked in tobacco, for a total of 1,897. Janiewski sees the failure to form class bonds between black and white workers in Durham factories as "sisterhood denied."

33. J. Jones, *Labor of Love*, 114, 110; Reiff, Dahlin, and Scott-Smith, "Rural Push and Urban Pull"; Katzman, *Seven Days a Week*, 77.

34. J. Jones, *Labor of Love*, 127.

35. When Catherine McNeill's great-grandmother washed clothes for a white family in Raleigh, she returned the clothes in a "basket on her head." Catherine McNeill, interview.

36. Katzman, *Seven Days a Week*, 195. Tera Hunter, who is researching Atlanta domestic workers, believes that the women took their "private labor" and made it a "public issue," as cited in Bonner, "Domestic Blacks," *Winston-Salem Journal*, March 3, 1996.

37. For southern servants in the Northeast, see Katzman, *Seven Days a Week*, viii, 77, and J. Jones, *Labor of Love*, 128.

38. Strasser, *Never Done*, 144. In 1900 seamstress was the fourth largest female occupation in North Carolina, and more than eight hundred women operated lodging houses. See Flowers, Employment Statistics, Women's History Exhibit, NCMOH.

39. Kessler-Harris, *Women Have Always Worked*, 76. Traditionally men had worked as sales clerks, but when they vacated those jobs during the Civil War, educated white women replaced them. Afterward women continued to work in retail positions. For the expansion of sales and clerical occupations as indicative of the separation of production and manual labor from consumerism and nonmanual work, and its relationship to the development of distinct social classes, see Blumin, "Hypothesis of Middle-Class Formation."

40. Rayne, *What Can a Woman Do?*, 123, as cited in Weiner, *From Working Girl to Working Mother*, 29; Baxandall, Gordon, and Reverby, *America's Working Women*, 235.

41. Ibid., 232–35; Davies, *Women's Place*, 30–38; Rayne, *What Can a Woman Do?*, 123, as cited in Weiner, *From Working Girl to Working Mother*, 29; Durham Business School advertisement; Bundy, "From State Normal School for Women to Coeducational University," 25, 43.

42. M. S. Smith, "Reynolda"; Weare, *Black Business*, 76–77, 88.

43. Riddick quoted from NCMOH files. More than thirty years later, when Riddick was appointed chief clerk to the State Utilities Commission after first being denied the post, which opened the way for the next four women chief clerks, she stated: "I was not a mother, but I did have nieces coming after me. I wanted to be able to think as I wanted, and I wanted them to be able to do the same thing." Ibid. See also Wayne K. Durrill, "Elsie Garnett Riddick," *DNCB* 5:219–21, and Harry Wilson McKown Jr., "Harriet Morehead Berry," *DNCB* 1:144–45.

44. B. J. Harris, *Beyond Her Sphere*, 85–86; Solomon, *In the Company of Educated Women*, 115–17; Glazer and Slater, *Unequal Colleagues*, 1–11; Flowers, Employment Statistics, Women's History Exhibit, NCMOH.

45. Noble, *Public Schools*, 411–13; Dean, "Women on the

Hill." Not until 1968 were women admitted to the University of North Carolina on equal terms with men.

46. Noble, *Public Schools*, 420, 423–24.

47. *Paths toward Freedom*, 34–35; Perdue, *Native Carolinians*, 50; Finger, *Eastern Band of Cherokees*, 130, 135–37 (quotation, 137); Dial and Eliades, *The Only Land I Know*, 90–95. Not until 1905 did the first Croatan Normal student graduate, and not until 1921 did a class of ten students graduate.

48. Noble, *Public Schools*, 438 (mission statement); Dean, "Learning to Be New Women," 287 (Randall), 289 (McIver); McCandless, "Progressivism"; M. L. Johnson, *Meredith College*, 31–32 (North Carolina Baptists); J. B. Cooper, "Meredith Alumnae." Dean notes that the State Normal students were daughters of yeoman farmers and planters, groups whose security was threatened by the new commercial farming and that would have to make their way in a new middle-class South. Claudia Colhoun, an intern for the North Carolina Women's History Project (1988–89), provided the research and statistical compilation and analysis for the discussion on higher education.

49. Noble, *Public Schools*, 439; Dean, "Learning to Be New Women." Subsequent State Normal graduates include good roads advocate Harriet Morehead Berry, preservationist Gertrude Carraway of New Bern, political activist Gladys Avery Tillett, pioneer lawyer Katherine Everett of Fayetteville, and supreme court justice Susie Sharp of Rockingham County, among others.

50. Percival Perry, "Alice Threatt Perry," *DNCB* 5:69–70.

51. *Fifty Years of Pioneering in North Carolina*, 61 (Alice Jones); Dean, "Women on the Hill," 5 (coed), 15–16 (Stockard).

52. Dean, "Learning to Be New Women," 289, 299–300; Gladys Avery Tillett, "Anna Maria Gove," *DNCB* 2:324–25; J. B. Cooper, "Meredith Alumnae," 11 (quotations); Warner Wells, "Elizabeth Delia Dixon-Carroll," *DNCB* 2:80–81.

53. Turrentine, *Romance of Education*, 121.

54. Gilmore, *Gender and Jim Crow*, 11.

55. Delany and Delany, *Having Our Say*, 79, 107–8; Gilmore, *Gender and Jim Crow*, 11; Scruggs, *Women of Distinction*, 265–66.

56. James Anderson, *Education of Blacks*, 238–39.

57. E. W. Knight, *Education in the South*, 2; Spring, *American School*, 120, 118. North Carolina Women's History Project intern (1988–89) Claudia Colhoun compiled and interpreted statistics derived from the biographies of the teachers profiled in *Some Pioneer Women Teachers*.

58. *Some Pioneer Women Teachers*, 97, 116–17, 98–99. Emma Lehman, in contrast, began teaching at age sixteen in free schools and switched to a private school seven years later. In 1864 she returned to her alma mater, Salem Academy, where she taught English, botany, art, and piano for fifty years, retiring in 1914. Ibid., 119–21; Richard Walser, "Emma Augusta Lehman," *DNCB* 4:49.

59. *AANC*, 153–56; J. Jones, *Labor of Love*, 142–46.

60. *AANC*, 156; Scruggs, *Women of Distinction*, 222–24, 298–300 (Smith). A Wilmington graded school was named in Howe's honor.

61. *Paths toward Freedom*, 123–25; Dial and Eliades, *The Only Land I Know*, 98.

62. Perdue, *Native Carolinians*, 42–44; Finger, *Eastern Band of Cherokees*, 130–38, 149–50, 158, 162.

63. Carmichael, "Women and North Carolina Libraries." See also Garrison, "Tender Technicians"; Anders, "Development of Public Library Service," 2, 29, 53, 67, 71, 82: Scott, "Women and Libraries"; and Carmichael, "Atlanta's Female Librarians."

64. Wyche, *Nursing in North Carolina*; Mitchell, "Raleigh's Rex Hospital"; William S. Powell, "Mary Lewis Wyche," *DNCB* 6:282–83.

65. Harold J. Dudley, "Annie Lowrie Alexander," *DNCB* 1:13; Annie L. Alexander, M.D., "Reports from the Various States, the South, 'The Carolinas,' " *Transactions of the Twenty-fifth Annual Meeting of the Alumnae Association of the Women's Medical College of Pennsylvania*, May 17–18, 1900, 131 (quotation). According to Alexander, there were seven white women and one black woman practicing medicine in the state in 1900. The census, however, shows twenty-two total women, and by 1910, fifty-six. See also Gilmore, *Gender and Jim Crow*, 21, and Scruggs, *Women of Distinction*, 265–66.

Dimock was born in Washington, N.C., but moved to Massachusetts after the Civil War. She received her early medical training at Boston's New England Hospital for Women and Children and practiced there after earning a medical degree with honors at the University of Zurich in 1871. Although Dimock never returned to North Carolina, she was received in 1872 as an "honorary" member of the state medical society through the influence of her childhood mentor, Washington's Dr. Solomon S. Satchwell, then board secretary. In April 1875 she drowned in a shipwreck off Cornwall, England, and was buried in Boston's Forest Hill Cemetery. See Pauline Worthy, "Susan Dimock," *DNCB* 2:70.

Born in Mecklenburg County, the daughter of a physician, Alexander practiced briefly in Baltimore, Md., before returning home in 1887 to a lifelong medical career in Charlotte; she also served for twenty-three years as the physician for the Presbyterian College for Women (later Queen's College). She was active in the YWCA, Florence Crittenton Home, Associated Charities, Cooperative Nursing Association, First Presbyterian Church of Charlotte, DAR, UDC, Charlotte Women's Club, and several regional and local medical societies.

In 1899 Dixon-Carroll became the first physician and professor of physiology at Meredith College, Raleigh, positions she held until her death thirty-five years later. She was a member of numerous medical societies and founding member and president of the Raleigh Women's Club, the North Carolina Federation of Women's Clubs (1930–34), and the Raleigh Garden Club. Cited by the *Raleigh News and Observer* as a "stern champion of good causes and an able advocate as well as exemplar of the proposition that as women are entitled to full citizenship, they should also be prepared to meet its obligations," she was active in woman suffrage and youth welfare, and in establishing in 1917 the State Home and Industrial School for Girls and Women, known as Samarcand Manor, in Moore County. See Warner Wells, "Elizabeth Delia Dixon-Carroll," *DNCB* 2:80–81.

66. The North Carolina women probably attended one of the two dental schools in Atlanta, Ga.: Southern Dental College,

founded in 1887, or Atlanta Dental College, begun in 1892. Southern Dental and Atlanta Dental combined in 1917 to form Atlanta-Southern Dental College, which merged in 1944 with Emory University's School of Dentistry. See L. A. W. Phillips, "Davis Brothers Store," 10–11.

67. As Wheeler (*New Women*) observes, the ideal southern lady was compassionate, virtuous, and *influential* and had been since plantation days, when her moral ministerings helped to keep slavery intact.

68. Eighty percent of black North Carolinians belonged to two denominations, the Baptist Church and the African Methodist Episcopal Zion Church, each of which had a women's group—the Baptist Women's Home Mission Convention and the African Methodist Episcopal Zion Women's Home and Foreign Missionary Society. See *AANC*, 98. The Methodists were the first of the white Protestant denominations to create ladies auxiliaries (1878–86), followed by the Episcopalians (1881), Baptists (1888), and Presbyterians (1912). The discussion of white women's church activities is based on Correll, " 'Women's Work for Women' "; Sims, "Feminism and Femininity," 27–31; Scott, *Natural Allies*, 85–93; C. B. Allen, *Women's Missionary Union*; and Hill, *The World Their Household*. Sims (p. 29) notes that the drive to spread Christianity to Africa and Asia coincided with the expansion of America's territorial and economic imperialism.

69. *AANC*, 96–98, 101; Scott, "Most Invisible of All"; Gilmore, *Gender and Jim Crow*, chap. 6. A study of black women's associations in Memphis demonstrates that many mutual aid groups were composed of women from all walks of life, from professionals to wives of businessmen to domestics and laundresses—a cross-class configuration that characterized the black women's club movement that came into existence in the 1890s. See Berkeley, " 'Colored Ladies Also Contributed.' "

70. Correll, " 'Women's Work for Women,' " 18–24; Ralph Hardee Rives, "Minnie Lee Hancock Hammer," *DNCB* 3:19.

71. Correll, " 'Women's Work for Women,' " 24–34.

72. Ibid., 47.

73. Memory F. Mitchell, "Fannie Exile Scudder Heck," *DNCB* 3:92. In 1846 Eliza and Matthew Yates were sent to China as missionaries.

74. *Western Recorder*, May 14, 1871.

75. Paula S. Jordan, "Frances Webb Bumpass," *DNCB* 1:268. See also Carter, "Sophie Stevens Lanneau."

76. Maud Thomas Smith, "Elizabeth Ann MacRae," *DNCB* 4:190–91.

77. Goodrich quotation from *Pratt Institute Monthly*, June 1898, as cited in Davidson, Introduction to *Mountain Homespun*, 32. This discussion is based on Davidson, Introduction; Boris, "Crafts Shop or Sweatshop?," and L. L. Pitman, "Frances Louisa Goodrich," *DNCB* 2:317–18.

78. WCTU Minutes, 1888, 17, as cited in Sims, "Feminism and Femininity," 64; Scott, *Southern Lady*, 141.

79. This discussion in based on Sims, "The Sword and the Spirit." For the WCTU generally, see Bordin, *Women and Temperance*, and Barringer, Barringer, and Chesson, *Rocky Mount*, 21. We are grateful to intern Lisa O'Neil for researching temperance activity in North Carolina.

80. In the 1870s temperance crusades had spread through the Midwest; as the WCTU's tenth anniversary approached, only Mississippi and North Carolina lacked state temperance unions.

81. Sims, "The Sword and the Spirit," 398.

82. Ibid., 398; O'Connel quoted in Sims, "Feminism and Femininity," 35, 246. Gilmore (*Gender and Jim Crow*, 45–59) provides an in-depth analysis of black women's participation in the WCTU. She notes that in the late nineteenth century, whites and blacks used the term "interracial cooperation" to signify working on common issues across race lines, but nothing about the term implied "a common commitment to civil rights, to racial equality, to working together cheerfully, or even to working together with civility" (p. 50).

83. C. Sylvester Green, "Laura Annie Ballinger Winston," *DNCB* 6:248–49. In addition to temperance reform, Woody worked for equal rights for women. She raised money for a gymnasium at Guilford College, possibly making it the first college in America to have a women's physical education department; worked with other Quaker women to establish the public woman's college (State Normal) in Greensboro; and convinced Philadelphia Quakers to fund a nursing school at the black Slater Industrial and State Normal School in Winston-Salem (now Winston-Salem State University). See Mary Edith Woody Hinshaw, "Mary Chawner Woody," *DNCB* 6:266–67.

84. Lu Ann Jones, " 'The Task That Is Ours,' " *Institute News*; Degler, *At Odds*, 337–42; Jeffrey, "Women in the Southern Farmers' Alliance"; Janiewski, *Sisterhood Denied*, 18–23; Lefler and Newsome, *North Carolina*, 528–29, 545–49; Powell, *North Carolina through Four Centuries*, 427–29.

85. Janiewski, *Sisterhood Denied*, 19. The first county alliance was established in April 1887 in Robeson County. By the year's end there were 12 county alliances, 250 subordinate alliances, a state organization, and about 30,000 members. See Lefler and Newsome, *North Carolina*, 528–29.

86. Lefler and Newsome, *North Carolina*, 528–29, 545–49; Powell, *North Carolina through Four Centuries*, 427–31.

87. Sims, "Feminism and Femininity," 36–41, 187–99; M. N. Price, "Development of Leadership"; Bishir, "Landmarks of Power."

88. Sims, "Feminism and Femininity," 39–40. For a "historical awakening," see Bishir, "Landmarks of Power," 18. Among the original organizers of the Literary and Historical Association were Mrs. John Van Landingham and Rebecca Cameron. Cameron's racial attitudes can be surmised by her comment that the white supremacy speech by her cousin Alfred Moore Waddell (prior to the Wilmington "race riots") "did me good." She and others had been "amazed, confounded, and bitterly ashamed of the acquiescence and quiescence of the men of North Carolina at the existing conditions, and more than once have asked wonderingly, Where are the white men and their shotguns?" Bishir, "Landmarks of Power," 16. See also Gilmore, *Gender and Jim Crow*, 108–10.

89. Bishir, "Landmarks of Power," 9.

90. Undated [February 1895] clipping, Scrapbook, Branch

Papers, NCDAH, as cited in Bishir, "Landmarks of Power," 10, 20; also Bishir, 18–35.

91. Bishir, "Landmarks of Power," 18–36. Wilmington also had strong claims to colonial history. In 1906 the North Carolina chapter of the Society of the Colonial Dames presented the city's first civic monument, commemorating local Revolutionary leader Cornelius Harnett.

92. Sims, "Feminism and Femininity," 192.

93. Ibid., chap. 6, "Handmaidens of History," 184–213 (quotations, 192).

94. Mary Hilliard Hinton (1869–1961) was the daughter of planter David Hinton and Mary Boddie Carr Hinton and the niece of Governor Elias Carr. She was active in Christ Episcopal Church, the Literary and Historical Association, UDC, Daughters of the Revolution, Colonial Dames, Daughters of the Barons of Runnymeade, Women's Club of Raleigh, and Association for the Preservation of Virginia Antiquities (APVA) and a leader in the Anti-Suffrage League. In Hinton's plans for the state's exhibit at the Jamestown Tercentenary in 1907, the first example of North Carolina history was the Roanoke voyages and Virginia Dare (Hinton took care to reassure Virginia that she cast no aspersions on that state's celebration, even though the Roanoke 1587 settlement did predate Jamestown's in 1607). Elvira Worth Jackson Walker Moffitt (1836–1930), the daughter of Governor Jonathan Worth (1865–68) and Martitia Daniel Worth, was thrice married and thrice widowed. Moffitt held positions in patriotic and reform causes, including UDC, Daughters of the Revolution, Literary and Historical Association, Women's Club of Raleigh, Wake County School Betterment Association, Women's Association for the Betterment of Public Schools, St. Luke's Circle of King's Daughters (to aid the sick and infirm and found St. Luke's Home), North Carolina Peace Society, Roanoke Colony Memorial Association, Virginia Dare Society, and (after she joined her son in Richmond) APVA. See Bishir, "Landmarks of Power," 24, 42, n. 36; Charles Hinton Silver, "Mary Hilliard Hinton," *DNCB* 3:150–51; William Underwood, "Elvira Worth Jackson Walker Moffitt," *DNCB* 4:284–85.

95. Quoted in Sims, "Feminism and Femininity," 97.

96. According to Sims, southern white women's organizations succeeded because they upheld the social order of the Old South and promoted the economic order of the New South. See Sims, "Feminism and Femininity," 100–32, and "Sallie Southall Cotten"; Scott, *Natural Allies*, 111–40; and Fischer, "Women's Organizations."

97. *AANC*, 97; Giddings, *When and Where I Enter*, 88–95; Scott, "Most Invisible of All"; Logan, *Negro in North Carolina*, 206–7. Sarah Dudley Petty (1869–1906), granddaughter of free blacks and slaves, daughter of a New Bern state legislator, and a mother active in temperance and church activities, attended Scotia Seminary in Concord; taught school in New Bern; and married AME Zion bishop Charles Petty, which enabled her to write a woman's column in the *Star of Zion* newspaper. She was optimistic about the prospects of women and blacks in the 1890s New South, but her expectations were dashed by 1900 disfranchisement and Jim Crow segregation. See Gilmore, *Gender and Jim Crow*, 156, 190–92.

98. Lucy Patterson was the wife of a prominent Winston-Salem attorney, J. Lindsay Patterson. In addition to her NCFWC work, she was active in the DAR and the Winston Embroidery Club and served as the state representative on the Republican National Executive Committee. See Rogers, *Tar Heel Women*, 169–74.

99. Sims, "Feminism and Femininity," 95, 100.

100. Ibid., 99–100.

101. Ibid., 126.

102. Leloudis, "School Reform in the New South."

103. See Wheeler, *New Women*; Scott, *Natural Allies* and "Most Invisible of All"; Blair, *The Clubwoman as Feminist*; and Sims, "Feminism and Femininity." North Carolina women's organized activity would be considered "domestic feminism" in that they expanded their domestic sphere without challenging its parameters, in contrast to "public feminism" which worked to obtain social, legal, and political rights for women as ends in themselves. See O'Neill, *Everyone Was Brave*, and C. T. Harris and Byers, "Social Backgrounds and Ideologies." Sociologists have observed that voluntary associations appear at times of dramatic socioeconomic change, when old systems of behavior and expectations are replaced by new, as in the shift from preindustrial to industrial society. Acting as bridges between old and new, voluntary groups help negotiate the change from dependence on family and kin to mutual aid. See G. E. Johnson, "Voluntary Associations."

ANNA JULIA HAYWOOD COOPER

1. Hutchinson, *Cooper*, 19.

2. Anna apparently received confirmation of her father's identity in 1934 from Haywood's nephew, who wrote that Haywood had had "one child by his slave Hannah without benefit of Clergy." Introduction by Mary Helen Washington to the Schomburg edition of *A Voice from the South*, xxxi.

3. Hutchinson, *Cooper*, 3–4.

4. Ibid., 19.

5. Annual Report of the Assistant Commissioner of North Carolina Bureau of Refugees, Freedmen, and Abandoned Lands for North Carolina Raleigh, October 9, 1867, Rare Book Room, Wake Forest University.

6. St. Augustine's College continues today as one of North Carolina's foremost historically black institutions. Delany and Delany's *Having Our Say* tells the story of living on the campus at St. Augustine's, where their father, Henry Beard Delany, was suffragan bishop of North Carolina and their mother, Nannie Logan Delany, was a teacher and matron.

7. A. J. Cooper, *A Voice from the South*, 76–77.

8. Hutchinson, *Cooper*, 34 (quotation). In the late 1860s an all-black community developed in western Raleigh and was called Oberlin Village, after Oberlin, Ohio, as one of the major stops on the Underground Railroad and the site of Oberlin College. Mary Jane Patterson's parents moved to Oberlin and enrolled her in the college. William E. Biggleston (*They Stopped in Oberlin*) observed that of the three hundred blacks who were in

Oberlin during the 1880s, the largest number were born in North Carolina. Today Oberlin Road is a major thoroughfare in Raleigh.

9. Churchill, "The Midwestern," OCA.

10. Hutchinson, *Cooper*, 67–83 ("industrializing wave," 83). See also Gabel, *From Slavery to the Sorbonne*, 46–59. Mary Helen Washington, in her introduction to the Schomburg edition of *A Voice from the South* (xxxv–xxxviii), discusses irresponsible charges made against Cooper, including rumors that she was having an affair with John Love, her foster son, who lived in her home.

11. Forten, *Journal of Charlotte Forten*. In the introduction, Billington writes: "Of those who have cooperated to make possible the publication of Miss Forten's diaries, none has been more helpful than Dr. Anna J. Cooper. It is my earnest hope that this book will contribute in some small way to that better racial understanding to which both Miss Forten and Dr. Cooper dedicated their lives" (p. 40).

12. Gabel, *From Slavery to the Sorbonne*, 35.

13. Ibid., 44; Hutchinson, *Cooper*, 132–38.

14. Cooper describes the challenges she faced in mothering five children while working toward her doctoral degree and during her summers in Paris in a short, unpublished autobiography, "The Third Step." See Alumni Records, December 20, 1957, pp. 3–16, OCA.

15. Cooper's *Personal Recollection of the Grimké Family and the Life and Writings of Charlotte Forten Grimké* was privately printed in 1951.

16. A. J. Cooper, *A Voice from the South*, Schomburg ed., 31. In 1991 Spelman College established its first endowed chair through a gift from the Charles Stewart Mott Foundation and William and Camille Cosby, who proposed that the professorship be named the Anna Julia Cooper Professorship in Women's Studies. In 1983 her Washington neighborhood, south of Howard University at LeDroit Park, was renamed the Anna J. Cooper Circle. Cooper Papers, OCA.

SALLIE SOUTHALL COTTEN

1. Cotten, *Journal of Mrs. R. R. Cotten (Chicago)*, NCC.

2. Scott, *Natural Allies*, 133–34.

3. Stephenson (*Cotten*) makes use of Cotten's extensive papers and provides readers with historic details of her life. Letters, journals, and other materials relating to Cotten are in the Sallie Southall Cotten Papers and the Cotten Family Papers, SHC.

4. Connor, "Sallie Southall Cotten," Cotten Family Papers, SHC.

5. Remembered by one of the Cotten children, Bruce, who wrote *As We Were*.

6. Cotten, *Journal*, NCC.

7. S. S. Cotten, *North Carolina Federation of Women's Clubs*, 127.

8. Ibid.

9. Clipping, Sallie Southall Cotten, NCC.

10. During her lifetime, women's residence halls were named for her at the present-day University of North Carolina at Greensboro and East Carolina University. After her death, she was accorded another honor when a World War II Liberty freighter was named for her and christened in Wilmington by a granddaughter. The North Carolina Federation of Women's Clubs maintains a scholarship fund in her honor.

JULIA WESTALL WOLFE

1. Donald, *Look Homeward*, 219. There are so many available sources about the Wolfe family that readers will have no difficulty pursuing their interests. See also Nowell, *Wolfe: A Biography* and her edited *Letters of Thomas Wolfe*; Holman and Ross, *Letters . . . to His Mother*; and Norwood, *The Marble Man's Wife*. Extensive Wolfe manuscripts are in the North Carolina Collection at the University of North Carolina at Chapel Hill, in Pack Memorial Library in Asheville, and in the Houghton Library of Harvard University. And, of course, the novels of Thomas Wolfe are readily available in a number of editions and languages. Quotations from *Look Homeward, Angel* in this biography are from the 1952 edition, published by Scribner's with illustrations by Douglas W. Gorsline and an introduction by Maxwell E. Perkins.

2. An interesting and useful document about Julia Wolfe's boardinghouse and other investments is the historical research report on "Thomas Wolfe and the Old Kentucky Home," by Wilson Angley (1975), NCDAH.

3. A xerox of the canceled check and a list of her properties from the Office of the Register of Deeds in Asheville were sent to the authors by Philip P. Banks, curator, Thomas Wolfe Collection, Asheville-Buncombe Library.

4. This narrative is based on Wilson Angley's study of Old Kentucky Home, which gives a more detailed account of the decline of her finances and the ultimate fate of the boardinghouse.

5. Julia Wolfe was interviewed seven years after Tom's death on radio, by Chet Huntley, who announced, "She is here to reveal for you, as only a mother could, the very personal and very dramatic story behind the writings of her son." See A. S. Harris, "The House on Spruce Street."

CHAPTER 8. MORE WAS EXPECTED OF US

1. Roydhouse, " 'Universal Sisterhood,' " 51. In 1900, 160,161 out of 685,003 women (22.9 percent) worked outside the home; in 1940, 323,601 women out of 1,283,853 (25 percent) did so. U.S. Census data, 1900, 1940, compiled for Women's History Exhibit, NCMOH. For the distribution of occupations, see Chapter 7, n. 1.

2. Nathans, *Quest for Progress*, 100. Degler (*At Odds*, 174) sees the rising divorce rate as part of the increasing individualization of women within the family; he notes (p. 181) that nationally white birthrates fell by 50 percent from 1800 to 1900.

3. Ware, *Holding Their Own*, 6–7. North Carolina's divorce and marriage records were not collected until the 1950s and 1960s. North Carolina created a Bureau of Vital Statistics by an act of the General Assembly in 1913 and started collecting birth and death records on October 1, 1913. Registration of divorces and annulments became effective on January 1, 1958, and registration of marriages on January 1, 1962. See North Carolina De-

partment of Health and Human Services, *Vital Statistics*, 1–17. The state's birthrate was 29.7 per 1,000 population in 1914 (the first year statistics were available) compared to 29.9 nationally, rose to 31.5 in 1920 compared to 27.7 nationally, fell to 22.4 in 1936 compared to 18.4 nationally, and was 23.1 in 1941 compared to 20.3 nationally. See North Carolina State Board of Health, *Annual Report of Public Health Statistics*, table 2, and U.S. Bureau of the Census, *Historical Statistics*, 49.

4. Gilmore, *Gender and Jim Crow*, 147–51. Racial segregation was the law until the 1954 Supreme Court decision declaring school desegregation unconstitutional, the 1964 Civil Rights Act, the 1965 Voting Rights Act, and the 1968 Fair Housing Act.

5. Barringer, Barringer, and Chesson, *Rocky Mount*, 37: Fripp, *Greensboro*, 75, 116, 118; Brownlee, *Winston-Salem*, 139.

6. Scott, *Natural Allies*, 111.

7. Jordan, *Women of Guilford County*, 88, 90.

8. Nathans, *Quest for Progress*, 62–67; "YWCA of Winston-Salem and Forsyth County Historical Timeline," mimeo.

9. M. S. Smith, "Reynolda," 295.

10. Ibid.

11. Gilmore, *Gender and Jim Crow*, 165–72.

12. Ibid., 169.

13. This discussion is based on Breen, "Southern Women in the War," and "Black Women and the Great War"; Henderson, "North Carolina Women in the World War"; and Sims, "Feminism and Femininity," 156, 201–4.

14. Breen, "Southern Women in the War"; Jordan, *Women of Guilford County*, 98–99. At least seventeen Guilford County women saw overseas duty during the war, including naval nurse Suzanne B. Hoskins, of Summerfield, who served with the Red Cross; Dolley Conyers, of Greensboro, on loan to the army; and Dr. Anna Gove, who took a 1918–20 leave of absence from her position at the State Normal School to work with French displaced children. For a list of North Carolina nurses who served in World War I, see Wyche, *Nursing in North Carolina*, app. D, 141–44. The only Eastern Cherokee officer in the war was Lula Owl Gloyne, of North Carolina, who was an army nurse. Finger, *Cherokee Americans*, 36.

15. Laura Holmes Reilley (1861–1941) was so well known for her women's club work on the local, state, and national levels that she was the first North Carolina woman to be included in *Who's Who in America*. Reilley was a charter member and first vice president of the Equal Suffrage League and represented North Carolina at the Southern Suffrage Conference in New Orleans in 1914. She was president of the Charlotte Women's Club, 1903–8 and 1920–22; president of the NCFWC, 1909–10; and on the board of the General Federation from 1910 (corresponding secretary, 1912–16; vice president, 1916–18; honorary vice president from 1924). She was active in her local Presbyterian church, the Mint Museum, the DAR, and the Mecklenburg County Committee of Colonial Dames. Eva Murphy, "Laura Holmes Reilley," *DNCB* 5:196–97. See also Breen, "Southern Women in the War" and "Black Women and the Great War"; Henderson, "North Carolina Women in the World War"; and Sims, "Feminism and Femininity," 156, 201–4.

16. Breen, "Southern Women in the War."

17. Ibid.

18. Ibid.

19. Breen, "Black Women and the Great War."

20. Jordan, *Women of Guilford County*, 98–99; Barringer, Barringer, and Chesson, *Rocky Mount*, 87.

21. McKimmon, *When We're Green We Grow*, 132–36. Rachel Martin caught meningitis and was the only one of the home demonstration force of ninety-eight to die during the influenza epidemic.

22. Berry (1877–1940) was born in Hillsborough, attended the Nash-Kollock School, and graduated first in her class at the State Normal and Industrial College in Greensboro. After her involvement with the good roads movement, she worked for the *Greensboro Daily News*, the North Carolina Credit Union Association, and the state Department of Agriculture; in 1927 she became state superintendent of savings and loans associations. She was a lifelong active Democrat on the local, state and national levels; a member of the Legislative Council of Women; and head of the Chapel Hill Equal Suffrage League and a vice president of the North Carolina Equal Suffrage League. See McKown, "Roads and Reform"; Harry Wilson McKown, "Harriet Morehead Berry," *DNCB* 1:144–45 (*Raleigh News and Observer*).

23. This discussion is based on E. Taylor, "Woman Suffrage Movement"; S. M. Evans, *Born for Liberty*, 164–72; and Wheeler, Keynote Address, NCMOH (quotations). See also Wheeler, *New Women of the New South*.

24. A. Elizabeth Taylor, "Helen Morris Lewis," *DNCB* 4:58–59.

25. Wheeler, Keynote Address, 12, NCMOH; E. Taylor, "Woman Suffrage Movement."

26. Anna Forbes Liddell (1891–1979) graduated from the University of North Carolina in 1918 with honors in English, received a M.A. from Cornell, in 1924 was the first woman to receive a Ph.D. from the University of North Carolina, and later studied at the University of Heidelberg. She taught philosophy at Chowan College (1925–26) and Florida State College for Women (1926–62). A lifelong Democrat and Baptist until her late-in-life conversion to Episcopalianism, she championed women's rights and in 1978 appeared in a wheelchair at a rally to chastise Florida legislators for not ratifying the Equal Rights Amendment in their state. See Barbara Elizabeth Lambert, "Anna Forbes Liddell," *DNCB* 4:64–65.

Barbara Bynum Henderson (1880–1955) was born into a family closely associated with the Episcopal Church; grew up in Salem, Charlotte, and Lincoln; attended St. Mary's in Raleigh, and graduated in 1902 (B.A., M.A.) from the University of North Carolina at Chapel Hill, where she was elected to Phi Beta Kappa. A translator and a poet, she married fellow student Archibald Henderson, who joined the faculty. See Carolyn Murray Happer, "Barbara Bynum Henderson," *DNCB* 3:100–101.

27. E. Taylor, "Woman Suffrage Movement" (quotation, no. 2, 178).

28. Wheeler, Keynote Address, 17–18, NCMOH (quotation); S. M. Evans, *Born for Liberty*, 165.

29. Jordan, *Women of Guilford County*, 100–102.

30. Green, "Those Opposed."

31. E. Taylor, "Woman Suffrage Movement," no. 2, 186 (Bickett); Wheeler, Keynote Address, 21, NCMOH (Lewis).

32. This discussion is based on Roydhouse, "'Our Responsibilities'" and "'Universal Sisterhood'"; Nasstrom, "'More Was Expected of Us'"; Wilkerson-Freeman, "From Clubs to Parties"; Kessler-Harris, *Out to Work*, chap. 7, "Protective Labor Legislation," 180–213.

33. Nasstrom, "'More Was Expected of Us.'"

34. Ibid.; Kessler-Harris, *Out to Work*, 206 (Alice Paul), and chap. 7 ("Protective Labor Legislation," 180–213). S. M. Evans (*Born for Liberty*, 192) sees the issue of protective legislation leading to the most direct conflict among feminists.

35. Nasstrom, "'More Was Expected of Us,'" 307 (Daniels); Houk, "In the Beginning, 1920–1950," 27–37. The North Carolina WCTU campaigned from 1883 to 1928 to have the legislature raise the age of female consent from ten years (1883) to fourteen (1895) to sixteen (1928). The WCTU did not always confine itself to temperance reform—to the discomfort of more conservative members—but cast a wide net that included child labor legislation as well as prison reform, eradication of prostitution, divorce reform, equal rights for women, and interracial cooperation.

36. Mollie C. Davis, "Kate Ancrum Burr Johnson," *DNCB* 3:295–96. Born in Morganton, Johnson (1881–1968) attended Queens College in Charlotte, lived in Raleigh with her husband and two sons, and was active in church, civic, and women's organizations, becoming in 1915 vice president of the North Carolina Conference for Social Service. Among the achievements of the Board of Charities and Public Welfare under her administration (1921–30) were a Mother's Aid program, institutions for juvenile offenders, a farm colony for women offenders, and appropriations for the institution for delinquent black girls established by the North Carolina Federation of Colored Women's Clubs.

37. Bost graduated from State Normal in 1903 and taught in Salisbury public schools until her marriage in 1909. Active in civic and club work, she served as president of the Raleigh Women's Club (1921–23), executive secretary of NCFWC, president of the North Carolina Conference for Social Service (1937–38), and delegate to the Democratic National Convention in 1944. See Thomas S. Morgan, "Annie Kizer Bost," *DNCB* 1:195–96.

38. Wilkerson-Freeman, "From Clubs to Parties," 330 (Molly Dewson on Jerman).

39. Ralph Hardee Rives, "Frances Blount Renfrow Doak," *DNCB* 2:81–82. Doak (1887–1974) also served in various offices in the Raleigh Women's Club and Raleigh WCTU and later as the executive secretary of the NCFWC (1941–51). She worked for prison reform, helped organize the first statewide Negro Parent-Teacher Association Congress, served as chair of her club's welfare department, and was instrumental in creating Raleigh's first day care center for black children. Active in the Democratic Party and League of Women Voters, she participated in international politics through her position as chair of the International Relations Committee of the National Federation of Women's Clubs and spoke in favor of the Dumbarton Oaks proposal for the formation of the United Nations.

40. Wilkerson-Freeman, "From Clubs to Parties."

41. Ibid.

42. See Ravi, *Notable North Carolina Women*, 48–51.

43. See Teresa Kay Beck, "Gertrude Dills McKee," *DNCB* 4:155–56. The daughter of a Jackson County state legislator, McKee graduated from Peace Institute in 1905 as president of her class, married Sylva businessman Ernest McKee, and had three children. She was active in her local Methodist church and in Liberty Loan and Salvation Army drives during World War I; president of the Southern Council of Federated Club Women (1926–28) and of the Southeastern Council of Federated Club Women (1927–30); chair of the Jackson County Board of Education; and a trustee of Western Carolina Teachers College, Peace College, the University of North Carolina, and Brevard College. For industrialists' view that compulsory education and employment of children were irreconcilable, see Wilkerson-Freeman, "From Clubs to Parties," 323.

44. Many of those elected to Congress were widows who carried out their husband's terms, and usually there were only four or five women in each session. Nationally, the number of women who won public office declined from the 1920s to the 1930s. In 1929 about 149 women were serving in thirty-eight state legislatures. By 1933 the number dropped slightly, to 132 women in thirty-four state legislatures. North Carolina had only Clements and McKee. See Ware, *Holding Their Own*, 95–96.

45. In 1910, of the 797,161 total women in North Carolina, 272,990 were in the workforce (34.2%): 130,380 white women (24.1% of 540,777) and 141,391 black women (55.7% of 253,755). In 1920, of the 926,790 total, 202,697 women were employed (21.9%): 105,622 white (16.4% of 642,642) and 96,309 black (34.4% of 280,284). In 1930, of 1,190,204 women, 272,968 were employed (22.9%): 151,243 white (18.1% of 833,679) and 120,065 black (34.4% of 343,026). In 1940, of 1,263,853 women, 323,601 were employed (25.6%): 213,040 white (23.4% of 918,275) and 109,149 black (32.2% of 338,962). Flowers, Employment Statistics, Women's History Exhibit, NCMOH.

46. Flowers, "Census of U.S. Manufacturers" chart (showing ages of females employed as spinners, 1910), Employment Statistics, Women's History Exhibit, NCMOH; Janiewski, *Sisterhood Denied*, 37–38; Hall et al., *Like a Family*, 310.

47. Hall et al., *Like a Family*, 158.

48. Ibid., 140, 143.

49. Ibid., 74–75.

50. Ibid., 76–77.

51. Ibid., 211–12.

52. Frederickson, "Summer School for Women Workers."

53. Hall et al., *Like a Family*, 327.

54. Janiewski, *Sisterhood Denied*, 122.

55. B. W. Jones, "Race, Sex, and Class," 446, 443–44; B. Jones and Egelhoff, *Working in Tobacco*, 4. The enforcement of the 1917 Child Labor Law by the late 1920s and early 1930s somewhat slowed the employment of children under sixteen, and black Durham households with working children decreased from 35 to 14 percent between 1919 and 1930.

56. Reiff, Dahlin, and Scott-Smith, "Rural Push and Urban

Pull"; B. W. Jones, "Race, Sex, and Class"; B. Jones and Egelhoff, *Working in Tobacco*," 14–15.

57. B. W. Jones, "Race, Sex, and Class," 444–45.

58. Mattie Sparks Shaw, interview; Byerly, *Hard Times Cotton Mill Girls*, 98–99.

59. Winston-Salem City Directory, 1884, 1921, 1930, 1940. For instance, in 1884 boardinghouse operator Mrs. E. T. Blair of High Point was listed in the city directory as providing "Hairworks."

60. Quoted in Hagood, *Mothers of the South*, 198.

61. This discussion of midwifery is based on E. H. Wilson, *Hope and Dignity*, 32–44; L. M. Hudson, "Midwifery"; and P. Starr, *Social Transformation of American Medicine*, 19.

62. L. M. Hudson, "Midwifery," 8, 15. According to "Births by Type of Attendance" (*Vital Statistics of the United States*, 1937, 95), midwives assisted in 21,553 out of more than 79,146 births. In 1981 less than 1 percent of all births were delivered by midwives, but that year the General Assembly enacted new provisions for licensing nurse-midwives to aid in home births. See "Live Births" (*Vital Statistics of the United States*, 1981).

63. Communication with Bertie Doughtery, Asheville, n.d.; L. Knight, "Midwife"; E. H. Wilson, *Hope and Dignity*, 39.

64. The proportion of North Carolina working women increased from 22.9 percent in 1930 to 25.6 percent in 1940. Ware, *Holding Their Own*, 21, 30, 35–40; Kessler-Harris, *Out to Work*, 252–72.

65. B. J. Harris, *Beyond Her Sphere*, 85–86; Solomon, *In the Company of Educated Women*; Glazer and Slater, *Unequal Colleagues*; Flowers, Employment Statistics, Women's History Exhibit, NCMOH. Of Meredith graduates, Mary Steel Smith (1913) was the first to receive a Ph.D. (English from Yale), Flossie Marshbank (1915) was the first lawyer, and Elizabeth Vann (1917) was the first physician. See J. B. Cooper, "Meredith Alumnae."

66. For how higher education, middle-class values, and professional mobility restructured late-nineteenth-century American society, see Bledstein, *The Culture of Professionalism*.

67. Littlefield, "Publicity from Neither Friend Nor Foe."

68. Disosway then went to Fort Yukon, Alaska, where she was the only doctor within hundreds of miles, returning home in 1948 to look after her mother, who was ill and died in 1954. Medical director of New Bern's Good Shepherd Hospital until it closed in 1967, she then practiced in the maternity ward "Stork Heaven" at Craven County Hospital. Ilene Disosway has been our principal source of information for her husband's aunt and has deposited many of Disosway's papers at the Joyner Library, East Carolina University. See also "Dr. Lula Disosway Receives Keys to Clinic," *Sun Journal*, August 28, 1972, 11, and E. H. Wilson, *Memories of New Bern*.

69. Dean, "Learning to Be New Women," 303–6 (Cott, 302); Ware, *Holding Their Own*, 60–66; S. M. Evans, *Born for Liberty*, 178.

70. Ware, *Holding Their Own*, 28–29; Interview with Sam Bowers, "We Makes Plenty," Federal Writers' Project, *These Are Our Lives*, 73–74.

71. Ware, *Holding Their Own*, 80; William S. Powell, "Sallie Belle Marks," *DNCB* 4:218; Dean, "Women on the Hill," 5, 7, 15–16, 24–26 (Hamilton); McCandless, "Progressivism," 319–22. Lynn Holdzkom and Barbara Kuligowski ("Organizing for Change: The Life and Work of Guion Griffis Johnson," paper presented at *Marching Through Time: North Carolina Women from Suffrage to Civil Rights: A Symposium of Southern Women's History*, November 1995) cite the numerous women's organizations that Johnson joined to promote social change from World War II until her death in 1989. See also Scott, *Unheard Voices*, 136–72 (Johnson), 111–35 (Spruill).

72. Carmichael, "Women and North Carolina Libraries."

73. Ibid. See also Garrison, "Tender Technicians"; Anders, "Development of Public Library Service," 2, 29, 53, 67, 71, 82: Scott, "Women and Libraries"; and Carmichael, "Atlanta's Female Librarians."

74. Elaine von Oesen, "Carrie Longee Broughton," *DNCB* 1:238.

75. Betty Young, "Lillian Baker Griggs," *DNCB* 2:373–74; Irene Hester, "Nellie Rowe (Mrs. William Cecil) Jones," *DNCB* 3:324; Fripp, *Greensboro*, 116.

76. Elaine von Oesen, "Helen Marjorie Beal," *DNCB* 1:123.

77. R. N. Moore, "Mollie Huston Lee." Not until the 1960s and desegregation did blacks truly have access to the same library resources as whites.

78. Boris, "Crafts Shop or Sweatshop?"; Hester, "Tryon Toymakers."

79. William S. Powell, "Lucy Calista Morgan," *DNCB* 4:323–24. Morgan (1889–1981) was educated at a private school in Hickory, a Michigan normal school, and the University of Chicago (two summers, 1916, 1917); taught in Illinois, Michigan, and Montana; and worked briefly for the Children's Bureau of Chicago.

80. George W. Troxler, "Juliana Royster Busbee," *DNCB* 1:289–90.

81. "North Carolina Women/Reclaiming Their Place in History" brochure.

82. Sims, "Feminism and Femininity," 102–9, 192 (Shuford). For Mary Myers Dwelle, see Wilkinson, *Mint Museum of Art*, 52–68.

83. Gertrude Carraway (1896–1993) graduated from State Normal in Greensboro and studied journalism at Columbia University in New York City. In addition to her longtime association with Tryon Palace, she founded the organization known today as the Historic Preservation Foundation of North Carolina, served forty years on the North Carolina Historical Commission, and was state regent, vice president, and president general (1953–56) of the national DAR. See *Raleigh News and Observer*, January 13, 1985.

Maude Moore Latham (1871–1951) was educated in New Bern and at Hunter College in New York City and married James Latham, a wealthy businessman. She was a longtime resident of Greensboro, where she attended the Presbyterian church; served on the City Planning and Zoning Board; belonged to local, state, and national cultural and civic organizations, including the North Carolina Art Society, North Carolina Folklife Society, State Literary and Historical Association, Historical Book Club of North Carolina, Euterpe Club, Garden

Club of North Carolina, National Council of State Garden Clubs, North Carolina Society for the Preservation of Antiquities, National Council for Historic Sites and Buildings (now the National Trust for Historic Preservation), and Women's Club of Greensboro. Latham was a trustee of the Presbyterian Home for the Aged, to which she donated generously as well as to the Latham Memorial Hospital and Masonic Home of Greensboro. She was the first and largest donor for the purchase of the Carolina Charter issued by Charles II to the Lords Proprietors in 1663. See Gertrude S. Carraway, "Maude Moore Latham," *DNCB* 4:27–28.

84. William S. Powell, "Adeline Denham McCall," *DNCB* 4:123-24; Powell, "Paul Eliot Green," *DNCB* 2:258–59; Richard Walser, "(Minna) Inglis Fletcher," *DNCB* 2:207–8; Walser, "Bernice (Christiana) Kelly Harris," *DNCB* 3:47–48. In 1990 the society celebrated its fiftieth anniversary with a new book written by state preservation historian Catherine Bishir and photographs by Tim Buchman that included yeoman farmhouses, slave cabins, and mill village housing, presenting a more complicated, textured, and complete historical picture of North Carolina.

85. Helen Dugan Allen, "Mary Bayard Morgan Wootten," *DNCB* 6:268–69. Wootten (1875–1959) attended State Normal and Industrial College in 1892, worked as an art instructor in schools for the deaf in Arkansas and Georgia, painted cards and calendars, and designed the first Pepsi-Cola trademark for New Bern pharmacist Caleb D. Bradham, a neighbor who invented the drink, before embarking on her photographic career. Her maternal grandmother was Mary Bayard Devereux Clarke, prolific author and poet whose writing supported her family in the aftermath of the Civil War.

86. Quoted in B. W. Jones, "Race, Sex, and Class," 443.

87. Pauli Murray, an attorney and one of the first women ordained in the Episcopal Church, also grew up in 1920s Durham and remembered its poorest black sections, the Bottoms, as "an odious conglomeration of trash piles, garbage dumps, cowstalls, pig-pens, and crowded humanity." See Parramore, *Express Lanes*, 62 (Durham), 58–61 (Raleigh). For a description of East Hargett Street, see Simmons-Henry and Edmisten, *Culture Town*, prologue, xvi.

88. Lefler and Powell, *North Carolina*, population figures, 576, 638.

89. Parramore, *Express Lanes*, 48.

90. In 1930 a YWCA committee headed by Mrs. Bryan Booe persuaded Winston-Salem merchants to lower the maximum workweek to fifty-five hours and provide stools behind the counters for retail clerks. See "YWCA of Winston-Salem and Forsyth County Historical Timeline," mimeo.

91. Cowan, *More Work for Mother*, 151–91; Strasser, *Never Done*, 243–62; Ware, *Holding Their Own*, 16 (Cowan quotations); Parramore, *Express Lanes*, 83.

92. In 1920 domestic service was the second highest occupation for black women at 33,537 (34.8%), in 1930 it was the highest occupation at 56,062 (46.7%), and highest again in 1940 at 61,483 (57.4%). Flowers, Employment Statistics, Women's History Exhibit, NCMOH.

93. When the REA was being developed in Washington D.C., the North Carolina General Assembly established the Rural Electrification Authority, a promotional agency charged with getting rural lines built by any organization, public or private, that would build them. See Ellis, *A Giant Step*, 44, and D. Clayton Brown, *Electricity for Rural America*, 13.

94. S. M. Evans, *Born for Liberty*, 177–79.

95. Ravi, *Notable North Carolina Women*, 104 (Mayer).

96. Janiewski, *Sisterhood Denied*, 81, 42–43.

97. Hagood, *Mothers of the South*.

98. Ibid., 100, 14; J. Jones, " 'Tore Up and A-Moving,' " 21.

99. Hagood, *Mothers of the South*, 88; Janiewski, *Sisterhood Denied*, 30, 195, n. 12.

100. Taylor and Zimmerman, 1921 Survey, 7. In the 1921 survey of farm families in three counties that included the Coast, Piedmont, and Mountains, not one tenant family, black or white, had indoor plumbing.

101. Hagood, *Mothers of the South*, 101–2.

102. Ibid., 93.

103. D'Emilio and Freedman, *Intimate Matters*, 246–48. Among the minority of rural southerners who tried to limit family size, blacks were more likely to rely on the female method of douching, and whites more often on male withdrawal and the use of condoms. For Hagood's discussion of family planning and contraception, see *Mothers of the South*, 118–21, 124, 127.

104. Terrill and Hirsch, *Such As Us*, 61. According to the 1921 survey, midwives attended 50 percent of landless births and 18 percent of landowning births; 70 percent of black births and 17 percent of white births. Physicians attended 70 percent of those of the landowning class and 48 percent of the landless, and 80 percent of white and 30 percent of black births. See Taylor and Zimmerman, 1921 Survey, 59.

105. Hagood, *Mothers of the South*, 120–21; Terrill and Hirsch, *Such As Us*, 87 (Mathews); D'Emilio and Freedman, *Intimate Matters*, 247.

106. J. Jones (" 'Tore Up and A-Moving' ") asserts that although poverty, common cause, and love of their families might have united rural black and poor white women, their races caused them to live in different worlds, with little interaction, sympathy, or understanding for the other. See also Hagood, *Mothers of the South*, 199.

107. Like Sarah Easton, Gracie Turner was illiterate ("all I learnt was to work in the field") and had stopped going to church because she had no dress "fittin' to wear." Federal Writers' Project, *These Are Our Lives*; J. Jones, " 'Tore Up and A-Moving,' " 20–21 (quotation).

108. Federal Writers' Project, *These Are Our Lives*, 3–17.

109. E. H. Wilson, *Hope and Dignity*, 5, 6, 8, 10.

110. A. R. Phillips, "Continuity and Change," 297–301, and " 'I Know How to Work.' " Landholdings were typically small, with the average farm size of sixty acres a constant from the mid-eighteenth century when Virginia settlers overflowed to the upper Carolina Piedmont.

111. Quoted in A. R. Phillips, "Continuity and Change," 7.

112. Quoted in A. R. Phillips, " 'I Know How to Work,' " 22.

Extended families were the norm in Stokes County, and newly married children often lived with their parents or in-laws, built their home on their parents' or inlaws' land, and considered the health and well-being of their parents or grandparents when deciding where they would live.

CHARLOTTE HAWKINS BROWN

1. Brown, "A Biography" [autobiography], 12, Brown Papers, NCDAH. Extensive papers are available at NCDAH, and selections are in the visitors' center at the Charlotte Hawkins Brown Historic Site in Sedalia. Among the important resources are William J. McCrea, National Register of Historic Places Report, and the research of Charles W. Wadelington for the North Carolina Historic Sites section.

2. Brown's story has been shaped by a complex and often contradictory mythology that Brown herself began to create during her lifetime. Among the most reliable sources of information are S. N. Smith, "Charlotte Hawkins Brown"; Wadelington, "What One Young African American Woman Could Do"; and Gilmore, *Gender and Jim Crow*, 178–95.

3. S. N. Smith, "Charlotte Hawkins Brown," 194–96.

4. Hunter, "The Correct Thing," 38.

5. Gilmore, *Gender and Jim Crow*, 186.

6. Brown letter, n.d., Brown Papers, NCDAH.

7. McCrea, "Palmer Memorial Institute," 7–8.

8. Gilmore (*Gender and Jim Crow*, 186–90) considers the dynamics of the Brown–McIver friendship and the "elusive" race ideologies of each.

9. Hunter, "The Correct Thing," 40.

10. Ibid., 41. For the Memphis speech and Brown's appeals to women, see S. N. Smith, "Charlotte Hawkins Brown," 200–203.

11. Gilmore, *Gender and Jim Crow*, 218.

12. Hunter, "The Correct Thing," 42–43.

13. Watts, telephone interview.

14. Gilmore, *Gender and Jim Crow*, 184–85. Gilmore's analysis of Brown's leadership is a closely argued study of Brown's ambitions, set in the context of racial and political history in the period 1896–1920.

15. Opinions about why trustees closed PMI differ. Hunter ("The Correct Thing," 43) observes: "The board of trustees, in an apparently retaliatory move against dissident students and in fear of the growing Black Power movement sweeping the nation's black college campuses, abruptly closed the school that summer in spite of the fact that a full staff had been employed and a record number of students enrolled."

JANE SIMPSON MCKIMMON

1. Home demonstration work in the 1990s was carried on through the cooperative extension programs of North Carolina State University. In 1979 the university dedicated the Jane S. McKimmon Center for Extension and Continuing Education.

2. McKimmon Papers, SHC. We are indebted to Lu Ann Jones for calling our attention to this small collection of Jane McKimmon's personal papers. In a letter to his son Billy, written in February 1918, Charles McKimmon confessed, "I am still unable to get anything in the way of work."

3. Gilmore, *Gender and Jim Crow*, 197.

4. Annual Report, 1924, Wayne County, p. 43, McKimmon Papers, NCDAH.

5. McKimmon, *When We're Green We Grow*, 139, 142.

OLIVE DAME CAMPBELL

1. ODC Journal, June 1906, Campbell Papers, SHC.

2. J. C. Campbell, *Southern Highlander*, xix.

3. "Statement for a Proposed Study Plan of the Southern Highland Section," attached to letter of May 15, 1908, to Mrs. John M. Glenn, Campbell Papers, SHC.

4. ODC Journal, vol. 3, October 1908–January 1909, Campbell Papers, SHC.

5. Ibid., March 1, 1909.

6. Ibid., March 11–12, 1909.

7. J. C. Campbell, *Southern Highlander*, 137.

8. ODC Journal, vol. 3, October 1908–January 1909, Campbell Papers, SHC.

9. Whisnant, *All That Is Native*, 293, n. 35.

10. Ibid., 115.

11. December 1911, Campbell Papers, SHC.

12. Campbell Papers, SHC.

13. J. C. Campbell, *Southern Highlander*.

14. Olive Dame Campbell Memorial Issue, *Mountain Life and Work*, 17–20.

GERTRUDE WEIL

1. For information on Gertrude Weil, see her extensive papers in the NCDAH; M. Rountree, *Strangers in the Land*, a family history; and Wilkerson-Freeman, "Emerging Political Consciousness." "The Legacy of Gertrude Weil" was the subject of a 1984 symposium organized by Jane De Hart Mathews and presented by the Women's Studies Program at the University of North Carolina in Chapel Hill. Papers were presented by Anne Firor Scott, Donald G. Mathews, Marion Roydhouse, Elsa Brown, and Rabbi Martin Beifield.

2. M. Rountree, *Strangers in the Land*, 136.

3. Wilkerson-Freeman, "Emerging Political Consciousness," 28–32.

4. M. Rountree, *Strangers in the Land*, 133.

5. Gilmore, *Gender and Jim Crow*, 205, 208–10.

6. Roydhouse, " 'Our Responsibilities,' " 12–13, 17.

7. M. Rountree, *Strangers in the Land*, 129.

8. Bluethenthal, interview.

9. In a conversation with Emily Herring Wilson, November 1997, Scott described visiting Weil in the last years of her life.

ELLA MAY WIGGINS

1. The best work on Wiggins is Haessley, " 'Mill Mother's Lament,' " on which this biography is based. Unless otherwise noted, Haessley's paper is the source of quotations. "Ella May" and "Ella May Wiggins" are variant names appearing in various publications about her.

2. A brief but useful study of Wiggins, particularly her involvement with the union, is included in Hall et al., *Like a Family*.

3. Larkin, "Ella May's Songs," *Nation*, 382.

4. Ibid.

5. Salmond's *Gastonia 1929* is a detailed history of the violence that plagued union activities; it includes the trials of the union leaders sentenced in the death of Gastonia's police chief and the acquittal of Wiggins's accused killers.

6. Lewis, "Ella May: A Triumph of North Carolina's Industrialism," in "Incidentally," *Raleigh News and Observer*, September 29, 1929. Battle later recanted her support for Wiggins and the union activities in Gastonia, claiming that she had been deluded by communist propaganda. The change in her attitude became obvious in the 1940s, when Lewis wrote about suspected Communist Party activities in Chapel Hill.

7. Graham's letter appeared in Lewis, "Incidentally," *Raleigh News and Observer*, September 29, 1929; "Ella May Wiggins Doesn't Count," *Raleigh News and Observer*, October 25, 1929.

8. Hall et al., *Like a Family*, 226.

MARY MARTIN SLOOP

1. With the help of journalist Legette Blythe, Sloop wrote *Miracle in the Hills* (1953). Readable, interesting, and personal, it is an introduction to Sloop as she wanted to be remembered. We also listened to Sloop's voice on cassette tapes transferred from the original interviews Blythe made on a wire recorder. In addition, individuals have greatly helped in our understanding of Crossnore School, especially Sloop's daughter, Dr. Emma Fink; Sloop's assistant, Bonnie Rash; Dr. Richard Zuber, a professor of history at Wake Forest University, who spent all twelve years at Crossnore School; and Dr. Elizabeth Phillips, emerita professor of English at Wake Forest and a native of Spruce Pine. We are also indebted to Joseph H. Mitchell, director, and students who made us copies of materials about Crossnore School, past and present.

2. Information on the early years of the college is from Shaw, *Davidson College*.

3. Ibid., 131–32.

4. Sloop, *Miracle in the Hills*, 13–14.

5. Ibid., 17–19.

6. Sloop, *Miracle in the Hills*, 26–27.

7. Ibid., 30–32.

8. Ibid., 36–37.

9. Yarbrough, "Interesting Carolina People."

10. *Crossnore School Bulletin*, April–June 1937, July–September 1934.

11. Rash, interview.

12. Fink, interview.

13. Sloop, *Miracle in the Hills*, 185.

14. The scene of Sloop speaking to students in the dining hall of Crossnore School was recalled by Richard Zuber (interview), professor of history, Wake Forest University.

CHAPTER 9. TURNING POINT OR TEMPORARY GAIN

1. E. Roosevelt, "We Have to Remember"; Gilbert, *Second World War*, 1; Jarrell, "Losses," 145–46.

2. Chafe, *American Woman*, 183; Hartmann, *The Home Front and Beyond*, 16; Rupp, *Mobilizing Women for War*, 176–81; K. Anderson, *Wartime Women*.

3. Lemmon, *North Carolina's Role in World War II*, 12.

4. Cecelski ("The Home Front's Dispossessed") describes what happened to a community of several hundred black people who were evicted from their homes near Havelock, N.C., to make way for the building of Cherry Point Marine Corps Air Station.

5. Baker, *Mrs. G.I. Joe*, 1.

6. E. H. Wilson, *Memories of New Bern*, 132–33.

7. Baker, *Mrs. G.I. Joe*, 242–47.

8. Williford, "Homefront Activities," 7.

9. "The Negro Woman Serves America," 159.

10. Lingeman, *Don't You Know There's a War On?* 36.

11. D'Ann Campbell, *Women at War with America*, 181.

12. E. H. Wilson, *Memories of New Bern*, 135.

13. Dial, *The Lumbee*, 90–93.

14. Larson, telephone interview.

15. Isabel Eggers Zuber, interview.

16. Gulick, *Cherokees at the Crossroads*.

17. E. H. Wilson, *Memories of New Bern*, 138.

18. Hewitt, "Beyond Rosie the Riveter," n. 9.

19. *Employment Service Review* 12, no. 10 (October 1945): 242–43.

20. Lingeman, *Don't You Know There's a War On?* 70.

21. Blood, "Negro Women War Workers," 176.

22. Theresa and Irwin Bland, interview.

23. Litoff and Smith, *American Women*, 167.

24. Lemmon, *North Carolina's Role in World War II*, 23–24.

25. Korstad, "Those Who Were Not Afraid."

26. "Tar Heel Women Training to Build Warplanes," *Raleigh News and Observer*, April 1, 1942.

27. From the transcript of a panel discussion at a symposium on World War II in Raleigh, September 23, 1995, sponsored by the North Carolina Division of Archives and History, North Carolina Literary and Historical Society, and Federation of North Carolina Historical Societies. The panel was introduced by Nancy A. Hewitt, professor of history at Duke University. Panel members were Kathryn Page Cloud, Dixie King Kennedy, and Mrs. Walton W. Smith.

28. S. M. Evans, *Born for Liberty*, 223.

29. Sawyer, "The Negro Woman in National Defense," 24–34.

30. Belton, "Westray Battle Boyce," 17.

31. Weatherford, *American Women and World War II*, 33.

32. "Salem in Service," 4.

33. "Women at War," *Winston-Salem Journal*, February 24, 1991.

34. "In a Support Position," *Greensboro News and Record*, March 17, 1990. See also "Mary Webb Nicholson," in Jordan, *Women of Guilford County*, 138–39.

35. Belton, "Westray Battle Boyce," 17–21. Westray Battle Boyce Long was married three times: in 1924 to James Stacy Boyce, from whom she was divorced in 1941; in 1948 to William Leslie, who died in 1962; and in 1964 to Willie Jones Long.

36. Ibid.

37. "Unsung Heroes," *Winston-Salem Journal*, February 27, 1994.

38. Weatherford, *American Women and World War II*, 54, 66; Holcomb (Crisanti), *Women Marines Make History*.

39. Litoff and Smith, *We're in This War, Too*, 43.

40. Lemmon, *North Carolina's Role in World War II*; Pyle, *Here Is Your War*, 82.

41. *Raleigh News and Observer*, June 2, 1997.

42. Weatherford, *American Women and World War II*, 306; Lingeman, *Don't You Know There's a War On?* 158–59.

43. K. Anderson, *Wartime Women*, 174–78.

44. Williford, "Homefront Activities," 44.

45. Flynn, "Women in the War," 12.

46. D'Ann Campbell, *Women at War with America*, 44.

47. Anderton, interview.

48. Chafe, *American Woman*, vii, 135–36, and *The Paradox of Change*, 233; Evans, *Born for Liberty*, 219, 229, 241; Rupp, *Mobilizing Women for War*, 163–64; D'Ann Campbell, *Women at War with America*; Hewitt, "Beyond Rosie the Riveter," 2.

49. Williford, "Homefront Activities," 29–30.

MINNIE EVANS

1. Studies of Minnie Evans include two publications prepared in conjunction with retrospective exhibitions of her work: Kahan's *Heavenly Visions*, published by the North Carolina Museum of Art (1986), and Lovell and Hester's *Minnie Evans: Artist*, edited for a 1993 exhibition organized by the Gray Gallery of East Carolina University. Each publication includes a bibliography, and each acknowledges its indebtedness to Nina Howell Starr, who first introduced Evans to a larger art world. Starr's interviews with Evans are the basis for her published articles and have been cited often by others. See N. H. Starr, "Minnie Evans: Innocent Surrealist" and "The Lost World of Minnie Evans."

2. This interview was conducted by Emily Herring Wilson as part of a project to collect oral histories of southern black women funded by the National Endowment for the Humanities. Minnie Evans was one of Wilson's subjects in *Hope and Dignity*. "Mrs. Starr," alluded to in Evans's interview, is Nina Howell Starr, who brought Evans to the attention of the art world in 1966. Unless otherwise noted, the quotations in this biography are from the Wilson interview.

3. B. D. Anderson, "Biography of Minnie Evans," 69.

4. Michele Wallace, a black woman writing in *Majority Report* (July 1975), objected to an exhibit of Evans's work at the Whitney Museum of American Art as playing to a stereotype of uneducated blacks. Kahan (*Heavenly Visions*, 30–37) analyzes Evans's use of white and her images of white faces as perhaps having associations apart from daily experiences.

5. Ashe, *Camelot*, 182–93 (quotation, 183).

6. Kahan, *Heavenly Visions*, 15–16.

7. E. H. Wilson, *Hope and Dignity*, 25.

8. Bearden and Henderson, *African-American Artists*, 346.

9. E. H. Wilson, *Hope and Dignity*, 28.

10. Lovell and Hester, *Minnie Evans*, 22.

ELIZABETH LAWRENCE

1. Lawrence introduced some of her favorite books by Gertrude Jekyll in *The Gardener's Essential Gertrude Jekyll*. Among the many books she often referred to are E. A. Bowles's *My Garden in Summer* and *My Garden in Autumn and Winter*; and Graffin von Arnim's *Elizabeth and Her German Garden*.

2. In addition to *Southern Garden*, Lawrence published *Little Bulbs* (1957) and *Gardens in Winter* (1961). She also wrote a small booklet about Carl Krippendorf's garden near Cincinnati, Ohio, entitled *Lob's Wood* (1971). Books appearing after her death include *Gardening for Love* (1987), ed. Allen Lacy; *Through the Garden Gate* (1990), ed. Bill Neal; *A Rock Garden in the South* (1990), ed. Nancy Goodwin with Allen Lacy; and *A Garden of One's Own* (1997), ed. Barbara Scott and Bobby J. Ward.

3. Lawrence, *Southern Garden*, 142.

4. Lawrence, *Through the Garden Gate*, 23.

5. Lawrence's niece, Elizabeth Way Rogers, and two Charlotte friends, Hannah Withers, who met Lawrence when she moved to Charlotte in 1948, and writer Dannye Romine Powell, a friend in Lawrence's later life, have shared some of their remembrances with Emily Herring Wilson.

6. For a copy of Lawrence's diary, we are indebted to Caroline Long Tillett, who knew her in Charlotte. As an adult Lawrence gave her childhood diary to Caroline's brother, William, who lived at the family home, Longview plantation in Northampton County, which Lawrence loved to visit.

7. Lawrence, *A Garden of One's Own*, 4.

8. Hannah Withers, interview, Charlotte, June 9, 1995.

9. Lawrence, *A Garden of One's Own*, 3.

10. Lawrence, *Southern Garden*, xi.

11. Ibid., xxv.

12. Ibid., 5.

13. K. S. White, *Onward and Upward in the Garden*, 325.

14. Lawrence, *Little Bulbs*, 1–3.

15. Lawrence, *A Rock Garden in the South*, 11.

16. Lawrence, *Gardening for Love*, 96–99.

17. Lawrence, *Through the Garden Gate*, 1.

PAULI MURRAY

1. The principal sources for this biography are Murray's own books, *Proud Shoes* and *Song in a Weary Throat*. Also useful is a 1975 interview with Murray, SHC. In 1979 Murray was interviewed by Emily Herring Wilson for *Hope and Dignity*; many personal impressions of Murray that inform this biography are based on that interview. Thurgood Marshall is quoted in *Song in a Weary Throat*, 289.

2. Murray, *Song in a Weary Throat*, 18.

3. Murray, interview by Genna Rae McNeil, February 13, 1976, p. 106, SHC, and *Song in a Weary Throat*, 369.

4. Murray, *Proud Shoes*, viii.

5. Murray, *Song in a Weary Throat*, 31.

6. Patricia Spacks, as quoted in Carolyn Heilbrun, *Writing a Woman's Life*, 23.

7. Murray, *Song in a Weary Throat*, 1, 12–13.

8. Murray, *Proud Shoes*, 269–70. "Stories told by oldtimers"

were heard by Emily Herring Wilson in visits to Durham in the fall and spring of 1979–80.

9. Murray, *Song in a Weary Throat*, 105.

10. Ibid.

11. For a detailed discussion of Murray's role regarding the ERA and the President's Commission on the Status of Women, see in Harrison, *On Account of Sex*, 126–30, 133–34.

12. Murray, *Song in a Weary Throat*, 368.

13. Ibid., 370, 435.

14. Ibid., 435.

15. Ibid., xi.

GLADYS AVERY TILLETT

1. Gladys Tillett, interview by Jacquelyn Hall, March 20, 1974, SHC. Unless otherwise noted, quotations attributed to Tillett are from the Hall interview.

2. Sara Tillett Thomas, telephone interview. The authors are especially indebted to Thomas for sharing materials, memories, and insights about her mother that inform this biography.

3. Gladys Tillett Papers, SHC.

4. Gladys Tillett to Charles Tillett, June 30, 1936, ibid.

5. For the work of Gladys and Charles Tillett in the Graham campaign, see Frank Porter Graham Materials, Gladys Tillett Papers, SHC.

6. For a history of the Graham senatorial race, see Pleasants and Burns, *Frank Porter Graham*, esp. 121–22.

7. Eleanor Roosevelt to Gladys Tillett, January 4, 1953, and Tillett to Roosevelt, January 29, 1953, Frank Porter Graham Materials, Gladys Tillett Papers, SHC.

8. United Nations, ibid.

9. Beth McAllister, telephone interview.

10. Gladys Tillett Papers, SHC.

11. *Charlotte Observer*, September 23, 1984. State representative Louise Brennan (D-Mecklenburg), a friend of twenty-five years, described Tillett as a "role model."

EPILOGUE

1. Discussion of the civil rights movement in Greensboro is based on Chafe, *Civilities and Civil Rights*.

2. Cantarow and O'Malley, "Ella Baker," as cited in Cantarow, *Moving the Mountain*, 84, 53.

3. Ruley, "Picking the Blues," 10–13.

4. Governor's Commission on the Status of Women, *The Many Lives of North Carolina Women*.

5. S. M. Evans, *Born for Liberty*, 275.

6. Ibid., 276.

7. Discussion of the ERA in North Carolina is based on Mathews and De Hart, *Sex, Gender, and the Politics of ERA*.

8. *Winston-Salem Journal*, September 9, 1995.

9. *What Is a Woman Worth?*, p. 5.

Bibliography

Manuscript and Archival Material

NORTH CAROLINA

Alamance County

Alamance Battleground State Historic Site
  Allen Family Files

Asheville

Pack Memorial Library
  Thomas Wolfe Collection

Chapel Hill

North Carolina Collection, University of North Carolina
  Sallie Southall Cotten Collection
  Journal of Mrs. R. R. Cotten (Chicago)
  Thomas Wolfe Collection

Southern Historical Collection, University of North Carolina
  Mary Jeffreys Bethell Diary
  John H. Bryan Papers
  Frances Bumpass Journal
  Cameron Family Papers
  John C. and Olive Dame Campbell Papers
  Cotten Family Papers
  Sallie Southall Cotten Papers
  Moses Ashley Curtis Papers
  DeRosset Family Papers
  Eccles Family Papers
  Edgeworth Female Seminary, Scrapbook 1176
  Hayes Collection
  Ernest Haywood Collection
  M. S. Henderson Diary, Henderson Papers
  Hicks-Parmelee-Williams Family Papers
  John DeBerniere Hooper Papers
  Chiliab Smith Howe Papers
  Susan Davis Nye Hutchison Diary
  Kimberly Papers
  Drury Lacy Collection
  Lenoir Family Papers
  Jane Simpson McKimmon Papers
  Meares-DeRosset Papers
  Mordecai Family Papers
  Pauli Murray Oral History
  Patterson Family Papers
  Alice Morgan Person Autobiography, 1840–1913
  Pettigrew Papers
  Polk, Badger, and McGehee Family Papers
  Polk and Yeatman Family Papers
  John Steele Papers
  Marcus Cicero Stephens Papers
  Gladys Tillett Oral History and Papers

Durham

Duke University
  Campbell Collection
  Samuel Smith Downey Papers
  James Iredell and James Iredell Jr. Papers
  Alexander McAllister Papers
  North Creek Primitive Baptist Church (Beaufort County) Records
  William Slade Papers
  John Buxton Williams Papers

Hillsborough

Burwell Female School
  Styron Collection

Raleigh

North Carolina Division of Archives and History
  Allen Family Papers
  John Gray Blount Papers
  James Boon Papers
  Charlotte Hawkins Brown Papers
  John H. Bryan Papers
  Henry K. Burgwyn Diary
  Clarke-Devereux Letters
  Devereux Family Papers
  William Dickson Papers
  Mary A. Gash and Gash Family Papers
  Governors' Papers
  J. Bryan Grimes Papers
  Samuel Johnston Papers
  M. Lewis Recipe Book
  Alonzo Mial Papers
  James Norcum Papers
  Richmond Manufacturing Co. Account Books
  John Wright Stanly Estate Papers, 1789, Craven County Records
  Treasurers' and Comptrollers' Papers, Executive Office
  Zebulon B. Vance Papers
  Gertrude Weil Papers
  Calvin H. Wiley Papers

North Carolina Museum of History
  Edward Flowers, comp., Employment and Population Statistics, Women's History Exhibit
  Women's History Files

North Carolina State University Archives
  Jane Simpson McKimmon Papers

Winston-Salem

Archives of the Moravian Church in America, Southern Province
  Boner Files

Jessop Family Papers, Private Collection

Museum of Early Southern Decorative Arts Archives

Reynolda House Museum of American Art
  Reynolds Family Papers

Z. Smith Reynolds Library, Wake Forest University
  Baptist Collection
  Sophie Stevens Lanneau Papers

OHIO

Oberlin

Oberlin College Archives

Alfred Vance Churchill Papers

Churchill, "The Midwestern," manuscript, n.d.

Anna Haywood Cooper Papers

PENNSYLVANIA

Philadelphia

Free Library of Philadelphia

H. L. Carson Papers

Government Publications

"Births by Type of Attendance." *Vital Statistics of the United States (1937), Part II: Natality and Mortality Data for the United States Tabulated by Place of Residence*. Washington, D.C.: GPO, 1939.

"Live Births by Attendant and Place of Delivery, etc." Local Area Statistics. *Vital Statistics of the United States (1981), Vol. 1: Natality*. Hyattsville, Md.: U.S. Department of Health and Human Services.

North Carolina Department of Health and Human Services, Division of Epidemiology, State Center for Health Statistics. *North Carolina Vital Statistics, Vol. 1: 1996*. Raleigh.

North Carolina State Board of Health, Epidemiology Division. *Annual Report of Public Health Statistics Section: Part 2, 1964*. Raleigh.

U.S. Bureau of the Census. *Historical Statistics of the United States, Colonial Times to 1970: Part 1*. Washington, D.C.: GPO, 1975.

U.S. Census Office. *Sixth Census of the United States, 1840*. Washington, D.C.: GPO, 1841.

—. *Seventh Census of the United States, 1850*. Washington, D.C.: GPO, 1853.

—. *Eighth Census of the United States, 1860*. Washington, D.C.: GPO, 1866.

U.S. Federal Census. *Mortality Statistics of the Seventh Census of the United States, 1850*. Edited by J. D. B. DeBow. Washington, D.C.: GPO, 1855.

Newspapers

Carolina Federal Republican (New Bern)

The Carolinian (New Bern)

Catawba Journal

Charlotte Bulletin

Charlotte Observer

Daily Conservative (Raleigh)

Edenton Gazette

Fayetteville Observer

Greensboro News and Record

Greensborough Patriot

Hall's Wilmington Gazette

Lynchburg Echo

Massachusetts Gazette

North Carolina Gazette

North Carolina Magazine

North Carolina Presbyterian

North Carolina Standard (Raleigh)

Raleigh News and Observer

Raleigh Register

Raleigh Star

Salisbury Daily Carolina Watchman

South Carolina and American General Gazette (Charleston)

Southern Weekly Post

Sun Journal (New Bern)

Tarborough Free Press

Western Carolinian

Wilmington Centinel and General Advertiser

Wilmington Gazette

Winston-Salem Journal

Interviews

Laura Anderton, interview by Emily Herring Wilson, Greensboro, April 3, 1996

Theresa and Irwin Bland, interview by Emily Herring Wilson, Goldsboro, February 8, 1980

Joan Bluethenthal, interview by Emily Herring Wilson, Greensboro, 1992

Reedie Lowry Chavis, interview by Emily Herring Wilson, Pembroke, December 14, 1993

Adolph L. Dial, interview by Emily Herring Wilson, Pembroke, December 13, 1993

Emma Sloop Fink, interview by Emily Herring Wilson, Crossnore, July 15, 1995

Bessie Sampson Larson, telephone interview by Emily Herring Wilson, Albuquerque, New Mexico, December 7, 1996

Beth McAllister, telephone interview by Emily Herring Wilson, Raleigh, August 15, 1995

Catherine McNeill, interview by Karen L. Cox for the Museum of the Cape Fear, January 13, 1989

Alice Patterson, telephone interview by Emily Herring Wilson, Chapel Hill, April 1, 1996

Bonnie Rash, interview by Emily Herring Wilson, Crossnore, July 15, 1995

Mattie Sparks Shaw, interview by Karen L. Cox for the Museum of the Cape Fear, Fayetteville, January 4, 1989

Sara Tillett Thomas, telephone interview by Emily Herring Wilson, Vienna, Virginia, August 22, 1996

Constance Merrick Watts, telephone interview by Emily Herring Wilson, Durham, January 18, 1990

Hannah Withers, interview by Emily Herring Wilson, Charlotte, March 1, 1998

Isabel Eggers Zuber, interview by Emily Herring Wilson, Winston-Salem, October 15, 1997

Richard Zuber, interview by Emily Herring Wilson, Winston-Salem, Fall 1994

Books, Articles, and Unpublished Sources

Adair, James. *The History of the American Indians*. 1775. Reprint, New York: Johnson Reprint Corp., 1968.

Adams, Robert G. *Nancy Ward: Beautiful Woman of Two Worlds*. Chattanooga, Tenn.: Hampton House Studios, 1979.

Alderman, Pat. *Nancy Ward: Cherokee Chieftainess*. Johnson City, Tenn.: Overmountain Press, 1978.

Alexander, Roberta Sue. *North Carolina Faces the Freedmen: Race Relations during Presidential Reconstruction, 1865–67*. Durham: Duke University Press, 1985.

Allen, Catherine B. *A Century to Celebrate: History of the Women's Missionary Union*. Birmingham, Ala.: Women's Missionary Union, 1987.

Allen, W. C. *History of Halifax County*. Boston, 1919.

Anders, Mary Edna. "The Development of Public Library Service in the Southeastern States, 1895–1950." D.L.S. thesis, Columbia University, 1958.

Anderson, Brooke D. "Biography of Minnie Evans." In Lovell and Hester, *Minnie Evans: Artist*.

Anderson, James. *The Education of Blacks in the South, 1860–1935*. Chapel Hill: University of North Carolina Press, 1988.

Anderson, Jean Bradley. *Piedmont Plantation: The Bennehan-Cameron Family and Lands in North Carolina*. Durham: Historic Preservation Society of Durham, 1985.

Anderson, Mrs. John Huske (Lucy London). *North Carolina Women of the Confederacy*. Fayetteville: N.p., 1926.

Anderson, Karen. *Wartime Women: Sex Roles, Family Relations, and the Status of Women during World War II*. Westport, Conn.: Greenwood Press, 1981.

Andrews, Evangeline Walker, ed. [Schaw, Janet.] *Journal of a Lady of Quality*. New Haven: Yale University Press, 1921.

Andrews, William L. *To Tell a Free Story: The First Century of Afro-American Autobiography, 1760–1865*. Urbana: University of Illinois Press, 1986.

Angle, Linda L. "Women in the North Carolina Courts, 1670–1739." M.A. thesis, University of North Carolina at Chapel Hill, 1975.

Angley, Wilson. "Thomas Wolfe and the Old Kentucky Home." Research Branch Report, North Carolina Division of Archives and History, Raleigh, 1975.

Anonymous. *Aunt Sally, or the Cross the Way of Freedom*. Cincinnati: American Reform Tract and Book Society, 1858. Reprint, Miami, Fla.: Mnemosyne, 1969.

Arthur, John P. *A History of Watauga County*. 1915. Reprint, Easley, S.C.: Southern Historic Press, 1976.

Ashe, Geoffrey. *Camelot and the Vision of Albion*. New York: St. Martin's Press, 1971.

Bacon, Margaret Hope. *Mothers of Feminism: The Story of Quaker Women in America*. San Francisco: Harper and Row, 1986.

Bakeless, John Edwin. *Daniel Boone: Master of the Wilderness*. New York: Morrow, 1939.

Baker, Blanche Egerton. *Mrs. G.I. Joe*. Raleigh: Graphic Press, 1951.

Barden, Mary Moulton. " 'Tenella': Mary Bayard Clarke, 1827–1886." Manuscript, January 29, 1990, courtesy of the author.

Bardolph, Richard. "Inconstant Rebels: Desertion of North Carolina Troops in the Civil War." *North Carolina Historical Review* 41 (1962): 163–89.

Barlowe, Arthur. "Narrative of the 1584 Voyage." In Quinn and Quinn, *The First Colonists*, 1–12.

Barringer, Bugs, Dot Barringer, and Lela Chesson. *Rocky Mount: A Pictorial History*. Norfolk: Donning Co., 1977.

Barton, Garry Lewis. *The Life and Times of Henry Berry Lowry*. Pembroke, N.C.: Lumbee Publishing Co., 1979.

Bartram, William. *Travels of William Bartram*. Edited by Mark Van Doren. 1791. Reprint, New York: Dover Publications, 1955.

Bassett, John Spencer. *Anti-Slavery Leaders of North Carolina*. Baltimore, Md.: Johns Hopkins Press, 1898.

Batson, Barbara C. "Daniel Welfare, 1796–1841: American Artist." M.A. thesis, University of Virginia, 1985.

Battle, Herbert Bemerton, Lois Yelverton, and William James Battle. *The Battle Book: A Genealogy of the Battle Family in America*. Montgomery, Ala.: Paragon Press, 1930.

Baxandall, Rosalyn, Linda Gordon, and Susan Reverby. *America's Working Women*. New York: Random Books, 1976.

Beach, S. A., N. O. Booth, and O. M. Taylor. *The Apples of New York*. Vol. 1. Albany: J. B. Lyon, 1905.

Bearden, Romare, and Harry Henderson. *A History of African-American Artists, from 1792 to the Present*. New York: Pantheon, 1993.

Beattie, Bess. "The Edwin Holt Family: Nineteenth-Century Capitalists in North Carolina." *North Carolina Historical Review* 63 (October 1986): 511–35.

Beecher, Catharine. In *Godey's Lady's Magazine*, January 1853, 176.

Belton, Tom. "Legendary Women." *Tar Heel Junior Historian* 33 (Fall 1992): 13–17.

—. "Westray Battle Boyce: The Story of a WAC." *Tar Heel Junior Historian* 26 (Spring 1986).

Benberry, Cuesta. *Always There: The African-American Presence in American Quilts*. Louisville: Kentucky Quilt Project, 1992.

Berkeley, Kathleen C. " 'Colored Ladies Also Contributed': Black Women's Activities from Benevolence to Social Welfare, 1866–1896." In *The Web of Southern Social Relations: Women, Family, and Education*, edited by Walter J. Fraser Jr., R. Frank Saunders Jr., and Jon L. Wakelyn, 181–203. Athens: University of Georgia Press, 1985.

Biggleston, William E. *They Stopped in Oberlin: Black Residents and Visitors of the Nineteenth Century*. Scottsdale, Ariz.: Innovation Group, Inc., 1981.

Bishir, Catherine W. "Landmarks of Power: Building a Southern Past, 1885–1915." *Southern Cultures* 1 (1993): 5–44.

—. *North Carolina Architecture*. Chapel Hill: University of North Carolina Press, 1990.

Bishir, Catherine W., Charlotte V. Brown, Carl R. Lounsbury, and Ernest H. Wood III. *Architects and Builders in North Carolina: A History of the Practice of Building*. Chapel Hill: University of North Carolina Press, 1990.

Bivins, Emma Carr. *Smiling through Seventy Years: A History of Dental Public Health in North Carolina*. Raleigh: Dental Public Health, 1988.

Bjorkman, Gwen Boyer. "Hannah (Baskel) Phelps Hill: A Quaker Woman and Her Offspring." *National Genealogical Society Quarterly* 75 (December 1987): 289–302.

Blair, Karen J. *The Clubwoman as Feminist: True Womanhood Redefined, 1868–1914*. New York: Holmes and Meier, 1980.

Blassingame, John W. *The Slave Community: Plantation Life in the Antebellum South*. New York: Oxford University Press, 1972.

Bledstein, Burton J. *The Culture of Professionalism: The Middle Class and the Development of Higher Education in America*. New York: Norton, 1976.

Blood, Kathryn. "Negro Women War Workers." In Litoff and Smith, *American Women in a World at War*, 175–89.

Blu, Karen I. *The Lumbee Problem: The Making of an American Indian People*. Cambridge: Cambridge University Press, 1980.

Blumin, Stuart M. "The Hypothesis of Middle-Class Formation in Nineteenth-Century America: A Critique and Some Proposals." *American Historical Review* 90 (April 1985): 313–38.

Bonner, Lynn. "Domestic Blacks." *Winston-Salem Journal*, March 3, 1996.

Bonvillain, Nancy. *Women and Men: Cultural Constructs of Gender*. Englewood Cliffs, N.J.: Prentice-Hall, 1995.

Bordin, Ruth. *Women and Temperance: The Quest for Power and Liberty, 1873–1900*. Philadelphia: Temple University Press, 1981.

Boris, Eileen. "Crafts Shop or Sweatshop? The Uses and Abuses of Craftsmanship in Twentieth-Century America." *Journal of Design History* 2 (1989): 175–92.

Boyd, William K., ed. *William Byrd's Histories of the Dividing Line betwixt Virginia and North Carolina*. 1929. Reprint, New York: Dover Publications, 1967.

Boylan, Anne N. "Evangelical Womanhood in the Nineteenth Century: The Role of Women in Sunday Schools." *Feminist Studies* 4 (1978): 62–80.

Braxton, Joanne M. *Black Women Writing Autobiography: A Tradition within a Tradition*. Philadelphia: Temple University Press, 1989.

Breen, William J. "Black Women and the Great War: Mobilization and Reform in the South." *Journal of Southern History* 44 (August 1978): 421–40.

—. "Southern Women in the War: The North Carolina Women's Committee, 1917–1919." *North Carolina Historical Review* 55 (July 1978): 251–81.

Brickell, John. *The Natural History of North Carolina*. 1737. Reprint, Murfreesboro, N.C.: Johnson Publishing Co., 1968.

"A Brief Sketch of the Life of Mrs. M. A. Burwell." *Voices of Peace* 1 (December 1889): 1–8.

Brinn, Susan H. "Blacks in Colonial North Carolina, 1660–1723." M.A. thesis, University of North Carolina at Chapel Hill, 1978.

Brown, Charlotte Hawkins. *The Correct Thing to Do, to Say, to Wear*. Boston: Christopher Publishing House, 1941.

Brown, D. Clayton. *Electricity for Rural America: The Fight for the* REA. Westport, Conn.: Greenwood Press, 1980.

Brown, Hugh Victor. *A History of the Education of Negroes in North Carolina*. Raleigh: Irving Swain Press, 1961.

Brownlee, Fambrough L. *Winston-Salem: A Pictorial History*. Norfolk: Donning Co., 1977.

Bundy, Emily B. "From State Normal School for Women to Coeducational University: The Evolution of Curriculum at the University of North Carolina at Greensboro." M.A.L.S. thesis, Wake Forest University, 1991.

Burkitt, Lemuel, et al. *A Concise History of the Kehukee Baptist Association, from its Original Rise to the Present Time*. Tarborough: George Howard, 1834.

Butler, Mrs. F. A., ed. *Frances Webb Bumpass: Autobiography and Journal*. Nashville, Tenn.: Methodist Episcopal Church, South, 1899.

Butler, Lindley Smith. "Life in Albemarle County, Carolina, 1663–1689." M.A. thesis, University of North Carolina at Chapel Hill, 1964.

—. *North Carolina Genesis: Seventeenth-Century Albemarle County*. Edited by Raymond A. Winslow Jr. Hertford, N.C.: Perquimans County Restoration Association, 1989.

Butler, Lindley Smith, and Alan D. Watson, eds. *The North Carolina Experience*. Chapel Hill: University of North Carolina Press, 1984.

Byerly, Victoria. *Hard Times Cotton Mill Girls: Personal Histories of Womanhood and Poverty in the South*. Ithaca: ILR Press, New York State School of Industrial and Labor Relations, Cornell University, 1986.

Bynum, Victoria E. *Unruly Women: The Politics of Social and Sexual Control in the Old South*. Chapel Hill: University of North Carolina Press, 1992.

Campbell, D'Ann. *Women at War with America: Private Lives in a Patriotic Era*. Cambridge: Harvard University Press, 1984.

Campbell, Edward D. C., Jr., and Kym S. Rice. *Before Freedom Came: African American Life in the Antebellum South*. Richmond: Museum of the Confederacy and Charlottesville: University Press of Virginia, 1991.

—. *A Woman's War: Southern Women, Civil War, and the Confederate Legacy*. Richmond: Museum of the Confederacy and Charlottesville: University Press of Virginia, 1996.

Campbell, John C. *The Southern Highlander and His Homeland*. New York: Russell Sage Foundation, 1921.

Campbell, Mildred. "Social Origins of Some Early Americans." In *Seventeenth-Century America: Essays in Colonial History*, edited by James Morton Smith, 63–89. Published for the Institute of Early American History and Culture at Williamsburg, Va., by the University of North Carolina Press, Chapel Hill, 1959.

Cantarow, Ellen. *Moving the Mountain: Women Working for Social Change*. Old Westbury, N.Y.: Feminist Press, 1980.

Capps, Gene. "Demographic Studies of Moravian Women." Paper, Old Salem, Inc., Winston-Salem, 1989.
—. "References to Women at Work in Salem, 1774–1833." Paper, Old Salem, Inc., Winston-Salem, 1989.
Carby, Hazel V. *Reconstructing Womanhood: The Emergence of the Afro-American Woman Novelist*. New York: Oxford University Press, 1987.
Carmichael, James V., Jr. "Atlanta's Female Librarians, 1883–1915." *Journal of Library History* 21 (Spring 1986): 377–99.
—. "Women and North Carolina Libraries: Promoting the Library Idea." *Tar Heel Junior Historian* 33 (Spring 1994): 28–31.
Carr, Lois Green, and Russell R. Menard. "Immigration and Opportunity: The Freedman in Early Colonial Maryland." In Tate and Ammerman, *The Chesapeake in the Seventeenth Century*, 206–42.
Carr, Lois Green, and Lorena S. Walsh. "The Planter's Wife: The Experience of White Women in Seventeenth-Century Maryland," *William and Mary Quarterly* 34 (October 1977): 542–71.
Carroll, Karen Cobb. *Windows to the Past: Primitive Watercolors from Guilford County, North Carolina, in the 1820s*. Greensboro: Greensboro Historical Museum, 1984.
Carson, Cary, Norman F. Barka, William M. Kelso, Garry Wheeler Stone, and Dell Upton. "Impermanent Architecture in the Southern American Colonies." *Winterthur Portfolio* 16 (Summer–Autumn 1981): 135–96.
Carter, Carolyn Howard. "Sophie Stevens Lanneau: Southern Baptist Missionary to Soochow China, 1907–1950." M.A. thesis, Wake Forest University, 1974.
Catesby, Mark. *The Natural History of Carolina, Florida, and the Bahama Islands*. London: Printed at the expense of the author, 1731–43.
Cecelski, David. "The Home Front's Dispossessed." *Southern Exposure* 23 (Summer 1995): 37–41.
Censer, Jane Turner. *North Carolina Planters and Their Children, 1800–1860*. Baton Rouge: Louisiana State University Press, 1984.
Chafe, William. *The American Woman: Her Changing Social, Economic, and Political Roles, 1920–1970*. New York: Oxford University Press, 1972.
—. *Civilities and Civil Rights: Greensboro, North Carolina, and the Black Struggle for Freedom*. New York: Oxford University Press, 1980.
—. *The Paradox of Change: American Women in the Twentieth Century*. New York: Oxford University Press, 1991.
Claassen, Cheryl P. "Gender, Shellfishing, and the Shell Mound Archaic." In Gero and Conkey, *Engendering Archaeology, Women, and Prehistory*, 276–300.
Claggett, Stephen R. "The First Colonists: 12,000 Years before Roanoke." *The Ligature: North Carolina Archaeology*, 1985.
Clark, Walter, ed. *The State Records of North Carolina*. 16 vols. numbered 11–26. Winston and Goldsboro: State of North Carolina, 1895–1906.
Clarke, Mary Bayard. *Wood Notes, or Carolina Carols*. 1854.
Clayton, Thomas H. *Close to the Land: The Way We Lived in North Carolina, 1820–1870*. Series edited by Sydney Nathans. Chapel Hill: University of North Carolina Press, 1983.
Clinton, Catherine. "Equally Their Due: The Education of the Planter Daughter in the Early Republic." *Journal of the Early Republic* 2 (April 1982): 39–60.
—. *The Plantation Mistress: Woman's World in the Old South*. New York: Pantheon, 1982.
Coe, Joffre L. *The Formative Culture of the Carolina Piedmont*. Transactions of the American Philosophical Society, n.s.v. 54, pt. 5, 1964. Reprint, 1980.
Coffin, Addison. *The Guilford Collegian* 3 (1890–91): 174–76.
Collins, P. "The Meaning of Motherhood in Black Culture." In *Double Stitch: Black Women Write about Mothers and Daughters*, edited by Patricia Bell-Scott et al., 42–60. New York: Harper Perennial, 1991.
Coon, Charles L. *North Carolina Schools and Academies, 1790–1840: A Documentary History*. Raleigh: Edwards and Broughton, 1915.
Cooper, Anna Julia. *A Voice From the South*. 1892. Reprint, with an introduction by Mary Helen Washington. The Schomburg Library of Nineteenth-Century Black Women Writers. New York: Oxford University Press, 1988.
Cooper, Jean Batten. "An Oral History of Meredith Alumnae." M.A.L.S. thesis, Wake Forest University, 1989.
Corkran, David S. *The Cherokee Frontier: Conflict and Survival, 1740–1762*. Norman: University of Oklahoma Press, 1962.
Correll, Emily Clair. " 'Women's Work for Women': The Methodist and Baptist Women's Missionary Societies in North Carolina, 1878–1930." M.A. thesis, University of North Carolina, 1977.
Cotten, Bruce. *As We Were: A Personal Sketch of Family Life*. Baltimore, Md.: Privately printed, 1935.
Cotten, Sallie Southall. *History of the North Carolina Federation of Women's Clubs, 1901–1925*. Raleigh: Edwards and Broughton, 1925.
Cowan, Ruth Schwartz. *More Work for Mother: The Ironies of Household Technology from the Open Hearth to the Microwave*. New York: Basic Books, 1983.
Cox, Karen Lynne. "To Be Good Wives and Mothers: The Education of Women in Nineteenth-Century North Carolina Female Academies." M.A. thesis, University of North Carolina at Greensboro, 1988.
Crabtree, Beth G., and James M. Patton, eds. *"The Journal of a Secesh Lady": The Diary of Catherine Ann Devereux Edmondston, 1860–1866*. Raleigh: North Carolina Division of Archives and History, 1979.
Crane, Verner. *The Southern Frontier, 1670–1732*. 1928. Reprint, New York: Norton, 1981.
Crow, Jeffrey J., Paul D. Escott, and Flora J. Hatley. *A History of African Americans in North Carolina*. Raleigh: North Carolina Division of Archives and History, 1992.
Crow, Jeffrey J., and Flora J. Hatley, eds. *Black Americans in North Carolina and the South*. Chapel Hill: University of North Carolina Press, 1984.
Crow, Terrell. " 'The Task That Is Ours': Planning the North

Carolina Women's History Project." Paper presented to the Historical Society of North Carolina, April 1986.
Cumming, Inez Parker. "The Edenton Ladies' Tea Party." *Georgia Review* 8 (Winter 1954): 389–94.
Daniel, Pete. *Standing at the Crossroads: Southern Life in the Twentieth Century*. New York: Hill and Wang, 1986.
Davies, Margery W. *Women's Place Is at the Typewriter: Office Work and Office Workers, 1870–1930*. Philadelphia: Temple University Press, 1982.
Davis, Charles T., and Henry Louis Gates. *The Slave's Narrative*. New York: Oxford University Press, 1985.
Davis, Curtis Carroll. "Another Echo of the Tea Party." *The State*, March 1982, 16–18.
Dean, Pamela. "Learning to Be New Women: Campus Culture at the North Carolina Normal and Industrial College." *North Carolina Historical Review* 68 (July 1991): 286–306.
—. "Women on the Hill: A History of Women at the University of North Carolina." Division of Student Affairs, University of North Carolina at Chapel Hill, 1987, 1–29.
"A Declaration and Proposal to All That Will Plant in Carolina." 1663. In Saunders, *Colonial Records of North Carolina*, 1:43–46.
Degler, Carl N. *At Odds: Women and the Family in America from the Revolution to the Present*. New York: Oxford University Press, 1980.
Delany, Sarah L., and A. Elizabeth Delany, with Amy Hill Hearth. *Having Our Say: The Delany Sisters' First 100 Years*. New York: Kodanska America, Inc., 1993.
D'Emilio, John, and Estelle B. Freedman. *Intimate Matters: A History of Sexuality in America*. New York: Harper and Row, 1988.
de Miranda, Francisco. *The New Democracy in America*. Norman: University of Oklahoma Press, 1963.
Demos, John. *A Little Commonwealth: Family Life in Plymouth Colony*. New York: Oxford University Press, 1971.
DePauw, Linda Grant, and Conover Hunt. *Remember the Ladies: Women in America, 1750–1815*. New York: Viking Press, in association with the Pilgrim Society, 1976.
"der [*sic*] Fremden Diener." Old Salem, Inc., June 1989.
Deutsch, Davida Tenenbaum. *The Luminary* [Museum of Early Southern Decorative Arts, Winston-Salem] 9 (August 1988): 3–4.
—. "The Polite Lady: Portraits of American Schoolgirls and Their Accomplishments, 1725–1830." *Antiques* (March 1989): 741–53.
Dial, Adolph L. *The Lumbee Indians of North America*. Edited by Frank W. Porter III. New York: Chelsea, 1993.
Dial, Adolph L., and David K. Eliades. *The Only Land I Know: A History of the Lumbee Indians*. San Francisco: Indian Historian Press, 1975.
Dixon, Eula. "Work Which the Women's Institutes May Do." *Bulletin of the North Carolina Department of Agriculture*, October 1908.
Donald, David Herbert. *Look Homeward: A Life of Thomas Wolfe*. Boston: Little, Brown, 1987.
Drake, Charles, ed. "Olive Dame Campbell Memorial Issue." *Mountain Life & Work* 30 (Autumn 1954). Berea, Ky.: Office of the Council of Southern Mountain Workers.
Drake, William Earle. *Higher Education in North Carolina before 1860*. New York: Carlton Press, 1964.
Dudden, Faye E. *Serving Women: Household Service in Nineteenth-Century America*. Middletown, Conn.: Wesleyan University Press, 1983.
Durrill, Wayne Keith. "Origins of a Kinship Structure in a Slave Community: The Blacks of Somerset Place, 1786–1862." M.A. thesis, University of North Carolina at Chapel Hill, 1980.
—. *War of Another Kind: A Southern Community in the Great Rebellion*. New York: Oxford University Press, 1990.
Edwards, Laura. "Sexual Violence, Gender, and Reconstruction in Granville County, North Carolina." *North Carolina Historical Review* 68 (July 1991): 237–60.
Ekirch, A. Roger. *"Poor Carolina": Politics and Society in Colonial North Carolina, 1729–1776*. Chapel Hill: University of North Carolina Press, 1961.
Ellis, Claye T. *A Giant Step*. New York: Random House, 1966.
Escott, Paul D. *Many Excellent People: Power and Privilege in North Carolina, 1850–1900*. Chapel Hill: University of North Carolina Press, 1985.
—. *Slavery Remembered: A Record of Twentieth-Century Slave Narratives*. Chapel Hill: University of North Carolina Press, 1979.
Evans, Phil, Nick Hodsdon, and Doug Barger. *America's 400th Anniversary Handbook*. Manteo, N.C.: Storie/McOwen Publishers, Inc., 1984.
Evans, Sara M. *Born for Liberty: A History of Women in America*. New York: Free Press, 1989.
Evans, W. McKee. *To Die Game: The Story of the Lowry Band, Indian Guerrillas of Reconstruction*. Baton Rouge: Louisiana State University Press, 1971.
Falk, Stanley L. "The Warrenton Female Academy of Jacob Mordecai, 1809–1818." *North Carolina Historical Review* 35 (July 1958): 281–98.
Faragher, John Mack. *Daniel Boone: The Life and Legend of an American Pioneer*. New York: Henry Holt, 1992.
—. "'White People That Live Like Savages': Daniel Boone in North Carolina." *Carolina Comments* 45 (May 1997): 63–71.
Farnham, Christie Anne. *The Education of the Southern Belle: Higher Education and Student Socialization in the Antebellum South*. New York: New York University Press, 1994.
Faust, Drew Gilpin. "Altars of Sacrifice: Confederate Women and the Narratives of War." *Journal of American History* 76 (March 1990): 1200–1228.
—. "Slavery in the American Experience." In Campbell and Rice, *Before Freedom Came*, 1–19.
Federal Writers' Project, Works Progress Administration. *These Are Our Lives*. Chapel Hill: University of North Carolina Press, 1939.
Felton, Harold W. *Nancy Ward: Cherokee*. New York: Dodd, Mead, 1975.
Fenn, Elizabeth A., and Peter H. Wood. *Natives and Newcomers: The Way We Lived in North Carolina before 1770*. Series

edited by Sydney Nathans. Chapel Hill: University of North Carolina Press, 1983.
Finger, John R. *Cherokee Americans: The Eastern Band of the Cherokees in the Twentieth Century*. Lincoln: University of Nebraska Press, 1991.
—. *The Eastern Band of Cherokees, 1819–1900*. Knoxville: University of Tennessee Press, 1984.
Fischer, Kirsten. "Women's Organizations in North Carolina, 1880–1930." North Carolina Women's History Project Intern Report, July 1989.
Fitzherbert, Master. *The Book of Husbandry*. 1534. Edited by Walter W. Skeat. London, 1832.
Fladmark, Knut R. "Times and Places: Environmental Correlates of Mid-to-Late Wisconsinan Human Population Expansion in North America." In *Early Man in the New World*, edited by Richard Stuller Jr., 13–42. Beverly Hills: Sage Publications, 1983.
Flowers, Linda. *Throwed Away: Failures of Progress in Eastern North Carolina*. Knoxville: University of Tennessee Press, 1990.
Flynn, Elizabeth Gurley. "Women in the War." In Litoff and Smith, *American Women in a World at War*, 11–24.
Foreman, Carolyn Thomas. *Indian Women Chiefs*. 1954. Reprint, Washington, D.C.: Zenger, 1976.
Forten, Charlotte L. *The Journal of Charlotte Forten: A Free Negro in the Slave Era*. Edited by Ray Allen Billington. 1951. Reprint, New York: Norton, 1981.
Foster, Gaines M. *Ghosts of the Confederacy: Defeat, the Lost Cause, and the Emergence of the New South, 1865 to 1913*. New York: Oxford University Press, 1987.
Fox, George. *A Journal of Historical Account of the Life, Travels, Sufferings . . . of . . . George Fox*. Vol. 2. 1831. Reprint, published by M. T. C. Gould, New York: AMS Press, 1975.
Fox-Genovese, Elizabeth. *Within the Plantation Household: Black and White Women of the Old South*. Chapel Hill: University of North Carolina Press, 1988.
Franklin, John Hope. *The Free Negro in North Carolina, 1790–1860*. New York: Russell and Russell, 1943.
Fraser, Walter J., Jr., R. Frank Saunders Jr., and Jon L. Wakelyn, eds. *The Web of Southern Social Relations: Women, Family, and Education*. Athens: University of Georgia Press, 1985.
Frazier, Lynne Howard. "Nobody's Children: The Treatment of Illegitimate Children in Three North Carolina Counties, 1760–1790." M.A. thesis, College of William and Mary, 1987.
Frederickson, Mary Evans. "The Southern Summer School for Women Workers." *Southern Exposure* 4 (Winter 1977): 70–75.
Friedman, Jean E. *The Enclosed Garden: Women and Community in the Evangelical South, 1830–1900*. Chapel Hill: University of North Carolina Press, 1985.
Fries, Adelaide L., Douglas L. Rights, Minnie J. Smith, and Kenneth G. Hamilton, eds. *Records of the Moravians in North Carolina*. 11 vols. Raleigh: North Carolina Historical Commission, 1922–69.
Fripp, Gayle Hicks. *Greensboro: A Chosen Center*. Woodland Hills, Calif.: Windsor Publications, Inc., 1982.
Fry, Gladys-Marie. *Stitched from the Soul: Slave Quilts from the Ante-bellum South*. New York: Dutton Books, 1990.
Gabel, Leona C. *From Slavery to the Sorbonne and Beyond: The Life and Writings of Anna J. Cooper*. Northampton, Mass.: Department of History, Smith College, 1982.
Gallman, James M. "Determinants of Age at Marriage in Colonial Perquimans County, North Carolina." *William and Mary Quarterly*, 3d ser., 39 (January 1982): 176–91.
Garrison, Dee. "Tender Technicians: The Feminization of Public Librarianship, 1876–1905." In *Clio's Consciousness Raised: New Perspectives on the History of Women*, edited by Mary S. Hartman and Lois Banner, 158–78. New York: Harper Colophon Books, 1974.
Gass, W. Conrad. "A Felicitous Life: Lucy Martin Battle, 1805–1874." *North Carolina Historical Review* 52 (October 1975): 367–93.
Gavins, Raymond. " 'A Sin of Omission': Black Historiography in North Carolina." In Crow and Hatley, *Black Americans in North Carolina*, 3–56.
Genovese, Eugene D. *Roll, Jordan, Roll: The World the Slaves Made*. New York: Pantheon, 1974.
Gero, Joan M., and Margaret W. Conkey, eds. *Engendering Archaeology, Women, and Prehistory*. Cambridge, Mass.: Basil Blackwell Ltd., 1991.
Giddings, Paula. *When and Where I Enter: The Impact of Black Women on Race and Sex in America*. New York: William Morrow, 1984.
Gilbert, Martin. *The Second World War: A Complete History*. New York: Henry Holt, 1989.
Gilmore, Glenda Elizabeth. "Gender and Jim Crow: Sarah Dudley Petty's Vision of the New South." *North Carolina Historical Review* 68 (July 1991): 261–85.
—. *Gender and Jim Crow: Women and the Politics of White Supremacy in North Carolina, 1896–1920*. Chapel Hill: University of North Carolina Press, 1996.
Ginns, Patsy Moore. *Rough Weather Makes Good Timber: Carolinians Recall*. Chapel Hill: University of North Carolina Press, 1977.
Glazer, Penina Megdal, and Miriam Slater. *Unequal Colleagues: The Entrance of Women into the Professions, 1890–1940*. New Brunswick: Rutgers University Press, 1987.
Goldin, Claudia. "Female Labor Force Participation: The Origin of Black and White Differences, 1870 and 1880." *Journal of Economic History* 37 (March 1977): 87–108.
Gollaher, David. *Voice for the Mad: The Life of Dorothea Dix*. New York: Free Press, 1995.
Goodrich, Frances Louisa. *Mountain Homespun*. A facsimile of the original, published in 1931, with a new introduction by Jan Davidson. Knoxville: University of Tennessee Press, 1989.
Green, Elna. "Those Opposed: The Antisuffragists in North Carolina, 1909–1920." *North Carolina Historical Review* 67 (July 1990): 315–33.
Green, Harvey. *The Light of the Home*. New York: Pantheon, 1983.
Green, Rayna. "Native American Women." *Signs* 6 (1980): 248–67.

Greenwood, Janette Thomas. *Bittersweet Legacy: The Black and White "Better Classes" in Charlotte, 1850–1910*. Chapel Hill: University of North Carolina Press, 1994.

Griffin, Frances. *Less Time for Meddling: A History of Salem Academy and College, 1772–1866*. Winston-Salem: Blair Publishing, 1979.

Grimes, J. Bryan. *North Carolina Wills and Inventories*. Raleigh: Edwards and Broughton for the Trustees of the Public Libraries, 1912.

Grumet, Robert Steven. "Sunksquaws, Shamans, and Tradeswomen: Middle Atlantic Coastal Algonkian Women during the 17th and 18th Centuries." In *Women and Colonization Anthropological Perspectives*, edited by Mona Etienne and Eleanor Leacock, 43–62. New York: Prager, 1980.

Gulick, John. *Cherokees at the Crossroads*. Chapel Hill: Institute for Research in Social Science, University of North Carolina, 1960.

Gutman, Herbert H. *The Black Family in Slavery and Freedom, 1750–1925*. New York: Pantheon, 1976.

Haessley, Lynn. "'Mill Mother's Lament': Ella May, Working Women's Militancy, and the 1929 Gaston County Textile Strikes." M.A. thesis, University of North Carolina at Chapel Hill, 1984.

Hagler, D. Harland. "The Ideal Woman in the Antebellum South: Lady or Farmwife?" *Journal of Southern History* 46 (August 1980): 405–18.

Hagood, Margaret Jarman. *Mothers of the South: Portraiture of the White Tenant Farm Woman*. Chapel Hill: University of North Carolina Press, 1939.

Haley, Dru Gatewood, and Raymond A. Winslow Jr. *The Historic Architecture of Perquimans County, North Carolina*. Raleigh: North Carolina Division of Cultural Resources and the Town of Hertford, 1982.

Hall, Jacquelyn Dowd, James Leloudis, Robert Korstad, Mary Murphy, Lu Ann Jones, and Christopher B. Daly. *Like a Family: The Making of a Southern Cotton Mill World*. Chapel Hill: University of North Carolina Press, 1987.

Hamburger, Robert. "A Stranger in the House." *Southern Exposure* 5 (Spring 1977): 22–31.

Hamilton, Joseph G. de R., ed. *Papers of Thomas Ruffin*. Raleigh: Edwards and Broughton, 1918–20.

Hancock, Beverlye H. "Skeletal Analysis of the Donnaha Site (31YD9), Yadkin County, North Carolina." M.A. thesis, Wake Forest University, 1987.

Handlin, Oscar, and Mary Handlin. "Origins of the Southern Labor System." *William and Mary Quarterly*, 3d ser., 7 (April 1950): 199–222.

Harper, C. W. "House Servants and Field Hands": Fragmentation in the Antebellum Slave Community." *North Carolina Historical Review* 55 (1978): 42–59.

Harriot, Thomas. "A briefe and true report of the new found land of Virginia (1588) as reprinted by Hakluyt in 1589." In Quinn and Quinn, *The First Colonists*, 46–76.

Harris, Arthur S., Jr. "The House on Spruce Street." *Antioch Review* 16 (Winter 1956–57): 506–11.

Harris, Barbara J. *Beyond Her Sphere: Women and the Professions in American History*. Westport, Conn.: Greenwood Press, 1978.

Harris, Catherine T., and Inzer Byers. "Social Backgrounds and Ideologies of Women Active in Woman Suffrage and Social Reform, 1870–1930." *Quarterly Journal of Ideology* 12 (1988): 61–84.

Harrison, Cynthia Ellen. *On Account of Sex: The Politics of Women's Issues, 1945–1968*. Berkeley: University of California Press, 1988.

Hartmann, Susan M. *The Home Front and Beyond: American Women in the 1940s*. Boston: Twayne Publishers, 1982.

Hassler, William W. *The General to His Lady: The Civil War Letters of William Dorsey Pender to Fanny Pender*. Chapel Hill: University of North Carolina Press, 1962.

Hatley, M. Thomas. "The Three Lives of Keowee: Loss and Recovery in Eighteenth-Century Cherokee Villages." In Wood, Waselkov, and Hatley, *Powhatan's Mantle*, 223–48.

Haywood, Marshall Delancey. "Jacob Marling: An Early North Carolina Artist." *North Carolina Booklet*, 1910.

Heilbrun, Carolyn G. *Writing a Woman's Life*. New York: Ballantine Books, 1988.

Heisner, Beverly. "Harriet Morrison Irwin's Hexagonal House: An Invention to Improve Domestic Dwellings." *North Carolina Historical Review* 58 (April 1981): 105–24.

Henderson, Archibald. "Elizabeth Maxwell Steel: Patriot." *North Carolina Booklet* 12 (October 1912): 67–103.

—. "North Carolina Women in the World War." *North Carolina Literary and Historical Association* (1920): 1–11.

Henle, Ellen, and Marlene Merrill. "Antebellum Black Coeds at Oberlin College." *Women Studies Newsletter* 7 (Spring 1979): 8–11.

Henretta, James. "Families and Farms: Mentalité in Pre-Industrial America." *William and Mary Quarterly* 35 (January 1978): 3–32.

Hester, Jim. "The Tryon Toymakers." *Tar Heel Junior Historian* 23 (Fall 1983): 17–19.

Hewitt, Nancy A. "Beyond Rosie the Riveter: Women on the Homefront in North Carolina." Paper presented at World War II Symposium sponsored by the North Carolina Division of Archives and History, Literary and Historical Society, and Federation of North Carolina Historical Societies, Raleigh, September 23, 1995.

Hickerson, Thomas Felix. *Echoes of Happy Valley*. Published by the author, distributed by Bull's Head Bookstore, Chapel Hill, 1962.

—. *Happy Valley: History and Genealogy*. Chapel Hill: Privately published, 1940.

Higginbotham, Don, ed. *The Papers of James Iredell*. 2 vols. Raleigh: North Carolina Division of Archives and History, 1976.

Hill, Patricia R. *The World Their Household: The American Woman's Foreign Mission Movement and Cultural Transformation, 1870–1920*. Ann Arbor: University of Michigan Press, 1985.

Hinshaw, Seth B., and Mary Edith Hinshaw, eds. *Carolina*

Quakers: Our Heritage, Our Hope. Greensboro: North Carolina Yearly Meeting, 1972.

Holcomb, Esther. *Women Marines Make History: Edenton, North Carolina*. 1943. Edenton, N.C.: Privately published (copyrighted under the name Esther Crisanti), 1988.

Holman, Hugh C., and Sue Fields Ross, eds. *The Letters of Thomas Wolfe to His Mother*. Chapel Hill: University of North Carolina Press, 1968.

Holt, Carrie. *An Autobiographical Sketch of a Teacher's Life*. Quebec: N.p., 1875.

Horn, James. "Servant Emigration in the Chesapeake in the Seventeenth Century." In Tate and Ammerman, *The Chesapeake in the Seventeenth Century*, 51–95.

Horne, Robert. *A Brief Description of the Province of Carolina on the Coasts of Floreda and More Particularly of A New-Plantation begun by the English at Cape-Feare . . .* 1666. Produced in facsimile with an introduction by John Tate Lanning. Charlottesville: Tracy W. McGregor Library, University of Virginia, 1944.

Houk, Annelle. "In the Beginning, 1920–1950." For the Citizen Education Foundation, an Educational Affiliation of the League of Women Voters of North Carolina. Raleigh, 1995.

Howard, John, ed. *Carryin' On in the Lesbian and Gay South*. New York: New York University Press, 1997.

Hudson, Charles M. *The Juan Pardo Expeditions: Explorations of the Carolinas and Tennessee, 1566–1568*. Washington, D.C.: Smithsonian, 1998.

—. *The Southeastern Indians*. Knoxville: University of Tennessee Press, 1976.

Hudson, Lynn M. "Midwifery in the Afro-American Community: A Question of Power." Paper, May 2, 1986.

Hulton, Paul. *America 1585: The Complete Drawings of John White*. Chapel Hill: University of North Carolina Press and British Museum Publications, 1984.

Hunter, Tera. "The Correct Thing: Charlotte Hawkins Brown and the Palmer Institute." *Southern Exposure* 5 (September–October 1983): 37–43.

Hutchinson, Louise Daniel. *Anna J. Cooper: A Voice from the South*. Washington, D.C.: Smithsonian Institution Press, 1981.

Inscoe, John C. "Coping in Confederate Appalachia: Portrait of a Mountain Woman and Her Community at War." *North Carolina Historical Review* 69 (October 1992): 388–413.

Jackson, Mary Anna. "High Hopes Waning," in *Heroines of Dixie*, compiled by Katharine M. Jones, 217–20. Indianapolis, Ind.: Bobbs-Merrill, 1955.

Jacobs, Harriet. *Incidents in the Life of a Slave Girl, Written by Herself*. 1861. Edited with an introduction by Jean Fagan Yellin. Cambridge: Harvard University Press, 1987.

James Sprunt Historical Monograph No. 4: The DeRosset Papers. Chapel Hill: University of North Carolina Press, 1903.

Janiewski, Delores E. *Sisterhood Denied: Race, Gender, and Class in a New South Community*. Philadelphia: Temple University Press, 1985.

Jarrell, Randall. "Losses." *The Complete Poems*. New York: Farrar, Straus and Giroux, 1969.

Jeffrey, Julie Roy. "Women in the Southern Farmers' Alliance: A Reconsideration of the Role and Status of Women in the Late-Nineteenth-Century South." *Feminist Studies* 3 (Fall 1975): 72–91.

Jensen, Joan M. "Cloth, Butter, and Boarders: Women's Household Production for the Market." *Review of Radical Political Economics* 12 (Summer 1980): 14–24.

Johnson, Graham E. "Voluntary Associations and Social Change: Some Theoretical Issues." *International Journal of Comparative Sociology* 16 (March–June 1975): 51–63.

Johnson, Guion Griffis. *Ante-Bellum North Carolina: A Social History*. Chapel Hill: University of North Carolina Press, 1937.

Johnson, Mary Lynch. *A History of Meredith College*. Raleigh: Edwards and Broughton, 1956.

Jones, Alice Hanson. *American Colonial Wealth*. New York: Aron Press, 1977.

Jones, Beverly W. "Race, Sex, and Class: Black Female Tobacco Workers in Durham, North Carolina, 1920–1940, and the Development of Female Consciousness." *Feminist Studies* 10 (Fall 1984): 441–51.

Jones, Beverly W., and Claudia Egelhoff, eds. *Working in Tobacco: An Oral History of Durham's Tobacco Factory Workers*. Durham: History Department, North Carolina Central University, 1988.

Jones, H. G. *North Carolina Illustrated, 1524–1984*. Chapel Hill: University of North Carolina Press, 1983.

Jones, Jacqueline. *Labor of Love, Labor of Sorrow: Black Women, Work, and the Family from Slavery to the Present*. New York: Basic Books, 1985.

—. *Soldiers of Light and Love: Northern Teachers and Southern Blacks, 1865–1873*. Chapel Hill: University of North Carolina Press, 1980.

—. " 'Tore Up and A-Moving': Perspectives on the Work of Black and Poor White Women in the Rural South, 1865–1940." In Wava G. Haney and Jane B. Knowles, *Women and Farming: Changing Roles, Changing Structures*. Boulder, Colo.: Westview Press, 1986, 15–34.

Jones, Kathi R. "That Also These Children May Become Useful People: Apprenticeships in Rowan County, North Carolina, from 1753 to 1795." M.A. thesis, College of William and Mary, 1984.

Jones, Lu Ann. " 'The Task That Is Ours': White North Carolina Farm Women and Agrarian Reform, 1888–1914." M.A. thesis, University of North Carolina, 1983.

—. " 'The Task That Is Ours': White North Carolina Farm Women and Agrarian Reform, 1888–1914." *Institute News: Newsletter of the North Carolina Institute of Applied History* 4 (March 1985): 3–8.

Jordan, Paula Stahls. *Women of Guilford County, North Carolina: A Study of Women's Contributions, 1740–1979*. Women of Guilford County, 1979.

Joyner, Charles. "The World of the Plantation Slaves." In Campbell and Rice, *Before Freedom Came*, 50–99.

Kahan, Mitchell D. *Heavenly Visions: The Art of Minnie Evans*. Raleigh: North Carolina Museum of Art, 1986.

Katzman, David M. *Seven Days a Week: Women and Domestic Service in Industrializing America*. New York: Oxford University Press, 1978.
Kay, Marvin L. Michael, and Lorin Lee Cary. "A Demographic Analysis of Colonial North Carolina with Special Emphasis upon the Slave and Black Populations." In Crow and Hatley, *Black Americans in North Carolina*, 71–121.
Kelly-Gadol, Joan. "Did Woman Have a Renaissance?" In *Becoming Visible: Women in European History*, edited by Renate Bridenthal, Claudia Koonz, and Susan Stuard, 175–201. Boston: Houghton Mifflin, 1987.
Kenzer, Robert C. *Kinship and Neighborhood in a Southern Community: Orange County, North Carolina, 1849–1881*. Knoxville: University of Tennessee Press, 1987.
Kerber, Linda K. "Daughters of Columbia: Educating Women in the New Republic, 1787–1805." In *The Hofstadter Aegis*, edited by Stanley Elkins and Eric McKitrick, 36–59. New York: Knopf, 1974.
—. *Women of the Republic: Intellect and Ideology in Revolutionary America*. Chapel Hill: University of North Carolina Press, 1980.
Kessler-Harris, Alice. *Out to Work: A History of Wage-Earning Women in the United States*. New York: Oxford University Press, 1982.
—. *Women Have Always Worked*. New York: Feminist Press and McGraw-Hill, 1981.
King, E. Sterling. *The Wild Rose of the Cherokee . . ., or Nancy Ward, the Pocahontas of the West*. Nashville: Nashville University Press, 1895.
Knight, Edgar W. *Education in the South*. Chapel Hill: University of North Carolina Press, 1924.
—. *Public Education in North Carolina*. Boston: Houghton Mifflin, 1916.
Knight, Laura. "Midwife." *Winston-Salem Journal*, June 30, 1991.
Kolodny, Annette. *The Land before Her: Fantasy and Experience of the American Frontiers, 1630–1860*. Chapel Hill: University of North Carolina Press, 1984.
Korstad, Bob. "Those Who Were Not Afraid: Winston-Salem 1943." In *Working Lives: The Southern Exposure History of Labor in the South*, edited by Marc S. Miller, 184–99. New York: Pantheon, 1980.
Kostyu, Joel A., and Frank A. Kostyu. *Durham: A Pictorial History*. Norfolk: Donning Co., 1978.
Kratt, Mary Norton. *Charlotte: Spirit of the New South*. Winston-Salem: John F. Blair, 1992.
Kupperman, Karen Ordahl. *Roanoke: The Abandoned Colony*. Totowa, N.J.: Rowman and Allanheld, 1984.
Larkin, Margaret. "Ella May's Songs." *Nation*, October 9, 1929, 382–83.
—. "Story of Ella May." *New Masses* 5 (November 1929): 3–4.
Lathrop, Virginia Terrell. *Educate a Woman: Fifty Years of Life at the Woman's College of the University of North Carolina*. Chapel Hill: University of North Carolina Press, 1942.
Lawrence, Elizabeth. *A Garden of One's Own: Writings of Elizabeth Lawrence*. Edited by Barbara Scott and Bobby J. Ward. Chapel Hill: University of North Carolina Press, 1997.
—. *Gardening for Love: The Market Bulletins*. Edited with an introduction by Allen Lacy. Durham: Duke University Press, 1987.
—. *Gardens in Winter*. New York: Harper and Brothers, 1961.
—. *The Little Bulbs: A Tale of Two Gardens*. 1957. Reprint, Durham: Duke University Press, 1986; introduction by Allen Lacy.
—. *A Rock Garden in the South*. Edited by Nancy Goodwin with Allen Lacy. Durham: Duke University Press, 1990.
—. *A Southern Garden: A Handbook for the Middle South*. Chapel Hill: University of North Carolina Press, 1942.
—. *Through the Garden Gate*. Edited by Bill Neal. Chapel Hill: University of North Carolina Press, 1990.
Lawson, John. *A New Voyage to Carolina*. 1709. Reprint, edited by Hugh T. Lefler, Chapel Hill: University of North Carolina Press, 1967.
Leary, Helen F. M. "Marriage, Divorce, and Widowhood: A Study of North Carolina Law Governing the Property and Person of Married Women, 1663–1869." *North Carolina Genealogical Society Journal* 16 (August 1990): 130–36.
—. "Women and the Law." *Tar Heel Junior Historian* 33 (Spring 1994): 11–13.
Lebsock, Suzanne. *The Free Women of Petersburg: Status and Culture in a Southern Town, 1784–1860*. New York: Norton, 1984.
Lebsock, Suzanne, with checklist and catalog entries by Kym S. Rice. *A Share of Honor: Virginia Women, 1600–1945*. Richmond: Virginia Women's Cultural History Project, 1984.
Lederer, John. *The Discoveries of John Lederer*. Edited with notes by William P. Cumming. Charlottesville: University of Virginia Press, 1958.
Lefler, Hugh T., ed. *North Carolina History Told by Contemporaries*. Chapel Hill: University of North Carolina Press, 1934, 1965.
Lefler, Hugh T., and Albert Ray Newsome. *North Carolina: The History of a Southern State*. Chapel Hill: University of North Carolina Press, 1973.
Lefler, Hugh T., and William S. Powell. *Colonial North Carolina: A History*. New York: Scribner's, 1973.
Leloudis, James L., II. "School Reform in the New South: The Women's Association for the Betterment of Public School Houses in North Carolina, 1902–1919." *Journal of American History* 59 (March 1983): 886–909.
Lemmon, Sarah McCulloh. *North Carolina's Role in World War II*. Raleigh: Department of Archives and History, 1964.
—, ed. *The Pettigrew Papers*. 2 vols. Raleigh: North Carolina Department of Archives and History, 1971, 1988.
Lennon, Donald R., and Ida Brooks Kellam, eds. *The Wilmington Town Book, 1743–1778*. Raleigh: Division of Archives and History, 1973.
Lewis, Johanna Miller. *Artisans in the North Carolina Backcountry*. Lexington: University Press of Kentucky, 1995.
—. "Women Artisans in Backcountry North Carolina, 1753–1790." *North Carolina Historical Review* 68 (July 1991): 214–36.

Lewis, Nell Battle. "Ella May Wiggins Doesn't Count." *Raleigh News and Observer*, September 25, 1929.
—. "Incidentally." *Raleigh News and Observer*, September 29, 1929.
Lindsay, Elizabeth Dick. *Diary of Elizabeth Dick Lindsay*. Edited by Jo White Linn. Salisbury: Salisbury Printing Co., 1975.
Lingeman, Richard R. *Don't You Know There's a War On? The American Home Front, 1941–1945*. New York: Putnam, 1976.
Litoff, Judy Barrett, and David C. Smith. *American Women in a World at War: Contemporary Accounts from World War II*. Wilmington, Del.: Scholarly Resources, Inc., 1997.
Litoff, Judy Barrett, and David C. Smith. *We're in This War, Too: Letters from American Women in Uniform*. New York: Oxford University Press, 1994.
Littlefield, Valinda W. "Publicity from Neither Friend Nor Foe: Annie W. Holland and African American Education in North Carolina, 1910–1934." Paper presented at the Women's Education Conference, North Carolina Museum of History, Raleigh, March 1995.
Logan, Frenise A. *The Negro in North Carolina, 1876–1894*. Chapel Hill: University of North Carolina Press, 1964.
Lonn, Ella. *Desertion during the Civil War*. New York: American Historical Association, 1928. Reprint, Gloucester, Mass.: Peter Smith, 1966.
Lossing, Benson J. *Pictorial Field Book of the Revolution*. 2 vols. New York: Harper, 1851.
Lounsbury, Carl R. "The Plague of Building: Construction Practices on the Frontier, 1650–1730." In Bishir et al., *Architects and Builders*, 9–47.
Lovell, Charles M., and Erwin Hester, eds. *Minnie Evans: Artist*. Greenville: Wellington B. Gray Gallery, East Carolina University, 1993.
Lucas, John Paul, Jr., and Bailey T. Groome. *The King of Scuffletown: A Croatan Romance*. Richmond: Garrett and Massie, 1940.
McCain, Diana Ross. "Women Tavernkeepers." *Early American Life* 21 (June 1990): 30–31, 61, 64.
McCall, Marguerite Butler. *Business as Usual: Edenton Merchant Ledgers, 1759–1819*. Edenton, N.C.: Published by the County of Chowan, printed by the *Chowan Herald*, 1988.
—. "Mystery Woman's Life Reads Like a Gothic Novel." *Chowan Herald*, n.d.
McCandless, Amy Thompson. "Progressivism and the Higher Education of Southern Women." *North Carolina Historical Review* 70 (July 1993): 302–25.
McCartney, Martha W. "Cockacoeske: Queen of Pamunkey, Diplomat, and Suzeraine." In Wood, Waselkov, and Hatley, *Powhatan's Mantle*, 173–95.
McClary, Ben Harris. "Nancy Ward." In *Notable American Women*, vol. 3, edited by Janet W. James and James T. Edwards, 491–93. Cambridge: Belknap Press, 1973.
—. "Nancy Ward: The Last Beloved Woman of the Cherokees." *Tennessee Historical Quarterly* 21 (1962): 352–64.
McCrea, William J. "Palmer Memorial Institute: A Southern Black Educator's Vision and Her New England Benefactors." Historic Sites Section, North Carolina Division of Archives and History, 1990.
McCulloch, Margaret Callender. "Founding the North Carolina Asylum for the Insane." *North Carolina Historical Review* 13 (July 1936): 185–201.
McKimmon, Jane Simpson. *When We're Green We Grow*. Chapel Hill: University of North Carolina Press, 1945.
McKinney, Gordon B. "Women's Role in Civil War Western North Carolina." *North Carolina Historical Review* 69 (January 1992): 37–56.
McKinney, Gordon B., and Richard M. McMurry, eds. *The Papers of Zebulon Baird Vance*. Frederick, Md.: University Publications of America, 1987.
McKown, Harry Wilson, Jr. "Roads and Reform: The Good Roads Movement in North Carolina, 1885–1921." M.A. thesis, University of North Carolina at Chapel Hill, 1972.
McMillan, Hamilton. *Sir Walter Raleigh's Lost Colony*. Raleigh: Edwards and Broughton, 1887.
McMillen, Sally G. *Motherhood in the Old South: Pregnancy, Childbirth, and Infant Rearing*. Baton Rouge: Louisiana State University Press, 1990.
—. *Southern Women: Black and White in the Old South*. Arlington Heights, Ill.: Harlan Davidson, 1992.
The Many Lives of North Carolina Women. Raleigh: Governor's Commission on the Status of Women, 1964.
Marriott, Alice, and Carol K. Rachlin. *American Indian Mythology*. New York: Thomas Y. Crowell, 1968.
Marshall, Helen. *Dorothea Dix: Forgotten Samaritan*. Chapel Hill: University of North Carolina Press, 1937.
Martin, M. Kay, and Barbara Voorhies. *Female of the Species*. New York: Columbia University Press, 1975.
Mason, Mrs. Mary (Ann Bryan). *The Young Housewife's Counsellor and Friend: Containing Directions in Every Department of Housekeeping, Including the Duties of Wife and Mother*. Philadelphia: J. B. Lippincott, 1871.
Mast, Greg. *State Troops and Volunteers: A Photographic Record of North Carolina's Civil War Soldiers*. Raleigh: North Carolina Division of Archives and History, 1995.
Mathews, Alice Elaine. "'A Plain Lively Methodist': The Circuit Rider's View of Women and the Family during the Second Awakening." *The Drew Gateway* 54 (Winter/Spring 1984): 65–75.
Mathews, Donald G. *Religion in the Old South*. Chicago: University of Chicago Press, 1977.
Mathews, Donald G., and Jane Sherron De Hart. *Sex, Gender, and the Politics of ERA: A State and the Nation*. New York: Oxford University Press, 1990.
Mathews, Jane De Hart. "The Status of Women in North Carolina." In *The North Carolina Experience*, edited by Lindley S. Butler and Alan D. Watson, 427–51. Chapel Hill: University of North Carolina Press, 1984.
Mathis, Mark A., and Jeffrey J. Crow, eds. *The Prehistory of North Carolina: An Archaeological Symposium*. Raleigh: North Carolina Division of Archives and History, 1983.
Melder, Keith. "Mask of Oppression: The Female Seminary

Movement in the United States." *New York History* 55 (1974): 261–79.

Merrell, James H. "Natives in a New World: The Catawba Indians of Carolina, 1650–1800." Ph.D. diss., Johns Hopkins University, 1982.

—. " 'Our Bonds of Peace': Patterns of Intercultural Exchange in the Carolina Piedmont, 1650–1750." In Wood, Waselkov, and Hatley, *Powhatan's Mantle*, 196–222.

—. " 'This Western World': The Evolution of the Piedmont." In *The Siouan Project: Seasons I and II*, edited by Roy S. Dickens, H. Trawick Ward, and R. P. Stephen Davis Jr., 19–27. Research Laboratories of Anthropology, University of North Carolina, Chapel Hill, Monograph Ser. 1, 1987.

Merrens, Harry Roy. *Colonial North Carolina in the Eighteenth Century: A Study in Historical Geography*. Chapel Hill: University of North Carolina Press, 1964.

Meyer, Duane. *The Highland Scots of North Carolina, 1732–1776*. Chapel Hill: University of North Carolina Press, 1957.

Miller, Marla R. "My Daily Bread Depends upon My Labor: Women and Work in an Eighteenth-Century Household in Rural New England." N.d., in the authors' possession.

Mitchell, Memory F. "A Half Century of Health Care: Raleigh's Rex Hospital, 1894–1944." *North Carolina Historical Review* 64 (April 1987): 162–98.

Montgomery, Carol Lemley. "Charity Signs for Herself: Gender and the Withdrawal of Black Women from Field Labor in Alabama, 1865–1876." Ph.D. diss., University of California at Irvine, 1991.

Montgomery, Lizzie Wilson. *Sketches of Old Warrenton, North Carolina: Traditions and Reminiscences of the Town and the People Who Made It*. Raleigh: Edwards and Broughton, 1924.

Mooney, James. *Myths of the Cherokee and Sacred Formulas of the Cherokee*. From the Nineteenth and Seventh Annual Reports, Bureau of American Ethnology. Nashville, Tenn.: Charles Elder, Bookseller, 1972.

Moore, Louis T. *Stories Old and New of the Cape Fear Region*. Wilmington: N.p., 1956.

Moore, Ray Nichols. "Mollie Huston Lee: A Profile." *Wilson Library Bulletin* (February 1975): 432–39.

Mordecai, Ellen. *Gleanings from Long Ago*. Savannah: Braid and Hutton, 1933.

Morgan, Lucy, with Legette Blythe. *Gift from the Hills*. Indianapolis: Bobbs-Merrill, 1958.

Morgan, Lynda Joyce. "The Status of Women in New Hanover County, 1750–1800." M.A. thesis, Western Carolina University, 1978.

Morley, Margaret W. *The Carolina Mountains*. Boston: Houghton Mifflin, 1913.

Moss, Kay, and Kathryn Hoffman. *The Backcountry Housewife*. Gastonia, N.C.: Living History Project, Schiele Museum of Natural History and Planetarium, 1985.

Murray, Elizabeth Reid. *Wake, Capital County of North Carolina: Prehistory through Centennial*. Vol. 1. Raleigh: Capital County Publishing Co., 1983.

Murray, Pauli. *Proud Shoes: The Story of an American Family*. New York: Harper and Row, 1978.

—. *Song in a Weary Throat: An American Pilgrimage*. New York: Harper and Row, 1987.

Nasstrom, Kathryn. " 'More Was Expected of Us': The North Carolina League of Women Voters and the Feminist Movement in the 1920s." *North Carolina Historical Review* 68 (July 1991): 307–19.

Nathans, Sydney. *The Quest for Progress: The Way We Lived in North Carolina, 1870–1920*. Series edited by S. Nathans. Chapel Hill: University of North Carolina Press, 1983.

Navey, Liane. "An Introduction to the Mortuary Practices of the Historic Sara." M.A. thesis, University of North Carolina, 1982.

"The Negro Woman Serves America." In Litoff and Smith, *American Women in a World at War*, 156–66.

Newbold, N. C., ed. *Five North Carolina Negro Educators*. Chapel Hill: University of North Carolina Press, 1939.

Newkirk, Judith A. "The Parker Site: A Woodland Site in Davidson County, North Carolina." M.A. thesis, Wake Forest University, 1978.

Noble, M. C. S. *History of Public Schools in North Carolina*. Chapel Hill: University of North Carolina Press, 1930.

Norment, Mary C. *The Lowrie History*. Wilmington: Daily Journal Printer, 1875. Reprint, Lumberton: Lumbee Publishing Co., 1990.

Norton, Mary Beth. *Liberty's Daughters: The Revolutionary Experience of American Women, 1750–1800*. Boston: Little, Brown, 1980.

—. " 'What an Alarming Crisis Is This': Southern Women and the American Revolution." In *The Southern Experience in the American Revolution*, edited by Jeffrey J. Crow and Larry E. Tise, 203–34. Chapel Hill: University of North Carolina Press, 1978.

Norwood, Hayden. *The Marble Man's Wife: Thomas Wolfe's Mother*. New York: Scribner's, 1947.

Nowell, Elizabeth, ed. *The Letters of Thomas Wolfe*. New York: Scribner's, 1956.

—. *Thomas Wolfe: A Biography*. Garden City, N.Y.: Doubleday, 1960.

Oldmixon, John. "The History of the British Empire in America." In *Narratives of Early Carolina, 1650–1708*, edited by Alexander Salley Jr. New York: Scribner's, 1911.

Olmsted, Frederick Law. *Our Slave States*. New York: Dix and Edwards, 1856.

Otto, John Solomon. "The Migration of Southern Plain Folk: An Interdisciplinary Synthesis." *Journal of Southern History* 51 (May 1985): 183–99.

Parker, Mattie Erma Edwards, ed. *North Carolina Higher Court Records, 1670–1696*. Vol. 2 of *Colonial Records of North Carolina*, 2d ser. Raleigh: North Carolina Department of Archives and History, 1968.

—. *North Carolina Higher Court Records, 1697–1701*. Vol. 3 of *Colonial Records of North Carolina*, 2d ser. Raleigh: North Carolina Department of Archives and History, 1971.

Parramore, Thomas C. *Express Lanes and Country Roads: The Way We Lived in North Carolina, 1920–1970*. Series edited by

Sydney Nathans. Chapel Hill: University of North Carolina Press, 1983.
—. "The Tuscarora Ascendancy." *North Carolina Historical Review* 59 (October 1982): 307–26.
Paths toward Freedom: A Biographical Dictionary of Blacks and Indians in North Carolina by Blacks and Indians, Illustrated by James and Ernestine Huff. Raleigh: Center for Urban Affairs, North Carolina State University, 1976.
Pattishall, Roy. "Plantation Voices." *Emory Magazine*, January 1988, 15–23.
Perdue, Theda. "Cherokee Women and the Trail of Tears." In *The American Indian Past and Present*, edited by Roger L. Nichols, 151–61. New York: McGraw-Hill, 4th ed., 1992. Reprinted from *Journal of Women's History* 1 (1989): 14–30.
—. "Nancy Ward." In *Portraits of American Women: From Settlement to the Present*, edited by G. J. Barker-Benfield and Catherine Clinton, 83–100. New York: St. Martin's Press, 1991.
—. *Native Carolinians: The Indians of North Carolina*. Raleigh: North Carolina Division of Archives and History, 1985.
—. *Slavery and the Evolution of Cherokee Society, 1540–1866*. Knoxville: University of Tennessee Press, 1979.
—. "Southern Indians and the Cult of True Womanhood." In Fraser, Saunders, and Wakelyn, *The Web of Southern Social Relations*, 35–51.
—. "The Traditional Status of Cherokee Women." *Furman Studies* 26 (1980): 19–25.
Perkins, Linda M. "The Black Female American Missionary Association Teacher in the South, 1861–1870." In Crow and Hatley, *Black Americans in North Carolina*, 122–36.
Peterson, Jacqueline, and Mary Druke. "American Indian Women and Religion." In *Women and Religion in America*. Vol. 2 of *The Colonial and Revolutionary Periods*, edited by Rosemary Radford Ruether and Rosemary Skinner Keller, 42–78. San Francisco: Harper and Row, 1983.
Phelps, David Sutton. "Archaeology of the North Carolina Coast and Coastal Plain: Problems and Hypotheses." In Mathis and Crow, *Prehistory of North Carolina*, 1–51.
Phifer, Edward. "Slavery in Microcosm: Burke County, North Carolina." *Journal of Southern History* 28 (1962): 137–57.
Phillips, Anne Radford. "Continuity and Change: Farm Women and the Production of Flue-Cured Tobacco, Stokes County, North Carolina, 1925–1955." Ph.D. diss., University of Maryland at College Park, 1990.
—. " 'I Know How to Work': Stories of Farm Women in Stokes and Surry County." *Tar Heel Junior Historian* 33 (Spring 1994): 19–22.
Phillips, Laura A. W. "Davis Brothers Store." National Register of Historic Places Nomination Form, 1993.
Pleasants, Julian M., and Augustus M. Burns III. *Frank Porter Graham and the 1950 Senate Race in North Carolina*. Chapel Hill: University of North Carolina Press, 1990.
Pope, Christie Farnham. "Preparation for Pedestals: North Carolina Antebellum Female Seminaries." Ph.D. diss., University of Chicago, 1977.
Powell, William S. "An Elizabethan Experiment." In *The North Carolina Experience*, edited by Lindley S. Butler and Alan D. Watson, 29–51. Chapel Hill: University of North Carolina Press, 1984.
—. *Higher Education in North Carolina*. Raleigh: North Carolina Department of Archives and History, 1964.
—. *The North Carolina Gazetteer*. Chapel Hill: University of North Carolina Press, 1968.
—. *North Carolina through Four Centuries*. Chapel Hill: University of North Carolina Press, 1989.
—. "Roanoke Colonists and Explorers: An Attempt at Identification." *North Carolina Historical Review* 34 (1957): 202–26.
—, ed. *Dictionary of North Carolina Biography*. 6 vols. Chapel Hill: University of North Carolina Press, 1979–96.
Price, Margaret Nell. "The Development of Leadership of Southern Women through Clubs and Organizations." M.A. thesis, University of North Carolina, 1945.
Price, William S., Jr., ed. *North Carolina Higher-Court Minutes, 1709–1723*. Vol. 5 of *The Colonial Records of North Carolina*. Raleigh: Division of Archives and History, 1977.
Purrington, Burton L. "Ancient Mountaineers: An Overview of the Prehistoric Archaeology of North Carolina's Western Mountain Region." In Mathis and Crow, *Prehistory of North Carolina*, 83–160.
Pyle, Ernie. *Here Is Your War*. New York: Henry Holt, 1943.
Quinn, David Beers. *Set Fair for Roanoke: Voyages and Colonies, 1584–1606*. Chapel Hill: Published for America's Four Hundredth Anniversary Committee by the University of North Carolina Press, 1985.
Quinn, David B., and Alison M. Quinn, eds. *The First Colonists: Documents on the Planting of the First English Settlements in North America, 1584–1590*. Raleigh: North Carolina Division of Archives and History, 1982.
Rable, George C. *Civil Wars: Women and the Crisis of Southern Nationalism*. Urbana: University of Illinois Press, 1989.
Rankin, Richard. *Ambivalent Churchmen and Evangelical Churchwomen: The Religion of the Episcopal Elite in North Carolina, 1800–1860*. Columbia: University of South Carolina Press, 1993.
Ravi, Jennifer. *Notable North Carolina Women*. Winston-Salem: Bandit Books, 1992.
Rawick, George P., gen. ed. *The American Slave: A Composite Autobiography*. 19 vols., 12 vols. in supplement. *North Carolina Narratives*, vols. 14–15. Westport, Conn.: Greenwood Publishing Co., 1972.
Rayne, Martha Louise. *What Can a Woman Do? or, Her Position in the Business and Literary World*. Petersburg, N.Y.: Eagle Publishing, 1893.
Redford, Dorothy Spruill, with Michael Dorso. *Somerset Homecoming: Recovering a Lost Heritage*. New York: Doubleday, 1988.
Reed, W. *Research on the African American Family*. Westport, Conn.: Greenwood Press, 1991.
Reeves, Eleanor Baker. *A Factual History of Early Ashe County, North Carolina*. West Jefferson, N.C.: E. B. Reeves, 1986.

Reid, John P. *A Law of Blood: The Primitive Law of the Cherokee Nation*. New York: New York University Press, 1970.
Reiff, Janice L., Michael R. Dahlin, and Daniel Scott-Smith. "Rural Push and Urban Pull: Work and Family Experiences of Older Black Women in Southern Cities, 1880–1900." *Journal of Social History* (1983): 39–45.
Rights, Douglas L. *The American Indian in North Carolina*. Durham: Duke University Press, 1947.
Roberson, Ruth Haislip, ed. *North Carolina Quilts*. Chapel Hill: University of North Carolina Press, 1988.
Rodman, Lida Tunstall, ed. *Journal of a Tour to North Carolina by William Attmore, 1787*. James Sprunt Studies in History and Political Science, vol. 17, no. 2. Chapel Hill: University of North Carolina Press, 1922.
Rogers, Lou. *Tar Heel Women*. Raleigh: Warren Publishing Co., 1949.
Rogers, Rhea J."The Clans of Passage." *Wake Forest University Magazine* 40 (December 1992): 14–17.
—. "The E. Davis Site and the Origins of the Woodland in Northwestern North Carolina." Paper presented at the Annual Southeastern Archaeological Conference, Tampa, Fla., 1989.
Roosevelt, Eleanor. "We Have to Remember." From "Our Day," *Indianapolis Times*, June 5, 1945.
Roosevelt, Theodore. *The Winning of the West*. Vol. 2. New York: Putnam, 1897.
Rosaldo, Michelle Zimbalist, and Louise Lamphere, eds. *Women, Culture, and Society*. Stanford, Calif.: Stanford University Press, 1974.
Ross, Isabel. *Child of Destiny: The Life Story of the First Female Doctor*. New York: Harper, 1949.
Roth, Rodris. "Tea Drinking in 18th-Century America: Its Etiquette and Equipage." Contributions from the Museum of History and Technology, paper 14, 63–91, *United States National Museum Bulletin* 225 (1961).
Rountree, Carlton White. "The Quaker Meeting near the Narrows of Pasquotank." *Southern Friend* 16 (Spring 1997): 64–76.
Rountree, Moses. *Strangers in the Land: The Story of Jacob Weil and His Tribe*. Philadelphia: Dorrance, 1969.
Roydhouse, Marion W. " 'Our Responsibilities Are Especially for Women': Gertrude Weil and Protective Legislation." Paper presented at the Gertrude Weil Seminar, University of North Carolina, Chapel Hill, 1984.
—. "The 'Universal Sisterhood of Women': Women and Labor Reform in North Carolina, 1900–1932." Ph.D. diss., Duke University, 1980.
Ruley, Melinda. "Picking the Blues." *The Independent*, July 6, 1994.
Rupp, Leila J. *Mobilizing Women for War: German and American Propaganda, 1936–1945*. Princeton: Princeton University Press, 1978.
Russell, Phillips. *The Woman Who Rang the Bell: The Story of Cornelia Phillips Spencer*. Chapel Hill: University of North Carolina Press, 1949.
Rutman, Darrett B., and Anita H. Rutman, " 'Now-Wives and Sons-in-Law': Parental Death in a Seventeenth-Century Virginia County." In Tate and Ammerman, *The Chesapeake in the Seventeenth Century*, 153–82.
"Salem in Service." *The Alumnae Record*. Vol. 67. Salem College. January 1944.
Salley, Katherine Batts, ed. *Life at Saint Mary's*. Chapel Hill: University of North Carolina Press, 1942.
Salmon, Marylynn. *Women and the Law of Property in Early America*. Chapel Hill: University of North Carolina Press, 1986.
Salmond, John A. *Gastonia 1929: The Story of the Loray Mill Strike*. Chapel Hill: University of North Carolina Press, 1995.
Saunders, William L., ed. *The Colonial Records of North Carolina*. 10 vols. Raleigh: State of North Carolina, 1886–90.
Sawyer, Annabel. "The Negro Woman in National Defense." In Litoff and Smith, *Women in a World at War*, 24–34.
Scarberry, Susan J. "Grandmother Spider's Lifeline." In *Studies in American Indian Literature: Critical Essays and Course Designs*, edited by Paula Gunn Allen, 100–107. New York: Modern Language Association of America, 1983.
Schweninger, Loren. "James Carruthers Stanly and the Anomaly of Black Slaveholding." *North Carolina Historical Review* 67 (April 1990): 159–99.
Scott, Anne Firor. "The Ever-Widening Circle: The Diffusion of Feminist Values from the Troy Seminary, 1822–1872." In A. F. Scott, *Making the Invisible Woman Visible*, 64–88. Urbana: University of Chicago Press, 1984.
—. "Most Invisible of All: Black Women's Voluntary Associations." *Journal of Southern History* 56 (February 1990): 3–22.
—. *Natural Allies: Women's Associations in American History*. Urbana: University of Illinois Press, 1991.
—. *The Southern Lady: From Pedestal to Politics, 1830–1930*. Chicago: University of Chicago Press, 1970.
—. *Unheard Voices: The First Historians of Southern Women*. Charlottesville: University of Virginia Press, 1993.
—. "Women and Libraries." In *Libraries, Books, and Culture*, edited by Donald G. Davis Jr., 400-405. Austin: Graduate School of Library and Information Science, University of Texas at Austin, 1986.
Scruggs, L. A. *Women of Distinction: Remarkable in Works and Invincible in Character*. Raleigh: L. A. Scruggs Publisher, 1893.
Sears Roebuck Catalogue, 1902 Edition. New York: Crown Publishers, 1969.
Sedgwick, Eve Kosofsky. *Epistemology of the Closet*. Berkeley: University of California Press, 1990.
Segrest, Mab. *My Mama's Dead Squirrel: Lesbian Essays in Southern Culture*. Ithaca, N.Y.: Firebrand Books, 1985.
Semple, Robert B. *A History of the Rise and Progress of the Baptists in Virginia*. Richmond: John O'Lynch Printer, 1810.
Sensbach, Jon F. *A Separate Canaan: The Making of an Afro-Moravian World in North Carolina, 1763–1840*. Chapel Hill: University of North Carolina Press, 1998.
Shammas, Carol. "The Domestic Environment in Early

Modern England and America." *Journal of Social History* 14 (1980–81): 3–24.
——. "How Self-Sufficient Was Early America?" *Journal of Interdisciplinary History* 13 (Autumn 1982): 247–72.
Sharp, Cecil J. *English Folk Songs from the Southern Appalachians*. Edited by Maud Karpeles. 1932. Reprint, New York: Oxford University Press, 1975.
Shaw, Cornelia Rebekah. *Davidson College: Intimate Facts*. New York: Fleming Revell Press, 1923.
Sheppard, Muriel Earley. *Cabins in the Laurel*. Chapel Hill: University of North Carolina Press, 1935.
Sigourney, Lydia H. *Letters to Young Ladies*. New York: Harper, 1837.
Sikorski, Rob. "Women in the New Republic." In *We, the People: North Carolinians Reconstruct Their Past, 1780–1800*. Durham, N.C.: Duke University, Office of Continuing Education, n.d.
Silver, Timothy. *A New Face on the Countryside: Indians, Colonists, and Slaves in South Atlantic Forests, 1500–1800*. Cambridge: Cambridge University Press, 1990.
Simmons-Henry, Linda, and Linda Edmisten. *Culture Town: Life in Raleigh's African American Communities*. Raleigh: Raleigh Historic Districts Commission, Inc., 1993.
Simmons-Henry, Linda, project director, Philip N. Henry, and Carl M. Speas, eds. *The Heritage of Blacks in North Carolina*. Vol. 1. Charlotte: African American Heritage Foundation in cooperation with the Delmar Co., 1990.
Sims, Anastatia. "Feminism and Femininity in the New South: White Women's Organizations in North Carolina, 1883–1930." Ph.D. thesis, University of North Carolina at Chapel Hill, 1985.
——. *The Power of Femininity in the New South: Women's Organizations and Politics in North Carolina, 1880–1930*. Columbia: University of South Carolina Press, 1997.
——. "Sallie Southall Cotten and the North Carolina Federation of Women's Clubs." M.A. thesis, University of North Carolina, 1976.
——. "The Sword and the Spirit: The WCTU and Moral Reform in North Carolina, 1883–1930." *North Carolina Historical Review* 64 (October 1987): 394–415.
Sklar, Kathryn Kish. *Catharine Beecher: A Study in American Domesticity*. New York: Norton, 1973.
Slocum, Sally. "Woman the Gatherer: Male Bias in Anthropology." In *Toward an Anthropology of Women*, edited by Rayna Rapp Reiter, 36–50. New York: Monthly Review Press, 1975. (Originally presented at the American Anthropological Association Meeting, San Diego, Calif., 1970, by Sally Linton.)
Sloop, Mary T. Martin, with Legette Blythe. *Miracle in the Hills*. New York: McGraw-Hill, 1953.
Smith, Daniel Scott. "Parental Power and Marriage Patterns: An Analysis of Historical Trends in Hingham, Massachusetts." In *The American Family in Social-Historical Perspective*, edited by Michael Gordon, 87–100. New York: St. Martin's Press, 1978.
Smith, Margaret Supplee. "Reynolda: A Rural Vision in an Industrializing South." *North Carolina Historical Review* 65 (July 1988): 287–313.
Smith, Sandra N. "Charlotte Hawkins Brown." *Journal of Negro Education* 51 (1982): 191–206.
Smith-Rosenberg, Carroll. "The Female World of Love and Ritual," in C. Smith-Rosenberg, *Disorderly Conduct: Visions of Gender in Victorian America*. New York: Knopf, 1985.
Solomon, Barbara Miller. *In the Company of Educated Women: A History of Women and Higher Education in America*. New Haven: Yale University Press, 1985.
Some Pioneer Women Teachers of North Carolina. Compiled by the Delta Kappa Gamma Society, North Carolina State Organization, 1955.
South, Stanley A. *Indians in North Carolina*. Raleigh: State Department of Archives and History, 1959.
Spector, Janet D., and Margaret W. Conkey. "Archaeology and the Study of Gender." *Advances in Archaeological Method and Theory* 7 (1984): 1–38.
Spencer, Cornelia Phillips. *First Steps in North Carolina History*. New York: American Book Co., 1888.
——. *The Last Ninety Days of the War in North Carolina*. New York: Watchman Publishing Co., 1866.
Spencer, Darrell. *The Gardens of Salem: Landscape History of a Moravian Town in North Carolina*. Winston-Salem: Old Salem, Inc., 1997.
Spindel, Donna J. *Crime and Society in North Carolina, 1663–1776*. Baton Rouge: Louisiana State University Press, 1989.
Spring, Joel. *The American School, 1642–1985: Varieties of Historical Interpretation of the Foundation and Development of American Education*. New York: Longmans, 1986.
Spruill, Julia Cherry. *Women's Life and Work in the Southern Colonies*. 1938. New York: Norton, 1972.
Stachiw, Myron O. *"Negro Cloth": Northern Industry and Southern Slavery*. Boston: Boston National Historical Park Visitor Center, September 1–November 1, 1981.
Starobin, Robert S., ed. *Blacks in Bondage: Letters of American Slaves*. New York: Marcus Werner, 1974.
Starr, Nina Howell. "The Lost World of Minnie Evans." *The Bennington Review* (Summer 1969): 40–58.
——. "Minnie Evans: Innocent Surrealist." In *Minnie Evans: Artist*, edited by Charles M. Lovell and Erwin Hester. Greenville: Wellington B. Gray Gallery, East Carolina University, 1993.
Starr, Paul. *The Social Transformation of American Medicine*. New York: Basic Books, 1982.
Stephenson, William E. "The Davises, the Southalls, and the Founding of Wesleyan Female College, 1854–1859." *North Carolina Historical Review* 57 (July 1980): 257–79.
——. *Sallie Southall Cotten: A Woman's Life in North Carolina*. Greenville, N.C.: Pamlico Press, 1987.
Stern, Madeleine B. *We the Women: Career Firsts of Nineteenth-Century America*. New York: Schulte Publishing Co., 1963.
Stick, David. *Roanoke Island: The Beginnings of English America*. Chapel Hill: University of North Carolina Press, 1983.
Stone, Lawrence. *The Family, Sex, and Marriage in England, 1500–1800*. New York: Harper and Row, 1977.

Stoops, Martha. *The Heritage: The Education of Women at St. Mary's College, Raleigh, North Carolina, 1842–1982*. Raleigh: St. Mary's College, 1984.

Stowe, Steven M. *Intimacy and Power in the Old South: Ritual in the Lives of the Planters*. Baltimore, Md.: Johns Hopkins Press, 1987.

Strasser, Susan. *Never Done: A History of American Housework*. New York: Pantheon, 1982.

Straub, Jean S. "Benjamin Rush's Views on Women's Education." *Pennsylvania History* 34 (1967): 147–57.

Swan, Susan Burrows. *Plain and Fancy: American Women and Their Needlework, 1700–1850*. New York: Holt, Rinehart, and Winston, 1977.

Swanton, John R. *The Indians of the Southeastern United States*. Washington, D.C.: Bureau of American Ethnology Bulletin, no. 137, 1946.

Sykes, John. "1805–1860: Extracts concerning Somerset Place and the Collins Family, from the Unpublished Portions of Manuscript Collections Associated with the Pettigrew and Bryan Families." Raleigh: Historic Sites Section, North Carolina Division of Archives and History, 1992.

—. "The James Iredell House: An Examination of the Documentary Evidence Relating to the Present Structure and the Iredell Family." Raleigh: Historic Sites Section, North Carolina Division of Archives and History, 1992.

—. "The Women of Somerset Place." *Tar Heel Junior Historian* 33 (Spring 1994): 14–18.

Tar Heel Authors. Raleigh: North Carolina Division of Archives and History, 1957.

Tarlton, William. *Somerset Place and Its Restoration*. Raleigh: North Carolina State Historic Sites, NDAH, 1954.

Tate, Thad W., and David L. Ammerman, eds. *The Chesapeake in the Seventeenth Century: Essays on Anglo-American Society*. Published for the Institute of Early American History and Culture, Williamsburg, Va., by the University of North Carolina Press, 1979.

Taylor, Elizabeth. "The Woman Suffrage Movement in North Carolina." *North Carolina Historical Review* 38, no. 1 (January 1961): 45–62; no. 2 (April 1961): 173–89.

Taylor, Gwynne Stephens. *From Frontier to Factory: An Architectural History of Forsyth County*. Raleigh: North Carolina Division of Archives and History, 1981.

Terrill, Tom E., and Jerrold Hirsch. *Such As Us: Southern Voices of the Thirties*. Chapel Hill: University of North Carolina Press, 1978.

Tessier, Mitzi Schaden. *Asheville: A Pictorial History*. Norfolk: Donning Co., 1982.

Thorp, Daniel B. *Moravian Community in Colonial North Carolina: Pluralism on the Southern Frontier*. Knoxville: University of Tennessee Press, 1989.

Timberlake, Henry. *Lieut. Henry Timberlake's Memoirs, 1756–1765*. Edited by Samuel Cole Williams. Johnson City, Tenn.: Watauga Press, 1927.

Townsend, George A., comp. *The Swamp Outlaws*. New York: Dewitt, 1872.

Troxler, Carole Waterson. *The Loyalist Experience in North Carolina*. Raleigh: North Carolina Division of Archives and History, 1976.

Turrentine, Samuel B. *A Romance of Education: A Narrative Including Recollections and Other Facts Connected with Greensboro College*. Greensboro: Piedmont Press, 1946.

Tusser, Thomas. *Five Hundred Points of Good Husbandrie*. 1573, 1577. Reprint, edited by W. Paine and Sidney Herrtage, London, 1878.

Ulrich, Laurel Thatcher. *Good Wives: Image and Reality in the Lives of Women in Northern New England, 1650–1750*. New York: Vintage Books, 1991.

Vinovskis, Maris A., and Richard M. Bernard. "Beyond Catharine Beecher: Female Education in the Antebellum Period." *Signs* 3 (1978): 856–69.

Vlach, John Michael. "Plantation Landscapes of the Antebellum South." In Campbell and Rice, *Before Freedom Came*, 20–49.

Vogel, Virgil J. *American Indian Medicine*. Norman: University of Oklahoma Press, 1970.

Wadelington, Charles W. Site Report, "Important Dates," and Charlotte Hawkins Brown Bibliography. North Carolina State Historic Sites, NCDAH, Raleigh.

—. "What One Young African American Woman Could Do: The Story of Charlotte Hawkins Brown and the Palmer Memorial Institute." *Tar Heel Junior Historian* 35 (Fall 1995): 22–26.

Walsh, Lorena S. " 'Till Death Us Do Part': Marriage and Family in Seventeenth-Century Maryland." In Tate and Ammerman, *The Chesapeake in the Seventeenth Century*, 126–52.

Ward, H. Trawick. "A Review of Archaeology in the North Carolina Piedmont: A Study of Change." In Mathis and Crow, *Prehistory of North Carolina*, 53–81.

Ware, Susan. *Holding Their Own: American Women in the 1930s*. Boston: Twayne, 1982.

Watson, Alan D. "Cornelius Harnett." In *Harnett, Hooper, & Howe: Revolutionary Leaders of the Lower Cape Fear*, by A. D. Watson, Dennis R. Lawson, and Donald L. Lennon, 1–31. Wilmington: Lower Cape Fear Historical Society, 1979.

—. "The Ferry in Colonial North Carolina: A Vital Link in Transportation." *North Carolina Historical Review* 51 (July 1974): 247–60.

—. "Household Size and Composition in Pre-Revolutionary North Carolina." *Mississippi Quarterly* 31 (Fall 1978): 551–69.

—. "Ordinaries in Colonial Eastern North Carolina." *North Carolina Historical Review* 45 (Winter 1968): 67–83.

—. "Women in Colonial North Carolina: Overlooked and Underestimated." *North Carolina Historical Review* 58 (January 1981): 1–22.

Watson, Elkanah. *Men and Times of the Revolution, or Memoirs of Elkanah Watson, Including Journals of Travels in Europe and America, from the Year 1777 to 1842, and His Correspondence with Public Men, and Reminiscences and Incidents of the American Revolution*. 2d ed. Edited by Winslow C. Watson. New York: Dana and Co., 1856.

Watson, Harry L. *An Independent People: The Way We Lived in North Carolina, 1770–1830*. Series edited by Sydney Nathans. Chapel Hill: University of North Carolina Press, 1983.

Watson, Patty Jo, and Mary C. Kennedy. "The Development of Horticulture in the Eastern Woodlands of North America: Women's Role." In Gero and Conkey, *Engendering Archaeology, Women, and Prehistory*, 255–75.

Weare, Walter B. *Black Business in the New South: A Social History of the North Carolina Mutual Life Insurance Company*. Urbana: University of Illinois Press, 1973.

Weatherford, Doris. *American Women and World War II*. New York: Facts on File, 1990.

Weiner, Lynn. *From Working Girl to Working Mother: The Female Labor Force in the United States, 1820–1980*. Chapel Hill: University of North Carolina Press, 1985.

Wellman, Manly Wade. *The County of Warren, North Carolina, 1586–1917*. Chapel Hill: University of North Carolina Press, 1959.

Welter, Barbara. "The Cult of True Womanhood, 1820–1860." *American Quarterly* 18 (1966): 151–74. Reprinted in *Dimity Connections: The American Woman in the Nineteenth Century*, 21–41. Athens: Ohio University Press, 1975.

Wetmore, Ruth Y. *First on the Land: The North Carolina Indians*. Winston-Salem: John F. Blair, 1975.

What Is a Woman Worth? North Carolina Women, Families, and the Economy in Transition. Raleigh: North Carolina Equity, Inc., 1991.

Wheeler, Marjorie Spruill. Keynote address presented at "Marching through Time: North Carolina Women from Suffrage to Civil Rights: A Symposium on Southern Women's History," November 13, 1995. North Carolina Museum of History, NCDAH, Raleigh.

——. *New Women of the New South: The Leaders of the Woman Suffrage Movement in the Southern States*. New York: Oxford University Press, 1993.

Whisnant, David E. *All That Is Native and Fine: The Politics of Culture in an American Region*. Chapel Hill: University of North Carolina Press, 1983.

White, Deborah Gray. *Ar'n't I a Woman?: Female Slaves in the Plantation South*. New York: Norton, 1985.

White, Katherine S. *Onward and Upward in the Garden*. Edited and with an introduction by E. B. White. New York: Farrar, Straus and Giroux, 1979.

"White's (John) Narrative of the 1587 Virginia Voyage." In Quinn and Quinn, *The First Colonists*, 93–109.

Wiley, Bell Irvin. *Confederate Women*. Westport, Conn.: Greenwood Press, 1975.

Wilkerson-Freeman, Sarah. "The Emerging Political Consciousness of Gertrude Weil: Education and Women's Clubs, 1879–1914." M.A. thesis, University of North Carolina at Chapel Hill, 1985.

——. "From Clubs to Parties: North Carolina Women in the Advancement of the New Deal." *North Carolina Historical Review* 68 (July 1991): 320–39.

Wilkinson, Henrietta H. *The Mint Museum of Art at Charlotte: A Brief History*. Charlotte: Heritage Printers, 1973.

Williams, Samuel Cole. *Early Travels in the Tennessee Country, 1540–1800*. Johnson City, Tenn.: Watauga Press, 1928.

——. *Tennessee during the Revolutionary War*. Nashville: Tennessee Historical Commission, 1944.

Williford, Jo Ann. "Homefront Activities in Wake County during World War II." M.A. thesis, University of North Carolina at Greensboro, 1977.

Wilson, Emily Herring. *Hope and Dignity: Older Black Women of the South*. Philadelphia: Temple University Press, 1983.

——. *Memories of New Bern*. An oral history based on interviews of New Bernians by New Bernians. New Bern: Memories of New Bern Committee, 1995.

Wilson, Joan Hoff. "The Illusion of Change: Women and the American Revolution." In *The American Revolution: Explorations in the History of American Radicalism*, edited by Alfred F. Young, 383–445. DeKalb: North Illinois University Press, 1976.

Wilson, Laurel E., and Lavina M. Franck. " 'She Had a Web of Cloth to Weave': Women's Roles in Nineteenth-Century Textile Production." *Clothing and Textile Research Journal* 8 (Spring 1980): 58–64.

Wilson, Louis R., ed. *Selected Papers of Cornelia Phillips Spencer*. Chapel Hill: University of North Carolina Press, 1953.

Winfree, Robin Schmitt. "A Different Picture: The Cameron Women of Fairntosh Plantation, Orange County, North Carolina, 1790–1843." M.A.L.S. thesis, Duke University, 1989.

Wolf, Jacquelyn H. "Patents and Tithables in Proprietary North Carolina, 1663–1729." *North Carolina Historical Review* 56 (July 1979): 263–77.

Wolfe, Thomas. *Look Homeward, Angel: A Story of the Buried Life*. 1929. Reprint, New York: Scribner's, 1952.

Woloch, Nancy. *Women and the American Experience*. New York: Knopf, 1984.

"Women in Late-Eighteenth-Century North Carolina: Politics and Private Lives." N.p., n.d.

Wood, Peter H. "The Changing Population of the Colonial South: An Overview by Race and Region, 1685–1790." In Wood, Waselkov, and Hatley, *Powhatan's Mantle*, 35–103.

——. "Digging Up Slave History." *Southern Exposure* (March–April 1983): 62–65.

Wood, Peter H., Gregory A. Waselkov, and M. Thomas Hatley, eds. *Powhatan's Mantle: Indians in the Colonial Southeast*. Lincoln: University of Nebraska Press, 1989.

Woodall, J. Ned. *Archeological Investigations in the Yadkin River Valley, 1984–1987*. Raleigh: Wake Forest University, Archeology Laboratory, North Carolina Archaeological Council, Publication no. 25, 1990.

Wright, Annette C. " 'The Grown-Up Daughter': The Case of North Carolina's Cornelia Phillips Spencer." *North Carolina Historical Review* 74 (July 1997): 260–83.

Wright, Rita P. "Women's Labor and Pottery Production in Prehistory." In Gero and Conkey, *Engendering Archaeology, Women, and Prehistory*, 194–223.

Wyatt-Brown, Bertram. "Black Schooling during Reconstruction." In Fraser, Saunders, and Wakelyn, *The Web of Southern Social Relations*, 146–65.

—. *Southern Honor: Ethics and Behavior in the Old South*. New York: Oxford University Press, 1982.
Wyche, Mary Lewis. *The History of Nursing in North Carolina*. Chapel Hill: University of North Carolina Press, 1938.
Yarbrough, Mrs. J. A. "Interesting Carolina People." *Charlotte Observer*, August 23, 1936.
Yarnell, Richard A., and M. Jean Black. "Temporal Trends Indicated by a Survey of Archaic and Woodland Plant Remains from Southeastern North America." *Southeastern Archaeology* 4 (1985): 93–106.
Yearns, W. Buck, and John G. Barrett. *North Carolina Civil War Documentary*. Chapel Hill: University of North Carolina Press, 1980.
Zuber, Richard L. "Conscientious Objectors in the Confederacy: The Quakers of North Carolina." *Journal of Quaker History* 67 (Spring 1978): 1-19.
—. *North Carolina during Reconstruction*. Raleigh: North Carolina Division of Archives and History, 1969.

Index

Illustrations and information in captions are indicated by italicized page numbers. Married women are indexed by their married names and some are also cross-referenced under birth name. For information on geographic places, check both county and town or city names.